The Five-Factor Model
of Personality Across Cultures

International and Cultural Psychology Series

Series Editor: **Anthony Marsella**, *University of Hawaii, Honolulu, Hawaii*

ASIAN AMERICAN MENTAL HEALTH
Assessment Theories and Methods
Edited by Karen S. Kurasaki, Sumie Okazaki, and Stanley Sue

THE FIVE-FACTOR MODEL OF PERSONALITY ACROSS CULTURES
Edited by Robert R. McCrae and Jüri Allik

A Continuation Order Plan is available for this series. A continuation order will bring delivery of each new volume immediately upon publication. Volumes are billed only upon actual shipment. For further information please contact the publisher.

The Five-Factor Model of Personality Across Cultures

Edited by

Robert R. McCrae

National Institute on Aging
Baltimore, Maryland

Jüri Allik

University of Tartu
Tartu, Estonia

Kluwer Academic / Plenum Publishers
New York, Boston, Dordrecht, London, Moscow

Library of Congress Cataloging-in-Publication Data

ISBN HB: 0-306-47354-2
    PB: 0-306-47355-0

©2002 Kluwer Academic / Plenum Publishers, New York
233 Spring Street, New York, New York 10013

http://www.wkap.nl/

10 9 8 7 6 5 4 3 2 1

A C.I.P. record for this book is available from the Library of Congress

Printed in the United States of America

CONTENTS

The Five-Factor Model
of Personality Across Cultures

INTRODUCTION

ROBERT R. McCRAE* & JÜRI ALLIK**

*National Institute on Aging, **University of Tartu, Estonia

Personality psychology has become an international enterprise. To take an example at random, the eight personality articles in the December, 2001, issue of the *Journal of Personality and Social Psychology* included contributions from the United States, Canada, Germany, Finland, and Israel. For the most part, international personality research is not cross-cultural; it is simply personality research conducted in different countries. The implicit assumption behind this practice is that personality processes are universal, and where they are studied is thus of no consequence. An insensitivity to cultural context once imputed mostly to Americans now appears to characterize the field worldwide.

Fortunately, recent years have also seen a rise of interest in studies of personality and culture (Church, 2001; Church & Lonner, 1998; Lee, McCauley, & Draguns, 1999; McCrae, 2000). What do these new studies show? Are personality processes indeed universal, or are there significant variations across cultures that necessitate a more nuanced approach to research? There is as yet no definitive answer to that question. In some respects, human personality does seem to transcend the boundaries of language and culture; in other respects, it is profoundly influenced by social and historical forces. Sorting these issues out must be a priority for our field if we are to understand the current personality literature.

The substantive focus of this book is the Five-Factor Model of personality (FFM; Digman, 1990; McCrae & John, 1992). The FFM is a hierarchical model of trait structure, in which relatively narrow and specific traits are organized in terms of five broad factors: Neuroticism, Extraversion, Openness to Experience, Agreeableness, and Conscientiousness. Proponents of the model claim that it is comprehensive—that is, that it encompasses all major dimensions of personality, and thus supercedes older trait models like Eysenck's (Eysenck & Eysenck, 1975) and Guilford's (Guilford & Zimmerman, 1976). This claim to comprehensiveness makes it a natural choice for cross-cultural research.

Although the model can be traced back at least to 1961 (Tupes & Christal, 1961/ 1992), it established itself as the dominant model of personality structure in the

1980s. At that time, cross-cultural replications (Amelang & Borkenau, 1982; Bond, 1979; Brokken, 1978) were vital in gaining widespread acceptance for the FFM. In fact, by 1992 Costa and McCrae (1992a) had identified *universality* as one of the reasons the five factors should be considered "basic"—although the evidence in favor of universality then was slim by today's standards.

As a general model of personality trait structure, the FFM can be assessed with a wide variety of instruments, including existing inventories such as the Personality Research Form (Jackson, 1984; Paunonen, Jackson, Trzebinski, & Forsterling, 1992) and new measures developed specifically to assess it (De Raad & Perugini, in press). Most of the articles in the present book, however, employ the Revised NEO Personality Inventory (NEO-PI-R; Costa & McCrae, 1992b). The NEO-PI-R assesses 30 specific traits or facets, six for each of the five factors. The NEO-PI-R (with its short form, the NEO Five-Factor Inventory) is the most widely used measure of the FFM, both in the United States and around the world. As this book documents, dozens of translations and adaptations have been made. Many of the chapters address the adequacy of translations and assess the universality of the model. By and large, the instrument appears to work well in translation.

NEO-PI-R translators have been encouraged to collaborate, and for the XXVIIth International Congress of Psychology in Stockholm, Jüri Allik organized a symposium on personality and culture and invited them to contribute (Allik & McCrae, 2000). So many researchers expressed interest that it was necessary to schedule two symposia. Many of the talks given there became the basis of chapters in this book. Other chapters were solicited to provide a balance of topics, perspectives, and geographical regions. The resulting chapters include data representing 40 cultures, 5 continents, and Indo-European, Altaic, Uralic, Hamito-Semitic, Malayo-Polynesian, Dravidian, Austro-Asiatic, Sino-Tibetan, and Bantu languages (plus Japanese and Korean).

Although the emphasis varies, there appear to be three recurring concerns in the chapters. The first is the psychometric properties of the personality measure. By and large, these analyses are familiar assessments of internal consistency, factor structure, and convergent and discriminant validity. Such analyses are the foundation for subsequent use of any translation and are understandably the first priority for many authors.

The second concern is with the generalizability or cultural specificity of various properties of the model. Most of the chapters in the first section of the book address this issue. The general conclusion seems to be that the basic features of the instrument—and thus of personality trait structure—seem to generalize well, but that there may be some interesting variations in specifics.

Finally, there is recurring interest in the issue of national character and its relation to mean personality profiles. Can one interpret mean personality trait scores as an indicator of common personality features, and can one compare cultures on these traits? If NEO-PI-R scores for Extraversion are higher in Norway than in Hong Kong, does that mean that Norwegians are really more extraverted? And might that fact be used to explain differences between the two cultures in customs and institutions? A few years ago, anyone trained in cross-cultural psychology would have answered with a quick and resounding "No!" There are many convincing reasons to doubt that different translations will have the scalar equivalence (Van de Vijver & Leung, 1997) that would be necessary to justify such comparisons.

But a recent, large-scale intercultural comparison (McCrae, 2001) provided evidence that personality scales may be more robust than methodologists had presumed. Perhaps because the many sources of error cancel out, it is possible to obtain meaningful results when raw scores are compared across cultures. By extension, it should be possible to interpret scores within a culture in terms of a universal metric.

However, evidence presented by McCrae (2001) and by Church and Katigbak in this volume suggests that these mean profiles do not match stereotypical judgments of national character, even when these judgments are provided by experts. How and why this should be so, and what it implies for the validity of personality measures, is open to debate. Given this uncertainty, most journal editors would probably discourage interpretation of mean levels. Here, however, we have adopted the opposite approach, encouraging contributors to speculate on the possible meaning of the personality profiles they find. We hope this exploration will provide clues to the real meaning of personality profiles in translation.

For Allik's Stockholm symposia, panelists were asked to address a "Five-Factor Theory Perspective." Five-Factor Theory (McCrae & Costa, 1996, 1999) is an attempt to make sense of the research results associated with the FFM in terms of a broader personality system. It was initially developed to account for personality stability and change (Costa & McCrae, 1994), but it can also illuminate cross-cultural research. The last section of this book is devoted to a critical overview of the book and to an assessment of its findings in terms of Five-Factor Theory.

As the chapters of this book show, international personality research is flourishing, and it is beginning to incorporate a sensitivity to cultural context that can only improve the quality of research. There is much more to personality than traits, but the traits of the FFM appear to offer a solid basis for cross-cultural research in personality.

REFERENCES

Allik, J., & McCrae, R. R. (2000, July). *Personality and culture: The Five-Factor Theory perspective.* Symposium presented at the XXVIIth International Congress of Psychology, Stockholm, Sweden.

Amelang, M., & Borkenau, P. (1982). Über die faktorielle Struktur und externe Validität einiger Fragebogen-Skalen zur Erfassung von Dimensionen der Extraversion und emotionaler Labilität [On the factor structure and external validity of some questionnaire scales measuring dimensions of extraversion and neuroticism]. *Zeitschrift für Differentielle und Diagnostische Psychologie, 3*, 119-146.

Bond, M. H. (1979). Dimensions used in perceiving peers: Cross-cultural comparisons of Hong Kong, Japanese, American, and Filipino university students. *International Journal of Psychology, 14*, 47-56.

Brokken, F. B. (1978). *The language of personality.* Unpublished doctoral dissertation, University of Groningen.

Church, A. T. (Ed.). (2001). Culture and personality [Special issue]. *Journal of Personality, 69*(6).

Church, A. T., & Lonner, W. J. (Eds.). (1998). Personality and its measurement in cross-cultural perspective [Special issue]. *Journal of Cross-Cultural Psychology, 29*(1).

Costa, P. T., Jr., & McCrae, R. R. (1992a). Four ways five factors are basic. *Personality and Individual Differences, 13*, 653-665.

Costa, P. T., Jr., & McCrae, R. R. (1992b). *Revised NEO Personality Inventory (NEO-PI-R) and NEO Five-Factor Inventory (NEO-FFI) professional manual.* Odessa, FL: Psychological Assessment Resources.

Costa, P. T., Jr., & McCrae, R. R. (1994). "Set like plaster"? Evidence for the stability of adult personality. In T. Heatherton & J. Weinberger (Eds.), *Can personality change?* (pp. 21-40). Washington, DC: American

Psychological Association.

De Raad, B., & Perugini, M. (Eds.). (in press). *Big Five assessment*. Göttingen, Germany: Hogrefe & Huber Publishers.

Digman, J. M. (1990). Personality structure: Emergence of the Five-Factor Model. *Annual Review of Psychology, 41*, 417-440.

Eysenck, H. J., & Eysenck, S. B. G. (1975). *Manual of the Eysenck Personality Questionnaire*. San Diego: EdITS.

Guilford, J. S., Zimmerman, W. S., & Guilford, J. P. (1976). *The Guilford-Zimmerman Temperament Survey handbook: Twenty-five years of research and application*. San Diego, CA: EdITS.

Jackson, D. N. (1984). *Personality Research Form manual (3rd. ed.)*. Port Huron, MI: Research Psychologists Press.

Lee, Y.-T., McCauley, C. R., & Draguns, J. G. (Eds.). (1999). *Personality and person perception across cultures*. Mahwah, NJ: Lawrence Erlbaum Associates.

McCrae, R. R., & Costa, P. T., Jr. (1996). Toward a new generation of personality theories: Theoretical contexts for the Five-Factor Model. In J. S. Wiggins (Ed.), *The Five-Factor Model of personality: Theoretical perspectives* (pp. 51-87). New York: Guilford.

McCrae, R. R., & Costa, P. T., Jr. (1999). A Five-Factor Theory of personality. In L. A. Pervin & O. P. John (Eds.), *Handbook of personality: Theory and research* (2nd ed., pp. 139-153). New York: Guilford.

McCrae, R. R., & John, O. P. (1992). An introduction to the Five-Factor Model and its applications. *Journal of Personality, 60*, 175-215.

McCrae, R. R. (Ed.). (2000). Personality traits and culture: New perspectives on some classic issues [Special issue]. *American Behavioral Scientist, 44(1)*.

McCrae, R. R. (2001). Trait psychology and culture: Exploring intercultural comparisons. *Journal of Personality*, 819-846.

Paunonen, S. V., Jackson, D. N., Trzebinski, J., & Forsterling, F. (1992). Personality structure across cultures: A multimethod evaluation. *Journal of Personality and Social Psychology, 62*, 447-456.

Tupes, E. C., & Christal, R. E. (1992). Recurrent personality factors based on trait ratings. *Journal of Personality, 60*, 225-251. (Original work published 1961)

Van de Vijver, F. J. R., & Leung, K. (1997). Methods and data analysis of comparative research. In J. W. Berry, Y. H. Poortinga, & J. Pandey (Eds.), *Handbook of cross-cultural psychology: Vol 1: Theory and method* (pp. 257-300). Boston: Allyn and Bacon.

AUTHOR NOTE

For generous and helpful comments on chapters in this book we thank Verónica Benet-Martínez, Michael H. Bond, Peter Borkenau, Sergey Budaev, Paul Costa, Boele De Raad, Geert Hofstede, Øyvind Martinsen, Ivan Mervielde, Sampo Paunonen, Larry Pervin, Ype Poortinga, V. S. Pramila, Harry Triandis, David Watkins, and Jian Yang. We thank Brenda VanAntwerp of Psychological Assessment Resources for prompt and expert administrative assistance in coordinating the licensing of translations.

SECTION I: INTERCULTURAL STUDIES

The five chapters in this Section are intercultural studies: All of them examine a phenomenon across a range of cultures, and most seek to relate cultural variation in personality to other culture-level variables. These studies capitalize on the spirit of collaboration that has developed among NEO-PI-R researchers around the world, and they lay the basis for future work.

Fittingly, the first chapter is Rolland's review of the generalizability of the Five-Factor Model in both lexical and questionnaire approaches. Varimax rotations of NEO-PI-R data from 16 cultures show clear replication of three factors (Neuroticism, Openness, and Conscientiousness), with alternative orientations of the Extraversion and Agreeableness factors. Although these findings do not preclude additional factors specific to different cultures, they do suggest that the FFM provides a viable common denominator for cross-cultural research.

Konstabel, Realo, and Kallasmaa investigate the possible sources of small variations in the FFM structure. In earlier work, the orientation of Extraversion and Agreeableness factors had been tentatively linked to Individualism-Collectivism. In this chapter, the authors explore possible links to other culture-level variables, including personality traits, values, and demographic indicators. They also look for cultural explanations of variations in the nature of Impulsiveness. These studies exemplify the vigorous exploration that is appropriate in these early stages of trait-psychology-and-culture studies.

Hřebíčková and colleagues examine the validity of the short form of the NEO-PI-R in three West-Slavic languages. Internal analyses of item structure are supplemented by a multitrait-multimethod analysis including three alternative measures of the FFM. Hřebíčková and colleagues also discuss national stereotypes and formulate hypotheses about mean level differences in personality traits among Czechs, Slovaks, and Poles. The limited support they find for their hypotheses anticipates results from a Filipino study reported by Church and Katigbak.

The affective correlates of FFM traits are addressed by Yik, Russell, Ahn, Fernández Dols, and Suzuki. In five languages, they replicate the familiar two-dimensional structure of affect and find similar, but not identical, personality correlates. This study adds a new perspective to the continuing controversy about which affective axes are truly basic.

Finally, McCrae reports an extension of earlier intercultural comparisons of mean levels of personality traits. These data make it clear that when scores from different translations are compared, lawfully ordered results are obtained. Whether differences should be taken at face value as an indication of differences in the mean level of true scores, however, remains a matter of controversy. Readers may wish to consult the chapter by Poortinga, Van de Vijver, and Van Hemert for a critical analysis of this point.

THE CROSS-CULTURAL GENERALIZABILITY OF THE FIVE-FACTOR MODEL OF PERSONALITY

JEAN-PIERRE ROLLAND

Université Paris X Nanterre

Abstract. A review of studies on the cross-cultural generalizability of the Big Five and the Five-Factor Model (FFM) of personality describes the convergent and divergent results of two main research traditions ("emic" and "etic") on this topic. The main divergent results relate to the Intellect-Openness dimension. The cross-cultural generalizability of the Intellect-Openness dimension is clearly problematic in the emic and psycho-lexical stream of research but firmly established by the etic stream using imported inventories. After this review of previous research, results of cross-cultural geralizability research on the FFM as assessed by the NEO-PI-R are presented and discussed. Comparisons of Varimax structures in 16 different cultures clearly show the cross-cultural generalizability of Neuroticism, Openness and Conscientiousness. Extraversion and Agreeableness, described as components of the interpersonal circumplex, appear to be more sensitive to cultural context. For some cultures—in Varimax structure—the factorial location of some facets of Extraversion and Agreeableness shift onto the other dimension. All these results are in line with previous research and suggest that the anthropological traditional that emphasizes cultural diversity and the impact of culture on individual psychology probably tends to underestimate the role of cross-cultural invariance in individual differences.

Keywords : Personality, Five-Factor Model, cross-cultural generalizability

1. THE FIVE-FACTOR MODEL OF PERSONALITY

Over the past decade, the psychology of personality has been heavily influenced by the Five-Factor Model (FFM or Big Five; see reviews by Deary & Matthews, 1993; Digman, 1990; John, 1990; John, Angleitner, & Ostendorf, 1988; McCrae & John, 1992; Rolland, 1993, 1996). The five-factor taxonomy of personality dimensions, in part due to the great amount of research that has contributed to establishing its validity, now stands as a model of reference amongst the hierarchical models of personality (Cattell, 1996; Eysenck, 1991, 1992). This model has, however, been challenged and finds itself at the center of fierce debate (Block, 1995a, 1995b, 2001; Brand, 1995; Briggs, 1992; Cattell, 1996; Costa & McCrae, 1992, 1995; Eysenck, 1992; Goldberg & Saucier, 1995; Loevinger, 1994; McAdams, 1992; Pervin, 1994). Nevertheless, most alternative solutions integrate this model to a large extent, being partly based on it, or regrouping its five dimensions, or adding extra dimensions (Rolland, 1996).

The five dimensions in the five-factor taxonomy are Neuroticism, Extraversion, Openness, Agreeableness and Conscientiousness.

Neuroticism (*vs*. Adjustment) is a classic dimension of personality represented in most models. It takes into account individual differences in the inclination to construct, perceive, and feel reality as being problematic, threatening, and difficult; and to feel negative emotions (such as fear, shame, and anger).

Extraversion (*vs*. Introversion) is also a classic dimension. Extraversion reflects the *quantity* and *intensity* of relationships with one's environment (notably social), and refers to a tendency to seek contacts with the environment with energy, spirit, enthusiasm, and confidence, and to live out experiences positively.

Openness is a dimension that the FFM, unlike its counterparts, deals with at the second order level. This dimension is independent of cognitive aptitudes and groups together different types of behavior related to an active search for and a love of new experiences. It describes cognitive and non-cognitive Openness to experience, which is manifested in a wide range of interests and an eagerness to seek out and live new and unusual experiences without anxiety and even with pleasure. The acceptance of new experiences may be relevant to various domains and different spheres (ideas, beliefs, values, actions) of behavior.

Agreeableness is also described uniquely in the FFM as a second order dimension. This dimension concerns the nature of one's relationships with others, and differs from Extraversion (another dimension with a strong interpersonal component) in that it refers more to the relational sphere and the tone of relationships with others (kindness, empathy *vs*. cynicism, hostility) whereas Extraversion refers more to the individual him/herself. Agreeableness deals with the quality of interpersonal relationships on a spectrum ranging from compassion to antagonism.

Conscientiousness is a dimension that focuses on issues such as orientation, persistency of behavior, and control of impulses. This dimension comprises dynamic elements (anticipation, success-orientation, task-orientation) and control and inhibition elements of behavior (organization, perseverance, thoroughness, respect for standards and procedures).

The FFM was originally developed in research founded on a psycho-lexical approach. From this perspective, it may be postulated that "Those individual differences that are of most significance in the daily transactions of persons with each other will eventually become encoded into their language. The more important is such a difference, the more people will notice it and wish to talk of it, with the result that eventually they will invent a word for it" (Goldberg, 1981, p. 141-142). Language provides a list of descriptors that enable us to describe the usual behavior of a person and differentiate between his/her behavior and that of others. An analysis of covariations of descriptions (of oneself or others) made by means of these descriptors can detect *traits* of personality (i.e. dimensions describing individual differences that are likely to be manifested in relatively stable and consistent patterns of cognition, feelings, and action) and covariation patterns between these traits: the *structure* of the personality. This method made it possible, initially in an Anglo-American semantic context, to extract with relative consistency the five dimensions of the Five-Factor Model (for reviews see Goldberg, 1993, 1995; John, 1990; Wiggins & Trapnell, 1997).

Over the past decade, the FFM has become a model of reference and the object of a large amount of research aiming to establish or confirm its validity. The five dimensions of this model have been systematically extracted by means of diverse instruments (lists of words in a psycho-lexical approach or classic personality inventories) and diverse assessment sources (assessment of oneself or others; McCrae & Costa, 1987; Mervielde, 1994; Somer & Goldberg, 1999) independently of the factorial procedures used (Goldberg, 1990), modes of assessment implemented (Botwin & Buss, 1989; Digman & Takemoto-Chock, 1981; McCrae & Costa, 1987; Mervielde & DeFruyt, 2000; Norman, 1963; Tupes & Christal, 1992) or affinity with the people assessed (Peabody & Goldberg, 1989; Somer & Goldberg, 1999), on samples of subjects of varying ages (Costa & McCrae, 1988; 1994; De Fruyt et al. 2000; Digman & Shmelyov, 1996; Mervielde & DeFruyt, 2000) including psychiatric populations (Yang et al., 1999) and from various cultures, using either a psycho-lexical approach (Anglo-American: Goldberg, 1990; 1992; Hofstee, De Raad, & Goldberg, 1992; Saucier, 1997; German: Ostendorf, 1990; Hungarian: Szirmak & De Raad, 1994; Italian: Caprara & Perugini, 1994; Polish: Szarota, 1996; Dutch: De Raad, 1992; De Raad, Hendriks, & Hofstee, 1992; Czech: Hřebíčková, 1995; Turkish: Somer & Goldberg, 1999), or lexical markers and standardized questionnaires (Benet-Martínez & John, 1998, 2000; Bond, 1979; Bond, Nakazato & Shiraishi, 1975; Chen & Piedmont, 1999 ; Costa & McCrae, 1992; Costa, McCrae, & Jónsson, 1999; Hendriks & Perugini, 2000; Hoekstra et al., 1996, 1997; John, 1990; Kallasmaa et al., 1999, 2000; Katigbak et al., 1996; Knežević, Radović, & Opačić, 1997; Martin et al., 1997; Marušić et al., 1996; McCrae & Costa, 1997; McCrae, Costa & Yik, 1996; McCrae et al., 1998; Montag & Levin, 1994; Ostendorf & Angleitner, 1994; Mastor, Cooper, & Jin, 1998; Paunonen et al., 1992, 1996; Piedmont & Chae, 1997; Pulver et al., 1995; Rolland, 1993, 1996, 1998; Rolland et al., 1998; Trull & Geary, 1997; Yang & Bond, 1990; Yang et al., 1999; Yik & Bond, 1993).[1]

2. CROSS-CULTURAL GENERALIZABILITY OF THE FFM

The validity of the structure of this model therefore seems to have been solidly established. However, the validity of structure is but one aspect, and insufficient in itself, of the validity of a model, which should take into account other elements such as concurrent validity, criterion validity, temporal stability, heritability, and cross-cultural generalizability. An examination of all of these elements is not within the realm of the present article; this study shall focus on cross-cultural generalizability. One important criterion of the validity of a model of personality is its cross-cultural validity (John, Goldberg & Angleitner, 1984), that is to say, the extent to which it is relatively independent of cultural systems. Given its origin (the psycho-lexical approach was founded on the analysis of Anglo-American linguistic terms), it is therefore relevant to ask whether the Five-Factor Model may not exclusively reflect the idiosyncrasies produced by the North-American language and culture. Juni, for example, explicitly

---

[1]Structures resembling the FFM have also been extracted in animals (King & Figueredo, 1997; Weiss, King, & Figueredo, 2000).

formulates this point of view: "The simplistic (a posteriori) basis of [its] FFM, as it is derived from colloquial usage of language, makes the model and its tools intrinsically bound to the culture and language that spawned it. Different cultures and different languages should give rise to other models that have little chance of being five in number nor of having any of the factors resemble those derived from the linguistic/ social network of Middle-class Americans" (Juni, 1996, p. 864). Criticism of this type has its roots in anthropological tradition and cross-cultural psychology, which tend to underline the diversity of cultures and their impact on the psychology of the individual (Markus & Kitayama, 1991, 1998). When discussing this problem, Church and Lonner (1998) pointed out that cultural psychology and social constructivism see the personality as an element that cannot be dissociated from culture; from this perspective "cross-cultural comparison of personality predispositions (is) futile" (p. 40). It is indeed important to know whether personality traits (i.e., the dimensions describing individual differences that are likely to be manifested in relatively stable and consistent patterns of cognition, feelings, and actions) are shaped by the culture (for example, educational practices, religious and moral values, or representation systems encoded in the language), because then personality traits and the structure of these traits should vary in keeping with the different cultural systems. On the other hand, if personality traits and the structure of these traits can be seen in terms of human universals, then the structure of these traits should show relative cross-cultural stability. This subject has been discussed both from a general point of view and within the framework of the Five-Factor Model; hence we envisage focusing here only on the Five-Factor Model.

A vast amount of research has focused on this essential element of validity of the FFM. If we refer to the classic distinction suggested by Berry (1969), we can divide research into two categories: the *emic*-type approach and the *etic*-type approach. The emic approach aims at discovering the constructs specific to each culture by gathering specific linguistic material in each culture. The etic approach, on the contrary, aims at verifying whether the constructs identified in a given culture can be found in another context, thereby attempting to detect universals. If we schematize, studies based on the psycho-lexical approach often incorporate what can be called an emic approach, whereas studies using lexical markers or standardized inventories use an etic-type approach. Some research combines both approaches in what is called an *integrated* method, thereby enabling both cross-cultural universals and specific dimensions to be identified (Yang & Bond, 1990; Yik & Bond, 1993; Katigbak, Church, & Akamine, 1996).

2.1 The Emic Perspective

From an emic perspective, although a certain number of psycho-lexical studies[2] have succeeded in extracting the Big Five by means of taxonomies implemented in diverse linguistic and cultural contexts (Anglo-American: Goldberg, 1990; Dutch: De Raad, 1994; Croatian: Mlacić, 2000; German; Ostendorf, 1990; Turkish: Somer &

---

[2]Constitution of a specific and hence unique linguistic corpus, elaboration of specific taxonomies, and extraction of specific dimensions of personality pertinent to each semantic and cultural context.

Goldberg, 1998), numerous studies have, in other contexts, obtained more problematic results. To briefly summarize some of these results:

• In numerous studies the Openness factor cannot be extracted (De Raad & VanHeck, 1994; Szirmak & De Raad, 1994; Di Blas & Forzi, 1998, 1999) as it seems to fluctuate very broadly depending on the cultural context (Somer & Goldberg, 1998) and the type of terms retained (Saucier & Goldberg, 1997; Di Blas & Forzi, 1999). This has led certain authors to discuss dropping it from taxonomies derived from psycho-lexical studies (De Raad, 1994, 1998; De Raad & VanHeck, 1994; Di Blas & Forzi, 1998, 1999).

• When purely evaluative terms (usually excluded following Allport and Odbert's initial decision) are included in the taxonomies, seven dimensions can reliably be extracted (Almagor, Tellegen, & Waller, 1995; Benet-Martínez & Waller, 1997).

• In certain linguistic and cultural contexts, even when evaluative terms are excluded more than five dimensions are normally necessary to cover the linguistic material retained (Church et al., 1997; Isaka, 1990; Katigbak, Church, & Akamine, 1996).

• Research combining emic and etic methods does not obtain exactly the same dimensions as those extracted by using the two sources separately (Di Blas & Forzi, 1999; Yang & Bond, 1990; Yik & Bond, 1993; Katigbak, Church, & Akamine, 1996).

• In certain cases, a psycho-lexical approach combined with an emic method is apparently not able to identify the essential dimensions (such as Neuroticism) that are found using an etic approach (Caprara, Barbaranelli, Borgogni, & Perugini, 1993; Caprara & Perugini, 1994; De Raad, Di Blas, & Perugini, 1998; Di Blas & Forzi, 1998, 1999). In cultural and linguistic contexts where the extraction of dimensions Openness and Neuroticism seems difficult or impossible using psycho-lexical methods, it is nevertheless possible to extract these dimensions using an etic (imposed) approach and the inventory method. Hence in the Italian context, although the five dimensions of the Big Five and notably the dimension Neuroticism were recovered using the inventory method (Caprara et al., 1992, 1993; Perugini & Leone, 1996), it seems that the dimension of Neuroticism cannot be extracted using classic methods incorporating a psycho-lexical approach (Caprara & Perugini, 1994; Di Blas & Forzi, 1998, 1999). This surprising result justifies criticisms formulated by McCrae (1994) and Loevinger (1994) in regards to the psycho-lexical approach, which they consider insufficiently comprehensive.

2.2 The Etic Perspective

From an etic perspective, the validity of the FFM in non Anglo-American linguistic and cultural contexts may be examined by using either validated markers or personality inventories. In most cases, studies using adjective markers have confirmed the existence of this model. This is the case, for example, for Germany (Borkenau & Ostendorf, 1990), Australia (Heaven, Connors, & Stones, 1994), France (Rolland, 1993), Italy (Di Blas & Forzi, 1999; Perugini & Leone, 1996), Japan (Bond, Nakazato, & Shiraishi, 1975), Taiwan (Yang & Bond, 1990), and Hong-Kong (Bond, 1979; Trull & Geary, 1997; Yik & Bond, 1990). Nevertheless, this is not always the case, for example, in the Philippines (Guthrie & Bennett, 1971)[3] and on a sample of Black South Africans (Heaven et al., 1994).

Nowadays there exist a large number of questionnaires developed to measure the dimensions of personality of the FFM. The Revised NEO Personality Inventory (NEO-PI-R; Costa & McCrae, 1992) is a questionnaire specifically conceived to assess this model. Out of all the personality inventories developed to assess the five dimensions of the FFM, to date this is the inventory that has been the most frequently adapted and validated in diverse linguistic and cultural contexts. The large number of validations of this inventory in different cultural contexts has made it possible to examine the general applicability of the FFM. Analysis of the factorial structure of the 30 facets of this questionnaire adapted in widely diverse linguistic and cultural contexts (Anglo-American, Chinese-Hong-Kong, Chinese-Mandarin, Korean, Croatian, French, German, Hebrew, Icelandic, Japanese, Dutch-Flemish, Malay, Philippine, Portuguese, Taiwanese [4]) has shown that, using Procrustes solutions, the general applicability of the Five-Factor Model is excellent. On the other hand, using Varimax solutions the structure of the dimensions Extraversion and Agreeableness is more problematic, because certain facets load on other dimensions. This is due to a combination of reasons: the type of rotations implemented in factorial analyses (McCrae & Costa, 1997; McCrae et al., 1996), the complex relationships that exist between Extraversion and Agreeableness (Church & Burke, 1994; Hofstee, De Raad, & Goldberg, 1992; McCrae & Costa, 1989; McCrae et al., 1998; Peabody & Goldberg, 1989), and also real cross-cultural differences (McCrae et al., 1996, 1998). After a series of cross-cultural validity studies based on the NEO-PI-R, McCrae and colleagues concluded that "personality, as measured by the NEO-PI-R, can be characterized in every culture so far examined in terms of N, O and C factors plus the interpersonal circumplex; and Procrustes rotation shows that the circumplex can always be interpreted in terms of E and A factors" (McCrae et al., 1998, p. 182).

Although the NEO-PI-R is a questionnaire that has been specifically designed to assess the Five-Factor Model, other questionnaires developed on the basis of other models can also be used to assess the dimensions of this model. This is notably the case for the Personality Research Form (PRF; Jackson, 1984) and the Nonverbal Personality Questionnaire (NPQ; Paunonen, Jackson, & Keinonen, 1990). Paunonen used these instruments to conduct a series of studies that tested the cross-cultural validity of the FFM (Paunonen & Ashton, 1998; Paunonen et al., 1992, 1996), and actually succeeded in extracting the five dimensions of the Five-Factor Model in widely varying linguistic and cross-cultural contexts (Germany, Canada, Finland, Poland, Russia). These results are all the more interesting because the NPQ is a non-verbal inventory that minimizes the possible structuring effect of language. The findings of this research were confirmed

---

[3] It must be mentioned that Guthrie and Bennett did not extract 5 factors.

[4] Anglo-American: Costa & McCrae, 1992; Chinese: McCrae, Costa, & Yik, 1996, McCrae, Zonderman, et al., 1996; Chinese-Mandarin: Yang et al., 1999; Korean: McCrae & Costa, 1997, Piedmont & Chae, 1997; Croatian: Marušić, Bratko, & Eterović, 1996; French: Rolland, Parker, & Stumpf, 1998, Rolland, 1998; Hebrew: Montag & Levin; 1994; Icelandic: Costa, McCrae, & Jónsson, 1999; Japanese: McCrae, Zonderman, et al., 1996; Malay: Mastor, Cooper, & Jin, 1998; Dutch-Flemish: Hoekstra, Ormel, & DeFruyt, 1996, 1997; Philippine: McCrae et al., 1998, Katigbak, Church, & Akamine, 1996; Portuguese: McCrae & Costa, 1997; Taiwanese: Chen & Piedmont, 1999.

by Stumpf (1993), who also used the PRF to replicate the dimensions of the Five-Factor Model in varying contexts (German, Anglo-American, Dutch, and Filipino).

2.3 Summary of Studies on Cross-Cultural Generalizability of the FFM

Using diverse approaches in different linguistic and cross-cultural contexts, it is therefore possible to come up with the same five dimensions as those interpreted as being the Five-Factor Model (Extraversion, Agreeableness, Conscientiousness, Adjustment and Openness) by using different instruments and approaches. Such proof of the generalizability of the Five-Factor Model is obviously an important element in its cross-cultural validity. The similarities that exist between the dimensions extracted in diverse linguistic and cultural contexts is another important element for the analysis of cross-cultural validity. In order to verify similarities between two constructs, it is not enough simply to make a subjective decision based on a visual examination of the results of the factorial analysis, it is also necessary to make cross-cultural comparisons of these constructs and quantify their proximity by means of Tucker's factorial coefficient of congruence (Tucker, 1951) or the coefficients of congruence suggested by McCrae, Zonderman, Costa, Bond, and Paunonen (1996).

Emic-type studies using a psycho-lexical approach focus on detecting dimensions specific to a given linguistic and cultural context and, because of their objectives and methodology, are not really suitable for cross-cultural comparisons based on quantitative indices. As the variables differ across lexical studies, one cannot ask if the factors are defined by the same variables in two different cultures, and congruence coefficients cannot be calculated. Emic studies that do allow for the empirical analysis of similarity indices on the extracted dimensions are relatively rare. Recent research is nevertheless succeeding in overcoming these obstacles (De Raad, Di Blas, & Perugini, 1998; De Raad, Perugini, Hřebíčková, & Szarota, 1998; De Raad, Perugini, & Szirmak, 1997; De Raad et al., 1998; Hofstee et al., 1997; Saucier, Ostendorf, & Peabody, 1998). Results from this research, which compares extracted dimensions in various contexts (German, Anglo-American, Hungarian, Italian, Dutch, Polish, Czech), have clearly established the cross-cultural validity of three dimensions: Extraversion, Agreeableness, and Conscientiousness (Ostendorf, 1990; De Raad, 1998, Di Blas et al. 1999, Saucier et al., 1998, Di Blas et al. 1999, Saucier et al., 1998). The cross-cultural validity of Neuroticism vs. adjustment is, in this type of study, rather poor and perhaps even insufficient (De Raad et al., 1998), whilst the cross-cultural validity of the Openness dimension remains highly problematic (De Raad & VanHeck, 1994; De Raad, Perugini, Hřebíčková, & Szarota, 1998; Di Blas & Forzi, 1999).

Emic studies raise some problems of comparability that are not encountered in etic-type studies, which use inventories created in one linguistic and cultural context and then validated in other cultures. With questionnaires, the variables remain the same across cultures, and consequently one can ask if the factors are defined by the same variables in two different contexts and examine the similarity of two factor structures through congruence coefficients. The NEO-PI-R was used in a series of studies to compare factorial structures obtained in widely diverse linguistic and cultural systems (German, Anglo-American, Hong Kong- and Mandarin Chinese, South Korean, Croatian, French, Hebrew, Icelandic, Italian, Japanese, Dutch-Flemish, Norwegian, Philippine, Portuguese, Russian, Serbian[5]). In all of the studies, the replicability of the model (in the Procrustes solutions) was very clear. Hendriks and Perugini (2000), using the Five-Factor Personality Inventory, extracted the five dimensions in 13 linguistic and cultural contexts (Belgium, England, Germany, Italy, Croatia, Czech Republic, Hungary, Israel, Japan, Slovakia, Spain, The Netherlands, U.S.A.). Furthermore, Paunonen et al. (1996, 2000), who compared the factorial structure of five dimensions obtained using the PRF and NPQ inventories in various linguistic and cultural contexts (Anglo-American, Canadian, Dutch, English, German, Norwegian, Israeli, Philippine), showed an excellent cross-cultural replicability for all of the dimensions of the FFM. Finally, Trull and Geary (1997) used a check-list (Goldberg's 50-BRS, 1992) and confirmatory methods to compare the structures obtained on two samples (Anglo-American and Chinese) and showed excellent cross-cultural generalizability for all five dimensions.

To summarize current results of cross-cultural validity studies on the Five-Factor Model of personality which use quantitative techniques to estimate factorial proximity:

• The cross-cultural validity of the dimensions Extraversion, Agreeableness, Conscientiousness is clearly established by the two approaches: emic-type research based on the psycho-lexical approach and also etic-type studies. Dimensions E and A nevertheless seem (in the Varimax solutions) more sensitive to cultural effects (McCrae Costa, 1997; McCrae et al., 1998; Yang et al., 1999).

• The cross-cultural validity of the dimension Neuroticism is established in all etic-type research, but seems more problematic in studies using emic methods. If we take into consideration the vast number of studies carried out using personality inventories, the cross-cultural validity of the dimension Neuroticism is hardly debatable. In addition to the studies carried out using the NEO-PI-R, the cross-cultural validity of central personality dimensions such as Extraversion and Neuroticism (or Anxiety) has been long and irrefutably established by a vast number of studies carried out using inventories such as the Eysenck Personality Inventory, the Sixteen Personality Factor Questionnaire, and the Minnesota Multiphasic Personality Inventory 2 (see, e.g., Barrett & Eysenck, 1984; Butcher, Lim, & Nezami, 1998; Eysenck, 1983; Eysenck & Eysenck, 1982; Paunonen & Ashton, 1998).

• The validity of the dimension O, which is very clearly established in etic type research, is very much more problematic in emic research. Problems of replication are such that some authors envisage dropping this dimension (De Raad et al., 1998; Di Blas & Perugini, 1999).

If we compare the results of cross-cultural validity studies using the psycho-lexical

[5]Anglo-American: McCrae & Costa, 1997; McCrae et al., 1998; Chinese-Hong Kong: McCrae & Costa, 1997, McCrae, Costa, & Yik, 1996, McCrae, Zonderman, et al., 1996; Chinese-Mandarin: Yang, McCrae, et al., 1999; German: Angleitner & Ostendorf, 2000, McCrae & Costa, 1997; Korean: McCrae & Costa, 1997, Piedmont & Chae, 1997; Croatian: Costa, McCrae, & Jónsson, 1999; French: McCrae et al., 1998, Rolland, Parker, & Stumpf, 1998; Hebrew: McCrae & Costa, 1997; Icelandic: Costa, McCrae, & Jónsson, 1999; Italian: Costa, McCrae, & Jónsson, 1999; Japanese: McCrae & Costa, 1997; Dutch-Flemish: Costa, McCrae, & Jónsson, 1999; Norwegian: Costa, McCrae, & Jónsson, 1999; Philippine: McCrae et al., 1998, Katigbak, Church, & Akamine, 1996; Portuguese: McCrae & Costa, 1997; Russian: Costa, McCrae, & Jónsson, 1999; Serbian: Costa, McCrae, & Jónsson, 1999.

approach on the one hand and the inventory approach on the other, differences on the dimensions Openness and Neuroticism are very noticeable. The lexical hypothesis has allowed for the extraction of the five dimensions (Big Five) in a variety of linguistic contexts (Anglo-American, Czech, German, Dutch, Turkish, etc.), and engendered a number of studies relative to the Five-Factor Model. The major difference in cross-cultural validity between the Big Five (five dimensions extracted using the lexical hypothesis and emic methods) and the FFM (five dimensions extracted using the questionnaire approach and etic methods) concern the dimension Openness, which certain authors discuss dropping, but eventually retain (De Raad, 1998; Di Blas & Perugini, 1999). The hypothesis most frequently put forward to account for the inability to extract Openness in certain linguistic and cultural contexts through psycho-lexical research is that—in certain cultures—adjectives, normally the major focus in taxonomic approaches, cover the domain insufficiently to allow for identification, thus affecting cross-cultural comparisons with Anglo-American taxonomies (De Raad et al., 1998; Di Blas & Forzi; Somer & Goldberg, 1999; Saucier, 1997). Given the importance of the issue at stake, it is essential that cross-cultural generalizability studies, and more notably those focusing on this dimension, be extended to include a greater number of samples from diverse linguistic and cultural contexts. The study which shall now be presented falls into this category.

3. A NEW META-ANALYSIS

Using as a basis findings from previous studies, the present study is intended to verify, on the one hand, the cross-cultural generalizability of the Openness dimension which has proven to be very problematic in emic studies adopting the psycho-lexical perspective and, on the other hand, the cross-cultural generalizability of the dimensions E and A which seem (in varimax solutions) problematic in the operationalization proposed by Costa and McCrae (1992). This study closely follows the lines adopted in previous research that uses the NEO-PI-R to assess the cross-cultural generalizability of the Five-Factor Model (McCrae & Costa, 1997; McCrae et al. 1998). The more specific contribution of the study is twofold. First, it significantly extends cross-cultural comparisons by integrating a larger sample of factorial structures from widely diverse linguistic and cultural contexts which, to date, have not been the object of comparative studies; and second, it analyses the cross-cultural generalizability of the FFM using dimensions derived from Varimax rotations. In most previous research Procrustes rotations toward an Anglo-American reference structure have been made before dimensions were compared. In the present analysis, Varimax solutions are compared to Anglo-American and French reference structures. Varimax rotations may allow for a better expression of cultural specificities than Procrustes rotations (McCrae et al., 1998)—although Varimax rotations may also reflect merely random error in the placement of the axes.

3.1. Approach to the Analysis

Etic method. The cross-cultural generalizability of the dimensions of the FFM was studied from an etic perspective, using an assessment made with the NEO-PI-R. In cross-cultural comparisons, the etic method allows for a constant set of parameters to be maintained (item selection method, items, scoring protocol), hence ensuring that the role of these parameters is, to a certain extent, controlled in terms of similarity of factors studied and thereby enabling the role of cross-cultural differences to be determined with greater precision (Paunonen et al., 1996, p. 341).

Instrument. The instrument used for this study is the NEO-PI-R (Costa & McCrae, 1992). This inventory, which measures the five domains of the FFM and comprises 30 facets (6 facets per domain), has become an instrument of reference (Cattell, 1996). A considerable body of research supports the hypothesis that the FFM covers a very large range of personality traits (McCrae, 1989), and no other major factors have so far been successfully proposed (McCrae & Costa, 1995). Moreover, as it measures 30 specific traits to describe the factors Neuroticism (N), Extraversion (E), Openness (O), Agreeableness (A), and Conscientiousness (C), the NEO-PI-R offers the advantage of rating the personality in both domains and facets (Costa & McCrae, 1995c). This inventory was specially designed to assess the five dimensions of the FFM, and has been the object of more adaptations and validations in diverse linguistic and cultural contexts than any other inventory[6]. The number of facets per domain allows for a finely-nuanced approach to the five dimensions. This inventory is therefore particularly well adapted for cross-cultural studies on the FFM.

Samples. In this study I compare 16 factor structures (Varimax rotations of five dimensions) extracted in diverse contexts using the 30 scales of the NEO-PI-R. Some of these factor structures come from other publications and some have been communicated to me by their authors. The wide diversity of these samples (described in Table 1), which includes a number of different linguistic and cultural contexts, allows a satisfactory examination of the role of linguistic and cultural contexts.

Factor comparison. A number of approaches exist for making empirical examinations of the proximity of two factors (Butcher & Han, 1996). Confirmatory analysis is rarely used, as it has been suggested by several studies that this method presents problems concerning the analysis of the structure of the personality (Church & Burke, 1994; McCrae, Zonderman et al., 1996). The method proposed by McCrae, Zonderman et al. (1996) is the one that is the most often used. These authors suggest using coefficients of congruence to make comparisons between the structure studied and a reference structure, after Procrustes rotation of the structure studied with the reference structure as target. The majority of cross-cultural validity studies compare dimensions derived from Procrustes rotations that target a normative Anglo-American sample (De Raad et al., 1998; Katigbak, Church, & Akamine, 1996; Marušić, Bratko, & Eterović, 1996; McCrae, Costa, & Yik, 1996; McCrae & Costa, 1997; McCrae et al., 1996, 1998; Pau-

---

[6]See Footnotes 4 and 5 and Table 1.

Table 1. Description of Sample and Sources.

Language	N	M	W	Family	Source
Chinese	352	161	191	Sino-Tibetan	McCrae, Costa, & Yik (1996)
Croatian	256	123	133	Indo-European	Marušić, Bratko, & Eterović (1996)
Dutch	621	323	348	Indo-European	Hoekstra, Ormel & DeFruyt (1997)
Estonian	711	225	486	Uralic	Kallasmaa, Allik, Realo & McCrae (2000)
French	801	334	467	Indo-European	Rolland (1998)
Hebrew	935	396	539	Hamito-semitic	Montag & Levin (1994)
Icelandic	337			Indo-European	Costa, McCrae, & Jónsson (P.C. 1999)
Italian	699	349	342	Indo-European	Barbaranelli & Comrey (P.C.. 1999)
Korean	2323	1234	1087	Not classified	McCrae & Costa (1997)
Malay	451	124	327	Austronesian	Mastor (P.C. 1999)
Norwegian	380			Indo-European	Martinsen (P.C. 1999)
Philippine	696	237	445	Austronesian	McCrae et al. (1998)
Portuguese	2000	861	1133	Indo-European	McCrae & Costa (1997)
Russian	350	142	208	Indo-European	Martin et al. (P.C. 1999)
Spanish	216	99	116	Indo-European	Sanz Fernandez (P.C., 1999).
English	1000	500	500	Indo-European	Costa & McCrae (1992)

Note. N = total, M = men, W = women, P.C. = personal communication.

nonen et al., 1996; Piedmont & Chae, 1997; Rolland, Parker, & Stumpf, 1998; Yang et al., 1999). Procrustes rotations define the upper boundary of factor replicability; they are thus good for falsifying the claim of replicability (generalizability) if in fact it is false. But Procrustes rotations make it is necessary to select a linguistic and cultural context as reference structure, and they may mask real cultural differences, as has been pointed out by McCrae and Costa (1997, p. 180). Consequently, in order to allow for a better expression of simple structure, I opted for comparisons of dimensions derived from Varimax rotations, which have a less constraining effect on data. Varimax rotations maximize the variance of loadings and hence allow for the identification of the most salient dimensions in the data, without reference to an external structure as with Procrustes rotations. I thus compiled Varimax results to see if there are discrepancies with the American and French targets and also consider whether one can detect some cultural patterns.

Coefficient of congruence. Given the objective of this study, it is indispensable that a replicability analysis be made of each factor independently of the others. For this purpose there is an index, Tucker's (1951) congruence coefficient (**TCC**), that has been very widely used in this type of study (Barrett, 1986; Haven & ten Berge, 1977). The factorial replication threshold is 0.85 (Haven & ten Berge, 1977).

Table 2. Coefficients of Congruence (TCC) for N, E, O, A, and C (Varimax Rotations) Comparing the French Sample with 15 Other Samples.

Sample	N	E	O	A	C	Mean
Chinese	.87	.87	.95	.88	.96	*.906*
Croatian	.91	.85	.94	.90	.94	*.908*
Dutch	.89	.95	.97	.96	.96	*.946*
Estonian	.90	*.80*	.95	.86	.96	*.894*
Hebrew	.87	.91	.96	.96	.97	*.934*
Icelandic	.93	.94	.95	.98	.96	*.952*
Italian	.88	.87	.96	.90	.98	*.918*
Korean	.89	.88	.96	.91	.96	*.920*
Malay	.87	.89	.86	.94	.94	*.900*
Norwegian	.91	*.82*	.91	.90	.95	*.898*
Philippine	.92	.87	.95	.93	.96	*.926*
Portuguese	.90	.90	.89	.95	.94	*.916*
Russian	.90	.88	.92	.94	.95	*.918*
U.S.	.89	.96	.97	.97	.97	*.952*
Spanish	.91	.91	.93	.89	.95	*.918*
Mean:	*.896*	*.887*	*.938*	*.925*	*.957*	

Note. Across all factors the mean is .92, the median .93, and the minimum .80.

3.2. Results

Descriptions of the samples are presented in Table 1. For each of the five dimensions (N, E, O, A, C) extracted after Varimax rotations in the 16 samples, comparisons (by means of Tucker's congruence coefficient) were carried out between the dimensions extracted in French and Anglo-American cultural contexts on the one hand, and the dimensions extracted in other contexts on the other (Tables 2 and 3).

In order to have a basis for the analysis of congruence coefficients, within the French Normative Sample ($N = 801$), we previously examined the congruence between Varimax structures computed on two subsamples from the total French Normative sample. For these two subsamples, **TCCs** are N = .97, E = .87, O = .96, A = .84, C = .95. These congruence coefficients from the same culture replicate findings in Korean (see McCrae & Costa, 1997; Piedmont & Chae, 1997)[7] and suggest that sources other than cultural differences can produce congruence coefficients < .85.

For the dimensions Neuroticism and Conscientiousness, all cross-cultural comparisons are above the .85 threshold proposed by Haven and ten Berge (1977). Out of the 30 comparisons made on the dimension Conscientiousness, the minimum value

---

[7]For these two different Korean samples, we obtained the following **TCCs**: N = .97, E = .79, O = .97, A = .78, and C = .96.

Table 3. Coefficients of Congruence (TCC) for N, E, O, A, and C (Varimax Rotations) Comparing the U.S. Sample with 15 Other Samples.

Sample	N	E	O	A	C	Mean
Chinese	.97	.93	.92	.94	.97	.946
Croatian	.95	.80	.92	.86	.94	.894
Dutch	.96	.98	.97	.98	.97	.972
Estonian	.95	.90	.95	.92	.96	.936
French	.89	.96	.97	.97	.97	.952
Hebrew	.98	.92	.96	.94	.95	.950
Icelandic	.93	.94	.95	.98	.96	.952
Italian	.92	.80	.94	.81	.98	.890
Korean	.97	.94	.94	.95	.96	.952
Malay	.94	.93	.83	.94	.97	.922
Norwegian	.96	.93	.90	.96	.94	.938
Philippine	.96	.86	.95	.89	.97	.926
Portuguese	.98	.89	.89	.93	.96	.930
Russian	.92	.93	.92	.96	.95	.936
Spanish	.94	.90	.92	.86	.95	.914
Mean:	.948	.907	.929	.926	.960	

Note. Across all factors the mean is .93, the median .94, and the minimum .80.

value is .94; the minimum value is .87 on the dimension Neuroticism. The cross-cultural validity of these two dimensions is clearly established; the structure of these two dimensions which were assessed on the facets retained by McCrae and Costa (1992) is therefore identical in the linguistic and cultural contexts studied here. 28 out of 30 coefficients of congruence reached the .85 threshold on the dimensions Openness and Agreeableness, and just two did not (Openness, Malay/US: .83; Agreeableness, Italy/US: .81). Overall, the cross-cultural validity of these two dimensions is therefore satisfactory, as the facets retained to measure these two dimensions formed similar patterns in the various cultures.

Lastly, 26 out of 30 coefficients reached the .85 threshold on the dimension Extraversion, and only four (French/Estonian: .80; French/Norwegian: .82; U.S./Croatian: .80; U.S./Italian: .80) did not. Here, as in earlier research (Kallasmaa et al., 1999; McCrae et al., 1998), the facets retained by McCrae and Costa in the Extraversion dimension seem somewhat more sensitive to linguistic and cultural context effects. We can detect these facets by making a detailed analysis of the loading of facets in the dimensions of Extraversion and Agreeableness on factors E and A. We notice that certain facets show loadings that are the reverse of what one would expect (Table 4). If we limit ourselves to the most obvious phenomena, E3: Assertiveness contributes in 8 out of the 16 cultural contexts analyzed here (8/16), not to the Extraversion factor as would be expected, but—with negative loadings—to the Agreeable-

Table 4. Frequency with which Extraversion and Agreeableness Facets
Load Chiefly on the Other Factor.

Extraversion facet	Frequency	Agreeableness facet	Frequency
E1: Warmth	0/16	A1: Trust	5/16
E2: Gregariousness	0/16	A2: Straightforwardness	0/16
E3: Assertiveness	8/16	A3: Altruism	6/16
E4: Activity	3/16	A4: Compliance	0/16
E5: Excitement	5/16	A5: Modesty	3/16
E6: Positive	0/16	A6: Tender-Mindedness	2/16

ness factor. In the cultural contexts concerned (Croatian, Spanish, French, Icelandic, Italian, Dutch, Philippine, Portuguese) Assertiveness therefore contributes more to the negative pole (Hostility-Antagonism) of the dimension Agreeableness than to the positive pole of Extraversion. Moreover, A3: Altruism, a component of Agreeableness in the model proposed by the authors, contributes more to the Extraversion factor in 6 contexts (Croatian, Philippine, Hebrew, Italian, Malay, Portuguese). Taking into account the links that are known to exist between the dimensions A and E (Kallasmaa et al., 1999; McCrae & Costa, 1989; McCrae et al., 1998; Wiggins, 1979) the origin of these discrepancies can at least be partially accounted for by the Varimax rotations, which are inappropriate for dimensions that are not orthogonal (Gurtman, 1997). However, they probably also reflect real cultural differences based on cultural/national emphasis on values.

4. DISCUSSION AND CONCLUSIONS

If we compare these results to findings produced in the psycho-lexical line of research, the divergence is clearly evident. In emic-type studies, the cross-cultural validity of the Neuroticism dimension is poor and the validity of the Openness dimension is even more problematic. The results obtained from an etic-type perspective following the lines of earlier research of a similar nature illustrate a strongly marked cross-cultural replicability for these two dimensions. Although these differences may be partially attributed to the radical differences in objectives and methodology of the two approaches, these results do lead us to ponder, like Church and Lonner, upon the validity of the assumptions underlying the lexical approach. For these authors: "Some individual differences may not be encoded in the natural language and the structure of the personality lexicon may not be identical to the structure of personality" (Church & Lonner, 1998, p. 36). This point of view is also expressed by McCrae and Costa, for whom "It is simply not the case that all personality traits are encoded as adjectives. . . . Cultures select a limited range from among the spectrum of personality traits to encode in their lexicon, and they may select differently. Languages differ not only in the precise trait terms they include (as every translator knows) but more broadly in the aspects of personality their vocabularies emphasize (Angleitner, Ostendorf, & John, 1990). Lexical studies thus confound differences in personality structure with differences in personality language" (McCrae & Costa, 1997, p. 510). It may still be a little too early for this type of conclusion. It is indeed not impossible that problematic results like these are partly due to the lexical materials, usually adjectives, that are used in psycho-lexical studies. The Anglo-American language, and also Dutch and German for example (and many others) seem to provide a sufficient set of adjectives that describe the Intellect (Openness) dimension, whereas other languages such as Italian (Di Blas & Forzi, 1999) and Hungarian (Szirmak & De Raad, 1994), don't seem to. Neither is it impossible, as suggested by Di Blas and Forzi (1999, pp. 462, 477), that it is due to the nouns and not the adjectives which, in certain types of languages, can be used for description and hence the extraction of this dimension.[8]

If the results of our study are added to those obtained in earlier research using the NEO-PI-R to assess the FFM (e.g., Angleitner & Ostendorf, 2000; Costa, McCrae, & Jónsson, 1999; McCrae & Costa, 1997; McCrae, Costa, del Pilar, Rolland, & Parker 1998; Katigbak et al., 2000), the cross-cultural generalizability of the dimensions N (Neuroticism), O (Openness), and C (Conscientiousness) is clearly evident. Our findings are all the more conclusive since they were obtained through the comparison of factors extracted after Varimax rotations (allowing for better expression of cultural specificities than the Procrustes rotation method) and comparisons of widely diverse cultures. Certain facets of the dimensions E (Extraversion) and A (Agreeableness), which both relate to the interpersonal sphere, seem to be more sensitive to cultural context, but a circumplex-type model allows for a better description of the structure of these two domains (Gurtman, 1997; McCrae et al., 1998; Wiggins, 1979). All of these finding support the conclusions already formulated by McCrae et al.: "We can assert that personality, as measured by the NEO-PI-R, can be characterized in every culture so far examined in terms of N, O, C factors plus the interpersonal circumplex; and Procrustes rotations shows that the circumplex can always be interpreted in terms of E and A factors" (McCrae et al. 1998, p. 182).

D'Andrade (1965), in a frequently quoted article, claimed that dimensions extracted from descriptions of self or others are only artifacts that reflect the structure of the language. Findings from cross-cultural validity studies show that the structure of the FFM can be replicated in very different languages. It is very unlikely that the structures of the languages in which this structure has been replicated are similar.

The Five-Factor Model of personality therefore shows good cross-cultural replicability, but this obviously doesn't signify that the model offers optimal representation in all cultures. Dimensions that are seemingly specific have, in fact, been described in a number of cultures and some of them do not appear to correspond directly to the dimensions of the FFM (Cheung & Leung, 1998; Church et al., 1997; Guanzon-Lapeña et al., 1998; Yang & Bond, 1990; Yik & Bond, 1993; Katigbak et al., 1996). It is essential to develop studies aimed at detecting specific dimensions, however such studies do not always bring the expected results. Guanzon-Lapena et al. (1998), for example, have drawn up a report on a considerable number of studies carried out in the Philippines, a country which has developed a long research tradition in indigenous psychology in the Tagalog language, and conclude that "Each of the Big Five domains is represented by one or more dimensions from each of the indigenous instruments.

---

[8]In some languages, nouns and adjectives may not be distinguishable.

None of the indigenous dimensions is so culturally unique that it is unrecognizable to non-Filipinos, or that it cannot be subsumed at least conceptually, under the Big Five dimensions. In other words, it appears that the general nature and range of personality concepts identified and assessed by these indigenous approaches can be encompassed by the western version of the Big Five model of personality" (p. 265).

Other structural models have been and will undoubtedly be developed, but in the meantime the FFM has proven its cross-cultural generalizability and its utility in a number of fields that are important in human behavior. Hence, its predictive and explanatory potential continues to be successfully exploited in fields such as job performance (Barrick & Mount, 1999; Salgado, 1997; 1999), clinical and psychiatric psychology (Matthews et al., 1998; O'Connor & Dyce, 2002; Yang et al., 1999, Yang et al., 2002), health (Lemos-Giraldez & Fidalgo-Aliste, 1997), and education and political psychology (Blickle, 1996; DeFruyt & Mervielde, 1996; De Raad & Schouwenbourg, 1996; Riemann et al., 1993). Finally, validity studies that extend beyond the internal structure of the NEO-PI-R are needed to discover if various links in the nomological network of the FFM are likewise generalizable.

REFERENCES

Almagor, M., Tellegen, A, & Waller, N. G. (1995). The Big-Seven model: A cross-cultural replication and further exploration of the basic dimensions of natural language trait-descriptors. *Journal of Personality and Social Psychology, 69*, 300-307.

Angleitner, A., Ostendorf, F., & John, O. P. (1990). Towards a taxonomy of personality terms in German: A psycho-lexical study. *European Journal of Personality, 4*, 89-118.

Angleitner, A., & Ostendorf, F. (2000, July). A comparison of German speaking countries (Austria, Former East and West Germany, and Switzerland). In J. Allik and R. R. McCrae (Chairs), *Personality and culture: The Five-Factor Theory perspective*. Symposium presented at the XXVII International Congress of Psychology, Stockholm, Sweden.

Barrett, P. (1986). Factor comparison: An examination of three methods. *Personality and Individual Differences, 7*, 32-340.

Barrett, P., & Eysenck, S. B. G. (1984). The assessment of personality factors across 25 countries. *Personality and Individual Differences, 5*, 615-632.

Barrick, M. R., & Mount, M. K. (1999, April). *The FFM personality dimensions and job performance: A meta-analysis of meta-analyses*. Paper presented at the 14th Annual Conference of the Society for Industrial and Organizational Psychology, Atlanta, Georgia.

Benet-Martínez, V., & John, O. P. (1998). "Los Cinco Grandes" across cultures and ethnic groups: Multitrait-multimethod analyses of the Big Five in Spanish and English. *Journal of Personality and Social Psychology, 75*, 729-750.

Benet-Martínez, V. & John, O. P. (2000). Towards the development of quasi-indigenous personality constructs. *American Behavioral Scientist, 44*, 141-157.

Benet-Martínez, V. & Waller, N. G. (1997). Further evidence of the cross-cultural generality of the Big-Seven model: Indigenous and imported Spanish personality constructs. *Journal of Personality, 65*, 567-598.

Berry, J. W. (1969). On cross-cultural comparability. *International Journal of Psychology, 4*, 119-128.

Blickle, G. (1996). Personality traits, learning strategies, and performance. *European Journal of Personality, 10*, 337-352.

Block, J. (1995a). A contrarian view of the five-factor approach to personality description. *Psychlogical Bulletin, 117*, 187-215.

Block, J. (1995b). Going beyond the five factors given: Rejoinder to Costa and McCrae (1995) and Goldberg and Saucier (1995). *Psychological Bulletin, 117*, 226-229.

Block, J. (2001). Millenial contrarianism: The five-factor approach to personality description five years later. *Journal of Research in Personality, 35*, 98-107.

Bond, M. H. (1979). Dimensions of personality in perceiving peers: Cross-cultural comparisons of Hong-Kong, Japanese, American and Filipino university students. *International Journal of Psychology, 14,* 47-56.

Bond, M. H., Nakazato, H., & Shiraishi, D. (1975). Universality and distinctiveness in dimensions of Japanese person perception. *Journal of Cross-Cultural Psychology, 6,* 346-357.

Borkenau, P., & Ostendorf, F. (1990). Comparing exploratory and confirmatory analysis: A study on the 5-factor model of personality. *Personality and Individual Differences, 11,* 515-524.

Botwin, M. D., & Buss, D. M. (1989). Structure of act-report data: is the Five-Factor Model of personality recaptured? *Journal of Personality and Social Psychology, 56,* 988-1001.

Brand, C. R. (1995). How many dimensions of personality? The "Big Five", the "Gigantic 3" or the "Comprehensive 6"? *Psychologica Belgica, 34,* 257-273.

Briggs, S. R. (1992). Assessing the Five-Factor Model of personality description. *Journal of Personality, 60,* 253-293.

Butcher, J. N., & Han. K. (1996). Methods for establishing cross-cultural equivalence. In J. N. Butcher (Ed.), *International adaptations of the MMPI-2: Research and clinical applications* (pp.43-63). Minneapolis: University of Minnesota Press.

Butcher, J. N., Lim. J., & Nezami, E. (1998). Objective study of abnormal psychology in cross-cultural settings: The MMPI-2. *Journal of Cross-Cultural Psychology, 29,* 189-211.

Caprara, G.V., Barbaranelli, C., Borgogni, L., & Perugini, M. (1993). The "Big Five Questionnaire": A new questionnaire to assess the Five-Factor Model. *Personality and Individual Differences, 15,* 281-288.

Caprara, G. V., & Perugini, M. (1994). Personality described by adjectives: Generalizability of the Big Five to the Italian lexical context. *European Journal of Personality, 8,* 357-369.

Cattell, H. E. P. (1996). The original Big Five: A historical perspective. *European Review of Applied Psychology, 46,* 5-14.

Chen, M. C., & Piedmont, R. L. (1999). Development and validation of the NEO-PI-R for a Taiwanese sample. In T. Sugiman, M. Karasawa, J.H. Liu, & C. Ward (Eds.), *Progress in Asian Psychology* (Vol. 2, pp. 105-119). Seoul: Kyoyook-Kwahak-Sa.

Cheung, F. M., & Leung, K. (1998). Indigenous personality measures: Chinese examples. *Journal of Cross-Cultural Psychology, 29,* 233-248.

Church, A. T., & Burke, P .J. (1994). Exploratory and confirmatory tests of the Big Five and Tellegen's three and four dimensional models. *Journal of Personality and Social Psychology, 66,* 93-114.

Church, A. T., & Lonner, W. J. (1998). The cross-cultural perspective in the study of personality: Rationale and current research. *Journal of Cross-Cultural Psychology, 29,* 32-62

Church, A .T., Reyes, J. A. S., Katigbak, M. S., & Grimm, S. D. (1997). Filipino personality structure and the Big Five model: A lexical approach. *Journal of Personality, 65,* 477-528.

Costa, P. T., Jr., & McCrae, R. R. (1988). Personality in adulthood: A six-year longitudinal study of self reports and spouse ratings on the NEO-PI. *Journal of Personality and Social Psychology, 54,* 853-863.

Costa, P. T., Jr., & McCrae, R. R. (1992). *Revised NEO Personality Inventory (NEO-PI-R) and NEO Five-Factor Inventory (NEO-FFI) professional manual.* Odessa, FL: Psychological Assessment Resources.

Costa, P. T., Jr., & McCrae, R. R. (1992). Four ways five factors are basic. *Personality and Individual Differences, 13,* 653-665.

Costa, P. T., Jr., & McCrae, R. R. (1994). Stability and change in personality from adolescence through adulthood. In C. F. Havelson, G. A. Kohnstamm, & R. P. Martin (Eds.), *The developing structure of temperament and personality from infancy to adulthood* (pp. 139-150). Hillsdale, NJ: Erlbaum.

Costa, P. T., Jr., & McCrae, R. R. (1995a). Solid grounds in the wetlands of personality: A reply to Block. *Psychological Bulletin, 117,* 216-220.

Costa, P. T., Jr., & McCrae, R. R. (1995b). Primary traits of Eysenck's PEN system: Three- and five-factor solutions. *Journal of Personality and Social Psychology, 69,* 308-317.

Costa, P. T. Jr., & McCrae, R. R. (1995c). Domains and facets: Hierarchical personality assessment using the Revised NEO Personality Inventory. *Journal of Personality Assessment, 64,* 21-50.

Costa, P. T., Jr., McCrae, R. R., & Jónsson, F. H. (1999, July) *A new measure of personality in the Old World: The NEO-PI-R in Europe.* Paper presented at the XVth International Congress of the International Association for the Cross-Cultural Psychology, Graz, Austria.

D'Andrade, R. B. (1965). Trait psychology and componential analysis. *American Anthropologist, 67,* 215-228

Deary, I. J., & Matthews, G. (1993). Traits are alive and well. *The Psychologist, 6,* 299-311.

De Fruyt, F., & Mervielde, I. (1996). Personality and interests as predictors of educational streaming and achievement. *European Journal of Personality, 10,* 405-426.

De Fruyt F., Mervielde, I., Hoekstra, H. A., & Rolland, J. P. (2000). Assessing adolescents' personality with the NEO-PI-R. *Assessment, 7,* 329-346.

De Raad, B. (1992). The replicability of the Big Five personality dimensions in three word-classes of the Dutch language. *European Journal of Personality, 6,* 15-29.

De Raad, B., Di Blas, L., & Perugini, M. (1998). Two independently constructed Italian trait taxonomies: Comparisons within Italian, and between Italian and Germanic languages. *European Journal of Personality, 12,* 19-41.

De Raad, B., Perugini, M., & Szirmak, Z. (1997). In pursuit of a cross-linguistic reference structure of personality traits: Comparisons between five languages. *European Journal of Personality, 11,* 167-185.

De Raad, B., Perugini, M., Hřebíčková M., & Szarota, P. (1998). Lingua franca of personality: Taxonomies and structures based on the psycho-lexical approach. *Journal of Cross-Cultural Psychology, 29,* 212-232.

De Raad, B., & Schouwenburg, H. C. (1996). Personality in learning and education. *European Journal of Personality, 10,* 303-336.

De Raad, B., & Van Heck, G. L. (1994). The Fifth of the Big Five: Editorial [Special Issue]. *European Journal of Personality, 8,* 225.

Di Blas, L., & Forzi, M. (1998). An alternative taxonomic study of personality descriptors in the Italian language. *European Journal of Personality, 12,* 75-101.

Di Blas, L., & Forzi, M. (1999). Refining a descriptive structure of personality attributes in the Italian language: The abridged Big Three circumplex structure. *Journal of Personality and Social Psychology, 76,* 451-481.

Digman, J. M. (1990). Personality structure: Emergence of the Five-Factor Model. *Annual Review of Psychology, 41,* 417-440.

Digman, J. M., & Shmelyov, A. S. (1996). The structure of temperament and personality in Russian children. *Journal of Personality and Social Psychology, 71,* 341-351.

Digman, J. M., & Takemoto-Chock, N. (1981). Factors in the natural language of personality: Re-analysis and comparison of six major studies. *Multivariate Behavioral Research, 16,* 149-170.

Eysenck, H. J. (1991). Dimensions of personality: 16, 5 or 3? Criteria for a taxonomic paradigm. *Personality and Individual Differences, 12,* 773-790.

Eysenck, H. J. (1992). Four ways five factors are *not* basic. *Personality and Individual Differences, 13,* 667-673.

Eysenck, H .J., & Eysenck, S. B. G. (1982). Recent advances in the cross-cultural study of personality. In C. D. Spielberger & J. N. Butcher (Eds.). *Advances in personality assessment* (pp. 42-69). Hillsdale, NJ: Erlbaum.

Eysenck, S. B. G. (1983). One approach to cross-cultural studies of personality. *Australian Journal of Personality, 35,* 381-391.

Goldberg, L. R. (1981). Language and individual differences: The search for universals in personality lexicons. In L. Wheeler (Ed.). *Review of personality and social psychology* (Vol. 2, pp. 141-165). Beverly Hills, CA: Sage.

Goldberg, L. R. (1990). An alternative "description of personality": the Big Five factor structure. *Journal of Personality and Social Psychology, 59,* 11216-1229

Goldberg, L. R. (1992). The development of markers for the Big-Five factor structure. *Psychological Assessment, 4,* 26-42.

Goldberg, L. R. (1993). The structure of phenotypic traits. *American Psychologist, 48,* 26-34.

Goldberg, L.R. (1995). What the hell took so long? Donald Fiske and the Big Five structure. In P. E. Shrout & S. T. Fiske (Eds.). *Personality research, methods and theory: A festschrift honoring Donald W. Fiske* (pp. 29-43). Hillsdale, NJ: Erlbaum.

Goldberg, L. R., & Saucier, G. (1995). So what do you propose we use instead? A reply to Block. *Psychological Bulletin, 117,* 221-225.

Guanzon-Lapeña, M. A., Church, A. T., Carlota, A. J., & Katigbak, M. S. (1998). Indigenous personality measures: Philippine examples. *Journal of Cross-Cultural Psychology, 29,* 249-266.

Gurtman, M.B. (1997). Studying personality traits: The circular way. In R. Plutchik & H. R. Conte (Eds.). *Circumplex models of personality and emotions* (pp. 81-102). Washington, DC: American Psychological Association.

Guthrie, G. M., & Bennett, A. B. (1971). Cultural differences in implicit personality theory. *International Journal of Psychology, 6*, 305-312.

Haven, S., & ten Berge, J. M. F. (1977). *Tucker's coefficient of congruence as a measure of factorial invariance: An empirical study.* Unpublished manuscript. University of Groningen.

Heaven, P. C. L., Connors, C. R., & Stones, C. R. (1994). Three or five personality dimensions? An analysis of natural language terms in two cultures. *Personality and Individual Differences, 17*, 181-190.

Hendriks, A. A. J., & Perugini, M. (2000, July). *A psycho-lexical structure of personality: Cross-cultural generalizability across 13 countries of the Five-Factor Personality Inventory.* Paper presented at the 10th European Conference on Personality, Krakow, Poland.

Hoekstra, H. A., Ormel, J., & De Fruyt, F. (1996). *Handleiding NEO Persoonlijkheids-vragenlijsten NEO-PI-R en NEO-FFI [Manual for NEO Personality Inventories NEO-PI-R and NEO-FFI].* Lisse, The Netherlands: Swets & Zeitlinger.

Hoekstra, H.A., Ormel, J., & De Fruyt, F. (1997). *NEO-Persoonlijkheidsvragenlijsten.* Lisse: Swets & Zeitlinger Publishers.

Hofstee, W. K. B., De Raad, B., & Goldberg, L. R. (1992). Integration of the Big Five and circumplex approaches to trait structure. *Journal of Personality and Social Psychology, 63*, 146-163.

Hofstee, W. K. B., Kiers, H. A. L., De Raad, B., Goldberg, L. R., & Ostendorf, F. (1997). Comparisons of the Big Five structures of personality in Dutch, English, and German. *European Journal of Personality, 11*, 15-31.

Hřebíčková, M. (1995). *The structural model of personality based on the lexical analysis: A Czech replication of the Five-Factor Model based on a comprehensive taxonomy of personality-descriptive adjectives.* Unpublished manuscript, Institute of Psychology, Academy of Sciences of the Czech Republic, Brno.

Isaka, H. (1990). Factor analysis of traits in everyday Japanese language. *Personality and Individual Differences, 11*, 115-124.

Jackson, D. N. (1984). *Personality Research Form manual.* Port Huron, MI: Research Psychologists Press.

John, O. P. (1990). The Big Five factor taxonomy: dimensions of personality in the natural language and in questionnaires. In L. A. Pervin (Ed.), *Handbook of personality: Theory and research* (pp. 66-100). New York: Guilford Press.

John, O. P., Angleitner, A., & Ostendorf, F. (1988). The lexical approach to personality: A historical review of trait taxonomic research. *European Journal of Personality, 2*, 171-203.

John, O. P., Goldberg, L., & Angleitner, A. (1984). Better than the alphabet: Taxonomies of personality descriptive terms in English, Dutch and German. In H. Bonarius, G. Van Heck, & N. Smith (Eds.). *Personality psychology in Europe: Vol.1. Theoretical and empirical developments* (pp. 88-100). Tilburg, the Netherlands: Tilburg University Press.

Juni, S. (1996). Review of the Revised NEO Personality Inventory. In J.C. Conoley & J.C. Impara (Eds.). *12th Mental Measurement Yearbook* (pp. 863-868). Lincoln, NB: University of Nebraska Press.

Kallasmaa, T., Allik, J., Realo, A., & McCrae, R. R. (1999). *The structure and properties of the Estonian-language NEO-PI-R.* Unpublished manuscript. University of Tartu.

Kallasmaa, T., Allik, J., Realo, A., & McCrae, R. R. (2000). The Estonian version of the NEO-PI-R: An examination of universal and culture-specific aspects of the Five-Factor Model. *European Journal of Personality, 14*, 265-278.

Katigbak, M. S., Church, A. T., Guanzon-Lapena, M. A., Carlota, A. J., & del Pilar, G. (2000, July). Indigenous Philippine dimensions and the Five-Factor Model. In J. Allik and R. R. McCrae (Chairs), *Personality and culture: The Five-Factor Theory perspective.* Symposium presented at the XXVII International Congress of Psychology, Stockholm, Sweden.

Katigbak, M. S., Church, A. T., & Akamine, T. X. (1996). Cross-cultural generalizability of personality dimensions: Relating indigenous and imported dimensions in two cultures. *Journal of Personality and Social Psychology, 70*, 1, 99-114.

King, J. E., & Figueredo, A. J. (1997). The Five-Factor Model plus dominance in chimpanzee personality. *Journal of Research in Personality, 31*, 257-271.

Knežević, G., Radović, B., & Opacić, G. (1997). *An evaluation of the "Big Five Model" of personality through an analysis of the NEO-PI-R Personality Inventory.* Unpublished manuscript. University of Belgrad.

Lemos-Giráldez, S., & Fidalgo-Aliste, A. M. (1997). Personality dispositions and health-related habits and attitudes: A cross-sectional study. *European Journal of Personality, 11*, 197-209.

Loevinger, J. (1994). Has psychology lost its conscience? *Journal of Personality Assessment, 62*, 2-8.

Marušić, I., Bratko, D., & Eterović, H. (1996). A contribution to the cross-cultural replicability of the five-factor personality model. *Review of Psychology, 3*, 23-35.

Markus, H. R., & Kitayama, S. (1991). Culture and the self: Implications for cognition, emotion and motivation. *Psychological Review, 98*, 224-253.

Markus, H. R., & Kitayama, S. (1998). The cultural psychology of personality. *Journal of Cross-Cultural Psycholog, 29*, 63-87.

Martin, T. A., Draguns, J. G., Oryol, V. E., Senin, I. G., Rukavishnikov, A. A., & Klotz, M. L. (1997, August). *Development of a Russian-language NEO-PI-R.* Paper presented at the Annual Convention of the American Psychological Association, Chicago, IL.

Mastor , H. R., Cooper, M., & Jin, P. (1998). *Malay personality structure: An etic approach using the Big Five model.* Paper presented at the XIVth International Congress of the International Association for the Cross-Cultural Psychology, Bellingham, WA.

Matthews, G., Saklofske, D. H., Costa, P. T., Jr., Deary, I. J., & Zeidner, M. (1998). Dimensional models of personality: A framework for systematic clinical assessment. *European Journal of Psychological Assessment, 14*, 36-49.

McAdams, D. P. (1992). The Five-Factor Model of personality: A critical appraisal. *Journal of Personality, 60*, 329-361.

McCrae, R. R. (1989). Why I advocate the Five-Factor Model: Joint analyses of the NEO-PI and other instruments. In D. M. Buss & N. Cantor (Eds.), *Personality psychology: Recent trends and emerging directions* (pp. 237-245). New York: Springer-Verlag.

McCrae, R. R. (1994). Openness to experience: Expanding the boundaries of Factor V. *European Journal of Personality, 8*, 251-272.

McCrae, R. R., & Costa, P. T., Jr., (1987). Validation of the Five-Factor Model of personality across instruments and observers. *Journal of Personality and Social Psychology, 52*, 81-90.

McCrae, R. R., & Costa, P. T., Jr., (1989). The structure of interpersonal traits: Wiggins's circumplex and the Five-Factor Model. *Journal of Personality and Social Psychology, 56*, 586-595.

McCrae, R. R., & Costa, P. T., Jr. (1995). Positive and negative valence within the Five-Factor Model. *Journal of Research in Personality, 29*, 443-460.

McCrae, R. R., & Costa, P. T., Jr., (1997). Personality trait structure as a human universal. *American Psychologist, 52*, 509-516.

McCrae, R R., & John, O. P. (1992). An introduction to the Five-Factor Model and its applications. *Journal of Personality, 60*, 175-215

McCrae, R. R., Costa, P. T., Jr., del Pilar, G., Rolland, J. P. & Parker, W. D. (1998). Cross-cultural assessment of the Five-Factor Model: The Revised NEO Personality Inventory. *Journal of Cross-Cultural Psychology, 29*, 171-188.

McCrae, R. R., Costa, P. T., Jr., & Yik, M. S. M. (1996). Universal aspects of the Chinese personality structure. In M. H. Bond (Ed.) *The handbook of Chinese psychology.* (pp. 190-207). Hong Kong: Oxford University Press.

McCrae, R. R., Zonderman, A. B., Costa, P. T., Jr., Bond, M. H., & Paunonen, S. V. (1996). Evaluating replicability of factors in the Revised NEO Personality Inventory: Confirmatory factor analysis versus Procrustes rotation. *Journal of Personality and Social Psychology, 70*, 552-566.

Mervielde, I., & De Fruyt, F. (2000). The "Big Five" personality factors as a model of structure of children's peer nominations. *European Journal of Personality, 14*, 91-106.

Mlacić, B. (2000, July). *Taxonomy and structure of Croatian personality-descriptive adjectives.* Paper presented at the 10th European Conference on Personality, Krakow, Poland.

Montag, I., & Levin, J. (1994). The five-factor personality model in applied settings. *European Journal of Personality, 8*, 1-11.

Norman, W. T. (1963). Towards an adequate taxonomy of personality attributes: Replicated factor structure in peer nomination personality ratings. *Journal of Abnormal and Social Psychology, 66*, 574-583.

O'Connor, B. P., & Dyce, J. A. (2002). Tests of general and specific models of personality disorder configuration. in P. T. Costa, Jr., & T. A. Widiger (Eds.), *Personality disorders and the Five-Factor Model of personality* (2nd. ed., pp. 223-246). Washington, DC: American Psychological Association.

Ostendorf, F. (1990). *Sprache und persönlichkeitsstruktur: Zur validität des Fünf-Faktoren-Modells der Persönlichkeit* [Language and personality structure: Validity of the Five-Factor Model of personality]. Regensburg, Germany: Roderer.

Paunonen, S. V., & Ashton, M. C. (1998). The structured assessment of personality across cultures. *Journal of Cross-Cultural Psychology, 29*, 150-170.

Paunonen, S. V., Jackson, D. N., & Keinonen, M. (1990). The structured non-verbal assessment of personality. *Journal of Personality, 58*, 481-502.

Paunonen, S. V., Jackson, D. N., Trzebinski, J., & Fosterling, F. (1992). Personality structure across cultures: A multimethod evaluation. *Journal of Personality and Social Psychology, 62*, 447-456.

Paunonen, S. V., Keikonnen, M., Trzebinski, J., Fosterling, F., Grishenko-Rose, N., Kouuznetsova, L., & Chan, D. W. (1996). The structure of personality in six cultures. *Journal of Cross-Cultural Psychology, 27*, 339-353.

Paunonen, S. V., Zeidner, M., Engvik, H. A., Oosterveld, P., & Maliphant, R. (2000). The non-verbal assessment of personality in five cultures. *Journal of Cross-Cultural Psychology, 31*, 220-239.

Peabody, D., & Goldberg, L. R. (1989). Some determinants of factor structures from personality trait-descriptors. *Journal of Personality and Social Psychology, 57*, 552-567.

Perugini, M., & Leone, L. (1996). Construction and validation of a short adjective checklist to measure the Big Five. *European Journal of Psychological Assessment, 12*, 33-42.

Pervin, L.A. (1994). A critical appraisal of current trait theory. *Psychological Inquiry, 5*, 552-567.

Piedmont, R .L., & Chae, J. H. (1997). Cross-cultural generalizability of the Five-Factor Model of personality: Development and validation of the NEO-PI-R for Koreans. *Journal of Cross-Cultural Psychology, 28*, 131-155.

Plutchik, R., & Conte, H. R. (Eds.). (1997). *Circumplex models of personality and emotions.* Washington, DC: American Psychological Association.

Pulver, A., Allik, J., Pulkkinen, L. & Hämäläinen, M. (1995). A Big Five personality inventory in two non-Indo-European languages. *European Journal of Personality, 9*, 109-124.

Riemann, R., Grubich, C., Hempel, S., Mergl, S., & Richter, M. (1993). Personality and attitudes towards current political topics. *Personality and Individual Differences, 15*, 313-321.

Rolland, J. P. (1993). Validité de construct de « marqueurs » des dimensions de personnalité du modèle en cinq facteurs [Construct validity of FFM dimensions markers]. *European Review of Applied Psychology, 43*, 317-337.

Rolland, J. P. (1996). Décrire la personnalité: La structure de second-ordre dans la perspective des Big Five [Describing personality: The second-order structure from Big Five perspective]. *Pratiques Psychologiques, 4*, 35-47.

Rolland, J. P. (1998). *Manuel de l'inventaire NEO-PI-R (Adaptation française)* [Manual of the NEO-PI-R, French adaptation]. Paris: ECPA.

Rolland, J. P. (2001). Validité interculturelle du modèle de personnalité en cinq facteurs. *Psychologie Française, 46*, 231-249.

Rolland, J. P., Parker, W. D., & Stumpf, H. (1998). A psychometric examination of the French translation of the NEO-PI-R and NEO-FFI. *Journal of Personality Assessment, 71*, 269-291.

Salgado, J. F. (1997). The Five-Factor Model of personality and job performance in the European Community. *Journal of Applied Psychology, 82*, 30-43.

Salgado, J. F. (1999, April). *Predicting job performance using personality measures based explicitly on the FFM.* Paper presented at the 14th Annual Conference of the Society for Industrial and Organizational Psychology, Atlanta, Georgia.

Saucier, G. (1997). Effects of variable selection on the factor structure of person descriptors. *Journal of Personality and Social Psychology, 73*, 1296-1035.

Saucier, G., Ostendorf, F., & Peabody, D. (2001). The non-evaluative circumplex of personality adjectives. *Journal of Personality, 69*, 537-582.

Somer, O., & Goldberg, L. R. (1999). The structure of Turkish trait-descriptive adjectives. *Journal of Personality and Social Psychology, 76*, 431-450.

Szirmak, Z., & De Raad, B. (1994). Taxonomy and structure of Hungarian personality traits. *European Journal of Personality, 8*, 95-118.

Stumpf, H. (1993). The factor structure of the Personality Research Form: A cross-national evaluation. *Journal of Personality, 61*, 27-48.

Trull, T. J., & Geary, D. C. (1997). Comparison of the Big Five factor structure across samples of Chinese and American adults. *Journal of Personality Assessment, 69*, 324-341.

Tucker, L. J. (1951). *A method for synthesis of factor analytic studies.* (Personnel Research Selection, Report No. 984). Washington, DC: Department of the Army.

Tupes, E. C., & Christal, R. E. (1992). Recurrent personality factors based on trait ratings. *Journal of Personality, 60*, 225-251. (Original work published 1961)

Weiss, A., King, J. E., & Figueiredo, A. J. (2000). The heritability of personality traits in chimpanzees (Pan troglodytes). *Behavior Genetics, 30*, 213-221.

Wiggins, J. S. (1979). A psychological taxonomy of trait-descriptive terms: The interpersonal domain. *Journal of Personality and Social Psychology, 37*, 395-412.

Wiggins, J. S., & Trapnell, P. D. (1997). Personality structure: The return of the Big Five. In R. Hogan, J. A. Johnson, & S. R. Briggs (Eds.), *Handbook of personality psychology* (pp. 737-765). San Diego, CA: Academic Press.

Yang, K. S., & Bond, M. H. (1990). Exploring implicit personality theories with indigenous or imported constructs: The Chinese case. *Journal of Personality and Social Psychology, 58*, 1087-1095.

Yang, J., McCrae, R. R., Costa, P. T., Jr., Dai, X., Yao, S., Cai, T., & Gao, B. (1999). Cross-cultural personality assessment in psychiatric populations: The NEO-PI-R in The People's Republic of China. *Psychological Assessment, 11*, 359-368.

Yang, J., Dai, X., Yao, S., Cai, T., Gao, B., McCrae, R. R., & Costa, P. T., Jr. (2002). Personality disorders and the Five-Factor Model of personality in Chinese psychiatric patients. In P.T. Costa, Jr., & T. A. Widiger (Eds.), *Personality disorders and the Five-Factor Model of personality* (2nd ed., pp. 215-221). Washington, DC: American Psychological Association.

Yik, M. S. M., & Bond, M. H. (1993). Exploring the dimensions of person perception with indigenous or imported constructs: Creating a culturally balanced scale. *International Journal of Psychology, 28*, 75-95.

AUTHOR NOTE

I would like to express my gratitude to all those researchers who generously agreed to send me their data, and also to those whose published data I have used: C. Ahn, J. Allik, C. Barbaranelli, D. Bratko, M. H. Bond, A. Comrey, P. T. Costa, F. De Fruyt, G. del Pilar, H. Eterović, H. A. Hoekstra, F. Jónsson, T. Kallasmaa, K. Lee, J. Levin, T. A. Martin, Ø. Martinsen, I. Marušić, K. A. Mastor, R. R. McCrae, I. Montag, J. Ormel, W. D. Parker, M. Pedroso de Lima, A. Realo, J. Sanz Fernandez, A. Simões, and M. S. M. Yik. A version of this chapter (in French) appeared as Rolland (2001). Email: Jean-Pierre.Rolland@u-paris10.fr

EXPLORING THE SOURCES OF VARIATIONS IN THE STRUCTURE OF PERSONALITY TRAITS ACROSS CULTURES

KENN KONSTABEL,[*] ANU REALO[**] & TALVI KALLASMAA[*]

University of Tartu, Estonia,
**University of Leuven, Belgium and University of Tartu, Estonia*

Abstract. In this chapter, two kinds of cross-cultural differences in the structure of personality traits are discussed. In Study 1, following preliminary findings that the position of the axes that define the interpersonal circumplex is related to the culture's position on the individualism-collectivism dimension (Kallasmaa et al., 2000a), our research addressed the questions of whether the angle of rotation is related (a) to any other country-level indices apart from individualism-collectivism across cultures (intercultural analysis) or (b) to the mean level of collectivism across various samples within a culture (intracultural analysis). At the intercultural level of analysis, significant correlations were found between the absolute angle of rotation and indices of life satisfaction and subjective well-being (negative) and a composite T-score of Neuroticism (positive). The results of Study 1 also suggested that the intercultural relationship between the orientation of varimax axes in the interpersonal plane and individualism-collectivism may also exist at the intracultural level. Study 2 was designed to address the question of the meaning of different degrees of association between Impulsiveness and two broad personality factors (Extraversion and Conscientiousness) in different cultures. In the intercultural part of the study, the relationship between Impulsiveness and Extraversion was found to be stronger in cultures scoring low in Conscientiousness, and high in individualism and Openness to Experience. In the intracultural part, we found that Conscientiousness moderated the relationship between Impulsiveness and Extraversion in two Russian samples, but not in the Estonian samples. In the latter, instead, Neuroticism was found to be a moderator variable.

Keywords: Factor structure, interpersonal axes, collectivism, impulsiveness

1. INTRODUCTION

The Five-Factor Model of personality is usually referred to as an empirical taxonomy of personality traits that has demonstrated considerable generalizability across different languages and cultures (see McCrae & Costa, 1997 for a review). Besides demonstrating basic similarity of the personality trait structure across many cultures, the model also provides a comprehensive framework for studying cross-cultural variation in the structure and manifestation of personality traits.

29

There is convincing evidence about cross-cultural similarities in the structure of personality traits as the adapted measures of the Five-Factor Model of personality have shown very similar structures in a number of diverse cultures and languages all over the world (e.g., Kallasmaa, Allik, Realo, & McCrae, 2000a; McCrae, Costa, del Pilar, Rolland, & Parker, 1998; Paunonen, Jackson, Trzebinski, & Forsterling, 1992; Rolland, 2000). Targeted rotation has become one of the most common procedures for demonstrating *above chance similarity* between two factor structures, computing factor and item congruence coefficients, and ensuring through a Monte Carlo simulation that the detected similarity is not due to chance (McCrae, Zonderman, Costa, Bond, & Paunonen, 1996). The method is excellent but unavoidably one-sided: It tells us about the presence of above chance similarity but does not rule out nonrandom, replicable, and interpretable differences or variations (Paunonen, 1997).

In several studies (McCrae et al., 1996, McCrae et al., 1998; Rolland, 2000), two of the five dimensions—Extraversion (E) and Agreeableness (A)—have been found to be relatively sensitive to cultural context. In Japanese (Gondo, Shimonaka, Nakazato, Ishihara, & Imuta, 1993), Korean (Piedmont & Chae, 1997), and Filipino samples (Katigbak, Church, & Akamine, 1996), for instance, the varimax dimensions of E and A were better interpreted as the interpersonal axes of *Love* and *Dominance*. Such findings have been further supported by Rolland (2000), who in his cross-cultural validity research on the Five-Factor Model (assessed by the Revised NEO Personality Inventory; Costa & McCrae, 1992) found that the factor congruence coefficients across 16 cultures (after varimax rotation) were somewhat lower for E than for the other four dimensions.

A second variation in the structure of personality traits concerns the primary loading of N5: Impulsiveness, which was originally meant to be a facet of Neuroticism (N; Costa & McCrae, 1992). Although this scale almost always has a considerable loading on the N factor, its loadings on E are notable in Germany (Angleitner & Ostendorf, 2000) and Russia (Martin, Oryol, Rukavishnikov & Senin, 2000), and it has its primary loading on Conscientiousness (C) in Estonia (Kallasmaa, Konstabel, & Realo, 2000b). These differences remain even after performing Procrustes rotation toward the North American structure. Moreover, it has been shown by means of a bilingual retest study (Konstabel, 1999) that at least in the case of the Russian and Estonian samples, it cannot be attributed merely to different properties of the test versions. (In that study, participants bilingual in Estonian and Russian filled up both versions of the NEO PI-R. Irrespective of the test version, Impulsiveness had its major loading on C in the ethnic Estonian group, and on E in the Russian group.)

1.1 Explaining Psychological Variation Across Cultures

The problem of the interpretation and explanation of psychological variation between cultures appears to be the central methodological and theoretical issue in current cross-cultural psychology. As outlined by several researchers (Berry, Poortinga, Segall, & Dasen, 1992; Georgas & Berry, 1995), one of the problems is a tendency to equate "culture" with "nation" or "ethnic group." For a study to be truly cross-cultural (and not merely "cross-country"), researchers must at least make an attempt to specify the aspects of culture that may produce the results that are obtained or expected. Culture can be conceptualized in many diverse ways (cf. Toomela, in press); among the most widespread ones in cross-cultural psychology is looking for comprehensive cultural indices (as, e.g., power distance or uncertainty avoidance) that would sum up aspects of culture related to individual psychological functioning. An important concern is the validity and range of application of such variables (cf. Fijneman, Willemsen, & Poortinga, 1996). The concept of individualism-collectivism, for example, has often been regarded as pertinent to explaining every difference or similarity in personality, self, and social behavior; it has been argued that this concept embodies the most significant differences between cultures (Triandis, 1988). Such popularity has led other authors to call for caution, as "there is a danger that Individualism/Collectivism is too readily used as an explanation for every behavioral variation between the so-called individualistic and collectivistic cultures—an all-purpose construct. If Individualism/Collectivism is used to explain everything, it may explain nothing" (Kağıtçıbaşı, 1997, p. 9).

Culture-level variables, including mean scores on personality scales, cannot always be taken at face value. As emphasized by Church (2000), "a challenge for cross-cultural psychologists will be separating out the many factors that can influence mean comparisons, including translation, structural, scalar, and sampling inequivalencies; cultural differences in response styles, self-presentation, and social judgments, and substantive personality differences based on biological or socio-cultural differences" (p. 659). Eysenck's cross-cultural comparisons, for instance, have been criticized for paying too little attention to issues of scalar equivalence and full-score comparability (cf. Van de Vijver & Leung, 1997).

While studying associations between mean levels of personality traits and cultural indices, a question of causal interpretation arises. According to McCrae (2000), there are not enough well documented associations yet to provide a reliable basis for assessing causal ordering in this area. When investigating the correlates of personality traits—or, as in the present case, variations in their structure—one must take into account that the interpretation of the results can proceed in either way: The cultural variables may help in interpreting variation in the structure of personality traits across cultures, and the latter may help in clarifying the meaning of the cultural indices.

1.2. Levels of Analysis

In cross-cultural psychology, it has been repeatedly argued that individuals and cultures need to be considered as two different units reflecting two different levels of analysis (Hofstede, 1980, 1994; Kim, Triandis, Kağıtçıbaşı, Choi, & Yoon, 1994; Smith & Schwartz, 1997). According to Hofstede (1980), an *ecological fallacy* is committed when culture-level scores or correlations are used to interpret individual behavior. Hui, Yee, and Eastman (1995), for example, found that the culture-level scores of Hofstede's individualism index correlated positively with mean scores of job satisfaction across 45 nations. Does it follow that individuals who emphasize individualistic values and attitudes are likely to be more satisfied with their jobs? Apparently not: Hui and colleagues' (1995) individual-level analysis in Hong Kong yielded a negative correlation between higher scores of job satisfaction and individualist attitudes. Conversely, when cultural or ecological indices are constructed on the basis of individual-level data, a *reverse ecological fallacy* occurs. As Hofstede has pointed out (1980), cultures should not be treated as individuals: "They are wholes, and their internal logic cannot be understood in the terms used for the personality dynamics of individuals" (p. 31).

Yet, despite the assertion that the cultural and individual levels must be separated for both conceptual and empirical purposes, in some studies the two levels have found to be functionally interrelated and highly congruent (Bond, 1988; McCrae, 2001; Schwartz, 1994) as they "interact through intermediate social structures, organizations, norms, and beliefs" (Kim et al., 1994, p. 6). Schwartz (1994), for example, has concluded, "culture-level values are organized into the same two basic dimensions that organize individual-level values" (p. 101). In line with Schwartz's results, McCrae (2001) found that the factor structure obtained in his cultural-level factor analysis of the 30 facets of the Revised NEO Personality Inventory (NEO-PI-R) showed "an unmistakable resemblance to the individual-level structure" (p. 832). In the context of the present study it is interesting to mention that one of the differences he found between the individual- and culture-level structures was that in the latter, the N5: Impulsiveness facet had its primary loading on E and only a small loading on N.

Taken together, although there is necessarily no one-to-one correspondence between a culture-level construct and an individual-level construct, one cannot exclude the existence of some relationship between the two levels as described above. Moreover, as proposed by Kim et al. (1994), "the degree of correspondence of interaction between the two levels is a research question worthy of further exploration in itself" (p. 6).

The classic distinction between cultural and individual levels is mostly about the level of measurement (job satisfaction and individualism, for instance, can be measured both at the cultural and individual levels); the problem is somewhat more complex when relationships between variables are concerned. Correlations and factor structures are always properties of groups, no matter whether the original measurements were carried out at the individual or cultural level. Although the original distinction does not directly apply to our study—variations in the structure of personality traits—the issue of levels of analysis emerges in an analogous form. The correlates of structural variations can be investigated in two ways: taking the cultural group as a unit of analysis and comparing different cultures with each other (*intercultural* level), or looking for the structural variations within a given culture (*intracultural* level; cf. McCrae, 2000). This distinction is mostly a methodological one: findings at both levels may be best explained by theories at the individual level; given the similarity of inter- and intracultural structures (McCrae, 2001), it is even possible that no separate culture-level *explanation* needs to be postulated in the domain of personality trait structure. If the results converge at the inter- and intracultural levels, then it is less probable that the variations in the structure of personality traits can be explained by purely culture-level variables.

1.3. The Present Study

In this chapter, two kinds of cross-cultural variation in the structure of personality traits are discussed. In Study 1, following preliminary findings that the position of the axes that define the interpersonal circumplex is related to the culture's position on the individualism-collectivism dimension (Kallasmaa et al., 2000a), our research addressed the questions of whether the angle of rotation is related (a) to any other country-level indices apart from individualism-collectivism across cultures (intercultural analysis) or (b) to the mean level of collectivism across various samples within a culture (intra-cultural analysis).

In Study 2, we investigate the correlates of different relationships between Impulsiveness and broad personality factors. We have preliminary results that the loadings of the Neuroticism facet N5: Impulsiveness of the NEO-PI-R on the Extraversion principal component may be related to the group's mean level of N (Kallasmaa et al., 2000b). The Russian participants in a study by Martin and colleagues (1997) scored about one standard deviation higher on N than the Estonian participants in a study by Kallasmaa and colleagues (2000a). Even after conducting Procrustes rotation towards the North American structure that should minimize the differences due to arbitrary location of axes, the loading of Impulsiveness on the E principal component was much higher in the first sample (.50) than in the second one (.22). For the loadings on C, an opposite pattern of results was obtained (−.29 *vs.* −.55, respectively). The results were similar when we compared high and low N scorers within the Estonian sample. One can thus hypothesize that N moderates the relationship between Impulsiveness and both E and C: the first one would be stronger and the second one weaker amongst individuals with higher N scores. If so, this might partly explain the observed intercultural variation in the magnitude of the loadings of Impulsiveness on E and C. In this chapter, we examine the correlates of the loadings of Impulsiveness on E and C at the intercultural level and test for the interactive effects of N, E, and C on Impulsiveness at the intracultural level. If results were similar at both levels, then the interpretation that some cross-cultural variations in the *structure* of traits result from different mean levels of basic dispositions in different countries would appear more plausible and merit further investigation.

2. ROTATIONAL ANGLE RECONSIDERED: INTERCULTURAL AND INTRACULTURAL ANALYSES

In most North American as well as in many other samples, varimax rotation of the NEO-PI-R factors has yielded standard E and A factors. However, in some samples (e.g., Japanese, Filipino) varimax rotations have recombined facets of E and A into interpersonal axes better interpreted as *Love* (L) versus *Hate* (H) (defined by E1: Warmth, E2: Gregariousness, E6: Positive Emotions, A1: Trust, A3: Altruism, and A6: Tender-Mindedness) and *Submission* (S) versus *Dominance* (D) (contrasting A4: Compliance, A5: Modesty, A2: Straightforwardness, and A3: Altruism with E3: Assertiveness, E4: Activity, and E5: Excitement-Seeking; McCrae et al., 1996). These two sets of factors (E and A; L *vs.* H and D *vs.* S), however, have been found to be

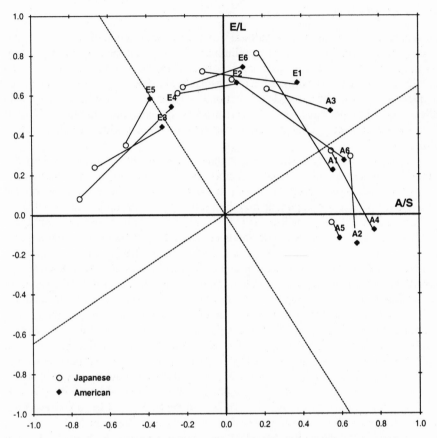

Figure 1. Factor plot of the NEO-PI-R Extraversion (E1-E6) and Agreeableness (A1-A6) facets using American (Costa & McCrae, 1992; filled boxes) and Japanese (Gondo, Shimonaka, Nakazato, Ishihara, & Imuta, 1993; empty circles) varimax-rotated factor loadings. The dashed lines represent the position of Procrustes axes in the Japanese data. L = Love; S = Submission.

rotational variants of each other. Namely, E and A factors appear to define the same plane as L *vs.* H and D *vs.* S but they differ in the angle of rotation that can range from 0 to 45 degrees, where 45 degrees represent the L *vs.* H and D *vs.* S position. In other words, the larger the angle of rotation, the more interpersonal the axes are.

Figures 1 illustrates this phenomenon by plotting E and A facets using Japanese (Gondo et al., 1993) and American normative (Costa & McCrae, 1992) varimax-rotated factor loadings (corresponding facets are joined with lines). In the American sample, the two varimax factors clearly represent E and A, whereas in the Japanese sample, the two axes are better interpreted as L and S, respectively. A targeted Procrustes rotation of Japanese factors towards the American normative structure shows that the Japanese axes are about 36 degrees away from the American position (McCrae et al., 1996). In Figure 1, the position of Procrustes axes in the Japanese data is represented by dashed lines.

Although such rotational differences might well be arbitrary, it was hypothesized (McCrae et al., 1998) that the position of the axes that define the interpersonal circumplex may be related to the culture's position on the individualism-collectivism dimension. More specifically, it was proposed that in collectivist cultures, where interpersonal relations are emphasized, L and S may be more salient axes than E and A. By combining data from their own study with findings from other cultures, Kallasmaa et al. (2000a) were able to test that hypothesis by calculating the angular degree of difference between E and A factors in the North-American sample and in 21 other available samples. Because American culture is prototypically individualistic, the degree of rotation away from the North-American position was hypothesized to be associated with the culture's degree of individualism-collectivism. The hypothesis was partially confirmed—a significant correlation was found between the Triandis ratings of individualism and the absolute angle of rotation (i.e., the absolute value of the angle of rotation that reflects closeness to one of the alternative axes): Cultures rated as more collectivistic tended to deviate more from the North-American position. Yet, the absolute angle of rotation was not significantly related to the other indices of individualism used in that study. Also, in some prototypically collectivistic cultures such as Peru and Malaysia, the varimax factor structures of the NEO-PI-R were almost identical to the North American one (Kallasmaa et al., 2000a).

2.1. Intercultural Analyses

Such mixed results intrigued us and led us to conduct further analyses and to seek other correlates of the variations in the position of the varimax axes in the interpersonal plane. More specifically, the present study—largely exploratory in its nature—sought to examine whether there exist any other cultural indices besides individualism-collectivism that show meaningful relationships with the absolute angle of rotation. A lack of previous research meant that we were unable to offer definitive hypotheses regarding the potential association between the angle of rotation and various personality-related constructs as well as social indicators amongst our sample.

Samples. Twenty-two samples as reported in Kallasmaa et al. (2000a, Table 2) were used in the intercultural analyses of this study. The range of samples was relatively broad, covering various cultural, geographical, and language contexts all around the world (Cassaretto, 1999; Chen & Piedmont, 1999; Costa, McCrae, & Jónsson, in press; Gondo et al., 1993; Hoekstra, Ormel, & De Fruyt, 1996; Kneževič, Radovič, & Opačić, 1997; Martin et al., 1997; Mastor, Jin, & Cooper, 2000; McCrae & Costa, 1997; McCrae, Costa, Piedmont et al., 1996; McCrae et al., 1998; Piedmont, Bain, McCrae & Costa, 2002; Piedmont & Chae, 1997; H. Nordvik, personal communication, May 5, 1999).

Procedure. The angular degrees of difference between E and A factors in the normative North-American sample and in 21 other samples were taken from Kallasmaa et al.

(2000a, Table 2). The mean absolute angle of rotation was 13.5 degrees ($SD = 11.7$), ranging from 0 to 38 degrees. To correlate the angle with cultural indices, a data-base was compiled including results from earlier cross-cultural studies on personality-related constructs as well as various social indicators across the samples. Altogether, the data-base included 63 variables covering a wide range of personality constructs such as the Big Five (McCrae, 2001) and Eysenck's (Lynn, 1981) personality traits, subjective well-being and life satisfaction (Diener & Diener, 1995; Diener, Diener, & Diener, 1995; Inglehart, 1990), Hofstede (1980, 1983) cultural dimensions, Schwartz (1994) and Rokeach (Bond, 1988) value dimensions, human mate preferences (Buss, 1989), and locus of control (Smith, Trompenaars, & Dugan, 1995), for instance. A number of socio-demographic indices were also included, such as total population, GNP per capita (1988), life expectancy at birth in years, percent of population urbanized, total fertility rate, and suicide rate per 100,000 inhabitants per country (UNICEF, 1991). As one may anticipate, it was not possible to find matches for all samples used in the present study across all variables in our database as the number and range of samples greatly varied in earlier cross-cultural projects. Thus, the number of present samples that could be matched with those in earlier studies ranged from 5 (indices of Protestant work ethic and spirit of capitalism in Furnham et al., 1993) to 20 (composite T-scores of the Big Five factors in McCrae, 2001).[1]

2.1.1. Results

In analyses with the absolute angle of rotation and multiple cultural indicators, six significant correlations emerged (uncorrected significance tests were used). Five correlations out of six marked relationships between the absolute angle of rotation and various indices of life satisfaction (Diener, Diener, & Diener, 1995) such as satisfaction with self for men and satisfaction with life both for men and women. Quite unfortunately, only nine of the present samples could be matched with those in Diener et al. (1995). Yet, the relationship between the absolute angle of rotation and life satisfaction was further confirmed in 16 of the present samples where corresponding data were available for the index of life satisfaction[2] (Diener & Suh, 1999) and an index of subjective well being (SWB)[3] (Diener et al., 1995). The correlations between the angle of rotation and the two variables were $r(16) = -.55$ ($p = .02$) and $-.66$ ($p = .01$), respectively.

Last but not least, there was a significant positive correlation between the absolute value of the degree of rotation and the composite T-score of the Neuroticism factor[4] (McCrae, 2001), $r(20) = .46$, $p = .04$. Table 1 lists the samples, the languages, the differences in degrees from the American position, and the scores of SWB (Diener et

---

[1]The samples employed in previous cross-cultural studies used in this research differ greatly in terms of subjects' age, gender, education, occupation, and social class.

[2]According to Diener and Suh (1999), life satisfaction is one the three major components of SWB.

[3]The score of SWB in Diener et al. (1995) "refers to the mean standardized value of four surveys (three national surveys plus student survey)" (p. 856).

[4]To control for age and gender differences and to make scores more easily interpretable, McCrae (2001) converted mean values of N to T-scores, using American norms for adult and college-age men and women (Costa & McCrae, 1992).

Table 1. Cultural Variations in Deviations of the NEO-PI-R Interpersonal Axes from American Normative Position and Ratings of Neuroticism, Subjective Well-Being, and Life Satisfaction by Country.

Country	Language	Absolute angle of rotation	SWB	Life satisfaction	N
Croatia	Croatian	10	−.81[b]	–	52.8
Estonia	Estonian	21	–	6.00	49.7
France	French	15	−.38	6.76	55.4
Hong Kong	Chinese	13	–	7.05	53.3
Iceland	Icelandic	3	1.11	8.02	–
Israel	Hebrew	10	−.18	–	–
Italy	Italian	33	−.44	7.24	55.6
Japan	Japanese	36	−.86	6.53	55.3
Malaysia	Malaysian	0	.08	–	54.2
Norway	Norwegian	1	.77	7.84	47.4
Peru	Spanish	2	–	7.41	50.8
Philippines	Filipino	23	.10	–	50.8
Portugal	Portuguese	17	−.41	7.10	55.5
Russia	Russian	15	–	5.37	53.7
Serbia	Serbian	9	−.81[b]	–	51.5
South Korea	Korean 1[a]	13	−1.15	6.69	53.6
South Korea	Korean 2[a]	38	−1.15	6.69	53.6
Taiwan	Chinese	8	–	–	51.5
The Netherlands	Dutch	3	.68	7.84	48.6
USA	English	0	.91	7.71	50.0
Germany	German	2	.18[c]	7.22[d]	52.8
Zimbabwe	Shona	26	–	6.40	50.9

Note. Absolute angle of rotation (in degrees) = absolute value of the deviation of interpersonal axes from American normative position (Kallasmaa, Allik, Realo, & McCrae, 2000a); SWB = Subjective well-being (Diener, Diener, & Diener. 1995, Table 1); Life satisfaction = Index of life satisfaction (Diener & Suh, 1999, Table 1); N = Composite *T*-score of Neuroticism (McCrae, 2001, Table 3). [a]Two published factor structures of the Korean-language NEO-PI-R are referred to as Korean 1 (McCrae & Costa, 1997) and Korean 2 (Piedmont & Chae, 1997). [b]Diener et al.'s (1995) ratings refer to Yugoslavia. [c]Diener et al.'s (1995) rating refers to West Germany. [d]Diener and Suh's (1999) rating refers to West Germany.

al., 1995), life satisfaction (Diener & Suh, 1999) and N (McCrae, 2001).[5] Taken together, it appears that not only decreases in individualism but also in SWB as well as increases in N are related to a greater salience of L *vs.* H and S *vs.* D axes.

Since both SWB and life satisfaction have been previously found to be highly and positively related with various indices of individualism (Diener & Diener, 1995; Diener et al., 1995), we conducted separate multiple regression analyses to predict the absolute angle of rotation from (a) the score of SWB and the individualism ratings of H. Triandis

---

[5]In those analyses, Diener and Suh's (1999) as well as Diener et al.'s (1995) scores for West Germany were matched with the NEO-PI-R data gathered in Germany. Diener et al.'s (1995) scores for Yugoslavia were matched with the NEO-PI-R data both from Croatia and Serbia.

as given in Kallasmaa et al. (2000a, Table 2) as well as from (b) the index of life satisfaction and the Triandis individualism ratings.[6] First, a standard multiple regression analysis indicated that although neither of the two variables attained statistical significance as a predictor, SWB ($\beta = -.48, p = .07$) seemed to play a slightly larger role than individualism ($\beta = -.32, p = .21$) in this linear equation. Similarly, in the second analysis neither life satisfaction ($\beta = -.32, p = .20$) nor individualism ($\beta = -.46, p = .07$) was a statistically significant predictor of the absolute angle of rotation. Yet, in this equation, the index of individualism appeared to be a better predictor of the angle of rotation.

2.1.2. Discussion

Combining data from a wide range of earlier cross-cultural studies allowed us to examine whether the orientation of axes in the interpersonal plane is related to other cultural variables besides individualism-collectivism. We set out without any specific hypotheses and found several significant correlations between the absolute angle of rotation and the cultural indicators included in our database. Three of the correlations deserved closer attention, as the number of matched cases in those analyses was higher than 50% of the total sample ($N = 22$) of this study. Significant negative correlations were found between the absolute angle of rotation (Kallasmaa et al., 2000a) and indices of life-satisfaction (Diener & Suh, 1999) and SWB (Diener et al., 1995) meaning that countries with lower SWB and life satisfaction tended to deviate more from the American position. The personality trait of Neuroticism (McCrae, 2001) showed a significant positive correlation with the absolute angle of rotation: The varimax factors of samples scoring high on N also tended to be farther away from the position of the standard American varimax axes.

An interesting issue to discuss here concerns the interrelations of the variables that showed significant correlations with the absolute angle of rotation. Both SWB and life satisfaction have shown strong positive relationships with individualism in earlier research (Diener et al., 1995; Diener & Diener, 1995). According to Suh, Diener, Oishi, and Triandis (1998), people in collectivist cultures not only report lower SWB than people in individualist cultures, they are also likely to judge their life satisfaction in different ways. Individualists, for instance, tend to weight their personal emotional experiences heavily, whereas collectivists emphasize interpersonal factors when they construct life-satisfaction judgments. Also, cultural norms that determine the correct and appropriate level of SWB influence a person's life satisfaction judgment in collectivist cultures, but not in individualist cultures (Suh et al., 1998).

Results of the multiple regression analyses showed that neither SWB nor life satisfaction was a significant predictor of the absolute angle of rotation after controlling for individualism. Yet SWB appeared to be a slightly better predictor than individualism. Thus, the relationships between the SWB and the absolute angle of rotation cannot be purely attributed to the main effect of individualism or life

---

[6]Due to incomplete overlap of the samples used in the analyses, the three variables could not be added to the equation simultaneously.

satisfaction. It appears that in collectivistic cultures where people also tend to report lower scores of SWB/life satisfaction, interpersonal relationships along axes of L vs. H and D vs. S are more salient. That goes well with research findings showing that in collectivist cultures, in-group harmony and acceptance of hierarchy in social behavior are emphasized (Triandis, 1995). Previous studies have shown, for instance, that collectivistic cultures tend to score high on the cultural dimension of Power Distance (Hofstede, 1991) that has close resemblance to the D vs. S axis of interpersonal behavior.[7] The second axis, L vs. H, finds its application in strong out-group-in-group distinctions in collectivistic societies. With an aim to maintaining in-group harmony and interdependence, people in collectivistic societies tend to be agreeable, pleasant, and non-critical in their relations with their in-group members but not with their out-group members (cf. Triandis, 1995), whereas such distinctions are usually not made in individualist cultures.

How should the association of N and the absolute angle of rotation be interpreted? Despite the fact that E and A are mainly related to interpersonal behavior, all five dimensions of personality "are in one sense interpersonal, because each influences the ways in which individuals interact" (McCrae & Costa, 1989, p. 586). Indeed, the Assured-Dominant subscale of the Revised Interpersonal Adjective Scales (IAS-R; Wiggins, Trapnell, & Philips, 1989) has been found to be highly related not only to E but also to two facets of N (Costa & McCrae, 1992). One may speculate that in cultures where people tend to be emotionally unstable and fearful as well as prone to feelings of insecurity and anxiety, interpersonal relationships along a well-defined status system tend to be emphasized.

While interpreting the results of this study, one needs to keep in mind that along with individualism-collectivism, the abovementioned three variables may not be the only or the most important cultural correlates of the absolute angle of rotation. First, it is possible that some of the significant correlations between the absolute angle of rotation and cultural indices may have occurred due to chance. Yet, it is not very likely that this is the case for all three variables (i.e., SWB, life satisfaction, and N). Secondly, the size and scope of our database was limited both in terms of variables and subjects. Probably many important culture-level criteria were not added to the database. Furthermore, for a great number of variables in our database there were data missing for cultures included in our study. Sampling itself raises another important question relating to the validity of our research—as mentioned earlier, the studies covered in our database differed greatly in size as well as across social class, gender, education and age of the subjects, ranging from national probability samples to small groups of college students.[8]

---

[7]In societies high in Power Distance, superiors (parents, teachers, bosses) and subordinates (children, students) consider each other as existentially unequal, with superiors having more status and respect than the subordinates; whereas in societies low in Power Distance, privileges and status symbols are frowned upon and subordinates treat superiors as equals (Hofstede, 1991).

[8]However, the samples of the studies where variables showed significant correlations with the absolute angle of rotation can be considered nearly ideal for any cross-cultural comparison. The index of SWB in Diener et al. (1995) was derived from three national surveys plus a student survey; the scores of life satisfaction were based on probability sample measurement in the World Value Survey (Diener & Suh, 1999) and McCrae (2001) used data standardized by age and gender from volunteer samples.

Our study answered some questions but also raised a few. We found that individualism-collectivism may indeed not be the only predictor of the absolute angle of rotation. Yet, the role of both SWB/life satisfaction and N in explaining variations in the position of the varimax axes in the interpersonal plane needs further exploration.

2.2. Intracultural Analyses

As outlined in the Introduction, a simple one-to-one correspondence between the cultural and individual levels may not exist. Furthermore, it has been also shown that a relationship between two constructs at the cultural level does not automatically apply to the parallel individual-level constructs. Yet, the results of several earlier studies in which the two levels were found to be highly congruent (Bond, 1988; McCrae, 2001; Schwartz, 1994), encouraged us to examine whether the negative correlation between the absolute angle of rotation and individualism-collectivism at the intercultural level can be also obtained using multiple samples within a culture.

Individualism and collectivism, most often, are seen as characteristics of cultures. Hofstede (1980), for instance, empirically derived individualism-collectivism as a unidimensional construct at the cultural level. Later research, however, has studied the constructs also at the individual level (see Triandis, 1995) and has shown that individualism and collectivism are not two opposite poles of a single dimension but rather two independent factors (see also Freeman, 1996; Gelfand, Triandis, & Chan, 1996; Rhee, Uleman, & Lee, 1996). Following the assumption that collectivism is not the opposite of individualism (at least at the individual level), our study concerns the relationship between the angle of rotation and collectivistic attitudes.

2.2.1. Intracultural Variability

Previous research has already shown some fluctuations in the position of the axes that define interpersonal plane across various subsamples within a culture. In one Korean sample (Piedmont & Chae, 1997), for instance, L and S factors emerged whereas standard E and A factors were found in another (McCrae & Costa, 1997). In their research using Filipino samples, McCrae et al. (1998) found L and S factors in the business school subsample while E and A factors emerged in the university student subsample.

The idea that the differences between various subgroups in a country may be even larger than those between different countries has been also supported by several studies on values and collectivistic attitudes (Verkasalo, Daun, & Niit, 1994; see also Marshall, 1997; Realo, Allik, & Vadi, 1997). For instance, Realo et al. (1997) showed that various cultural and socio-demographic groups within Estonia have very different patterns of collectivism, meaning that groups exist within a national culture which differ considerably in the strength of their collectivistic attitudes.

Taken together, in line with the results of the intercultural-level study by Kallasmaa et al. (2000a), we hypothesized that in more collectivist subsamples within a culture, L vs. H and D vs. S may be more salient axes than E and A. As in studies at the intercultural level (Kallasmaa et al., 2000a; McCrae et al., 1996; McCrae et al., 1998),

Table 2. *Intracultural Variations in Deviations of the NEO-P-R*
Interpersonal Axes and Mean Scores of the General Collectivism Index.

Sample	Absolute angle of rotation	COL	n
S1	1.9	24.9	174
S2	7.7	38.6	185
S3	17.8	48.1	176
S4	15.1	60.3	187

Note. Absolute angle of rotation (in degrees) = absolute value of the deviation of interpersonal axes from American normative position (Costa & McCrae, 1992). COL = General Collectivism Index.

the angular degree of difference from E and A factors in the American normative sample was calculated since the U.S. is typically seen as a yardstick of individualism (cf. Hofstede, 1980). In our intracultural study we hypothesized that the degree of rotation away from the American position would be associated with the subsample's degree of collectivism.

Sample. The sample for this study consisted of 747 Estonians (557 females and 190 males) with mean age 23.0 ($SD = 9.8$) ranging from 12 to 83 years. Forty-eight percent of the respondents were tested during their entrance examinations to the Faculty of Social Sciences of the University of Tartu, 27% of the respondents were already students at the University of Tartu and the remaining 25% of the respondents were individuals with diverse socio-demographical and educational background. The data were collected in 1996-1997 and in 1999.

Measures. Among various other measures, the respondents were asked to complete the Estonian version (Kallasmaa et al., 2000a) of the NEO-PI-R (Costa & McCrae, 1992) and the ESTCOL Scale (Realo et al., 1997). The ESTCOL Scale consists of 24 items that measure three subtypes of collectivism related to family, peers, and society. According to the tripartite model used in this study, collectivism consists of at least three distinct yet interrelated subtypes focused on relations with family (*Familism*), peers (*Companionship*), and society (*Patriotism*) (Allik & Realo, 1996; Realo et al., 1997). *Familism* implies dedication of one's life to the family and putting its interests higher than one's personal aspirations. *Companionship* is exemplified by tight relations between an individual and his/her neighbors, friends, or co-workers, and by the individual's focus on the needs of his/her in-group. Finally, *Patriotism* means dedication to serve one's nation by surrendering one's personal comforts to the latter (cf. Realo et al., 1997). The Cronbach alphas were .80, .72, and .83 for Family, Peers, and Society subscales, respectively.

Procedure. First, with an aim to have subsamples for our research that would differ in their strength of collectivistic attitudes, the sample was divided into quartiles on the General Collectivism Index (Family + Peers + Society) of the ESTCOL Scale. The mean scores of the General Collectivism Index and the size of four subsamples are shown in Table 2. Secondly, the angular degrees of difference between E and A factors in the American normative sample and in the total sample of our study as well as in four subsamples were calculated. The degrees of rotation were estimated as inverse cosines of appropriate entries in the factor transformation matrix from the Procrustes analysis in which the varimax structure was rotated to best approximate the ideal simple structure.

2.2.2. Results

The mean of the General Collectivism Index for the total sample was 43.2 ($SD = 14.0$) and the difference from the American normative simple structure was −14.4 degrees. Table 2 lists the differences in degrees from the American position across the subsamples.

As can be seen from Table 2, there indeed appears to be a visible tendency for the degree of rotation away from the American normative position to increase along with increase in the subsample's degree of collectivism. While in the least collectivistic subsample (S1), the E and A varimax factors had nearly an identical location with the respective American factors (about 2 degrees), the axes were about 15-17 degrees away from the American position in more collectivistic subsamples (S4 and S3, respectively).

2.2.3. Discussion

The results of intracultural analyses provided preliminary support to our hypothesis that the degree of rotation away from the American normative structure would be associated with the subsample's degree of collectivism. Yet, one must be somewhat cautious in interpreting these findings due to the following reasons.

First, we had only four subsamples in our study. If compared to the findings at the intercultural level, the angles of rotation across our subsamples were relatively small, showing that in all subsamples, more or less, the standard E and A factors in varimax rotation emerged. Thus, in order to get a statistically valid proof for the relationship between the absolute angle of rotation and collectivistic attitudes, more subsamples with diverse scores of collectivism at the intracultural level would be needed.

Secondly, the analyses were conducted only within one culture. Similar studies in other cultures (which should be ideally located at the opposite ends of the individualism and collectivism dimensions) should be conducted to establish the universality of the relationship between the angle of rotation and collectivistic attitudes at the intracultural level.

3. CORRELATES OF IMPULSIVENESS: INTER- AND INTRACULTURAL VARIATIONS

Many NEO-PI-R facet scales have secondary loadings on factors other than that to which they are nominally assigned. However, these patterns of secondary loadings tend to be similar across cultures (McCrae & Costa, 1997). One facet for which cultural variation in secondary loadings has been observed is N5: Impulsiveness. Study 2 was designed to address the question of the meaning of different degrees of association between Impulsiveness and two broad personality factors (E and C) in different cultures. In the intercultural part of the study, we examined whether the loadings of N5 on the E and C factors have any meaningful culture-level correlates. In the intracultural part of the study, we investigated—using four samples from two different cultures—whether there are moderating variables affecting the relationship between Impulsiveness and E or C.

3.1. Intercultural Analyses

Samples. Eighteen cultural samples used in this study are listed in Table 3. Sixteen samples were the same as those analyzed in Rolland's (2000) study. Additionally, we included data from Germany (Angleitner & Ostendorf, 2000) and South Africa (Heuchert, Parker, Stumpf, & Myburgh, 2000).

Analyses. To check the preliminary hypothesis (derived from intercultural comparison between Russia and Estonia; Kallasmaa et al., 2000b) that the degree of association of

Table 3. Loadings of N5: Impulsiveness on N, E, and C in 18 Samples.

Country	N5 on N	N5 on E	N5 on C
Belgium	.41	.48	−.30
Croatia	.51	.19	−.36
Estonia	.43	.22	−.55
France	.45	.38	−.34
Germany	.41	.46	−.32
Hong Kong	.54	.29	−.36
Italy	.36	.43	−.28
Japan	.45	.40	−.40
Malaysia	.51	.26	−.32
Netherlands	.41	.48	−.30
Norway	.33	.36	−.42
Philippines	.54	.20	−.28
Portugal	.39	.33	−.34
Russia	.41	.45	−.33
South African Blacks	.49	.24	−.39
South Korea	.51	.31	−.45
Spain	.46	.30	−.26
U. S.	.49	.35	−.32

Note. These are loadings of N5: Impulsiveness facet on factors after orthogonal Procrustes rotation targeted toward the North American normative structure (Costa & McCrae, 1992).

Table 4. *Rank Order Correlations between Cultural Indices and Loadings of N5: Impulsiveness on the E and C Factors.*

	N	r
N5 on E & C	18	−.61**
N5 on E & O	18	.52*
N5 on E & Hofstede[a]	12	.68*
N5 on E & Triandis[a]	15	.49
N5 on E & Composite index[a]	15	.62*
N5 on C & Life satisfaction[b]	15	.55*
N5 on C & Normative life satisfaction[b]	13	.57*

Note. N5 on E and N5 on C = the loadings of N5: Impulsiveness facet on the Extraversion and Conscientiousness principal components from orthogonal Procrustes rotation toward the North American normative structure. C and O = mean factor scores on the Conscientiousness and Openness factors (McCrae, 2001). Hofstede = individualism ratings from Hofstede (1980); Triandis = individualism ratings from Triandis; Composite index = combined individualism ratings from Hofstede and Triandis (Kallasmaa et al., 2000a). [a]From Kallasmaa et al. (2000a). [b]From Diener and Suh (1999). *p < .05. **p < .01.

N5 with different broad personality factors is moderated by the group's mean level of N, we correlated the loadings of N5 on E and C factors with mean levels of broad personality factors as measured by the NEO-PI-R (data from McCrae, 2001) across the 18 cultural samples. We also included in our analyses the indices of Individualism (namely, ratings by Geert Hofstede and Harry Triandis, see Kallasmaa, et al., 2000), life-satisfaction, and normative life-satisfaction (Diener & Suh, 1999)— variables that have often been used in cross-cultural research and that were found to be related to the position of interpersonal axes in Study 1.

3.1.1. Results.

The correlations between the cultural level indices and the loadings of N5 on Procrustes-rotated E and C components are shown in Table 4. (We used Procrustes rather than Varimax loadings to assure maximal comparability of the factor structures.) Most notably, there was a significant negative correlation between the N5 loading on the E principal component, and sample's mean level of C. There was also a tendency for samples with higher levels of Openness to Experience (O) and individualism to have higher loadings of N5 on E. Contrary to our initial hypothesis, there was no correlation between the sample's mean level of N and the loadings of N5 on E.

The loading of N5 on C was found to be associated with life-satisfaction and normative life-satisfaction. (Note that N5 typically has a negative loading on C; thus, in cultures with higher mean levels of life-satisfaction, there tends to be a weaker association between C and Impulsiveness.)

In sum, the intercultural variability in the loadings of N5 shows some meaningful relationships with culture-level indices. In particular, the result that we can attempt to replicate at the intracultural level is that in cultures low in Conscientiousness or high in

Openness, Impulsiveness shows a stronger relationship with E (extraverted people tend to be impulsive). The hypothesized association with N, however, was not supported.

3.2 Intracultural Analyses

In this section, we intend to replicate the results from the intercultural analyses at the intracultural level in four Russian and Estonian samples. As we have no within-culture data on individualism in the Russian samples, and on life satisfaction in either sample, the only effects that we can try to replicate are related to C and O, the hypothesis being that in groups scoring low on C and high on O there would be a stronger association between N5: Impulsiveness and E than in groups scoring high on C and low on O. To allow a comparison between levels, we divide each sample into two parts (according to scores on C and O) and perform a principal components analysis in each of these subsamples. It is expected, thus, that in low C scoring subsamples, the loadings of N5 on E would be higher than in high scoring subsamples, and that in high O subsamples, the respective loadings would be lower than in low O subsamples.

Samples. The first sample (henceforth referred to as the first Estonian sample or "EE1" in Table 5) consisted of 711 Estonians (225 men and 486 women) whose age ranged from 18 to 82 (M = 31.2, SD = 14.3). The participants represented a wide range of educational, cultural, and social background. Data from this sample have been analyzed in Kallasmaa et al. (2000a). The second sample (henceforth referred to as the first Russian sample or "RU1" in Table 5) consisted of 350 participants living in Yaroslavl and surrounding regions of Central Russia. They were university students, medical students, and workers in educational, industrial, and commercial enterprises. The age of 208 females and 142 males ranged from 16 to 63 years (*M* = 28.7, *SD* = 10.5). These data have been analyzed in a study by Martin and colleagues (2000), and were kindly made available by Thomas A. Martin.

To check replicability of the results, data from two additional samples were included in some analyses. The second Estonian sample (labeled "EE2" in Table 5) consisted of 1,144 applicants to the Faculty of Social Sciences of the University of Tartu, Estonia; data were collected during the period of application examinations in 1999 and 2000. The sample consisted of 895 women and 246 men (3 participants did not report their gender) whose age ranged from 17 to 37 years (*M* = 19.4, *SD* = 1.8). The second Russian sample (labeled "RU2" in Table 5) consisted of ethnic Russians (153 women and 32 men) living in various parts of Estonia whose age ranged from 17 to 59 years (*M* = 22.5, *SD* = 7.6). They originally participated in four different unpublished studies (including Konstabel, 1999).[9]

Measures. The Estonian (Kallasmaa et al., 2000a) or Russian (Martin et al., 2000) versions of the NEO-PI-R (Costa & McCrae, 1992) were administered to participants. Among the 30 facet scales of the NEO-PI-R, N5: Impulsiveness is of principal interest

---

[10]The data were kindly provided by Hillar Matto, Kätlin Nummert, and Helle Pullmann.

Table 5. Factor Loadings for N5: Impulsiveness in Four Samples Split by Conscientiousness and Openness.

Sample	N	Split	Loadings[a]				
			N	E	O	A	C
EE1	351	C < 118	.38	.29	.11	−.18	−.37
	353	C > 118	.42	.29	.08	−.13	−.42
EE2	534	C < 120	.42	.33	.14	−.32	−.36
	561	C > 120	.49	.36	.06	−.28	−.31
RU1	175	C < 111.5	.41	.48	.04	−.37	−.14
	175	C > 111.5	.44	.30	.29	−.30	−.28
RU2	86	C < 113	.12	.50	.28	−.18	−.34
	87	C > 113	.63	.36	.02	−.15	−.31
EE1	347	O < 115	.44	.21	.06	−.16	−.57
	351	O > 115	.47	.17	.00	−.21	−.51
EE2	561	O < 128	.49	.24	.15	−.29	−.46
	542	O > 128	.44	.26	.09	−.33	−.48
RU1	169	O < 110	.46	.35	−.02	−.36	−.36
	167	O > 110	.40	.36	.05	−.31	−.41
RU2	85	O < 118	.44	.38	.22	−.22	−.44
	92	O > 118	.46	.40	.21	−.13	−.32

Note. See text for a description of the Russian and Estonian samples (RU1, RU2, EE1 and EE2) used in the present analysis. N = Neuroticism; E = Extraversion; O = Openness to Experience; A = Agreeableness; C = Conscientiousness. [a]Loadings of N5: Impulsiveness on Procrustes-rotated principal components targeted toward American normative structure.

here. This scale is not intended to comprehend all aspects of the lay concept of impulsivity; rather, its content is defined more specifically as "inability to control cravings and urges" (Costa & McCrae, 1992, p. 16).

3.2.1. Results

All four samples were first split into two approximately equal halves according to the scores on C, using the median as a cut point. In the resulting 8 samples, separate principal component analyses were conducted. To ensure maximal comparability of loadings, the matrices were first target rotated towards the North American normative structure (Costa & McCrae, 1992). Then, the procedure was repeated splitting the samples by the median scores on O. The results (see Table 5) showed that in the Russian samples, the loadings of N5 on the E principal component were higher in the below-median than in the above-median C group, whereas there were no systematic differences when the samples were divided according to the scores on O. In the Estonian samples, neither splitting by C nor by O produced any systematic differences in the factor loadings of N5.

3.2.2. Discussion

At the intercultural level, the loadings of N5 on the E principal component appear to decrease with higher mean levels of C, and increase with higher mean levels of O and individualism. In other words, in countries where people tend to be less conscientious, and more open and individualistic, extraverted people tend to be impulsive, and this relationship is weaker in countries with higher mean levels of C and lower mean levels of O and individualism. The relationships of impulsiveness to O and individualism are easily interpretable, especially as the latter two constructs have been found to be positively related at the intercultural level of analysis (McCrae, 2001). As one of the most important attributes of collectivism (as an opposite to individualism at the cultural level) is an emphasis on social norms and duty defined by the group (Triandis, 1995), the expression of extraversion in impulsive behavior may be inhibited by norms and rules in collectivistic and less open cultures. The moderating role of C also supports the validity of the culture-level mean scores; it can be speculated that higher levels of C may hinder the expression of extraversion in impulsive behavior. (The results of factor analyses suggested a similar moderating role of C in the two Russian samples.) The only cross-cultural correlates of the loading of N5: Impulsiveness on C were life-satisfaction and norms for life-satisfaction. It appears that conscientious people, who live in countries where people are satisfied with their life and/or think that people should be satisfied with life, may or may not be impulsive; in countries where people are less satisfied with their life, conscientious people tend not to be impulsive.

The intercultural results were only weakly replicated at the intracultural level. In both Russian samples—but in neither Estonian sample—the loading of N5 on E followed the predicted pattern.

4. SUMMARY AND CONCLUSIONS

To sum up, we would like to discuss two issues that are relevant to both studies reported in this chapter. The first issue concerns the correspondence of our results at the intercultural and intracultural levels of analysis. In some results, we saw a fair correspondence between the two levels, yet in another part, inconclusive findings emerged.

The second issue concerns directions for further investigations. As expressed in the title, our study is exploratory in nature, and cannot thus provide definitive answers to any substantial questions. We feel, however, that some preliminary conclusions can and should be drawn from the results of our study and these conclusions can be expressed in the form of hypotheses that can either be confirmed or rejected by subsequent studies.

4.1. Correspondence of the Results at the Intercultural and Intracultural Levels

All in all, the results of our study provided diverse and inconsistent evidence about the correspondence of the constructs at the intercultural and intracultural level. In Study 1 we found that the intercultural relationship between the orientation of varimax axes in the interpersonal plane and the bipolar dimension of individualism-collectivism may also exist at the intracultural level. We calculated the angular degree of difference between E and A factors in the American normative sample and in four subsamples of Estonian data and found a clear trend for the increase of the absolute angle of rotation to parallel the increase of the mean score of collectivistic attitudes. Thus, it appears that both in collectivist cultures (intercultural level of analysis) and in more collectivist subsamples within a culture (intracultural level of analysis), there is a tendency for the interpersonal axes of L vs H and D vs S to be more salient than E and A.

In Study 2, we found that C moderates the relationship between E and N5: Impulsiveness: In cultures with higher mean levels of C, this relationship tends to be weaker. The results of the factor analysis suggested a tendency in this direction within the Russian samples, but not in the Estonian samples. Thus, it is unclear whether there is a strict correspondence between the intercultural and intracultural levels in this case, especially as at the intracultural level, results may have been affected by different variability of C in our samples.

4.2. Directions for Further Investigation

Obviously, the present study leaves many questions about the meaning and implication of the variations in the position of the varimax axes in the interpersonal plane for further explorations. First, the relationships of the position of axes with N and SWB/life satisfaction at the intercultural level are far from clear—further research is needed to explain why cultures with higher scores of N and lower scores of SWB/life satisfaction tend to deviate more from the standard American position. Secondly, the emergence of interpersonal axes (L vs H and D vs S) in collectivist samples calls for further analyses of the differences in the impact of contextual factors such as roles, norms, specific relationships, and situational contexts on personality at various levels of analysis (cf. Church, 2000). There is also a need to clarify the meaning of rotational differences. If, as it has been proposed, greater deviation of the axes from the North American position means greater salience of the interpersonal categories of L vs H and D vs S, then one may speculate that collectivists (or those scoring low on SWB or high on N) should describe (or encode) acts and person impressions more readily in those terms, rather than in terms of E and A. This hypothesis can be tested empirically, although it clearly needs further elaboration before the investigation can proceed.

Considering the results of our second study, we should first bear in mind that both inter- and intracultural results may reflect individual-level functioning (as well as the culture-individual relationship), and the fact that inter- and intracultural results did not converge may partly derive from insufficient power in our intracultural study. At this point, one may therefore consider both inter- and intracultural results in deriving hypotheses on individual functioning

Secondly, one should take into account that we only used a self-report measure of impulsiveness. It is therefore unclear whether the results are specific to self-reports, or whether they can be extended to impulsive behavior. On the other hand, the items in the N5 facet of the NEO-PI-R are rather concretely worded, all tapping the issues related to the "inability to control cravings and urges" (Costa & McCrae, 1992). It would therefore be natural to expect that the results of behavioral and self-report methods should point in the same direction. Impulsivity is known to have various cognitive correlates and behavioral expressions (e.g., Newman, 1987; Brunas-Wagstaff, Bergquist, Morgan, & Wagstaff, 1995). Among these, the ones that seem to be most closely related to the content of the NEO-PI-R N5: Impulsiveness facet are susceptibility to interference in cognitive tasks (Brunas-Wagstaff et al., 1995) and delay of gratification (Mischel, Shoda, & Rodriguez, 1989). Thus, one possible way to examine the generality of the moderating effects found in the present study would be to investigate whether they also hold for cognitive correlates of Impulsiveness.

At the intercultural level, we found a clear relationship between mean factor scores on C and the loading of N5 on the E principal component. We cannot be sure, though, what this association means because we do not know what aspects of C are relevant for this effect. One possibility would be to concentrate on more specific facet scales rather than overall C. Another, possibly more informative, option would be to compare cultural norms concerning impulsive behavior and their relation to the ideas of duty and self-discipline in different cultures.

Paying attention to variations in the structure of personality traits may help in clarifying the possible culture-specific ways in which personality dispositions are expressed in characteristic adaptations. At the very least, we hope to have shown that in such a way, one can produce interesting and specific hypotheses about the relationship between individual and culture.

REFERENCES

Allik, J., & Realo, A. (1996). The hierarchical nature of individualism-collectivism: Comments on Matsumoto et al. (1996). *Culture and Psychology, 2,* 109-117.

Angleitner, A., & Ostendorf, F. (2000). *The FFM: A comparison of German-speaking countries.* Paper presented at the XXVIIth International Congress of Psychology, July 23-28, Stockholm, Sweden.

Berry, J. W., Poortinga, Y. H., Segall, M. H., & Dasen, P. R. (1992). *Cross-cultural psychology: Research and applications.* New York: Cambridge University Press.

Bond, M. H. (1988). Finding universal dimensions of individual variation in multicultural studies of values: The Rokeach and Chinese Value Surveys. *Journal of Personality and Social Psychology, 55,* 1009-1015.

Brunas-Wagstaff, J., Bergquist, A., Morgan, K., & Wagstaff, G. F. (1995). Impulsivity, interference on perceptual tasks and hypothesis testing. *Personality and Individual Differences, 20,* 471-482.

Buss, D. M. (1989). Sex-differences in human mate preferences: Evolutionary hypothesis tested in 37 cultures. *Behavioral and Brain Sciences, 12,* 1-14.

Cassaretto, M. (1999). *Adaptacion del inventario de personalidad NEO Revisado (NEO-PI-R) Forma S en un grupo de estudiantes universitarios.* [Adaptation of the Revised NEO Personality Inventory (NEO-PI-R) Form S, in a Peruvian university student sample]. Unpublished thesis, Pontificia Universidad Catolica del Peru, Lima.

Chen, M. C., & Piedmont, R. L. (1999). Development and validation of the NEO-PI-R for a Taiwanese sample. In T. Sugiman, M. Karasawa, J. H. Liu, & C. Ward (Eds.), *Progress in Asian social psychology,* (Vol. 2, pp. 105-119). Seoul, South Korea: Kyoyook-Kwahak-Sa Publishing.

Church, A. T. (2000). Culture and personality: Toward an integrated cultural trait psychology. *Journal of Personality, 68,* 651-703.

Costa, P. T., & McCrae, R. R. (1992). *Revised NEO Personality Inventory (NEO-PI-R) and NEO Five-Factor Inventory (NEO-FFI) professional manual.* Odessa, FL: Psychological Assessment Resources.

Costa, P. T., Jr., McCrae, R. R., & Jónsson, F. H. (in press). Validity and utility of the Revised NEO Personality Inventory: Examples from Europe. In B. DeRaad & M. Perugini (Eds.), *Big Five assessment.* Göttingen, Germany: Hogrefe & Huber.

Diener, E., & Diener, M. (1995). Cross-cultural correlates of life-satisfaction and self-esteem. *Journal of Personality and Social Psychology, 68,* 653-663.

Diener, E., Diener, M., & Diener, C. (1995). Factors predicting the subjective well-being of nations. *Journal of Personality and Social Psychology, 69,* 851-864.

Diener, E., & Suh, E. M. (1999). National differences in subjective well-being. In D. Kahneman, E. Diener, & N. Schwarz (Eds.), *Well-being: The foundations of hedonic psychology* (pp. 434-450). New York, NY: Russell Sage Foundation.

Fijneman, Y. A., Willemsen, M. E., & Poortinga, Y. H. (1996). Individualism-collectivism: An empirical study of a conceptual issue. *Journal of Cross-Cultural Psychology, 27,* 381-402.

Freeman, M. A. (1996). Factorial structure of individualism-collectivism in Sri Lanka. *Psychological Reports, 78,* 907-914.

Furnham, A., Bond, M., Heaven, P., Hilton, D., Lobel, T., Masters, J., Payne, M., Rajamanikam, R., Stacey, B., & Vandaalen, H. (1993). A comparison of Protestant Work Ethic beliefs in thirteen nations. *Journal of Social Psychology, 133,* 185-197.

Gelfand, M. J., Triandis, H. C., & Chan, D. K. S. (1996). Individualism versus collectivism or versus authoritarianism? *European Journal of Social Psychology, 26,* 397-410.

Georgas, J., & Berry, J. W. (1995). An ecocultural taxonomy for cross-cultural psychology. *Cross-Cultural Research: The Journal of Comparative Social Science, 29,* 121-157.

Gondo, Y., Shimonaka, Y., Nakazato, K., Ishihara, O., & Imuta, H. (1993, September). *Preliminary study for the standardization of the Japanese version of NEO-Pi-R.* Paper presented at the 57th Meeting of the Japanese Psychological Association, Tokyo.

Heuchert, J. W. P., Parker, W. D., Stumpf, H., & Myburgh, C. P. (2000). The Five-Factor Model of personality in South African college students. *American Behavioral Scientist, 44,* 112-125.

Hoekstra, H. A., Ormel, J., & De Fruyt, F. (1996). *Handleiding NEO Persoonlijkheids-vragenlijsten NEO-PI-R en NEO-FFI [Manual for NEO Personality Inventories NEO-PI-R and NEO-FFI].* Lisse, The Netherlands: Swets & Zeitlinger.

Hofstede, G. (1980). *Culture's consequences: International differences in work-related values.* Beverly Hills, CA: Sage.

Hofstede, G. (1983). Dimensions of national cultures in fifty countries and three regions. In J. Deregowski, S. Dziurawiec, & R. C. Annis (Eds.), *Expisications in cross-cultural psychology* (pp. 335-355). Lisse, Netherlands: Swets & Zeitlinger.

Hofstede, G. (1991). *Cultures and organizations: Software of the mind.* London: McGraw-Hill.

Hofstede, G. (1994). Foreword. In U. Kim, H. C. Triandis, Ç. Kağıtçıbaşı, S. C. Choi, & G. Yoon (Eds.), *Individualism and collectivism: Theory, method, and applications* (pp. ix-xiii). Thousand Oaks, CA: Sage.

Hui, C. H., Yee, C., & Eastman, K. L. (1995). The relationship between individualism-collectivism and job satisfaction. *Applied Psychology: An International Review, 44:* 276-282.

Inglehart, R. (1990). *Culture shift in advanced industrial societies.* Princeton, NJ: Princeton University Press.

Kağıtçıbaşı, Ç. (1997). Individualism-collectivism. In J. W. Berry, M. H. Segall, & Ç. Kağıtçıbaşı (Vol. Eds.), *Handbook of cross-cultural psychology: Vol. 3. Social behavior and applications* (2nd ed., pp. 1-49). Boston, MA: Allyn and Bacon.

Kallasmaa, T., Allik, J., Realo, A., & McCrae, R. R. (2000a). The Estonian version of the NEO-PI-R: An examination of universal and culture-specific aspects of the Five-Factor Model. *European Journal of Personality, 14,* 265-278.

Kallasmaa, T., Konstabel, K., & Realo A. (2000b). Five-Factor Model of personality in Estonian: Universal and culture-specific aspects. *International Journal of Psychology, 35,* 279.

Katigbak, M. S., Church, A. T., & Akamine, T. X. (1996). Cross-cultural generalizability of personality dimensions: Relating indigenous and imported dimensions in two cultures. *Journal of Personality and Social Psychology, 70,* 99-114.

Kim, U., Triandis, H. C., Kağıtçıbaşı, Ç., Choi, S. C., & Yoon. G. (1994). Introduction. In U. Kim, H. C. Triandis, Ç. Kağıtçıbaşı, S. C. Choi, & G. Yoon (Eds.), *Individualism and collectivism: Theory, method, and applications* (pp. 1-16). Thousand Oaks, CA: Sage.

Kneževič, G., Radovič, B., & Opačić, G. (1997). An evaluation of the "Big Five Model" of personality through an analysis of the NEO-PI-R Personality Inventory. *Psihologija, 1-2,* 3-24

Konstabel, K. (1999). *A bilingual retest study of the Revised NEO Personality Inventory: A comparison of Estonian and Russian versions.* Unpublished master's thesis, University of Tartu.

Lynn, R. (1981). Cross-cultural differences in neuroticism, extraversion, and psychotism. In R. Lynn (Ed.), *Dimensions of personality* (pp. 263-286). New York: Pergamon.

Marshall, R. (1997). Variances in levels of individualism across two cultures and three social classes. *Journal of Cross-Cultural Psychology, 28,* 490-495.

Martin, T. A, Draguns, J. G., Oryol, V. E., Senin, I. G., Rukavishnikov, A. A., & Klotz, M. L. (1997, August). *Development of a Russian-language NEO-PI-R.* Poster presented at the 105th Convention of the American Psychological Association, Chicago.

Martin, T. A., Oryol, V. E., Rukavishnikov, A. A., & Senin, I. G. (2000, July). *Applications of the Russian NEO-PI-R.* Paper presented at the XXVIIth International Congress of Psychology, Stockholm, Sweden.

Mastor, K. A., Jin, P., & Cooper, M. (2000). Malay culture and personality: A Big Five perspective. *American Behavioral Scientist, 44,* 95-111

McCrae, R. R. (2000). Trait psychology and the revival of personality and culture studies. *American Behavioral Scientist, 44,* 10-31.

McCrae, R. R. (2001). Trait psychology and culture: Exploring intercultural comparisons. *Journal of Personality, 69,* 819-846.

McCrae, R. R., & Costa, P. T., Jr. (1989). The structure of interpersonal traits: Wiggins's Circumplex and the Five-Factor Model. *Journal of Personality and Social Psychology, 56,* 586-595.

McCrae, R. R., & Costa, P. T., Jr. (1996). Toward a new generation of personality theories: Theoretical contexts for the Five-Factor Model. In J. S. Wiggins (Ed.), *The Five-Factor Model of personality: Theoretical perspectives* (pp. 51-87). New York, NY: The Guilford Press.

McCrae, R. R., & Costa, P. T., Jr. (1997). Personality trait structure as a human universal. *American Psychologist, 52,* 509-516.

McCrae, R. R., Costa, P. T., Jr., del Pilar, G. H., Rolland, J.-P., & Parker, W. D. (1998). Cross-cultural assessment of the Five-Factor Model: The Revised NEO Personality Inventory. *Journal of Cross-Cultural Psychology, 29,* 171-188.

McCrae, R. R., Costa, P. T., Jr., Piedmont, R. L., Chae, J.-L., Caprara, G. V., Barbaranelli, C., Marusic, I., & Bratko, D. (1996, November). *Personality development from college to midlife: A cross-cultural comparison.* Paper presented at the 49th Annual Scientific Meeting of the Gerontological Society of America, Washington, DC.

McCrae, R. R., Zonderman, A. B., Costa, P. T., Bond, M. H., & Paunonen, S. V. (1996). Evaluating replicability of factors in the Revised NEO Personality Inventory: Confirmatory factor analysis versus Procrustes rotation. *Journal of Personality and Social Psychology, 70,* 552-566.

Mischel, W., Shoda, Y., & Rodriguez, M. L. (1989). Delay of gratification in children. *Science, 244,* 933-938.

Newman, J. P. (1987). Reaction to punishment in extraverts and psychopaths: Implications for the impulsive behavior of disinhibited individuals. *Journal of Research in Personality, 21,* 464-480.

Paunonen, S. V. (1997). On chance and factor congruence following orthogonal Procrustes rotation. *Educational and Psychological Measurement, 57,* 33-59.

Paunonen, S. V., Jackson, D. N., Trzebinski, J., & Forsterling, F. (1992). Personality structure across cultures: A multimethod evaluation. *Journal of Personality and Social Psychology, 62,* 447-456.

Piedmont, R. L., Bain, E., McCrae, R. R., & Costa, P. T., Jr. (2002). The applicability of the Five-Factor Model in a Subsaharan culture: The NEO-PI-R in Shona. In R. R. McCrae & J. Allik (Eds.), *The Five-Factor Model of personality across cultures* (pp. 155-173). New York: Kluwer Academic/Plenum Publishers.

Piedmont, R. L., & Chae, J. H. (1997). Cross-cultural generalizability of the Five-Factor Model of personality: Development and validation of the NEO-PI-R for Koreans. *Journal of Cross-Cultural Psychology, 28,* 131-155.

Realo, A., Allik, J., & Vadi, M. (1997). The hierarchical structure of collectivism. *Journal of Research in Personality, 31,* 93-116.

Rhee, E., Uleman, J. S., & Lee, H. K. (1996). Variations in collectivism and individualism by in-group and culture: Confirmatory factor analyses. *Journal of Personality and Social Psychology, 71,* 1037-1054.

Rolland, J. P. (2000, July). Cross-cultural validity of the Five-Factor Model of personality. In J. Allik and R. R. McCrae (Chairs), *Personality and culture: The Five-Factor Theory perspective.* Symposium presented at the XXVII International Congress of Psychology, Stockholm, Sweden.

Schwartz, S. H. (1994). Beyond individualism/collectivism: New cultural dimensions of values. In U. Kim, H. C. Triandis, Ç. Kağıtçıbaşı, S. C. Choi, & G. Yoon (Eds.), *Individualism and collectivism: Theory, method, and applications* (pp. 85-119). Thousand Oaks, CA: Sage.

Smith, P. B., & Schwartz, S. H. (1997). Values. In J. W. Berry, M. H. Segall, & Ç. Kağıtçıbaşı (Vol. Eds.), *Handbook of cross-cultural psychology: Vol. 3. Social behavior and applications* (2nd ed., pp. 77-118). Boston, MA: Allyn and Bacon.

Smith, P. B., Trompenaars, F., & Dugan, S. (1995). The Rotter locus of control scale in 43 countries: A test

of cultural relativity. *International Journal of Psychology, 30,* 377-400.
Suh, E., Diener, E., Oishi, S., Triandis, H. C. (1998). The shifting basis of life satisfaction judgments across cultures: Emotions versus norms. *Journal of Personality and Social Psychology, 74,* 482-493.
Toomela, A. (in press). Culture as semiosphere: On the role of culture in the culture-individual relationship. In I. E. Josephs and J. Valsiner (Eds.), *Dialogicality in development.* Westpoort, CT: Greenwood.
Triandis, H. C. (1988). Collectivism and individualism: A reconceptualization of a basic concept in cross-cultural psychology. In G. K. Verma & C. Bagley (Eds.), *Personality, attitudes, and cognitions* (pp. 60-95). London: MacMillan.
Triandis, H. C. (1995). *Individualism and collectivism.* Boulder, CO: Westview Press.
UNICEF (1991). *The state of the world's children 1991.* Oxford: Oxford University Press.
Van de Vijver, F. J. R., & Leung, K. (1997). *Methods and data analyses for cross-cultural research.* Thousand Oaks, CA: Sage.
Verkasalo, M., Daun, Å., & Niit, T. (1994). Universal values in Estonia, Finland, and Sweden. *Ethnologia Europaea, 24,* 101-117.

AUTHOR NOTE

This research was supported by grant 4423 from the Estonian Science Foundation (2000-2001). While writing this article, the second author was supported by a fellowship (F/00/036) and a grant (GOA/00/02) from the Research Council of the Katholieke Universiteit Leuven. Portions of this article were presented at the XXVIIth International Congress of Psychology, July 2000, Sweden. We thank an anonymous reviewer for constructive criticism and helpful comments on earlier drafts of what became this chapter. We are also grateful to Jean-Pierre Rolland and Thomas A. Martin for kindly sharing their data with us. Address correspondence to Kenn Konstabel, Department of Psychology, University of Tartu, Tiigi 78, Tartu 50410, Estonia. E-mail: nek@psych.ut.ee.

THE NEO FIVE-FACTOR INVENTORY IN CZECH, POLISH, AND SLOVAK CONTEXTS

MARTINA HŘEBÍČKOVÁ,* TOMÁŠ URBÁNEK,* IVO ČERMÁK,* PIOTR SZAROTA,** EMÍLIA FICKOVÁ*** & LUCIA ORLICKÁ***

*Institute of Psychology, Academy of Sciences of the Czech Republic, **Polish Academy of Sciences and Warsaw School of Advanced Social Psychology, ***Slovak Academy of Sciences*

Abstract. The principal aim of this chapter is to investigate the validity and the generalized applicability of the NEO Five-Factor Inventory (NEO-FFI) across three different countries and languages. These countries represent West Slavic branches of the Indo-European languages. We first examine the psychometric characteristics of the NEO-FFI (reliabilities, factor structure of the items, and congruence coefficients). Next, we compare four instruments proposed to measure the five personality dimensions, namely the NEO Five-Factor Inventory, the Five-Factor Personality Inventory, the Big Five Questionnaire, and the Czech Big Five Markers. We report data regarding their reliability and convergent and discriminant validity using multitrait-multimethod analysis and structural equation modeling. Finally, we compare Czech, Polish, and Slovak adolescents on the scales of the NEO-FFI.

Keywords: Factor structure, multimethod assessment, national character, adolescent personality

1. PERSONALITY IN THE SLAVIC WORLD

1.1. Language

There is one obvious similarity between Czechs, Slovaks, and Poles. They all speak very similar languages—from the Western perspective almost indistinguishable. At the present time the Slavic world comprises 13 languages, each with a distinct literary standard (Jakobson, 1955). In the usual classification they are divided into three groups: Eastern, Western, and Southern Slavic. Czech, together with Polish, Slovak and Upper and Lower Serbian (Lusatian), is a member of the West-Slavic group within the Slavonic branch of Indo-European languages (Stone, 1990). The long evolution of Protoslavonic (Primitive Slavonic), which took around three millennia, can be traced up to its final stage—the entrance of the Slavs onto the historical scene (ca. 6th Century), the oldest foreign records of Slavonic proper and common nouns (ca. 7th Century), the formation of the first hereditary Slavonic states (10th century), the appearance of Slavonic written literature (9th Century), and the final dissolution of the Slavonic linguistic unity toward the beginning of the second millennium. However, many similarities have persisted up to the present time.

The dissolution of linguistic unity was accompanied by historical changes in Central and Eastern Europe, which resulted in the division of the region into two different cultural worlds founded on different religious systems: the world of Latin culture—*Slavia Romana*, and the world of Byzantine culture—*Slavia Orthodoxae* (Bobrownicka, 1995). This division can be easily recognized even in modern times. Thus, the Czech Republic, together with Poland, Slovakia, Croatia, and Slovenia, comprise Slavia Romana, while Russia, the Ukraine, Belarus, Bulgaria, Serbia (Yugoslavia) and Macedonia constitute Slavia Orthodoxae. Bosnia and Herzegovina comprise three cultural worlds, Latin, Byzantine, and Muslim.

Linguistic similarity does not imply cultural similarity (Bobrownicka, 1995). In the case of the Czech Republic, Slovakia and Poland, however, linguistic similarities are accompanied by similarities in both distant and more recent history and cultural heritage that connect this region to Western civilization (cf. Huntington, 1996).

Czech, Polish and Slovak languages are flexible languages—nouns and numerals are declined and verbs conjugated, there is de facto only one past tense, and there is a well-developed system of verbal aspects and voices. Around 10 million people speak the Czech language in the Czech Republic, about 5 million people speak Slovak in Slovakia, and about 39 million people speak Polish in Poland.

1.2. The Five-Factor Model of Personality in Czech, Polish, and Slovak Contexts

In the framework of the Five-Factor Model of personality two approaches are usually differentiated: lexical (taxonomic) and dispositional (questionnaire; John & Srivastava, 1999; Wiggins, 1997). For lexical researchers, the Five-Factor Model has been derived from lexical data; it is a model of personality attributes and it is, therefore, descriptive rather than explanatory (Saucier & Goldberg, 1996). In contrast, the Five-Factor Model in a dispositional approach is based on factor analyses of questionnaire scales. It is assumed that the five factors correspond to biological traits, which can explain behavior (McCrae & Costa, 1996; McCrae & Costa, 1999). Both approaches share another similarity as well: striving after completeness (in case of the questionnaire approach through the collection of many items from different questionnaires). From this point of view there is no theoretical distinction, because both are lexical in spirit. Both these approaches have been implemented in research on the Five-Factor Model in Czech, Polish, and Slovak. At the end of the last century Professor Alois Angleitner from the University of Bielefeld coordinated research projects aimed at verification of the validity of the Five-Factor Model of personality description in the Czech, Polish, and Slovak languages. Lists of personality-relevant adjectives and nouns were formed (in Czech, moreover, personality-relevant verbs were also listed) in the first phase of the lexical projects. The lists were reduced in the second phase according to the German classification system (Angleitner, Ostendorf, & John, 1990). Several studies concerning this stage of the lexical project have been published in Czech (Hřebíčková, 1995), in Polish (Szarota, 1996), and in Slovak (Ruisel, 1997). The existence of the five-factor structure of personality description was confirmed in Czech by Hřebíčková (1997), and in Polish by Szarota (1997); lexical studies in the Slovak Republic have not been completed yet. Representative lexical studies have been performed in two other Slavonic languages as well: Russian (Shmelyov & Pokhil'ko, 1993) and Croatian (Mlačić, 2000).

The factors of the Czech five-factor structure were labeled Extraversion/Surgency (I), Agreeableness (II), Conscientiousness (III), Emotional Stability (IV), and Intellect (V) and provide a fairly typical version of the five-factor structure. Although some subtle differences may be observed, the Polish five-factor structure also seems to be a fair version of the Big Five. Agreeableness (II), Conscientiousness (III) and Intellect (V) were virtually identical to the American-English structure. However, the Extraversion (I) factor had no sociability facet, and Emotional Stability (IV) included content related to self-control.

Czech and Polish five-factor structures have been used in cross-cultural comparisons. De Raad in recent times has instigated several studies comparing five-factor structures in different languages (De Raad, Perugini, & Szirmák, 1997; De Raad, Di Blas, & Perugini, 1998, De Raad, Perugini, Hřebíčková, & Szarota, 1998). In a recent review De Raad, Perugini, Hřebíčková, and Szarota (1998) compared seven languages (English, Dutch, German, Hungarian, Italian, Czech, and Polish). Within each language, terms that had clear English equivalents in the Goldberg (1992) structure were identified, and congruence coefficients were calculated in the different languages, using the American English solution as a benchmark. The Polish five-factor structure corresponds with the American English better than the Czech one. Peabody and De Raad (2000) chose another strategy for a comparison of structures across languages. They used a qualitative examination of factor content, looking carefully at the content of factors derived from the five-factor structures in different languages (Hungarian, Dutch, Polish, Czech, and two independent Italian lexical studies were used). The overall framework within which the comparisons were carried out was a version of the Big Five presented in Peabody and Goldberg (1989). From this comparison it followed that the contents of the Agreeableness (II) and Intellect (V) factors are similar whereas the contents of Conscientiousness (III), Extraversion (I), and Emotional Stability (IV) differ in the Czech and Polish models. The Polish Extraversion factor contains characteristics of persistence, which in the Czech are incorporated in the Conscientiousness factor. Irritableness and fearfulness are included in one factor— Emotional Stability—in the Czech. The Polish fourth factor represents only Irritableness, and the Polish five-factor structure does not comprise Fearfulness.

The dispositional (questionnaire) approach to the Five-Factor Model has been elaborated primarily by Costa and McCrae. Their Five-Factor Theory of personality (McCrae & Costa, 1999) and their instrument, the NEO Personality Inventory, were originally developed in the context of longitudinal studies of personality and aging. The short version, the NEO Five-Factor Inventory (NEO-FFI; Costa & McCrae, 1992), has been translated into Czech, Polish, and Slovak, and has been used in several research projects. The NEO-FFI was first applied as a validity criterion in the Czech

(Hřebíčková, 1993) and the Polish (Szarota, 1997) lexical studies. The correlations of the NEO-FFI scales with factors derived from the representative Czech and Polish five-factor structures were examined. The Czech version of the instrument was used in further research (e.g. Blatný, in press; Macek, Osecká, Hřebíčková & Bernard, 1998; Macek, Hřebíčková & Čermák, 1999; Řehulka & Řehulková, 1999; Štěpaníková & Macek, 1997), and a *Professional Manual* of the Czech version of the NEO-FFI by Hřebíčková and Urbánek (2001) is available for Czech psychologists. Zawadzki, Strelau, Szczepaniak, and Sliwinska (1998) are the authors of the Polish NEO-FFI *Manual*. A Slovak version of the NEO-FFI was developed by Ruisel (1998) and was used by Ficková (1999; 2000), Orlická (2001), Ruiselová (2000), and Stríženec and Ruisel (1998).

2. PSYCHOMETRIC PROPERTIES OF THE CZECH, POLISH, AND SLOVAK NEO FIVE-FACTOR INVENTORIES

The purpose of the first study is to evaluate the psychometric integrity of the Czech, Polish, and Slovak translations of the NEO-FFI. For each national version of the NEO-FFI, internal consistency of the scales was examined. Item-level principal component analysis was performed, and factor congruence coefficients were calculated to compare the similarity of the NEO-FFI across cultures.

Subjects. The Czech version of the NEO-FFI was administered to 945 subjects (417 males, 518 females, 10 did not indicate their gender). Mean age of the sample was 24.34 years (range = 14-81, 15 subjects did not indicate their age, SD = 13.16). The participants represented a wide range of educational, cultural, and social backgrounds. The Polish sample consisted of 350 subjects (157 boys and 193 girls) with mean age 16.6 years, SD = 1.1. The Slovak subjects were 516 adolescents (209 boys, 300 girls, 7 did not indicate their gender); mean age of the sample was 16.49 years (range = 14-23, SD = 1.8).

Measure. The scales of the NEO Five-Factor Inventory (Costa & McCrae, 1992) are: a) Neuroticism, reflecting anxiety, hostility, depression, self-consciousness, impulsiveness, and vulnerability; b) Extraversion, comprising warmth, gregariousness, assertiveness, activity, excitement-seeking, and positive emotions; c) Openness to Experience in the areas of fantasy, aesthetics, feelings, actions, ideas, and values; d) Agreeableness, reflecting altruism, sympathy, trust, and nurturing tendencies and; e) Conscientiousness, comprising organization, punctuality, achievement, and honesty.

The NEO-FFI is a shortened version of the NEO Personality Inventory and includes many of its better aspects. The NEO-FFI comprises 60 self-report items, 12 items for each of the personality domains.

Two psychologists independently translated the original version of the NEO-FFI. The preliminary Czech version of the items was formulated through comparison of both translations. Afterwards, the back translation of the NEO-FFI was done by the translator and reviewed by the authors of the original version. Eight problematic items were

Table 1. Reliability (Cronbach alpha) of NEO-FFI Scales in Six National Samples.

NEO-FFI Scales	C	P	S	G	Can	US	M
Neuroticism	.81	.82	.79	.85	.87	.86	**.83**
Extraversion	.79	.80	.78	.80	.84	.77	**.79**
Openness	.60	.69	.66	.71	.73	.73	**.68**
Agreeableness	.70	.73	.69	.71	.75	.68	**.71**
Conscientiousness	.84	.84	.83	.85	.81	.81	**.83**
Mean	**.75**	**.77**	**.75**	**.78**	**.80**	**.77**	

Note. C = Czech sample, P = Polish sample, S = Slovak sample, G = German sample (Borkenau &Ostendorf, 1993), Can = Canadian sample (Holden & Fekken, 1994), US = American sample (Costa & McCrae, 1992).

reformulated and the final Czech version of the NEO-FFI was used in this research. Analogous strategies were used in the formulation of the Polish and Slovak versions.

2.1. Results

Reliability. Table 1 gives the internal consistencies for the five scales of the NEO-FFI in six national samples, namely Czech, Polish, Slovak, German, Canadian, and American. None of the scales showed an alpha lower than 0.60. The mean alpha reliability of the NEO-FFI scales was highest in Canadian sample (.80), followed by German sample (.78). Mean reliability of the Polish NEO-FFI was as high as the mean reliability obtained for the American normative data (.77). The lowest mean reliabilities were found in the Czech and Slovak versions of the NEO-FFI (.75). The most reliable scales in the NEO-FFI are Neuroticism and Conscientiousness (mean reliability = .83), while Openness showed lowest mean reliability in the six samples (.68).

Factor analysis. An explanatory principal components analysis with five components rotated by varimax was undertaken on the item intercorrelations. We were interested in comparing five-factor solutions across national samples so we did not address the issue of alternative numbers of factors. The first ten eigenvalues in the Czech sample were 7.51, 4.22, 3.69, 3.49, 2.47, 1.57, 1.41, 1.35, 1.16, and 1.11; in the Polish sample they were 7.57, 4.51, 3.98, 3.65, 2.40, 1.80, 1.52, 1.38, 1.37, and 1.32; and in the Slovak sample, 7.45, 4.39, 3.58, 3.02, 2.47, 1.86, 1.66, 1.40, 1.30, and 1.27. The percentages of variance explained by the five factors were 35.68% (Czech), 36.85% (Polish), and 34.85% (Slovak). The varimax-rotated factor structures are shown in Table 2.

In the Czech sample, 52 of 60 items had loadings greater than or equal to .30 on the correct NEO-FFI factor. Eight of the Czech items did not load on the expected factor. The discrepancies were due to two items expected to measure Extraversion (27, 57), four items from the Openness to Experience scale (8, 18, 28, 38), and two items from the Agreeableness scale (29, 34). With the exception of two items from the Openness

Table 2. Item Factor Analysis of the Czech, the Polish, and the Slovak NEO-Five-Factor Inventory.

Factor	Item	N			E			O			A			C			h^2		
		C	P	S	C	P	S	C	P	S	C	P	S	C	P	S	C	P	S
Neuroticism	1	**.43**	**.41**	**.41**	-.17	-.28	-.07	.01	.17	-.04	.11	.01	.22	-.07	.02	-.06	.24	.28	.23
	6	**.62**	**.60**	**.57**	-.02	-.08	-.19	.06	.00	.01	.07	.16	-.07	-.10	-.13	-.03	.41	.42	.38
	11	**.53**	**.55**	**.65**	-.11	.11	.04	.01	.11	.11	.10	.00	-.06	.19	-.01	-.03	.35	.34	.44
	16	**.36**	**.48**	**.31**	-.30	-.47	-.26	.23	.10	.13	-.06	-.09	.09	-.11	-.17	-.07	.30	.52	.20
	21	**.66**	**.74**	**.67**	-.14	-.07	-.12	-.03	.01	.02	-.12	-.02	-.05	.01	.03	-.04	.48	.56	.47
	26	**.65**	**.59**	**.67**	-.13	-.14	-.17	.11	.11	.11	-.02	.12	-.07	-.11	-.23	-.12	.47	.46	.52
	31	**.53**	**.50**	**.42**	-.13	-.29	-.24	.08	.04	.16	.18	.04	.14	-.16	-.13	-.06	.37	.36	.29
	36	**.38**	**.55**	**.42**	.14	.01	.05	-.06	-.07	.01	-.40	-.31	-.13	.01	-.03	-.00	.34	.41	.20
	41	**.56**	**.42**	**.48**	-.03	.00	-.02	-.13	-.00	-.02	-.00	-.09	.12	-.27	-.32	-.27	.41	.30	.32
	46	**.42**	**.50**	**.36**	-.36	-.47	-.34	.14	.06	.15	-.04	-.10	.09	-.07	-.09	-.08	.34	.51	.29
	51	**.66**	**.60**	**.66**	.07	-.08	.05	.02	.05	-.01	.00	.11	.06	-.16	-.23	-.12	.48	.45	.46
	56	**.56**	**.52**	**.52**	-.06	.00	.04	.10	-.05	-.01	-.10	.16	-.02	-.17	-.17	-.03	.38	.34	.28
Extraversion	2	.03	.10	.02	**.66**	**.64**	**.60**	-.01	.15	-.03	-.02	-.01	.10	.06	-.14	.03	.45	.47	.38
	7	.04	.12	.11	**.64**	**.57**	**.63**	.07	-.03	.03	.07	.14	.16	-.03	-.14	-.03	.43	.38	.44
	12	-.18	-.25	-.20	**.63**	**.31**	**.54**	-.02	.04	.03	.03	-.13	.28	-.14	-.30	-.01	.45	.27	.42
	17	-.02	-.03	.02	**.68**	**.59**	**.69**	.07	.24	-.01	.00	.07	.10	.10	.04	.10	.49	.42	.51
	22	-.04	-.08	-.11	**.61**	**.59**	**.55**	.03	.17	.11	-.12	-.13	-.21	.00	-.08	.04	.40	.42	.38
	27	.03	-.07	.07	.19	.39	.17	-.13	-.02	-.12	.21	.20	.27	-.24	-.21	-.18	.16	.25	.16
	32	-.15	-.06	-.08	**.50**	**.55**	**.60**	.15	.19	.10	-.30	-.09	-.11	.13	.17	.24	.42	.39	.45
	37	-.20	-.15	-.17	**.70**	**.74**	**.67**	.06	-.05	-.09	.06	-.04	-.11	.11	.11	.12	.56	.59	.52
	42	-.33	-.30	-.26	**.55**	**.52**	**.37**	.04	.03	.12	.12	.08	.13	.01	.05	.08	.44	.38	.25
	47	-.14	.02	-.03	**.33**	**.50**	**.50**	-.02	.17	-.06	-.35	-.11	-.27	.15	.24	.11	.29	.35	.35
	52	-.17	-.04	-.08	**.47**	**.65**	**.49**	.20	.17	.02	-.21	-.20	-.13	.33	.29	**.38**	.45	.59	.42
	57	-.15	-.06	-.05	.19	**.43**	.28	-.05	-.08	.13	.18	-.31	.10	.13	.12	-.04	.12	.31	.12
Openness	3	.15	.10	.22	-.06	.07	-.04	**.36**	**.36**	**.36**	.10	.10	.25	-.29	-.09	-.18	.26	.17	.29
	8	-.00	-.16	-.04	-.11	-.02	-.01	-.03	.22	**.69**	.03	-.06	.05	-.39	-.20	.09	.17	.12	.50
	13	.05	-.01	.17	.04	-.01	.19	**.69**	**.67**	**.56**	.07	.02	-.07	.10	.06	.10	.50	.45	.40
	18	-.23	-.09	-.18	.00	.06	-.01	**.28**	**.31**	**.32**	.10	-.03	.13	-.18	-.13	.08	.18	.13	.16
	23	-.02	.07	.11	.06	.08	.08	**.58**	**.69**	**.50**	.11	-.01	-.01	.04	.00	.02	.36	.50	.28
	28	.03	-.09	-.05	.33	.22	.32	.15	**.34**	.21	-.25	-.20	-.13	.07	.08	.02	.21	.23	.17
	33	.07	.01	.07	.05	.07	.01	**.36**	**.40**	.27	.27	.18	.19	-.01	.10	.04	.22	.22	.12

Table 2 (continued)

Factor	Item	N C	N P	N S	E C	E P	E S	O C	O P	O S	A C	A P	A S	C C	C P	C S	h² C	h² P	h² S
	38	-.10	-.13	-.15	-.01	.04	.08	-.16	.12	-.06	-.03	-.31	.16	-.04	-.14	-.12	.04	.15	.08
	43	.04	.06	.12	.04	.05	.13	**.67**	**.73**	**.64**	.01	.01	-.02	.05	.03	.02	.46	.55	.45
	48	-.00	.04	.05	-.00	-.05	-.08	**.59**	**.62**	**.51**	-.04	-.02	.10	-.08	.07	.02	.36	.40	.28
	53	-.13	.09	-.05	.09	.14	.13	**.48**	**.49**	**.40**	-.15	-.18	-.17	**.32**	.28	**.45**	.40	.39	.42
	58	.10	.11	-.02	.05	.07	-.00	**.58**	**.48**	**.68**	-.24	-.01	-.14	-.09	-.00	-.03	.42	.25	.49
Agreeableness																			
	4	.07	.03	.20	.05	.02	**.35**	.21	-.00	.05	**.37**	**.49**	.26	**.43**	.27	**.33**	.38	.32	.35
	9	-.29	-.38	-.22	-.10	-.07	-.00	.02	.03	.07	**.43**	**.35**	**.33**	.26	.19	.29	.36	.32	.25
	14	-.08	-.17	-.10	.17	.02	.15	-.05	-.16	.02	**.56**	**.53**	**.58**	.13	.02	.07	.37	.35	.38
	19	.23	.16	.20	.14	.00	**.30**	.00	.03	.03	**.39**	**.57**	.24	.15	.03	.11	.25	.36	.21
	24	-.17	-.08	-.06	.00	.15	.23	.08	.16	.17	**.38**	**.50**	**.42**	.20	.16	-.11	.23	.34	.28
	29	-.24	-.04	-.17	.15	-.01	.12	.22	.12	-.07	.18	.25	**.37**	-.21	-.07	.00	.22	.09	.19
	34	-.08	.16	-.06	**.42**	**.34**	**.51**	.02	-.06	.01	.29	.24	.24	.14	.20	.26	.29	.25	.40
	39	-.03	.01	-.05	.22	.17	.16	.04	-.12	.12	**.62**	**.56**	**.66**	.04	-.13	.06	.44	.38	.49
	44	-.00	.05	.24	.20	-.08	-.00	.01	.07	.05	**.52**	**.59**	**.40**	-.09	-.27	-.16	.33	.44	.25
	49	.09	.22	.28	.14	.27	.22	.27	.26	.22	**.40**	**.45**	.21	**.32**	.26	**.32**	.38	.47	.34
	54	.05	.04	.09	-.09	-.18	-.22	.01	-.11	-.06	**.37**	**.52**	**.40**	-.07	.00	.09	.15	.32	.24
	59	.09	.00	.19	-.08	-.13	-.15	.04	.03	.05	**.55**	**.64**	**.59**	-.03	-.02	-.01	.33	.44	.42
Conscientiousness																			
	5	.01	-.09	.13	.02	-.12	.06	-.07	.03	.00	.18	.07	.15	**.64**	**.45**	**.56**	.45	.24	.36
	10	-.12	-.08	-.16	.03	.15	.16	-.06	-.01	-.08	.00	-.05	-.02	**.63**	**.63**	**.60**	.42	.44	.42
	15	-.16	-.10	-.16	.05	-.06	.03	-.10	-.06	.06	.06	.14	.16	**.52**	**.60**	**.47**	.32	.39	.29
	20	.11	-.00	.12	-.05	.06	.01	.02	.02	.12	.14	.14	.05	**.69**	**.60**	**.71**	.52	.39	.55
	25	-.06	-.18	-.09	.09	.05	.12	.04	-.01	-.04	-.23	-.07	-.25	**.64**	**.65**	**.63**	.48	.47	.49
	30	-.31	-.24	-.23	-.06	-.09	-.00	-.04	.06	-.04	.13	.11	.04	**.51**	**.56**	**.46**	.39	.40	.28
	35	-.06	.07	-.05	.18	.05	.15	.03	.00	-.05	-.32	.03	-.20	**.58**	**.69**	**.71**	.49	.49	.58
	40	-.07	-.09	-.04	.02	.17	.14	.05	.00	.05	.17	.00	.08	**.56**	**.51**	**.62**	.35	.30	.43
	45	-.15	-.28	-.17	-.08	.01	-.09	-.07	-.01	.07	.21	-.02	.29	**.46**	**.41**	**.45**	.30	.25	.34
	50	-.13	-.15	-.18	.08	.07	.17	-.00	.01	.05	-.03	-.03	-.10	**.64**	**.70**	**.60**	.45	.52	.45
	55	-.27	-.25	-.23	.13	.03	.00	-.01	.06	.03	.22	.01	**.34**	**.43**	**.59**	**.43**	.33	.43	.36
	60	-.00	.01	-.00	.14	.21	.04	.13	.19	.08	-.28	-.17	-.20	**.53**	**.48**	**.60**	.38	.35	.42

Note. Loadings ≥ 0.30 are listed in bold. $Ns = 945$ for Czech (C), 350 for Polish (P), and 516 for Slovak (S) samples.

Table 3. Comparison of Czech, Polish, Slovak, American,
And German NEO-FFI Item Factors.

	N	E	O	A	C	M
C – P	0.94	0.92	0.90	0.84	0.95	**0.91**
C – S	0.96	0.94	0.83	0.89	0.93	**0.91**
C – U	0.95	0.93	0.91	0.86	0.95	**0.92**
C – G	0.95	0.93	0.85	0.92	0.95	**0.92**
P – S	0.94	0.91	0.85	0.75	0.93	**0.88**
P – U	0.94	0.94	0.90	0.85	0.93	**0.91**
P – G	0.95	0.92	0.90	0.88	0.96	**0.92**
S – U	0.91	0.91	0.83	0.79	0.93	**0.88**
S – G	0.94	0.93	0.90	0.86	0.96	**0.92**
U – G	0.94	0.93	0.88	0.93	0.93	**0.92**
Mean	**0.94**	**0.93**	**0.88**	**0.86**	**0.94**	**0.91**

Note: C = Czech, P = Polish, S = Slovak, U = United States, G = German. These are congruence coefficients between five rotated factors derived from principal component analysis of the 60 NEO-FFI items in each country.

scale (8, 38) and two items from the Agreeableness scale (29, 34), the items of the Polish NEO-FFI loaded most highly on the appropriate factor. In the Slovak sample, 51 of the 60 items marked the appropriate factors with loadings ≥ 0.30; nine items did not load on the intended factor: two from Extraversion (27, 57), three from Openness (28, 33, 38), and four from Agreeableness (4,19,34, 49).

Congruence coefficients. The similarity of the NEO-FFI item factor structures in five languages was assessed by means of congruence coefficients (McDonald, 1991) between the varimax-rotated principal components. We compared the varimax-solutions in the three West Slavic languages with the results of a previous factor analysis carried out by Borkenau and Ostendorf (1993) on German normative data and with a factor analysis of American data published by Parker and Stumpf (1998). In the latter study academically talented young people (mean age of 12 years) were used as subjects.

The results (see Table 3) showed the highest mean congruence was between German and other NEO-FFI structures. When the congruence coefficients among the three West Slavic languages were compared, the highest congruence was observed between the Czech and the Slovak factors, and between the Czech and the Polish factors, whereas a slightly lower congruence was found between the Polish and Slovak factors. The Neuroticism and Conscientiousness factors showed the highest mean congruences, the Agreeableness factor the lowest.

2.2. Discussion

The present results indicate that almost all scales fulfilled the .70 level criterion recommended by Nunnally (1978) for an alpha coefficient. The Openness to Experience scale does not exceed this level in any of the three national samples, consistent with the results of factor analyses reported above. The Agreeableness scale also has a low internal consistency in the Slovak sample. If we compare these findings with the German, Canadian, and American results, we can see that alpha coefficients of these two scales are also lowest in these samples. Items 27 and 57 from the Extraversion scale did not load highly on the factor in the Czech and Slovak samples, whereas in the Polish, American, and German structures they have adequate factor loadings. Both items indicate that the respondent prefers individual work over work with others. For Czechs and Slovaks, these items are probably not suitable as indicators of (low) Extraversion.

Four items of the Openness to Experience scale have factor loadings less then 0.30 and thus they are not included in Openness to Experience in the Czech sample; similarly, two in the Polish and three in the Slovak sample fail to load as intended. This finding led us to think over again the cultural adequacy of these "bad" items. It seems to us that the content of item 18 is experience-based in Western cultures, but does not express the real life experience of people in post-communist countries. We can suppose that people from former communist countries will differ from persons living in democratic countries mainly on the Openness to Experience scale. Angleitner and Ostendorf (2000) compared personality traits in residents of the former East and West Germanys. Personality profiles for the two samples were virtually identical, but former East Germans scored about one quarter standard deviation lower in Openness than former West Germans. For example, item 18, "I believe letting students hear controversial speakers can only confuse and mislead them," is clear for people living in Western countries. But an individual who has lived 40 years under a totalitarian regime can feel that acceptance of different approaches and views is difficult. This item is not included in any factor in the Czech sample and has a lower loading in the Polish and Slovak samples in comparison to American and German factor loadings. Item 28, asking whether respondents often taste new and exotic meals, makes sense only in countries where the availability of exotic meals and travel opportunities has not been interrupted by political development. These items are problematic in the Czech and Slovak NEO-FFI versions, but also in the German sample. We can also speculate about the national mentality as an interpretation of very divergent findings related to this item in individual nations. Item 38, asking whether people are guided in their decisions by the opinions of religious authorities, does not load on the Openness to Experience factor in any five-factor structure, including the adolescent American structure (see Parker & Stumpf, 1998) and the Russian version of the questionnaire (R. R. McCrae, personal message, March 1996). We can carefully form a tentative conclusion that (church) authorities are not so important in the life of adolescents (or, when they are, adolescents deny it). The weak internal reliability of the Openness to Experience scale was largely caused by the four items, 8, 18, 28, and 38. A similar set of potentially weak NEO-FFI items also exists within the Agreeableness scale. Item 29 failed to mark the factor in the all matrices except Slovak and item 34 is problematic in all four matrices except German. For the new revision of the NEO-FFI Parker and Stumpf (1998) suggest replacing problematic items of Openness to Experience and Agreeableness scales with more appropriate items from the rich item pool of the NEO-PI-R. We can agree with this statement. Eight problematic items in the Czech NEO-FFI version were reformulated and the revised version was used in several research studies (Hřebíčková & Urbánek, 2001). In this new study 55 of the 60 items had loadings ≥ .30 on the correct NEO-FFI factor. Four of these five reformulated items—57 (E), 8, 38 (O) and 29 (A)—are still problematic.

Results showed higher congruence between the German and the American factors than among Slavonic languages. Low mean congruence of the factors Agreeableness and Openness to Experience was already expected on the basis of an inspection of the factor patterns reported in Table 2.

3. A COMPARISON OF FOUR MEASURES OF THE FIVE-FACTOR MODEL

In addition to increasing interest in the application of the Five-Factor Model not only in research but also in clinical and applied settings, there is interest in instruments for reliably measuring individual dimensions. These instruments can be classified into two major groups. Self-rating inventories belong to the first group, in which adjectives are used. Examples are Goldberg's Big Five adjective markers (Goldberg, 1990, 1992) and their reduced version (Saucier, 1994), the Revised Interpersonal Adjective Scales-Big Five (IAS-R-B5; Trapnell & Wiggins, 1990), the 23 Bipolar Big Five questionnaire (23BB5; Duijsens & Diekstra, 1995), the Short Adjective Checklist to measure the Big Five (SACBIF; Perugini & Leone, 1996) and the Czech Big Five Markers (CBFM; Hřebíčková, Urbánek, & Čermák, 2000). Instruments in the second group use items formulated as short sentences. Internationally, the Revised NEO Personality Inventory (NEO-PI-R; Costa & McCrae, 1992) is the most widely validated instrument to assess the Five-Factor Model. In Europe two others five-factor based inventories have arisen : in The Netherlands the Five-Factor Personality Inventory (FFPI; Hendriks, 1997) and in Italy the Big Five Questionnaire (BFQ; Caprara, Barbaranelli, Borgogni, & Perugini, 1993). John, Donahue, and Kentle (1991) constructed the Big Five Inventory (BFI) containing a short-phrase item format more concrete than Goldberg's single adjective items but of lower complexity than the sentence format used by NEO questionnaires. A number of studies have reported on the psychometric characteristics of each instrument and some studies have compared two or more instruments with each other (e.g. Goldberg, 1992; McCrae & Costa, 1987; Benet-Martínez & John, 1998; John & Srivastava, 1999; Perugini & Ercolani, 1998; Mooradian & Nezlek, 1996; Rosendahl, 1977; Scharf, Tuente, Brinkmeier, & Benne, 1996).

The goal of our second study is to assess convergent and discriminant validity of the five personality dimensions as measured by several questionnaires. The Czech version of the NEO-FFI was compared with three other instruments to assess five basic personality dimensions. Two of them are translated instruments—the FFPI and the BFQ—and one was originally developed in the Czech language, the CBFM. We examined a multitrait-multimethod (MTMM) correlation matrix and used structural equation modeling on a covariance matrix. We also addressed the question of the orthogonality of the Big Five-Factors.

3.1. Method

Sample and procedure. The sample included 253 individuals (135 males, 116 females, 2 did not indicate their sex; age18-62, M = 35.51 years, SD = 12.53 years). The educational level was above average.

Instruments. The revised Czech version of the NEO-FFI, together with FFPI, BFQ, and CBFM were used in the study. *The Five-Factor Personality Inventory* (FFPI) by Hendriks (1997) was based on the Abridged Big Five Circumplex taxonomic model of traits (AB5C model; Hofstee, De Raad & Goldberg, 1992). The model accounts for the fact that a simple structure in which traits are associated with just one underlying dimension is generally not encountered in the area of personality and individual differences. However, few traits have more than two sizeable factor loading. The AB5C model therefore represents trait variables by their projections in a circumplexical plane defined by the two factors on which they have their highest loadings. The FFPI consists of 100 brief and concrete statements, 20 items for each scale. Items were written in the third person singular. This formulation may stimulate the respondent to take an objective perspective. Elementary sentences were constructed (e.g. "helps others") and negations were excluded. In contrast to all other personality questionnaires, the authors excluded all dispositional adjectives and nouns, and used only observable, concrete, and behavioral items, which were represented by verbs. The fifth basic factor was called Autonomy (for Intellectual Autonomy), and the items emphasize the capability to make independent decisions, to resist social pressures to conform, and to maintain an independent opinion on topics. The cross-cultural replicability and generalizability of the five-factor structure shows that the relationships among the 100 trait variables in the FFPI are largely invariant across 13 cultures (Hendriks et al., in press).

The Big Five Questionnaire was constructed by Caprara, Barbaranelli, Borgogni, and Perugini (1993). The BFQ comprises 132 phrases equally distributed over its 10 facet scales, plus a Lie scale, which contains 12 items. The Lie scale was designed to assess socially desirable responding. The Italian authors labeled the first of the Big Five dimensions *Energy.* This dimension is organized into the following two facets: Dynamism, which refers to expansiveness and enthusiasm, and Dominance, which refers to assertiveness and confidence. The dimension usually labeled Agreeableness is labeled Friendliness in the Italian questionnaire and is organized into two facets: Cooperativeness/Empathy, which refers to concern and sensitiveness towards others and their needs, and Politeness, which refers to kindness, civility, docility, and trust. The Conscientiousness dimension is organized into two facets: Scrupulousness, which refers to dependability, orderliness, and precision, and Perseverance, which refers to the capability of fulfilling one's own tasks and commitments. The Emotional Stability dimension was organized into two facets: Emotion Control, which refers to the capacity to cope adequately with one's own anxiety and emotionality, and Impulse Control, which refers to the capacity to control irritation, discontent, and anger. The Openness dimension is organized into two facets: Openness to Culture, which refers to the broadness or narrowness of one's own cultural interests, and Openness to Experiences, which refers to openness to novelty and tolerance of different values. Each facet scale contains 12 items; half are positively worded, half negatively.

Czech Big Five Markers. The fourth instrument in our study was the Czech Big Five markers by Hřebíčková, Urbánek and Čermák (2000). The CBFM contains 60 bipolar rating scales, 12 for each of the 5 factors, and they were selected from two sources. The first source was a representative taxonomy of Czech personality descriptive adjectives (Hřebíčková, 1995; 1997). From the Dictionary of Standard Czech (Academia, 1989) containing approximately 28,000 adjectives, all 4,145 potentially personality-relevant adjectives were selected using the German classification system (Angleitner, Ostendorf, & John, 1990). In a classification task, six judges assigned the 4,145 terms to the 13 categories. Only those adjectives assigned by a majority of the judges to the category of Dispositions were chosen to represent the domain of trait terms. This procedure resulted in 366 adjectives that were rated by 397 subjects. A principal components analysis was performed and five varimax-rotated factors were retained. The major factors of the Czech personality language could be interpreted as the Big Five. The analysis con-firmed the generalizability of the Five-Factor Model in the Czech language as well as the robustness of the Big Five across different samples of variables, rating inventories, and groups of raters (Hřebíčková, 1997). The second source was an analysis of a comprehensive sample of bipolar adjective rating scales (Big Five markers) previously used by several American authors (Goldberg, 1989; John, 1983; McCrae & Costa, 1987; Norman, 1963; Peabody, 1984; Peabody & Goldberg, 1989). Altogether 171 scales were translated into the Czech language and self-ratings from 418 Czech subjects were collected. A principal component analysis with varimax rotation was performed. The five-factor solution represented a clear demonstration of the Big Five factors. From these two sources three experts selected 60 bipolar adjective rating scales representing the Big Five in the Czech language. Adjectives with the highest factor loading for each dimension were chosen and, in addition, facets for Extraversion, Agreeableness, and Intellect/Openness were determined in advance. Adjectives representing Extraversion describe sociability, activity, and talkativeness, which are the main facets of the Czech Extraversion/Surgency factor. Adjectives representing Agreeableness describe relationships to other people and morality. Six bipolar adjective rating scales represent Intellect and six represent Openness to Experience.

3.2. Results

The reliabilities of the scales are given in Table 4. All alpha coefficients are at satisfactory levels. Overall, the reliabilities were impressive for these relatively short rating scales, with the CBFM (mean of .88), followed by the FFPI (.86), the BFQ (.80), and the NEO-FFI (.79). Across instruments, Conscientiousness, Neuroticism (vs. Emotional Stability) and Extraversion (Energy) were measured most reliably, whereas Openness (Autonomy, Intellect/Openness) and Agreeableness were measured less reliably.

Table 5 is the MTMM correlation matrix. Simple inspection of the matrix reveals the similarities of pattern in the submatrices of intercorrelations of the individual methods. There are always quite high correlation values at the diagonal and rather small values (although sometimes statistically significant) in the off-diagonal cells. The

Table 4. Reliability of the NEO-FFI, FFPI, BFQ, and CBFM.

Instrument	N	E	O	A	C	*M*
NEO-FFI	.81	.81	.75	.73	.83	**.79**
FFPI	.88	.86	.85	.82	.86	**.86**
BFQ	.86	.78	.79	.77	.80	**.80**
CBFM	.86	.92	.83	.86	.93	**.88**
Mean	**.85**	**.84**	**.81**	**.80**	**.86**	**.83**

Note. N = Neuroticism or Emotional Stability, E = Extraversion or Energy, O = Openness, Intellect, or Autonomy, A = Agreeableness or Friendliness, C = Conscientiousness.

values in the diagonals of the submatrices are indicators of the convergent validity (negative values are due to reversed orientation of the correlated scales). The values imply a reasonable degree of convergent validity. The values in the off-diagonal cells are indicators of discriminant validity. In our opinion it is not realistic to expect zero correlations between different Big Five scales but rather similar patterns of scale intercorrelations in each submatrix. Although results of factor analyses of the Big Five data are usually reported in orthogonally rotated form, we suppose that nonzero correlations between scales can be expected.

Across all five factors and all instruments, the mean of the convergent validity correlations was .60. The FFPI/CBFM showed the strongest convergence (mean $r = .64$), followed by the NEO-FFI/BFQ and NEO-FFI/FFPI (both mean $r = .63$). The lowest convergence was found between the FFPI and the BFQ (mean $r = .53$). Across instruments mean validities ranged from .69 (Neuroticism) to .48 (Openness). In fact, the correlations are attenuated by less-than-perfect reliabilities of the instruments and disattenuation would raise them.

Overall, the discriminant correlations were low; the absolute values averaged .17 for the NEO-FFI, .19 for the FFPI, .18 for the BFQ, and .20 for the CBFM. Ten of the discriminant correlations reached .40, with the largest correlation (.57) between BFQ Energy and FFPI Autonomy.

As a more formal test of convergent and discriminant validity, we used structural equation modeling for the analysis of this MTMM matrix. The covariance matrix was used in these analyses. Several models were estimated, but during the estimation phase problems with inappropriate parameter values were encountered in some of them, which often happens in this type of model, due to identification problems probably caused by two mutually orthogonal sets of factors (Wothke, 1996). We report three models: a model with orthogonal trait factors (model M1), a model with correlated trait factors (model M2), and a model with correlated trait factors and correlated method factors (M3). Model M1 corresponds with the standard Big Five model, model M2 represents its alternative with correlated factors and model M3 assumes the existence of method factors. The latter model also assumes that these method factors are correlated; it is possible to argue that three self-report questionnaires and one rating inventory in fact do not represent distinct methods.

Table 6 summarizes the overall fit of the three models. Models M2 and M3 are nested in model M1, so we can directly compare their chi-square values. Improvement

Table 5. Multitrait-Multimethod Matrix for NEO-FFI, FFPI, BFQ, and CBFM.

	NEO-FFI					FFPI					BFQ					CBFM				
	N	E	O	A	C	ES	E	Au	A	C	ES	En	O	F	C	ES	E	I/O	A	C
NEO-FFI N																				
E	-.31																			
O	-.02	.18																		
A	-.12	.04	.04																	
C	-.29	.06	-.07	.00																
FFPI ES	**-.72**	.26	.03	.16	.33															
E	-.23	**.74**	.03	.10	.06	.20														
Au	-.49	.30	.30	-.19	.45	.52	.28													
A	-.09	-.10	.14	**.67**	.17	.27	-.03	.04												
C	-.11	-.16	-.27	.16	**.73**	.22	-.02	.22	.34											
BFQ ES	**-.69**	.09	-.09	.20	.25	**.71**	-.02	.30	.23	.12										
En	-.23	.54	.25	-.31	.26	.17	**.46**	.57	-.29	-.06	.05									
O	-.19	.30	**.68**	.01	.15	.17	.13	**.48**	.09	-.12	.12	.51								
F	-.10	.41	.26	**.58**	.03	.15	.44	.05	**.48**	.02	.14	.16	.31							
C	-.06	-.05	.12	-.06	**.64**	.11	-.10	.33	.13	**.54**	.09	.32	.34	.06						
CBFM ES	**-.63**	.32	-.05	.22	.31	**.73**	.22	.37	.22	.17	**.69**	.19	.17	.25	.17					
E	-.16	**.71**	-.01	-.01	.09	.08	**.78**	.30	-.21	-.03	-.12	**.55**	.15	.30	-.05	.19				
I/O	-.26	.39	**.40**	.06	.32	.27	.28	**.48**	.13	.01	.13	.42	**.56**	.24	.25	.35	.35			
A	-.04	.27	-.01	**.56**	.24	.11	.33	.04	**.53**	.28	.08	.03	.10	**.48**	.15	.35	.33	.42		
C	-.18	.09	-.14	.11	**.76**	.26	.12	.34	.24	**.68**	.15	.18	.07	.12	**.61**	.38	.20	.33	.42	

Note: NEO-FFI = NEO Five-Factor Inventory, FFPI = Five Factor Personality Inventory, BFQ = Big Five Questionnaire, CBFM = Czech Big Five Markers, N = Neuroticism, ES = Emotional stability, E = Extraversion, En = Energy, O = Openness to Experience, I/O = Intellect/Openness to Experience, Au = Autonomy, A = Agreeableness, F = Friendliness, C = Conscientiousness. *N* = 252 subjects.

Table 6. Summary of the Model Fit.

Model	Description	Par.	df	χ^2	GFI	RMSEA
M1	Uncorrelated trait factors	40	170	1371.13	0.64	0.167
M2	Correlated trait factors	50	160	1288.73	0.65	0.167
M3	Correlated trait factors and correlated method factors	76	134	590.33	0.83	0.116

Note. Par. = number of parameters, GFI = goodness of fit index, RMSEA = root mean square error of approximation.

of the model fit from M1 to M2 is statistically significant (χ^2 = 82,4; df = 10; p = 0.000), but other reported overall fit indices (GFI = .83 and RMSEA = .116) do not indicate substantial improvement. Improvement of the model fit from M2 to M3 is considerable (χ^2 = 698,4; df = 26; p = 0.000). This result suggests the presence of method variance in the data. However, there is still the possibility of substantial improvement in model fit in Model 3 (GFI = .83 and RMSEA = .116). The sources of model misfit can be attributed to insufficient discriminant validity. Modification indices suggest some overlap of the Agreeableness and Extraversion scales and even Agreeableness and Conscientiousness scales of several methods (see the correlation matrix in Table 5).

More detailed results of the model M3 are given in Table 7, including standardized regression coefficients (factor loadings), residual variances of individual variables, intercorrelations of the latent variables (factors) and variances of latent variables. There are only two statistically non-significant regression weights (A from NEO-FFI on the NEO-FFI factor and Au from FFPI on O factor). All variances of latent variables are significant as are most of the intercorrelations of latent variables. Despite low internal consistency NEO-FFI Openness to Experience and Agreeableness factors are the strongest indicators of their respective factors. Low reliability does not necessarily compromise validity.

All signs of the regression weights are in agreement with orientation of the scale; in fact, only weights of the N from NEO-FFI are negative. This can be expected, because this scale is focused on Neuroticism as opposed to Emotional stability in the other three methods.

3.3 Discussion

Across all four instruments the scales with the lowest reliability were the NEO-FFI scales Agreeableness and Openness. A study by John and Srivastava (1999) that compared data from three instruments used for measurement of five personality dimensions in the United States (BFI, John, et al 1994; Trait Descriptive Adjectives, Goldberg 1992; and NEO-FFI, Costa & McCrae, 1992) found comparable results. The NEO-FFI scale Openness to Experience was least reliable, followed by the Agreeableness scale. Similar findings in another sample were published by Benet-Martínez and John (1998). The Openness to Experience and Agreeableness NEO-FFI scales tended to

Table 7. Detailed Results of the Model M3.

Method	Scale	–N	E	O	A	C	NEO	FFPI	BFQ	CBFM	Residual variance
		\multicolumn{5}{c	}{Trait}	\multicolumn{4}{c	}{Method}	
NEO–	N	–.63					–.54				16.02
FFI	E		.68				.48				9.83
	O			.73			.43				13.18
	A				.89		.02				5.82
	C					.69	.63				6.65
FFPI	ES	.69						.60			2.02
	E		.83					.37			18.79
	Au			–.02				.87			22.55
	A				.77			.20			28.49
	C					.84		.36			19.62
BFQ	ES	.82							.38		35.22
	En		.32						.79		31.63
	O			.54					.73		25.43
	F				.70				.36		46.22
	C					.56			.61		45.11
CBFM	ES	.70								.58	13.58
	E		.76							.47	21.06
	I/O			.32						.74	15.63
	A				.67					.46	15.73
	C					.67				.62	16.17

	\multicolumn{4}{c}{Correlations}	Variance
N					126.99
E	–.11				11.40
O	–.22	–.16			39.60
A	.36	.17	.33		58.92
C	.11	–.28	–.42	.30	44.70
NEO–FFI					8.49
FFPI	.89				69.15
BFQ	.88	.75			72.81
CBFM	.80	.73	.72		25.13

Note: NEO–FFI = NEO Five–Factor Inventory, FFPI = Five Factor Personality Inventory, BFQ = Big Five Questionnaire, CBFM = Czech Big Five Markers, N = Neuroticism, ES = Emotional stability, E = Extraversion, En = Energy, O = Openness to experience, I/O = Intellect/Openness to experience, Au = Autonomy, A = Agreeableness, F = Friendliness, C = Conscientiousness. $N = 252$ subjects.

be less reliable in the Polish and Slovak NEO-FFI versions (see Table 1). John and Srivastava (1999) suggested that items involving trying new and foreign foods and looking to religious authorities for decision on moral issues do not discriminate in adolescents as well as in Costa and McCrae's samples of older adults.

The lowest regression value was for Autonomy on the Openness trait factor, suggesting that this is not equivalent to other measures of that trait. Similar results were obtained by Perugini and Ercolani (1998) in an Italian version of the FFPI. They stated that Autonomy can be an additional alternative for the fifth factor so far labeled as Openness to Experience (Costa & McCrae, 1992), Intellect (Goldberg, 1992), Culture (Norman, 1963), or Creativity and Imagination (Saucier, 1992).

Correlations between method factors are all positive and high (from 0.89 to 0.72). This is caused, in our opinion, by the fact that the methods in fact do not really differ (questionnaires and self–rating scales). More interesting are correlations between individual trait factors (see Table 7). Seven of them are significant, suggesting that people who are emotionally stable score lower on Openness and higher on Agreeableness; that people with higher Extraversion ratings score higher on Agreeableness and lower on Conscientiousness; and that people who are open to experience tend to be agreeable but not conscientious. Finally, more agreeable people see themselves as more conscientious. In our opinion these findings need corroboration in further research.

Although we can conclude that the model M3 represents a description of data that is consistent with present knowledge, there is the possibility of further improvement of the model fit. Inspection of the residual covariances reveals that there are probably some other sources of variation in the data not accounted for by this model.

4. COMPARISONS OF CZECH, POLISH AND SLOVAK ADOLESCENTS

4.1. The Czech National Character

Opinions of historians, politicians, philosophers, and psychologists relating to Czech national character are contradictory, and therefore it is difficult to formulate hypotheses about levels of the five general personality dimensions in the case of Czechs. Paulus Stránský (1643/1840) collected ideas of his contemporary colleagues—historians who noted various faults among the Czech inhabitants: rapacity in wars, cruelty, inebriation. German writers asserted, according to Stránský, that Czech people are restless and quarrelsome by nature. These characteristics suggest a higher level of Neuroticism and lower level of Agreeableness. Contradictory opinions about the agreeableness of the Czech people can often be found in relevant literature. Stránský appreciates in Czechs their hospitality, magnanimity, and self-confidence. About Czech people it is said that they are of a dove-like nature, are mild, and yield rather than stand up to opposition. Avoiding conflicts is usual for people scoring high on Agreeableness. Masaryk (1895), the first president of Czechoslovakia, wrote one paper about the faults of the Czech character, in which he stressed rather its passivity, manifesting itself in the fact that Czechs believe in martyrdom and celebrate it. It is significant that the most brilliant pages of Czech history begin and end with martyrdom—Saint Wenceslas and John Huss. Moreover, Masaryk wrote about a special type of intrigue. "Since the intriguers are unable to behave as lions, they become foxes. Since they can not act as heroes, they become lackeys and help themselves by servile cunning." They use manipulation of others to obtain some advantage that suggests low scores on Agreeableness. According to Hyhlík (1969), Czech people tend to be individualistic and appreciate privacy, and therefore a low score on Extraversion can be hypothesized. Their attitude to work includes characteristics like conscientiousness, responsibility, and pride of accomplishment, as well as a strong sense of duty; for those reasons we can expect higher scores on Conscientiousness. Hyhlík also presents a long list of traits that express intellectual capabilities, abilities, and talents. In his opinion Czech people are rational, industrious, active, inventive, and teachable, think logically, and have the ability of improvisation. In addition, Mahen (1924) considered playfulness as a typical feature of the Czech people. Sýkora (1939) mentioned the musical talent of the whole nation. We can expect higher score of Openness to Experience.

4.2. Polish Cultural Norms and Scripts

Although stereotypes regarding Poles are widespread and well known, little research has been done concerning Polish cultural norms and cultural scripts, which would be reflected in people's behavior. However, some of them have been identified and might be observable at the level of personality traits.

Although Poles are not as expressive as Russians or Brazilians, there is clearly a norm of spontaneity when it comes to expressing their own emotions. Wierzbicka (1994) suggested that in Polish culture "emotional spontaneity is valued more highly than a desire to make someone else feel good;" thus, it encourages the showing of good feelings toward the addressee as well as bad feelings. However, it seems that bad feelings are expressed more readily. Disagreement, disapproval, or irritation can be expressed quite openly, which might shock foreigners from more "agreeable" cultures. Poles would rather be seen as rude and aggressive than as agreeable and self-controlled. As Ronowicz (1995, p. 80) puts it: "an argument is not only considered a good way of exchanging ideas, but also an enjoyable form of conversation." There is also a cultural script for complaining. When two friends meet, they often start a conversation by discussing their own health problems. In a study by Dolinski (1997), Polish subjects usually define their moods as worse than usual, in contrast to American subjects, who always feel better than usual. This might also result in a relatively high level of reported Neuroticism.

The importance of the Roman Catholic Church in Polish history cannot be overestimated. This applies even in the 20th century, despite an almost universal trend to secularization. In Communist Poland, the Church was oppressed, but not under such strong control as in U.S.S.R. or in Czechoslovakia, and it became a strong force in people's struggle for freedom, especially after Karol Wojtyla became Pope John Paul II. At the individual level, the Catholic Church has advocated "family values." According to them, family life has to be more important than individual career. In Poland, marriage is often considered "ever-lasting," and it has one of the smallest divorce rates in Europe (19% in 1996; for the Czech Republic and Slovakia the figures are 61% and 34%, respectively). There is also strict condemnation of pre- and extra-marital sex, contraceptives, and abortion. Generally, the Catholic Church advocates conservative values, which prescribe following traditional rules, suspicion of everything that is new or unknown, honoring elders, and showing respect to national history and cultural heritage. Little wonder that Polish subjects had one of the highest rates of conservatism in Schwartz's (1994) cross-cultural comparison. One might also expect relatively low scores in the case of Openness to Experience.

Boski et al. (1999) has listed the following elements of Polish culture that could be interpreted as a femininity syndrome: a) a cult of the Virgin Mary as the principal Catholic deity and a symbolic queen of Poland; b) women's high participation rate in the workforce; c) marginality of sexual crimes such as harassment and rape; and d) great diversity of diminutives in the spoken language, which personalize the human interaction and make it affectionate. In feminine cultures dominant values are caring for others and preservation: People work in order to live, not vice versa, preferring co-operation to competition; and in politics the welfare state is the ideal. The position of Poland among feminine societies has been confirmed by research of Hofstede (1998). He found that there is a strong modesty rule in Poland; thus Polish subjects, in contrast to American and Canadian ones, rated their skills "moderate" or "good," rather than "excellent." As Hofstede (1998, p. 85) put it: "In feminine countries, both boys and girls learn to be nonambitious and modest. Assertive behavior and attempts at excelling that are appreciated in masculine cultures are easily ridiculed in feminine ones. Excellence is something one keeps to oneself." And this is also true of success. Throughout post war times, material success in Poland has been associated with fraud and corruption, and the situation changes very slowly. This rule of modesty might also be evident in personality scores, especially if dimensions are evaluative (e.g. Conscientiousness).

4.3. On the Character of Slovaks

The politician Fishof (Mahen 1924) noted the following differences among Czech, Polish, and Slovak people. The Czech people are, in his opinion, ambitious, consistent, enthusiastic, but bitter. Polish people are dreamers, hot-blooded and proud. They do not spare time, money, or blood. Slovaks are, in Fishof's opinion, self-confident and short-tempered. Jurovský (1943) supposed that Slovaks are able to experience more emotions in comparison with members of other nations; they are more emotional and excitable; and they easily change from one emotion to another, although they are able to control themselves. Slovaks are characterized by sanguine temperament, cohering with impulsiveness, generosity, flexibility, and the capacity to be enthusiastic about something new (Stavěl, 1982). Thus, lower scores on Neuroticism and higher levels of Extraversion and Openness to Experience can be hypothesized. No relevant references were found on which to base hypotheses about levels of Agreeableness and Conscientiousness.

4.4. An Empirical Study

On the basis of relevant literature, the following hypotheses were formulated. We expected that Czechs would reach higher scores on Openness and Conscientiousness, Polish people higher on Neuroticism, and Slovaks higher on Extraversion, in comparison with the other two countries. Our third study was directed at a comparison of Czech, Polish, and Slovak adolescents on the five personality dimensions measured by the NEO-FFI. We expected some differences between individual nations and between boys and girls but no interaction of gender and nation.

The sample consists of 1,538 adolescents (age 14-23, $M = 16.95$, $SD = 1.8$), including 279 boys and 400 girls from the Czech Republic, 157 boys and 193 girls from Poland, and 209 boys and 300 girls from Slovakia. Members of each national sample completed a NEO-FFI translated into their native language.

The analysis conducted was MANOVA with the vector of Big Five scales as set of dependent variables and nation and gender as fixed factors (in our opinion the sample is not so unbalanced that dummy variable contrast coding is needed).

4.5. Results

To make scores more easily interpretable, all mean values were converted to T-scores (which have a mean of 50 and standard deviation of 10 in the normative group), using American norms for college-age men and women (Costa & McCrae, 1992). Differences

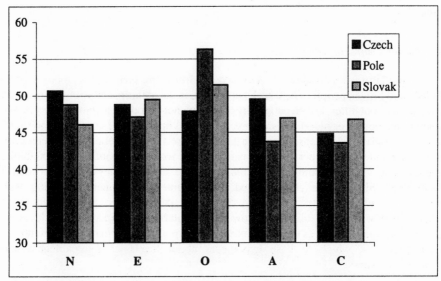

Figure 1. Differences among Czech, Polish, and Slovak adolescents on NEO-FFI scales. Mean T-scores were computed within each culture using means and standard deviation from the American normative college age sample. N = Neuroticism, E = Extraversion, O = Openness to Experience, A = Agreeableness, C = Conscientiousness.

Table 8. Summary of the Post Hoc Comparisons.

	Czech					Polish					Slovak				
Czech	N	E	O	A	C	**N**	E	O	**A**		**N**	E	O	A	C
Polish	N	E	**O**	A	C	N	E	O	A	C	N	E	**O**	A	C
Slovak	N	E	**O**	A	**C**	N	**E**	O	**A**	**C**	N	E	O	A	C

between the nations on the Big Five scales are plotted in Figure 1. The greatest differences can be seen in the self-reports concerning Openness to Experience and Neuroticism. Czech adolescents describe themselves as most neurotic (followed by Poles and Slovaks) and least open (followed by Slovaks and Poles who describe themselves as most open). Compared to American college-age respondents, most scores are in the average range. The most striking findings are the uniformly low levels of Conscientiousness (compared to the U.S.) and the variation in Openness to Experience among cultures.

Further analysis assessed the statistical significance of these differences. The results showed significant differences between boys and girls on all personality traits with the exception of Conscientiousness. Girls reported higher Neuroticism, Extraversion, Openness, and Agreeableness than boys. These differences are consistent with findings using German data (Borkenau & Ostendorf, 1993).

MANOVA with NEO-FFI scales as dependent variables and country and gender as fixed factors (and their interaction) showed significant differences in the profiles of the NEO-FFI scales for individual countries (Wilks' lambda = 0.817, p = 0.000) and gender (Wilks' lambda = 0.877, p = 0.000). Their interaction was not statistically significant. Differences among countries are statistically significant on all scales, and the same holds true in the case of gender (with the exception of Conscientiousness scale).

In order to carry out a fine-grained discussion of the national differences, we performed post hoc comparisons (with Bonferroni correction) of individual countries on each NEO-FFI scale. The results are summarized in the Table 8. Boldface entries in individual cells mean that subjects from the nation in the corresponding row rate themselves higher on the particular NEO-FFI scale than subjects from the country in the corresponding column (e.g. Czech adolescents rate themselves as more neurotic then Poles and Slovaks and more agreeable than Poles).

4.6. Discussion

From the MANOVA results it follows that there are significant differences in the national self-ratings among Czech, Polish, and Slovak adolescents. The most extreme self-ratings were shown by Slovak adolescents—they are more emotionally stable, extroverted, and conscientious than Czech and Polish adolescents. Only one hypothesis was confirmed, namely, that Slovaks would achieve a higher score on Extraversion in comparison with adolescents from the other countries. The basic assumption that Polish people would achieve lower scores on the Openness scale was not confirmed; on the contrary, Polish adolescents rated themselves as most open in comparison with Czechs and Slovaks. The hypothesis of a high score of Neuroticism in the Polish sample was also not confirmed; Czech adolescents rated themselves as most neurotic. Further, we expected that Czech adolescents would rate themselves as more conscientious in comparison with Polish and Slovak adolescents, but Slovak adolescents rated themselves as the most conscientious. Evaluations of various nationalities, which were provided by psychologists, historians, philosophers, and politicians seem to differ significantly from how members of these nations rated themselves.

Hřebíčková, Macek, and Ostendorf (2000) compared Czech and German adolescents on the NEO-FFI scales and found that Czech adolescents reported significantly higher Neuroticism, Extraversion, and Conscientiousness, and lower Openness to Experience, when compared to the German sample. Possible explanations of the cross-cultural differences include non-equivalent translations of the instruments.

5. SUMMARY

The principal aims of this study were to investigate the validity and applicability of the NEO Five-Factor Inventory across three countries and languages, to compare four different instruments proposed to measure the five-factor structure, and to compare mean levels of personality traits in Czech, Polish, and Slovak adolescents.

The results in the first study give an overall impression of the psychometric qualities of the NEO-FFI in Czech, Polish, and Slovak contexts. It was corroborated that the same traits were measured by the instrument when it was translated into other languages and administered to subjects from cultures different from the one in which it was originally developed. For four scales, results strongly supported the reliability of the NEO-FFI in these three West Slavic languages. The Openness scale demonstrated lower reliability. This result is probably not greatly affected by cultural or language differences. As noted by John and Srivastava (1999), some items from the Openness scale do not discriminate well in an adolescent sample. Our results and the results reported by Parker and Stumpf (1998) support this statement. The comparison of factor patterns by means of congruence coefficients showed that the structures in the three Slavonic languages converge to a lesser degree than the structures in American English and German.

The Five-Factor Model has been conceptualized as an orthogonal factor model (Borkenau & Ostendorf, 1993). However, the consistent pattern of nonzero correlations among the domain scales seems to imply the possibility of an oblique factor structure in the FFM. Caprara, Barbaranelli, Bermudez, and Maslach (2001) revealed non-negligible cross loadings in Italian, Spanish, and American versions of the BFQ. We determined that this is not a problem of a specific instrument such as BFQ, because the same findings apply in the cases of the NEO-FFI, FFPI, and CBFM.

Across all five factors and all instruments, convergent validity is satisfactory. Although the mean convergence validity correlation was only .60, the correlation values are attenuated due to the unreliability of the scales. Overall, mean discriminant correlations were low, although some correlations were higher than they should have been. The parameters estimated for Model 3 suggest three major conclusions. First, all scales except one (Autonomy from FFPI) have substantial loadings on the relevant latent variables, with an average loading of .64, suggesting that all four measures generally tap the same five dimensions. Second, there are significant loadings on the method factors that are strongly correlated, suggesting that the methods are rather similar. Third, however, there is still variation not accounted for by this model.

We assumed that people from these three countries who speak similar languages and live in similar cultural conditions would not differ in the level of personality traits. Our results showed otherwise: Among Czech, Slovak, and Polish adolescents there are statistically significant differences. Slovak adolescents provide the most extreme self-ratings—they are more emotionally stable, extroverted, and conscientious then Czech and Polish adolescents. Polish adolescents describe themselves as more open in comparison with Czech and Slovak adolescents.

REFERENCES

Angleitner, A., Ostendorf, F., & John, O.P. (1990). Towards a taxonomy of personality descriptors in German: A psycho-lexical study. *European Journal of Personality, 4*, 89-118.

Angleitner, A., & Ostendorf, F (2000, July). The FFM: A comparison of German speaking countries (Austria, Former East and West Germany, and Switzerland). In J. Allik (Chair), *Personality and culture: The Five-Factor Theory perspective*. Symposium conducted at the XXVIIth International Congress of Psychology, Stockholm, Sweden.

Benet-Martínez, V., & John O. P. (1998). *Los Cinco Grandes* across cultures and ethnic groups: Multitrait-multimethod analyses of the Big Five in Spanish and English. *Personality and Social Psychology, 75*, 729-750.

Blatný, M. (in press): Osobnostní předpoklady sebehodnocení a životní spokojenosti: Shody a rozdíly [Personality assumptions of self-esteem and life satisfaction]. In I. Čermák, P. Macek, & M. Hřebíčková (Eds.), *Agrese, identita, osobnost* [Aggression, identity, personality]. Brno: Sdružení Scan.

Bobrownicka, M. (1995). *Narkotyk mitu* [A drug of myth]. Kraków: Universitas.

Borkenau, P., & Ostendorf, F. (1993). *NEO Fünf-Faktoren Inventar (NEO-FFI) nach Costa und McCrae* [NEO Five-Factor Inventory (NEO-FFI) by Costa and McCrae]. Göttingen: Hogrefe.

Boski, P., van de Vijver, F., Hurme, H., & Miluska, J. (1999). Perception and evaluation of Polish cultural femininity in Poland, the United States, Finland, and the Netherlands. *Cross-Cultural Research, 33*, 131-161.

Campbell, D. T., & Fiske, D. W. (1959). Convergent and discriminant validation by the multitrait–multimethod matrix. *Psychological Bulletin, 56*, 81-105.

Caprara, G. V., Barbaranelli, C., Borgogni, L., & Perugini, M. (1993). "The Big-Five Questionnaire": A new questionnaire to assess the Five-Factor Model. *Personality and Individual Differences, 15*, 281-288.

Caprara, G. V., Barbaranelli, C., Bermudez, J., & Maslach, C. (2001). *A cross-cultural comparison of the psychometric characteristics of the Big Five Questionnaire*. Unpublished manuscript, University of Rome.

Costa, P.T., Jr., & McCrae, R.R. (1992). *Revised NEO Personality Inventory (NEO-PI-R) and NEO Five-Factor Inventory (NEO-FFI) professional manual*. Odessa, FL: Psychological Assessment Resources.

De Raad, B., Perugini, M., & Szirmák, Z. (1997). In pursuit of a cross-lingual reference structure of personality traits: Comparisons among five languages. *European Journal of Personality, 11*, 167-185.

De Raad, B., Di Blas, L., & Perugini, M. (1998). Two independently constructed Italian trait taxonomies: Comparisons among Italian and between Italian and Germanic languages. *European Journal of Personality, 12*, 19-41.

De Raad, B., Perugini, M., Hřebíčková, M., & Szarota, P. (1998). Lingua franca of personality: Taxonomies and structures. *Journal of Cross-Cultural Psychology, 29*, 212-232.

Dolinski, D. (1996). The mystery of the Polish soul. B.W. Johnson's effect a rebour. *European Journal of Social Psychology, 26*, 1001-1005.

Duijsens, I. J., & Diekstra, F. W. (1995). The 23BB5: A new Bipolar Big Five Questionnaire. *Personality and Individual Differences, 19*, 753-755.

Ficková, E. (1999). Personality dimensions and self-esteem indicators relationships. *Studia Psychologica, 41*,

76   HŘEBÍČKOVÁ, URBÁNEK, ČERMÁK, SZAROTA, FICKOVÁ & ORLIKÁ

323-328.

Ficková, E. (2000, October). *Osobnostné dimenzie adolescentov vo vzťahu ku každodenným problémom (HASSLES)* [Personality dimensions of adolescents in relation to daily problems (HASSLES)]. Poster presented at the Conference *Sociální procesy a osobnost*. Brno, Czech Republic.

Goldberg, L. R. (1989). *Standard markers of the Big-Five factor structure*. Paper presented at the Invited Workshop on Personality Language, Groningen, The Netherlands.

Goldberg, L. (1990). An alternative "description of personality": The Big-Five factor structure. *Journal of Personality and Social Psychology, 59*, 1216-1229.

Goldberg, L. R. (1992). The development of markers for the Big-Five factor structure. *Psychological Assessment, 4*, 26-42.

Hendriks, A. A. J. (1997). *The construction of the Five-Factor Personality Inventory (FFPI)*. Groningen: University of Groningen.

Hendriks, A. A. J., Perugini. M., Angleitner, A., Bratko, D., Conner, M., De Fruyt, F., Hřebíčková, M., Johnson, J. A., Murakami, T., Nagy, J., Nussbaum, S., Ostendorf, F., Rodríguez-Fornells A., & Ruisel, I. (in press). The Five-Factor Personality Inventory: Cross-cultural generalizability across 13 countries. *European Journal of Psychological Assessment.*

Hofstede, G. (1998). The cultural construction of gender. In G. Hofstede (Ed.), *Masculinity and femininity. The taboo dimension of national cultures* (pp. 77-105). Thousand Oaks: Sage.

Hofstee, W. K. B., De Raad, B., & Goldberg, L. R. (1992). Integration of the Big Five and circumplex approaches to trait structure. *Journal of Personality and Social Psychology, 63*, 146-163.

Holden, R. R., Fekken, C. G. (1994). The NEO Five-Factor Inventory in a Canadian context: Psychometric properties for a sample of university women. *Personality and Individual Differences, 17*, 441-444.

Hřebíčková, M.(1993). *Česká verze NEO pětifaktorového inventáře (NEO-FFI)* [The Czech version of the NEO Five-Factor Inventory (NEO-FFI)]. Unpublished manuscript, Institute of Psychology, Academy of Sciences of the Czech Republic, Brno.

Hřebíčková, M. (1995). *Osobnostní deskriptory: Přídavná jména pro popis osobnosti* [Personality descriptors: Adjectives for personality description]. Brno: Psychologický ústav AV ČR.

Hřebíčková, M. (1997). *Jazyk a osobnost: Pětifaktorová struktura popisu osobnosti* [Language and personality: Five-Factor structure of personality description]. Brno: Vydavatelství Masarykovy univerzity a Psychologický ústav AV ČR.

Hřebíčková, M., Macek, P., & Ostendorf, F. (2000, September). *How the Czech and German adolescents rate themselves in the five personality domains.* Poster presented at the 42nd Kongress Deutsche Gesellschaft für Psychologie, Jena, Germany.

Hřebíčková, M., Urbánek, T., & Čermák, I. (2000). Inventář přídavných jmen pro posouzení pěti obecných dimenzí osobnosti [Inventory of adjectives for assessment of five general personality dimensions]. *Československá. psychologie, 44*, 317-329.

Hřebíčková, M., & Urbánek, T. (2001). *NEO pětifaktorový osobnostní inventář podle NEO Five-Factor Inventory P. T. Costy a R. R. McCrae* [NEO Five-Factor Personality Inventory according to NEO Five-Factor Inventory by P. T. Costa and R. R. McCrae]. Praha: Testcentrum.

Hyhlík, F. (1969). Český člověk [The Czech character]. *Forum zahraničních studentů, 2* (7), 1-2.

Jakobson, R. (1955). *Slavic languages: A condensed survey*. New York: King's Crown Press.

John, O. P. (1983). *Effects of language and culture on trait attribution and evaluation: A preliminary report of methodology and some results.* Unpublished manuscript, University of Oregon.

John, O. P., Donahue, E. M., & Kentle, R. L. (1991). *The Big Five Inventory – Versions 4a and 54.* Unpublished manuscript. University of California, Berkley.

John, O.P., & Srivastava, S. (1999). The Big Five trait taxonomy: History, measurement, and theoretical perspectives. In L. A. Pervin & O. P. John (Eds.), *Handbook of personality theory and research* (pp. 102-138). New York: The Guilford Press.

Jurovský, A. (1943). Slovenská národná povaha [Slovak national character]. In *Slovenská vlastiveda II. diel* [Slovak national history and geography]. Bratislava: Slovenská akadémia vied a umení.

Macek, P., Osecká, L., Hřebíčková, M., & Bernard, J. (1998, February). *Identity of Czech adolescents: Empirical types, personality and values context.* Poster presented at the 7th Biennial Meeting of the Society for Research on Adolescence, San Diego.

Macek, P., Hřebíčková, M., & Čermák, I. (1999). Identita, vývoj a osobnostní charakteristiky adolescentů [Identity, development and personality characteristics of adolescents]. In M. Blatný & M. Svoboda (Eds.), *Sociální procesy a osobnost. Sborník příspěvků* [Social processes and personality. Proceeding of contributions] (pp. 78-84). Brno: PsÚ AV ČR, PsÚ FF MU.

Mahen, J. (1924). *Kniha o českém chrakteru* [The book about Czech character]. Vyškov na Moravě: František Obzina.

Masaryk, T. G. (1895): Vady českého charakteru [The faults of Czech character]. In *Česká otázka* (pp. 216-219). Praha: Čas.

McCrae, R. R., & Costa, P. T., Jr. (1987). Validation of the Five-Factor Model of personality across instruments and observers. *Journal of Personality and Social Psychology, 52,* 81-90.

McCrae, R. R., & Costa, P. T., Jr. (1996). Toward a new generation of personality theories: Theoretical contexts for the Five-Factor Model. In J. S. Wiggins (Ed.), *The Five-Factor Model of personality: Theoretical perspectives* (pp. 51-87). New York: Guilford Press.

McCrae, R. R., & Costa, P. T., Jr. (1999). A Five-Factor Theory of personality. In L. A. Pervin & O. P. John (Eds.), *Handbook of personality* (pp. 139-153). New York: Guilford.

McDonald, R. P. (1991). *Test theory: A unified treatment.* London: Lawrence Erlbaum Associates.

Mlačić, B. (2000, July). *Taxonomy and structure of Croatian personality-descriptive adjectives.* Paper presented at the 10th European Conference on Personality, Krakow, Poland.

Mooradian, T. A., & Nezlek, J. B. (1996). Comparing the NEO-FFI and Saucier's mini-markers as measures of the Big Five. *Personality and Individual Differences, 21,* 213-215.

Norman, W. T. (1963). Toward an adequate taxonomy of personality attributes: Replicated factor structure in peer nomination personality ratings. *Journal of Abnormal and Social Psychology, 66,* 574-583.

Nunnally, J. (1978). *Psychometric theory.* New York: McGraw Hill.

Orlická, L. (2001). Prvé skúsenosti s diagnostikou intelektových štýlov pomocou dotazníka TSI (Thinking Styles Inventory, Stenberg-Wagner) [The first experiences with diagnostic of intellectual styles by means of the TSI (Thinking Styles Inventory, Stenberg-Wagner) questionnaire]. In M. Blatný, M. Svoboda, I. Ruisel & J. Výrost (Eds.), *Sociální procesy a osobnost 2000: Sborník příspěvků.* Brno: Psychologický ústav AV ČR and Masarykova univerzita.

Parker, W. D., & Stumpf, H. (1998). A validation of the Five-Factor Model of personality in academically talented youth across observers and instruments. *Personality and Individual Differences, 25,* 1005-1025.

Peabody, D. (1984). Personality dimensions through trait inferences. *Journal of Personality and Social Psychology, 46,* 384-403.

Peabody, D., & Goldberg, L. R. (1989). Some determinants of factor structures from personality-trait descriptors. *Journal of Personality and Social Psychology, 57,* 552-567.

Peabody, D., & De Raad, B. (2000, July). *The substantive nature of personality factors: A comparison across languages.* Paper presented at the 10th European Conference on Personality, Krakow, Poland.

Perugini, M., & Ercolani, A. P. (1998). Validity of the Five-Factor Personality Inventory (FFPI): An investigation in Italy. *European Journal of Psychological Assessment, 14,* 234-248.

Perugini. M., & Leone, L. (1996). Construction and validation of a Short Adjective Checklist to measure Big Five (SACBIF). *European Journal of Psychological Assessment. 12,* 33-42.

Ronowicz, E. (1995). *Poland: A handbook in intercultural communication.* Sydney: National Center for English Language Teaching and Research.

Rosendahl, M. (1997). *Ein Vergleich verschiedener Instrumente zur Erfassung fünf zentraler Persönlichkeitsdimensionen* [A comparison of different instruments to assess the five basic personality dimensions]. Unpublished master's thesis, Department of Psychology, University of Bielefeld, Germany.

Ruisel, I. (1997). Analysis of personality descriptors in the Slovak language. *Studia Psychologica, 39,* 233-245.

Ruisel, I. (1998). *Inteligencia v kognitívnom a osobnostnom kontexte* [Intelligence in context of cognition and personality]. Bratislava: ÚEPs SAV.

Ruiselová, Z. (2000). Salutogenetic approach in the context of the Big Five factors. *Studia Psychologica, 42,* 157-161.

Řehulka, E., & Řehulková, O. (1999).Učitelky základních škol: Charakteristiky osobnosti a zvládání zítěže [Elementary school female teachers: Personality characteristics and coping with stress]. In E. Řehulka & O. Řehulková (Ed.), *Učitelé a zdraví* (pp. 123-132). Brno: PsÚ AV ČR a Nakladatelství Pavel Křepela.

Saucier, G. (1992). Openness versus intellect: Much ado about nothing? *European Journal of Personality, 6,* 381-386.

Saucier, G. (1994). Mini-markers: A brief versions of Goldberg's unipolar Big-Five markers. *Journal of Personality Assessment, 63,* 506-516.

Saucier, G., & Goldberg, L. R. (1996). The language of personality: Lexical perspectives on the Five-Factor Model. In: J. S. Wiggins (Ed.), *Theoretical perspectives for the Five-Factor Model* (pp.21-50). New York: Guilford.

Scharf, D., Tuente, A., Brinkmeier, H., & Benne, A. (1996). *Ein Vergleich von verschidenen Verfahren zur Messung der fünf zentralen Persönlichkeitsfaktoren (Big Five)* [A comparison of different instruments for assessing the five basic dimensions of personality (Big Five)]. Unpublished manuscript, University of Bielefeld.

Shmelyov, A.G., & Pokhil'ko, V.I. (1993). A taxonomy-oriented study of Russian personality-trait names. *European Journal of Personality, 7*, 1-17.

Schwartz, S. H. (1994). Beyond individualism/collectivism: New cultural dimensions of values. In U. Kim (Ed.), *Individualism and collectivism: Theory, method, and applications* (pp. 85-119). London-New Delhi: Sage.

Slovník spisovného jazyka českého I. – VIII [Dictionary of Standard Czech I-VII] (1989). Praha: Academia.

Stavěl, J. (1982). *Autobiografické texty* [Autobiographical texts]. Praha: Academia.

Stránský, P. (1840). O obyvatelích Čech a jejich mravech [On the inhabitants of Bohemia and their conduct]. In: *O státě českém* (pp.79-84). Praha: Evropský literární klub. (Original work published 1643)

Stríženec, M., & Ruisel, I. (1998). Religious coping styles and personality in Slovak adolescents. *Studia Psychologica, 40*, 303-307.

Sýkora, V. (1939). *O povaze českého člověka* [About the nature of Czech persons]. Praha: Český svaz pro spolupráci s Němci.

Szarota, P. (1995). *Taxonomy and structure of Polish personality-relevant adjectives.* Unpublished manuscript, University of Warsaw.

Szarota, P. (1996). Taxomomy of the Polish personality-descriptive adjectives of the highest frequency of use. *Polish Psychological Bulletin, 27*, 342-351.

Štěpaníková, I., & Macek, P. (1997). Osobnostní charakteristiky u pacientek s psychogenními poruchami příjmu potravy ve světle pětifaktorového modelu osobnosti [Personality characteristics of patients with psychogenic defects of receiving food in the light of Five-Factor Model of personality]. *Československá psychologie, 41*, 513-524.

Trapnell, P. D., & Wiggins, J. S. (1990). Extension of the interpersonal adjective scales to include the Big Five dimensions of personality. *Journal of Personality and Social Psychology, 59*, 781-790.

Wierzbicka, A. (1994). Emotion, language, and cultural scripts. In W. H. Markus & S. Kitayama (Eds.), *Emotion and culture* (pp. 133-196). Washington, DC: American Psychological Association.

Wiggins, J. S. (1997). In defense of traits. In R. Hogan, J. Johnson & S. Briggs (Eds.), *Handbook of personality psychology* (pp. 95-115). San Diego: Academic Press.

Wothke, W. (1996). Models for multitrait-multimethod matrix analysis. In G. A. Marcoulides & R. E. Schumacker (Eds.), *Advanced structural equation modeling issues and techniques* (pp. 7-56). Mahwah, NJ: Erlbaum.

Zawadzki, B., Strelau, J., Szczepaniak, P., & Sliwinska, M. (1998). *Inwentarz osobowosci NEO-FFI Costy i McCrae. Adaptacja polska. Podrecznik.* [Personality inventory NEO-FFI by Costa and McCrae. Polish adaptation. Handbook]. Warszawa: Pracownia Testow Psychologicznych PTP.

AUTHOR NOTE

This research was supported by Grant 406/01/1507 from the Grant Agency of the Czech Republic and is related to research plan AV 0Z7025918 of the Institute of Psychology, Academy of Sciences of the Czech Republic. We wish to thank two anonymous reviewers for useful comments on a prior draft. Address correspondence to Martina Hřebíčková, Institute of Psychology, Academy of Sciences of the Czech Republic, Veveří 97, 602 00 Brno, Czech Republic. E-mail: martina@psu.cas.cz

RELATING THE FIVE-FACTOR MODEL OF PERSONALITY TO A CIRCUMPLEX MODEL OF AFFECT

A Five-Language Study

MICHELLE S. M. YIK,* JAMES A. RUSSELL,**
CHANG-KYU AHN,*** JOSE MIGUEL FERNÁNDEZ DOLS† &
NAOTO SUZUKI‡

*Hong Kong University of Science and Technology, China, **Boston College, USA,
***Pusan National University, Korea, †Universidad Autonoma de Madrid, Spain,
‡Doshisha University, Japan

Abstract. This chapter examines the relation between the Five-Factor Model of personality and momentary affect in five languages, based on a pooled sample of 2070 (Ns = 535 for English, 233 for Spanish, 487 for Chinese, 450 for Japanese, 365 for Korean). Affect is described with a two-dimensional space that integrates major dimensional models in English and that replicates well in all five languages. Personality is systematically linked to affect similarly (although not identically) across languages, but not in a way consistent with the claim that Positive Activation and Negative Activation are more basic; indeed, Pleasant vs. Unpleasant and Activated vs. Deactivated came closer to the personality dimensions.

Keywords: Affect, circumplex models, personality correlates, cross-cultural comparisons

1. INTRODUCTION

In recent years, psychologists have witnessed the emergence of the Five-Factor Model (FFM) as a consensual descriptive map for assessing personality (Costa & McCrae, 1992; Digman, 1990; Goldberg, 1993; Wiggins & Trapnell, 1997). Much of what psychologists mean by "personality" can be succinctly summarized by the FFM. In a narrow sense, the FFM represents an umbrella of replicable factor structures resulting from hundreds of validation studies conducted in different cultures (McCrae & Costa, 1997) and with different measurement devices (McCrae & John, 1992). The FFM was regarded as "the Christmas tree on which findings of stability, heritability, consensual validation, cross-cultural invariance, and predictive utility are hung like ornaments"

(Costa & McCrae, 1993, p. 302). In a broader sense, psychologists are now moving beyond the descriptive structure of the FFM to the Five-Factor Theory (FFT) of personality (McCrae & Costa, 1996). This theory promises to serve as a stimulus to an integrated understanding of personality, to organize myriad empirical findings into a coherent story, and to establish connections between personality and all other aspects of the human condition.

The present chapter examines the link between the FFM and such momentary affective feelings as happiness, nervousness, and relaxation. One typically feels happy with good news, nervous before an interview, and relaxed on vacation: Affect obviously can be predicted from the immediate context. What is less obvious, one's affect can also be predicted from one's enduring personality traits (Diener, 1984; Larsen & Ketelaar, 1991; McCrae & Costa, 1991). It is this latter link on which we focus. The viability of the FFT relies partly on its ability to predict and explain affect (as well as behavior, cognition, and other psychological processes). Indeed, some personality dimensions might predict behavior via its associations with affect (Lucas & Fujita, 2000). Some writers believe that Extraversion and Neuroticism are fundamentally affective in nature (Lucas, Diener, Grob, & Suh, & Shao, 2000; Tellegen, 1985; Watson & Clark, 1997) and recent analyses point to the affective nature of the other dimensions of the Big Five as well (McCrae & Costa, 1991; Watson 2000).

The study of affect, too, is enhanced through establishing its links to personality. For instance, our understanding of the nature of affect will depend on the degree to which it is more context- or more personality-dependent, and it has been proposed that correlations between personality and affect can help locate the fundamental axes in the structure of affect.

1.1. A Circumplex Model of Affect

In this chapter, we use as a tool a structure of affect that integrates the traditional pleasure and arousal axes, the circular ordering of affect, Thayer's (1996) dimensions of activation, and the dimensions that Watson and Tellegen (1985) called Positive Affect and Negative Affect (changed by Watson, Wiese, Vaidya, & Tellegen [1999] to Positive Activation and Negative Activation).

As in the study of personality, the study of affect requires a comprehensive descriptive structure. It is also highly desirable to have the whole or part of such a structure be a common framework for describing affect across languages and cultural groups. If such a universal "etic" structure can be found, it would be a unifying tool allowing us to compare and contrast affective feelings in different groups. In that way, both universal and language/culture-specific aspects of affect could be delineated.

In the past decade, various dimensional models have been proposed to characterize the covariations of self-reported momentary affective feelings. Major models include Russell's (1980) circumplex, Thayer's (1996) energetic and tense arousal, Larsen and Diener's (1992) eight combinations of pleasantness and activation, and Watson and Tellegen's (1985) positive and negative affect. Each has achieved psychometric success and inspired a line of supportive research. Each is continuing to be improved through empirical research. And the four are converging on one another.

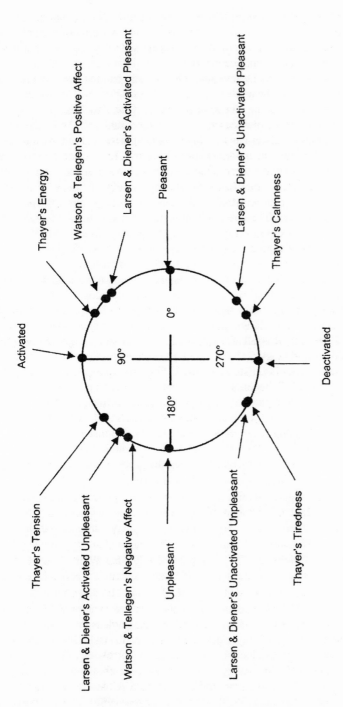

Figure 1. A Circumplex Model of Affect. 14 unipolar affect constructs empirically placed in an integrated two-dimensional space via CIRCUM (Browne, 1992). Results are obtained from a study of 535 English-speaking Canadians. Adopted from Russell, Yik, and Steiger (2002).

Recently, attempts have been made to integrate these four specific models. Results have shown that all four fit comfortably within the same two-dimensional affective space. Figure 1 shows an empirical example of one proposed integrated space (Russell, Yik, & Steiger, 2002), which is characterized by two bipolar axes of Pleasant versus Unpleasant and Activated versus Deactivated. On the right hand side are the pleasant states; on the left hand side are the unpleasant states. On the upper half are the activated states; on the lower half are the deactivated states. One can find any possible combination of different doses of Pleasant versus Unpleasant and Activated versus Deactivated affect. Affective states can thus fall at any angle throughout the integrated space of Figure 1. In this way, the model includes Thayer's, Larsen and Diener's, and Watson and Tellegen's constructs as specific vectors within the space. The model is thoroughly bipolar in that any state has a bipolar opposite 180° away. It is also a circumplex in which affective dimensions fall in a circular ordering along the perimeter rather than cluster at the axes. The circumplical nature of momentary affective states has received good empirical support (Remington, Fabrigar, & Visser, 2000). We do not assume that the structure of Figure 1 captures all of affect, but we do propose it as a means of representing affect at the most general level of description.

Various questions immediately arise: For instance, is this integrated structure of affect limited to English-speaking societies where it was developed? Or can it be generalized to those speaking other languages? Current evidence suggests similar dimensions of affect in different languages. Russell and his colleagues (1983; Russell, Lewicka, & Niit, 1989; Yik, Russell, & Ahn, 2002; Yik, Russell, Oceja, & Fernández Dols, 2000; Yik, Russell, & Suzuki, 2002) reported cross-cultural replications of their circumplex in Chinese, Croatian, Estonian, Greek, Gujarti, Japanese, Korean, Polish, and Spanish. Watson and Tellegen's (1985) Positive Affect and Negative Affect structure was replicated in Japanese (Watson, Clark, & Tellegen, 1984), Hebrew (Almagor & Ben-Porath, 1989), Castillian Spanish (Joiner, Sandín, Chorot, Lostao, & Marguina, 1997), and Tagalog (Church, Katigbak, Reyes, & Jensen, 1999).

Another question concerns the structure itself. Although there is widespread agreement on a two-dimensional structure of affect, the proper rotation of the two axes remains controversial. Pleasure and arousal are used as the horizontal (0°) and vertical axes (90°) in our model (Figure 1); this rotation is one of the viable alternatives, but any other pair of non-redundant axes explains the same amount of variance and defines the space equally well—mathematically. Some investigators have argued that the basic dimensions are at approximately 45° and at 135°. The diagonal at 45° (and, assuming bipolarity, its opposite number at 225°) is approximately what Watson and Tellegen (1985) defined as Positive Activation (i.e., Pleasant Activated versus Unpleasant Deactivated) and what Thayer defined at Energetic Arousal. The diagonal at 135° (and its opposite number at 315°) is independent of the first and is approximately what Watson and Tellegen defined as Negative Activation (i.e., Unpleasant Activated versus Pleasant Deactivated) and what Thayer defined as Tense Arousal. One argument for this latter rotation centers on the location of personality correlates of affect: Affect dimensions at 45° and 135° are basic, it is said, because they correlate with the personality dimensions of Extraversion and Neuroticism (Costa & McCrae, 1996; Meyer & Shack, 1989; Tellegen, 1985; Watson & Tellegen, 1985). The emergence of the FFM indicates that it is essential to extend the discussion beyond simply Extraversion and Neuroticism to include the remaining three major personality dimensions. For example, Watson (2000) recently showed that Conscientiousness and Agreeableness too are related to affect. Furthermore, if the location of personality dimensions can locate the fundamental axes in a universal structure of affect, then that location should be the same in different societies. Here, we present data on this question gathered in five different societies speaking five different languages.

1.2. Predicting Affect from Personality

Various questions arise about the relation of affect to personality (e.g., Allik & Realo, 1997; Carver, Sutton, & Scheier, 2000; Fossum & Feldman Barrett, 2000; Gross, Sutton, & Ketelaar, 1998; Lucas & Fijita, 2000; Moskowitz, Brown, & Côté, 1997). Arguably, the first question is whether affect can be predicted from personality, and that is our topic.

The superfactors of Extraversion (E) and Neuroticism (N) have long been argued as temperamental traits that influence feelings and emotional behaviors (H. J. Eysenck, 1992; H. J. Eysenck & M. W. Eysenck, 1985; Tellegen, 1985). Much research has been reported to show that these two are related to affect (Costa & McCrae, 1980, 1984; Diener & Emmons, 1984; Izard, Libero, Putnam, & Haynes, 1993; Meyer & Shack, 1989; O'Malley & Gillett, 1984; McCrae & Costa, 1991; Thayer, Takahashi, & Pauli, 1988; Warr, Barter, & Brownbridge, 1983; Watson & Clark, 1992, 1997; Williams, 1981).

Fewer studies have been conducted on the predictive utility of Agreeableness (A), Conscientiousness (C), and Openness to Experience (O) on affect. Positive relations were reported between O and positive affective states (Costa & McCrae, 1984; McCrae & Costa, 1991; Watson & Clark, 1992). Both A and C were found to correlate positively with positive affective states and negatively with negative affective states (McCrae & Costa, 1991; Watson, 2000; Watson & Clark, 1992).

In short, both empirical and conceptual considerations indicate reliable and meaningful links between affect and all five basic dimensions of personality. However, the evidence available does not indicate clearly what the precise relation is between affect and each personality trait, how large that relation is, how best to represent those relations, or how these links can be used to determine the best rotation of the affective space. Here, we consider these questions. In addition, previous research has been focused mostly on English-speaking participants (see Lucas et al., 2000 for an exception). To advance our understanding of interlocking relations between personality and affect, research in non-English-speaking societies is much needed. Indeed, to our knowledge, we offer here the first empirical examination of the link between affect and personality with data from several different languages simultaneously.

2. FIVE LANGUAGE SAMPLES

The present chapter relies on previous studies conducted by our laboratory to examine the relations between the FFM and momentary affect in five different languages, each belonging to a distinct language family. By sampling different languages, we test the limits of the generalizability of the nomological network of the FFM. Language families are groups of languages that share a common historical origin and similar grammar and syntax (Crystal, 1997). Spanish, like English, belongs to the Indo-European language family, although the former is under the Italic branch and the latter the Germanic branch. Chinese belongs to the Sino-Tibetan family. Although many Westerners might assume that Chinese, Japanese, and Korean are similar languages, they actually represent different language families. Japanese is actually a language family of its own and is very different from any other language. Korean is a member of the Altaic family (which includes Turkish and Mongolian).

Participants. Participants were undergraduate student volunteers. Test administration took place either during class time or in a laboratory. The English data came from 535 participants (241 men, 294 women) from the University of British Columbia (mean age = 19.61, SD = 3.22; Russell, Yik, & Steiger, 2002). The Spanish data came from 233 partici-pants (96 men, 137 women) from Universidad Autonoma de Madrid (mean age = 19.83, SD = 4.29; Yik, Russell, Oceja, & Fernández Dols, 2000). The Chinese data came from 487 participants (164 men, 323 women) from the Chinese University of Hong Kong and the City University of Hong Kong (mean age = 19.74, SD = 2.04; Yik & Russell, 2002). The Japanese data came from 450 participants (228 men, 222 women) from Doshisha University (mean age = 19.69, SD = 1.15; Yik, Russell, & Suzuki, 2002). Finally, the Korean data came from 365 participants (176 men, 189 women) from Pusan University (mean age = 21.16, SD = 4.28; Yik, Russell, & Ahn, 2002).

Personality scales. All five studies relied on the NEO FFI (Costa & McCrae, 1992), which is a 60-item questionnaire designed to measure the Five-Factor Model of personality. Each of the five factors is represented by 12 items. Responses are made on a 5-point rating scale ranging from *strongly disagree* through *neutral* to *strongly agree.* Data on reliability and other psychometric properties of the original English version are given by Costa and McCrae (1992). We used the Spanish translation developed by Sanz, Silva, and Avia (1999), the Chinese translation developed by Liu (1991) and revised by Ho (1994), the Japanese translation developed by Shimonaka, Nakazato, Gondo, & Takayama (1999), and the Korean translation developed by Ahn and Chae (1997). All versions of the scales show adequate psychometric properties.

Psychometric data for the NEO from our five samples are given in Table 1. Cronbach's alphas ranged from .62 to .83, indicating that the scales are internally consistent. The five dimensions showed the expected small but reliable correlations with each other. These psychometric properties resemble those found with the original English version (McCrae et al., 1998).

Remembered Moments Questionnaire. In much previous research, participants were asked to rate how they felt so far today, this week, this month, or "in general." All of these instructions rely on memory and have the disadvantage of covering a large span

Table 1. Psychometric Properties of the NEO-FFI in Five Different Languages.

NEO-FFI Scale	Correlation				Mean	SD	α
	N	E	O	A			
ENGLISH (N = 535)							
Neuroticism					22.80	8.40	.87
Extraversion	−.32*				29.76	8.40	.81
Openness	.02	.04			29.16	6.48	.74
Agreeableness	−.15*	.24*	.04		31.32	5.88	.74
Conscientiousness	−.26*	.15*	−.07	.12	30.60	6.84	.84
SPANISH (N = 233)							
Neuroticism					25.20	8.64	.86
Extraversion	−.41*				28.08	6.48	.76
Openness	−.05	.03			32.16	5.40	.67
Agreeableness	−.20*	.35*	.10		31.08	5.64	.68
Conscientiousness	−.13*	.17*	−.05	.18*	27.84	7.20	.84
CHINESE (N = 487)							
Neuroticism					26.16	7.32	.83
Extraversion	−.42*				25.92	5.76	.72
Openness	.04	.02			27.96	5.40	.64
Agreeableness	−.19*	.19*	−.07		27.12	4.92	.62
Conscientiousness	−.32*	.25*	.08	.11	28.20	6.12	.80
JAPANESE (N = 450)							
Neuroticism					29.88	8.04	.85
Extraversion	−.26*				26.40	7.08	.81
Openness	.09	−.04			30.36	5.52	.63
Agreeableness	−.24*	.41*	.04		28.56	5.76	.69
Conscientiousness	−.24*	.26*	−.04	.21*	26.52	6.48	.76
KOREAN (N = 365)							
Neuroticism					27.36	7.56	.84
Extraversion	−.45*				28.80	7.32	.85
Openness	−.07	.21*			27.60	5.76	.67
Agreeableness	−.22*	.29*	.19*		29.76	5.76	.72
Conscientiousness	−.32*	.27*	.08*	.03	29.52	6.96	.85

Note. Each scale score is the sum of 12 items, scored 0 to 4. Possible scores range from 0 to 48. *$p \le .05$.

of time during which many different feelings might have occurred. One alternative is to ask respondents to rate how they feel "right now." This method too has its drawbacks. As participants proceed through a multi-item affect questionnaire, they can either try to remember how they felt when first asked (and thus rely on memory) or they can report their affect at each moment as it shifts from item to item. Over the course of a long questionnaire, presumably some respondents get bored or annoyed or offended or become less tense; if so, we are no longer measuring "momentary affect" but a changing stream. In addition, if participants are in a classroom or laboratory completing a questionnaire, variance on affective dimensions is likely restricted because the immediate context is kept constant.

With these considerations in mind, we are exploring the complementary technique of asking respondents to describe a moment in the recent past that they remember well. On the front page of the affect questionnaire were general instructions under the title "Remembered Moments Questionnaire." Each participant was asked to return in memory to a well-remembered point during a specified time during the preceding day. There were six possible times: some time "before breakfast," "after breakfast," "before lunch," "after lunch," "before dinner," and "after dinner." Participants were randomly assigned to one of the six times. For instance, one-sixth of the participants were asked to search their memory to find one specific well-remembered moment yesterday "before breakfast." They were allowed to continue searching their memory until one clear, well-remembered moment came to mind. That moment was then defined as "the remembered moment" and all affect questionnaires were to be answered with respect to that specific moment. The five studies with this technique reported in this chapter all found basically the same structure of affect as found with "right now" instructions but had the advantage of greater range and variance on all the affective variables.[1]

Affect scales. In all five studies, affect was assessed with four questionnaires, each in a different format, in the following order: (a) Semantic differential scales; (b) Adjective format, which was an adjective list accompanied by a five-point Likert scale ranging from 1, *not at all,* to 5, *extremely;* (c) Agree-Disagree format, which was a list of statements with which participants were asked to indicate their degree of agreement, ranging from 1, *strongly disagree,* to 5, *strongly agree,* and (d) Describes Me format, which was a list of statements, for each of which participants were asked to indicate how well it described their feelings, ranging from 1, *not at all,* to 4, *very well.*

The semantic differential scales consisted of bipolar measures of Pleasure and Arousal translated directly from Mehrabian and Russell (1974). The remaining three questionnaires were unipolar in format and each questionnaire included translated items from (a) Feldman Barrett and Russell's (1998) Current Mood Questionnaire (CMQ) assessing Pleasant, Unpleasant, Activated, and Deactivated affect; (b) Larsen and Diener's (1992) Activated Unpleasant, Unactivated Unpleasant, Activated Pleasant, and Unactivated Pleasant affect; (c) Thayer's (1996) Energy, Tiredness, Tension, and Calmness; and (d) Watson, Clark, and Tellegen's (1988) Positive Affect and Negative Affect. Therefore, three scores (one from each format) could be estimated for these

---

[1] In the English sample, a total of 44 affect scales (14 constructs of Figure 1, each assessed in three different ways, plus two semantic differential scales) were administered to a sample of 535 participants. These 44 scales had also been administered by Yik, Russell, and Feldman Barrett (1999) to one or both samples of their article focusing on "current mood" measurements. Therefore we could examine our anticipation of greater variance in the present study relative to the variance observed by Yik et al. Our hypothesis was generally correct. In 39 of 44 comparisons, variance in the present study was greater than that reported by Yik et al.

various dimensions.

Original English versions of the affect scales were translated into the target language through a translation and back-translation procedure. In each language, the affect measures were first translated by a native speaker of the target language (one of the co-authors of this chapter). After the translation was completed, a second translator (blind to the original English version) back-translated the questionnaire into English. Discrepancies between the back-translated version and the original English version were reviewed and translations were revised on the basis of joint consultation of the translator, back-translator, and the first two authors. Translators were advised to maintain the affective meaning of the items even though that might require changes in the literal content.[2]

3. STRUCTURE OF AFFECT IN THE FIVE LANGUAGES

Affect data within each sample have been analyzed separately and reported in previous studies (Russell, Yik, & Steiger, 2002; Yik & Russell, 2002; Yik, Russell, & Ahn, 2002; Yik, Russell, Oceja, & Fernández Dols, 2000; Yik, Russell, & Suzuki, 2002). Even though the scales were created simply through translation and had not been refined through repeated revision, the hypothesized structure provided a reasonable fit to the data in every case. The affect scales themselves then underwent a conservative process of revisions. By "conservative," we mean that no item was allowed to move from one construct to another; the pleasure and displeasure scales were not changed, and no new items were added. In other words, the scales were changed simply by dropping items that weakened the psychometric properties of the scales.[3] Here we use data from these revised scales.

We report three additional analyses, all cross-language comparisons: (a) a measurement model for our proposed affective space integrated across the five languages; (b) an assessment of how well various affect constructs from different prior models can be integrated within that space; and (c) the linear prediction of affect from the FFM.

3.1. Horizontal and Vertical Axes

Our model rests on four cornerstone constructs—Pleasant, Unpleasant, Activated, and Deactivated. To obtain a single affective structure for data from all 5 samples, we conducted a multi-sample confirmatory factor analysis with these four as latent

---

[2]Translation was guided by the theoretical assumptions of the Affect Circumplex, especially that all affect items are made up different degrees of the two axes: pleasure and arousal. In order to help in the translation, a handbook was created for the first translator defining each word or phrase used in the original English version in terms of pleasure and arousal. For each affect item, synonyms were provided where possible. For instance, *ecstatic* and *joyful* were given besides *elated*. Finally, translators were asked to provide different translations for different terms. Only one translation could be used for each term and that translation had to be adopted throughout the whole questionnaire.

[3]For the scales designed to measure CMQ, no items were dropped in English; five were dropped in Spanish; six in Chinese; 14 in Japanese; and 10 in Korean. For the scales designed to measure other affect dimensions, one item was dropped in Chinese and one was dropped in Japanese.

Table 2. Interfactor Correlations Among Pleasant, Unpleasant, Activated, and Deactivated in a Multi-sample Confirmatory Factor Analysis.

	Pleasant	Unpleasant	Activated
Unpleasant	−.88*		
Activated	.09	.09	
Deactivated	−.03	.00	−.69*

Note. Ns = 535 (English), 233 (Spanish), 487 (Chinese), 450 (Japanese), 365 (Korean). *$p \leq .001$.

constructs. Each construct was indicated by 3 unipolar scales (the semantic differential scales were omitted from this analysis). The interfactor correlations among the four constructs (given in Table 2) were constrained to be equal across the five languages. Factor loadings and error variances were estimated for each language separately, however. The hypothesized model fit the data well: χ^2 (174, Ns =535, 233, 487, 450, 365) = 805.12, and RMSEA = .09. Factor loadings between the manifest variables and their intended constructs (Pleasant, Unpleasant, Activated, and Deactivated) were all statistically significant in each language.

The reader may have noted that although our structural model of affect is thoroughly bipolar, the four constructs in the preceding analysis were unipolar and that all of the manifest variables were in a unipolar format. This makes our analysis quite conservative (Russell & Carroll, 1999). The unipolar format was adopted (a) so that unipolar constructs (such as Watson and Tellegen's Positive and Negative Activation) could be assessed (as shown in Figure 1) and (b) so that bipolarity could be tested empirically rather than simply presupposed in the rating scale. One simple test of bipolarity is provided by the interfactor correlation matrix from the multi-sample confirmatory factor analysis given in Table 2. Negative correlations of sizable magnitude were found between the hypothesized bipolar opposites: Pleasant and Unpleasant correlated −.88; Activated and Deactivated correlated −.69. All other correlations were expected to be near zero and were, in fact, below .10 in magnitude. These results are consistent with the variables being thoroughly bipolar. Russell and Carroll (1999) analyzed empirical tests of bipolarity and showed that the more strictly unipolar the actual response format, the further from −1.00 is the expected correlation between bipolar opposites. Thus, the linear correlations estimated here are unlikely to be −1.00, even in error-free data. (Russell, Yik, and Steiger [2002] described various ways of examining bipolarity. Analyses within each of the five data sets showed that these data passed these additional tests as well.) Based on these considerations, we then redefined the two axes as bipolar continua.

3.2. Placing Other Affect Constructs within the Integrated Space

The next question is how well other major affective dimensions fit within this integrated space. We used two ways to explore this question. One way was to use Pleasant versus Unpleasant and Activated versus Deactivated axes (now defined and assessed as bipolar) as exogenous variables to predict all other (unipolar) affect constructs. By treating all other constructs as endogenous variables, we could test the

Table 3. Variance Explained by the Pleasant versus Unpleasant and Activated versus Deactivated Axes: A Cross-Language Comparison.

Construct	% Variance Explained					
	English	Spanish	Chinese	Japanese	Korean	Mean
Activated Pleasant[a]	69 (2.5)	73 (3.5)	86 (1.8)	75 (2.8)	75 (3.1)	76
Positive Affect[b]	79 (1.9)	79 (3.0)	78 (2.2)	68 (3.4)	68 (3.3)	74
Energy[c]	81 (1.9)	82 (2.9)	77 (2.5)	76 (2.5)	83 (2.6)	80
Tension[c]	69 (2.3)	79 (2.9)	82 (1.8)	72 (2.8)	77 (2.7)	76
Activated Unpleasant[a]	77 (2.0)	83 (2.5)	86 (1.5)	80 (2.2)	88 (1.8)	83
Negative Affect[b]	78 (1.8)	84 (2.2)	83 (1.6)	74 (2.4)	86 (1.8)	81
Unactivated Unpleasant[a]	69 (2.5)	80 (3.1)	72 (2.5)	79 (2.4)	72 (3.1)	74
Tiredness[c]	60 (2.8)	63 (4.4)	64 (3.1)	74 (2.8)	60 (3.8)	64
Calmness[c]	83 (2.0)	77 (3.6)	86 (3.2)	81 (2.4)	75 (3.1)	80
Unactivated Pleasant[a]	78 (1.9)	78 (3.0)	86 (2.1)	83 (2.0)	86 (2.2)	82

Note. Figures in parentheses are the standard errors. RMSEAs for the 10 structural equation models ranged from .08 to .11 in English; .06 to .11 in Spanish; .07 to .11 in Chinese; .08 to .11 in Japanese; and .08 to .10 in Korean. CFIs for the 10 structural equation models ranged from .94 to .97 in English; .94 to .98 in Spanish; .94 to .97 in Chinese; .93 to .97 in Japanese; and .95 to .97 in Korean. [a]Larsen and Diener (1992). [b]Watson and Tellegen (1985). [c]Thayer (1996).

hypothesis that the two axes explain most of the reliable variance in them. For each language sample, we conducted a separate analysis for each of 10 unipolar affect constructs (four from Thayer, four from Larsen and Diener, and two from Watson and Tellegen) in each language. Hence, there were 50 analyses in all. The resulting variance explained is given in Table 3. The mean variance explained across five languages ranged from 64% to 83%, with a mean of 77%. The two bipolar axes in all five languages were able to explain most, although not all, the reliable variance in constructs from other structural models of affect.

To examine language differences in the variance explained by the Pleasant versus Unpleasant and Activated versus Deactivated axes, we conducted a one-way ANOVA with language as the between-group variable and variance explained as the dependent variable. The main effect of language was not statistically significant, $F(4, 45) = .90$, n.s. To examine whether there were differences in variance explained between affect variables, we conducted another ANOVA with affect as the between-group variable. The main effect was significant, $F(9, 40) = 6.21$, $p<.001$. Post-hoc tests indicated that Thayer's Tiredness (unpleasant deactivated affect) yielded significantly lower variance explained that did affective feelings in the remaining quadrants of the proposed integrated space.

Our second way of examining the structure of affect across languages focused on their representation as a circumplex. Within each separate data set, all 14 constructs had been modeled with a structural equation modeling program (CIRCUM) developed by Browne (1992). This program provides fit indices and angular position for each input variable. In all five languages examined separately, results indicated that the 14 constructs conform approximately to a circumplex, which explained much of the common variance. Within each sample, results resembled those shown in Figure 1.

To provide a cross-cultural comparison of the circumplexity results, the 14 affect constructs were rank-ordered by their angular positions on the circumplex in each language. For instance, Pleasant was always designated as the reference variable and was given the rank of 1. Rank 2 was given to the construct that came closest to Pleasant in the anti-clockwise position. Spearman's rank order correlations were computed pairwise for the five samples. All correlations were above .97, indicating that the 14 constructs were arrayed in much the same order on the circumplex in each language. English, Spanish, and Chinese had identical positions for all 14 constructs. (A stricter test comes from Pearson correlations between the actual angles, which were even higher, ranging from .99 to 1.00)

3.3. Core Affect and Beyond

One of the vexing problems in the study of personality/affect connections has been the lack of a consensual descriptive map for affect. The Cartesian space in Figure 1 is a possible solution to this problem. Within this two-dimensional space occur differing doses of Pleasant versus Unpleasant and Activated versus Deactivated dimensions. Many different affect dimensions can therefore be found or placed within this space. Our data provided support for the viability of our proposed space as a means to integrate affect constructs, and this hypothesis was supported in all five samples.

We do not want to be misunderstood as claiming that all there is to affect is captured in our two-dimensional space. Rather, the two-dimensional space captures the *core* of affect (Russell, 2002). We find it convenient to describe that core in terms of Pleasantness versus Unpleasantness and Activation versus Deactivation. Other researchers have found it useful to define other dimensions within that space. Whatever the resolution of that debate (to which we return in Section 4), many researchers agree on the importance of some two-dimensional space. Our evidence here showed that the two-dimensional models of Thayer, Watson and Tellegen, Russell, and Larsen and Diener have all captured the same space; empirically, variables from different models are so highly interrelated that they cannot be treated as independent. These substantial interrelations cry out for a common space. Further, the space they have all captured can be demonstrated in different languages, indeed in all the languages we have so far tested.

Beyond this core of affect, other ingredients within emotions can be identified. For example, a prototypical emotional episode consists not only of changes in core affect, but also specific expressive and instrumental actions, specific accompanying central and peripheral physiological changes, cognitive process of attribution and appraisal, and subjective experiences of discrete categories of emotion. In proposing that the two-dimensional space (core affect) is universal, we do not assume that these other ingredients are necessarily universal. There might be, for example, discrete categories of prototypical emotional episodes that occur frequently within one culture but that are rare or nonexistent within another. This possibility is illustrated by the work on the Japanese concept of *amae* (Doi, 1973). To emphasize the distinction between what is captured in Figure 1 and the remaining ingredients that make up emotional episodes, we shall now refer to the space of Figure 1 as *core affect*.

4. RELATING CORE AFFECT TO THE FFM

So far, we have offered or referred to evidence that the structure of personality as represented by the FFM and the structure of core affect as represented by our proposed integrated model both serve well across societies and languages. In this section, we can at last turn to questions on the relations of personality to affect: What is the magnitude of relations? What is the pattern of relations? And what is the implication of these relations for finding the proper reference axes in the structure of affect? Can these relations be modeled in a simple way?

To explore such questions, we report here two complementary sets of analyses. First, we created a series of structural equation models, each using the FFM dimensions as exogenous variables and one affect construct as endogenous. With 8 bipolar affect constructs (our two axes plus two each from Thayer, Larsen & Diener, and Watson & Tellegen) and 5 languages, there were 40 structural equation models in all, which are shown in Table 4. This analysis assumes a very simple way to model the personality/affect link, namely, that each affect dimension is a simple linear function of the five factors of the FFM.

Second, we used Browne's (1999) CIRCUM-Extension procedure, which builds on the circumplex model of affect described above. This analysis assumes an even simpler way to model the personality/affect link, namely, that each personality dimension can be represented as a single vector within the affect circumplex. This is equivalent to saying that the relation of that personality variable to any affect variable can be predicted from the affect variable's position on the circumplex. Browne's procedure provides a maximum likelihood estimate of the angular location of each personality variable within the affect circumplex. This is a new technique that, we believe, has large advantages over the common research practice of calculating a zero-order correlation between one affect dimension and one personality dimension. Browne's CIRCUM-Extension provides three figures for each personality dimension. An *angle* estimates the location within the entire circumplex for that personality variable. (In the affect space, Pleasant was fixed at 0° and degrees increase counter-clockwise.) The *zeta* estimates the correlation between the personality dimension and the affect vector at the angle specified. It corresponds to the maximal correlation of that personality trait with any affective dimension, whether or not the affective dimension was actually measured. Finally, the VAF estimates model fit for placing that personality variable within the circumplex model. With the exception of O in the Japanese sample, the VAF ranged from 43% to 99% and showed that the CIRCUM-Extension procedure generally provided a good fit to the data.

4.1. Magnitude of Relations

Both analyses showed that there is a significant relation between personality and momentary affect, modest in magnitude, and varying somewhat with affective dimen-

Table 4. Predicting Affect from FFM: A Cross-Language Examination.

| Language | Regression Weight | | | | | % Variance |
	N	E	O	A	C	
Endogenous variable: Pleasant versus Unpleasant[a]						
English	−.32**	.04	.06	.06	.05	14 (2.8)
Spanish	−.23**	.18**	.02	−.04	.23**	19 (4.7)
Chinese	−.44**	.03	.00	.08	.02	23 (3.4)
Japanese	−.15**	.01	.02	.17**	.04	7 (2.5)
Korean	−.16**	.16**	−.06	.13*	.12*	14 (3.5)
Mean	**−.26**	**.08**	**.01**	**.08**	**.09**	**15.4**
Endogenous variable: Activated Pleasant versus Unactivated Unpleasant[b]						
English	−.20**	.07	.10*	.01	.07	8 (2.3)
Spanish	−.07	.20**	.13*	−.07	.20**	12 (4.1)
Chinese	−.30**	.12*	.04	.03	.10*	18 (3.2)
Japanese	−.13**	.14**	.07	.05	.08	8 (2.5)
Korean	−.17**	.18**	.06	.07	.03	12 (3.3)
Mean	**−.17**	**.14**	**.08**	**.02**	**.10**	**11.6**
Endogenous variable: High versus Low Positive Affect[c]						
English	−.21**	.06	.13**	.01	.12	10 (2.5)
Spanish	−.10	.18*	.15*	−.08	.22**	13 (4.2)
Chinese	−.31**	.09*	.06	.02	.14**	19 (3.3)
Japanese	−.13**	.13*	.08	.04	.08	7 (2.4)
Korean	−.18**	.16**	.04	.08	.06	13 (3.4)
Mean	**−.19**	**.12**	**.09**	**.01**	**.12**	**12.4**
Endogenous variable: Energy versus Tiredness[d]						
English	−.17**	.04	.06	−.01	.07	5 (1.8)
Spanish	.01	.18*	.16*	−.10	.19**	9 (3.7)
Chinese	−.25**	.11*	.05	−.02	.11*	14 (3.0)
Japanese	−.12*	.14**	.05	.05	.11*	8 (2.5)
Korean	−.16**	.17**	−.02	.07	.05	11 (3.1)
Mean	**−.14**	**.13**	**.06**	**.00**	**.11**	**9.4**
Endogenous variable: Activated versus Deactivated[a]						
English	.08	.18**	.05	−.03	.06	4 (1.6)
Spanish	.13	.10	.24**	−.09	.09	8 (3.6)
Chinese	.20**	.16**	.03	−.05	.12*	5 (2.2)
Japanese	.01	.20**	.05	−.03	.08	5 (2.3)
Korean	−.03	.09	.05	−.00	−.02	1 (1.3)
Mean	**.08**	**.15**	**.08**	**−.04**	**.07**	**4.6**
Endogenous variable: Tension versus Calmness[d]						
English	.34**	.08	−.02	−.04	.04	10 (2.6)
Spanish	.27**	−.05	.18**	−.02	−.07	12 (4.2)
Chinese	.47**	.09	−.03	−.04	.04	19 (3.3)
Japanese	.15**	.08	−.03	−.12*	−.03	4 (1.9)
Korean	.16**	−.12*	.10	−.12*	−.08	11 (3.1)
Mean	**.28**	**.02**	**.04**	**−.07**	**−.02**	**11.2**

Table 4 (continued)

Language	N	E	O	A	C	% Variance
			Regression Weight			
Endogenous variable: Activated Unpleasant versus Unactivated Pleasant[b]						
English	.38**	.07	−.05	−.04	.00	14 (2.8)
Spanish	.29**	−.09	.12*	.01	−.14*	16 (4.5)
Chinese	.46**	.04	−.02	−.06	.01	21 (3.4)
Japanese	.19**	.04	−.01	−.14**	.01	6 (2.2)
Korean	.17**	−.16**	.08	−.14**	−.07	13 (3.4)
Mean	**.30**	**−.02**	**.02**	**−.07**	**−.04**	**14.0**
Endogenous variable: High versus Low Negative Affect[c]						
English	.38**	.07	−.04	−.06	−.01	14 (2.8)
Spanish	.29**	−.10	.10	−.00	−.14*	16 (4.5)
Chinese	.46**	.05	−.02	−.07	−.01	21 (3.4)
Japanese	.19**	.04	−.03	−.14**	−.02	6 (2.3)
Korean	.17**	−.15*	.08	−.13*	−.08	13 (3.4)
Mean	**.30**	**−.03**	**.02**	**−.08**	**−.05**	**14.0**

Note. Ns = 535 (English), 233 (Spanish), 487 (Chinese), 450 (Japanese), 365 (Korean). N = Neuroticism, E = Extraversion, O = Openness to Experience, A = Agreeableness, C = Conscientiousness. [a]Yik et al. (1999). [b]Larsen and Diener (1992). [c]Watson and Tellegen (1985). [d]Thayer (1996). *$p \le .05$. **$p \le .01$.

sion, personality dimension, and language. The 40 structural equation models, summarized in Table 4, estimated the percentage of variance in each bipolar affect variable that was explained by the FFM dimensions taken together. These results showed that all affect dimensions are predictable from the FFM, but that some affect variables are more predictable than others. The horizontal Pleasant versus Unpleasant axis was generally the most predictable; the vertical Activation versus Deactivation axis least predictable, and diagonal dimensions intermediate. This pattern was obtained in each language. One interpretation of variation in predictability is that Activation versus Deactivation is more context dependent, whereas Pleasantness versus Unpleasantness more personality dependent, with the diagonal dimensions falling in between because they are a combination of the horizontal and vertical axes.

The structural equation models in Table 4 also showed that the magnitude of the personality/affect relation varied with language: Variance accounted for was 17.5% in Chinese, 13.1% in Spanish, 11.0% in Korean, 9.9% in English, and 6.4% in Japanese. Although one might anticipate the greatest variance explained to occur in English (simply because all scales were psychometrically developed in English), this was not the case. The zetas of the CIRCUM–Extension procedure led to a similar conclusion. Mean zeta calculated across personality dimensions was .29 in Spanish, .27 in Chinese, .27 in Korean, .22 in English, and .20 in Japanese.

Finally, the CIRCUM-extension results showed that the magnitude of relation varied with personality dimension. The zeta of Table 5 is the estimated maximum correlation of a specific personality variable with any one affective variable. Averaging across languages, the mean zeta was .43 for Neuroticism, .29 for Extraversion, .24 for Conscientiousness, .18 for Agreeableness, and .10 for Openness to Experience.

Table 5. *Empirical Location of Personality Dimensions in the Two-Dimensional Affective Space via CIRCUM-Extension.*

Personality Dimension	Language	Angle	Zeta	VAF
Neuroticism	English	176°	.47	98
	Spanish	159°	.42	97
	Chinese	174°	.54	99
	Japanese	176°	.31	97
	Korean	184°	.39	98
Extraversion	English	28°	.22	84
	Spanish	357°	.35	98
	Chinese	19°	.31	97
	Japanese	24°	.21	84
	Korean	7°	.38	97
Openness to Experience	English	32°	.10	86
	Spanish	83°	.20	95
	Chinese	65°	.05	66
	Japanese	63°	.07	0[a]
	Korean	68°	.09	43
Agreeableness	English	355°	.13	75
	Spanish	339°	.13	85
	Chinese	347°	.17	79
	Japanese	352°	.24	87
	Korean	357°	.25	85
Conscientiousness	English	18°	.17	84
	Spanish	0°	.33	97
	Chinese	19°	.27	94
	Japanese	15°	.18	90
	Korean	359°	.23	93

Note. Ns = 535 (English), 233 (Spanish), 487 (Chinese), 450 (Japanese), 365 (Korean). *Angle* refers to the estimated angular position of the personality dimension within the two-dimensional affective space. *Zeta* refers to the estimated communality index for the personality dimension and indicates the correlation between the personality dimension and the common score. Model fit for placing a personality dimension within the circumplex was assessed by the Variance Accounted For (VAF). [a]Since the VAF was computed as zero, the result for Openness to Experience in Japanese was discarded from further discussion.

Compared with past findings, the reported personality/affect connections in the present investigation might appear modest in size. We do not view them as small, or even smaller than past research indicates, for several reasons. First, previous research relied heavily on zero-order correlations.[4] Shared systematic (method) variance may

---

[4]For comparison purposes, we re-examined the personality/affect relations using the traditional multiple regressions in the English data. The Pleasant versus Unpleasant and Activated versus Deactivated affect variables served, respectively, as the dependent variable while the Big Five served as the independent variables. Three regression equations were computed for each bipolar affect variable, one for each scale (response format). Results resembled those in Table 4: The mean variance explained for Pleasant versus Unpleasant affect was 12%; Neuroticism yielded significant relations in all three scales (mean regression weight = -.31). The mean variance explained for Activated versus Deactivated was 2%; Extraversion yielded significant relations in all three scales (mean regression weight = .15).

have inflated past estimations of personality/affect relations (see Jaccard & Wan, 1985). For example, if both affect and personality are assessed with self-report questionnaires in a similar unipolar format, some of the overlap between personality and affect might stem from an acquiescent response style (see Tellegen, Watson, & Clark, 1999). In our analyses, relying on structural equation modeling, we allowed correlated errors. Thus, systematic variance was estimated and removed. The estimates of personality/affect correlations here are thus likely more conservative.

Second, the affective ratings collected in past research often stemmed from participants' describing how they "generally feel" (e.g., Watson & Clark, 1992) or felt in the last two weeks (e.g., McCrae & Costa, 1991). The personality/affect relations may be exaggerated by the shared trait rating instructions, as well as the scale content overlap between the two domains. In effect, the participant is asked to average across a series of moments to arrive at an average affect state—just as, in completing a personality questionnaire, the participant is asked to average across past times and situations to arrive at a characteristic average. Thus, both measures might rely on self schemas or memory biases. In contrast, our data concerned affect at a thin slice of time at a randomly chosen moment. In characterizing the affect of a given well-remembered moment, there is less room for the participant to rely on generalized schematic knowledge of the self. Thus artifacts due to shared rating instructions between personality and affect were minimized. Situational influence on the momentary affect is maximal. In light of these considerations, we are impressed that the FFM can predict a person's momentary affect at an arbitrarily chosen point in time with the variance explained ranging from 6.4% to 17.5%. (These figures correspond to correlations between .25 and .42.)

Third, although we used multiple measures of momentary affect, we relied here on a single measure of the FFM. When, in an earlier study, we had used multiple measures of the FFM, the magnitude of the relation between affect and personality was substantially larger (variance explained in affect by the FFM ranged from 17.8% to 38.5%). Multiple measures coupled with structural equation modeling allow better elimination of method variance and thus a purer measure of trait variance. In agreement with arguments made by other researchers (Green, Goldman, & Salovey, 1993; Lucas & Fujita, 2000), we suggest that the FFM is best operationalized with multiple and maximally distinct formats.

Finally, because the relation of FFM to momentary affect is uniformly reliable, we can invoke standard psychometric principles (as captured, for example, in Epstein's [1979] aggregation procedure or in the Spearman-Brown prophesy formulae) to interpret the magnitude. These principles predict that as one aggregates different instances of momentary affect (across multiples times and situations for the same individual), then the correlation of the FFM with that aggregate will rise. The more instances aggregated, the higher the correlation. (Conversely, the thinner the slice in time for affect, the lower the correlation.)

4.2. Pattern of Relations

The pattern of relations between affect and personality can be seen in the regression

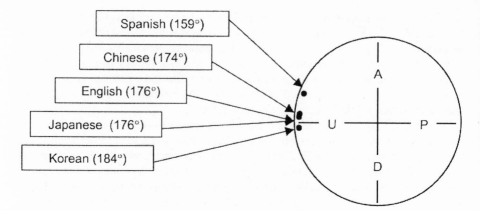

Figure 2. Locating Neuroticism within the Integrated Two-Dimensional Space Portrayed in Figure 1.

weights predicting momentary affect from the FFM (Table 4) and also in the angles estimated in CIRCUM-Extension procedure (*Angle* in Table 5). Both of these analyses tell a similar story and indeed, perhaps the most interesting story we have to offer. Here we focus on the angles from the CIRCUM-Extension procedure. Figures 2 to 6 display, for each language, the location of each personality variable in the integrated affective space.

For instance, consider Neuroticism. Figure 2 shows that those high in Neuroticism tend to experience unpleasant affect in all five samples. Yet there were subtle differences as well. In the Spanish sample, neurotics tended to experience unpleasant affect coupled with high activation. In all the other samples, especially Korean, however, neurotics were just as likely to experience low or medium as high activation. This pattern of results replicates an earlier finding with an English-speaking Canadian sample (Yik & Russell, 2001) and is important to the definition of Neuroticism. Much past research has reported a significant correlation between N and Watson and Tellegen's Negative Activation, and this result has been interpreted as showing that high Ns typically experience high and negative activation. By placing N within the entire affective space, this interpretation is challenged, at least in the majority of our samples.

The results in Figure 3 with E tell an equally fascinating story. In all five samples, extraverts tend to experience pleasant affect, as found in prior research (Lucas et al., 2000). Yet, again, we found subtle differences. In English, Japanese, and Chinese, that pleasant affect was coupled with high activation. This result is also consistent with our prior work (Yik & Russell, 2001) and with the general findings of others (Meyer & Shack, 1989; Watson & Clark, 1992). Yet, in Spanish and Korean, Extraversion was not associated with differences in activation. This result reminds us of Lucas et al.'s (2000) argument that the essence of Extraversion is simply positive affect.

Openness showed the greatest range of angles of any personality trait (Figure 4). In Japanese, the magnitude of the relation between O and affect was too low to justify

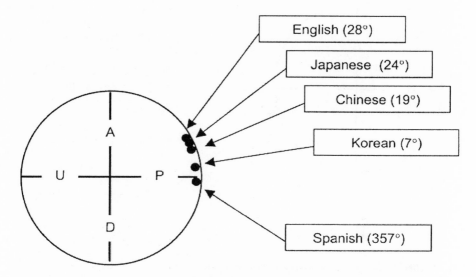

Figure 3. Locating Extraversion within the Integrated Two-Dimensional Space
Portrayed in Figure 1.

calculating an angle. The remaining four languages showed that people high in Openness tend to experience pleasant and activated affect, but mainly activated in Spanish and mainly pleasant in English. Again, however, the low magnitude of the relations suggest caution in assuming the replicability of these results.

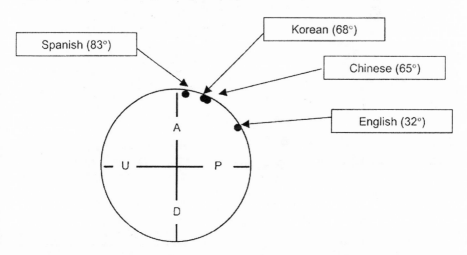

Figure 4. Locating Openness to Experience within the Integrated Two-Dimensional
Space portrayed in Figure 1. Japanese data omitted.

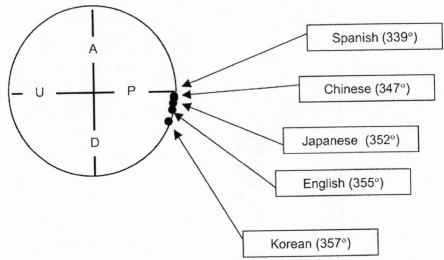

Figure 5. Locating Agreeableness within the Integrated Two-Dimensional Space Portrayed in Figure 1.

Finally, those high in A and C tend to experience positive affect. Both A and C showed similar angles across languages, suggesting a reliable pattern (see Figures 5 and 6). Both are principally related to Pleasant versus Unpleasant axis with only a slight difference in Activation.

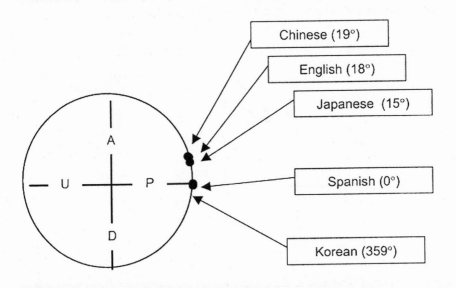

Figure 6. Locating Conscientiousness within the Integrated Two-Dimensional Space portrayed in Figure 1.

4.3. Proper Reference Axes within Affective Space

One of the vexing controversies even among those who agree on a two-dimensional structure of affect concerns the proper rotation of the axes. The two competing rotations are, on the one hand, the horizontal and vertical axes as shown in Figure 1 and, on the other, the diagonal axes, namely Pleasant Activated versus Unpleasant Deactivated and Unpleasant Activated versus Pleasant Deactivated. From a statistical point of view, any pair of non-redundant axes explains the same amount of variance as any other pair. Therefore, comparing the variance explained by the two competing rotations does not help decide which rotation is more "proper" or "basic" than the other.

Researchers therefore turned to external correlates for help. Meyer and Shack (1989) provided evidence in support of the basicness of the diagonal axes in their high correlations with Extraversion and Neuroticism. Larsen (1989) examined a broader range of personality dimensions and did not find them clustered at the 45° and 135° diagonals, but scattered in various places around the circumplex. A number of personality dimensions were found near the horizontal axis of Pleasant versus Unpleasant and the vertical axis of Activated versus Deactivated.

Our analysis assumes that all five dimensions of the FFM should be examined and is summarized in Table 5. Across the five languages, Neuroticism fell at the Unpleasant quadrant (range: 159° to 184°) on the circumference; Extraversion fell at Pleasant Activated/Activated quadrant (range: 357° to 28°); Openness fell at the Pleasant Activated quadrant (range: 32° to 83°); Agreeableness fell at the Pleasant Deactivated quadrant (range: 339° to 357°); and Conscientiousness fell at the Pleasant quadrant (range: 359° to 19°). Each FFM dimension was associated with a range of angles—the spread ranged from 51° for Openness to 17° for Neuroticism. Thus, the same personality dimension might fall at a different angle in different languages; if this result can be replicated, then it would speak loudly against using personality correlates to locate the fundamental axes of a universal affective space. Equally telling and contrary to what Tellegen (1985) and Meyer and Shack (1989) predicted, most personality dimensions do not point to 45° or 135° as fundamental. Although O did, neither E nor N pointed to these angles and, indeed, fell closer to the horizontal axis. In fact, four of the five personality dimensions included the horizontal pleasant-unpleasant axis (0° and 180°) within the range; whereas only O included 45° within its range. Earlier we showed that the horizontal axis was more predictable from the FFM than were the diagonal dimensions. Consistent with Larsen's (1989) findings, personality dimensions fall at different locations around affective space. In short, although a stronger case can be made for our rotation than the alternative 45°/135° rotation, we believe that personality correlates offer no clear guidance on just where the "basic" rotation lies in the two-dimensional space. Rather, the selection of the proper rotation has to be based on other criteria. Larsen and Diener (1992) and Reisenzein (1994) offered conceptual arguments in favor of the Pleasure and Arousal rotation.

5. CONCLUDING REMARKS

The present chapter examined the relations between brief affective states and the fundamental enduring characteristics of personality. We found the results exciting, pointing to the possibility of a simple pancultural description of at least one level of affect and of a simple, even elegant model of the links of affect so described with the FFM of personality. On the other hand, one might view our results with skepticism. The correlations were modest in magnitude. Different personality dimensions bore somewhat different relations to affect in different languages. We relied heavily on translations. For the affect measures, we adopted the expedient of translating scales developed in English into four languages. For personality, only one personality inventory—the NEO-FFI (Costa & McCrae, 1992)—was used. The four language versions available for the present study had been validated and found to have sound psychometric properties. However, psychometric properties do not guarantee complete accuracy of the translated measures. And accuracy of translation is a key factor in the interpretation of the personality/affect connections reported in the present chapter. The first author was involved in the Chinese translation of the NEO-PI-R, and this experience raised questions about simply equating scales in different languages. Similar concerns apply to our scales for affect, which similarly began in English. The present personality/affect connections are therefore best regarded as tentative. More research efforts are needed to extend and replicate the present results with different and improved personality and affect measures.

The present study adopted the "imposed-etic" approach (Berry, 1969; Church & Katigbak, 1989) in which translations of scales originating from the West were administered to participants speaking Spanish, Chinese, Japanese, and Korean. This approach emphasizes similarities across cultures and can be blind to indigenous constructs or processes. Given the richness of the emotion lexicon in each language (e.g., Russell & Yik, 1996), the possibility remains that additional affect dimensions or even different structural models would emerge with more indigenous items. Results obtained in the present study represent a first step towards studying affect and its external correlates in languages other than English. Expanding the current investigation to other languages is necessary to advance our understanding of cross-language similarities and differences. Here affect was studied at a broad general level high in the affect hierarchy, and further studies are much needed to examine more specific affective dimensions at a lower level in a hierarchy. We suspect that cultural differences will be more obvious the lower one goes in that hierarchy.

On the other hand, some of these limitations were self-imposed. Consider the seemingly small magnitude of the relations found. We deliberately obtained ratings of momentary affect rather than ratings of affect across large blocks of time for which participants would necessarily have had to aggregate their remembered feelings. Momentary affect can be influenced by diurnal variations in hormones, current situation, weather and very many other factors in addition to personality. In other words, our Remembered Moments technique maximized the contextual variance and minimized personality variance in affect. Had we held context constant or aggregated over contexts, we would have seen stronger correlations with personality (but at the cost of possibly introducing artifacts). Therefore, being able to predict small but reliable variance in momentary affect represents an important contribution of personality.

Progress has been made in the psychology of personality, moving from divided opinions on how the covariations of personality traits should be described to a near-consensus on the Five-Factor Model as a comprehensive descriptive map. In parallel fashion, progress is being made in the psychology of affect. The present research adds to the existing literature by providing evidence on the viability of a two-dimensional affective space as a common denominator for studying affect across languages and its links to personality. It also provides a springboard to examine affect's connections to other variables. So, whether one views these results with excitement or skepticism, they point to areas of much needed research.

REFERENCES

Ahn, C. K., & Chae, J. H. (1997). Standardization of the Korean version of the Revised NEO Personality Inventory. *The Korean Journal of Counseling and Psychotherapy, 9*, 443-473.

Allik, J., & Realo, A. (1997). Emotional experience and its relation to the Five-Factor Model in Estonian. *Journal of Personality, 65*, 625-647.

Almagor, M., & Ben-Porath, Y. (1989). The two-factor model of self-reported mood: A cross-cultural replication. *Journal of Personality Assessment, 53*, 10-21

Berry, J. W. (1969). On cross-cultural comparability. *International Journal of Psychology, 4*, 119-128.

Browne, M. W. (1992). Circumplex models for correlation matrices. *Psychometrika, 57*, 469-497.

Browne, M. W. (1999). *CIRCUM-Extension.* Unpublished manuscript, Ohio State University.

Carver, C. S., Sutton, S. K., & Scheier, M. F. (2000). Action, emotion, and personality: Emerging conceptual integration. *Personality and Social Psychology Bulletin, 26*, 741-751.

Church, A. T., & Katigbak, M. S. (1989). Internal, external, and self-report structure of personality in a non-Western culture: An investigation of cross-language and cross-cultural generalizability. *Journal of Personality and Social Psychology, 57*, 857-872.

Church, A. T., Katigbak, M. S., & Reyes, J. A. S., & Jensen, S. M. (1999). The structure of affect in a non-Western culture: Evidence for cross-cultural comparability. *Journal of Personality, 67*, 503-532.

Costa, P. T., Jr., & McCrae, R. R. (1980). Influence of Extraversion and Neuroticism on subjective well-being: Happy and unhappy people. *Journal of Personality and Social Psychology, 38*, 668-678.

Costa, P. T., Jr., & McCrae, R. R. (1984). Personality as a lifelong determinant of wellbeing. In C. Z. Malatesta, & C. E. Izard (Ed.), *Emotion in adult development* (pp. 141-157). Beverly Hills: Sage.

Costa, P. T., Jr., & McCrae, R. R. (1992). *The Revised NEO Personality Inventory (NEO-PI-R) and NEO Five-Factor Inventory (NEO-FFI) professional manual.* Odessa, FL: Psychological Assessment Resources.

Costa, P. T., Jr., & McCrae, R. R. (1993). Bullish on personality psychology. *The Psychologist, 6*, 302-303.

Costa, P. T., Jr., & McCrae, R. R. (1996). Mood and personality in adulthood. In C. Magai & S. H. McFadden (Eds.), *Handbook of emotion, adult development, and aging* (pp. 369-383). San Diego, California: Academic Press.

Crystal, D. (1997). *The Cambridge encyclopedia of language* (2nd ed.). New York: Cambridge University Press.

Diener, E. (1984). Subjective well-being. *Psychological Bulletin, 95*, 542-575.

Diener, E., & Emmons, R. A. (1984). The independence of positive and negative affect. *Journal of Personality and Social Psychology, 47*, 1105-1117.

Digman, J. (1990) Personality structure: Emergence of the Five-Factor Model. *Annual Review of Psychology, 41*, 417-440.

Doi, T. (1973). *The anatomy of dependence.* Tokyo: Kodansha.

Epstein, S. (1979). The stability of behavior: I. On predicting most of the people much of the time. *Journal of Personality and Social Psychology, 37*, 1097-1126.

Eysenck, H. J. (1992). Four ways five factors are *not* basic. *Personality and Individual Differences, 13*, 667-673.

Eysenck, H. J., & Eysenck, M. W. (1985). *Personality and individual differences: A natural science approach.* New York: Plenum Press.

Feldman Barrett, L. F., & Russell, J. A. (1998). Independence and bipolarity in the structure of current affect. *Journal of Personality and Social Psychology, 74*, 967-984.

Fossum, T. A., & Feldman Barrett, L. F. (2000). Distinguishing evaluation from description in the personality- emotion relationship. *Personality and Social Psychology Bulletin, 26,* 669-678.

Goldberg, L. R. (1993). The structure of phenotypic personality traits. *American Psychologist, 48,* 26-34.

Green, D. P., Goldman, S. L., & Salovey, P. (1993). Measurement error masks bipolarity in affect ratings. *Journal of Personality and Social Psychology, 64,* 1029-1041.

Gross, J. J., Sutton, S. K., & Ketelaar, T. (1998). Relations between affect and personality: Support for the affect-level and affective-reactivity views. *Personality and Social Psychology Bulletin, 24,* 279-288.

Ho, E. K. F. (1994). *Validating the Five-Factor Model of personality: The Hong Kong case.* Unpublished bachelor's thesis, Chinese University of Hong Kong.

Izard, C. E., Libero, D. Z., Putname, P., & Haynes, O. M. (1993). Stability of emotion experiences and their relations to traits of personality. *Journal of Personality and Social Psychology, 64,* 847-860.

Jaccard, J., & Wan, C. K. (1995). Measurement error in the analysis of interaction effects between continuous predictors using multiple regression: Multiple indicator and structural equation approaches. *Psychological Bulletin, 117,* 348-357.

Joiner, T. E., Jr., Sandín, B., Chorot, P., Lostao, L., & Marquina, G. (1997). Development and factor analytic validation of the SPANAS among women in Spain: (More) cross-cultural convergence in the structure of mood. *Journal of Personality Assessment, 68,* 600-615.

Larsen, R. J. (1989, August). Personality as an affect dispositional system. In L. A. Clark & D. Watson (Chair), *Emotional Bases of Personality.* Symposium conducted at the meeting of the American Psychological Association, New Orleans.

Larsen, R. J., & Diener, E. (1992). Promises and problems with the circumplex model of emotion. In M. S. Clark (Ed.), *Review of Personality and Social Psychology: Emotion* (Volume 13, pp. 25-59). Newbury Park, CA: Sage.

Larsen, R., & Ketelaar, T. (1991). Personality and susceptibility to positive and negative affect. *Journal of Personality and Social Psychology, 61,* 132-140.

Liu, F. Y. (1991). *The generalizability of the NEO Personality Inventory to an university sample in Hong Kong.* Unpublished Bachelor's thesis, Chinese University of Hong Kong.

Lucas, R. E., Diener, E., Grob, A., Suh, E. M., & Shao, L. (2000). Cross-cultural evidence for the fundamental features of Extraversion. *Journal of Personality and Social Psychology, 79,* 452-468.

Lucas, R. E., & Fujita, F. (2000). Factors influencing the relation between Extraversion and pleasant affect. *Journal of Personality and Social Psychology, 79,* 1039-1056.

McCrae, R. R., & Costa, P. T., Jr. (1991). Adding *Liebe und Arbeit*: The full Five-Factor Model and well-being. *Personality and Social Psychology Bulletin, 17,* 227-232.

McCrae, R. R., & Costa, P. T., Jr. (1996). Toward a new generation of personality theories: Theoretical contexts for the Five-Factor Model. In J. S. Wiggins (Ed.), *The Five-Factor Model of personality: Theoretical perspectives* (pp. 51-87). New York: Guilford.

McCrae, R. R., & Costa, P. T., Jr. (1997). Personality trait structure as a human universal. *American Psychologist, 52,* 509-516.

McCrae, R. R., Costa, P. T., Jr., Ostendorf, F., Angleitner, A., Hřebíčková, M., Avia, M. D., Sanz, J., Sánchez-Bernardos, M. L., Kusdil, M. E., & Smith, P. B. (1998, August). *Adult age differences in personality: Five factors in five cultures.* Poster presented at the 106th Annual Convention of the American Psychological Association, San Francisco, CA.

McCrae, R. R., Costa, P. T., Jr., & Yik, M. S. M. (1996). Universal aspects of Chinese personality structure. In M. H. Bond (Ed.), *The handbook of Chinese psychology* (pp. 189-207). Hong Kong: Oxford University Press.

McCrae, R. R., & John, O. P. (1992). An introduction to the Five-Factor Model and its applications. *Journal of Personality, 60,* 175-215.

Mehrabian, A., & Russell, J. A. (1974). *An approach to environmental psychology.* Cambridge, MA: MIT Press.

Meyer, G. J., & Shack, J. R. (1989). Structural convergence of mood and personality: Evidence for old and new directions. *Journal of Personality and Social Psychology, 57,* 691-706.

Moskowitz, D. S., Brown, K. W., & Côté, S. (1997). Reconceptualizing stability: Using time as a psychological dimension. *Current Directions in Psychology Science, 6,* 127-132.

O'Malley, M. N., & Gillette, C. S. (1984). Exploring the relations between traits and emotions. *Journal of Personality, 52,* 274-284.

Reisenzein, R. (1994). Pleasure-activation theory and the intensity of emotions. *Journal of Personality and Social Psychology, 67,* 525-539.

Remington, N. A., Fabrigar, L. R., & Visser, P. S. (2000). Reexamining the circumplex model of affect.

Journal of Personality and Social Psychology, 79, 286-300.

Russell, J. A. (1980). A circumplex model of affect. *Journal of Personality and Social Psychology, 39,* 1161-1178.

Russell, J. A. (1983). Pancultural aspects of the human conceptual organization of emotions. *Journal of Personality and Social Psychology, 45,* 1281-1288.

Russell, J. A. (2002). *Core affect and the psychological construction of emotion.* Unpublished manuscript, Boston College.

Russell, J. A., & Carroll, J. M. (1999). On the bipolarity of positive and negative affect. *Psychological Bulletin, 125,* 3-30.

Russell, J. A., Lewicka, M., & Niit, T. (1989). A cross-cultural study of a circumplex model of affect. *Journal of Personality and Social Psychology, 57,* 848-856.

Russell, J. A., & Yik, M. S. M. (1996). Emotions among the Chinese. In M. H. Bond (Ed.), *The handbook of Chinese psychology* (pp. 166-188). Hong Kong: Oxford University Press.

Russell, J. A., Yik, M. S. M., & Steiger, J. H. (2002). *A 12-point circumplex model of affect.* Unpublished manuscript, Boston College.

Sanz, J., Silva, F., & Avia, M. D. (1999). La evaluacion de la personalidad desde el modelo de los Cinco Grandes: El Inventario de Cinco Factores NEO (NEO-FFI) de Costa y McCrae [Personality assessment from Big Five model: Costa and McCrae's NEO Five-Factor Inventory (NEO-FFI)]. In F. Silva (Ed.), *Avances en evaluacion psicologica* [Advances in psychological assessment] (pp. 171-234). Valencia: Promolibro.

Shimonaka, Y., Nakazato, K., Gondo, Y., & Takayama, M. (1999). *Revised NEO Personality Inventory (NEO-PI-R) and NEO Five-Factor Inventory (NEO-FFI) manual for the Japanese Version [in Japanese].* Tokyo: Tokyo Shinri.

Tellegen, A. (1985). Structures of mood and personality and their relevance to assessing anxiety, with an emphasis on self-report. In A. H. Tuma & J. D. Maser (Eds.), *Anxiety and anxiety disorders* (pp. 681-706). Hillsdale, New Jersey: Erlbaum.

Tellegen, A., Watson, D., & Clark, L. A. (1999). On the dimensional and hierarchical structure of affect. *Psychological Science, 10,* 297-303.

Thayer, R. E. (1996). *The origin of everyday moods: Managing energy, tension, and stress.* New York: Oxford University Press.

Thayer, R. E., Takahashi, P. J., & Pauli, J. A. (1988). Multidimensional arousal states, diurnal rhythms, cognitive and social processes, and Extraversion. *Personality and Individual Differences, 9,* 15-24.

Warr, P., Barter, J., & Brownbridge, G. (1983). On the independence of positive and negative affect. *Journal of Personality and Social Psychology, 44,* 644-651.

Watson, D. (2000). *Mood and temperament.* New York: Guilford.

Watson, D., & Clark, L. A. (1992). On traits and temperament: General and specific factors of emotional experience and their relation to the Five-Factor Model. *Journal of Personality, 60,* 441-476.

Watson, D., & Clark, L. A. (1997). Extraversion and its positive emotional core. In R. Hogan, J. Johnson, & S. Briggs (Eds.), *Handbook of personality psychology* (pp. 767-793). San Diego: Academic Press.

Watson, D., Clark, L. A., & Tellegen, A. (1984). Cross-cultural convergence in the structure of mood: A Japanese replication and a comparison with U.S. findings. *Journal of Personality and Social Psychology, 47,* 127-144.

Watson, D., Clark, L. A., & Tellegen, A. (1988). Development and validation of brief measures of positive and negative affect: The PANAS scales. *Journal of Personality and Social Psychology, 54,* 1063-1070.

Watson, D., & Tellegen, A. (1985). Toward a consensual structure of mood. *Psychological Bulletin, 98,* 219-235.

Watson, D., Wiese, D., Vaidya, J., & Tellegen, A. (1999). The two general activation systems of affect: Structural findings, evolutionary considerations, and psychobiological evidence. *Journal of Personality and Social Psychology, 76,* 820-838.

Wiggins, J. S. & Trapnell, P. D. (1997). Personality structure: The return of the Big Five. In R. Hogan, J. Johnson, & S. Briggs (Eds.), *Handbook of personality psychology* (pp. 737-765). San Diego: Academic Press.

Williams, D. G. (1981). Personality and mood: State-trait relationships. *Personality and Individual Differences, 2,* 303-309.

Yik, M. S. M. (1998). *A circumplex model of affect and its relation to personality: A five-language study.* Unpublished doctoral dissertation, University of British Columbia.

Yik, M. S. M., & Russell, J. A. (2001) Predicting the Big Two of affect from the Big Five of personality.

Journal of Research in Personality, 35, 247-277.

Yik, M. S. M., & Russell, J. A. (2002). *Relating momentary affect to the Five-Factor Model of personality: A Chinese case.* Unpublished manuscript, Hong Kong University of Science and Technology.

Yik, M. S. M., Russell, J. A., & Ahn, C. (2002). *Momentary affect in Korean: Scales, their structure, and their relation to Five-Factor Model of personality.* Unpublished manuscript, Hong Kong University of Science and Technology.

Yik, M. S. M., Russell, J. A., & Feldman Barrett, L. F. (1999). Structure of current affect: Integration and beyond. *Journal of Personality and Social Psychology, 77*, 600-619.

Yik, M. S. M., Russell, J. A., Oceja, L. V., & Fernández Dols, J. M. (2000). Momentary affect in Spanish: Scales, structure, and relation to personality. *European Journal of Psychological Assessment, 16*, 160-176.

Yik, M. S. M., Russell, J. A., & Suzuki, N. (2002). *Relating momentary affect to the Five-Factor Model of personality: A Japanese case.* Unpublished manuscript, Hong Kong University of Science and Technology.

AUTHOR NOTE

Michelle S. M. Yik, Division of Social Science, Hong Kong University of Science and Technology; James A. Russell, Department of Psychology, Boston College; Chang-kyu Ahn, Department of Education, Pusan National University; Jose Miguel Fernández Dols, Facultad de Psicologia, Universidad Autonoma de Madrid; Naoto Suzuki, Department of Psychology, Doshisha University. Data reported in this article are based on Michelle Yik's doctoral dissertation. Correspondence can be directed to Michelle Yik, Hong Kong University of Science and Technology, Division of Social Science, Clear Water Bay, Kowloon, Hong Kong. Fax: (852) 2335-0014. E-mail: myik@ust.hk

NEO-PI-R DATA FROM 36 CULTURES

Further Intercultural Comparisons

ROBERT R. McCRAE

National Institute on Aging

Abstract. This chapter presents reanalyses of data originally reported in McCrae (2001) in an enlarged sample of cultures. Analyses of age and gender differences, the generalizability of culture profiles across gender and age groups, and culture-level factor structure and correlates are replicated after the addition of 30 new subsamples from 10 cultures. Cross-cultural variations in the standard deviations of NEO-PI-R scales are also examined. Standardized factor- and facet-level means are provided for use by other researchers.

Keywords: Personality traits, cultures, variance, factor structure

1. INTERCULTURAL COMPARISONS

For centuries, people have characterized their own group and their neighbors in the language of personality traits (usually more flattering to themselves than others); more recently, psychologists and anthropologists have attempted to provide scientific assessments of national character. Personality scales provide an obvious candidate, because mean levels of representative groups from different cultures can be compared quantitatively. This approach, however, has drawn extensive criticism, because raw scores obtained in different cultures, often from instruments in different languages, may not be directly comparable. Critics (e.g., Marsella, Dubanoski, Hamada, & Morse, 2000; Van de Vijver & Leung, 1997) have pointed to a number of potential problems: Translations may not be equivalent, response styles may confound results, samples may not be representative of the culture as a whole.

Although all of these points are well taken, until recently they were largely moot, because, with rare exceptions (Barrett & Eysenck, 1984), extensive collections of cross-cultural personality data were simply not available. In the last decade, however, worldwide interest in the Five-Factor Model (FFM) has resulted in numerous translations of the Revised NEO Personality Inventory (NEO-PI-R; Costa & McCrae, 1992), and McCrae (2001) used data from these translations to explore intercultural comparisons.

105

Encouraged by results from bilingual studies that showed minimal evidence of distortion due to translation per se (e.g., McCrae, Yik, Trapnell, Bond, & Paulhus, 1998), McCrae proposed that, in a large sample of traits and cultures, all the various sources of bias might cancel out, leaving reasonably comparable scores. That was a radical hypothesis that clashes with conventional wisdom in the field; most cross-cultural psychologists would have expected such comparisons to be meaningless. Yet analyses of the data showed clearly meaningful patterns. It was possible that different groups from the same culture would show very different personality profiles, but in fact, McCrae (2001) found agreement on all five factors when college-age samples were compared to adult samples of the same culture, and when men were compared to women. It was possible that factor structure at the culture level (where group means are analyzed instead of individuals' scores) would bear no resemblance to the individual-level FFM, but in fact, strikingly similar factors were found. It was possible that those factors would lack construct validity, but in fact they were strongly related to national levels of subjective well-being and personality, and to Hofstede's (2001) dimensions of culture. Those data convincingly demonstrated that intercultural comparisons of personality scores are feasible even when the available data are less than optimal.

Since publication, data from an additional 30 age- and gender subsamples from 10 cultures have become available. This chapter replicates earlier analyses in this larger and more representative sample of cultures and provides a summary of the data for use by other investigators.

2. NEW CULTURES AND REPLICATIONS

2.1. Samples

As in McCrae (2001), the data presented here were obtained from the published litera-ture or from colleagues with unpublished data. All data were from volunteers guaranteed confidentiality; separate values were tabulated for men and women and for (roughly) college-age and adult subsamples. Table 1 lists the complete set of 36 samples; new cultures are listed in at the bottom in boldface, and briefly described here. Most of the new cultures are from Europe, but it should be noted that they include among them representatives of five language families: Indo-European (e.g., Danish), Uralic (Hungarian), Altaic (Turkish), Dravidian (Telugu), and Sino-Tibetan (Chinese).

Data from Austria and Switzerland were collected by a variety of researchers as part of the standardization of the German NEO-PI-R (Angleitner & Ostendorf, 2000). Similarly, Czech, Hungarian, Swedish, and Turkish data were intended to serve as the basis for norms in those countries. In the Swedish case, a random national sample was recruited. Only the student data were used for Turkey, because the adults were tested in an employment context that may have affected their responses (Gülgöz, 2002). Twin studies in Canada (Jang, Livesley, & Vernon, 1996) and Denmark were the source of the data reported here from those countries. Data from the People's Republic of China were collected at a variety of sites from normal controls for a study of personality in psychiatric patients (Yang et al., 1999).

The Telugu-speaking Indian sample is of particular interest. These data were collected from adolescents aged 15 to 18, and thus stand in clear contrast to the

Table 1. Characteristics of the Samples.

Country	Language	Subsample Size (Men/Women)		Source/Reference
		College	Adult	
Hong Kong	Chinese	60/62		McCrae, Yik et al., 1998
Taiwan	Chinese	173/371		Chen, 1996
Croatia	Croatian	233/233	123/133	Marušić et al., 1997
Netherlands	Dutch	615/690		Hoekstra et al., 1996
United States	English	148/241	500/500	Costa & McCrae, 1992
S. Africa-Bl.	English	19/46		W. Parker
S. Africa-Wh.	English	41/168		W. Parker
Philippines	English	152/236		A. T. Church
	Filipino	134/375		G. del Pilar
Estonia	Estonian	119/398	189/331	J. Allik
Belgium	Flemish	34/68	527/490	F. De Fruyt
France	French	54/338	279/395	Rolland, 1998
Germany	German	290/454	1185/1801	F. Ostendorf
Indonesia	Indonesian	34/138		L. Halim
Italy	Italian	26/41	315/308	G. V. Caprara
Japan	Japanese	176/177	164/164	Shimonaka et al., 1999
South Korea	Korean-1	1257/1096		Lee, 1995
	Korean-2		278/315	R. L. Piedmont
Malaysia	Malay	124/327		Mastor et al., 2000
India	Marathi	107/107		Lodhi et al., 2002
Norway	Norwegian-1	74/18	397/295	H. Nordvik
	Norwegian-2		148/210	Ø. Martinsen
Portugal	Portuguese	205/253	606/816	M. P. de Lima
Russia	Russian	26/91	201/192	T. Martin
Yugoslavia	Serbian	72/547	256/245	G. Knežević
Zimbabwe	Shona	36/35	135/106	R. L. Piedmont
United States	Spanish	24/49		PAR, 1994
Peru	Spanish	274/165		Cassaretto, 1999
Spain	Spanish		89/107	M. Avia
China	**Chinese**		**115/86**	**Yang et al., 1999**
Czech Rep.	**Czech**	**90/152**	**161/167**	**M. Hřebíčková**
Denmark	**Danish**	**52/40**	**545/576**	**E. L. Mortensen**
Canada	**English**		**282/566**	**K. Jang**
Austria	**German**	**28/110**	**120/186**	**F. Ostendorf**
Switzerland	**German**		**44/63**	**F. Ostendorf**
Hungary	**Hungarian**	**36/56**	**92/128**	**Z. Szirmak**
Sweden	**Swedish**	**21/30**	**286/383**	**H. Bergman**
India	**Telugu**	**157/102**		**V. S. Pramila**
Turkey	**Turkish**	**123/137**		**S. Gülgöz, 2002**

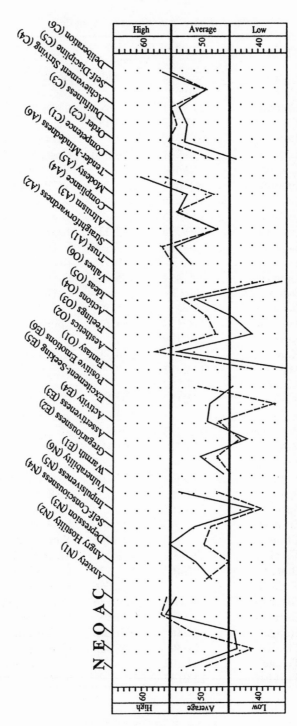

Figure 1. Mean NEO-PI-R profiles for Telugu-speaking adolescents (solid line) and Marathi-speaking graduate students (dashed line), plotted using U.S. college-age norms. Profile form reproduced by special permission of the Publisher, from the Revised NEO Personality Inventory, by Paul T. Costa, Jr., and Robert R. McCrae. Copyright 1978, 1985, 1989, 1992 by PAR, Inc. Further reproduction is prohibited without permission of PAR, Inc.

Marathi-speaking Indian sample in McCrae (2001), which was composed of graduate students (Lodhi, Deo, & Belhekar, 2002). In addition to age and education, these two groups differ not merely in language, but in language family: Marathi is an Indo-European language, whereas Telugu is Dravidian. A comparison of these two samples provides a first test of the hypothesis that personality scores are a robust indicator of the personality profile of a culture. Despite the differences in these two groups and the translations used to assess them, their shared Indian culture ought to be reflected in similar profiles.

Figure 1 plots combined-sex data for these two samples on U.S. college-age norms. The Marathi speakers appear to be slightly lower in N and E and higher in A and C, probably reflecting their greater age (Costa & McCrae, 2002); they are substantially higher in O, probably because of both age and educational differences. Much more striking, however, are the similarities, especially in the facets of Openness, Agreeableness, and Conscientiousness. For some purposes it might make sense to combine them into an Indian profile; here they will be treated separately. Figure 1 attests to the meaningfulness of personality scores in translation.

2.2. Age and Gender Standardization

As in McCrae (2001), analysis of raw domain scores showed evidence of familiar age and gender differences (Costa & McCrae, 2002; Costa, Terracciano, & McCrae, 2001). Analyses of the 30 new subsamples (see Table 1, boldface) showed that women scored higher than men in Neuroticism, Openness, and Agreeableness (all $p < .05$), and that college-age men and women scored higher in Neuroticism and Extraversion and lower in Conscientiousness than adults (all $p < .01$). There was a trend for adults to score higher in Agreeableness ($p < .10$), but no age difference in Openness. When analyses were repeated in the full set of 114 subsamples, the same gender and age differences were found; in addition, across all 36 cultures, adults scored lower in Openness and higher in Agreeableness.

To test the feasibility of combining subsamples to generate culture-level personality profiles, I assessed the generalizability of profiles across age and gender groups. Scores for each of the five domains from men were matched with those from women of the same culture and age group. The resulting correlations ranged from .71 to .93 ($N = 15$, $p < .01$) in the subset of new cultures, and from .77 to .88 ($N = 57$, $p < .001$) across all cultures. Men and women of the same age and culture clearly show similar personality profiles.

To test generalizability of profiles across age groups, I matched scores of adults with scores of college-age samples of the same culture and gender. Because some samples had only one age group, the number of cases was reduced to 10 for the new cultures and 40 for the full sample. Nevertheless, significant correlations were found for Neuroticism (.90), Openness (.92), and Agreeableness (.97; all $p < .001$) even among the new cultures. Across all 36 cultures, the correlations for Neuroticism, Extraversion, Openness, Agreeableness, and Conscientiousness were .81, .54, .60, .79, and .48, respectively, all $p < .01$. These data provide support for generalizing across age groups. It should be noted that the age groups in this study often differ in ways other than age.

For example, almost all the college-age subsamples are composed of college students, whereas the adult samples often have a wider range of educational levels.

For subsequent analyses, to correct for age and gender differences, all raw facet score means were standardized using the age- and gender-appropriate U.S. norms (Costa & McCrae, 1992). NEO-PI-R factor scores were calculated from these standardized facets, using the scoring weights provided in the *Manual*, Table 2.

2.3. The Culture-Level Factor Structure

The 30 subsamples available from the 10 new cultures were too few to allow a factor analysis. However, the full set of 114 subsamples was factored. In this analysis, each age- and gender-defined subsample was treated as a case. Seven eigenvalues exceeded 1.0, but a parallel analysis (Horn, 1965) confirmed that only five should be retained. After varimax rotation, these showed a broad Extraversion factor, but all the other factors were close to the usual structure seen in analyses of individual-level data. Table 2 reports the results of a Procrustes rotation of the factors (McCrae, Zonderman, Costa, Bond, & Paunonen, 1996). This solution is almost identical to that found in the smaller set of 26 cultures; the most notable changes are increases in the intended loadings for O4: Actions and A5: Modesty, and a decrease for O6: Values. All of the factor congruences reach the .85 criterion recommended by Haven and ten Berge (1977). Thus, the culture-level analysis replicates the individual-level structure.

2.4. Culture Profiles and Correlates

To characterize cultures, unweighted means of the data from each subsample were calculated. Note that the Norwegian profiles are based on six subsamples, and that the Filipino profiles combine English and Filipino administrations. However, Telegu and Marathi, general American and Hispanic American, Hong Kong and PRC Chinese, and Black and White South Africans are retained as separate cultures. Table 3 reports values of the five factors across the 36 cultures; values for the 30 individual facets are given in Appendix I.

Because factor comparabilities (Table 2, last row) are uniformly high, the means of individual-level factors (Table 3) are comparable to culture-level factor scores. To validate such factors, McCrae (2001) correlated them with culture-level values for the Eysenck Personality Questionnaire (EPQ; Lynn & Martin, 1995) and with Hofstede's (2001) dimensions of culture. Table 4 reports these correlations in the expanded sample.[1] As in the earlier analysis, Neuroticism and Extraversion are significantly related to their EPQ counterparts, but no other EPQ correlations reach significance. (The Indian EPQ data were omitted in these analyses because they appear to be outliers.) At the facet level, EPQ Neuroticism is chiefly related to N1: Anxiety, N2: Angry Hostility, N3: Depression, and N6: Vulnerability ($rs = .69–.70$, $p < .01$), although the largest correlation, unexpectedly, is with O6: Values ($r = -.78$, $p < .001$). EPQ Extraversion is significantly correlated with E1: Warmth, E3: Assertiveness, and

---

[1]For somewhat different results, using a different source of EPQ data, see Poortinga et al. (2002).

Table 2. *Culture-Level Factor Structure of NEO-PI-R Facet Scales after Procrustes Rotation.*

NEO-PI-R Facet Scale	Procrustes-Rotated Principal Component					VC[a]
	N	E	O	A	C	
N1: Anxiety	**.86**	−.05	.04	−.07	−.14	.99**
N2: Angry Hostility	**.74**	−.03	−.03	**−.55**	−.04	.99**
N3: Depression	**.83**	−.21	−.25	−.05	−.25	.95**
N4: Self-Consciousness	**.64**	**−.42**	−.14	−.11	−.08	.92*
N5: Impulsiveness	.28	**.66**	.25	−.16	**−.47**	.86*
N6: Vulnerability	**.70**	−.33	−.11	−.16	**−.40**	.96**
E1: Warmth	−.13	**.64**	.34	.29	.07	.97**
E2: Gregariousness	−.14	**.75**	−.07	−.13	−.02	.95**
E3: Assertiveness	−.13	**.61**	.19	−.31	.08	.88*
E4: Activity	.11	**.70**	.05	−.36	.27	.94**
E5: Excitement Seeking	.11	**.65**	−.22	**−.43**	.09	.88*
E6: Positive Emotions	−.34	**.71**	.34	.11	−.05	.91*
O1: Fantasy	.20	**.45**	**.61**	−.30	−.35	.95**
O2: Aesthetics	.31	−.23	**.70**	−.27	.22	.78
O3: Feelings	.25	**.58**	**.66**	−.08	−.08	.94**
O4: Actions	−.26	.09	**.67**	.25	−.18	.92*
O5: Ideas	−.08	−.09	**.83**	−.03	.27	.98**
O6: Values	−.06	**.60**	**.42**	−.02	−.33	.72
A1: Trust	**−.55**	.10	−.16	**.49**	.02	.85
A2: Straightforwardness	−.21	−.11	−.17	**.70**	.08	.94**
A3: Altruism	−.09	**.66**	.12	.34	.35	.93*
A4: Compliance	−.38	**−.43**	−.08	**.67**	−.02	.88*
A5: Modesty	.26	.36	−.25	**.63**	−.02	.80
A6: Tender-Mindedness	.03	.07	−.13	**.63**	.32	.79
C1: Competence	**−.44**	**.51**	.09	.02	**.50**	.90*
C2: Order	−.15	−.22	−.04	.18	**.69**	.87*
C3: Dutifulness	−.05	.13	−.14	.28	**.73**	.94**
C4: Achievement Striving	−.04	−.26	.12	−.14	**.76**	.82
C5: Self-Discipline	**−.45**	.11	−.03	.22	**.64**	.96**
C6: Deliberation	−.01	−.33	**−.51**	.22	**.54**	.79
Factor Congruence[b]	.94**	.85**	.87**	.92**	.94**	.90**
Factor Comparability	.97	.96	.95	.95	.95	

Note: These are principal components from 114 subsamples targeted to American normative factor structure. Loadings greater than .40 in absolute magnitude are given in boldface. [a]Variable congruence coefficient; total congruence coefficient in the last row. [b]Congruence with American normative factor structure. *Congruence higher than that of 95% of rotations from random data. **Congruence higher than that of 99% of rotations from random data.

Table 3. Composite Factor T-scores and Mean SD for Peoples from 36 Cultures.

Group	N	E	O	A	C	SD[a]
Indonesians	48.6	43.3	49.9	51.9	50.3	8.1
Telugu Indians	52.3	43.5	44.0	55.9	54.0	8.5
South African Blacks	49.1	41.4	47.7	50.4	47.9	8.6
Zimbabweans	50.9	42.3	47.0	51.0	51.8	8.8
Malaysians	54.2	42.5	46.6	58.5	54.2	8.9
Taiwan Chinese	51.5	42.0	50.2	54.5	48.1	9.2
South Koreans	53.6	40.0	51.4	52.3	48.8	9.2
Danes	46.5	52.8	46.5	52.0	47.5	9.3
Filipinos	50.8	43.8	51.8	52.9	51.5	9.5
Portuguese	55.5	46.3	49.2	51.2	50.3	9.6
Hong Kong Chinese	53.3	37.6	49.2	54.6	49.2	9.7
Japanese	55.3	41.7	51.7	47.7	42.6	9.7
Marathi Indians	49.1	40.7	51.4	56.7	55.7	9.8
Peruvians	50.8	45.5	50.0	48.6	49.0	9.8
Russians	53.6	45.2	49.1	46.7	46.5	9.9
Americans	50.0	50.0	50.0	50.0	50.0	10.0
Dutch	48.6	43.9	55.7	54.6	48.6	10.2
South African Whites	51.9	47.2	54.4	52.2	47.9	10.2
Norwegians	47.4	53.6	51.5	49.9	45.7	10.2
Belgians	53.0	47.7	51.8	50.0	46.6	10.3
Hispanic Americans	49.5	47.5	51.2	47.1	51.6	10.3
German Swiss	53.2	48.5	58.9	47.0	49.6	10.4
PRC Chinese	53.1	44.5	48.3	47.8	50.3	10.5
Germans	52.8	47.3	56.7	49.1	46.7	10.6
Yugoslavians	51.1	47.6	56.0	48.4	51.7	10.7
Croatians	52.8	45.1	49.0	47.5	53.2	10.8
Swedes	46.3	50.6	46.0	56.5	45.7	10.8
French	55.4	47.3	54.1	52.1	47.4	10.9
Austrians	52.9	48.4	59.1	48.2	46.7	11.0
Canadians	50.5	51.7	51.6	51.9	49.2	11.0
Turks	50.9	50.3	50.8	48.5	50.4	11.1
Spaniards	57.1	48.3	48.0	49.4	48.3	11.2
Italians	55.6	46.6	52.6	48.9	50.4	11.6
Czechs	54.2	47.4	52.3	50.7	47.5	11.8
Hungarians	53.8	47.1	53.7	47.9	50.0	12.3
Estonians	49.7	49.9	52.6	50.8	49.6	12.8

[a]Mean standardized standard deviation across 30 NEO-PI-R facet scales.

E6: Positive Emotions. It is also related to O4: Actions, and A3: Altruism, and, inversely, to N4: Self-Consciousness and C6: Deliberation. EPQ Psychoticism is related only to low A1: Trust.

Hofstede indices were taken from the second edition of *Culture's Consequences*

Table 4. *Correlations Between Eysenck Personality Questionnaire (EPQ) Means, Hofstede (1991) Dimensions, and NEO-PI-R Factors.*

			Factor		
Criterion	N	E	O	A	C
EPQ					
Neuroticism	.80***	−.40	−.38	−.42	−.04
Extraversion	−.24	.51*	.18	.22	.03
Psychoticism	.18	−.28	.12	−.11	.22
Hofstede Index					
Power Distance	.28	−.58***	−.40*	.19	.52***
Uncertainty Avoidance	.58***	.03	.31	−.56***	−.25
Individualism	−.12	.64***	.34*	−.07	−.30
Masculinity	.55***	−.27	.37*	−.32	.06
Long-Term Orientation	.08	−.51**	−.16	.11	−.04

Note. N = 35 cultures for Hofstede indices (25 for Long-Term Orientation), 18 for EPQ (India omitted as an outlier). *p < .05. **p < .01. ***p < .001.

(Appendix 5), and differ slightly from earlier sources. In particular, the present analyses use values for Dutch-speaking Belgians rather than all Belgians, and for German-speaking Swiss. Table 4 shows correlations, which in general resemble in size and pattern those reported earlier (McCrae, 2001). Power Distance, which refers to an acceptance of status differences, is associated with Conscientiousness, Closedness, and Introversion; at the facet level, it is positively related to Achievement Striving and Deliberation, and negatively related to Impulsiveness, Gregariousness, Activity, Positive Emotions, and Openness to Fantasy, Feelings, and Values (all *p* < .01). Cultures with high Power Distance appear to have members who are serious, traditional, task-minded workers.

Uncertainty Avoidance is associated with both Neuroticism and low Agreeableness. Anxiety, Angry Hostility, and Openness to Fantasy are positive correlates; Trust, Straightforwardness, Achievement Striving and Deliberation are inversely related. Strict rules and routines may serve as defenses in populations where such volatile temperaments prevail. Individualism-Collectivism is associated with Extraversion and Openness at the factor level and, at the facet level, with Impulsiveness, Warmth, Activity, Positive Emotions, Openness to Fantasy, Feelings, and Values, and Altruism versus Self-Consciousness, Achievement Striving, and Deliberation. Note that this complex pattern of facet associations resembles the pattern of loadings on the E factor in Table 2; indeed, one might argue that that factor would be better labeled *Individualism* than *Extraversion*.

In McCrae (2001), Masculinity was unrelated to any of the factors. In the present analyses, it is associated with both Neuroticism and Openness. Its facet correlates include high Angry Hostility, Vulnerability, and Openness to Aesthetics and Ideas, as well as low Modesty. These correlates bear no resemblance to masculine personality traits as seen in gender differences (Costa et al., 2001). That is not surprising, however, because Hofstede's Masculinity index reflects egoistic versus social work goals. In practice, significant correlations with Masculinity appeared in the expanded sample because the new cultures included Austria and German-speaking Switzerland, which rank in the top four cultures for Masculinity scores, and Sweden and Denmark, which rank in the bottom three. In essence, Hofstede's Masculinity contrasts agentic Germanic work styles with communal Scandinavian work styles. Because German-speaking people are also comparatively higher in Neuroticism and Openness than their Scandinavian neighbors, N and O become the correlates of Masculinity. In a larger sample of cultures, it is not clear that these associations would remain.

In the second edition of *Culture's Consequences*, Hofstede also lists a fifth dimension of culture, Long-term Orientation, based on work by Bond and associates (Chinese Culture Connection, 1987). Long-Term Orientation implies valuing persistence, thrift, and modesty over protecting "face" and reciprocating favors. Only a subset of cultures had indices for this dimension, and only Introversion was associated with it at the factor level. Two facets were significantly ($p < .01$) related to Long-Term Orientation: Low Positive Emotions and low Openness to Actions.

3. CROSS-CULTURAL TRENDS IN VARIABILITY ABOUT THE MEAN

Previous intercultural comparisons in this sample of cultures have focused on mean levels, but it is also possible to examine variances or standard deviations. A first step is to establish whether variances are consistent within cultures—that is, whether the variance estimates can be generalized across age and gender groups. Standard deviations for each of the thirty facets from men were matched with those from women of the same culture and age group. Correlations ranged from .42 to .88 ($N = 57$, $p < .001$), with a median correlation of .68. Similar correlations calculated across age groups ranged from .33 to .85 ($N = 38$, $p < .05$) with a median of .66. It appears that, for all NEO-PI-R facets, variance is a characteristic feature. It is not yet clear whether the consistency is due to the culture or to the language. In the Filipino subsamples, facet standard deviations were, on average, 14% larger when the NEO-PI-R was administered in Filipino than when it was administered in English.

In examining the intercorrelation of facet *SD*s, it became clear that the magnitude of variances were consistent across facets. Cultures that had low *SD*s for some facets tended to have low *SD*s for all. This could be seen most clearly in factor analyses. In men, principle component analysis of the 30 *SD*s yielded a first factor accounting for 55% of the variance, and on which all variables showed loadings greater than .40. The first factor in women accounted for 52% of the variance, and again, all variables had substantial loadings. It appears that variance is a cross-trait characteristic of cultures (or languages).

To characterize variability in each culture, *SD*s were first standardized using data from the age- and gender-appropriate U.S. norms. They are thus expressed in terms of American *T*-scores. Because values were generalizable across age and gender, facet *SD*s for each culture were calculated as the unweighted mean values across subsamples. These values are reported in Appendix II. Because variances were generalizable across all 30 facets, a grand mean was calculated. This value is presented in the last column of Table 3, where the entries are ordered from lowest to highest value.

The range of SDs is substantial, especially considering that these are averages across 30 different traits. Conveniently, Americans fall near the center of the distribution. It is clear that the data are geographically ordered: Except for China, all Asian cultures fall in the lower half of the distribution, as do the two Black African cultures. Variability is most pronounced among Europeans. Mean SD is significantly related to Power Distance ($r = -.39$, $p < .05$) and Individualism ($r = .54$, $p < .01$), presumably because Europeans are lower in Power Distance and higher in Individualism than Asians.

Costa, Terracciano, and McCrae (2001) reported that the magnitude of gender differences followed a similar pattern, with the largest gender differences in European countries and the smallest in Asian. These two effects are independent, because the data in Table 3 were standardized within gender, and the gender differences Costa et al. (2001) reported were standardized within culture. If variability among raw scores were examined, the two effects would reinforce each other, and the differences between European/American and Asian/African cultures would be even more pronounced.

3.1 Some Possible Explanations

Descriptively, these findings mean that self-reported trait scores show more within-culture variability in European than in Asian cultures. Several explanations are possible. For example, Asians might avoid the use of extreme response options, leading to a narrower range of scores. This is a serious concern, because it could in principle contribute artifact in comparisons of mean levels (Cheung & Rensvold, 2000). We can understand this phenomenon by considering the most extreme case: If all the individuals in a culture endorsed the *neutral* response option for every item, they would have raw scores of 96 on each NEO-PI-R domain. In comparison to American norms, they would appear to be high in Neuroticism, low in Extraversion and Openness, and very low in Agreeableness and Conscientiousness. Although Asians do score low in Extraversion, Table 3 shows that they are not low in either Agreeableness or Conscientiousness. A neutral response style might account for differences in SDs, but it is unlikely that it is responsible for mean level differences in these data.

Lower standard deviations might also be due to problems in the translations. Piedmont, Bain, McCrae, and Costa (2002) reported difficulties in preparing a Shona translation of the NEO-PI-R, and the median alpha reliability of the facet scales was only .49 (compared to .71 in the American normative sample; Costa & McCrae, 1992). Random error of measurement reduces variance, so the low mean SD found in Zimbabwe and some Asian countries might be attributed to this source. (Conversely, coefficient alpha depends to some extent on the range of variation; if Asian cultures do in fact show a relative restriction of range, they would also tend to report lower alphas.)

Again, individual differences might be muted in collectivistic cultures, either because individuals avoid emphasizing their distinctive personal attributes, or, more profoundly, because individual traits are less important and salient in these cultures (see Church & Katigbak, 2000). Where social interactions are governed by social convention instead of personal preferences, the differences between introverts and extraverts may not be obvious, even to them.

Finally, it is possible that the data accurately portray the distribution of traits within cultures. Perhaps there is more homogeneity of personality among Asians and Africans than among European groups. That fact in turn might be due to genetic or to environmental factors at which we can only guess. The distribution of cultures in Table 3 is a phenomenon awaiting an explanation.

4. SOME APPLICATIONS

This chapter extends the database reported earlier by McCrae (2001) to 36 cultures, adding two new language families, Dravidian and Altaic. The new or combined samples replicated virtually all previous findings, suggesting that results are likely to be widely generalizable. New findings about the consistency of variability across facets and the geographical ordering of mean *SD*s provide new interpretive challenges.

At the beginning of this project there were many reasons to expect that comparisons of personality scores across cultures would be meaningless. Translation problems, response sets, varying standards of comparison and self-presentation, and the unrepresentativeness of most available samples might have yielded uninterpretable and meaningless data. The analyses reported here, however, show patterns that are beyond a doubt lawful. This does not mean that they necessarily show the scalar equivalence of scores. Analyses by Church and Katigbak (2002) showing major discrepancies between mean self-reported personality traits and pervasive national stereotypes of Filipinos call into question the validity of one or both of these characterizations of culture-level personality profiles. New perspectives and new methodologies, such as peer reports (Martin, Costa, Oryol, Rukavishnikov, & Senin, 2002) or participant observations (Leininger, 2002) will be needed to resolve these issues. Clearly, however, intercultural explorations of personality data are well worth pursuing.

Analyses are underway to extend the range of correlates of culture-level factors to include economic and cultural variables (Inglehart,1997) and national values (Schwartz, 1999). Other researchers may find the data in Table 3 and in Appendices I and II useful in other intercultural comparisons.

The data may also be useful in attempting to understand individual cultures. Some of the chapters in this volume (e.g., Hřebíčková et al., 2002; Lima, 2002) have begun to use FFM data to interpret national character. The personality profiles provided here may suggest research questions or hypotheses. Consider the Indian data presented in Figure 1. In both Telugu and Marathi samples, Indians describe themselves as low in Openness to Fantasy, but high in Openness to Aesthetics—two facets that are positively related at both the individual and cultural level. What are the causes and consequences of this discordance? Might a love of art but a lack of imagination explain why India produces a huge number of films, most made "according to a predictable formula" (Taj, 1994)?

Finally, consider the implications of the current findings for the assessment of individuals. In recent years psychologists have been sensitized to the need to consider cultural background in psychological assessment (e.g., Sue, Kuraski, & Srinivasan, 1999), and one common presumption is that scales can only be properly interpreted in terms of culture- or subculture-specific norms (Marsella et al., 2000). The present analyses suggest something very different. At least one interpretation of the pattern of findings is that translations of the NEO-PI-R, when made by competent psychologists who understand the language and culture involved, have reasonable scalar equivalence. If that is so, it is legitimate to compare not only cultures, but also individuals in terms of a common metric, such as U.S. norms (Costa & McCrae, 1992).

Consider an example. Values in Table 3 suggest that an Austrian woman whose raw score on the German NEO-PI-R Openness domain was 127 would be average in Openness for an Austrian, but high in Openness compared to Americans. Both of these assessments are correct; which is to be preferred depends on the frame of reference. An American psychologist might correctly predict that she would be willing to try a new approach to therapy, because she is so open. An Austrian psychologist might make the same prediction, on the grounds that new methods of therapy are acceptable to the average Austrian.

This proposal is not so ethnocentric as it may appear. The hypothesized scalar equivalence applies to all versions, and thus, in principle it would be possible to use any set of norms to interpret scores for any individual. A Danish psychologist interpreting scores from a Peruvian client might do well to use Danish norms to enhance his own understanding of the client; if he wished to provide feedback that the client could understand, however, he should probably use Peruvian norms. Eventually, as larger and more representative samples are obtained from a wider range of cultures, it may be feasible to pool data to obtain world norms, with reference to which all people—and peoples—could be compared.

REFERENCES

Angleitner, A., & Ostendorf, F. (2000, July). *The FFM: A comparison of German speaking countries (Austria, Former East and West Germany, and Switzerland).* Paper presented at the XXVIIth International Congress of Psychology, Stockholm, Sweden.

Barrett, P., & Eysenck, S. B. G. (1984). The assessment of personality factors across 25 countries. *Personality and Individual Differences, 5,* 615-632.

Cassaretto, M. (1999). *Adaptacion del Inventario de personalidad NEO Revisado (NEO-PI-R) Forma S en un grupo de estudiantes universitarios.* Unpublished thesis, Pontificia Universidad Catolica del Peru, Lima.

Chen, M. C. (1996). *Psychosocial correlates of prosocial behavior among college students in Taiwan.* Unpublished doctoral dissertation, Loyola College in Maryland.

Cheung, G. W., & Rensvold, R. B. (2000). Assessing extreme and acquiescence response sets in cross-cultural research using structural equations modeling. *Journal of Cross-Cultural Psychology, 31,* 187-212.

Church, A. T., & Katigbak, M. S. (2000). Trait psychology in the Philippines. *American Behavioral Scientist, 44,* 73-94.

Church, A. T., & Katigbak, M. S. (2002). The Five-Factor Model in the Philippines: Investigating trait structure and levels across cultures. In R. R. McCrae & J. Allik (Eds.), *The Five-Factor Model of personality across cultures* (pp. 129-154). New York: Kluwer Academic/Plenum Publishers.

Chinese Culture Connection. (1987). Chinese values and the search for culture-free dimensions of culture. *Journal of Cross-Cultural Psychology, 18,* 143-174.

Costa, P. T., Jr., & McCrae, R. R. (1992). *Revised NEO Personality Inventory (NEO-PI-R) and NEO Five-Factor Inventory (NEO-FFI) professional manual.* Odessa, FL: Psychological Assessment Resources.

Costa, P. T., & McCrae, R. R. (2002). Looking backward: Changes in the mean levels of personality traits from 80 to 12. In D. Cervone & W. Mischel (Eds.), *Advances in personality science* (pp. 219-237). New York: Guilford Press.

Costa, P. T., Jr., Terracciano, A., & McCrae, R. R. (2001). Gender differences in personality traits across cultures: Robust and surprising findings. *Journal of Personality and Social Psychology, 81,* 322-331.

Gülgöz, S. (2002). Five-Factor Theory and the NEO-PI-R in Turkey. In R. R. McCrae & J. Allik (Eds.), *The*

Five-Factor Model of personality across cultures (pp. 175-196). New York: Kluwer Academic/Plenum Publishers.

Haven, S., & ten Berge, J. M. F. (1977). *Tucker's coefficient of congruence as a measure of factorial invariance: An empirical study* (Heymans Bulletin 290 EX): University of Groningen.

Hoekstra, H. A., Ormel, J., & De Fruyt, F. (1996). *Handleiding NEO Persoonlijkheids-vragenlijsten NEO-PI-R en NEO-FFI [Manual for NEO Personality Inventories NEO-PI-R and NEO-FFI].* Lisse, The Netherlands: Swets & Zeitlinger.

Hofstede, G. (2001). *Culture's consequences: Comparing values, behaviors, institutions, and organizations across nations* (2nd. ed.). Thousand Oaks, CA: Sage.

Horn, J. L. (1965). A rationale and test for the number of factors in factor analysis. *Psychometrika, 30,* 179-185.

Hřebíčková, M., Urbánek, T., Čermák, I., Szarota, P., Ficková, E., & Orlická, L. (2002). The NEO Five-Factor Inventory in Czech, Polish, and Slovak contexts. In R. R. McCrae & J. Allik (Eds.), *The Five-Factor Model of personality across cultures* (pp. 53-78). New York: Kluwer Academic/Plenum Publishers.

Inglehart, R. (1997). *Modernization and postmodernization: Culture, economic, and political change in 43 societies.* Princeton, NJ: Princeton University Press.

Jang, K. L., Livesley, W. J., & Vernon, P. A. (1996). Heritability of the Big Five personality dimensions and their facets: A twin study. *Journal of Personality, 64,* 575-591.

Lee, K.-I. (1995). *Factor structure and maladaptive group profiles of the Revised NEO Personality Inventory for Koreans.* Unpublished doctoral dissertation, Pusan National University.

Leininger, A. (2002). Vietnamese-American personality and acculturation: An exploration of relationships between personality traits and cultural goals. In R. R. McCrae & J. Allik (Eds.), *The Five-Factor Model of personality across cultures* (pp. 197-225). New York: Kluwer Academic/Plenum Publishers.

Lima, M. P. (2002). Personality and culture: The Portuguese case. In R. R. McCrae & J. Allik (Eds.), *The Five-Factor Model of personality across cultures* (pp. 249-260). New York: Kluwer Academic/Plenum Publishers.

Lodhi, P. H., Deo, S., & Belhekar, V. M. (2002). The Five-Factor Model of personality: Measurement and correlates in the Indian context. In R. R. McCrae & J. Allik (Eds.), *The Five-Factor Model of personality across cultures* (pp. 227-248). New York: Kluwer Academic/Plenum Publishers.

Lynn, R., & Martin, T. (1995). National differences for thirty-seven nations in extraversion, neuroticism, psychoticism and economic, demographic and other correlates. *Personality and Individual Differences, 19,* 403-406.

Marsella, A. J., Dubanoski, J., Hamada, W. C., & Morse, H. (2000). The measurement of personality across cultures: Historical, conceptual, and methodological issues and considerations. *American Behavioral Scientist.*

Martin, T. A., Costa, P. T., Jr., Oryol, V. E., Rukavishnikov, A. A., & Senin, I. G. (2002). Applications of the Russian NEO-PI-R. In R. R. McCrae & J. Allik (Eds.), *The Five-Factor Model of personality across cultures* (pp. 261-277). New York: Kluwer Academic/Plenum Publishers.

Marušić, I., Bratko, D., & Eterović, H. (1997). A contribution to the cross-cultural replicability of the five-factor personality model. *Review of Psychology, 3,* 23-35.

Mastor, K. A., Jin, P., & Cooper, M. (2000). Malay culture and personality: A Big Five perspective. *American Behavioral Scientist, 44,* 95-111.

McCrae, R. R. (2001). Trait psychology and culture: Exploring intercultural comparisons. *Journal of Personality, 69,* 819-846.

McCrae, R. R., Yik, M. S. M., Trapnell, P. D., Bond, M. H., & Paulhus, D. L. (1998). Interpreting personality profiles across cultures: Bilingual, acculturation, and peer rating studies of Chinese undergraduates. *Journal of Personality and Social Psychology, 74,* 1041-1055.

McCrae, R. R., Zonderman, A. B., Costa, P. T., Jr., Bond, M. H., & Paunonen, S. V. (1996). Evaluating replicability of factors in the Revised NEO Personality Inventory: Confirmatory factor analysis versus Procrustes rotation. *Journal of Personality and Social Psychology, 70,* 552-566.

Piedmont, R. L., Bain, E., McCrae, R. R., & Costa, P. T., Jr. (2002). The applicability of the Five-Factor Model in a Sub-Saharan culture: The NEO-PI-R in Shona. In R. R. McCrae & J. Allik (Eds.), *The Five-Factor Model of personality across cultures* (pp. 155-174). New York: Kluwer Academic/Plenum Publishers.

Poortinga, Y. H., Van de Vijver, F., & Van Hemert, D. A. (2002). Cross-cultural equivalence of the Big Five: A tentative interpretation of the evidence. In R. R. McCrae & J. Allik (Eds.), *The Five-Factor Model of*

personality across cultures (pp. 281-302). New York: Kluwer Academic/Plenum Publishers.
Psychological Assessment Resources. (1994). *The Revised NEO Personality Inventory: Manual Supplement for the Spanish Edition.* Odessa, FL: Author.

Rolland, J. P. (1998). *NEO-PI-R: Inventaire de Personnalité-Révisé (Adaptation française).* Paris: Les Editions du Centre de Psychologie Appliquée.

Schwartz, S. H. (1999). A theory of cultural values and some implications for work. *Applied Psychology: An International Review, 48,* 23-47.

Shimonaka, Y., Nakazato, K., Gondo, Y., & Takayama, M. (1999). *Revised NEO Personality Inventory (NEO-PI-R) and NEO Five-Factor Inventory (NEO-FFI) manual for the Japanese Version [in Japanese].* Tokyo: Tokyo Shinri.

Sue, S., Kuraski, K. S., & Srinivasan, S. (1999). Ethnicity, gender, and cross-cultural issues in clinical research. In P. C. Kendall, J. N. Butcher, & G. N. Holmbeck (Eds.), *Handbook of research methods in clinical psychology* (pp. 54-71). New York: Wiley.

Taj, A. (1994). *A brief overview of the Indian cinema.* University of Virginia. Retrieved December, 2001, from the World Wide Web: http://www.virginia.edu/~soasia/newsletter/Fall94/1.0.html

van de Vijver, F. J. R., & Leung, K. (1997). Methods and data analysis of comparative research. In J. W. Berry, Y. H. Poortinga, & J. Pandey (Eds.), *Handbook of cross-cultural psychology: Vol 1: Theory and method* (pp. 257-300). Boston: Allyn and Bacon.

Yang, J., McCrae, R. R., Costa, P. T., Jr., Dai, X., Yao, S., Cai, T., & Gao, B. (1999). Cross-cultural personality assessment in psychiatric populations: The NEO-PI-R in the People's Republic of China. *Psychological Assessment, 11,* 359-368.

AUTHOR NOTE

For providing new data for this chapter, I thank V. S. Pramila, Sami Gülgöz, Erik Lykke Mortensen, Hans Bergman, Jian Yang, Zsofia Szirmak, Janos Nagy, Kerry Jang, W. John Livesley, Martina Hřebíčková (supported by Grant 406/01/1507 from the Grant Agency of the Czech Republic and Research Plan AV 0Z7025918 of the Institute of Psychology, Academy of Sciences of the Czech Republic), and Alois Angleitner and Fritz Ostendorf and their collaborators: Christian Antl, André Beauducel, Peter Becker, Gerhard Blickle, Peter Borkenau, Claudia Dziallas, Doris Fay, Jürgen Guthke, Tobias Haupt, Sabine Helmdach, Philipp Y. Herzberg, Otmar Kabat vel Job, Silvia Knobloch, Gabriele Köhler, Denis Köhler, Klaus Kubinger, Bernd Marcus, Erhard Olbrich, Beatrice Rammstedt, Hellgard Rauh, Ricarda Reinhard, Rainer Reisenzein, Rainer Riemann, Melanie Rosendahl, Willibald Ruch, Harald Schaub, Manfred Schmitt, Peter Schmolck, Miriam Schuler, Günter Schulter, Alexander Seiwald, Frank M. Spinath, Regine Steiner, Carolin Wahl, Hannelore Weber, Oliver Wilhelm, Friedrich Wilkening, and Winfried Zinn. German data were collected under a 1992 Max-Plank-Research Award to Alois Angleitner and Jan Strelau. For providing unpublished data in McCrae (2001), I thank Filip De Fruyt, Ivan Mervielde, Hans Hoekstra, Wayne Parker, Jüri Allik, Talvi Kallasmaa, Anu Realo, Gregorio del Pilar, A. Timothy Church, Marcia Katigbak, Jean-Pierre Rolland, Jean-Michel Petot, Fritz Ostendorf, Alois Angleitner, Lena Halim, Gian-Vittorio Caprara, Claudio Barbaranelli, Savita Deo, P. H. Lodhi, Hilmar Nordvik, Øyvind Martinsen, Margarida Pedrosa de Lima, Ralph L. Piedmont, Maria Avia, Jesús Sanz, María Sánchez-Bernardos, Goran Knežević, B. Radović, and Thomas Martin. Address correspondence to Robert R. McCrae, Box #03, NIA Gerontology Research Center, 5600 Nathan Shock Drive, Baltimore, MD 21224-6825, USA. Email: jeffm@lpc.grc.nia.nih.gov

	N1	N2	N3	N4	N5	N6	E1	E2	E3	E4	E5	E6	O1	O2
1. Austrians	52.5	51.6	50.7	51.8	50.7	53.4	48.9	52.2	48.5	49.2	44.1	53.0	58.1	58.0
2. Belgians	52.4	50.6	54.9	50.8	51.0	53.0	43.3	52.7	46.7	48.8	47.9	50.5	52.8	52.8
3. Black S. Africans	49.0	49.3	53.3	52.4	44.5	50.3	44.7	48.0	46.6	43.6	42.8	46.3	45.0	50.7
4. Canadians	50.4	49.4	50.5	50.8	50.7	48.9	50.4	50.2	49.7	51.3	51.3	52.5	52.0	51.6
5. PRC Chinese	49.7	54.1	54.0	54.9	47.2	56.3	45.7	53.2	46.4	49.3	46.8	45.3	45.8	53.6
6. Croatians	50.5	52.2	52.1	51.8	46.7	50.5	43.0	49.6	45.3	51.7	44.7	48.0	48.9	53.2
7. Czechs	51.1	51.3	51.9	49.0	52.0	59.9	50.5	48.3	47.9	47.8	42.4	52.3	52.4	52.0
8. Danes	46.4	44.9	49.2	48.4	49.8	47.6	49.5	55.9	48.0	56.8	47.1	52.2	47.6	46.8
9. Estonians	49.0	45.7	49.9	48.7	50.1	44.8	49.1	48.0	51.5	52.0	50.3	51.3	54.4	53.4
10. Filipinos	50.4	47.4	51.4	53.4	46.7	51.7	45.8	48.7	49.6	45.7	44.3	48.0	46.0	54.8
11. French	55.1	51.2	54.6	52.1	51.9	53.7	48.1	49.2	46.7	50.5	45.4	49.0	54.1	52.7
12. Germans	51.6	50.8	51.3	52.4	50.7	54.1	47.2	51.1	48.4	49.9	41.5	51.4	54.7	56.9

	O3	O4	O5	O6	A1	A2	A3	A4	A5	A6	C1	C2	C3	C4	C5	C6
1.	55.8	54.1	54.0	53.0	46.0	43.0	45.6	46.3	46.4	53.8	47.2	47.4	46.7	49.4	43.7	47.6
2.	50.2	49.3	48.6	52.1	47.7	48.9	44.7	46.4	53.6	53.8	43.8	47.2	48.7	48.5	46.1	49.1
3.	42.0	48.2	49.9	42.6	44.9	48.4	41.9	54.8	49.9	50.2	44.2	48.9	45.7	48.1	47.0	53.5
4.	51.9	49.5	50.4	52.7	51.6	52.4	53.7	50.1	48.9	52.5	50.7	49.3	49.8	47.5	48.3	50.8
5.	44.7	43.1	47.6	49.7	50.0	48.4	41.7	40.9	47.2	54.2	44.0	47.7	50.5	49.7	47.2	57.2
6.	47.7	44.5	49.7	44.9	45.5	46.2	47.6	47.0	48.5	50.6	47.6	50.2	51.5	54.6	48.5	51.8
7.	51.6	53.7	49.8	49.9	41.0	51.7	48.3	48.1	51.0	50.1	40.3	47.7	50.1	49.7	45.2	49.8
8.	47.4	51.5	46.4	48.9	54.2	52.7	48.6	50.6	51.2	51.5	48.2	48.7	50.6	48.5	49.4	48.5
9.	53.9	49.3	50.1	47.2	52.1	46.8	45.0	46.9	55.3	56.6	44.6	50.3	52.4	50.2	49.6	50.6
10.	46.4	51.5	52.3	45.3	49.5	50.4	46.9	54.9	49.7	53.6	47.1	50.7	49.0	52.4	49.4	54.7
11.	50.9	53.8	52.7	51.9	43.0	50.1	48.9	49.8	55.4	54.7	42.1	48.3	49.2	48.2	44.7	48.0
12.	54.3	54.9	50.9	51.9	46.2	44.8	44.7	48.1	46.7	54.1	45.3	48.7	46.7	48.2	44.6	47.0

APPENDIX I: STANDARDIZED FACET MEANS FOR 36 CULTURES

	N1	N2	N3	N4	N5	N6	E1	E2	E3	E4	E5	E6	O1	O2
13. Hispanic Americans	50.9	49.1	50.4	48.0	46.1	51.2	46.5	50.5	51.6	50.3	48.0	50.6	49.4	53.7
14. Dutch	48.5	45.5	50.9	47.9	48.6	48.2	43.9	49.3	46.9	47.6	40.1	49.3	51.4	54.1
15. HK Chinese	53.1	48.4	52.8	55.2	46.0	59.2	45.0	43.7	43.9	45.5	36.5	40.1	45.6	52.1
16. Hungarians	49.8	50.6	53.7	51.1	50.4	53.9	46.2	50.2	47.4	51.0	48.6	49.1	53.3	56.4
17. Indonesians	48.3	45.2	49.2	49.1	45.5	52.6	46.6	48.8	46.8	46.6	45.0	47.6	46.5	53.9
18. Italians	55.1	53.8	53.8	50.1	52.4	55.4	47.6	50.8	48.2	52.6	44.3	46.8	54.1	56.4
19. Japanese	56.0	52.4	56.7	53.5	52.3	62.6	41.3	47.2	45.3	45.4	44.5	46.0	52.2	52.6
20. S. Koreans	53.1	50.0	54.6	56.7	45.9	57.3	41.3	48.5	46.0	45.6	40.3	43.0	48.4	52.9
21. Malaysians	52.3	46.4	53.0	57.6	46.0	51.5	45.1	45.9	46.9	45.1	38.6	47.8	42.2	49.3
22. Marathi Indians	48.9	44.9	49.3	48.1	39.1	47.2	44.7	47.1	43.1	46.8	37.0	50.5	40.8	57.9
23. Norwegians	47.3	46.5	49.6	47.7	54.7	47.7	47.5	56.6	50.7	53.1	50.7	54.4	52.9	50.7
24. Peruvians	53.5	47.7	51.5	49.5	48.9	52.8	45.0	48.7	49.6	46.7	45.8	48.7	50.6	52.3

	O3	O4	O5	O6	A1	A2	A3	A4	A5	A6	C1	C2	C3	C4	C5	C6
13.	45.9	49.6	53.7	44.9	45.7	45.6	47.2	49.2	46.5	50.5	49.6	49.7	49.8	53.8	50.4	49.3
14.	50.5	54.2	51.0	55.3	51.5	51.9	45.5	51.5	54.0	57.9	45.6	48.7	52.5	49.6	50.0	51.2
15.	43.6	47.0	46.6	47.4	48.6	55.4	40.7	57.4	48.1	52.4	40.3	48.6	48.6	48.7	48.7	53.4
16.	53.4	48.9	52.6	49.0	45.6	47.0	48.4	47.2	49.3	47.0	42.5	51.8	51.2	50.3	45.8	49.5
17.	45.8	51.2	49.6	43.1	52.2	52.1	44.8	52.3	50.7	46.3	42.0	52.1	49.2	54.3	45.9	56.4
18.	49.8	49.9	49.2	47.5	44.6	52.9	48.1	43.6	49.8	48.9	44.1	45.0	51.3	49.3	48.2	51.9
19.	48.4	51.2	49.2	43.9	47.9	49.7	35.9	51.2	46.4	44.7	34.9	45.6	43.2	45.9	39.8	48.0
20.	46.5	47.3	48.7	48.9	51.2	52.1	43.2	50.4	46.7	53.3	42.1	47.6	52.8	47.9	44.9	52.5
21.	43.8	52.1	49.9	34.4	51.1	54.6	46.5	57.4	53.0	64.6	44.9	56.3	53.2	55.0	44.5	56.9
22.	47.4	48.9	53.2	39.5	54.7	56.7	47.1	54.2	47.7	56.2	47.7	55.5	54.0	55.0	48.8	55.1
23.	50.1	53.2	49.6	53.0	51.5	50.1	48.6	48.5	49.7	52.8	47.8	48.2	49.0	48.8	45.8	48.6
24.	45.4	47.0	49.6	45.4	45.5	48.1	45.4	49.6	46.0	51.9	47.8	46.5	49.4	53.1	44.8	50.9

	N1	N2	N3	N4	N5	N6	E1	E2	E3	E4	E5	E6	O1	O2
25. Portuguese	56.9	51.0	54.5	52.8	49.8	54.8	47.2	48.8	45.7	47.3	50.0	46.0	49.1	54.0
26. Russians	51.7	51.8	54.1	54.0	49.5	58.6	45.9	48.8	47.6	48.0	46.4	47.2	49.8	53.6
27. Serbians	49.7	49.6	48.8	47.1	50.5	49.3	47.6	52.5	46.9	51.2	47.1	49.0	53.5	59.1
28. Zimbabweans	48.5	49.5	53.4	51.2	44.0	53.9	42.4	48.9	46.3	48.4	43.8	48.2	41.5	50.7
29. Spaniards	58.6	50.1	56.5	54.0	52.0	57.6	43.3	50.6	45.6	50.1	48.3	49.2	52.4	51.1
30. Swedes	45.6	45.5	49.8	46.3	47.8	49.6	47.8	54.8	46.9	46.1	45.0	53.4	48.4	45.6
31. German Swiss	51.0	50.6	50.1	53.1	51.6	53.4	47.3	51.1	49.8	52.8	46.2	52.5	57.0	57.3
32. Taiwan Chinese	51.1	46.4	52.6	53.9	45.4	56.0	46.1	46.5	45.6	43.4	41.4	46.8	46.2	54.7
33. Telugu Indians	47.9	50.7	55.2	50.9	40.8	53.8	45.9	50.0	41.8	48.8	48.4	44.4	34.6	54.0
34. Turks	47.9	50.7	50.9	53.1	49.0	51.6	47.7	52.8	48.8	50.7	50.2	53.1	49.8	53.0
35. Americans	50.0	50.0	50.0	50.0	50.0	50.0	50.0	50.0	50.0	50.0	50.0	50.0	50.0	50.0
36. White S. Africans	49.1	50.4	53.1	51.6	50.7	49.9	49.2	48.6	48.1	48.8	47.0	49.5	52.4	54.6

	O3	O4	O5	O6	A1	A2	A3	A4	A5	A6	C1	C2	C3	C4	C5	C6
25.	47.4	51.1	47.6	42.8	46.1	47.1	45.6	52.3	52.9	52.9	44.9	50.8	50.2	51.7	46.4	51.4
26.	47.4	50.6	46.8	43.5	47.0	43.2	41.3	46.9	49.6	46.0	40.6	50.2	46.0	46.8	43.8	50.3
27.	54.5	51.2	53.9	48.4	47.1	49.5	48.9	46.4	46.0	49.5	46.9	50.3	51.3	54.2	47.7	51.0
28.	41.0	55.2	48.1	39.9	44.6	52.0	40.1	54.5	48.7	56.2	40.9	53.1	49.3	55.3	48.1	55.2
29.	47.7	44.6	45.4	48.5	47.0	43.8	45.8	44.8	53.1	57.2	44.6	48.1	47.8	51.4	44.3	51.8
30.	48.4	49.7	43.9	50.7	52.9	51.8	51.7	52.7	54.6	59.1	48.8	49.8	52.7	42.7	47.0	54.5
31.	56.4	55.4	54.8	53.6	46.0	44.7	46.5	45.1	46.7	51.5	48.9	50.6	48.6	50.6	45.6	48.7
32.	47.4	47.3	46.2	47.1	50.4	51.3	45.4	56.9	45.6	53.1	42.5	47.3	48.9	49.7	45.7	54.4
33.	40.9	44.5	50.9	35.6	51.6	54.5	47.1	53.9	52.2	60.5	43.8	52.7	52.2	53.6	49.0	56.6
34.	50.5	52.0	47.4	51.5	47.2	53.5	51.6	45.5	44.3	48.0	49.5	47.3	50.2	52.0	48.2	51.4
35.	50.0	50.0	50.0	50.0	50.0	50.0	50.0	50.0	50.0	50.0	50.0	50.0	50.0	50.0	50.0	50.0
36.	53.3	52.7	52.3	49.0	47.5	52.7	48.1	50.7	52.1	52.3	45.4	46.8	48.5	47.3	47.1	50.1

	N1	N2	N3	N4	N5	N6	E1	E2	E3	E4	E5	E6	O1	O2
1. Austrians	11.2	9.8	12.2	10.9	10.4	12.1	10.4	11.4	11.2	11.3	11.0	13.0	10.6	9.7
2. Belgians	10.6	9.4	9.6	10.4	11.3	10.6	9.6	10.5	10.6	10.7	10.5	11.2	10.9	9.6
3. Black S. Africans	7.6	8.2	7.3	8.3	8.4	9.4	8.6	9.2	7.2	7.8	9.4	10.2	8.8	8.5
4. Canadians	10.8	11.2	11.6	11.2	10.7	11.7	10.5	10.5	11.2	10.1	10.7	11.0	10.6	11.4
5. PRC Chinese	10.9	10.6	10.1	10.9	11.6	13.0	10.8	10.8	9.7	9.9	9.9	11.0	8.2	9.2
6. Croatians	11.2	9.8	9.9	10.9	10.2	11.7	11.0	11.4	10.0	9.9	10.5	11.3	11.3	11.2
7. Czechs	11.2	11.6	10.8	11.3	12.4	11.0	10.8	12.8	11.2	10.6	13.2	13.1	11.8	11.4
8. Danes	9.9	8.2	8.9	8.2	7.9	9.4	8.4	8.5	9.7	10.8	9.6	8.4	9.3	10.1
9. Estonians	12.3	12.0	11.7	12.4	12.6	13.3	11.8	13.3	12.8	15.7	12.4	14.4	13.3	12.7
10. Filipinos	9.5	9.9	8.4	9.1	9.6	10.3	9.9	9.5	9.3	10.4	10.6	9.8	9.5	8.1
11. French	11.0	10.4	10.2	10.2	10.5	12.6	11.2	11.4	10.0	11.1	10.2	11.9	10.9	10.3
12. Germans	11.0	9.4	10.7	10.6	9.9	11.9	9.7	10.6	10.8	10.6	10.8	12.2	11.0	9.9

	O3	O4	O5	O6	A1	A2	A3	A4	A5	A6	C1	C2	C3	C4	C5	C6
1.	10.8	12.5	10.3	9.0	10.9	9.9	12.0	10.1	11.6	11.3	10.3	11.0	10.4	11.4	12.5	10.8
2.	9.7	11.3	9.3	9.5	10.3	10.4	9.9	10.4	10.3	10.6	9.6	10.6	9.9	10.7	10.2	11.2
3.	7.9	6.3	7.9	9.2	6.2	9.0	12.2	10.6	9.6	11.1	7.5	8.1	8.2	7.1	8.7	8.7
4.	10.7	10.6	11.4	10.6	11.1	10.8	10.5	11.9	11.2	10.9	10.9	11.3	11.2	11.6	11.5	11.0
5.	9.7	9.1	9.7	11.2	9.2	11.2	11.3	11.4	10.7	10.5	11.7	9.8	11.0	9.5	9.6	11.8
6.	10.8	10.5	11.1	9.6	11.5	10.2	12.2	12.0	12.1	10.6	11.0	9.5	10.0	10.3	10.9	11.5
7.	11.9	13.0	11.6	9.0	11.8	12.8	11.7	12.4	12.5	11.3	11.2	11.6	12.4	12.1	11.5	13.3
8.	9.6	10.6	10.5	7.9	8.6	9.7	8.7	9.3	10.4	10.2	9.4	7.8	8.8	10.1	9.5	9.5
9.	12.3	15.1	14.3	11.6	12.2	12.8	11.8	12.4	13.2	12.2	13.0	12.1	11.8	12.8	12.0	13.4
10.	9.1	9.4	9.3	9.0	9.2	9.2	10.0	10.3	9.2	10.2	9.9	9.5	9.3	9.2	9.6	9.3
11.	9.5	10.9	10.2	10.0	11.5	12.2	11.1	11.5	10.7	11.7	9.7	12.3	11.1	11.0	11.1	11.1
12.	10.6	12.4	10.4	9.6	10.7	9.5	11.3	10.3	10.4	10.2	9.9	10.5	10.8	10.9	11.5	10.8

APPENDIX II: STANDARDIZED FACET STANDARD DEVIATIONS
FOR 36 CULTURES

	N1	N2	N3	N4	N5	N6	E1	E2	E3	E4	E5	E6	O1	O2
13. Hispanic Americans	8.5	10.4	9.0	8.9	9.6	11.0	11.0	9.9	8.3	10.7	10.6	12.5	9.5	9.3
14. Dutch	11.0	9.1	9.2	8.7	11.2	10.4	9.4	10.5	10.6	11.2	11.3	12.7	10.3	9.5
15. HK Chinese	10.4	9.6	9.6	8.5	10.1	12.2	10.8	10.3	9.1	9.1	11.5	12.1	8.7	8.1
16. Hungarians	11.4	11.3	11.1	11.4	10.8	14.0	12.0	11.7	11.7	13.0	12.3	14.6	11.7	11.5
17. Indonesians	9.7	8.0	7.9	8.3	8.4	8.5	6.9	6.9	7.6	9.9	10.4	9.4	6.4	8.3
18. Italians	11.2	10.6	10.9	11.8	11.2	12.3	11.6	12.0	9.6	10.6	11.6	12.9	13.0	10.3
19. Japanese	10.1	9.7	9.4	9.1	10.0	10.6	10.3	9.5	9.3	10.5	9.6	10.3	9.0	9.2
20. S. Koreans	9.6	8.1	8.9	9.1	10.0	10.3	9.5	9.5	8.8	8.9	8.6	9.5	8.8	8.9
21. Malaysians	9.1	9.5	7.0	7.1	10.0	9.9	9.5	8.8	8.6	8.7	8.0	11.1	7.1	8.0
22. Marathi Indians	9.3	9.9	8.7	9.6	10.8	11.8	10.7	10.2	9.5	9.7	10.5	10.1	8.1	8.4
23. Norwegians	10.6	8.6	10.0	10.2	9.7	10.0	9.5	10.0	10.6	9.8	10.5	11.8	10.0	10.9
24. Peruvians	8.9	9.2	9.4	10.1	10.4	11.0	9.9	10.0	9.8	8.7	10.4	12.4	9.7	9.2

	O3	O4	O5	O6	A1	A2	A3	A4	A5	A6	C1	C2	C3	C4	C5	C6
13.	10.4	10.0	10.2	11.5	11.2	10.6	13.5	10.4	11.1	12.6	9.4	10.0	9.4	8.3	10.6	10.2
14.	9.6	11.6	9.2	9.6	10.4	10.4	10.5	9.9	10.2	11.2	8.4	9.2	10.0	9.9	9.6	10.7
15.	8.7	10.6	12.1	8.3	9.6	8.6	10.6	8.6	9.6	8.8	10.6	8.6	8.4	9.1	8.2	10.2
16.	12.6	14.5	11.8	10.6	12.8	12.0	13.2	13.4	13.6	12.9	13.1	12.0	12.1	12.5	11.4	11.9
17.	8.2	9.2	7.2	6.4	8.6	8.5	8.2	9.1	7.0	9.0	7.0	8.1	8.2	6.3	7.3	8.6
18.	11.3	12.5	11.8	10.3	12.9	11.4	11.7	12.5	12.8	10.7	11.0	11.9	11.1	11.3	11.7	12.9
19.	8.8	10.4	9.8	8.4	9.5	9.5	10.9	9.6	9.1	9.7	9.7	10.2	9.4	9.6	8.8	10.7
20.	8.8	10.0	9.4	8.0	8.5	8.7	10.3	9.0	8.0	9.7	9.4	10.1	9.3	9.9	8.4	9.7
21.	8.2	9.3	8.3	8.9	8.5	9.4	10.2	10.1	9.2	10.0	9.1	8.9	10.2	9.0	7.6	9.2
22.	9.3	11.0	9.5	8.5	9.6	9.9	10.0	10.7	8.0	11.9	10.0	10.4	9.8	9.3	9.1	8.8
23.	10.9	12.1	11.6	8.2	9.3	10.3	9.8	10.1	9.7	10.6	9.4	10.1	10.4	9.6	10.4	10.8
24.	9.0	8.3	10.3	9.2	10.9	10.6	10.9	9.6	9.8	9.0	9.3	8.5	9.4	9.7	8.5	10.9

	N1	N2	N3	N4	N5	N6	E1	E2	E3	E4	E5	E6	O1	O2
25. Portuguese	8.7	8.9	8.9	9.6	8.9	10.7	9.5	9.9	8.1	8.3	9.6	10.0	9.7	9.2
26. Russians	9.7	8.9	7.7	9.0	9.9	10.4	9.8	11.2	10.3	11.7	10.6	10.7	9.8	8.2
27. Serbians	11.0	10.0	10.2	10.1	11.1	11.9	10.1	10.7	9.0	11.4	11.2	11.9	11.9	9.3
28. Zimbabweans	7.7	8.9	6.9	6.9	9.4	10.9	10.1	8.5	8.3	5.0	8.0	9.3	8.3	8.3
29. Spaniards	9.8	10.3	10.9	11.2	9.4	12.1	11.9	11.6	9.9	11.3	10.3	11.6	11.8	10.8
30. Swedes	11.0	9.8	9.8	10.5	9.0	11.2	10.4	10.7	10.8	9.9	11.9	13.1	10.4	11.5
31. German Swiss	10.3	10.3	10.2	10.1	9.5	11.0	9.7	10.8	12.1	10.2	9.6	11.3	10.4	8.7
32. Taiwan Chinese	9.7	8.9	8.9	9.5	9.5	10.1	9.6	8.8	8.1	9.2	10.8	11.4	8.1	7.9
33. Telugu Indians	8.4	8.2	6.9	6.9	9.0	9.2	10.4	10.6	7.0	8.8	9.8	9.7	7.6	7.5
34. Turks	10.2	10.3	9.2	9.3	10.5	11.5	10.2	11.1	9.8	11.8	11.5	14.4	8.6	10.5
35. Americans	10.0	10.0	10.0	10.0	10.0	10.0	10.0	10.0	10.0	10.0	10.0	10.0	10.0	10.0
36. White S. Africans	10.9	9.4	9.8	9.8	9.0	10.6	10.2	10.6	10.1	10.3	11.5	12.9	9.5	10.1

	O3	O4	O5	O6	A1	A2	A3	A4	A5	A6	C1	C2	C3	C4	C5	C6
25.	9.7	9.9	10.3	9.1	10.2	9.3	11.1	10.9	9.5	10.3	9.5	10.0	10.2	9.2	9.1	10.9
26.	9.7	10.5	9.5	8.5	9.6	9.8	10.8	9.8	10.9	10.2	9.6	9.8	10.1	11.3	10.0	10.4
27.	10.1	11.6	10.5	9.4	11.7	10.4	11.0	10.6	11.4	10.4	10.5	9.5	10.9	9.5	11.0	11.9
28.	8.7	8.3	7.8	8.7	7.3	10.6	11.1	9.6	6.7	12.3	10.0	8.2	11.3	9.5	8.9	9.0
29.	9.6	11.2	10.8	10.5	11.1	10.8	10.8	11.8	11.9	10.2	13.0	11.9	11.0	11.5	12.6	13.2
30.	11.4	12.9	11.6	9.5	10.2	10.3	10.6	10.7	10.8	11.4	10.1	10.1	11.5	11.0	11.9	11.7
31.	10.3	11.4	11.3	9.7	10.6	9.9	9.5	10.9	12.3	9.8	8.7	10.1	10.7	11.6	11.6	10.7
32.	8.9	8.7	10.0	8.8	9.2	9.1	10.5	9.0	8.3	10.3	9.5	8.8	9.1	8.8	7.7	9.2
33.	6.8	10.1	8.1	7.4	8.4	9.2	10.4	9.6	7.7	9.8	8.5	8.0	8.6	8.4	7.2	7.4
34.	9.8	15.0	11.9	10.4	10.9	12.8	11.9	11.6	11.7	11.6	9.8	14.1	11.2	10.3	10.2	10.4
35.	10.0	10.0	10.0	10.0	10.0	10.0	10.0	10.0	10.0	10.0	10.0	10.0	10.0	10.0	10.0	10.0
36.	8.6	11.3	9.2	10.1	9.9	10.7	11.0	11.5	9.6	10.3	9.7	9.0	11.0	10.0	9.7	10.9

SECTION II: CASE STUDIES
IN PERSONALITY AND CULTURE

When an instrument created in one culture is used in another, the results are often profoundly ambiguous. A failure to replicate might be evidence of a real cultural difference, but it might also indicate only a poor translation. The interpretation of raw scores is questionable until scalar equivalence has been established. Associations between features of culture and differences in mean scores are usually speculative, because any two cultures differ in many ways, any one of which might be associated with the mean difference.

Faced with these difficulties, researchers have two options: They can conduct studies of the validity and scalar equivalence of the imported instrument in the new culture, essentially beginning from scratch; or they can rely on generalizations from other cross-cultural studies. The chapters in this Section adopt both strategies.

Church and Katigbak continue a distinguished series of papers on personality in the Philippines in a chapter that directly addresses the correspondence between trait mean levels and judgments of national character. Bicultural judges from the U.S. and the Philippines concur in describing the personality of Filipinos, but their judgments do not correspond to mean NEO-PI-R profiles. Both descriptions of Filipino personality are apparently reliable, but they cannot both be valid. Clearly, additional systematic studies of national character are needed, and this chapter provides an excellent model.

Piedmont, Bain, McCrae, and Costa report data from Zimbabwe, where a Shona translation was prepared. Assessments of reliability, factor structure, cross-language equivalence, and construct validity show marginally acceptable evidence of validity. Rolland's review shows that the FFM is highly generalizable across cultures; in that context, the relatively poor performance of the Shona NEO-PI-R is perhaps best attributed to limitations of the translation. It is unfortunate that political instability in Zimbabwe has prevented further efforts to refine the translation.

Personality research in Turkey is reviewed by Gülgöz. His translation of the NEO-PI-R shows excellent psychometric properties in both student and adult samples. However, mean levels of traits differ markedly for these two groups, even after accounting for age differences. Because McCrae has shown that profiles of adults and students from the same culture are usually similar, it seems likely that this difference is due to contextual effects: Adults completed the instrument at work, and their responses may have been colored by this context. Certainly future research needs to attend to the circumstances of test administration and their possible effects on scores.

Leininger brings an anthropologist's perspective to the study of personality among Vietnamese-Americans. Surprisingly, the members of this achievement-oriented group score low, on average, in Conscientiousness. More surprising, Leininger's participant observations have led her to believe that the trait scores are accurate. Perhaps this is an instance in which cultural imperatives simply override personal dispositions. It will be of interest to follow these immigrants through the next several generations, to see if over-achievement declines as American norms increasingly allow the expression of personality traits.

India is soon to become the world's most populous country, and it encompasses a number of subcultures, defined in part by language. Lodhi, Deo, and Belhekar report on the internal structure and external correlates of a Marathi translation. It is of considerable interest that their sample, drawn from university graduate students, shows a striking resemblance to a sample of adolescents who completed a Telegu translation of the NEO-PI-R (see Figure 1 in McCrae's chapter in this volume). Perhaps subcultural differences are less important determinants of personality profiles than we might imagine.

Lima reports on the Portuguese version of the NEO-PI-R. She notes that, in comparison to Americans, Portuguese score high on Depression and low on Openness to Values. But, in contrast to the Slavic and Filipino studies, Lima finds that these are precisely the qualities ascribed to the Portuguese by their writers. Here national character and mean personality profiles do appear to match.

Martin, Costa, Oryol, Rukavishnikov, and Senin provide a progress report on use of the Russian NEO-PI-R. Their data include studies of Russian couples, with both self-reports and spouse ratings. The cross-observer correlations reported here contribute to the growing cross-cultural literature on the consensual validation of personality traits. The data are of particular interest because this team of researchers is planning a longitudinal follow-up that will shed new light on the stability of individual differences.

THE FIVE-FACTOR MODEL IN THE PHILIPPINES

Investigating Trait Structure and Levels Across Cultures

A. TIMOTHY CHURCH & MARCIA S. KATIGBAK

Washington State University

Abstract: The Five-Factor Model is a prominent exemplar of the trait psychology perspective, one of several theoretical perspectives in the study of personality across cultures. Research indicates that the trait psychology perspective provides a viable theoretical basis for understanding Filipino personality and behavior. Structure-oriented studies in the Philippines using the Revised NEO Personality Inventory (NEO-PI-R) indicate that the Five-Factor Model generalizes well to the Philippine context, particularly when targeted factor rotations are used. Indigenous dimensions, derived using lexical and inventory approaches, resemble, or overlap with, dimensions of the FFM and are not very culture-specific, but sometimes carve up the personality space somewhat differently. In a study of mean trait levels with the NEO-PI-R, hypotheses about average cultural differences between Filipinos and Americans derived from the literature converged well with the personality comparison judgments of 43 bicultural judges. However, the resulting predictions of average cultural differences received only limited or partial support in an examination of Filipino mean profiles on the NEO-PI-R, plotted using U.S. norms. These results highlighted the uncertain nature of direct score comparisons, and concerns about measurement equivalence, in investigations of mean differences in personality traits across cultures.

Keywords: Five-Factor Model, Philippines, personality structure, cross-cultural

1. CURRENT THEORETICAL PERSPECTIVES ON PERSONALITY AND CULTURE

In a book dedicated to cross-cultural investigations of the Five-Factor Model (FFM) of personality (McCrae & Costa, 1996) it is worth reminding ourselves that the trait psychology perspective, of which the FFM is a prominent exemplar, is only one of several theoretical perspectives in the study of personality across cultures. Alternative perspectives differ in their views on the nature of the relationship between culture and personality, the means to study this relationship, and the extent to which cultural universals versus specifics are anticipated. In the present chapter we briefly address (a) current theoretical perspectives on personality and culture and (b) trait psychology in the Philippines, before turning to (c) structure-oriented and (d) level-oriented studies of the FFM in the Philippines.

Trait psychology perspectives. Cross-cultural trait psychologists tend to treat culture as an independent variable, and thus as implicitly outside of, and distinguishable from, the individual personality (Church & Lonner, 1998). They tend to focus on, and be optimistic about, the identification of cultural universals in personality structure (e.g., McCrae & Costa, 1997; Paunonen & Ashton, 1998), and view culture as affecting primarily the level, expression, and perhaps correlates of traits across cultures. For example, in McCrae and Costa's (1996, 1999) Five-Factor Theory, inherited basic tendencies, including the traits of the FFM (i.e., Neuroticism, Extraversion, Openness to Experience, Agreeableness, and Conscientiousness) and external influences (including culture) are viewed as independent co-determiners of characteristic adaptations such as acquired competencies, attitudes, goals, and self-concepts. The traits of the FFM are viewed as cultural universals.

Evolutionary perspectives. Evolutionary perspectives try to explain both universal human nature and individual differences in terms of evolved psychological mechanisms that are selectively activated depending on cultural contexts (Buss, 2001). Evolutionary perspectives on personality are generally compatible with cross-cultural trait perspectives, particularly when they address individual differences. Indeed, evolutionary theorists have proposed evolutionary bases for the dimensions of the FFM (Buss, 1996; MacDonald, 1998). However, they have also investigated universal individual-differences dimensions in the sexuality domain and have considered whether these dimensions are "beyond the FFM" or "a reapportionment of Big Five variation along more evolution-relevant, sexual dimensions of personality description" (Schmitt & Buss, 2000, p. 168).

Indigenous perspectives. Proponents of indigenous perspectives tend to be skeptical about the relevance of imported personality theories, constructs, methods, and measures. They emphasize instead the development of psychologies that are rooted in the experiences, ideas, and orientations of indigenous cultures (Enriquez, 1992; Ho, 1998; Sinha, 1997). Although some indigenous approaches make use of trait perspectives and measures (e.g., Cheung & Leung, 1998; Guanzon-Lapeña, Church, Carlota, & Katigbak, 1998), the emphasis is on identifying culture-relevant constructs that may or may not be generalizable outside the local context. In the Asian context, indigenous psychologists have noted the relational nature of salient personality constructs and have suggested that the unit of analysis in personality research should be the *person-in-relations*—that is, the person in different relational contexts—rather than the individual person in isolation (Ho, 1998).

Cultural psychology perspectives. The cultural psychology perspective may be the least compatible with the trait perspective. Cultural psychologists emphasize the mutually constitutive nature of culture and personality (Miller, 1997; Shweder & Sullivan, 1993) and argue that the very concept of the person or self is socially constructed and hence variable across cultures (Markus & Kitayama, 1991). The result is considerable skepticism about (a) whether personality can be meaningfully described in terms of context-free traits (Shweder, 1991); (b) whether comparable factor structures across cultures imply that "personality" in the Western sense of an "internal package of attributes" is a cultural universal (Markus & Kitayama, 1998, p. 7); and (c) whether trait measures will be useful in predicting behavior in collectivistic cultures (Markus & Kitayama, 1998; Triandis, 1995). Like indigenous psychologists, cultural psychologists tend to emphasize the context of behavior, and, in this respect, resemble situationist or interactionist approaches to personality (e.g., Mischel & Shoda, 1995; Poortinga & Van Hemert, 2001). Cultural psychologists tend to study conceptions and processes of self in different cultures rather than traits. Also, while some cultural psychology measures resemble traditional trait measures, ethnographic, qualitative, and constructivist methods of assessment are probably more consistent with cultural psychology perspectives (Church, 2001; Greenfield, 1997).

In sum, although trait psychology perspectives—and cross-cultural studies of the FFM—can significantly advance our understanding of the relationship between personality and culture, the viewpoints of alternative perspectives should be kept in mind. Given these challenges to trait approaches, particularly imported ones, and as a context for our own Philippine studies of the FFM, it is worth briefly considering the viability of the trait psychology perspective for the Philippines.

2. TRAIT PSYCHOLOGY IN THE PHILIPPINES

Church and Katigbak (2000a, b) reviewed trait psychology literature in the Philippines and concluded that it "supports the viability of trait psychology as a theoretical basis for understanding Filipino personality and behavior" (Church & Katigbak, 2000b, p. 87). The viability of the trait perspective in the Philippines can be summarized in terms of the following conclusions:

1) Filipinos readily use trait terms to describe persons and to evaluate and understand their behavior.
2) Trait assessments are widely used in the Philippines, and there is some evidence of their predictive validity.
3) Based on evidence to date, the structure of Filipino personality traits can be approximated by Big Five-like dimensions.
4) There is limited evidence of replicable and meaningful cultural differences in mean trait scores involving Filipinos.
5) There is limited evidence of interjudge agreement in trait ratings involving Filipino samples.

We turn now to a review of Philippine literature that has addressed the FFM. Most of this research has involved structure-oriented studies, which we address first. Then, we investigate the meaningfulness or likely validity of mean level comparisons with the FFM and Filipino samples.

3. STRUCTURE-ORIENTED STUDIES OF THE FFM IN THE PHILIPPINES

3.1. Early Research

Perhaps the first attempt to test the generalizability of the Big Five or Five-Factor model in a non-Western culture was a study by Guthrie and Bennett (1971) in the Philippines. These authors conducted a factor analysis of peer-rating data obtained with Passini and Norman's (1966) 20 Big Five marker scales. The Extraversion and Agreeableness factors were replicated well, but additional scales loaded highly on the Agreeableness factor. The Culture (or Openness to Experience) factor and the Conscientiousness factor blended into a single Sophistication factor. The Emotional Stability scales divided into separate Anxiety and Physical Symptom factors. Given the small number of marker scales used and the fact that the instrument was administered in English, a language of instruction, rather than a native language, the results of this early study were not definitive regarding the replicability of the FFM in the Philippines.

Guthrie, Jackson, Estilla, and Elwood (1983) did research with Jackson's Personality Research Form in the Philippines. They found six comparable factors in Filipino and North American samples, but Filipino judges were able to enumerate cultural differences in the subtle meanings and connotations of the PRF trait definitions and items. Stumpf (1993) later reanalyzed Guthrie et al.'s (1983) data and showed that Philippine five-factor solutions could be rotated into fairly good congruence with Costa and McCrae's (1988) joint PRF-NEO factor structure, whose dimensions were interpreted in terms of the FFM.

3.2. Studies with the Revised NEO Personality Inventory

3.2.1. Samples

In our review of NEO-PI-R studies in the Philippines we will refer to three samples. *Sample 1* consisted of 514 college students (242 men, 270 women, 2 not reporting gender) from five Philippine universities, whose ages ranged from 18 to 27 ($M= 19.5$; $SD = 1.4$). These students were part of a larger sample described by Katigbak, Church, and Akamine (1996). Katigbak et al. (1996) reduced this sample to 432 students by eliminating 46 students with high scores on inconsistency scales constructed by the authors and 36 students who lacked scores for some facet scales because of missing data. The Sample 1 reliability and factor analyses summarized here were based on this reduced sample. However, to make the mean profile results for Sample 1 more comparable to those in Samples 2 and 3, in which screening for inconsistency was not done by the authors, the mean profile results for Sample 1 are based on all 512 students who had scores for most or all facet scales (514 minus 2 who did not report gender).

Sample 2 consisted of 398 Filipino college students (131 men, 245 women, 22 not reporting gender) from three Philippine universities and a seminary. These students were part of a larger sample described by Katigbak, Church, Guanzon-Lapeña, Carlota, and del Pilar (2002). The ages of the students ranged from 15 to 25 ($M = 18.9$; $SD = 1.4$).

Sample 3 consisted of 696 Filipino college students (237 men, 445 women, 14 not reporting gender) from two universities in the Philippines (del Pilar, 1998). Ages ranged from 15 to 50 ($M = 18.8$; $SD = 2.5$). Principal components analysis of the NEO-PI-R scales with this data set were previously reported by McCrae, Costa, del Pilar, Rolland, and Parker (1998).

Students in Sample 1 filled out the NEO-PI-R in English, a language of instruction. Students in Samples 2 and 3 filled out a Filipino (Tagalog) version developed by del Pilar (1998; see also McCrae, Costa, et al., 1998). McCrae, Costa, et al. (1998) described the backtranslation process used and noted that near word-for-word translation of NEO-PI-R items was "virtually never possible in Filipino" (p. 176). Four items were replaced entirely because of problems with cultural relevance.

3.2.2. Comparative Reliability

Alpha (α) coefficients address the extent to which the behaviors referred to in the NEO-PI-R items cohere to the same extent across cultures. Table 1 shows the α reliabilities for the three Philippine samples and the American normative sample (Costa & McCrae, 1992). At the domain level, the α values in the three Philippine samples were quite similar to each other, and generally comparable to, or just slightly lower than, the U.S. values. The primary exception involves the Openness to Experience domain, for which the Philippine α values (.78 - .80) were consistently lower than the U.S. values, although still acceptable. Relatively lower α values have been reported for this domain in some other Asian cultures, including Malaysia (Mastor, Jin, & Cooper, 2000) and Hong Kong (McCrae, Costa, & Yik, 1996), but this was not the case in a Korean sample (Piedmont & Chae, 1997).

The reliabilities of the facet scales were usually lower in the Philippine samples than in the American normative sample, suggesting that some behavioral exemplars of the traits are less relevant or cohere less well in the Philippines. The most consistently low values were for three Openness facets—Feelings, Actions, and Values. These three facets had low α values for both the English and Filipino versions of the instrument; this suggests that the problem may be as much with the relevance or coherence of the items for these facets as with their translation. The Openness to Actions and Openness to Values facets have been among those with the lowest α values in other Asian cultures as well (Mastor et al., 2000; Piedmont & Chae, 1997).

3.2.3. Factor Structure: Cultural Universals and Specifics

Although confirmatory factor analysis is often preferred as a method for testing structural hypotheses, the method has proven too stringent when applied to the NEO-PI-R Five-Factor Model, probably in part because of the many facets involved and the limited simple structure of the personality domain (Church & Burke, 1994; Katigbak et al., 1996; McCrae, Zonderman, Costa, Bond, & Paunonen, 1996). Instead, principal components analyses have been used, with varimax and Procrustes rotations.

Principal components analyses of the NEO-PI-R facet scales have been conducted in all three Philippine samples and the results have been very similar (Katigbak et al., 1996; Katigbak et al., 2002; McCrae, Costa, et al., 1998). When varimax rotations

Table 1. Reliabilities for NEO-PI-R Domains and Facets in Three Philippine Samples and the U.S. Normative Sample.

| | Philippines | | | |
Scales	Sample 1	Sample 2	Sample 3	U.S.[a]
Domains				
Neuroticism	.89	.88	.89	.92
Extraversion	.83	.85	.87	.89
Openness to Experience	.80	.78	.79	.87
Agreeableness	.78	.81	.83	.86
Conscientiousness	.89	.90	.92	.90
Facets				
N: Anxiety	.67	.64	.71	.78
Angry Hostility	.65	.77	.75	.75
Depression	.69	.68	.72	.81
Self-Consciousness	.62	.51	.61	.68
Impulsiveness	.50	.58	.63	.70
Vulnerability	.66	.64	.74	.77
E: Warmth·	.67	.68	.70	.73
Gregariousness	.65	.74	.77	.72
Assertiveness	.67	.62	.74	.77
Activity	.47	.59	.69·	.63
Excitement-Seeking	.55	.54	.62	.65
Positive Emotions	.60	.62	.67	.73
O: Fantasy	.69	.61	.70	.76
Aesthetics	.72	.61	.65	.76
Feelings	.62	.34	.48	.66
Actions	.28	.50	.45	.58
Ideas	.70	.74	.75	.80
Values	.48	.24	.31	.67
A: Trust	.49	.72	.77	.79
Straightforwardness	.58	.53	.58	.71
Altruism	.65	.56	.62	.75
Compliance	.54	.60	.65	.59
Modesty	.66	.51	.56	.67
Tender-Mindedness	.26	.58	.56	.56
C: Competence	.55	.61	.72	.67
Order	.62	.71	.73	.66
Dutifulness	.54	.53	.59	.62
Achievement Striving	.69	.70	.79	.67
Self-Discipline	.73	.70	.76	.75
Deliberation	.63	.67	.73	.71

Note. Sample 1 completed the English version of the NEO-PI-R, Samples 2 and 3 completed the Filipino NEO-PI-R. [a]α reliabilities in U.S. normative sample. Reprinted with permission from Table 5 in Costa & McCrae (1992). Copyright 1992 by Psychological Assessment Resources.

have been applied, Neuroticism, Openness to Experience, and Conscientiousness factors have clearly emerged, but the Agreeableness and Extraversion facet scales have realigned into factors that Katigbak et al. (1996) labeled Affiliation and Surgency and McCrae, Costa, et al. (1998) labeled Love and Submission (inverse Surgency). In all three samples, the Extraversion facets of Warmth, Gregariousness, and Positive Emotions have combined with the Agreeableness facets of Trust, Altruism, and Tender-Mindedness to define the Affiliation factor, and the Extraversion facets of Assertiveness, Activity, and (in two of the three samples) Excitement-Seeking have combined with (inverse) Straightforwardness, Compliance, and Modesty to define the Surgency factor. The congruence coefficients between matched factors in these three varimax solutions have ranged from .91 to .97. The realignment of Extraversion and Agreeableness facets is not unique to the Philippines (Rolland, 2000).

Cross-cultural differences in the orientation of the Extraversion and Agreeableness factors are afforded in part by the circumplex nature of the space defined by the Extraversion and Agreeableness facets (Katigbak et al., 1996; McCrae, Costa, et al., 1998). In the Philippines, another contributing factor is probably the reduced cohesion, or average intercorrelations, among the Agreeableness facet scales, making them more prone to depart from their intended factor in the context of significant correlations with some Extraversion facets. In the U.S. normative sample (Costa & McCrae, 1992), the mean intercorrelation among the Agreeableness facets was .33, but in the three Philippine samples the mean intercorrelations ranged from .24 to .27. The cohesion of the Extraversion facets is somewhat more comparable in the U.S. (mean $r = .35$) and in the three Philippine samples (mean r's from .30 to .34).

In all three Philippine samples the intended factor alignments of all five factors were attained using Procrustes rotations, in which the varimax solutions were rotated toward a U.S. varimax solution (Costa & McCrae, 1992). The congruence coefficients relating the Procrustes factor solutions in the three Philippine samples to the U.S. varimax solution have ranged from .93 to .98, with the exception of a .86 value for the Openness to Experience factor in Sample 1 (Katigbak et al., 1996). This suggests that the FFM provides an adequate representation of Filipino personality structure, at least as assessed with an imported instrument.

3.3. Indigenous Approaches

3.3.1. Filipino Trait Lexicon and the FFM

Cross-cultural support for the FFM would be even more persuasive if the Big Five dimensions emerged independently in a variety of cultures using indigenous approaches. Relevant, therefore, are studies that have examined the composition and structure of indigenous personality lexicons (Saucier & Goldberg, 2001). Lexical approaches have limitations. For example, it is conceivable that some important personality dimensions are not encoded in some languages, or only sparsely so. Nonetheless, the following assumptions of the lexical approach seem plausible: (a) important phenotypic attributes of personality become encoded in the natural language; and (b) the most important attributes will be represented more extensively in person-ality lexicons, within and across cultures (Saucier & Goldberg, 2001).

We investigated the indigenous structure of Filipino personality in a series of lexical studies that involved (a) the culling of 6,900 person-descriptive adjectives from a Filipino dictionary; (b) classifications by trained judges of adjectives into person-descriptive categories (e.g., personality traits, experiential states, roles and statuses, physical characteristics, etc.); (c) trait prototypicality judgments of Filipino college students; (d) classification of a master list of 1,297 Filipino trait adjectives into a Big Five taxonomy; and (e) factor analyses of self ratings on large and representative sets of trait adjectives (Church, Katigbak, & Reyes, 1996, 1998; Church, Reyes, Katigbak, & Grimm, 1997; Katigbak et al., 2002). Most relevant to the FFM are the following conclusions based on these studies:

1) The Filipino trait lexicon is well subsumed by the Big Five domains.
2) The relative sizes of the Big Five domains, as measured by the number of adjectives in each domain, is similar across cultures, with the interpersonal domains of Agreeableness and Extraversion/Surgency being the largest.
3) The following seven indigenous dimensions provide a rather comprehensive and replicable representation of Filipino personality structure, as derived from the Filipino trait lexicon: Concerned for Others versus Egotism, Gregariousness, Temperamentalness, Self-Assurance, Conscientiousness, Intellect, and Negative Valence.
4) These indigenous dimensions show considerable overlap with the Big Five dimensions, but do not carve up the personality space in precisely the same manner. Although good one-to-one correspondence has been found between Philippine Concerned for Others and Agreeableness, Philippine Conscientiousness and Big Five Conscientiousness, Philippine Gregariousness and Extraversion, and, to a lesser extent, Philippine Intellect and Big Five Intellect or Openness to Experience, the Philippine Temperamentalness and Self-Assurance dimensions have tended to be multidimensional in Big Five terms.

3.3.2. Indigenous Philippine Inventories and the FFM

Indigenous inventories provide a promising source of data on the cross-cultural universality versus specificity of personality structure (e.g., Church, 2001; Cheung & Leung, 1998; Katigbak et al., 1996; Guanzon-Lapeña et al., 1998). In one series of studies, we used interviews and open-ended questionnaires to derive Filipino conceptions of healthy personality or "good psychological functioning" (Church & Katigbak, 1988). Factor analyses of items written to assess these conceptions resulted in six dimensions that showed fairly good conceptual overlap with the lexical dimensions described earlier: Responsibility, Social Potency, Emotional Control, Concern for Others, Broad-Mindedness, and Affective Well-being (Church & Katigbak, 1989; Katigbak et al., 1996). We found moderate to strong associations between these indigenous dimensions and dimensions of the FFM, as assessed with the NEO-PI-R (Katigbak et al., 1996).

In a recent study with Filipino colleagues, we collected data with a Filipino trait adjective measure, two indigenous inventories, and the Filipino NEO-PI-R (Katigbak et al., 2002). We used factor analyses and regression analyses to show that (a) most of the dimensions measured by Philippine personality inventories overlap considerably with the FFM; (b) a few Philippine scales (Social Curiosity, Risk-Taking, Religiosity) were less well accounted for by the FFM; these constructs may be particularly salient or comprised somewhat differently in the Philippines, although the constructs are not unknown in Western cultures; and (c) Philippine inventories do not generally outperform the NEO-PI-R in predicting scores on selected culture-relevant criteria, but they do add modest incremental validity.

In summary, structure-oriented studies, particularly with imported measures, support the generalizability of the FFM in the Philippine context. Studies of indigenous lexical and inventory dimensions also suggest that Big-Five-like dimensions are relevant in the Philippines, although the imported and indigenous dimensions generally do not carve up the personality space in precisely the same way. Nonetheless, there is enough support for the relevance of the FFM to warrant consideration of how Filipinos, on average, might compare to persons in other cultures on these dimensions. Thus, we now turn to level-oriented studies with the FFM in the Philippines.

4. LEVEL-ORIENTED STUDIES WITH THE FFM IN THE PHILIPPINES

4.1. Construct and Measurement Equivalence Issues

When scale scores are compared across cultures, issues of construct and measurement equivalence (versus bias) become important. Van de Vijver and Leung (1997) provided the following definitions. *Construct equivalence* exists when construct definitions and behavioral exemplars are equivalent across cultures. *Measurement unit equivalence* is present when the measure has the same unit of measurement across cultures, but different origins, as might occur when sources of method bias cause shifts in mean scores in one or more cultures. *Scalar or full scale equivalence* (or *full score comparability*) is present when the measure has the same measurement unit and origin across cultures.

The structural studies reviewed earlier are most relevant to the issue of construct equivalence. These studies suggested that the dimensions of the FFM, or similar dimensions, may be universal or etic in nature, although the most relevant behavioral exemplars may not be equally sampled in each culture. The most likely sources of method bias in the application of the NEO-PI-R in the Philippines might be inequivalent samples and differential response styles. For example, college students may be a more elite group in the Philippines than in the United States. Possible sources of item bias, which would impact full score comparability, would include translation inequivalencies and differences in the cultural appropriateness of some items.

Backtranslation procedures were used in translating the NEO-PI-R into Filipino, probably reducing item bias due to translation inequivalence (del Pilar, 1998; McCrae, Costa, et al., 1998). Grimm and Church (1999) investigated response styles in multiple Philippine and U.S. data sets with multiple instruments, including the NEO-PI. They concluded that Americans show a greater tendency to respond in a socially desirable manner when rating themselves on trait adjectives. Across instruments, no consistent differences were found between the two cultural groups in acquiescent, extreme, or neutral/midpoint responding. However, Filipinos did show modest tendencies to agree (acquiesce) more in their NEO-PI responses than did Americans, while also showing less variability (i.e., smaller item standard deviations) in their use of the rating scales. Church and Katigbak (1992) found that Filipinos gave higher mean ratings than Americans on all of the 16 Likert-type motive scales investigated. Regarding item bias, Huang, Church, and Katigbak (1997) found that about 40% of NEO-PI items showed differential item functioning (DIF) in a comparison of Filipino and American college student samples and that many apparent cultural differences were eliminated after DIF items were removed. These few studies present a mixed picture regarding the likely impact of method and item bias on cross-cultural mean comparisons involving Filipinos and the NEO-PI-R, but they do suggest the need for caution.

Researchers differ in their optimism regarding the appropriateness of comparing mean scores on inventories such as the NEO-PI-R across cultures. Poortinga and Van Hemert (2001) expressed doubt that full score comparability can ever be established, making the interpretation of cultural mean differences hazardous. On the other hand, McCrae (2001), while sensitive to the problems of measurement equivalence involved, suggested that cross-cultural assessments may be more robust than methodologists expect. Indeed, McCrae (2001) reported sensible correlations between culture-level scores on the dimensions of the FFM and other culture-level variables. However, when given a list of high and low scoring cultures for each FFM dimension, a panel of judges with extensive cross-cultural experience showed only a chance level of ability to select which of the FFM dimensions had been used to rank the cultures on each dimension. This may indicate, as McCrae (2001) suggested, the questionable accuracy of national stereotypes. However, it might also suggest that the task was too difficult: It may not be reasonable to expect judges to be familiar enough with the full range of cultures to successfully perform the task. It might be more realistic, however, to ask judges who are familiar with two specific cultures (e.g., the Philippines and the U.S.) to make predictions about average cultural differences in trait scores.

We implemented a two-fold strategy here. First, we examined the literature on Filipino personality in an attempt to infer those facets of the FFM for which Filipinos and Americans might differ, on average. Second, we asked relatively bicultural judges, that is, individuals with significant experience living in both the Philippines and the U.S., to consider each of the 30 NEO-PI-R facet scales and judge whether Filipinos or Americans would tend to average higher on the trait, or whether they would exhibit no average differences. By combining hypotheses from the literature with the judgments of bicultural individuals, we hoped to predict which facets would show cultural mean differences and in which direction. If these predictions were largely validated in an examination of actual Filipino mean profiles on the NEO-PI-R, plotted using U.S. norms, it might be reasonable to conclude that the mean score differences reflected valid average differences in trait levels.

4.2. Filipino Personality Literature and the FFM

Space considerations do not allow a review here of the extensive literature on Filipino personality. Instead, we drew on our previous reviews and critiques of this literature

(Church, 1986, 1987; Church & Katigbak, 2000a, b) to formulate hypotheses about which NEO-PI-R facets would show mean differences between Filipinos and Americans. In the first column of Table 2 we summarize these predictions by indicating whether the literature suggests that Filipinos (F) or Americans (A) would average higher on the trait (facet scale). More definitive predictions are shown in boldface. For some facets the literature provided no basis for predictions.

A number of limitations of the literature should be noted. First, many of the studies and writings are not culture-comparative in nature. Rather, purported Filipino traits or values have been described based on the results of ethnographic observations, interviews, questionnaires, thematic apperception techniques, clinical observations in therapy, linguistic analyses, and, in some cases, the apparent perceptions or opinions of native or foreign scholars. A smaller percentage of studies have involved direct empirical comparisons across cultures using personality inventories such as the Edwards Personal Preference Schedule, Jackson's Personality Research Form, and Cattell's High School Personality Questionnaire. Second, even when empirical comparisons have been made, the cross-cultural equivalence of the instruments has been uncertain. Third, cultural mean scores may depend on which gender, social strata, or regional groups are sampled; however, there is not much Philippine literature on subgroup differences in personality, so we did not offer group-specific hypotheses here. Fourth, with the greater focus in recent years on indigenous Philippine psychology (Enriquez, 1992; Pe-Pua & Protacio-Marcelino, 2000), even fewer studies have addressed Filipino personality in a culture-comparative sense. As a result, many of the studies that are potentially relevant to the FFM are now somewhat dated. On the other hand, although Filipino culture and personality may have changed over time—for example, in response to Western influences—Pe-Pua and Protacio-Marcelino (2000) have argued that the core of Filipino personality is still Asian, and includes such characteristics as deference to authority, modesty and humility, and concern for others.

4.3. Personality Comparisons by Bicultural Judges

4.3.1. Judgment Procedure

Our bicultural judges included 43 adults (19 men, 24 women) with a mean age of 48 ($SD = 16.7$; range = 22 to 76). Twenty-three were ethnic Filipinos and 20 were white Americans. Twenty-eight (65.1%) grew up primarily in the Philippines; 13 (30.2%) grew up primarily in the U.S.; 1 lived in both countries while growing up; 1 grew up in Indonesia prior to living in the U.S. and the Philippines. Judges were required to have lived in both countries for three or more years. The mean number of years lived in the Philippines was 22 ($SD = 10.5$; range = 3 to 44 years); the mean number of years lived in the U.S. was 26 ($SD = 16.6$; range = 5 to 59). The sample included native Filipinos who had immigrated to the U.S., native Filipinos studying in the U.S., American missionaries who had served in the Philippines or their family members, and a few other Americans who had worked in other capacities in the Philippines. All judges were highly proficient in English.

Judges were given brief English descriptions, adapted from the NEO Job Profiler (Costa, McCrae, & Kay, 1995), of each of the 30 traits (facets) in the NEO-PI-R (e.g.,

Anxiety: Worrying, tense, and apprehensive). They were asked to:

read each trait description and then decide whether you think Filipinos (particularly in the Philippines) or Americans (particularly in the United States), tend, on average, to exhibit or show the trait more, or whether you think Filipinos and Americans will tend to exhibit or show the trait about equally.

Judges used the following 7-point rating scale to indicate their judgments:

1 = Americans, on average, exhibit this trait *much more* than Filipinos.
2 = Americans, on average, exhibit this trait *somewhat more* than Filipinos.
3 = Americans, on average, exhibit this trait *slightly more* than Filipinos.
4 = Americans and Filipinos, on average, exhibit this trait *to about the same extent*.
5 = Filipinos, on average, exhibit this trait *slightly more* than Americans.
6 = Filipinos, on average, exhibit this trait *somewhat more* than Americans.
7 = Filipinos, on average, exhibit this trait *much more* than Americans.

The composite inter-rater reliability of the judges' ratings was excellent (.97; Tinsley & Weiss, 1975, Formula 6).

4.3.2. Agreement between Literature and Judges

For each facet scale, Table 2 shows the mean and standard deviation of the ratings for the judges as a group, as well as the percentages of raters who judged Americans to exhibit each trait more, the same, or less than Filipinos. In a MANOVA with judges' ethnicity (Filipino versus American) as the independent variable and the 30 traits as dependent variables, the effect of judges' ethnicity was not statistically significant (Wilks' Lambda = .16, $F[30, 12] = 2.1, p > .05$). For each FFM domain, we will consider the judges' mean ratings in Table 2, and their consistency with the hypotheses based on the review of literature.

In the Neuroticism domain, our review of literature suggested that Filipinos, as compared to Americans, would average higher in Self-Consciousness and lower in Angry Hostility and Depression. The most definitive finding in the judges' ratings was the strong consensus that Filipinos, on average, indeed exhibit more Self-Consciousness than Americans; 88.4% of the raters judged Filipinos to be more self-conscious than Americans. Although the literature regarding Angry Hostility and Depression was less definitive, the judges, on average, did tend to view Filipinos as exhibiting slightly less angry hostility and depression than Americans, and slightly less of the remaining Neuroticism traits.

In the Extraversion domain, the most definitive hypothesis from our review of literature was that Filipinos would average lower than Americans on the Assertiveness facet. We also expected that Filipinos might average higher than Americans in the Warmth, Gregariousness, and Positive Emotions facets. The judges' ratings were generally consistent with these expectations. Large percentages of the judges opined that Filipinos exhibit less assertiveness than Americans (86.0%), but greater warmth (79.1%) and positive emotions (76.7%). There was less consensus regarding the Gregariousness facet (e.g., see large SD of 1.94). In addition, Americans were clearly

Table 2. Descriptive Statistics for Bicultural Judges' Ratings.

Trait	H^a	M	SD	US>	US=	US<	T-score[b]
				Percentages			

Trait	H^a	M	SD	Percentages US>	Percentages US=	Percentages US<	T-score[b]
Anxiety	-	3.12	1.73	56	23	21	50.56
Angry Hostility	A>F	3.19	1.45	58	19	23	46.99
Depression	A>F	3.33	1.36	47	37	16	50.89
Self-Consciousness	**F>A**	5.95	1.11	2	9	88	53.85
Impulsiveness	-	3.40	1.55	44	30	26	45.85
Vulnerability	-	3.35	1.38	56	30	14	51.49
Warmth	**F>A**	5.51	1.44	12	9	79	45.70
Gregariousness	**F>A**	4.74	1.94	26	16	58	49.42
Assertiveness	**A>F**	2.16	1.41	86	7	7	49.28
Activity	-	3.40	1.40	56	30	14	45.92
Excitement-Seeking	-	2.60	1.53	79	9	12	44.28
Positive Emotion	**F>A**	5.33	1.21	5	19	77	48.44
Fantasy	-	4.26	1.36	21	42	37	45.61
Aesthetics	-	4.16	1.40	33	26	42	54.88
Feelings	**F>A**	4.95	1.69	23	9	67	46.14
Actions	A>F	2.72	1.14	74	19	7	52.12
Ideas	A>F	2.93	1.30	65	28	7	52.89
Values	**A>F**	2.91	1.85	63	19	19	44.36
Trust	-	4.86	1.26	12	26	63	49.65
Straightforwardness	**A>F**	2.58	1.68	74	12	14	50.11
Altruism	**F>A**	5.70	1.17	2	9	88	46.83
Compliance	**F>A**	5.93	1.12	5	7	88	56.17
Modesty	**F>A**	5.93	.99	0	9	91	49.88
Tender-Mindedness	**F>A**	5.42	1.03	5	9	86	54.98
Competence	-	3.44	1.39	49	33	19	46.66
Order	**F>A**	3.67	1.44	44	28	28	50.76
Dutifulness	-	4.07	1.47	30	37	33	49.28
Achievement Striving	**F>A**	3.14	1.77	58	23	19	53.48
Self-Discipline	-	3.16	1.60	56	26	19	49.87
Deliberation	-	4.02	1.50	37	16	47	54.80

Note. US = United States (Americans). Mean ratings indicate whether judges viewed Americans as exhibiting the traits much more (1), somewhat more (2), slightly more (3), or about the same (4) as Filipinos; or Filipinos as exhibiting the traits slightly more (5), somewhat more (6), or much more (7) than Americans. Percentages column shows the percentages of bicultural judges who viewed Americans as exhibiting the trait more, the same, or less than Filipinos. Percentages were rounded to the nearest integer value, so that not all row percentages total exactly 100. [a]Hypothesized direction of cultural mean differences between Filipinos (F) and Americans (A) based on a review of the Philippine personality literature. The most definitive predictions are indicated in boldface. [b]Mean *T*-score for each facet across three male and three female samples.

viewed as higher in Excitement-Seeking and there was a modest tendency for Americans to be viewed as higher in Activity. Thus, Filipinos were judged to be higher in more communal and affective aspects of the domain (i.e., warmth, gregariousness, positive emotions), while Americans were judged to be higher in the more agentic and adventuresome aspects of the domain (assertiveness, activity, excitement-seeking).

In the Openness to Experience domain, our review of literature suggested that Filipinos would average lower than Americans in the Values facet and possibly the Actions and Ideas facets, but higher than Americans in the Feelings facet. These expectations were all consistent with the judges' ratings. The literature did not address much the Fantasy and Aesthetics facets and the judges showed no strong tendency to view Filipinos and Americans as different on these two traits.

In the Agreeableness domain, our review of the literature suggested that Filipinos might average higher than Americans on most of the trait facets in this domain, except for Straightforwardness. This expectation was supported by the judges' ratings. Indeed, there was considerable consensus for nearly all of the traits in this domain; for 5 of the 6 traits nearly 75% or more of the judges agreed on which cultural group would exhibit the trait more. Only for the Trust facet were the judges somewhat less definitive in their judgments.

In our review of the literature, it was most difficult to form hypotheses about cultural differences in the Conscientiousness domain. With limited confidence, we suggested that Filipinos might average higher in the Order and Achievement-Striving facets. The judges also exhibited little consensus regarding most of the facets in this domain (e.g., see the even distribution of percentages for most Conscientiousness traits). The most definitive judgments involved the Achievement Striving and Self-Discipline facets; for both facets, Americans were judged to be higher than Filipinos, on average.

In summary, we observed considerable convergence between our literature-based hypotheses and the ratings of the bicultural judges. Will these hypothesized cultural differences concur with actual NEO-PI-R mean scores for these traits? For some of the 30 traits, the predictions of cultural differences were not very definitive. In these cases, failure to find corresponding cultural mean differences in actual trait scores would probably not increase skepticism much about the validity of the mean profiles. However, for other traits, definitive predictions were suggested by high convergence among the judges, high convergence between the judges and the literature, or both. These include the predictions that Filipinos, relative to U.S. norms, will score above average on the Self-Consciousness, Warmth, Positive Emotions, Altruism, Compliance, Modesty, and Tender-Mindedness facets, and below average on the Assertiveness, Excitement-Seeking, Openness to Actions (and perhaps Openness to Ideas and Values), and Straightforwardness facets. If many of these predictions proved to be inaccurate then it would raise questions about (a) the cross-cultural equivalence of the NEO-PI-R, or at least the functioning of particular scales in the Philippines; and (b) the meaningfulness of cross-cultural mean comparisons with the instrument. Thus, we turn now to an inspection of mean profiles.

4.4. Mean Profiles in Three Philippine Samples

In Figures 1 and 2 we show the NEO-PI-R profiles obtained by plotting the mean raw scores of men and women in each of the three Philippine samples of college students using U.S. college student norms. McCrae (2001, Figure 1) previously reported male profiles for Samples 1 and 3. Our samples are slightly different from those profiled by McCrae (2001) because we did not exclude the relatively small number of Filipino college students who were outside the traditional age for U.S. college student samples (i.e., 18-21 years old). The inclusion of these additional students had only trivial effects on mean scores, however.

In Figures 1 and 2 we note the considerable similarity between the three profiles for each gender. We quantified this similarity by correlating the *T*-scores for the various sample profiles across the 30 facets. The correlations among the three male profiles ranged from .71 to .86 (*p* < .01 in all cases). The correlations among the three female profiles ranged from .81 to .97. For both the male and female profiles the highest correlation was between the profiles for the two samples that completed the Filipino version of the instrument (i.e., Samples 2 and 3). The correlations between the opposite-gender profiles ranged from .64 to .85. These results suggest that the NEO-PI-R scales are functioning in a generally consistent manner across samples and across language versions of the instrument. Given the generally similar profiles within and across genders, we computed, for each facet scale, the mean *T*-score across all six samples (i.e., the three male and three female samples). These overall facet means are shown in the last column of Table 2. In the following discussion of results readers can refer to the sample profiles in Figures 1 and 2, which retain information about modest sample differences, or to the mean *T*-scores in Table 2, which provide a reasonable summary of the facet scores across all of the samples.

We first examined the score levels of those facet scales for which definitive predictions had been made. Our predictions based on the literature, the bicultural judges, or both, received some support for the Self-Consciousness, Tender-Mindedness, and (especially) Compliance facets, for which Filipino mean scores tended to be above average to high compared to U.S. norms, and for the Excitement-Seeking and Openness to Values facets, for which Filipino mean scores tended to be below average compared to U.S. norms. For some of these facets, support for our predictions was better when the Filipino version of the instrument was used (i.e., in Samples 2 and 3). On the other hand, our definitive predictions did not receive much support for the Warmth, Assertiveness, Positive Emotions, Altruism, Modesty, Straightforwardness, Openness to Actions, and Openness to Ideas facets. For these facets, the Filipino samples scored near the U.S. mean, or in some cases, slightly opposite the direction of our prediction. The latter was the case for the Warmth, Positive Emotions, and Altruism facets, on which Filipinos averaged slightly below average in some profiles, and the Openness to Actions and Ideas facets, on which Filipinos scored slightly above average in some profiles.

Looking next at those facets for which less definitive predictions had been made, we again see a mixed picture. Consistent with our expectations from the literature, the judges, or both, Filipinos did average slightly below the American mean on the Angry Hostility and Activity facets. Contrary to expectations, Filipinos were not above average on the Gregariousness, Openness to Feelings, Trust, and Order facets, nor were they below average on the Depression or Self-Discipline facets. Based on the literature

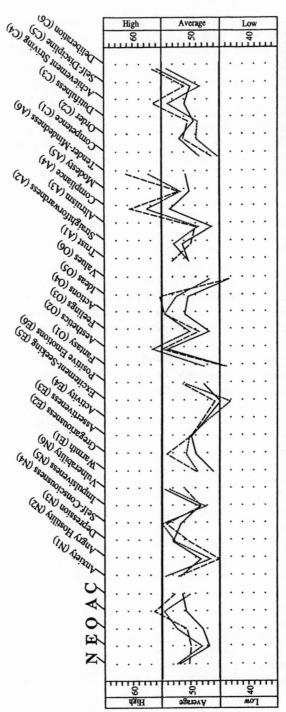

Figure 1. Mean NEO-PI-R profiles for three samples of Filipino male (M) college students, plotted using U.S. norms. Sample 1M (solid line) completed the English version of the NEO-PI-R. Samples 2M (dashed line) and 3M (dotted line) completed the Filipino version. Profile form reproduced by special permission of the Publisher, from the Revised NEO Personality Inventory, by Paul T. Costa, Jr., and Robert R. McCrae. Copyright 1978, 1985, 1989, 1992 by PAR, Inc. Further reproduction is prohibited without permission of PAR, Inc.

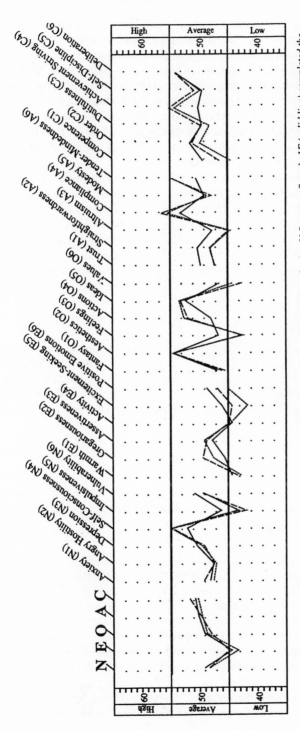

Figure 2. Mean NEO-PI-R profiles for three samples of Filipino female (F) college students, plotted using U.S. norms. Sample 1F (solid line) completed the English version of the NEO-PI-R. Samples 2F (dashed line) and 3F (dotted line) completed the Filipino version. Profile form reproduced by special permission of the Publisher, from the Revised NEO Personality Inventory, by Paul T. Costa, Jr., and Robert R. McCrae. Copyright 1978, 1985, 1989, 1992 by PAR, Inc. Further reproduction is prohibited without permission of PAR, Inc.

we had predicted that Filipinos might average higher than Americans in Achievement Striving (although the judges tended to expect the opposite result). The actual mean scores for this facet tended to support our hypothesis based on the literature.

Our judges generally rated Americans as higher in the Neuroticism facets (except for Self-Consciousness) but these judgments were not much supported by the Neuroticism domain scores (means of 51.5 for males and 48.6 for females across samples). The judges also rated Filipinos as higher in the Agreeableness facets (except for Straightforwardness). This received some support in the profiles for the Filipino males ($M = 53.9$), especially when the instrument was completed in Filipino ($M = 55.5$ for Samples 2 and 3), but not for the females ($M = 49.9$).

A few other observations are noteworthy. Filipino women, but not men, scored below average in Impulsiveness (see Figures 1 and 2), which might be consistent with traditional morality expectations for Philippine women. Filipinos scored slightly below average in Openness to Fantasy. This might be inconsistent with Bulatao's (1978) description of Filipinos as being open to altered states of consciousness, but the Fantasy scale also assesses imaginativeness, creativity, and a tendency to daydream. Filipinos were slightly above average on Openness to Aesthetics, which is consistent with the stereotype of Filipinos as artistic and musical; however, our bicultural judges did not predict this cultural difference. Filipinos also scored above average on Deliberation. If this is a valid finding, it might suggest a careful and planful approach to achievement striving in the context of difficult economic conditions.

Given the inconsistent relationship between the judges' ratings and the T-scores for the various facets, it is not surprising that the correlations between the judges' mean facet ratings and the six T-score profiles in Figures 1 and 2 were low. The correlations for the three female profiles ranged from .10 to .12, for the three male profiles .00 to .35. In only one case did the correlation approach statistical significance (for Sample 2 males, $r = .35$, $p < .06$).

5. GENERAL DISCUSSION

We discuss here the structure- and level-oriented results reviewed, while considering some potential limitations of cross-cultural trait approaches.

5.1. Structure-Oriented Studies

Most cross-cultural studies of the NEO-PI-R have focused on (a) the replicability of the five dimensions of the FFM and (b) the internal consistency reliabilities of the domain and facet scales. We consider here what these studies may or may not be able to tell us. Good replication of the NEO-PI-R factor structure does suggest that this structure provides an adequate representation of Filipino trait structure. However, three considerations lead us to question whether this structure necessarily provides the most optimal, comprehensive, or culture-relevant representation of Filipino personality structure.

First, setting aside for now the potential limitations of imported approaches, the alternative orientation of the Extraversion and Agreeableness dimensions (i.e., Affiliation and Surgency), suggests the possibility of at least minimal cultural differences in the optimal representation of Filipino personality structure. We are not sure how much or how little to make of this replicable cultural difference, and probably will remain uncertain until some persuasive explanation for the alternative factor orientations is found. McCrae, Costa, et al. (1998) speculated that the alternative factors might be more prevalent in collectivistic cultures in which affiliation and status are more important, but a direct test of this hypothesis by Kallasmaa, Allik, Realo, and McCrae (2000) found only mixed support. Rolland (2000) also failed to discern any patterns in the cultures that did or did not show shifts in facet loadings between the Extraversion and Agreeableness dimensions. In the Philippine samples examined here, the alternative factor orientations might be accounted for, in large part, by the reduced coherence (intercorrelations) among the Agreeableness facets. However, it is not clear whether this reduced coherence is the result of (a) problems of measurement equivalence (e.g., the α reliabilities for some facets were lower in the Philippines than in the U.S.) or (b) a true cultural difference in the structural coherence of traits in the Agreeableness domain.

Second, cross-cultural structural analyses of the NEO-PI-R have been conducted solely at the facet level of analysis. The moderate size intercorrelations found among the facet scales suggests that they represent distinguishable "lower-order" traits in various cultures. Nonetheless, researchers have not tested directly whether the nature and number of distinct facets or more specific traits within the domains of the FFM are the same across cultures by examining the item-level structure of the instrument. Even in U.S. samples perhaps only half of the facets can be reproduced in item-level factor analyses (Church & Burke, 1994).

Finally, two potential limitations of imported approaches should be considered. First, imported instruments could miss salient culture-specific constructs. Second, imported instruments could tend to "impose" their structure in new cultural contexts to some extent. In using the term "impose" we do not intend to imply ethnocentric or other motives in the application of "imposed-etic" (imported) models across cultures. We simply mean that any particular manner of carving up the personality space into dimensions is probably facilitated to some extent by the inclusion of sufficient numbers of markers of those dimensions. This phenomenon is suggested by the finding that the four dimensions of the Eysenck personality inventories (e.g., Barrett, Petrides, Eysenck, & Eysenck, 1998), the eight dimensions of the Comrey Personality Scales (Brief, Comrey, & Collins, 1994), and the ten dimensions of the Multidimensional Personality Questionnaire (Ben-Porath, Almagor, Hoffman-Chemi, & Tellegen, 1995) all replicate well across cultures. These alternative models may assess traits at different levels in a personality hierarchy and their structures are probably not incompatible with each other or with the FFM. Nonetheless, the fact remains that each instrument organizes the personality space somewhat differently yet replicates across cultures. This suggests that each model facilitates the emergence of its structure to some extent.

Studies of indigenous structure are valuable because they address these limitations of imported approaches. They can give some indication of (a) whether the organization of traits provided by the FFM might be imposed to some extent; and (b) whether additional dimensions beyond the FFM are needed. Studies of indigenous Philippine dimensions tend to provide additional support for the generalizability of the FFM, or at least Big Five-like dimensions, for the Philippine setting. These studies tend to show that indigenous dimensions derived with lexical or inventory approaches resemble or overlap with dimensions of the FFM, although they do not always carve up the personality space in precisely the same manner (again suggesting that the NEO-PI-R FFM may not provide the optimal or only representation of Filipino personality structure). Equally important, indigenous Philippine studies have yet to identify any dimensions that are clearly culture-specific or outside the FFM (e.g., Katigbak et al., 2002).

Another interesting feature of indigenous lexical studies is that they may provide information about the relative salience in person perception of various traits or trait domains across cultures, assuming that basic assumptions of the lexical approach are valid (Saucier & Goldberg, 2001). Indeed, contrary to the impression one might get from the fixed number of facet scales in each FFM domain, our lexical studies suggest that the degree of nuance or refinement of person perception categories may differ quite a bit across different FFM domains, but with the relative sizes of each domain being comparable across cultures.

In short, indigenous or emic studies serve as an important complement to imported or imposed-etic studies of the FFM. In the Philippines, indigenous studies actually provide further support for dimensions resembling those of the FFM, while also reminding us of the potential limitations of imported approaches. Of course, indigenous approaches also have limitations (Church, 2001).

Cultural psychologists' criticisms of trait approaches should be considered and are particularly relevant in considering directions for future cross-cultural research with the FFM. As noted earlier, some cultural psychologists question whether findings of replicable personality factors really imply that personality is conceived similarly across cultures or that traits have a comparable role in understanding or predicting behavior in all cultures (Markus & Kitayama, 1998; Triandis, 1995). For these psychologists, the repeated replications of the NEO-PI-R dimensions across cultures will always be of limited persuasiveness. Even psychologists who are more amenable to trait approaches should probably now be feeling a strong need to go beyond structural replication to cross-cultural investigations of (a) the behavioral correlates of the FFM and (b) the role that traits play in understanding personality, self, and behavior in different cultural contexts. It is possible, for example, that both implicit beliefs about the traitedness of behavior, as well as the actual traitedness of behavior, will differ across cultures (Church. 2000).

Similarly, additional studies of the behavioral indicators or manifestations of traits across cultures would be important (Church, 2000; Huang et al., 1997; McCrae, 2000). For example, current reliability analyses with the NEO-PI-R only address whether the behavioral indicators that comprise the current item pool are relevant in particular cultures; these analyses do not consider whether other—perhaps culture-unique— indicators might be important to include.

5.2. Level-Oriented Studies

The results of our level-oriented study were much more mixed. There are other ways that one might try to validate cultural differences in mean profiles. For example, one could compare mean profiles derived from self-ratings and peer ratings, or compare mean profiles of individuals differing in acculturation (McCrae, Yik, Trapnell, Bond, & Paulhus, 1998). However, the strategy used here seemed reasonable. Had our hypotheses based on the literature, the ratings of the bicultural judges, and the mean profiles largely concurred regarding the direction of mean cultural differences, we believe it would have made a fairly persuasive case for the validity of these differences. There was, in fact, rather good convergence between the literature-based hypotheses and the bicultural judges. However, because less than half of the resulting predictions were verified in the mean profiles, one is left with limited confidence in the validity of the generally modest cultural differences identified.

What might account for the rather good convergence between the literature and bicultural judges on the one hand, but only limited or partial convergence with the mean profiles? As we noted earlier, the literature itself is limited in several ways, including the small number of direct empirical comparisons involving Filipinos and Americans. On the other hand, the backgrounds of our bicultural judges would seem to be fairly ideal for their task. Thus, if their judgments of average cultural differences are not valid, it is not clear whose judgments would be.

Some possible limitations of the judgment task itself can be noted, however. First, the judges were asked to compare Americans and Filipinos in general. To the extent that personality profiles differ as a function of age, gender, social class, geographical region, or other demographic characteristics, or that judges considered different subgroups when making their comparisons, their judgments might fail to converge with the mean profile differences exhibited by college student samples (e.g., Filipino college students may be more Open to Ideas and more Assertive than the population as a whole). The high agreement among the judges, including between American and Filipino judges, would seem to reduce this concern, however. Second, the judged differences between Americans and Filipinos may be more stereotypic than valid, resulting from lay persons' tendencies to form impressions of ethnic groups or to inaccurately infer traits from limited samples of behavior or with inadequate consideration of contextual information. Indeed, it is possible that the convergence of the literature and bicultural judges merely reflects a common source in questionable ethnic or national stereotypes.

We believe that the lack of support for at least some of our hypotheses is the result of (a) measurement inequivalence problems, or (b) how some traits were operationalized (e.g., the item content of the facet scales). Differential item functioning is one form of measurement inequivalence that could result in misleading mean level comparisons (Huang et al., 1997). Although McCrae (2001) has suggested that DIF might average out across the items in a scale, we are less optimistic about this possibility. When Huang et al. (1997) deleted DIF items, it affected the number of cultural mean differences found with the NEO-PI scales.

Predictions involving the interpersonal domains of Extraversion and Agreeableness may be complicated by the greater importance of the in-group versus out-group distinction in the Philippines than in the U.S. For example, although Filipinos may be warm, gregarious, playful, and cheerful with in-group members, their interpersonal behavior can be more reserved and distant with strangers or out-group members. Consistent with this interpretation, Bulatao (1963) attributed the lower average score of Filipinos on the EPPS Affiliation scale to Filipinos' fear of face-to-face relations with strangers. Thus, the findings that Filipinos did not average higher than Americans in Warmth, Gregariousness, Positive Emotions, Altruism, and Trust may be the result of the following: Many items in these scales refer to people or emotions in general and do not distinguish between behavior with in-group versus out-group members. If the Filipino students did not respond in reference to in-group members, there might not be any reason to expect them to average higher in these traits than Americans.

The definitions that we gave to the bicultural judges were based closely on those contained in the NEO Job Profiler (Costa et al., 1995). In retrospect, however, we suspect that a few cases of disagreement between our judges and the mean profiles were the result of imperfect congruence between these definitions and the items in the corresponding facet scales. For example, for the Straightforwardness facet, judges received the following definition: *Frank, sincere, and candid; does not manipulate others or conceal information.* Our judges may have focused on the "frank" and "candid" elements of this definition when they judged Filipinos to be lower on this trait than Americans; Filipinos are often perceived to be less direct and frank than Americans in interpersonal communication. This could lead the judges to disagree with the mean profile differences because most of the items in the Straightforwardness facet scale assess more general Machiavellian or manipulative behaviors, which are the focus of only the latter half of the definition given to the judges. Similarly, our judges may have expected Filipinos to average higher than Americans on the Openness to Feelings facet based on their perceptions that Filipinos exhibit greater openness to, and empathy with, others' feelings (at least with in-group members). Although these characteristics were part of the definition given to the judges, the majority of the items in the Openness to Feelings scale refer instead to the experiencing of one's own strong emotions; indeed, only one item refers to other persons. It can be difficult to summarize a set of items or a construct in a few words or phrases; in retrospect, we suspect that the match between the definitions given to the judges and the item content of the corresponding facet scales was less than optimal in a few cases.

Finally, we have considered whether the failure of some of our hypotheses might support the contention of some cultural psychologists that introspection about one's own personality characteristics or behavior is an unnatural task for persons in collectivistic cultures and that, as a result, such assessments might not be genuine or accurate. As we summarized earlier, there is evidence in the Philippine literature for the validity of trait measures, but further evidence of the accuracy and validity of trait assessments is needed.

Given these results, we continue to be somewhat skeptical about the viability of direct mean score comparisons across cultures. Although differences on some scales may reflect valid personality differences across cultures, other differences may be contaminated by construct, method, or item bias. And unfortunately, it may be difficult to know which of the apparent cultural differences are valid versus invalid in any given study or sample. It will probably require multiple studies using diverse samples, instruments, and methods in each culture before confident conclusions can be drawn about personality differences across cultures.

REFERENCES

Barrett, P. T., Petrides, K. V., Eysenck, S. B. G., & Eysenck, H. J. (1998). The Eysenck Personality Questionnaire: An examination of the factorial similarity of P, E, N, and L across 34 countries. *Personality and Individual Differences, 25,* 805-819.
Ben-Porath, Y. S., Almagor, M., Hoffman-Chemi, A., & Tellegen, A. (1995). A cross-cultural study of personality with the Multidimensional Personality Questionaire. *Journal of Cross-Cultural Psychology, 26,* 360-373.
Brief, D. E., Comrey, A. L., & Collins, B. E. (1994). The Comrey Personality Scales in Russian: A study of concurrent, predictive, and external validity. *Personality and Individual Differences, 16,* 113-122.
Bulatao, J. C. (1963). Personal preferences of Filipino students. *Philippine Sociological Review, 11,* 168-178.
Bulatao, J. C. (1978, July). *An Asian approach to transpersonal counseling.* Paper presented at the Convention of the Association of Psychological and Educational Counselors in Asia, Hong Kong University, Hong Kong.
Buss, D. M. (1996). Social adaptation and five major factors of personality. In J. S. Wiggins (Ed.), *The Five-Factor Model of personality: Theoretical perspectives* (pp. 180-207). New York: Guilford.
Buss, D. M. (2001). Human nature and culture: An evolutionary psychological perspective. *Journal of Personality, 69,* 955-978.
Cheung, F. M., & Leung, K. (1998). Indigenous personality measures: Chinese examples. *Journal of Cross-Cultural Psychology, 29,* 233-248.
Church, A. T. (1986). *Filipino personality: A review of research and writings* (Monograph Series No. 6). Manila: De La Salle University Press.
Church, A. T. (1987). Personality research in a non-Western culture. *Psychological Bulletin, 102,* 272-292.
Church, A. T. (2000). Culture and personality: Towards an integrated cultural trait psychology. *Journal of Personality, 68,* 651-703.
Church, A. T. (2001). Personality measurement in cross-cultural perspective. *Journal of Personality, 69,* 979-1006.
Church, A. T., & Burke, P. J. (1994). Exploratory and confirmatory tests of the Big Five and Tellegen's three- and four-dimensional models. *Journal of Personality and Social Psychology, 66,* 93-114.
Church, A. T., & Katigbak, M. S. (1988). The emic strategy in the identification and assessment of personality dimensions in a non-Western culture: Rationale, steps, and a Philippine illustration. *Journal of Cross-Cultural Psychology, 19,* 140-163.
Church, A. T., & Katigbak, M. S. (1989). Internal, external, and self-report structure of personality in a non-Western culture: An investigation of cross-language and cross-cultural generalizability. *Journal of Personality and Social Psychology, 57,* 857-872.
Church, A. T., & Katigbak, M. S. (1992). The cultural context of academic motives: A comparison of American and Filipino college students. *Journal of Cross-Cultural Psychology, 23,* 40-58.
Church, A. T., & Katigbak, M. S. (2000a). *Filipino personality: Indigenous and cross-cultural studies.* Manila: De La Salle University Press.
Church, A. T., & Katigbak, M. S. (2000b). Trait psychology in the Philippines. *American Behavioral Scientist, 44,* 73-94.
Church, A. T., Katigbak, M. S., & Reyes, J. A. S. (1996). Toward a taxonomy of trait adjectives in Filipino: Comparing personality lexicons across cultures. *European Journal of Personality, 10,* 3-24.
Church, A. T., Katigbak, M. S., & Reyes, J. A. S. (1998). Further exploration of Filipino personality structure using the lexical approach: Do the Big-Five or Big-Seven dimensions emerge? *European Journal of Personality, 12,* 249-269.
Church, A. T., & Lonner, W. J. (1998). The cross-cultural perspective in the study of personality: Rationale and current research. *Journal of Cross-Cultural Psychology, 29,* 32-62.
Church, A. T., Reyes, J. A. S., Katigbak, M. S., & Grimm, S. D. (1997). Filipino personality structure and the Big Five model: A lexical approach. *Journal of Personality, 65,* 477-528.
Costa, P. T. Jr., & McCrae, R. R. (1988). From catalog to classification: Murray's needs and the Five-Factor Model. *Journal of Personality and Social Psychology, 55,* 258-265.

Costa, P. T. Jr., & McCrae, R. R. (1992). *Revised NEO Personality Inventory (NEO-PI-R) and NEO Five-Factor Inventory (NEO-FFI) professional manual*. Odessa, FL: Psychological Assessment Resources.

Costa, P. T., Jr., McCrae, R. R., & Kay, G. G. (1995). Persons, places, and personality: Career assessment using the Revised NEO Personality Inventory. *Journal of Career Assessment, 3*, 123-139.

del Pilar, G. H. (1998). *L'extraversion en psychologie differentielle et l'extratension au Test De Rorschach* [Extraversion in differential psychology and Rorschach extratension]. Doctoral dissertation, University of Paris X-Nanterre.

Enriquez,V. G. (1992). *From colonial to liberation psychology: The Philippine experience*. Quezon City, Philippines: University of the Philippines Press.

Greenfield, P. M. (1997). Culture as process: Empirical methods for cultural psychology. In J. W. Berry, Y. H. Poortinga, & J. Pandey (Eds.), *Handbook of cross-cultural psychology: Theory and method* (2nd ed., Vol. 1, pp. 301-346). Needham Heights, MA: Allyn & Bacon.

Grimm, S. D., & Church, A. T. (1999). A cross-cultural investigation of response biases in personality measures. *Journal of Research in Personality, 33*, 415-441.

Guanzon-Lapeña, M. A., Church, A. T., Carlota, A. J., & Katigbak, M. S. (1998). Indigenous personality measures: Philippine examples. *Journal of Cross-Cultural Psychology, 29*, 249-270.

Guthrie, G. M., & Bennett, A. B., Jr. (1971). Cultural differences in implicit personality theory. *International Journal of Psychology, 6*, 305-312.

Guthrie, G. M., Jackson, D. N., Astilla, E., & Elwood, B. (1983). Personality measurement: Do the scales have similar meanings in another culture? In S. H. Irvine & J. W. Berry (Eds.), *Human assessment and cultural factors* (pp. 377-392). New York: Plenum Press.

Ho, D. Y. F. (1998). Indigenous psychologies: Asian perspectives. *Journal of Cross-Cultural Psychology, 29*, 88-103.

Huang, C. D., Church, A. T., & Katigbak, M. S. (1997). Identifying cultural differences in items and traits: Differential item functioning in the NEO Personality Inventory. *Journal of Cross-Cultural Psychology, 28*, 192-218.

Kallasmaa, T., Allik, J., Realo, A., & McCrae, R. R. (2000). The Estonian version of the NEO-PI-R: An examination of universal and culture-specific aspects of the Five-Factor Model. *European Journal of Personality, 14*, 265-278.

Katigbak, M. S., Church, A. T., & Akamine, T. X. (1996). Cross-cultural generalizability of personality dimensions: Relating indigenous and imported dimensions in two cultures. *Journal of Personality and Social Psychology, 70*, 99-114.

Katigbak, M. S., Church, A. T., Guanzon-Lapeña, M. A., Carlota, A. J., & del Pilar, G. H. (2002). Are indigenous personality dimensions culture-specific? Philippine inventories and the Five-Factor Model. *Journal of Personality and Social Psychology, 82*, 89-101.

MacDonald, K. (1998). Evolution, culture, and the Five-Factor Model. *Journal of Cross-Cultural Psychology, 29*, 119-149.

Markus, H. R., & Kitayama, S. (1991). Culture and the self: Implications for cognition, emotion, and motivation. *Psychological Review, 98*, 224-253.

Markus, H. R., & Kitayama, S. (1998). The cultural psychology of personality. *Journal of Cross-Cultural Psychology, 29*, 63-87.

Mastor, K. A., Jin, P., & Cooper, M. (2000). Malay culture and personality: A Big Five perspective. *American Behavioral Scientist, 44*, 95-111.

McCrae, R. R. (2000). Trait psychology and the revival of personality and culture studies. *American Behavioral Scientist, 44*, 10-31.

McCrae, R. R. (2001). Trait psychology and culture: Exploring intercultural comparisons. *Journal of Personality, 69*, 803-846.

McCrae, R. R., & Costa, P. T., Jr. (1996). Toward a new generation of personality theories: Theoretical contexts for the Five-Factor Model. In J. S. Wiggins (Ed.), *The Five-Factor Model of personality: Theoretical perspectives* (pp. 51-87). New York: Guilford.

McCrae, R. R., & Costa, P. T., Jr. (1997). Personality trait structure as a human universal. *American Psychologist, 52*, 509-516.

McCrae, R. R., & Costa, P. T., Jr. (1999). A Five-Factor Theory of personality. In L. A. Pervin & O. P. John (Eds.), *Handbook of personality* (2nd ed., pp. 139-153). New York: Guilford.

McCrae, R. R., Costa, P. T., Jr., del Pilar, G. Y., Rolland, J.-P., & Parker, W. D. (1998). Cross-cultural assessment of the Five-Factor Model: The Revised NEO Personality Inventory. *Journal of Cross-Cultural Psychology, 29*, 171-188.

McCrae, R. R., Costa, P. T. Jr., & Yik, M. S. M. (1996). Universal aspects of Chinese personality structure. In M. Bond (Ed.), *Handbook of Chinese psychology* (pp. 189-207). Hong Kong: Oxford University Press.

McCrae, R. R., Yik, M. S. M., Trapnell, P. D., Bond, M. H., & Paulhus, D. L. (1998). Interpreting personality profiles across cultures: Bilingual, acculturation, and peer rating studies of Chinese undergraduates. *Journal of Personality and Social Psychology, 74,* 1041-1055.

McCrae, R. R., Zonderman, A. B., Costa, P. T., Jr., Bond, M. H., & Paunonen, S. V. (1996). Evaluating replicability of factors in the Revised NEO Personality Inventory: Confirmatory factor analysis versus Procrustes rotation. *Journal of Personality and Social Psychology, 70,* 552-566.

Miller, J. G. (1997). Theoretical issues in cultural psychology. In J. W. Berry, Y. H. Poortinga, & J. Pandey (Eds.), *Handbook of cross-cultural psychology: Vol. 1. Theory and method* (2nd ed., pp.85-128). Boston: Allyn and Bacon.

Mischel, W., & Shoda, Y. (1995). A cognitive-affective system theory of personality: Reconceptualizing situations, dispositions, dynamics, and invariance in personality structure. *Psychological Review, 102,* 246-268.

Passini, F. T., & Norman, W. T. (1966). A universal conception of personality structure? *Journal of Personality and Social Psychology, 4,* 44-49.

Paunonen, S. V., & Ashton, M. C. (1998). The structured assessment of personality across cultures. *Journal of Cross-Cultural Psychology, 29,*150-170.

Pe-Pua, R., & Protacio-Marcelino, E. (2000). *Sikolohiyang Pilipino* (Filipino psychology): A legacy of Virgilio G. Enriquez. *Asian Journal of Social Psychology, 3,* 49-71.

Piedmont, R. L., & Chae, J. H. (1997). Cross-cultural generalizability of the Five-Factor Model of personality: Development and validation of the NEO-PI-R for Koreans. *Journal of Cross-Cultural Psychology, 28,* 131-155.

Poortinga, Y. P., & Van Hemert, D. A. (2001). Personality and culture: Demarcating between the common and the unique. *Journal of Personality, 69,* 1033-1060.

Rolland, J. P. (2000, July). Cross-cultural validity of the Five-Factor Model of personality. In J. Allik and R. R. McCrae (Chairs), *Personality and culture: The Five-Factor Theory perspective.* Symposium presented at the XXVII International Congress of Psychology, Stockholm, Sweden.

Saucier, G., & Goldberg, L. R. (2001). Lexical studies of indigenous personality factors: Premises, pro-ducts, and prospects. *Journal of Personality, 69,* 847-879.

Schmitt, D. P., & Buss, D. M. (2000). Sexual dimensions of person description: Beyond or subsumed by the Big Five? *Journal of Research in Personality, 34,* 141-177.

Shweder, R. A. (1991). *Thinking through cultures: Expeditions in cultural psychology.* Cambridge, MA: Harvard University Press.

Shweder, R. A., & Sullivan, M. A. (1993). Cultural psychology: Who needs it? *Annual Review of Psychology, 44,* 497-523.

Sinha, D. (1997). Indigenizing psychology. In J. W. Berry, Y. H. Poortinga, & J. Pandey (Eds.), *Handbook of cross-cultural psychology: Vol. 1. Theory and method* (2nd ed., pp. 129-169). Boston: Allyn & Bacon.

Stumpf, H. (1993). The factor structure of the Personality Research Form: A cross-national evaluation. *Journal of Personality, 61,* 27-48.

Tinsley, H. E. A., & Weiss, D. J. (1975). Interrater reliability and agreement of subjective judgments. *Journal of Counseling Psychology, 22,* 358-376.

Triandis, H. C. (1995). *Individualism and collectivism.* Boulder, CO: Westview Press.

Van de Vijver, F., & Leung, K. (1997). *Methods and data analysis for cross-cultural research.* Thousand Oaks, CA: Sage.

AUTHOR NOTE

We express appreciation to Gregorio del Pilar for providing a copy of his data set, which was used to make comparisons with other Philippine samples, and to Shellah Imperio and Debi Thomas-Jones for assistance in collecting data from bicultural judges in the personality comparison study. Preparation of this chapter was supported by National Institute of Mental Health grant R01-MH59941. Correspondence concerning this chapter should be addressed to A. Timothy Church, Department of Educational

Leadership and Counseling Psychology, Cleveland Hall, Washington State University, Pullman, WA, 99164-2136. E-mail: church@mail.wsu.edu

THE APPLICABILITY OF THE FIVE-FACTOR MODEL IN A SUB-SAHARAN CULTURE

The NEO-PI-R in Shona

RALPH L. PIEDMONT,* ELAINE BAIN,* ROBERT R. McCRAE** & PAUL T. COSTA, JR.**

*Loyola College in Maryland, **National Institute on Aging*

Abstract. This chapter examines the Five-Factor Model of personality in Shona, a native tongue of Zimbabwe. One hundred and sixty-five women and 193 men participated in this study; all were bilingual in English and Shona. The Shona version of the Revised NEO Personality Inventory (NEO-PI-R) and the English version of the Adjective Check List (ACL) were completed by 199 participants. The remaining 159 participants took English or Shona versions of the NEO-PI-R on two occasions, with a mean retest interval of seven days. Alpha reliabilities for the facet scales were quite low, but retest reliabilities and cross-language correlations were considerably higher. Targeted factor analyses showed that the factors and most of the specific facets had a structure similar to that found in Americans, and correlations with the ACL generally supported the construct validity of the new translation. The Openness (O) factor proved weakest in translation. The viability of trait approaches in collectivistic societies and the possible role of sociological context on personality development are discussed.

Keywords: traits, Africa, collectivistic culture

1. THE UNIVERSALITY OF TRAITS

Are personality traits relevant only in modern industrial societies? That might be asserted by some proponents of cultural psychology, who argue that the notion of enduring characteristics within the individual, independent of cultural context, is meaningful only in the highly individualistic cultures of the West (Cross & Markus, 1999; Shweder & Sullivan, 1993). In the extreme, such a position would lead to the prediction that personality trait models and instruments could never be successfully imported into truly collectivistic cultures. Questionnaire items could not be translated, because collectivistic languages would lack the vocabulary to express trait constructs. Collectivistic respondents, who presumably define themselves in terms of their relation to the social situation, would not have a consistent self-image of their traits on which to

156   PIEDMONT, BAIN, MCCRAE & COSTA

base self-reports; in consequence, trait measures would lack internal consistency and retest reliability. Surely one would not expect the network of trait associations that underlie factor structure to be preserved in such circumstances.

In a careful and balanced review of these issues, Church (2000) concluded that evidence to date does not support so radical a view of personhood in non-Western societies: Any cultural differences in the validity and utility of trait constructs "will be at most a matter of degree" (p. 662). Evidence to date, however, is limited largely to Western and industrialized Far Eastern countries. In the present paper we examine the applicability of the Five-Factor Model (FFM) of personality in an agrarian society from southern Africa. Although the respondents are fully literate and have had extensive exposure to Western culture through the popular media, they do represent one of the furthest generalizations of the FFM attempted so far.

Researchers have translated instruments measuring the FFM into a variety of languages and have found it surprisingly robust (McCrae & Costa, 1997). However, the bulk of this work has been with either European cultures (e.g., Italian—Capara, Barbaranelli, Borgogni, & Perugini, 1993; German—Borkenau & Ostendorf, 1990; Finnish and Polish—Paunonen, Jackson, Treebinski, & Forsterling, 1992) or with modern industrial non-European nations (e.g., Japanese—Bond, Nakazato, & Shiraishi, 1975; Chinese—Bond, 1979; Korean—Piedmont & Chae, 1997). The purpose of the current study was to evaluate the utility of the FFM in Shona, a native language of Zimbabwe, which is a mostly agrarian, Sub-Saharan African nation.

Some psychometric research has already been done on psychological constructs in Zimbabwe. Wilson, Doolabh, Cooney, Khalpey and Siddiqui (1990) evaluated the reliability and validity of the Jackson (1974) Personality Research Form among Zimbabwean students. They found mixed support for this English version: Scale reliabilities and validities were of an acceptable magnitude overall, although convergence with peer ratings was quite small. Patel, Simunyu, Gwanzura, Lewis, and Mann (1997) employed an emic paradigm for developing a measure of psychological distress among the Shona. Using idioms and symptoms obtained from local focus groups, a measure of psychological distress was developed that evidenced good internal consistency and predictive validity. Given that the dimensions of Neuroticism (N) and (low) Conscientiousness have been shown to be linked with symptom experience (Piedmont & Ciarrocchi, 1999), the Patel et al. (1997) study suggests that, at a minimum, it should be possible to recover these two factors in native Shona.

Direct tests of the generalizability of the FFM in Africans have been limited to South Africa. Further, most of these studies either employed samples that were mostly White or used instruments that were written in English. The results have not always been a consistent replication of the five-factor structure. Heaven, Connors, and Stones (1994) gave a list of English adjectives to a sample of 230 South Africans from a predominantly Black university and 186 Australian university students. This list contained 112 adjectives identified as markers of the FFM. Although the five dimensions were nicely reproduced in the Australian sample, factor analyses did not provide much support for a five-factor solution in the African sample. Most items loaded on a first factor defined by evaluatively positive items from Agreeableness (A), Consciousness (C), and Openness/Intellect factors. Two methodological reasons for this failure to obtain a five-factor structure are possible. First, the use of English terms with individuals whose primary language generally was not English could have created problems with interpretation and understanding. Second, response sets may operate more strongly in South African samples than in Australian or American samples, especially when an adjective checklist format is used. However, it is also possible that the FFM does not adequately represent the personality structure of Black South Africans.

Heuchert, Parker, Stumpf and Myburgh (2000) gave the Revised NEO Personality Inventory (NEO-PI-R; Costa & McCrae, 1992) in English to a mixed racial group of 408 South African students. Their results gave far more support to the replicability of the FFM. Overall the expected five-factor structure was obtained, although more clearly among White students than among Black students. For the Black students, Openness to Experience was weakly replicated in the data. In this case, the small sample size (N = 92) and the exclusive reliance on the English version of the NEO-PI-R might have been responsible for problems with O. Those for whom English is not a first language may have difficulty in understanding the relatively abstract constructs represented in this domain. Such an imposed etic paradigm does not allow one to determine whether there are true cultural differences in the nature of the factor, or whether the English terms fail to convey the construct in this language community (see Yang & Bond, 1990).

An unpublished thesis (Horn, 2000) examined a Xhosa translation of the NEO-PI-R. Xhosa is a Bantu language spoken in southern South Africa. Horn reported that translation was difficult, in part because "the Xhosa language has a restricted vocabulary" (p. 73). This caused particular problems for items measuring O, especially O1: Fantasy and O6: Values. In a sample of 75 bilingual undergraduates, correlations between the Xhosa and English versions administered three weeks apart were significant but modest in magnitude, ranging from .30 for A to .54 for O. Internal consistency estimates for the Xhosa version were smaller than typically seen in American samples, ranging from .57 to .83 for the five domains. Given the small sample size, no factor analysis was conducted.

This study will report on the translation of the NEO-PI-R into Shona, a native language of Zimbabwe. An overview of the culture as well as some of the challenges encountered in the translation process are discussed and the resulting implications for personality assessment are highlighted. From a psychometric perspective, the new translation will be evaluated in terms of internal consistency, retest reliability, and cross-language comparability. Targeted factor analysis (McCrae, Zonderman, Costa, Bond, & Paunonen, 1996) will be used to evaluate replicability of the American structure. McCrae et al. (1999) have noted cross-cultural age differences on these personality dimensions, and age and gender effects will be evaluated in this sample. Finally, associations with the scales of the Adjective Check List (ACL; Gough & Heilbrun, 1992) will be used to evaluate the construct validity of the new Shona scales.

1.1. Zimbabwe Culture and the Shona

The Shona are the largest ethnic group in Zimbabwe, comprising 80% of the total population. Shona and Ndebele are the two most frequently spoken native languages. Like most of the major languages of central and southern Africa, Shona is from the

Bantu branch of the Niger-Congo language family, and is unrelated to any European or Asian language.

Economically, Zimbabwe is a poor country by world standards, although it is above average for southern Africa ("Zimbabwe," 1993). More than two-thirds of the labor force is employed in agriculture. Zimbabwe was a former British colony, Rhodesia, and English remains the official language. Sociologically, the Shona are very similar to many other East African cultures, which are regarded as collectivistic cultures. (For example, on a 1 to 10 scale of individualism, Kenya and Tanzania are both rated "3;" see Diener, Diener, & Diener, 1995). As a people, the Shona are very sociable and gregarious. Much of their time is spent in the company of others, either with their extended family or with other villagers and neighbors. The interpersonal, sharing-based nature of their daily life precludes any sense of personal privacy. Parin and Parin-Mathèy (1964) suggested that African social behavior is controlled by a group ego, and this might well describe Shona life. As Okeke, Draguns, Sheku, and Allen (1999, p. 149) have noted about African culture, "The sphere of private experience . . . is not explicitly heeded in daily interactions . . . the boundaries between public and private domains are porous and easily penetrated."

The stress placed upon social relationships and interpersonal contacts creates a psychosocial reality that cannot understand individuality or separateness from the group. This sociocentric orientation of the Shona permeates all aspects of living. By living and working among the Shona for many years, the second author (EB) has become acquainted with the many subtleties in behavior that reinforce this connectedness. For example, when talking with a single individual, it is important that both speak loud enough to be heard by others in the immediate environs. Such loudness helps to assure others that the pair is not talking about them. This constant connectedness is also reflected in Shona sculpture (see Figure 1). A frequent theme is a circle of people who are all holding hands or hugging, or of birds with intertwined necks.

However, this interpersonal closeness also brings with it high levels of envy, jealousy, and vengefulness. Despite frequent contact, there is always a background level of wariness and distrust. For example, when meeting someone and shaking hands, it is important that *both* hands are involved in the contact. Having one hand behind your back or at your side is seen as threatening, suggesting that one has something to hide or is trying to deceive. Thus, there is a high degree of social comparison operating; the group politic wanting to ensure the equality of each member. As a result, conformity and interpersonal sophistication are highly valued and respected.

As Okeke et al. (1999) pointed out, Africans in general are more inclined towards global, intuitive, and expressive cognitive functions than to the more detail-oriented, analytic approaches that characterize Western thought processes (cf. Nisbett, Peng, Choi, & Norenzayan, 2001). This holistic style focuses more on immediate experiences than on abstract concepts and ideas. Okeke et al. noted that field-dependence (Witkin & Berry, 1975) rather than field independence is the more prevalent cognitive style.

This necessarily brief and general overview of the Shona sets the stage for some of the difficulties that were experienced in translating the NEO-PI-R into this language and culture. Items relating to low Extraversion (E), particularly low Gregariousness, were difficult to construct because being alone, or wanting to be alone, is perceived as a sign of psychological illness. As a result, it was difficult to find items that would reflect

Figure 1. "Family" by Henry Munyaradzi. Serpentine, 89 ×48 ×20 cm.
From the Richard Handelsman collection of Shona Sculpture at
www.scholars.nus.edu.sg/landow/post/zimbabwe/art/handelsman/handelsmanov.html.
Image © Richard and Susan Handelsman and may be used freely for any
educational or scholarly purpose. All other uses require prior written permission.

low E without also containing a high degree of Neuroticism (N). Another difficulty was found with the O domain. The cognitive style of the Shona is at odds in many ways with the abstract concepts reflected by this construct. This was particularly true with the Fantasy facet, a trait defined as a propensity to engage in internal and solitary activity. For the Shona, the world of fantasy and daydreaming is very much wrapped up in their external behaviors. Other difficulties were encountered with Aesthetics, which again stresses intraindividual experiences and activities (such as reading poetry or listening to music). In many instances there were no single Shona words that could convey the more abstract ideas and concepts represented in the English.

Thus, in making this translation, we were concerned with our ability to assess some of the domains in this language, specifically O. Clear O factors were found neither by Heuchert et al. (2000) nor by Heaven et al. (1994) in predominantly Black African samples, and Horn (2000) reported difficulty in translating O items into the related Xhosa language. We were also concerned with the factor structure of E and A facets. In some other socially oriented societies, such as Korean, the facets from these two domains frequently form hybrid factors that are a rotational variant of those seen in the America normative structure (Piedmont & Chae, 1997). With the Shona, the strong linkage between E and mental health may force a realignment of these two factors. The underlying suspicion and wariness that pervades social interactions may affect A in ways not anticipated.

It is exactly such concerns that highlight the value of cross-cultural research of this type. Although it would be very significant to recover intact the five-factor structure of the NEO-PI-R in this culture, failures in replicability may, ultimately, be of more theoretical importance. Extending the FFM to non-Western, agrarian cultures offers an opportunity to contrast how personality comes to be organized in various sociological contexts. From a psycho-anthropological perspective, we may begin to address questions as to how the socioeconomic development of a culture may affect the structure and content of personality.

2. THE NEO-PI-R IN ZIMBABWE

The NEO-PI-R was translated into Shona using a multi-step process. Initially, the original English items were translated into Shona. This version was then sent to two bilingual individuals unfamiliar with psychological constructs, who backtranslated the items into English. Next, the backtranslated versions were compared with the original English. Items which were not clear or did not satisfactorily capture the constructs being assessed were identified and new translations were made. These changes were sent to the backtranslators who retranslated the second Shona version into English. At this point, the translations were forwarded to the authors of the NEO-PI-R for their review. They identified 43 items they believed unclear. Those items were again retranslated and sent to the two bilinguals for backtranslation. Review of this final version showed some remaining problems; however, because the opportunity for data collection was limited, it was decided to proceed with this version.

It should be noted that this translation posed more difficulties than most translations of the NEO-PI-R. Typically, fewer than 20 questionable items are identified in the authors' review of the backtranslation (e.g., McCrae, Costa, del Pilar, Rolland, & Parker, 1998). One explanation is that the Shona translator was not a personality psychologist, as most previous NEO-PI-R translators had been (Costa, McCrae, & Jónsson, in press), and was less successful in conveying the psychological sense of the items. It is also possible, however, that some of the constructs assessed by the NEO-PI-R have no direct equivalents in Shona language and culture.

We also administered the Adjective Check List (ACL). Developed by Gough and Heilbrun (1983), this measure consists of 300 adjectives from which individuals select those which are viewed as most self-descriptive. The ACL can be scored for 33 scales from diverse theoretical orientations, including Murray's (1938) needs, Berne's (1961) Transactional Analysis, Welsh's (1976) Intellectence and Originence scales and several scales developed by Gough and Heilbrun (1983) to measure salient interpersonal qualities. Piedmont et al. (1991) have shown the scales of the ACL to be meaningfully related to the domains of the FFM in American samples. The results of the Piedmont et al. study will be used as a benchmark for evaluating the construct validity of the Shona version of the NEO-PI-R. As in that earlier study, ACL scale scores were adjusted for gender and total number of items checked as recommended in the Manual.

These instruments were administered to 165 women and 193 men, aged 17 to 80 ($M = 30, SD = 9.7$). All were volunteers. The sample consisted of native Zimbabweans, all bilingual in both their native tongue of Shona and English. Participants were recruited from a variety of sources, including university students, personnel from an all-girls parochial high school, and a general sample of convenience. These individuals can be considered Zimbabwean middle-class, coming mostly from villages (suburban to rural areas) rather than from cities. Villages, on average, have about 700 people (100 households of extended families) and do have basic amenities (e.g., electricity, television).

Of these 358 participants, 199 completed the Shona version of the NEO-PI-R and the English version of the Adjective Check List. The remaining 159 participants were involved in the test-retest phase of the study; these individuals took the NEO-PI-R twice, with a retest interval, on average, of 7 days (range 0 to 39 days). Participants were randomly assigned to one of four testing groups: Group 1 took the Shona version twice ($n = 42$); Group 2 took the Shona version of the NEO-PI-R first, then the English version ($n = 41$); Group 3 took the English version first, followed by the Shona version ($n = 32$); and Group 4 took the English version twice ($n = 44$). College students who participated in this study completed the Shona version of the NEO-PI-R and the ACL under controlled circumstances at their university. Nonstudents completed their materials at home in their own time.

2.1. Psychometric Analyses

As the first step in evaluating the translation, item-total correlations were examined to determine whether specific items failed to converge with other items constituting their putative personality domain. A total of 19 items were identified which had negative item-total correlations (two each for N, O, and C, eight for E, and five for A). Inspection of these items, which included "In dealing with other people, I always dread

Table 1. Descriptive Statistics and Alpha Reliabilities for the Shona NEO-PI-R.

NEO-PI-R Scale	Men		Women		α	r_{tt}	Age r
	Mean	SD	Mean	SD			
Domains:							
N: Neuroticism	86.94	16.43	84.82	17.53	.82	.87	−.21***
E: Extraversion	106.37	12.81	105.20	13.07	.73	.92	.07
O: Openness	104.19	12.34	99.94ª	12.02	.64	.77	−.14*
A: Agreeableness	120.04	17.72	120.44	16.55	.80	.80	.26***
C: Conscientiousness	122.05	18.90	125.81	19.28	.88	.81	.28***
Facets:							
N1: Anxiety	15.05	3.93	14.89	4.01	.41	.69	−.07
N2: Angry Hostility	13.45	4.26	13.35	4.68	.60	.70	−.23***
N3: Depression	15.90	4.19	14.52ª	3.98	.49	.78	−.16**
N4: Self-Consciousness	15.82	3.25	15.55	3.13	.27	.69	−.12*
N5: Impulsiveness	13.88	3.92	14.09	4.54	.46	.71	−.17**
N6: Vulnerability	12.83	4.14	12.42	4.70	.59	.57	−.10
E1: Warmth	19.91	3.91	20.09	4.16	.51	.85	.07
E2: Gregariousness	17.57	4.21	17.34	4.32	.53	.85	.05
E3: Assertiveness	15.10	3.46	14.06ª	4.43	.41	.66	.07
E4: Activity	17.28	1.81	17.94ª	2.02	.21	.64	.21***
E5: Excitement Seeking	16.78	3.41	15.43ª	3.32	.36	.71	−.09
E6: Positive Emotions	19.73	3.60	20.35	4.00	.53	.81	.01
O1: Fantasy	13.34	3.90	13.57	4.35	.41	.48	−.19***
O2: Aesthetics	18.91	4.38	17.95	4.59	.57	.75	.01
O3: Feelings	17.61	3.10	17.19	3.57	.24	.76	−.16***
O4: Actions	17.90	3.13	17.97	2.85	.22	.49	−.01
O5: Ideas	19.39	3.98	16.93ª	3.74	.45	.77	−.03
O6: Values	17.02	3.10	16.32	3.45	.13	.48	−.08
A1: Trust	18.13	2.97	17.65	3.66	.42	.51	.10
A2: Straightforwardness	21.30	4.56	21.66	5.26	.60	.70	.23***
A3: Altruism	19.91	3.71	20.07	3.85	.50	.59	.05
A4: Compliance	19.19	3.93	20.59ª	4.86	.56	.57	.30***
A5: Modesty	18.45	3.15	17.89	2.83	.30	.71	.15*
A6: Tendermindedness	23.06	4.06	22.58	4.04	.49	.78	.18**
C1: Competence	18.67	3.47	19.04	3.88	.38	.71	.14*
C2: Order	19.87	3.84	20.60	3.66	.52	.58	.21***
C3: Dutifulness	22.72	4.71	22.75	4.63	.65	.72	.28***
C4: Achievement Striving	21.40	4.01	22.65ª	4.36	.61	.72	.22***
C5: Self-Discipline	19.43	4.25	20.92ª	4.35	.62	.68	.22***
C6: Deliberation	19.95	3.93	19.85	3.83	.52	.78	.22***

Note. N = 312 for age correlations, 314 for coefficients alpha, and 42 for retest correlations. The time interval between test and retest was approximately 7 days. All retest correlations are significant at *p* < .001. ªSignificant (*p* < .05) difference between men and women. * *p* < .05; ** *p* < .01; *** *p* < .001.

making a social blunder" and "My work is likely to be slow but steady," did not suggest any pattern that could account for their poor performance. These items were treated as missing data; in order to maximize comparability to the English version, respondents' scores on these items were all recoded to the *neutral* category before scale scores were calculated.[1]

Descriptive statistics for each gender and reliability coefficients are presented in Table 1 for 314 participants. This includes 199 who took the NEO-PI-R only once and 115 who took the Shona version as part of the test-retest phase (for those who took the Shona twice in this paradigm, only their initial scores were used).

Although scalar equivalence of the Shona NEO-PI-R scales has not yet been established, it is worth pointing out that the means and SDs are roughly comparable to those found in American samples. Internal consistency, however, is not. Alpha reliabilities for the domains are acceptable, ranging from .64 for O to .88 for C, but lower than seen in American samples. Values for the facet scales are uniformly lower than their American counterparts, ranging from a low of .13 for Openness to Values to .65 for Dutifulness (Median = .49); only 5 of the 30 facets have an alpha above .60. Especially at the facet level, these values suggest that the trait constructs are only weakly represented in Shona, or that these specific items are poor trait indicators in this culture, or that there are significant problems in the translation. Somewhat more encouraging is the one-week retest reliability. These values range from .48 to .92, and suggest that respondents generally gave similar responses on the two occasions.

The last column of Table 1 reports correlations with age. Consistent with most literature on adult personality development, these correlations are uniformly small, because personality changes very slowly after adolescence. The direction of the correlations is generally consistent with the cross-cultural literature (Costa et al., 2000; McCrae et al., 1999): N and O decline, whereas A and C increase with age. Somewhat surprisingly, E is unrelated to age, although in most cultures it declines. At the facet level, the declines in Impulsiveness and Openness to Fantasy and Feelings and the increases in Straightforwardness, Modesty, Dutifulness, Self-Discipline, and Deliberation match findings from nine other cultures, from Estonia to South Korea (Costa et al., 2000). Alone among these cultures, however, the Shona data do not show declines in Excitement Seeking, Positive Emotions, or Openness to Values. In part, this may be due to the translation, because Excitement Seeking shows a strong relation to age ($r = -.30$, $N = 115$, $p < .01$) when assessed by the English version. However, even in English, Positive Emotions and Openness to Values are unrelated to age in this Shona sample.

In contrast to age effects, where Shona results largely mirror those found in other cultures, associations of gender with personality are apparently different in Shona. In most cultures (Costa, Terracciano, & McCrae, 2001), women score higher than men in N and A, but as Table 1 shows, women do not differ from men in these two domains. Instead, women score somewhat lower in O, and especially in Openness to Ideas. Similar results are seen when the English version is analyzed in this sample.

Table 2 presents domain-level results of a bilingual study. Subjects were assigned to one of four groups, and each completed either the Shona or the English version on two occasions one week apart. Both versions had acceptable internal consistency on both occasions, with generally higher coefficients for the English version. As the t-values in

---

[1]This procedure had little impact on overall results. For example, a targeted factor analysis based on the original scoring of the scales gave congruence coefficients of .95, .85, .78, .85, and .93 for the five factors, only marginally worse than the values in Table 3.

Table 2. Descriptive Statistics and Reliability Estimates for the Four Testing Groups.

Domain	Time 1			Time 2			r_{tt}	t
	Mean	SD	α	Mean	SD	α		
				SHONA/SHONA				
Neuroticism	88.8	14.5	.76	89.7	14.0	.77	.87	−.75
Extraversion	106.5	14.7	.81	106.4	13.4	.80	.92	.13
Openness	98.6	12.9	.68	97.7	12.4	.69	.78	.65
Agreeableness	122.9	14.4	.78	122.2	12.0	.72	.80	.55
Conscientiousness	130.5	15.6	.83	130.1	14.7	.81	.81	.28
				SHONA/ENGLISH				
Neuroticism	82.5	17.6	.86	84.8	15.6	.81	.78	-1.32
Extraversion	109.1	12.2	.74	108.8	11.0	.63	.66	−.35
Openness	106.0	13.2	.73	107.0	13.3	.75	.77	−.73
Agreeableness	124.4	14.5	.80	122.4	13.1	.75	.80	1.45
Conscientiousness	129.5	18.6	.90	130.0	14.6	.82	.70	−.22
				ENGLISH/SHONA				
Neuroticism	91.0	16.9	.84	86.3	16.6	.84	.77	2.35*
Extraversion	107.1	13.1	.75	106.0	13.0	.77	.82	1.95
Openness	103.8	13.3	.74	103.9	12.8	.71	.75	−.08
Agreeableness	126.9	14.3	.78	127.5	13.2	.77	.56	−.25
Conscientiousness	124.7	15.6	.85	125.4	18.2	.90	.83	−.40
				ENGLISH/ENGLISH				
Neuroticism	85.2	18.6	.87	84.1	19.5	.89	.92	.93
Extraversion	111.3	17.1	.83	110.7	15.4	.80	.95	.66
Openness	105.7	12.9	.71	106.0	13.6	.76	.87	−.24
Agreeableness	121.5	19.1	.87	122.4	18.7	.88	.93	−.87
Conscientiousness	122.6	22.5	.92	122.9	23.5	.93	.93	−.22

Note. The time interval between test and retest was approximately 7 days. All retest correlations are significant at $p < .001$. *$p < .05$.

the last column show, neither order of presentation nor language itself had much effect on mean levels. (The English version of N showed a higher mean level in Group 3, but this finding was not replicated in Group 2.) Retest correlations for the Shona version (shown in the top panel) are all lower than those for the English version (bottom panel), but still reasonably high. Of particular importance in this table are results for the Shona-English and English-Shona groups (middle panels). The retest correlations, ranging from .59 to .86, reflect the cross-language-and-time convergence of the two versions. Corrected for retest unreliability (estimated in the other two groups), these values ranged from .69 to .97, suggesting that factors from the two versions measure closely related constructs. These values are comparable to those seen in a similar study of a Korean translation (Piedmont & Chae, 1997), but lower than those reported in a Hong Kong study (McCrae et al., 1998).

The cross-language correlation for Activity (only three of whose items survived

Table 3. *Principal Components Analysis of the Shona NEO-PI-R Facet Scales Using an Orthogonal Procrustes Rotation.*

Shona NEO-PI-R Scale	Factor					Facet
	N	E	O	A	C	Con.
N1: Anxiety	**.66**	−.04	−.04	.01	−.14	.99**
N2: Angry Hostility	**.53**	−.18	.06	−.39	−.16	.96**
N3: Depression	**.60**	−.17	.15	.01	**−.40**	.94**
N4: Self-Consciousness	**.58**	−.11	.13	.13	−.19	.94**
N5: Impulsiveness	**.58**	.20	−.03	−.34	−.36	.96**
N6: Vulnerability	**.57**	.05	−.26	.03	**−.46**	.93*
E1: Warmth	−.24	**.61**	.03	.39	.21	.96**
E2: Gregariousness	−.14	**.59**	−.01	.39	−.07	.89*
E3: Assertiveness	**−.51**	.22	.27	−.26	.14	.88*
E4: Activity	−.15	.35	.05	.01	**.42**	.85
E5: Excitement Seeking	−.02	.35	**.52**	−.04	−.30	.59
E6: Positive Emotions	.04	**.65**	.30	.25	.09	.96**
O1: Fantasy	.27	.25	.28	**−.54**	−.07	.69
O2: Aesthetics	.01	**.40**	**.53**	.10	.16	.83
O3: Feelings	**.47**	.32	.22	−.08	.21	.90*
O4: Actions	−.03	.15	.38	.09	.14	.89*
O5: Ideas	−.22	−.07	**.73**	.04	.21	.98**
O6: Values	−.18	.00	**.59**	.18	−.02	.87**
A1: Trust	**−.46**	.22	.07	**.46**	−.02	.97**
A2: Straightforwardness	−.13	−.04	−.10	**.61**	.38	.96**
A3: Altruism	−.34	.28	.25	.26	.39	.72
A4: Compliance	−.12	.20	−.27	**.61**	.31	.78
A5: Modesty	.10	−.32	.12	**.61**	.09	.82
A6: Tender-Mindedness	.10	.24	.25	**.54**	**.42**	.82
C1: Competence	−.29	.22	.10	−.09	**.57**	.97**
C2: Dutifulness	−.12	.03	.10	.27	**.72**	.86*
C3: Order	−.25	.13	.06	**.44**	**.65**	.96**
C4: Achievement Striving	−.06	.14	.10	.31	**.72**	.84
C5: Self-Discipline	−.29	.10	−.04	.30	**.67**	.95**
C6: Deliberation	−.29	−.02	.15	.34	**.63**	.89*
Factor Congruence	.94**	.89**	.80**	.83**	.93**	.89**

$N = 314$. Factors were rotated toward the American normative structure (Costa & McCrae, 1992). Loadings above .40 in absolute magnitude are in bold. * Congruence higher than that of 95% of rotations from random data. ** Congruence higher than that of 99% of rotations from random data (McCrae et al., 1996).

item analysis) was .17. Cross-language correlations for the remaining 29 facet scales ranged from .42 to .77, with a median of .61. Corrected for retest unreliability, these correlations would suggest substantial similarity between the Shona and English scales.

2.2 Factor Structure

In order to determine if the five-factor structure can be replicated in this data set, facet scores were factor analyzed using a principal components analysis. The first seven eigenvalues were 8.0, 2.7, 2.3, 1.5, 1.3, 1.0, 1.0, and 1.0. Parallel analysis suggested four factors, whereas the scree test clearly suggested five. To evaluate replicability with the FFM, the five-factor solution was examined. Varimax rotation of these factors showed a clear N factor and a recognizable E factor. Facets of O loaded on two different factors, and A and C facets were combined on a large first factor. Although this shows limited resemblance to the American varimax structure, it is possible that similarities are masked by essentially arbitrary factor rotations. As recommended by McCrae et al. (1996), these factors were therefore subjected to an orthogonal Procrustes rotation (Schönemann, 1966) using the normative data presented by Costa and McCrae (1992) as the target. The results of this analysis are presented in Table 3.

Congruence coefficients were calculated for each factor and for each facet scale (see McCrae et al., 1996). These values reflect the degree to which the rotated solution matches the target matrix. McCrae et al. (1996) presented values for determining the significance of these coefficients. As can be seen in Table 3, all five factors have statistically significant congruence values, and facet congruence coefficients indicate that 21 of the 30 facets significantly replicate patterns found in the normative data. Although the resemblance of these factors to the American structure is far greater than chance, it is not strong except in the cases of N and C. Indeed, by one criterion (MacCallum, Widaman, Zhang, & Hong, 1999), the replications of E and A would be considered *borderline* and that of O *poor*. Given the low internal consistencies of many of the facet scales, this is perhaps not surprising. To determine whether the relatively weak fit is due to problems with the Shona translation or whether it reflects real differences between American and Shona personality structures, we factored the English NEO-PI-R. Although the English version shows somewhat higher reliability, the sample size (n = 117) is marginal for a factor analysis. Thus, this cannot be considered a definitive test of the structure of personality in Shona-speaking people. The first eight eigenvalues were 6.7, 3.3, 2.6, 2.2, 1.5, 1.4, 1.1. and 1.1. Parallel analysis suggested four factors, the scree test, six. A five-factor solution was examined. Results are presented in Table 4.

All five domains and 26 of the 30 facets show better-than-chance replication of the American structure. Only E and O are borderline replications in this small sample; N, A, and C would be considered good replications. In both Shona and English analyses, the weakest factor is O, which has small loadings on both O1: Fantasy and O3: Feelings, and an unexpected large loading on E5: Excitement Seeking. The O factor in Shona culture thus shows some resemblance to Zuckerman's (1979) sensation seeking, which combines experience seeking with thrill and adventure seeking.

It might be argued that the relatively poor fit of the FFM in these data is evidence that some other factor structure is more suitable for Shona respondents. One way to explore that possibility is by conducting comparability analyses comparing structures from the English and Shona administrations. As Everett (1983) argued, the correct number of factors can be determined by noting the solution in which all factors are replicable in two different samples. Table 5 shows the results of such an analysis.

Everett suggested that all comparabilities should be greater than .90; by that criter-

Table 4. Principal Components Analysis of the English NEO-PI-R Facet Scales Using an Orthogonal Procrustes Rotation.

| English NEO-PI-R Scale | Factor | | | | | Facet |
	N	E	O	A	C	Con.
N1: Anxiety	**.68**	.18	−.09	−.06	−.24	.95**
N2: Angry Hostility	**.64**	−.12	−.13	−.37.	.06	.95**
N3: Depression	**.76**	.08	−.01	−.08	−.14	.96**
N4: Self-Consciousness	**.65**	−.17	.22	−.14	.06	.86*
N5: Impulsiveness	**.51**	.19	−.02	−.19	**−.49**	.95**
N6: Vulnerability	**.52**	−.16	−.10	.01	**−.56**	.95**
E1: Warmth	−.19	**.69**	.09	.27	.14	.98**
E2: Gregariousness	−.10	.34	.28	.05	−.14	.79
E3: Assertiveness	**−.56**	.29	**.40**	−.22	.16	.88*
E4: Activity	−.05	**.48**	−.13	−.30	.18	.86*
E5: Excitement Seeking	.28	.32	**.50**	−.17	−.12	.64
E6: Positive Emotions	.19	**.58**	.31	.24	.15	.90*
O1: Fantasy	−.10	.39	.33	−.18	−.37	.80
O2: Aesthetics	.21	−.02	**.64**	.16	**.41**	.93*
O3: Feelings	.30	.39	.29	−.14	.21	.94*
O4: Actions	−.25	.04	**.51**	−.02	−.14	.94*
O5: Ideas	−.06	.03	**.69**	.07	.37	.93*
O6: Values	−.31	.19	.30	.15	−.19	.78
A1: Trust	−.15	.38	.05	**.57**	.00	.92*
A2: Straightforwardness	−.14	−.28	.05	**.66**	.26	.95**
A3: Altruism	−.31	.55	.07	**.44**	.27	.93*
A4: Compliance	−.13	.17	−.03	**.67**	.22	.90*
A5: Modesty	.14	**−.50**	.06	**.60**	−.04	.82
A6: Tender-Mindedness	−.07	.18	.04	**.71**	.19	.94**
C1: Competence	−.33	.34	.06	.03	**.59**	.96**
C2: Dutifulness	−.13	−.19	.11	.08	**.70**	.85*
C3: Order	−.22	.12	−.02	**.44**	**.60**	.95**
C4: Achievement Striving	−.01	−.01	.18	.17	**.75**	.88*
C5: Self-Discipline	−.26	−.01	−.04	.21	**.76**	.96**
C6: Deliberation	−.21	−.21	−.01	.21	**.68**	.99**
Factor Congruence	.93**	.86**	.83**	.94**	.94**	.91**

N = 117. Factors were rotated toward the American normative structure (Costa & McCrae, 1992). Loadings above .40 in absolute magnitude are in bold. * Congruence higher than that of 95% of rotations from random data. ** Congruence higher than that of 99% of rotations from random data (McCrae et al., 1996).

ion only the two-factor solution is considered replicable. One of these factors contrasts N facets with A and C facets; the other combines E and O facets. These factors nicely replicate the higher-order structure proposed by Digman (1997) and interpreted by McCrae and Costa (1995) as negative and positive valence, respectively. In other

Table 5. Comparabilities for Varimax-Rotated Factors in English
And Shona Versions.

Factors	Factor Comparabilities after Varimax Rotation							
Rotated	1st	2nd	3rd	4th	5th	6th	7th	8th
8	.96	.87	.86	.77	.75	.66	.56	.20
7	.95	.91	.85	.64	.53	.42	.35	
6	.94	.91	.78	.68	.67	.20		
5	.88	.86	.82	.76	.72			
4	.78	.74	.73	.67				
3	.88	.86	.84					
2	.94	.90						

words, when fewer than five factors are retained, the result is no longer a substantive description of personality, but an artifact of evaluative bias.

However, Everett's rule-of-thumb was intended for comparisons of the same instrument in two different samples. Here two significantly different instruments—English and Shona—are compared, and a lower level of comparability might appropriately be accepted as evidence of replicability. It is clear that the five-factor solution is superior to the four-factor solution as well as to solutions with more than five factors. Together with results of scree tests, these analyses suggest that the FFM provides the optimal structure for the facets of the NEO-PI-R in Shona culture.

2.3. Correlations with ACL Scales

One reason the Shona results are less than perfect replications of the American structure may be that Shona respondents are more susceptible to effects of response sets such as social desirability. Evidence of this can be seen in correlations between domains. Both A and C are positively evaluated, and in American samples show a small positive correlation ($r = .24$; Costa & McCrae, 1992). By contrast, in the present sample, the correlation between A and C domains was .67. Similarly, the correlation between N and A is $-.25$ in the normative American sample, but $-.48$ in the Shona. Because of these large correlations, domain scores may be expected to show limited evidence of discriminant validity. In examining external correlates, it is probably better to use orthogonal factor scores.

In order to evaluate the construct validity of the Shona version of the NEO-PI-R, factor scores from the orthogonal Procrustes rotation were correlated with the scales of the ACL. Table 6 presents a summary of the correlates, organized by domain. For each domain, the ACL scales most highly (and distinctively) correlated with that domain in an American sample (Piedmont et al., 1991) were chosen as hypothesized convergent correlations. Few ACL scales are related to O—only three had correlations exceeding .30 in the Piedmont et al. study—but the other domains had a range of relevant scales, correlations with which provide evidence of validity.

As the Table shows, 22 of 23 convergent correlations were significant, showing a similar pattern of results in Zimbabwe as in America. There is also some evidence of

Table 6. Selected ACL Scale Correlates of NEO-PI-R Factor Scores.

	Shona NEO-PI-R Factor				
Domain/ACL Correlate	N	E	O	A	C
Neuroticism					
Adapted Child (.56)	**.44*****	−.16*	.16*	−.24***	−.40***
Succorance (.50)	**.38*****	−.19*	.10	.02	−.25***
Nurturant Parent (−.47)	**−.38*****	.14*	−.22**	.35***	.45***
Ideal Self (−.46)	**−.46*****	.16*	−.19**	.18*	.36***
Personal Adjustment (−.40)	**−.35*****	.18*	−.22**	.29***	.34***
Extraversion					
Self-Confidence (.51)	−.30***	**.33*****	−.12	.02	.24***
Dominance (.51)	−.27***	**.25*****	−.06	−.09	.19**
Heterosexuality (.50)	−.10	**.20****	.02	−.02	−.05
Free Child (.49)	−.28***	**.27*****	−.01	−.10	−.06
Exhibitionism (.44)	−.06	**.20****	.00	−.32***	−.15**
Openness					
Creative Personality (.42)	−.29***	.18*	**−.09**	−.13	.13
Change (.34)	.08	.10	**.20****	−.22**	−.16*
Welsh A-2 (.30)	.24***	−.13	**.19****	−.33***	−.24***
Agreeableness					
Critical Parent (−.55)	.31***	−.10	.15*	**−.35*****	−.18*
Autonomy (−.54)	.10	−.08	.14*	**−.38*****	−.19**
Aggression (−.49)	.20**	.02	.16*	**−.37*****	−.26***
Deference (.48)	−.16*	.07	−.15*	**.33*****	.20**
Nurturance (.46)	−.30***	.14*	−.18*	**.39*****	.29***
Conscientiousness					
Endurance (.53)	−.26***	.09	−.15*	.32***	**.46*****
Order (.51)	−.28***	.06	−.08	.34***	**.47*****
Military Leadership (.44)	−.17*	.05	−.08	.36***	**.39*****
Achievement (.44)	−.23**	.17*	−.09	.21**	**.42*****
Welsh A-4 (.42)	−.30***	.24***	−.22**	.28***	**.25*****

Note. N = 196. Correlation of the ACL scale with the NEO-PI-R factor in an American sample (Piedmont et al., 1991) is given in parentheses. Hypothesized convergent correlations are given in boldface. $*p < .05$; $**p < .01$; $***p < .001$.

discriminant validity: For most ACL scales (15 of 23), the convergent correlation is larger than any other in the row. Convergence is strongest for N, A, and C, perhaps because these correlations are inflated by shared evaluative bias.

3. PERSONALITY TRAITS IN AGRARIAN CULTURES

Overall the results of this study seem to support Church's (2000) conclusion that trait models are universally applicable, although they may work better in some cultures than in others. It was possible, though difficult, to translate the NEO-PI-R into Shona. Self-reports showed evidence of a consistent and stable self-image, although more at the domain than the facet level, and more in retest reliability than in internal consistency. Targeted factor analyses indicated that the Shona version of the NEO-PI-R gave better-than-chance replications of the factor structure for all factors and most facets. Expected age differences were found for four of the domains, and correlations with ACL scales generally replicated those reported by Piedmont et al. (1991), suggesting construct validity for the factors.

A more critical perspective on the results would point to many weaknesses. Coefficient alpha for most facet scales was lower than would normally be considered acceptable. By some criteria, factor replicability, especially of the O factor, would be considered poor or borderline at best. Domain scales intercorrelated strongly in ways that suggested the operation of evaluative biases.

There are three plausible explanations for these findings, which are, of course, not mutually exclusive. The first, and least interesting, blames the Shona translation. The translator was not a personality psychologist and may have missed the essential meaning of items. The fact that the English version appeared psychometrically superior is consistent with that interpretation. A new or revised translation, constructed by psychologists, might substantially improve the psychometric qualities of the instrument. However, it is also possible that the problems are inherent in the Shona language, which may lack equivalent terms for some English items. In that case, it might be necessary to write new items that assess the same constructs as they are expressed in Shona language (cf. Benet-Martínez & John, 2000).

A second possibility is that self-reports of personality are systematically distorted by response styles and biases. As Van de Vijver and Leung (2001) have observed, "the likelihood of finding method bias due to response styles may increase with the cultural distance of the groups" (p. 1020). In the present case, this is strongly suggested by the sizeable correlations among A, C, and (low) N domains. It is noteworthy that Heaven et al. (1994) also found that adjectives related to A and C formed a single large factor in a predominantly Black South African sample. Perhaps Sub-Saharan Africans tend to assess themselves chiefly in evaluative terms, regarding themselves as "good" (high A, high C) or "bad" (low A, low C). Such a relatively undifferentiated response might be due to the global cognitive style attributed to Africans (Okeke et al., 1999), and it might introduce error into the measurement of many constructs.

A third, and perhaps most interesting possiblity, is that some of the constructs measured by the NEO-PI-R, especially at the facet level, simply have no counterpart in Shona culture. For example, as in other collectivist cultures (McCrae, Yik et al., 1998), Altruism (generosity toward outgroup members) seems very alien. The Shona cannot understand why someone would donate time, energy, and money to a cause without receiving anything in return. Similarly, the thrill seeking, careless abandon of high Excitement Seeking—an essentially self-centered motivation—is also foreign to this very sociocentric, group cohesive culture. Although the broad personality domains of the FFM can be captured in this culture, especially if an English questionnaire is used, the localized failures in replication may offer some interesting points of departure for speculating about the cross-cultural generalizability of personality.

Extending research on the FFM to nonindustrialized, agrarian cultures may offer an opportunity to examine how personality traits arise and are shaped by cultural experience. Consider, for example, Openness to Experience, the factor least well replicated in the present study. There is ample evidence from Western cultures that O is strongly heritable (Riemann, Angleitner, & Strelau, 1997), and there is no reason to believe that the Shona lack variation in the relevant genes. But in a traditional society, where options and innovations are distinctly limited, individual differences in O may not be perceived, or may not be sufficiently important in daily life to warrant the development of a relevant vocabulary. Without the words to express it, men and women in traditional cultures may never develop well-defined self-concepts with respect to O. The Shona participants in the present study, of course, do not live in a strictly traditional society, but the relative weakness of the O factor may reflect the residual effects of centuries of collective experience in the preindustrialized world.

The salience of O as an individual difference variable in the West may be a recent response to urbanization and industrialization. The many new adaptive pressures these sociological changes incurred may have highlighted individual differences in reactions to novelty, distinguishing innovators from laggards (Rogers, 1983). That hypothesis can be tested in two ways. First, studies like the current one can examine personality in preindustrial, preferably preliterate, cultures. Are individual differences in O consistently overlooked in such cultures? Second, one might evaluate personality lexicons at different points in their development (cf. Benjafield & Muckenheim, 1989). It would be possible to examine the presence of various trait adjectives in Old, Middle, and Modern English. Do adjectives related to O increase over this time period? Do they appear chronologically later than adjectives related to E or A? This would be an intriguing finding, suggesting that observable personality structure may evolve as qualities of the cultural environment change and afford new opportunities for the expression of inherent but latent basic tendencies (McCrae & Costa, 1999).

At a more practical level, the data presented here encourage continued research on the FFM and the NEO-PI-R in a wide variety of cultures. Even the imperfect translation evaluated here would be useful for psychological research in Zimbabwe, and better instruments could doubtless be developed. We have not yet encountered a culture in which the trait approach is not applicable.

REFERENCES

Benet-Martínez, V., & John, O. P. (2000). Toward the development of quasi-indigenous personality constructs: Measuring Los Cinco Grandes in Spain with indigenous Castilian markers. American Behavioral Scientist, 141-157.

Benjafield, J., & Muckenheim, R. (1989). A further historicodevelopmental study of the interpersonal circumplex. Canadian Journal of Behavioural Science, 21, 83-93.

Berne, S. L. (1961). Transactional analysis in psychotherapy. NY: Grove Press.

Bond, M. H. (1979). Dimensions used in perceiving peers: Cross-cultural comparisons of Hong Kong, Japanese, American, and Filipino university students. International Journal of Psychology, 14, 47-56.

Bond, M. H., Makazato, H., & Shiraishi, D. (1975). Universality and distinctiveness in dimensions of Japanese person perception. Journal of Cross-Cultural Psychology, 6, 346-357.

Borkenau, P., & Ostendorf, F. (1990). Comparing exploratory and confirmatory factor analysis: A study on the 5-factor model of personality. Personality and Individual Differences, 11, 515-524.

Capara, B. V., Barbaranelli, C., Borgogni, L., & Perugini, M. (1993). The "Big Five Questionnaire": A new questionnaire to assess the Five-Factor Model. Personality and Individual Differences, 18, 193-200.

Church, A. T. (2000). Culture and personality: Toward an integrated cultural trait psychology. Journal of Personality, 68, 651-703.

Costa, P. T., Jr., & McCrae, R. R. (1989). Personality, stress, and coping: Some lessons from a decade of research. In K. S. Markides & C. L. Cooper (Eds.), Aging, stress, and health (pp. 267-283). New York: John Wiley.

Costa, P.T., Jr., & McCrae, R.R. (1992). *Revised NEO Personality Inventory: Professional manual.* Odessa, FL: Psychological Assessment Resources.

Costa, P. T., Jr., McCrae, R. R., & Dye, D. A. (1991). Facet scales for Agreeableness and Conscientiousness: A revision of the NEO Personality Inventory. *Personality and Individual Differences, 12,* 887-898.

Costa, P. T., Jr., McCrae, R. R., & Jónsson, F. H. (in press). Validity and utility of the Revised NEO Personality Inventory: Examples from Europe. In B. DeRaad & M. Perugini (Eds.), *Big Five assessment.* Göttingen, Germany: Hogrefe & Huber.

Costa, P. T., Jr., McCrae, R. R., Martin, T. A., Oryol, V. E., Senin, I. G., Rukavishnikov, A. A., Shimonaka, Y., Nakazato, K., Gondo, Y., Takayama, M., Allik, J., Kallasmaa, T., & Realo, A. (2000). Personality development from adolescence through adulthood: Further cross-cultural comparisons of age differences. In V. J. Molfese & D. Molfese (Eds.), *Temperament and personality development across the life span* (pp. 235-252). Hillsdale, NJ: Erlbaum.

Costa, P. T., Jr., Terracciano, A., & McCrae, R. R. (2001). Gender differences in personality traits across cultures: Robust and surprising findings. *Journal of Personality and Social Psychology, 81,* 322-331.

Cross, S. E., & Markus, H. R.. (1999). The cultural constitution of personality. In L. A. Pervin & O. P. John (Eds.), *Handbook of personality: Theory and research* (2nd. ed., pp. 378-396). New York: Guilford.

Diener, E., Diener, M., & Diener, C. (1995). Factors predicting the subjective well-being of nations. *Journal of Personality and Social Psychology, 69,* 851-864.

Digman, J. M. (1990). Personality structure: Emergence of the Five-Factor Model. *Annual Review of Psychology, 41,* 417-440.

Digman, J. M. (1997). Higher-order factors of the Big Five. *Journal of Personality and Social Psychology, 73,* 1246-1256.

Everett, J. E. (1983). Factor comparability as a means of determining the number of factors and their rotation. *Multivariate Behavioral Research, 18,* 197-218.

Gough, H. G., & Heilbrun, A. B. (1983). *The Adjective Check List manual.* Palo Alto, CA: Consulting Psychologists Press.

Heaven, P. C. L., Connors, J., Stones, C. R. (1994). Three or five personality dimensions? An analysis of natural language terms in two cultures. *Personality and Individual Differences, 17,* 181-189.

Heuchert, J. W. P., Parker, W. D., Stumpf, H., & Myburgh, C. P. H. (2000). The Five-Factor Model in South African college students. *American Behavioral Scientist, 44,* 112-125.

Horn, B. S. (2000). *A Xhosa translation of the Revised NEO Personality Inventory: A pilot study.* Unpublished master's thesis, University of Port Elizabeth.

Jackson, D. N. (1974). *Personality Research Form manual.* Port Huron, MI: Research Psychologists Press.

MacCallum, R. C., Widaman, K. F., Zhang, S., & Hong, S. (1999). Sample size in factor analysis. *Psychological Methods, 4,* 84-99.

McCrae, R. R., & Costa, P. T., Jr. (1995). Positive and negative valence within the Five-Factor Model. *Journal of Research in Personality, 20,* 443-460.

McCrae, R. R., & Costa, P. T., Jr. (1997). Personality trait structure as a human universal. *American Psychologist, 52,* 509-516.

McCrae, R. R., & Costa, P. T., Jr. (1999). A Five-Factor Theory of personality. In L. A. Pervin & O. P. John (Eds.), *Handbook of personality: Theory and research* (2nd ed., pp. 139-153). New York: Guilford.

McCrae, R. R., Costa, P. T., Jr., del Pilar, G. H., Rolland, J.-P., & Parker, W. D. (1998). Cross-cultural assessment of the Five-Factor Model: The Revised NEO Personality Inventory. *Journal of Cross-Cultural Psychology, 29,* 171-188.

McCrae, R. R., Costa, P. T., Jr., Pedroso de Lima, M., Simões, A., Ostendorf, F., Angleitner, A., Marušić, I, Bratko, D., Caprara, G. V., Barbaranelli, C., Chae, J-H, & Piedmont, R.L. (1999). Age differences in personality across the adult life span: Parallels in five cultures. *Developmental Psychology, 35,* 466-477.

McCrae, R. R., & John, O. P. (1992). An introduction to the Five-Factor Model and its applications. *Journal of Personality, 60,* 175-215.

McCrae, R. R., Yik, M. S. M., Trapnell, P. D., Bond, M. H., & Paulhus, D. L. (1998). Interpreting personality profiles across cultures: Bilingual, acculturation, and peer rating studies of Chinese undergraduates. *Journal of Personality and Social Psychology, 74,* 1041-1055.

McCrae, R. R., Zonderman, A. B., Costa, P. T., Jr., Bond, M. H., & Paunonen, S. B. (1996). Evaluating replicability of factors in the Revised NEO Personality Inventory: Confirmatory factor analysis versus Procrustes rotation. *Journal of Personality and Social Psychology, 70,* 552-566.

Murray, H. A. (1938). *Explorations in personality.* NY: Oxford University Press.

Nisbett, R. E., Peng, K., Choi, I., & Norenzayan, A. (2001). Culture and systems of thought: Holistic versus analytic cognition. *Psychological Review, 108,* 291-310.

Okeke, B. I., Draguns, J. G., Sheku, B., & Allen, W. (1999). Culture, self, and personality in Africa. In Y-H. Lee, C. R. McCauley, & J. G. Draguns (Eds.), *Personality and person perception across cultures* (pp. 139-162). Mahwah, NJ: Lawrence Erlbaum.

Ozer, D. J., & Riese, S. P. (1994). Personality assessment. *Annual Review of Psychology, 45,* 357-388.

Parin, P., & Parin-Mathèy, G. (1964). Ego and orality in the analysis of West Africans. *Psychoanalytic Study of Society, 3,* 197-203.

Patel, V., Simunyu, E., Gwanzura, F., Lewis, G., & Mann, A. (1997). The Shona Symptom Questionnaire: The development of an indigenous measure of common mental disorders in Harare. *Acta Psychiatrica Scandinavica, 95,* 469-475.

Paunonen, S. V., Jackson, D. N., Trzebinski, J., Forsterling, F. (1992). Personality structure across cultures: A multi-method evaluation. *Journal of Personality and Social Psychology, 62,* 447-456.

Piedmont, R. L. (1993). A longitudinal analysis of burnout in the health care setting: The role of personal dispositions. *Journanl of Personality Assessment, 61,* 457-473.

Piedmont, R. L., & Chae, J-H. (1997). Cross-cultural generalizability of the Five-Factor Model of personality: Development and validation of the NEO-PI-R for Koreans. *Journal of Cross-Cultural Psychology, 28,* 131-155.

Piedmont, R. L., & Ciarrocchi, J. W. (1999). The utility of the NEO-PI-R in an outpatient, drug rehabilitation context. *Psychology of Addictive Behaviors, 13,* 213-226.

Piedmont, R. L., McCrae, R. R., & Costa, P. T., Jr. (1991). Adjective Check List scales and the Five-Factor Model. *Journal of Personality and Social Psychology, 60,* 630-637.

Piedmont, R. L., & Weinstein, H. P. (1993). A psychometric evaluation of the new NEO-PI-R facet scales for Agreeableness and Conscientiousness. *Journal of Personality Assessment, 60,* 302-318.

Riemann, R., Angleitner, A., & Strelau, J. (1997). Genetic and environmental influences on personality: A study of twins reared together using the self-and peer report NEO-FFI scales. *Journal of Personality, 65,* 449-475.

Rogers, E. M. (1983). *Diffusion of innovations* (3rd ed.). New York: The Free Press.

Schöneman, P. H. (1966). A generalized solution of the orthogonal Procrustes problem. *Psychometrica, 31,* 1-10.

Shweder, R. A., & Sullivan, M. A. (1993). Cultural psychology: Who needs it? *Annual Review of Psychology, 44,* 497-523.

Van de Vijver, F., & Leung, K. (2001). Personality in cultural context: Methodological issues. *Journal of Personality, 69,* 1005-1031.

Welsh, G. S. (1975). *Creativity and intelligence: A personality approach.* Chapel Hill, NC: University of North Carolina, Institute for Research in Social Issues.

Wiggins, J. S. (1996). *The Five-Factor Model of personality: Theoretical perspectives.* New York: Guilford .

Wilson, D., Doolabh, A., Cooney, J., Khalpey, M., & Siddiqui, S. (1990). A cross-cultural validation of the Personality Research Form in Zimbabwe. *International Journal of Psychology, 25,* 1-12.

Witkin, H. A., & Berry, J. W. (1975). Psychological differentiation in cross-cultural perspective. *Journal of Cross-Cultural Psychology, 6,* 4-87.

Yang, K-S., & Bond, M. H. (1990). Exploring implicit personality theories with indigenous or imported constructs: The Chinese case. *Journal of Personality and Social Psychology, 58,* 1087-1095.

Zimbabwe. (1993). In *The new encyclopedia Britannica* (Vol. 12, pp. 916-917). Chicago: Encyclopedia Britannica.

Zuckerman, M. (1979). *Sensation seeking: Beyond the optimal level of arousal.* Hillsdale, NJ: Erlbaum.

AUTHOR NOTE

The authors would like to thank Mr. George Nyakupinda for translating NEO-PI-R items into Shona and Mr. A. Madukeko and Ms. Pelagia Chiwayi for backtranslating into English, as well as Ronald Mcainsh and Peter Chiroro for their assistance in the collection of data. Address correspondence to Ralph L. Piedmont, Department of Pastoral Counseling, Loyola College in Maryland, 7135 Minstrel Way, Columbia, MD, 21045. E-mail: rpiedmont@loyola.edu

FIVE-FACTOR MODEL AND NEO-PI-R IN TURKEY

SAMI GÜLGÖZ

Koç University, Istanbul, Turkey

Abstract. Personality testing in Turkey has escalated in recent years even though the number of tests with solid psychometric properties is very low. Tests developed or adapted in recent years show a tendency to reveal a structure similar to that of Five-Factor Model. The Turkish version of the NEO-PI-R produced a factor structure that had five factors and that was congruent with the original factor structure. The scores from the adult sample showed some discrepancies from the original normative sample. Correlations with age and gender differences were similar to those obtained in other studies. The discrepancies between the Turkish adult sample and the American normative sample are possibly functions of cultural differences as well as the contextual factors that were influential on the response patterns of the Turkish sample. A second study with bilingual respondents displayed high correlations between the scores on the English and Turkish versions of the NEO-PI-R, and there were significant differences between the two versions on four facet scores. These differences are interpreted in the framework of cultural contexts triggered by language.

Keywords: Language, context effects, factor structures, psychological assessment

1. INTRODUCTION

Personality theories have dual purposes. One purpose is to reach a general description of human personality characteristics that are relatively stable and that depict all human beings. The second purpose is to identify the sources of variation between people and to define dimensions of such variation. Today, many of the personality theories seem to focus on the sources of variation rather than invariant characteristics. If some particular tendency is basic and present in all humans at the same magnitude, then it does not account for any variation and therefore is less relevant to many of the current personality theories.

Studying variation and invariance in personality across cultures can be a tricky endeavor. First, in order to determine the invariant characteristics across cultures, researchers need to develop measurement devices that will produce the same category of responses irrespective of the language and the cultural context in which the device is presented. Second, in every culture, the measurement device must be composed of items that reflect the ordinary behavior of the respondents in. Third, the response patterns of the respondents must not be under the influence of any culturally directed tendency such as a tendency to agree or disagree, to respond in the extremes, to respond in a socially desirable manner (at least more so than other cultures), or to undervalue certain traits. Given these possible confounding circumstances, to achieve invariance across cultures is a highly remote possibility. Therefore, the consistency attained by the Five-Factor Model in different cultures, using various personality tests, cannot be regarded as coincidental. The aim of this chapter is to present the results of the recent standardization process of the NEO-PI-R in Turkey with the dual perspective of discovering invariant components and revealing the divergence.

2. PERSONALITY ASSESSMENT IN TURKEY

The history of personality testing is not very long in Turkey (Kağıtçıbaşı, 1994). Adequate test development or standardization began in early seventies leading to published tests within the same decade. Well-known examples of the seventies and the eighties are the MMPI (Savaşır, 1981), which is limited to clinical populations; Hacettepe Personality Inventory (Özgüven, 1992), a multi-purpose test that was developed using rather small sample sizes for reliability and validity studies; the Eysenck Personality Questionnaire (Bayar, 1983); California Psychological Inventory (Demirtürk, 1987), composed of 18 subtests; and Symptom Distress Checklist (Kılıç, 1987), also a clinically-oriented checklist type test. Between the early 1970s and mid-1990s there have been several translations and adaptations generally characterized by small sample size and restricted populations, generally in theses and dissertations (Öner, 1994). Many of these tests on limited samples do not meet the minimum standards for being considered adequate adaptations.

Recent years have rekindled interest in personality testing partly due to the developments in personnel selection and career planning and the demand associated with these trends. Although companies reportedly use a large number of personality tests that were developed locally and a number that are translations of tests developed elsewhere, documentation for many of these tests is not available. Therefore, the discussion in this chapter will be limited to those tests for which there is documentation and sufficient research.

The Adjective Check List (ACL; Gough & Heilbrun, 1983) is one of the tests developed outside Turkey that has been adapted to Turkey (Savran, 1993). In its adaptation study, where the sample consisted of 350 males and 350 females, the Turkish version of the ACL showed the same factorial structure as the original version, with substantial reliability and validity. In a subsequent study with managers using the ACL (Sinangil, Savran, Öneş, & Balcı, 1997), the researchers found differences on the dimensions of order, military leadership, endurance, ideal self, and achievement, between first line, middle, and upper-level managers. They also observed correlations between age and order (.41), endurance (.39), military leadership (.31), change (–.25), and personal adjustment (.23). In another study, Savran and Balcı (1998) tested for differences in ACL factors in studies after studying counseling. They tested students in their freshmen and senior years and found that in their senior year, students scored higher in thirteen of the 24 dimensions, and they scored lower in four dimensions. Recently, the 28 scales of the ACL were subjected to a factor analysis and resulted in a five-factor solution approximating the factors of the Five-Factor Model (Savran, 2001).

In another adjective-based test, Tevrüz and Türk Smith (1996) developed a self-rating scale of 43 adjectives. They presented it to 236 undergraduate students and obtained a six-factor solution. In a second study (Türk Smith & Tevrüz, 1998), the authors revised the scale to contain 36 of the items in the previous version and presented these items to 120 undergraduate students. The participants of the study rated themselves, a disliked person, a liked person, the ideal person, and the typical person in their peer group. The final factor structure contained six factors that included Talent (*clever, brave, strong, perfect, superior, creative, talented*), Compliance (*humble, patient, calm, silent, easygoing, gentle*), Liveliness (*active, close, dynamic, cheerful, comical, talkative, joyful, loving, warm, teasing*), Restlessness (*conflicted, capricious, pessimist, aggressive, worried, nervous, impatient*), Determination (*determined, ambitious*), and Egoism (*selfish, egoistical*). Despite the limited number of items, small number of participants, and the fact that all the participants were undergraduate students, the factor structure resembled closely that of the Five-Factor Model. Two factors, Talent and Determination, represent Conscientiousness. Two other factors, Compliance and (low) Egoism, seem to match Agreeableness. The factors Liveliness and Restlessness have their exact matches in Extraversion and Neuroticism, respectively. One factor in the Five-Factor Model, Openness, has no counterpart in this particular study, but that is probably due to the limited range of adjectives in the initial item pool.

Somer (1998; Somer & Goldberg, 1999) has developed another test, based on adjectives descriptive of personality. After a thorough and meticulous selection of adjectives from the Turkish language lexicon, Somer and Goldberg (1999) developed a 235-item personality inventory. The development and validation of the test spanned three studies. The first study helped determine the adjectives, and in the second study the items were applied to 945 university students. In the third study (Somer, 1998), the inventory was given to 538 adults with an age range of 19-65. All three studies produced a factor structure similar to the five factors of McCrae and Costa (1997). Even though Somer and Goldberg (1999) expressed an expectation that the fifth factor would be closer to Intellect, the item clustering resembled the Openness factor. The order of emergence was consistent in both studies: Extraversion, Conscientiousness, Agreeableness, Neuroticism, and Openness.

Sümer, Sümer, Çifçi, and Demirutku (2000) developed a personality test specialized for personnel selection in the Turkish military. As a first step, they conducted a job analysis, and they had the personality characteristics resulting from the job analysis rated for relevance and importance. Factor analysis of these ratings revealed five factors: Conscientiousness, Military Factor, Self-Confidence, Agreeableness-Extraversion, and Leadership. As a next step, they developed a 242-item scale and applied them to 519 active officers. The analysis of these items revealed four factors similar to the previous factors except that Self-Confidence was subsumed under the Leadership factor.

In a separate study, Sümer et al. (2000) made modifications to the 242-item scale and applied the resulting 248-item version to 698 active officers. This final version of the test had 16 sub-factors that were organized under four major factors and three independent sub-factors. The first factor was the Military Factor and it included orderliness, commitment, military discipline, and strength of character. The second factor was Leadership, which included persuasion, group leading, tolerance of stress, determinedness, decision-making and problem solving. Conscientiousness was the third factor, subsuming work discipline, planning, and openness to development. The fourth factor was called Extraversion-Agreeableness and it included sociability, Agreeableness, and relationship with superior. Communication, monitoring task progress, and self-confidence sub-factors each loaded on a different factor. Some of the factors in this test seem to be agreeing with the trends in personality dimensions of various trait theories (e.g., Costa & McCrae, 1992; Goldberg, 1990). However, there seems to be more agreement between Sümer et al. (2000) and Costa and McCrae (1992) at the sub-factor level than at the level of the main factors. Conscientiousness was a main factor in Sümer et al.'s research but one of the sub-factors, openness to development, was more relevant to the Openness factor, which did not emerge in their study. Sümer et al.'s Military Factor includes sub-factors that may be associated positively with Conscientiousness and negatively with Neuroticism and Agreeableness. Leadership factor includes sub-factors that were associated positively with Extraversion and Conscientiousness, and negatively with Neuroticism. Thus, the configuration of the sub-factors indicated that for a very specific population (predominantly male, young military officers), a different set of factors might be generated. However, one needs to bear in mind that the items were rated for relevance and kept if they met the condition of relevance for the task. The task-oriented test items may have shifted away from the purpose of measuring personality towards measuring acquired habits that are appropriate for the military tasks.

Sümer et al. (2000) have competently developed a tool to measure the necessary characteristics for military personnel. Their tool may not qualify completely as a personality test but it is appropriate for their purposes and their findings may provide some information specific to a particular segment of the Turkish population. The items were selected for relevance to military activity and therefore any item that was deemed to be irrelevant was left out. The personality characteristics not included in the resulting structure may be those characteristics perceived to be irrelevant to functioning in the military environment. Their work may also exemplify the cultural differences within a group for which uniformity is incorrectly assumed. The evidence from Sümer et al. (2000) is not sufficient to warrant such a conclusion because item pool is purposive. However, the possibility that the structure of the test items for the military may not reflect the same structure for the overall Turkish population may suggest that there is possibly as much variation within Turkish sub-populations as between Turkish and other populations.

The recent trend in personality testing in Turkey has been towards adjective-based tests with the exception of Sümer et al.'s (2000) test for a limited population. The NEO-PI-R has gone through the adaptation process concurrently with some of the other tests indicated in this section. The development of another test composed of items in the spirit of NEO-PI-R is currently underway by O. Somer (personal communication, January 16, 2001) based on Goldberg's International Personality Item Pool. With the presence of these two tests, substantial research with the five-factor perspective should be possible in the future.

3. THE TURKISH NEO-PI-R

For the Turkish version of the NEO-PI-R, the translation was performed by the author, who is Turkish, has studied English beginning in secondary school, and has studied and worked in the U.S. for nine years. The translation of the items was double-checked by a colleague who has studied, taught, and published in English in the area of clinical psychology. Once the translation was considered adequate, a faculty member in the History Department of Koç University who was not familiar with theories of personality, who was multilingual, and for whom both English and Turkish were foreign languages, backtranslated it into English. The back translation was then sent to Robert McCrae, and upon his comments, modifications were made and the final backtranslations were sent for final approval. Most of the comments about the translation reflected problems with the backtranslation or wordings that were open to multiple interpretations. The final approved version was free of such problems.

One of the difficulties in translation is rooted in the structure of language. Turkish is a Ural-Altaic language that was influenced by Arabic and Persian during the Ottoman Empire and has undergone a purification process after the establishment of the Turkish Republic in 1923. The sentence structure is Subject-Object-Verb, although there is much flexibility in that ordering. The major difficulty in translating test items in English to Turkish is the lack of as many verbs with nuances in Turkish. The verb in Turkish for *like, enjoy,* or *love* is the same word: *sevmek.* According to Talmy's (1985) typology, verb-framed languages like Turkish indicate path of action more than manner of action. The rarity of manner verbs necessitates an indirect description of the state by adjectives and adverbs in the translation so that the spirit of the item is preserved. The same is true for words that do not have a direct translation. It has always been a question whether the lack of a word in one language is indicative of the lack of that concept in that culture (Whorf, 1956). For example, if there is no single word in Turkish for the word *apprehensive,* does that mean speakers of Turkish never feel apprehensive, although they do feel anxious? The chapters in this volume present an answer to this question as well as the issue of how basic are our basic tendencies.

Another set of items that presented difficulty were those that were culturally American in content. For example, vacationing in Las Vegas, starting a self-improvement program, vacationing in an isolated cabin in the woods, and the new morality of permissiveness may be considered specific to a particular culture. Fortunately, the NEO-PI-R contained few items in that category. In some of these items, alternative situations that preserved the spirit of the item were presented.

The translation process did not produce any other difficulties, but there were minor modifications afterwards based on the wording recommendations by test takers or the research team.

There was an unforeseen predicament in the application of the scale to Turkish people, which may be related to the unfamiliarity of the five-point scales. In previous research with illiterate or semi-literate participants, we had observed participants having difficulty in fine-tuning between *disagree* and *strongly disagree* or *agree* and *strongly agree* responses. The participants responding to the NEO-PI-R were all literate and most were high school graduates or better. Still, some of them had problems in distinguishing between the two gradations of a response, especially when the item contained a qualifying adverb such as *rarely, seldom, often,* or *occasionally.* The participants in our sample frequently asked what the difference was between disagreeing and strongly disagreeing with a statement saying that you do something infrequently. With careful explanation by the research team, the respondents were able to respond using the whole scale. However, it remains an empirical issue to ascertain whether a three-point scale would produce the same outcome. Indeed, this may not be a language-specific problem but a logical problem present in many or all languages.

3.1. Psychometric and Normative Data for the Turkish NEO-PI-R

In the first study, the Turkish translation of the NEO-PI-R was given to participants for the purpose of observing its psychometric properties as well as obtaining normative data. The sample in this study included 804 participants, 301 undergraduate students and 503 working adults. Among the students, 137 were females, 123 were males and 41 did not indicate gender. They were representative samples from three consecutive entering groups at Koç University, Istanbul. The adult sample consisted of employees of a large company with various positions and levels of education. The company did not employ any selection procedure that included testing, except skill tests for positions requiring specific skills. Among the working adults 216 were females and 287 were males. For the 464 participants reporting age in this group, the age range was between 18 and 54 with the mean age of 29.2 ($SD = 5.6$). Together with the student sample, the mean age was 24.8 ($SD = 7.0$).

The test booklets and the answer sheets were designed to resemble the original version but they were printed in black on one side of the sheets.

The students were tested in groups of 10 to 24 people. They were invited to participate for 90 minutes so that they could respond without rushing. A member of the research team gave instructions verbally in addition to the written instructions. Most participants completed in approximately 45 minutes. The employees were verbally instructed on how to respond, with the specific instruction that they should complete the inventory alone whenever they could spare the necessary uninterrupted time. A member of the research team was available in person or by telephone at all times. The respondents were asked whether they had responded alone without interruption when they returned the tests. There were no reported problems in the administration of the tests.

3.1.1. Descriptive Statistics and Correlations

Table 1 shows the descriptive statistics for each of the domains and facets. The results for college students closely resemble the statistics for their American counterparts. The adults, however, show major differences in all five factors. Overall, Turkish adults show lower averages for Neuroticism and Agreeableness and higher averages for Extraversion, Openness, and Conscientiousness factors. For Neuroticism and Openness, the differences appear to stem from the female adult participants, because there are only minor differences between Turkish and American adult males on these factors.

Next, correlations between the facets were examined. There are several patterns in

Table 1. Means and Standard Deviations for NEO-PI-R Domains and Facets.

	Student						Adult					
	Female		Male		Total		Female		Male		Total	
Scale	M	SD	M	SD	M	SD	M	SD	M	SD	M	SD
N	99.1	20.9	94.6	20.0	97.0	20.6	72.2	17.8	68.8	16.5	70.3	17.1
E	122.3	22.3	121.8	21.3	122.0	21.8	128.1	16.6	123.8	18.2	125.7	17.6
O	120.8	18.5	114.7	17.9	117.9	18.4	123.5	16.3	115.5	18.0	119.0	17.7
A	109.0	20.4	107.5	17.4	108.3	19.1	114.4	13.8	112.6	14.8	113.3	14.4
C	112.4	23.0	115.0	23.0	113.6	23.0	144.3	17.6	145.4	16.5	144.9	17.0
N1	16.6	5.3	15.6	4.6	16.1	5.0	11.3	4.3	10.7	4.1	11.0	4.2
N2	16.6	5.0	16.0	5.4	16.3	5.2	12.5	4.4	11.7	4.4	12.1	4.4
N3	16.2	5.3	15.1	5.2	15.7	5.3	10.2	4.3	10.2	4.2	10.2	4.2
N4	18.1	4.6	17.5	4.3	17.8	4.5	16.0	4.5	15.9	3.9	15.9	4.2
N5	17.8	4.7	17.7	4.0	17.7	4.4	13.8	4.0	13.2	3.6	13.5	3.8
N6	13.6	4.8	13.0	5.0	13.3	4.9	8.4	4.0	7.4	3.6	7.8	3.8
E1	22.3	4.2	21.7	4.4	22.0	4.3	21.6	3.8	20.6	4.2	21.0	4.0
E2	20.5	5.3	20.3	5.9	20.4	5.6	22.5	4.2	21.0	5.0	21.6	4.8
E3	15.9	5.3	16.8	4.5	16.4	4.9	19.0	4.4	19.4	4.4	19.2	4.4
E4	18.8	4.4	19.0	4.6	18.9	4.5	20.7	3.8	19.9	3.5	20.3	3.7
E5	22.1	4.7	21.1	4.5	21.6	4.7	20.4	4.3	20.7	4.3	20.5	4.3
E6	23.0	6.4	22.1	5.1	22.6	5.8	23.9	3.9	22.3	4.3	23.0	4.2
O1	19.8	4.2	20.1	4.2	19.9	4.2	17.6	5.0	17.9	4.8	17.8	4.9
O2	21.2	5.8	19.0	6.0	20.2	6.0	22.4	4.2	19.5	5.1	20.8	5.0
O3	22.5	4.2	22.2	3.8	22.4	4.0	21.8	3.7	20.0	4.2	20.8	4.1
O4	17.1	6.2	15.7	4.2	16.4	5.4	19.8	4.2	18.0	4.3	18.8	4.4
O5	18.6	5.6	17.0	6.4	17.8	6.0	19.7	4.6	18.6	5.3	19.1	5.0
O6	21.7	3.7	20.8	4.0	21.3	3.9	22.2	3.2	21.4	3.4	21.7	3.3
A1	17.1	4.6	17.4	4.9	17.2	4.7	18.2	4.3	17.8	4.6	18.0	4.4
A2	20.0	5.7	19.4	6.3	19.7	6.0	21.8	4.2	21.1	4.3	21.4	4.3
A3	23.5	4.4	23.5	3.9	23.5	4.2	25.9	3.4	25.2	3.4	25.5	3.4
A4	13.5	5.2	13.5	4.9	13.5	5.1	15.3	4.1	15.4	4.3	15.4	4.2
A5	15.9	5.4	14.5	5.2	15.3	5.3	15.3	4.0	15.4	4.3	15.3	4.2
A6	19.3	3.8	18.7	3.8	19.0	3.8	17.9	3.1	17.8	3.6	17.8	3.4
C1	20.9	3.9	21.0	4.0	21.0	4.0	24.6	3.0	24.6	3.2	24.6	3.1
C2	16.0	6.9	17.0	6.9	16.5	6.9	22.0	5.3	22.5	4.8	22.2	5.1
C3	21.4	4.4	21.0	4.8	21.2	4.6	26.7	3.1	26.6	3.1	26.7	3.1
C4	19.4	5.1	20.2	5.0	19.8	5.1	25.3	3.9	25.5	4.0	25.4	3.9
C5	17.5	5.3	18.3	5.2	17.9	5.3	25.2	3.6	25.1	3.2	25.2	3.3
C6	17.1	4.8	17.3	4.7	17.2	4.7	20.5	4.0	21.1	4.0	20.9	4.0

Note. N = Neuroticism, E = Extraversion, O = Openness to Experience, A = Agreeableness, C = Conscientiousness. See Table 2 for facet scale labels.

the correlation matrix that are worth mentioning. First, the intercorrelations among the facets of Agreeableness were generally low, especially the correlations of the other facets with A5: Modesty and A6: Tender-Mindedness. Other noticeably low correlations within domains were those between N4: Self-Consciousness and N5: Impulsiveness and between O1: Fantasy and O4: Actions. The intercorrelations among the facets of Conscientiousness were the highest. These facets also showed large negative correlations with N1: Depression and N6: Vulnerability. (The complete correlation matrix is available from the author.)

3.1.2. Factor Structure

A principal components factor analysis was conducted in the full sample ($N = 804$). The scree plot and the eigenvalues both clearly suggested five factors. Table 2 displays the factor structure obtained after a Varimax rotation, the variance accounted for by each factor, and congruence coefficients with the American normative structure for the five factors. The resulting factor structure supports the five factors intended in the original NEO-PI-R. Except for one facet, N5: Impulsiveness, which loads somewhat more highly on Conscientiousness than it does on Neuroticism, the largest loading of all the facets are on the same factors as in the original structure. Procrustes rotation produced variable congruence coefficients between 0.88 and 1.00 for the facets, with only three facets having coefficients less than 0.95.

This is indicative of a successful adaptation process for the NEO-PI-R as well as support for the cross-cultural validity of the Five-Factor Model. The order of emergence in the analysis is worth noting as well: Conscientiousness, Extraversion, Neuroticism, Openness, and Agreeableness. Other research with Turkish samples such as Somer (1998), Somer and Goldberg (1999), and Türk Smith and Tevrüz (1998) all culminate in the same structure. The five-factor structure is supported not only by adaptations of tests (e.g., the Adjective Check List by Savran, 1993), but also by tests developed from a pool of personality-descriptive adjectives in Turkish (Somer, 1998; Somer & Goldberg, 1999) and one developed from a limited number of selected adjectives (Türk Smith & Tevrüz, 1998).

In the Varimax factor structure of the Turkish NEO-PI-R, the factor with the highest portion of the variance was Conscientiousness. In addition to the expected facets of Conscientiousness, four more facets had high loadings (> .4) on this factor. A3: Altruism loaded in the same direction with the Conscientiousness facets and N3: Depression, N5: Impulsiveness, and N6: Vulnerability loaded negatively.

The loading of Altruism with other Conscientiousness facets may not be surprising to those familiar with the Turkish culture, where helping others is considered a civic responsibility as well as being part of the customs. It is equally likely that conceptualization of altruism may vary according to the culture and the level of relatedness among the individuals in that culture (Kağıtçıbaşı, 1996a). Altruism is a natural necessity when there is a high level of connectedness among the members of a culture. In cultures where the self is construed in relationship to the community, helping behavior is the norm rather than the exception. Many visitors to countries like Turkey are surprised (and sometimes annoyed) by the extent of assistance they receive from

Table 2. *Factor Structure of the Turkish NEO-PI-R, Congruence with the Original Factor Structure, and Internal Consistency Coefficients for the Facets.*

NEO-PI-R Facet	N	E	O	A	C	Alpha
	\multicolumn{5}{c}{Varimax-Rotated Component}	
N1: Anxiety	**.74**	−.10	.00	−.10	−.38	.75
N2: Angry Hostility	**.62**	.09	−.07	**−.43**	−.26	.70
N3: Depression	**.67**	−.25	−.04	.00	**−.46**	.77
N4: Self-Consciousness	**.69**	−.23	−.12	.11	−.02	.44
N5: Impulsiveness	**.42**	.27	.13	−.17	**−.53**	.59
N6: Vulnerability	**.62**	−.09	−.04	.00	**−.58**	.78
E1: Warmth	−.01	**.71**	.16	.33	−.07	.66
E2: Gregariousness	−.27	**.70**	−.02	.08	.12	.75
E3: Assertiveness	**−.41**	**.49**	.13	−.28	.38	.73
E4: Activity	−.03	**.62**	.15	−.22	.27	.56
E5: Excitement-Seeking	−.03	**.68**	.13	−.20	−.10	.62
E6: Positive Emotions	−.14	**.71**	.25	.08	.09	.67
O1: Fantasy	.05	.23	**.51**	−.10	−.36	.68
O2: Aesthetics	.13	.13	**.75**	.11	.16	.74
O3: Feelings	.22	.39	**.62**	−.03	−.07	.66
O4: Actions	−.32	.15	**.51**	−.18	.15	.63
O5: Ideas	−.19	−.04	**.74**	−.02	.13	.77
O6: Values	−.34	.08	**.48**	.04	−.09	.45
A1: Trust	−.19	.27	.09	**.63**	−.01	.72
A2: Straightforwardness	−.01	−.18	−.02	**.61**	.26	.66
A3: Altruism	−.02	.31	.03	**.60**	.41	.72
A4: Compliance	−.19	−.26	−.06	**.68**	.13	.64
A5: Modesty	.14	−.34	−.14	**.51**	−.05	.72
A6: Tender-Mindedness	.25	.30	.00	**.55**	−.15	.44
C1: Competence	−.25	.29	.14	−.03	**.73**	.69
C2: Order	−.05	−.02	.01	.08	**.78**	.84
C3: Dutifulness	−.06	.03	.01	.27	**.82**	.72
C4: Achievement Striving	−.12	.29	.09	−.15	**.76**	.81
C5: Self-Discipline	−.30	.12	.02	.04	**.83**	.83
C6: Deliberation	−.17	−.21	−.03	.15	**.74**	.73
Percent of Variance	11.2	12.5	8.4	9.5	18.0	
Congruence coefficient	.96	.96	.97	.98	.96	

Note. N = 804. Factors have been reordered.

total strangers, let alone individuals they have met. Farmers often rely on solidarity among members of the community for seasonal help. Similarly, preparation for a wedding in traditional communities is an activity in which all the members of the community give a hand to the parents of the bride and the groom.

Impulsiveness is naturally contradictory with Conscientiousness because an impulsive person would lack self-discipline and deliberation. Similar loadings for Impulsiveness and Vulnerability were present in findings reported by McCrae (2000), McCrae and Costa (1997a), and Piedmont and Chae (1997). Finally, Depression items may be considered somewhat contradictory with those of Competence, Achievement-Striving, and Self-Discipline, which are the facets of Conscientiousness.

The Extraversion domain was the second largest factor, defined only by the expected facets. The third factor, Neuroticism, contained a high negative loading of Assertiveness in addition to all the Neuroticism facets. This indicates that lack of assertiveness can be considered a sign of neurotic behavior, although intuitively in the Turkish culture, one would expect extreme assertiveness to be considered neurotic. McCrae and Costa (1997a) have also reported similar negative correlations between Assertiveness and Neuroticism in several cultures, supporting a link between assertiveness and dominance and the perception of dominance as a trait of emotionally stable individuals. Heuchert, Parker, Stumpf, and Myburgh (2000) and Mastor, Jin, and Cooper (2000) have also observed that Assertiveness loaded on Neuroticism in South Africans and Malays. Agreeableness was the fourth factor with all the expected facets loading on it. Agreeableness also included Angry Hostility as a secondary loading, in the reverse direction. This outcome resembles that obtained by Costa and McCrae (1992) in the factor structure of the original inventory as well as those by Heuchert et al. (2000), Mastor et al., (2000), McCrae and Costa (1997a), and McCrae (2000). Finally, Openness emerged as a clear factor with the expected facets loading on it without any secondary loadings.

3.2. Effects of Age, Gender, and Other Sample Characteristics

The sample included both college students and adults, but a portion of the adult sample was as young as the college sample. Age was studied as a variable only within the adult sample, because contextual factors had the potential to confound the outcome if the two samples were combined. The correlation between age and scores using only the adult group ($N = 460$) revealed a general lack of significant correlations, and those that were significant were very low. Three factors, Extraversion ($r = -.12, p < .01$), Openness ($r = -.16, p < .001$), and Agreeableness ($r = .13, p < .01$) showed significant correlations with age, whereas there were no correlations between age and Neuroticism or Conscientiousness. The correlations between age and individual facet scores reflected the overall tendency observed in the correlations with the factors. None of the Neuroticism and Conscientiousness facets correlated with age. In Extraversion, three of the facet scores correlated significantly with age: Activity ($r = -.12, p < .01$), Excitement-Seeking ($r = -.15, p < .01$) and Positive Emotions ($r = -.14, p < .01$). In the Openness factor, Fantasy ($r = -.15, p < .01$), Aesthetics ($r = -.13, p < .01$), Feelings ($r = -.19, p < .001$), and Actions ($r = -.13, p < .01$) correlated significantly with age.

Finally, among the facets of the Agreeableness factor, Trust ($r = .12, p < .01$) and Compliance ($r = .17, p < .001$) correlated significantly with age.

In order to determine group differences (student vs. adult) that were not accounted for by age, a MANCOVA was conducted where the group was used as an independent variable and age was used as a covariate. Age was a significant covariate on Extraversion ($F (1, 731) = 5.55, p < .05$), Openness ($F (1, 731) = 10.91, p < .005$), and Agreeableness ($F (1, 731) = 4.90, p < .05$). However, group differences between adults and students were sustained as shown in subsequent univariate analyses. Students were higher in Neuroticism ($F (1, 731) = 124.82, p < .001$), whereas adults were higher on Extraversion ($F (1, 731) = 7.37, p < .01$), Openness ($F (1, 731) = 6.68, p < .05$), and Conscientiousness ($F (1, 731) = 178.40, p < .001$).

The correlations and age effects reported here agreed with those reported by McCrae et al.'s (2000) findings in German, British, Czech, Spanish, and Turkish samples using the NEO-FFI. They also found decreases in Neuroticism, Extraversion, and Openness and increases in Conscientiousness and Agreeableness with age. Consistent age differences across cultures may point to a natural maturational progression that is biologically determined. On the other hand, cohort effects cannot be ruled out easily because even though these cohorts across cultures do not share identical historical forces, there is increasing homogenization of experiences across cultures. (A discussion of homogenization will take place later in this chapter as a possibility to investigate.) Twenge (2001) has performed a meta-analysis on the data from the Extraversion scores from the Eysenck Personality Inventory and Eysenck Personality Questionnaire given to college students between 1966 and 1993. The analysis indicated a clear cohort effect with a large effect size. This result may help resolve the seemingly contradictory findings of age differences in Extraversion (or any other trait) and long-term stability of such traits.

Besides age differences, gender differences were investigated, together with the group differences because major group differences were found in the previous analyses. The two-way MANOVA on five factors investigated whether there were gender differences along the same lines as in other research and whether these gender differences were consistent across the two groups of participants. There were no interactions between gender and group indicating gender differences to be consistent across student and adult samples (all $Fs < 1$).

Univariate analyses indicated gender main effects on Neuroticism ($F (1, 729) = 7.47, p < .01$) and Openness ($F (1, 729) = 26.59, p < .001$). Females scored higher ($M = 82.58, SD = 23.09$) in Neuroticism than males ($M = 76.53, SD = 21.19$) and they also scored higher ($M = 122.47, SD = 17.23$) in Openness than males ($M = 115.27, SD = 17.92$). The higher scores of females on Neuroticism is consistent with other research (e.g., Costa & McCrae, 1992; Tevrüz & Türk Smith, 1996; Lynn & Martin, 1997). In a study that included participants from 26 cultures, Costa, Terracciano, and McCrae (2001) also reported higher scores by females in all facets of Neuroticism and three facets of Openness: Aesthetics, Feelings, and Actions.

Age, group, and gender differences resemble the overall patterns obtained in other studies. Age patterns were virtually identical to those obtained by McCrae et al. (2000) with British, Czech, German, Spanish, and Turkish participants.

The group differences that were observed in addition to age effects point to the fact that the adult sample and the student sample reflected differences beyond those explained by age. The group differences between student and adult samples are in agreement with the Costa and McCrae (1994) for the domains of Neuroticism, Agreeableness, and Conscientiousness. In the current study with Turkish adults and students, adult were higher in the domains of Extraversion and Openness, which was a reversal of the pattern in Costa and McCrae (1994). Whether these dissimilarities can be immediately attributed to cultural differences is a difficult question. The transition from being a student to adulthood is not only a change in age. The analyses above showed differences were not attributable to age. Thus, this transition in social standing may result in certain changes in adaptations. When one is in college one does not need Extraversion, because enthusiastic peers are easily available, and the university environment is less competitive and friendlier. However, the workplace is quite different. Competition is increasingly a part of reality, and people are not drawn automatically to each other as they are in campus settings. Therefore, in adult life, Extraversion is a more requisite characteristic. It may be argued that people who have the basic tendency of Extraversion begin to activate or display this tendency when they move to an adult life. Similarly, the college environment is characterized by relative homogeneity. In contrast, the work environment brings together a more varied sample of people. Consequently, Openness may emerge in the context of interaction with different types of people.

It is also possible that the differences between adults and students in Extraversion and Openness was a function of their respective cohorts as indicated in Twenge's (2001) research on Extraversion, although the trend in her research is in the opposite direction from the current findings. İmamoğlu and Aygün (1999) have provided some results that corroborate the possibility of a cohort effect. They have shown, for example, that Turkish university students in the 1970s valued intellectual characteristics, independence, and imaginativeness more than students in the 1990s. Finally, the fact that the adults and the students responded to the items in very distinct settings and contexts may have led to different types of pressures and response biases. Specifically, the adults may have exaggerated qualities they thought would make a favorable impression at work.

The gender differences in the current study showed females to be higher than males in Neuroticism and Openness. The outcome regarding Openness seems in agreement with the findings reported in Costa et al. (2001). Higher Openness in females is also supported by cultural elements. In the characterization of the Turkish culture, males are depicted as more conservative and more resistant to change (İmamoğlu & Yasak-Gültekin, 1993). Males are also expected to preserve and protect the value system of the society (İmamoğlu & Aygün, 1999). Thus, the argument here is that the source of the difference may be the lower Openness level of the males as a consequence of cultural demands.

3.3. Comparison with the American Normative Sample

In order to describe the general profile of a culture, a comparison is necessary; therefore we can describe the Turkish adult profile as plotted on the American adult profile forms. A word of caution is necessary here. As I shall discuss below, the adult sample may be somewhat affected by contextual factors present when responding to the NEO-PI-R, and their scores may not be representative of all contexts.

Both Turkish males and females scored average on the Neuroticism factor (T-scores of 47 and 45, respectively). Both groups scored at about equal levels and high on Extraversion (T-scores of 60 for females and 58 for males). On Openness, females scored high and males were in the high range of average (T-scores around 58 and 52, respectively). Turkish males were in the lower part of the average range on Agreeableness with a T-score of 46. Females scored low on Agreeableness with an average score approaching the very low range (T-score of 40). On Conscientiousness, both Turkish males and females scored on the upper range of high Conscientiousness (T-scores for both groups around 62).

When the facet scores were examined, some scores that were in the low or high ranges were observed. Turkish females were particularly lower than American females on Anxiety, Trust, Compliance, Modesty, and Tender-Mindedness. They were also higher than their American counterparts on Gregariousness, Assertiveness, Excitement-Seeking, Aesthetics, Actions, and all of the Conscientiousness facets, particularly, Achievement Striving. Turkish males displayed similar tendencies such that they also scored high on Gregariousness and all the facets of Conscientiousness. Similarly, they scored low on Trust, Compliance, and Modesty.

Explaining the differences. These differences were surprising in most cases for those who are familiar with both Americans and Turks. For example, Turkish females scored very low on Agreeableness when compared with their American counterparts. Although their raw scores would be considered average when compared with the American males or the Turkish males, they remain considerably below the American sample. Several explanations could be offered. First, the sample consisted of professional women who may have been selected for certain characteristics that would make them successful in the workplace. Second, they may have adopted more masculine characteristics to exist in a man's world. A third explanation could be that the social pressures present in the workplace may have selected those characteristics as the adaptive ones over time. Early demographic research (Blitz, 1975) has shown that as early as the 1960s, 38.2% of the labor force in Turkey was female as opposed to 32.7% in the U.S. Moreover, the proportion of females in high-prestige professional jobs was 25%, whereas in the US it was 2.3%. These figures are functions of the encouragement of females to participate in the workforce with the establishment of the republic, which may have turned into some sort of social pressure for professional identity. Turkish women may have developed more masculine tendencies in interpersonal relations, being less submissive and less Agreeable and more dominant and more extraverted (Costa, Terracciano, & McCrae, 2001).

In addition, conceptualization of the facets may be an important factor in comprehension of discrepancies between judgments about a culture and descriptive scores obtained in a study. Trust is a good example. Trust is inherent in the American system where declared information is assumed to be correct. In Turkey, on the other hand, in many official transactions one needs to obtain documentation for even insignificant information like home address through government offices. In contrast, one can go to a neighborhood bazaar and buy a rug, paying in installments. The merchant, who is there only one day a week, asks for a name and address and arranges for dates of payments assuming that the information provided is correct and that the buyer will return periodically to make the payments. Moreover, this situation takes place not in a small village but in a large, cosmopolitan city like Istanbul with a population of over 10 million.

More examples of trust and mistrust can be provided from either country. The cultural differences lie in the context and the type of trust. As McCrae and Costa (1999) argue, the culture may determine the context and type of a particular individual tendency. When items of a personality test are developed in one cultural frame, the items may be a representative sample of contexts and types for that specific culture. The adaptation, however, just like the present one, may translate the original set of items and if they are valid for some contexts in the adaptation sample, the items will work. The missing component will be that the items may not constitute a representative sampling of contexts for the adaptation group. In addition, members of some cultures may possess a higher need to think about their responses in a context. Our research team reported that a good number of our respondents felt uncomfortable in responding to some items because they wanted to respond as "it depends," contextualizing their responses. Kağıtçıbaşı (1996b) comments that there are cultural differences in the conceptualization of people such that when Americans describe people, they tend to use more trait descriptions whereas Indians describe a changeable person whose behavior is dependent upon situational context. Then, if that is true, one should expect considerable difficulty in using personality tests, especially the adjective-based tests, in cultures like India. On the other hand, there seems to be a set of studies with consistent findings of five-factor structure even in countries where contextualization is expected such as Turkey and India (Lodhi, Deo, & Belhekar, 2002).

Furthermore, it is possible that many of our respondents responded to the items having in mind the job context (or the school context for the student respondents) because that was where they were taking the inventory. For example, both male and female adult respondents had high average Conscientiousness scores. Thus, the level of the trait represented here may be representative of their behavior only in the job context. Findings supporting the presence of such influences have been reported by Schmit, Ryan, Stierwalt, and Powell (1995). Therefore, it would be misleading at this point to assume that the scores in this report represent the profiles of Turkish adults in general. The observations regarding contextual factors introduce questions of the extent and type of context effects present in all types of research. Because all data collection takes place in some context, estimating the magnitude of context influence, if any, becomes a major issue. The context may influence responses to test questions by defining a set of desirable characteristics. The respondents may be inadvertently responding in a way they consider more desirable in that context, or they may feel the pressure of being assessed by people in positions of authority such as managers or professors, even if they have been specifically informed that this would not be the case.

4. A BILINGUAL STUDY

In order to provide information on the equivalence of the Turkish version of the NEO-PI-R to the English version, a group of bilingual participants were given both versions with a two-week interval between the two administrations. Although bilingual studies provide valuable information, the outcome of such research is not definitive because multiple explanations are possible for any differences between the results of the two versions.

One reason the test results may be different is the obvious reason that the two versions are not equivalent. The translation process may have shifted the test items in various directions. The second possible reason is that the bilingual participants of the research are not equally fluent in both languages, and consequently, their responses may be affected by the incorrect interpretation of the items in their less fluent language. A third reason is the possibility that the language of the test creates a cultural frame and the participants respond within the expectations created by that culture. If the cultural frames are sufficiently distinct then the response patterns will be different. The different response patterns would be expected to vary in one direction for all participants in this case. Finally, the languages may create individual cultural contexts in which the individuals have different selves. This is distinct from the cultural frame in that the emphasis is on the individual's representation of self in a particular language rather than the general cultural frame. Gradually, evidence from research has accumulated indicating that there are differences in the representation of self in different languages (see Schrauf, 2000, for a review). It is plausible that in responding to the test items the participants are retrieving information about self from different culture-specific and language-specific pools.

The absence of any differences between the results in the two languages would support both the identity of the two versions and stability of personality characteristics regardless of cultural contexts. In that case, self is a singular unit not affected by the cultural context.

The participants were 15 faculty or staff between the ages of 23 and 53 at Koç University, where the medium of instruction is English and many faculty members are Americans. The call for participation stated the necessity of being equally comfortable in both languages. Participation was voluntary and confidentiality was ensured. All the participants reported Turkish to be their native languages except one, who reported both languages as native tongues.

The participants were given two envelopes each containing either the English version or the Turkish version of the NEO-PI-R. The envelopes indicated that one was to be completed immediately and the other two weeks later. The order of taking the tests was counterbalanced across participants. These envelopes were given in a larger envelope that also contained a questionnaire about language behaviors in each language. The participants were asked to seal each envelope after completing the test in it and to return both envelopes and the questionnaire to the author's mailbox in the larger envelope.

The first analysis performed on the data obtained from bilingual participants was the correlation between the scores in each language. Table 3 shows that the correlations between the scores of the Turkish and English versions are in general significant and

Table 3. *Mean Domain and Facet Scores of Bilingual Participants in Turkish and English Versions and the Correlations Between the Two Versions.*

| NEO-PI-R Scale | Turkish | | English | | | |
	M	SD	M	SD	d	r
Neuroticism	86.1	27.1	86.4	29.8	−.01	.95**
Extraversion	116.1	27.4	117.1	25.9	−.04	.98**
Openness	131.2	14.1	130.3	17.2	.06	.87**
Agreeableness	116.2	12.7	112.2	13.6	.30	.81**
Conscientiousness	125.6	24.9	126.3	25.3	−.03	.93**
Anxiety	15.7	6.9	16.1	6.5	−.06	.94**
Angry Hostility	14.3	5.2	13.5	6.6	.14	.88**
Depression	13.5	6.4	13.5	6.3	.00	.91**
Self–Consciousness	16.1	4.4	14.9	5.2	.25	.74**
Impulsiveness	16.5	5.7	16.7	4.1	−.04	.70**
Vulnerability[a]	9.8	6.3	11.7	6.6	−.29	.91**
Warmth	20.7	4.4	21.1	4.9	−.09	.91**
Gregariousness	17.8	7.2	18.7	6.7	−.13	.94**
Assertiveness	16.5	5.5	17.3	7.2	−.13	.94**
Activity	20.1	4.2	20.3	3.5	−.05	.80**
Excitement–Seeking	18.7	6.3	18.0	4.2	.14	.89**
Positive Emotions	21.7	5.4	22.4	4.7	−.14	.91**
Fantasy[b]	21.3	3.9	18.7	5.0	.59	.77**
Aesthetics	22.1	4.5	23.0	4.6	−.20	.75**
Feelings	24.3	3.3	23.8	4.3	.13	.69**
Actions	17.8	3.9	17.3	4.3	.12	.72**
Ideas	21.6	4.3	22.7	3.5	−.29	.72**
Values	24.0	3.2	24.9	3.0	−.29	.78**
Trust	19.3	4.7	19.7	5.3	−.08	.79**
Straightforwardness[b]	23.1	5.9	20.0	4.8	.59	.91**
Altruism[b]	23.1	3.6	21.2	3.8	.51	.87**
Compliance	15.6	4.5	15.9	4.2	−.07	.69**
Modesty	15.9	4.2	15.2	4.3	.16	.76**
Tender–Mindedness	19.2	3.0	20.2	2.4	−.38	.48
Competence	22.3	3.9	23.2	4.4	−.22	.77**
Order	17.7	5.8	17.9	5.9	−.03	.88**
Dutifulness	24.8	4.1	24.7	3.3	.03	.78**
Achievement Striving	22.6	4.3	21.5	4.1	.26	.74**
Self–Discipline	21.5	6.4	21.7	5.8	−.03	.90**
Deliberation	16.8	5.1	17.3	5.8	−.09	.95**

Note. $N = 15$. [a]The difference between the Turkish and English versions is significant, $p < .05$. [b]The difference between the Turkish and English versions is significant, $p < .01$. ** $p < .01$.

very high, except for one of the facets (A6: Tender-mindedness). The facets of Extra-version seem to have highest correlations and the facets of Openness the lowest.

The next set of analyses involved comparing the scores on the English version with those on the Turkish version. Before the analyses, any effect of receiving the test in one language first was tested and no such effect was found on any of the factors. The within-subjects *t*-test revealed that the English and Turkish versions of the tests led to similar outcomes. The means and standard deviations for each version are also presented in Table 3. The only significant differences were observed in N6: Vulner-ability, O1: Fantasy, A2: Straightforwardness, and A3: Altruism. For Vulnera- bility, participants had higher scores when they took the NEO-PI-R in English. In Straight-forwardness, Altruism, and Fantasy, the scores were higher for the Turkish version. When individual differences were examined, it was observed that 10 to 12 of the parti-cipants had differences in the direction shown by the overall group.

The results obtained with a limited sample lean towards the similarity of the two versions of the tests, although in four of the 30 facets, there were significant dif-ferences. It is possible to attempt an interpretation of the differences solely in the context of the differences obtained here, but more convincing arguments may be developed if the results from Study 1 and Study 2 are combined.

5. CULTURE, LANGUAGE, AND THE FIVE-FACTOR MODEL

In the previous sections, the standardization process of the Turkish version of the NEO-PI-R and a study on a limited and select group of bilinguals were described. The results indicated that the five factors emerged in yet another culture and the factor structure is, with minor variations, congruent with that of the original inventory.

The study with the bilinguals is another way of approaching cultural differences. The bilingual study demonstrated, to a certain degree, the linguistic equivalence of the English and Turkish versions, although further research with larger and more repre-sentative groups is needed. A wealth of research is beginning to accumulate, dealing with the relationship between language and self in bilinguals. Our research (Gülgöz, Schrauf & Rubin, 2001), as well as others' (Schrauf & Rubin, 1998; Marian & Neisser, 2000) on autobiographical memory shows that linguistic context determines the auto-biographical memory retrieved by participants. These studies consistently observed congruence between the language of research context and the language of event in memory. Other reports indicate that during therapy, retrieval of events of childhood is easier when the therapy is conducted in the language spoken during childhood (Schrauf, 2000).

These findings point towards a differential conceptualization of self according to language. The consistency in the second study between the responses in two languages becomes a strong statement when examined on the background of such research. It may mean that the traits remain stable across the contexts of two languages and two cultures. Even though cultural shaping through language was expected to modify responses across the two languages, research by Watkins and Gerong (1999) has also failed to show such differences using the Twenty Statements Test.

Comparisons of the facets showing a significant difference across the two languages with those that are different in the Turkish and American samples may add to our understanding of cultural differences. The differences between the scores in two languages were in the facets of Vulnerability, Fantasy, Straightforwardness, and Altruism. Vulnerability and Straightforwardness seem to have equal means in American and Turkish samples. The Turkish sample has means that are in the upper part of the average range for the American sample in Altruism and Fantasy, and this is in agreement with the difference between the bilinguals' responses. Turkish culture has often been characterized as altruistic, and therefore the context of Turkish language may have stimulated the cultural responses. This is also consistent with the observation in the first study that the Altruism facet correlated with the Conscientiousness domain. Altruism represents social Conscientiousness in this culture, which is characterized by emotional interdependence (Kağıtçıbaşı, 1990). Research by Kuşdil and Kağıtçıbaşı (2000) has shown that values like benevolence are among those with the highest ratings among Turkish teachers. Other highly rated values were universalism, security, achievement, conformity, and openness to change. These ratings are in agreement with high means of the Turkish participants using the American norms on Openness and Conscientiousness domains and Achievement Striving facet. The high value placed on security may be related to the lower levels of Trust among the Turkish participants.

Those facets for which the Turkish sample had a higher or lower mean compared to the American sample did not show a difference in the bilingual study. The absence of differences in the bilingual study should be interpreted with caution because of the small sample size, but it is also true that the sample is a distinct group from the general Turkish sample. They are highly educated, bilingual or multilingual, many had lived in the U.S., some for more than 10 years, and many were academicians. Therefore, it should come as no surprise that their results were considerably different from the overall sample.

Interpreting similarities. When we examine the results of the two studies reported here, we observe that there are minor variations in the cultural and linguistic representations of personality traits between Turkish and American groups. This also means that the Turkish sample fits well among other countries where similar findings were obtained (e.g., Heuchert, Parker, Stumpf, & Myburgh, 2000; Mastor, Jin, & Cooper, 2000; Piedmont & Chae, 1997). There are obvious difficulties in interpreting cultural similarities, just as there are in interpreting differences. Berry, Poortinga, Segall, and Dasen (1992) indicate three ways of interpreting cultural differences in trait means. These interpretations can be applied to the factor structures of a trait model. One interpretation is that the difference in the factor structure reflects the differences between cultures in the conceptualization of the trait. A second interpretation is that the difference resulted from errors made in the translation of the items, or from the fact that some items have no corresponding verbalization in that particular culture. Finally, the difference may result from the complete irrelevance of the dimensions, traits, or the way personality is conceptualized. This may be the case, for example, if a culture regards behavior as totally variable, dependent on the contextual or situational factors without any stability of patterns. The real mistake would be to assume that all these interpretations are not called for if the factor structure appears to be similar, as it did in many studies. If there are no differences in the factor structures between cultures, can we automatically assume that the factor structure reflects identical underlying trait structures, that the test is identical in capturing the measures of interest in all cultures, and that behavior is conceptualized the same way in all cultures? No doubt, other corroborating evidence is sought for the similarities across cultures and across languages for the validity of the Five-Factor Model.

McCrae and Costa (1999) take the position of defending the biological deterministic perspective for personality traits, arguing that the five dimensions are universal, and individual levels on these dimensions are biologically determined. Zuckerman (1995) had taken a similar position with five factors that were slightly different in identity than those of the Five-Factor Model (McCrae & Costa, 1999). Zuckerman's (1995) argument relied on the biological correlates of certain personality traits. He presented evidence that the monoamine systems played a significant role in personality. For example, low levels of MAO were related to Sociability (i.e., Extraversion), Impulsive Sensation-seeking (i.e., the reverse of Conscientiousness), and Aggression–Hostility (i.e., reverse of Agreeableness), and MAO levels were stable over long periods of time, increasing gradually with age. It is interesting to note that the increase in MAO levels coincides with a decrease in Extraversion, and increases in Conscientiousness and Agreeableness, as would be expected from the correlations. Zuckerman (1995) states that traits are not inborn or inherited, but they are affected by the chemicals produced by the brain structures and chemical composition, which *are* inherited. In a similar vein, it can be argued that happiness is determined by the chemical composition in the brain, and optimists and extroverts are happier. However, there is also research casting doubt on such an argument. For example, there are substantial differences between nations in their subjective well-being such that happiness correlates well with GNP per capita (Myers & Diener, 1995).

Are there any explanations for the similarities across cultures besides the assumption that there is some form of biological determination? Kağıtçıbaşı (1996) emphasized the adaptive function of certain personality characteristics to account for the similarities in personality within a culture. Certain personality characteristics were reinforced because they had adaptive value in that culture. If we pursue the same line of reasoning, it is possible that certain dimensions of personality become salient in societies because they have high adaptive value. It is also possible that in all human social life, regardless of cultural variations, there are unchanging characteristics, and the dimensions emerging in factor analyses are five dimensions of adaptation to all societies. All societies may have the same dimensions of adaptation and in all societies there would be individuals with varying degrees of adaptation to the society as a consequence of multiple causalities, biological and environmental.

An additional argument would be the transitions in cultures in the last century, in the midst of an era of globalization. The effects of globalization have been argued by some to be in the direction of homogenization and by some to be in the direction of polarization (Holton, 2000). The homogenization thesis is generally simplified as the standardization of the global culture around a Western or American pattern. The polarization argument counters this thesis with the argument that culture is harder to standardize than economic organization and technology. Even though there seems to be a convergence in economic systems around the world, nationalist and separatist movements are stronger than ever. Holton (2000) presents an alternative view called hybridization. It is the idea that cultures are in constant contact and interaction with each other. During this contact, which has been going on for centuries, the cultures borrow elements from each other and incorporate them into their own meaning system. It has become so hybrid in time that it is difficult to define an authentic culture that is pure and distinct from others. The multiplicity of meaning systems developed within a culture limits the ability to define the culture, whether it is the Turkish, German, South African, Malay, or American. An excellent case is language, an important aspect of culture. It is virtually impossible to find a pure language unaffected by any other. Experts on the Turkish language vary in their estimation of foreign words in Turkish, but the most conservative estimate has been around 40%. It is clear that the definition of *foreign* is also problematic because it is impossible to find a point in time when a culture has not been in contact with any other. Even within one individual, language (and culture) changes with exposure to other languages. When an individual learns a second language, the result is not a person with two distinct languages but a person with a hybrid form of two languages (Grosjean, 1992) who switches between languages, borrows words from the other language, and uses idioms translated from the other language.

In investigating cultural differences, we may be examining differences between different forms of hybrids, not differences between cultures. The hybrids encompass a wide range of variations but they do not have the characteristics of any of the variations. The characteristics of hybrids resemble each other by virtue of being averages and that average may not be true of any single individual forming the hybrid. Consequently, the five domains that emerge in factor analysis may be the common-alities of the hybrids, the characteristics of the averages, but they may not be appropriate descriptions of individual personalities.

In conclusion, culture has been neglected in many areas of psychology for years. Validation and generalization of our theories necessitate research in many cultures and meticulous examination of the results of these studies. Cross-cultural comparisons may suggest universality or major differences but the interpretation of both types of outcomes requires extreme caution.

REFERENCES

Bayar, P. (1983). *Atletlerin kişilik özellikleri* [Personality characteristics of athletes]. Unpublished master's thesis, Ankara University, Ankara, Turkey.

Berry, J. W., Poortinga, Y. H., Segall, M. H., & Dasen, P. R. (1992). *Cross-cultural psychology: Research and applications.* Cambridge, England: Cambridge University Press.

Blitz, R. C. (1975). An international comparison of women's participation in the professions. *The Journal of Developing Areas, 9,* 499-510.

Costa, P. T., Jr., & McCrae, R.R. (1992). *Revised NEO Personality Inventory (NEO-PI-R) and NEO Five-Factor Inventory (NEO-FFI) professional manual.* Odessa, FL: Psychological Assessment Resources.

Costa, P. T., Jr., Terracciano, A., & McCrae, R. R. (2001). Gender differences in personality traits across cultures: Robust and surprising findings. *Journal of Personality and Social Psychology, 81,* 322-331.

Demirtürk, P. (1987). *A preliminary study towards the development of the Turkish form of the California Psychological Inventory.* Unpublished master's thesis. Boğaziçi University, Istanbul, Turkey.

Goldberg, L.R. (1990). An alternative "description of personality": The Big Five factor structure. *Journal of*

Personality and Social Psychology, 59, 1216-1229.

Gough, H. G., & Heilbrun, A. B., Jr. (1983). *Adjective Check List manual.* Palo Alto, CA: Consulting Psychologists Press.

Grosjean, F. (1992). Another view of bilingualism. In R. J. Harris (Ed.), *Cognitive processing in bilinguals* (pp. 51-62). Amsterdam, The Netherlands: Elsevier Science Publishers.

Gülgöz, S., Schrauf, R., & Rubin, D. R. (2001). *Autobiographical memory in bilinguals.* Unpublished manuscript, *Koç University.*

Heuchert, J. W. P., Parker, W. D., Stumpf, H., & Myburgh, C. P. H. (2000). The Five-Factor Model of personality in South African college students. *American Behavioral Scientist, 44,* 112-125.

Holton, R. (2000). Globalization's cultural consequences. *Annals of the American Academy of Political and Social Science, 570,* 140-152.

İmamoğlu. E. O., & Aygün, Z. K. (1999). 1970'lerden 1990'lara değerler: Üniversite düzeyinde gözlenen zaman, kuşak ve cinsiyet farklılıkları [Value preferences from 1970s to 1990s: Cohort, generation and gender differences at a Turkish university]. *Türk Psikoloji Dergisi, 14,* 1-18.

İmamoğlu, O. & Yasak-Gültekin, Y. (1993). Gazetelerde kadın ve erkeğin temsil edilişi [Representations of men and women in newspapers]. *Türk Psikoloji Dergisi, 8,* 23-30.

Kağıtçıbaşı, Ç. (1990). Family and socialization in cross-cultural perspective: A model of change. In J. Berman (Ed.), *Cross-cultural pespectives: Nebraska symposium on motivation, 1989* (pp. 135-200). Lincoln, NE: Nebraska University Press.

Kağıtçıbaşı, Ç. (1994). Psychology in Turkey. *International Journal of Psychology, 29,* 729-738.

Kağıtçıbaşı, Ç. (1996a). *Family and human development across cultures.* Mahwah, NJ: Lawrence Erlbaum.

Kağıtçıbaşı, Ç. (1996b). The autonomous-relational self: A new synthesis. *European Psychologist, 1,* 180-186.

Kılıç, M. (1987). *Değişik psikolojik arazlara sahip olan ve olmayan öğrencilerin sorunları [Problems of students with or without various psychological disorders.]* Unpublished doctoral dissertation, Hacettepe University, Ankara, Turkey.

Kuşdil, M. E., & Kağıtçıbaşı, Ç. (2000). Türk öğretmenlerin değer yönelimleri ve Schwartz değer kuramı [Value orientations of Turkish teachers and Schwartz's theory of values]. *Türk Psikoloji Dergisi, 15,* 59-76.

Lodhi, P. H., Deo, S., & Belhekar, V. M. (2002). The Five-Factor Model of personality: Measurement and correlates in the Indian context. In R. R. McCrae & J. Allik (Eds.), *The Five-Factor Model of personality across cultures* (pp. 227-248). New York: Kluwer Academic/Plenum Publishers.

Lynn, R. & Martin, T. (1997). Gender differences in Extraversion, Neuroticism, and Psychoticism in 37 nations. *Journal of Social Psychology, 137,* 369-373.

Marian, V. & Neisser, U. (2000). Language-dependent recall of autobiographical memories. *Journal of Experimental Psychology: General, 129,* 361-368.

Mastor, K. A., Jin, P., & Cooper, M. (2000). Malay culture and personality. *American Behavioral Scientist, 44,* 95-111.

McCrae, R. R. (2001). Trait psychology and culture: Exploring intercultural comparisons. *Journal of Personality, 69,* 819-846.

McCrae, R.R., & Costa, P. T., Jr. (1997a). Personality trait structure as a human universal. *American Psychologist, 52,* 509-516.

McCrae, R.R., & Costa, P. T., Jr. (1997b). Conceptions and correlates of Openness to experience. In R. Hogan, J. A. Johnson, & S. R. Briggs (Eds.), *Handbook of personality psychology* (pp. 825-847). San Diego, CA: Academic Press

McCrae, R. R., Costa, P. T., Jr., Ostendorf, F., Angleitner, A., Hřebičková, M., Avia, M. D., Sanz, J., Sánchez-Bernardos, M. L., Kuşdil, M. E., Woodfield, R., Saunders, P. R., & Smith, P. B. (2000). Nature over nurture: Temperament, personality, and lifespan development. *Journal of Personality and Social Psychology, 78,* 173-186.

Myers, D. G., & Diener, E. (1995). Who is happy? *Psychological Science, 6,* 10-19.

Öner, N. (1994). *Türkiye'de kullanılan psikolojik testler [Psychological tests used in Turkey].* Istanbul, Boğaziçi University Press.

Özgüven, I. E. (1992). *Hacettepe kişilik envanteri el kitabı [Hacettepe personality inventory manual].* Ankara, Turkey: Odak Matbaacılık.

Piedmont, R. L., & Chae, J. (1997). Cross-cultural generalizability of the Five-Factor Model of personality: Development and validation of the NEO-PI-R for Koreans. *Journal of Cross-Cultural Psychology, 28,* 131-155.

196   GÜLGÖZ

Savaşır, I. (1981). *Minnesota çok yönlü kişilik envanteri el kitabı (Turk standardizasyonu) [Minnesota Multiphasic Personality Inventory manual (Turkish standardization)]*. Ankara, Turkey: Sevinç Matbaası.

Savran, C. (1993). *Sıfat listesinin Türkiye koşullarına uygun dilsel eşdeğerlilik, geçerlik, güvenirlik ve norm çalışması [The linguistic equivalence, validity, reliability, and norm study for the Adjective Check List for Turkey]*. Unpublished doctoral dissertation, Marmara University, Istanbul, Turkey.

Savran, C., Balcı, Z. (1996, September). *Psikolojik danışma ve rehberlik eğitiminin danışman adaylarının kişilik özellikleri üzerindeki etkisi [The effect of psychological counseling education on the personality characterisitcs of counselor candidates]*. Paper presented at the Ninth National Congress of Psychology, Boğaziçi University, Istanbul, Turkey.

Savran, C. (2001). *Factor analysis of the dimensions of the Turkish adjective checklist*. Unpublished manuscript, Marmara University, Istanbul, Turkey.

Schmit, M. J., Ryan, A. M., Stierwalt, S. L., & Powell, A. B. (1995). Frame-of-reference effects on personality scale scores and criterion-related validity. *Journal of Applied Psychology, 80*, 607-620.

Schrauf, R. W. (2000). Bilingual autobiographical memory: Experimental studies and clinical cases. *Culture & Psychology, 6*, 387-417.

Schrauf, R. W., & Rubin, D. C. (1998). Bilingual autobiographical memory in older adult immigrants: A test of cognitive explanations of the reminiscence bump and the linguistic encoding of memories. *Journal of Memory and Language, 39*, 437-457.

Schrauf, R. W. & Rubin, D. C. (2000). Internal languages of retrieval: The bilingual encoding of memories for the personal past. *Memory and Cognition, 28*, 616-623.

Sinangil, H. K., Savran, C., Ones, D. S., & Balcı, Z. (1997) Public and private sector managers: Factors influencing personality characteristics and performance. *Quaderni di Psicologia del Lavoro, 5*, 194-201

Somer, O. (1998). Türkçe'de kişilik özelliği tanımlayan sıfatların yapısı ve beş-faktör modeli [The structure of trait descriptive adjectives in Turkish language and the five-factor model]. *Türk Psikoloji Dergisi, 13*, 17-32

Somer, O., & Goldberg, L. R. (1999). The structure of Turkish trait-descriptive adjectives. *Journal of Personality and Social Psychology, 76*, 431-450

Sümer, H. C., Sümer, N., Çifci, D.S., & Demirutku, K. (2000). Subay kişilik özelliklerinin ölçülmesi ve yapı geçerliği çalışması [Measurement of officer personality attributes: A construct validity study]. *Turk Psikoloji Dergisi, 15*, 15-36.

Talmy, L. (1985). Lexicalization patterns: Semantic structure in lexical forms. In T. Shopen (Ed.), *Language typology and syntactic description: Vol 3. Grammatical categories and the lexicon* (pp. 57-149). Cambridge: Cambridge University Press.

Tevrüz, S., & Türk Smith, Ş. (1996). Üniversite gençliğinin kişilik profilleri [Personality profiles of the university students]. In Y. Topsever & M. Göregenli (Eds.), *Proceedings of the Eight National Congress of Psychology* (pp. 99-113). Ankara: Turkish Psychological Association.

Türk Smith, Ş., & Tevrüz, S. (1998). Marmara Üniversitesi Öğrencileri Üniversite Gençliğini değerlendiriyor: Sevilen, sevilmeyen, tipik ve ideal öğrenci hangi özellikleri taşıyor? [Marmara University students evaluate university students: What characteristics do liked, disliked, typical, and ideal students have?]. In G. Okman-Fişek (Ed.), *Proceedings of the Ninth National Congress of Psychology* (pp. 421-430). Ankara: Turkish Psychological Association.

Twenge, J. M. (2001). Birth cohort changes in extraversion: A cross-temporal meta-analysis, 1966-1993. *Personality and Individual Differences, 30*, 735-748.

Watkins, D. & Gerong, A. (1999). Language of response and the spontaneous self-concept. *Journal of Cross-Cultural Psychology, 30*, 115-121.

Whorf, B.L. (1956). *Language, thought, and reality*. Cambridge: MIT Press.

Zuckerman, M. (1995). Good and bad humor: Biochemical bases of personality and its disorders. *Psychological Science, 6*, 325-332.

AUTHOR NOTE

Address correspondence to Sami Gülgöz, Koç University, Sariyer 80910 Istanbul, Turkey. Email: sgulgoz@ku.edu.tr

VIETNAMESE-AMERICAN PERSONALITY AND ACCULTURATION

An Exploration of Relations Between Personality Traits and Cultural Goals

APRIL LEININGER

University of California, Los Angeles

Abstract. This chapter reports the personality profile of Vietnamese Americans and some central components of Vietnamese culture, and explores relationships between Vietnamese personality, culture, and acculturation in the United States. Vietnamese Americans in California and North Carolina took a Vietnamese translation of the International Personality Item Pool version of the NEO-PI-R (NEO-IPIP; Goldberg, 1999). Procrustes rotation shows a close fit between Vietnamese and U.S. factors structures (factor congruences = .89-.95). Interview, participant observation, and personality measure results provide evidence that Vietnamese Americans are low in C4. Unacculturated Vietnamese Americans are low in Openness relative to Americans and acculturated Vietnamese Americans. Hypocognition (Levy, 1984) and canalization (D'Andrade, 1992) provide models for possible cultural effects on trait expression.

Keywords: Acculturation, personality traits, Conscientiousness, goal hierarchies, participant observation

1. THE VIETNAMESE IN AMERICA

Since the fall of Saigon in 1975, hundreds of thousands of Vietnamese citizens have left their home country. The United States has been a common destination for many of these refugees and immigrants: In 1991, the estimated population of Vietnamese Americans was 850,000 (about 250,000 American-born; Daeg de Mott, 1997). This chapter reports the personality profile of Vietnamese Americans and some central components of Vietnamese culture, and explores relationships between Vietnamese personality, culture, and acculturation in the United States.

The personality profile was collected as one component of an ethnographic study of Vietnamese-American families in California and North Carolina. Several research assistants and I distributed questionnaire packets containing the Vietnamese NEO-IPIP, a cultural values questionnaire, and a demographic questionnaire to participants at their homes or in public meeting places. Participants were asked to fill out the questionnaires at home during the next week; the research assistants and I retrieved the questionnaires from participants after they had completed them. In addition to administering the personality inventory, my research included living with two Vietnamese-American families, conducting participant observation both in these and other families throughout their daily activities, and conducting depth interviews with a range of Vietnamese Americans.

California and North Carolina represent two distinct types of sociocultural environments in which immigrants find themselves in the United States: a region with bustling ethnic enclaves, on the one hand, and a region with a relatively scarce Asian- or Vietnamese-American population, on the other. As even a casual visit to the San Diego area will reveal, scores of Vietnamese restaurants, groceries, and other businesses dot the landscape. The metropolis lies within easy driving distance of Westminster, California's Little Saigon, the neighborhood widely considered the capital of Vietnamese America. With its bountiful immigrant population, thriving ethnic businesses, and several Vietnamese-language newspapers, modern San Diego bears some resemblance to the eastern cities of the late-19th and early-20th Centuries, large urban centers where immigrant groups carved out zones of social and cultural autonomy within the larger fabric of American life.

Not all Vietnamese immigrants to the United States move to cities or regions with such well-established or numerically dense Vietnamese-American communities. Initially, U.S. policy was to spread Vietnamese refugee resettlement equally across the 50 states, in hopes of avoiding greater economic impact on any one state or region. The concentration of Vietnamese Americans in California (45.6% of Vietnamese Americans live in California, according to the 1990 census) is a result of their voluntary, secondary migration there. Smaller, yet sizable, Vietnamese populations continue to exist, though, across the United States. Raleigh, North Carolina, like its sister cities across the state, Greensboro and Charlotte, is one such metropolitan area containing a relatively small Vietnamese-American population. Although it supports a handful of Vietnamese-owned businesses and stages large annual Tet celebrations, Raleigh's Vietnamese-American population remains scattered across the city rather than clustered in ethnic enclaves.

Despite these differences in geography and population density, Vietnamese-American family life in both San Diego and Raleigh resembles the patterns of family life described in earlier studies of Vietnamese Americans. In both regions, education is highly valued and family obligations play a central role in educational pursuits (Caplan, Choy, & Whitmore, 1989; Zhou & Bankston, 1994). Vietnamese-American families across the country are also characterized by important differences in experiences of Generation 1, 1.5, and 2 family members (Rumbaut, 1991; Zhou & Bankston, 1998), and the difficulties encountered by individuals and families as a result of these generational differences (Freeman, 1989; Kibria, 1993)—that is, of differences in acculturation level resulting from age at the time of immigration. In Vietnamese-American families in both regions, it is also typical for Generation 1 parents to have experienced post-migration downward mobility and for this trend to be in the process of being reversed by the high frequency of Generation 1.5 Vietnamese Americans who earn engineering, DDS, PharmD, and MD degrees.

Because of the war and migration-related traumas Vietnamese Americans have endured, most previous studies of Vietnamese-American personality have focused on mental health. Studies of Vietnamese refugees in the United States have shown elevated levels of depression, assumed to result from the trauma of the refugee experience, that may gradually decrease as Vietnamese Americans learn English, find stable employment, and otherwise become integrated into the new social world surrounding them (Rumbaut, 1989; Rumbaut, 1985). The purpose of the present chapter is to provide a more general view of Vietnamese-American personality by reporting the results from the administration of a personality measure and interpreting these results in the context of evidence from participant observation and interviews.

2. SELF-REPORTED PERSONALITY TRAITS

2.1. Characteristics of the Vietnamese-Americans in this Study

The 233 respondents (119 female, 114 male) were Vietnamese Americans living in North Carolina (n = 57) and California (n = 176). The age range was 17-88, with a mean of 39.7. The respondents were relatively recent immigrants: eighty-nine percent of my sample left Vietnam in 1979 or later, and the average time an informant had been in the United States was 11 years. Some of the findings reported in this chapter may be relevant to the earlier immigrants, but there are important demographic differences between the waves of immigrants from Vietnam. First-wave immigrants (those fleeing Vietnam in 1975) tended to be part of the urban, intellectual elite. The post-1979 immigrants on which this study focuses tend to be from more rural, lower-SES backgrounds. In general, these later immigrants face greater difficulty in acclimating to the United States, due in part to the United States' "compassion fatigue" and in part to shifts in the U.S. economy (Freeman, 1995). Twenty percent of informants' household incomes fell in the range of $30,000 to $49,000 total annual household income—this was the overall modal income category. While the percentage of households below the poverty line was not small—30.1% reported incomes of $19,000 or below—26% of my informants reported annual household incomes over $50,000. Numerous factors are at play here—households have multiple income sources, and income levels tend to rise steadily with time spent in the United States.

2.2. A Vietnamese Translation of the NEO-IPIP

The instrument used is the International Personality Item Pool (IPIP; Goldberg, 1999) version of the NEO-PI-R (Costa & McCrae, 1992). In the English version, the average correlation between NEO-IPIP scales and the corresponding NEO-PI-R scales was .73 (.94 when corrected for scale unreliability) in a sample of 501 adults in Oregon. The average alpha for the 30 English NEO-IPIP scales was .80. One scale, O6: Values, failed to achieve a reasonable alpha in the Vietnamese version.[1] For the other 29

---

[1]This is consistent with other researchers' difficulty in translating this particular facet into Chinese (McCrae et al. 1998, p.1044). Individual items in this facet (e.g. "I tend to vote for conservative political candidates;" "I believe criminals should receive help rather than punishment") seemed to translate reasonably well, and further, O6 did have a clean loading on the O factor (see Table 1). Perhaps some underlying trait like O6 exists in Vietnamese culture, but the items are too culturally specific and therefore do no share the underlying

Vietnamese scales reported here, the average alpha was .70, with facet alphas ranging from .43-.83. In the IPIP questionnaire, respondents are asked to rate how accurately each item describes them. The English items are brief verbal phrases, e.g. "lose my temper," "seldom get lost in thought," "look at the bright side of life." The Vietnamese translation adds the pronoun *toi* ("I") to each item. Respondents rate themselves on a 5-point scale, from 1 (very inaccurate) to 5 (very accurate). This paper uses results from Goldberg's administration of the NEO-IPIP to a sample in Oregon as a point of comparison; those results are referred to as the U.S. American norms.

I worked with Vietnamese-English bilingual research assistants to translate the NEO-IPIP into Vietnamese. Translators were all Vietnamese-Americans who had been born in and attended school in Vietnam and whose first language was Vietnamese, and who were attending college in the United States. We often worked in groups of three to make an initial translation. A different translator would then provide a backtranslation. We then worked in groups again to discuss and revise items for which backtranslations indicated difficulties.

The large majority of items had obvious, equivalent translations in Vietnamese. Seventy-six percent of the backtranslations produced word-for-word or otherwise equivalent English. Sixteen percent of the backtranslations indicated that the Vietnamese translation was not a perfect equivalent to the original English, but that the meaning was preserved. In some cases this was due to readily recognized sociocultural differences.[2] About 7% of the items were conceptually difficult to translate and produced backtranslations indicative of this difficulty. For example, one of the items on the trust scale, "believe people are basically moral" backtranslated as, "even though people sometimes do something bad, I believe everyone has morals." In cases like this, the translation seems roughly accurate, but translators appeared not to fully understand the meaning of the item in either its English or Vietnamese version. This suggests the item is too culturally specific and future work on the questionnaire may need to improve the scales by eliciting scale items that are readily understandable by Vietnamese respondents. The facet alpha mean of .70 and the five factor structure (discussed below) suggest that on the whole, the translation was successful, although there is certainly some room for improvement.

---

meaning they do in U.S. American culture. To develop a set of items that measure the Vietnamese equivalent to O6, more ethnographic and translation work are required. Based on the literature and my fieldwork, I suspect that the closest dimension might involve evaluations not only of Communism versus democracy and capitalism, but also of dimensions such as: government control vs. local level control, bureaucracy vs. simple village social organization, strong government vs. weak government, nationalism vs. identity politics, and belief that governments are usually corrupt vs. belief that those in power deserve power.

[2]For example, we translated one of the excitement-seeking items, "Would never go hang-gliding or bungee jumping" to "I would never jump from a waterfall or go motorcycle racing." The underlying meaning—the assertion that one would not put oneself in physical danger by engaging in "extreme sports" that some people engage in in order to challenge themselves, feel a physical rush, etc.—is preserved by substituting activities that are more familiar in Vietnam but that are similar to hang-gliding and bungee jumping in the risk-taking they require.

2.3. The Conceptualization and Measurement of Culture

Advancing the study of personality and culture requires that we attend to the characteristic adaptations that are culturally-shaped manifestations of basic tendencies (McCrae & Costa, 1999), and to be aware of the integration of psychological and cultural factors in beliefs, values, and other components of the psyche (McCrae, 2000). Recent work in psychological anthropology develops theoretical constructs that can serve as the units of culture of interest for personality and culture studies. One of the most widely accepted constructs among psychological anthropologists is the cognitive schema (D'Andrade, 1995; Strauss & Quinn, 1997), conceptualized as a unit of culture that becomes part of the personality when internalized (c.f. D'Andrade, 1990). The methods by which cultural schemas are identified usually involve a kind of content analysis of speech, either speech elicited in formal interviews or recorded during participant observation (D'Andrade, in press; Quinn, in press).

Cultural schemas can be typologized according to their psychological, cultural, and social functions. The type of cultural schemas I will focus on in this chapter are goal schemas (D'Andrade, 1992)—schemas infused with motivational force. A cultural goal is a culturally learned schema for something that is experienced as a wish or a want. Using this definition, cultural goals are one type of characteristic adaptation (McCrae & Costa, 1999)—they are culturally learned ways of expressing endogenous personality traits.

One of the central Vietnamese cultural goals I will discuss in this chapter is the goal of *Obeying my parents*. The precept that one should obey one's parents is a culturally transmitted ideal, but also a goal that functions as part of the personality of the Vietnamese Americans who internalize it. The Vietnamese Americans who internalized this goal schema experienced themselves as wanting to obey their parents. This was evidenced both in their direct report of this desire and in their actions. The goal of *Obeying my parents* is thus a frequently recurring motivational state, a culturally shaped part of many Vietnamese Americans' personality.

Using this conceptualization of culture makes the operationalization of acculturation relatively straightforward. If U.S. Americans and Vietnamese have different characteristic adaptations or cultural goals, the degree of acculturation of Vietnamese Americans can be conceptualized as the degree to which they internalize Vietnamese or U.S. American cultural schemas (e.g. Minoura, 1992). The component of culture I focus on in this study is cultural goal schemas; therefore Vietnamese Americans' acculturation is operationalized here as the degree to which Vietnamese Americans want the things that Vietnamese people typically want and the degree to which they want the things that Americans typically want. This approach is compatible with but distinct from models of acculturation developed by psychologists (Flannery, Reise, & Yu, 2001). The present approach does not offer an indicator of level of acculturation along global dimensions, but instead focuses on small units of personality and culture, thereby providing a detailed portrait of some of the characteristic adaptations of acculturated and non-acculturated individuals.

3. COMPARATIVE INTERCULTURAL ANALYSES

3.1. Factor Structure

Though cross-cultural comparative work on personality traits is in its early stages, evidence so far suggests that the five-factor structure is very similar across cultures (McCrae & Costa, 1997b; McCrae, Costa, del Pilar, Rolland, & Parker, 1998). However, this evidence is based on direct comparisons of the NEO-PI-R. Because the present study uses the NEO-IPIP, a two-step process was used to compare the Vietnamese-American and U.S. American factor structures. First, a Procrustes rotation (McCrae, Zonderman, Costa, Bond, & Paunonen, 1996) was performed to align the NEO-IPIP with the NEO-PI-R in the U.S. American data. Results of this rotation yielded a close fit between the two structures: All factor and item congruence scores are above .90, indicating that on the whole, the NEO-IPIP replicates the structure found using the NEO-PI-R.[3] In step two, a Procrustes rotation was again performed, this time aligning the Vietnamese data to the structure yielded by step one (the American NEO-IPIP targeted to the American NEO-PI-R). Table 1 shows the results of step two, the Procrustes solution for the Vietnamese-American data. All five factors are readily recognizable in the Procrustes rotation. Factor loadings with an absolute value of .40 or higher are in bold.

One of the trends in the slight difference in the Vietnamese-American structure is that some A and C facets have high loadings on the C and A factors. Facets C3: Dutifulness and C6: Deliberation have high loadings not only on the C factor but also on the A factor. A2: Straightforwardness and A3: Altruism have high loadings on C as well as on A. One way of interpreting these secondary loadings would be to notice that there is much basis in the Confucian-influenced aspects of Vietnamese culture[4] to consider the facets A2, A3, C3, and C6 as composing a dimension along which someone with high amounts of these qualities would fit the ideal of the *chuu tzu* (noble man; profound person; "Chung yung," 1995)—honest, *jen* (humanity; feeling connection to all living things and therefore having kindness to others; Shun 1995), righteous, obedient, benevolent, humane, deferential, trustworthy, *co hieu*[5] (having filial piety), and judicious.

The Confucian look of the Vietnamese factor loadings has a number of possible interpretations. The differences could be the result of cultural factors (e.g. Confucian-influenced social judgments) rather than of a truly distinct personality structure. This seems consistent with the findings, because the slight differences in loadings do not create a previously unrecognized factor; instead they consist of double loadings on expected factors and another of the already recognized factors. One could argue, though, that these shifts in loadings would resolve into a clearer factor if the measure were better—if, for example, Vietnamese personality concepts were used to develop the measure (c.f. Yang & Bond, 1990).

---

[3]Facets with high loadings on factors other than those they were targeted to include E4, O3, A1, and C6.

[4]Certain aspects of Chinese Confucianism were both appropriated by and forced upon Vietnamese people (Nguyen Ngoc Huy, 1998).

[5]*Co hieu* is a Vietnamese term; *chuu tzu* and *jen* are Chinese terms.

Table 1. Procrustes Rotation of Vietnamese-American FactorLoadings.

NEO-IPIP Facet	N	E	O	A	C	VC[a]
N1: Anxiety	**86**	–07	–05	01	–05	99
N2: Angry Hostility	**78**	–04	03	–30	–12	96
N3: Depression	**64**	–35	13	–27	–22	96
N4: Self-Consciousness	**69**	–14	–14	11	–22	95
N5: Impulsiveness	20	37	–04	–36	**–66**	86
N6: Vulnerability	**71**	–04	–26	17	**–42**	99
E1: Warmth	**–43**	**53**	24	30	18	97
E2: Gregariousness	–22	**83**	–01	–07	–07	95
E3: Assertiveness	–24	**66**	21	–23	36	96
E4: Activity	–22	32	15	–35	**53**	98
E5: Excitement-Seeking	–13	38	38	**–43**	–27	91
E6: Positive Emotions	–15	**57**	**42**	07	01	92
O1: Fantasy	26	10	**74**	–03	–02	93
O2: Aesthetics	–01	38	**60**	40	27	92
O3: Feelings	**44**	34	39	32	33	93
O4: Actions	–23	**44**	**51**	–17	–04	94
O5: Ideas	–24	10	**68**	–15	35	97
O6: Values	–07	01	**47**	16	–10	92
A1: Trust	–07	35	–03	**41**	04	84
A2: Straightforwardness	05	–11	–04	**57**	**49**	96
A3: Altruism	–15	23	34	**54**	**46**	92
A4: Compliance	00	–11	–06	**74**	04	96
A5: Modesty	02	**–50**	–05	**60**	18	79
A6: Tender-Mindedness	08	17	39	**54**	30	90
C1: Competence	**–44**	23	21	13	**64**	95
C2: Order	04	03	10	28	**67**	76
C3: Dutifulness	–04	–07	05	**62**	**61**	98
C4: Achievement Striving	–13	23	27	14	**73**	95
C5: Self-Discipline	–37	11	13	–01	**73**	95
C6: Deliberation	–24	–17	01	**57**	**57**	85
Factor congruence	93	95	89	92	95	93

Note. Vietnamese-American NEO-IPIP targeted to (U.S. NEO-IPIP targeted to U.S. NEO-PI-R). Decimals are removed; loadings with an absolute value of 40 or greater are in bold. N = Neuroticism, E = Extraversion, O = Openness, A = Agreeableness, C = Conscientiousness. [a]Variable congruence.

No matter how these loadings are interpreted, the evidence here shows slight differences from the U.S. norm in a factor structure that is overwhelmingly similar to that of the U.S. The Procrustes rotation reveals that 25 of the 30 facets have variable congruence coefficients above .90, and factor congruences for the five factors range from .89 to .95.

3.2. Facet Comparisons

Similarity across facets. Before comparing factor and facet means, let us consider some summary statistics that can speak to the overall amount of difference and similarity between Vietnamese Americans and U.S. Americans. This comparison is based on the means for my Vietnamese-American sample and the U.S. American means for Goldberg's Oregon sample (L. Goldberg, personal communication, January 24, 2001). If we compare Vietnamese Americans with U.S. Americans across all facets, we find that absolute differences in terms of standard deviations range from 0 to .8, with an average of .39. In other words, there are a number of facets for which the difference between the two groups is negligible, and among the facets on which they do differ, the difference is never greater than one standard deviation.

The finding that the average standard deviation unit difference between Vietnamese-American and U.S. American facet scores is .39 indicates that the two groups are relatively similar with respect to NEO profiles. This amount of difference is consistent with measures of cross-cultural difference and similarity in other studies. For example, it has been shown that there are slight but interpretable differences in the meanings of Japanese and English emotion terms (Romney, Moore, & Rusch, 1997) and Chinese and English color terms (Moore, Romney, Hsia, & Rusch, 1999). The differences are the smallest in the domain of color terms, slightly greater in the domain of emotion terms, and slightly greater again in the case of NEO profiles. In each of these cases, variability within groups is quite large relative to variability between groups, and yet there are small but consistent and interpretable differences between the groups. I will now turn to those differences between Vietnamese Americans and U.S. Americans.

Concerns about comparing mean levels. Psychologists and anthropologists alike are wary about translating instruments and then comparing means from the two different translations of the same instrument. Anthropologists emphasize semantic differences in translations that are considered near equivalents. For example, while there is little doubt that the most direct translation of "sad" into Vietnamese is "*buon*," such anthropologists have argued that the two are far from equivalent and can be fully translated only by further unpacking the senses of these terms using semantic universals (Wierzbicka, 1999). While any concept can be translated into any human language, these anthropologists argue, rigorous translation techniques should be applied, and cross-cultural research should progress using *decentered translation* (e.g. Werner & Campbell, 1970), which would entail not only using backtranslation in order to find a near-equivalent expression that both retains the meaning and sounds natural in the target language, but also to alter the wording of the original scale (in this case, the English version) when backtranslation indicates that another wording would be more

Table 2. Mean Differences Between
Vietnamese Americans and U.S. Americans.

NEO-IPIP Scale	Vietnamese Mean T-score	t
Neuroticism	53	3.39***
N1: Anxiety	56	7.15***
N2: Angry Hostility	53	4.22***
N3: Depression	53	4.04***
N4: Self-consciousness	52	2.89**
N5: Impulsiveness	45	6.06***
N6: Vulnerability	56	8.13***
Extraversion	48	2.60**
E1: Warmth	48	2.20*
E2: Gregariousness	51	1.06
E3: Assertiveness	47	4.15***
E4: Activity	48	2.27*
E5: Excitement-Seeking	49	1.04
E6: Positive Emotions	44	6.98***
Openness	44	7.59***
O1: Fantasy	42	9.96***
O2: Aesthetics	45	5.70***
O3: Feelings	45	6.59***
O4: Actions	45	6.76***
O5: Ideas	43	8.94***
Agreeableness	50	0.30
A1:Trust	42	10.64***
A2:Straightforwardness	56	8.05***
A3:Altruism	48	2.70**
A4:Cooperation	48	2.70**
A5: Modesty	56	7.55***
A6: Tender-mindedness	49	1.35
Conscientiousness	48	2.11*
C1: Competence	44	7.40***
C2: Order	50	0.60
C3: Dutifulness	49	1.53
C4: Achievement Striving	46	5.55***
C5: Self-discipline	47	4.05***
C6: Deliberation	54	5.29***

Note. Vietnamese-American T- scores are normalized with respect to American scores: mean = 50, standard deviation = 10. Vietnamese Americans n = 233; U.S. Americans n = 501. *p < .05. **p < .01. ***p < .001.

directly comparable to the closest equivalents in the target language. The work reported in this chapter represents a good first effort in using backtranslation to achieve a translation that is close enough in meaning to the English version to warrant mean level comparisons.

The factor analysis reported above would seem to provide evidence for cross-language validity of the Vietnamese and English versions used here. Feeling sad may not be the same thing as feeling *buon*—there may be different social settings particular to each, slightly different cognitions characterizing each, and so on—but in both the Vietnamese and English versions of the NEO-IPIP, items using these terms or close synonyms generated high alphas for N3, and N3 in both cases had a high loading on the N factor. In other words, "sad" and "*buon*" may not be equivalent, but they are very similar—similar enough that items like "Often feel blue" and "*Toi thuong khi cam thay buon chan*," and the facets that these items compose, can be meaningfully compared. When anthropologists caution about the non-equivalence of "sad" and "*buon*," they are rightly directing our attention to differences in display rules, social norms, cultural connotations of an emotion, and other sociocultural factors influencing the activation, experience, and meaning of an emotion. I would argue that anthropology can also benefit from the very different, but equally useful, task of cross-cultural comparison that assumes near-cross-cultural-equivalence of small conceptual units such as the concepts of "sad" and "*buon*."

A further concern about comparing mean facet scores is that source and target translations of an instrument may lack scalar equivalence (McCrae, Yik, Trapnell, Bond, & Paulhus, 1998). The participant observation component of my research project provides some evidence bearing on this concern. My English-version NEO-IPIP ratings of some of the Vietnamese-Americans I knew best showed high agreement with their own self-ratings on the Vietnamese version (Leininger, 2000). This finding gives some evidence for cross-language validity and scalar equivalence. A test-retest design in which bilingual respondents take the questionnaire in both languages would provide even more confidence about the closeness of the equivalence of the two versions (McCrae et al., 1998). In light of my access to personality data from independent sources (participant observation and depth interviews), I proceed in the following section to compare mean scores, drawing on these multiple sources of data.

Comparison of Vietnamese-American and U.S. American mean facet scores. Table 2 shows the Vietnamese-American differences from the U.S. for each factor and facet. The U.S. sample consisted of 501 adults, all but twelve of whom were Caucasian. The Vietnamese-American and U.S. American samples are comparable in terms of age and gender composition. They also appear to be comparable in terms of their education level, though equivalent indexes were not collected for the two samples. Forty-five percent of the U.S. American sample reported having a college or post-college degree, while 55% of the Vietnamese-American sample reported having or planning to achieve a post-high school degree.[6]

---

[6]The 45% of U.S. Americans includes those who indicated they were college graduates (20.2%) and those who indicated they had a post-college degree (24.8%). In comparison, 25% of Vietnamese Americans had or

To facilitate comparison with other chapters in this volume, I use NEO-PI-R facet names rather than NEO-IPIP facet names; t values and p levels are listed next to each facet. The following discussion focuses on mean level differences in Openness and Conscientiousness.

Openness to experience and Vietnamese traditionalism. Vietnamese Americans were consistently lower than U.S. Americans on Openness.[7] The Vietnamese-American Openness average was 44 and Vietnamese-American Openness facet scores were all at least half a standard deviation below the U.S. American average (all $ps < .001$). The O factor measures openness to experience, the degree to which a person is driven to pursue complexity, change, and difference, as opposed to being motivated to avoid these and to pursue sameness, regularity, and the familiar (McCrae & Costa, 1997a). In speculating about possible explanations for the Vietnamese Americans' low scores on all O facets, one thinks first of the predominantly traditionalistic nature of Vietnamese society—a society in which, generally speaking, social structure, culture, and person-ality have been oriented toward conformity with a hierarchical social order that is assumed to be natural and unchanging.[8] Of course, major change has taken place in Vietnam over the past decades, and Vietnamese Americans now find themselves in a new social system and are finding ways to preserve Vietnamese institutions as well as adopt some U.S. American practices (Kibria, 1993). Still, it is safe to say that relative to the United States, Vietnamese society has been more traditionalistic—has been composed of sociocultural formations in which human action is largely constrained by previously held, relatively rigid norms and values (Parsons, 1949/1966).

My participant observation and fieldwork provide evidence that indeed tradition-alism-related goals were deeply internalized (D'Andrade, 1992; Strauss & Quinn, 1997) by many Vietnamese Americans. Some of the central Vietnamese cultural goals for the immigrants in my sample included: *Obeying my parents, Taking care of my parents,* and *Having a successful family.* These goals are conceptually related to Openness to Experience in that they share with facets that load negatively on the Openness factor the concept of the perpetuation of tradition and an aversion to change.

A further reason these goals are related to Openness to Experience is that they tend to be internalized as parts of goal hierarchies (D'Andrade, 1992) that are relatively rigid. For example, a subgoal of each of the upper-level goals listed above is *Marrying a good husband or wife,* where a good spouse is defined as one who is respected in the community, comes from a good family, and has a good education and a good job. This goal is very different from its U.S. American counterpart, according to which marriage is most centrally about falling in love with and marrying someone you feel is right for

---

planned to get a four-year college degree; 14% had or planned to get a post-college degree. The 55% of Vietnamese Americans includes those who indicated a number of degrees, ranging from two-year technical school degrees to medical, law, and other graduate and professional degrees.

[7] As reported earlier in this chapter, the alpha for the O6: Values facet was only .10; this facet is therefore not considered in the present discussion of other Openness facets.

[8] Scholars of Confucianism point out that Confucian philosophy emphasizes doing right over following tradition. However, in the normative behavior, internalized values, and use of cultural ideology among Vietnamese people there is a tendency to equate what is right with what those in authority (parents or men) want.

you or whom you feel you were meant to be with (McCollum, 2000). Marriage in Vietnam, though no longer arranged, is still held to be a family matter, not solely an individual matter. In order to *Obey one's parents*, one must marry someone of whom one's parents approve—one they recognize as fitting the standards of a good spouse.

The following interview excerpt illustrates how strongly these goals can be internalized, both by Vietnamese-American young adults and their parents. The excerpt begins with my asking Thuy, one of the Vietnamese Americans with whom I conducted a case study based on intensive interviewing, whether her mother is still encouraging her to call Hien, whom her mother hopes she will date. (All case materials have been disguised to protect confidentiality.)

AL: Is [your mom] still bugging you about calling that guy, Hien?

Thuy: Ohhhh, daily! [pause] I don't know. Yeah. I don't know. He's okay.

AL: He's okay? But you're not really sure if you like him that much, or—

Thuy: No. I'm not sure. [giggles]

AL: Is he nice looking? Is he good looking?

Thuy: Well, he's [sighs] he's okay, you know. Average.

AL: Avèrage?

Thuy: The one [guy] I like, not really like, but is more good looking than Hien, but—My parents doesn't, my parents don't approve. So. [pause]

AL: Mmmm.

Thuy: Forget that guy. [snickers]

AL: It's someone that you know right now?

Thuy: Well not right now, because since they not approve, so what's the use of continuing.

AL: Mmmm.

Thuy: Never work out, so. Why mess up our whole family and go through all that. Even if—maybe my parents knows better. Maybe they can see something we cannot see. Maybe even if I marry that guy, it's like—but no, they—We just, you know, we still keep in contact but it's long distance. Just friends, really.

AL: So you tried to start seeing him, but—

Thuy: No. No.

AL: You were just friends, but you found out that your parents—

Thuy: We—no, because even if—you know, when I decided someone to be my friend, I try to keep them as far away from—like—if he's, like—if—not, you know, the normal friends that I have, but if he's like, if I like that guy a little bit, I don't think it's fair, you know, to keep him around me. So I just keep him as far away from me as possible so nothing will happen. . . . He's okay. I like him. . . . But I don't want to, ah—have conflicts in the family.

AL: yeah.

Thuy: Maybe [the relationship] never works out. You know, why do you want to create so much conflict.

AL: yeah.

Thuy: I don't feel like other people, like you know, when they lost some kind of love, they go kill themself. I don't feel like that. I just let my parents raise me up from—since I was born, so. I owe them a lot. I don't do that kind of thing. The other guy, he—you know, even if you marry him, you die, he's going to remarry someone else. So.

AL: Mmhmm.

Thuy: Yeah. But my parents will always be there for me.

AL: Mmmm.

Thuy: So. They're more important.

AL: [pause]. Makes sense.

Thuy: I don't get when someone suicide and kill themselves over a guy or girl. I don't get it. What about their parents, their family? They don't think about their family any more? Is that person going to—what can that person do for them? Only when you—only when you in trouble or you in some kind of pain that you know who's really care for you. And usually at that time your girlfriend or boyfriend will desert you. Go somewhere else, right? But your family stay there. That's what I think; I don't know. I value family a lot.

The above interview is one example of many instances in which Thuy and Vietnamese Americans like her asserted the importance of family and of obeying one's parents. Thuy, a 25-year old dental student, conveys in the above excerpt that she is not particularly attracted to Hien, the man her parents have been trying to set her up with. She had been attracted to another young man, but immediately stopped seeing him when her parents expressed their disapproval of him. My interviews with her parents and siblings confirmed the details of the above narrative. In stark contrast to U.S. American young adults, Thuy gives her parents' wishes with respect to her future spouse priority over her own personal preferences. In addition to the conceptual consonance between low Openness and Vietnamese goals of traditionalism, then, there appears to be an empirical relationship: Vietnamese goals appear to be negatively correlated with Openness.

Competence, achievement striving, and self-discipline. Interestingly, Vietnamese Americans were about half a standard deviation lower than the American norms on the facets of C1: Competence, C4: Achievement Striving, and C5: Self-Discipline, with scores of 44, 46, and 47, respectively (all $ps < .001$). This result is surprising in view of the large literature describing numerous Asian groups, including the Vietnamese, as particularly conscientious in these very regards (e.g. Caplan, Choy, & Whitmore, 1989; Zhou & Bankston, 1994), and attributing Vietnamese and other recent Southeast Asian immigrants' educational and economic success in large part to Vietnamese cultural values of hard work and achievement in service of the family.

In a study addressing the low level of C1: Competence among Hong Kong students taking the NEO-PI-R in Chinese, McCrae et al. (1998) show that low C1, high N6: Vulnerability, and average C4: Achievement Striving seen among HK Chinese may be social judgment artifacts. The study found that when Chinese Canadians rate themselves, recent immigrants' self-ratings on C1 are in the low range, like their counterparts who still live in Hong Kong, whereas Canadian-born Chinese rate themselves in the average range of C1. This might be interpreted as an acculturation effect; however, when Hong Kong-born Chinese Canadian peers rate others, Canadian-born targets are rated as low in C1 as well. In other words, Canadian-born targets' C1, C4, N, and N6 levels shift as a function of whether they are rating themselves or are being rated by Hong Kong-born peers. This result is interpreted as a social judgment effect—a tendency for Hong Kong-born raters to give lower C1, C4, N, and N6 ratings to both themselves and others. The low C1 scores of Hong Kong Chinese, then, can be interpreted as an effect of high Chinese standards for judging Competence rather than an indication of truly low Competence.

Something like this may explain Vietnamese Americans' low and average means on the Conscientiousness facets as well: Vietnamese standards for these traits may be especially high, resulting in attenuated scores due to social judgment. Another possibility is that because the sample is largely relatively recent immigrants, they have a decreased sense of competence due to the difficulties of life in a new country. Data from Vietnamese living in Vietnam and a peer rating design like that used by McCrae et al. for the Hong Kong Chinese could help shed light on the Vietnamese-American case.

Perhaps a peer rating study will show that Vietnamese Americans are in fact higher than the U.S. norms on these C facets. But based on the currently available data—my participant observation and interview results—I would judge these NEO-IPIP results to be accurate: The Vietnamese Americans I know are sometimes about like an average U.S. American with respect to C1, C4, and C5, and in some cases a little lower.

As mentioned previously in this chapter, after conducting six months of fieldwork, I rated two of the Vietnamese-American individuals I knew best on the NEO-IPIP. I made these ratings before calculating the self-report results. My ratings generally agreed with the self-reports: Coefficients of profile agreement (McCrae, 1993) were .53 and .59. This small study suggests that information derived from questionnaires may be corroborated by participant observations. I also made ratings of Vietnamese Americans in general, based on my impressions after hundreds of hours of observing their behavior and engaging interpersonally with them. My impression is that the mean profile shown in Table 2—including merely average levels of C—is for the most part an accurate reflection of Vietnamese-American personality.

To be sure, Vietnamese Americans are generally hard workers and good students. Vietnamese-American students have high grades and test scores, high rates of college attendance, and high projected socioeconomic status (Caplan et al., 1989).[9] Previous studies depict Generation 1 Vietnamese Americans as extremely hardworking and as valuing hard work at school and at one's job (Caplan et al., 1989). However, while Vietnamese Americans do highly value educational success and hard work for the good of one's family, depth interviewing and participant observation illustrate that these values and their enactment are not equivalent to high levels of Achievement Striving or related C traits.

Again, I will turn to an example from my interviews with Thuy, who was introduced above. In my interviews with her, Thuy made it clear that she has long been anxious about getting good enough grades, but that she is not particularly motivated to excel.

---

[9]Caplan et al. (1989) report results from a national sample of Southeast Asian refugees in aggregate—the sample includes Chinese-Vietnamese, Laotian, and Vietnamese refugees. They find, for example, that 27% of the children had a GPA in the 3.6-4.0 range, 52.1% in the 2.6-3.5 range, and only 3.7% of the children had a GPA in the D range (1.5 or lower). These are strikingly high grades for children whose first language is not English; their math grades are even higher.

Thuy: When I was in high school, sometimes I worried about getting into college, too. [inaud] high enough GPA to go to college. And then I didn't know that they have community college that you can go to and transfer to UC. So I don't know who put that in my head, but I heard some people say you have to get a 3.8 to a 4.0 to get into UC. Shoot! Only thing I did all day was works! One works after the other. Oh, Jesus! Four years—terrible! No life at all! Even in high school. I didn't go to any parties, no dancing, nothing! Mostly I just go and then go home, study. Yeah, so after four years, finally get to UCSD. And then somebody said studying, getting a BA is easy, but when you come out you have graduate school to go to. So there's a new worry. To get my GPA high enough to go to graduate school. . . . I think my most enjoy moments in life is when I'm–like right now, when I'm in dental school.

AL: Oh really.

Thuy: Yeah. Because when you in there, you know what you studying. You have no pressure any more. You know you're going to get out. As long as you pass the board. There's no more pressure for you. . . . You know you're going to find a good job. So it's really very nice going to dental school. That's the time that I relax most. Enjoy life. But not before that. Eight years prior to this was hell. . . . But even right now if I try to tell myself to relax, I can't. There's always a test somewhere in the back of my head. . . . It's keep popping up. When you have the nicest time of your life and suddenly that big board exam pop up and destroy the whole thing. You have to start thinking about studying for the exam. So I really wish I could get it over with.

AL: Yeah, so you don't have to worry about it.

Thuy: But the unfortunate thing is that I have to wait for a year before I can take it. . . . So I'll have to survive for the next year. The next long year. And then hopefully with the board exam I'll pass it the first time. And then I won't have to worry about it. If I don't pass it the first time, oh my God. For the next half a year I'll have to concentrate on studying for that exam.

AL: Are you worried about not passing? Is it hard?

Thuy: I know lots of people who failed . . . so that kinds of get me worried. They're pretty smart, and they fail. [laughs]

The above interview excerpt illustrates that Thuy's anxiety is not the result of wanting to excel, but is instead a fear of failing—failing to get into college, or into dental school, or failing to pass her board exam. Her motivation is not to be the top in her class; instead she wants to be able to "enjoy life," secure in the knowledge that she will also be able to "find a good job." Thuy's actions were in accord with her self-description: Thuy spent a substantial amount of time watching television, playing computer games, and socializing with friends. I would estimate that she spent more hours per week on leisure than on studying or working. She worked as hard as she had to in order to reach her goals of passing a test, getting into dental school, and so on. These are not the self-descriptions and behaviors of an individual high on C4.

I gathered a number of case studies similar to Thuy's from other informants, male and female, young and old, who worked hard enough to succeed in getting through professional school or to put their children through professional school, but who did not exhibit high levels of Achievement Striving. There are no doubt some Vietnamese Americans high in C4. One such individual, a Vietnamese American named Doan who immigrated to the U.S. around age 10, appears in a case study presented by Tenhula (1991). At the time of the interview, Doan had an MD and a DDS, and was studying for an engineering degree. In interviews, he expressed a love for studying, excelling, getting the best grades he could, pushing himself, getting things right, getting ahead, and other C4-related traits. Doan appears to be an outlier, though: I came across no one like him during my fieldwork. Instead, my informants tended to resemble Thuy. These case studies suggest that Vietnamese Americans' educational and socioeconomic success is not the result of elevated levels of C4.

There is the possibility that Vietnamese Americans' success is the result of something like what DeVos (1973) argued was the case for Japanese Americans: that they have elevated levels of achievement motivation, but that this motivation is tightly linked to their family relationships, such that they are highly motivated to achieve only in ways that advance their family's well-being. Possibly, Vietnamese Americans have average or low Conscientiousness levels in general, but high Conscientiousness levels in activities related to their family's success. My impression, based on interview and participant observation evidence like that presented above, is that even family-related success is not underlain by high C4.

I suggest we consider another possibility: that no one personality profile, C or otherwise, underlies Vietnamese Americans' success. Other studies of Vietnamese Americans' success (Caplan, Choy, & Whitmore, 1991; Zhou & Bankston, 1994) have concluded the success results from Vietnamese cultural values and family practices. My fieldwork generally confirms this conclusion—my fieldnotes are filled with examples of family practices enabling and promoting educational and occupational success. I would add, however, that such an explanation does not mean that personality has no causal role in the outcome of success. Rather, the Vietnamese family is a social system with norms that can take individuals with a wide range of personality profiles and turn these individuals into successful students and professionals.

4. COMPARATIVE INTRACULTURAL ANALYSES

4.1. Generational and Regional Differences in Immigrant Adaptation

Acculturation-related intracultural variation presents another opportunity for investigating relationships between culture and personality. Previous research shows that recent immigrants are more culturally and psychologically similar to members of their home society than immigrants who have lived for longer periods in their new country (McCrae et al., 1998). Research has also shown that as is the case for language, there is a sensitive period for the acquisition of culture, after which some aspects of culture are internalized problematically or with difficulty (Minoura, 1992). Immigrants and children of immigrants can be divided into three groups according to their age at the time they immigrated: Generations 1, 1.5, and 2 (Rumbaut, 1991; Zhou & Bankston, 1998). Generation 1 immigrants are those who were adults at the time of immigration. The prototypic member of Generation 1 was, at the time of immigration, aged 30-45 and already had a family and career. Members of Generation 1.5 are those who were past the acculturation sensitive period but not yet adults when they immigrated. The prototypical member of Generation 1.5 was aged 11-16 at the time of immigration, speaks his/her second language with a slight accent, and is only partially acculturated. These Vietnamese Americans, who came after the sensitive period is over, but before personality development ends, offer a unique window into the processes of acculturation and personality development.

For the purpose of this generational analysis, members of Generation 1 ($n = 164$) are those who immigrated to the United States when they were age 20 or older. Generation

1.5 ($n = 61$) are those who immigrated to the U.S. when they were aged 8-19. Generation 2 ($n = 8$) were between the ages of 0 and 7 when they came to the United States, or were born in the U.S. to immigrant parents (these are excluded from the present analysis.)

4.2. High N and O Among Generation 1.5 North Carolinians

Among the most interesting results in this study are those found when comparing Generation 1 Californians ($n = 122$), Generation 1.5 Californians ($n = 40$), Generation 1 North Carolinians ($n = 37$), and Generation 1.5 North Carolinians ($n = 21$). A two-way analysis of variance yielded only a few significant F ratios; this comes as little surprise, given the relatively small cell n's in the North Carolina sample. However, a series of t tests helps bring the pattern of results into focus, and Figure 1 highlights some of the most interesting mean differences.

A Region × Generation analysis shows that the North Carolinians, and particularly the Generation 1.5 North Carolinians, were especially high on Neuroticism. The Generation 1.5 North Carolinians' N score (57.6) is not only significantly higher than the U.S. norm ($t = 3.8, p < .001$), but is also higher than expected relative to the other Vietnamese Americans (the Californians and the Generation 1 North Carolinians), whose average N was 53.2 ($t = 2.05, p < .05$).

On the O factor, the Generation 1.5 North Carolinians again stand out, this time with higher Openness scores than the other three groups. There is no difference between U.S. and Generation 1.5 North Carolinians ($t = .67, p = .51$), whereas the other three Vietnamese subgroups, whose means range from 45.2 to 47.6, each differ significantly from the U.S. norm (t's ranging between 3.8 and 5.1, p levels all < .001). In other words, Generation 1.5 North Carolinians' Openness scores indicate they are no different than U.S. Americans with respect to Openness, but that they and U.S. Americans do differ from the other three Vietnamese-American groups.

4.3. Lower Acculturation Among Generation 1.5 Californians

As discussed above, culture is conceptualized here as cognitive schemas, measured by means of content analysis of interviews and participant observation. Acculturation is operationalized as the presence and level of internalization of Vietnamese and American cultural goal schemas. The Vietnamese goal schemas of interest here were introduced previously: *Obeying my parents, Taking care of my parents, Being taken care of by my parents*, and *Having a successful family*. The contrasting U.S. American goal schemas to be examined here are: *Pursuing a career that fits my interests and talents, Being autonomous and independent*, and *Having a close, loving, friendship with my romantic partner*.

Results of a comparative analysis of these goal schemas among the Generation 1.5 respondents indicate that the Generation 1.5 North Carolinians tend to be more acculturated than the Generation 1.5 Californians. Californian members of that generation, like Thuy, deeply internalized Vietnamese goals and had not acquired U.S.

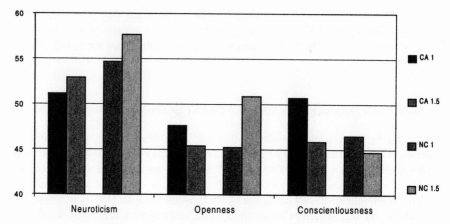

Figure 1. Vietnamese-American normalized Neuroticism, Openness, and Conscientiousness scores by region and generation.

American goals. Members of Generation 1.5 in North Carolina, in contrast, deeply internalized American, not Vietnamese, goals.

To illustrate this difference in acculturation, I will elaborate here on the case material from Thuy, the Generation 1.5 Californian introduced earlier in this chapter. Case material presented above provides an illustration of Thuy's desire to obey her parents—her interest in an attractive dating partner was unimportant relative to her parents' assessment of his potential as a husband. Similarly, Thuy de-emphasized any misgivings she had about living with her parents. As the following interview excerpt shows, Thuy may have disliked aspects of the Vietnamese norms, but she readily complied with them.

AL: How do you like living in San Diego as opposed to living [away from home]?

[long pause]

Thuy: It has its up and down side.

AL: Mmhmm.

Thuy: In San Diego the weather's pretty decent. The scenery is more beautiful. But—[pause] I have a curfew now. So I have to be home before eight.

AL: Before eight.

Thuy: So anytime after eight [my parents] call me like every 5 minutes.

AL: On your cell phone?

Thuy: On my cell phone. . . . Yeah, when I'm at school, I'm out until two, three in the morning. When I get back home everyone go to sleep and I just go on my way. Here I cannot do that.

AL: Does it take you awhile to get used to having a curfew?

Thuy: Well, I'm used to it for 20-something years. So now it just coming back. Nothing new. . . . I guess I probably s—stay—live with my parents until I get married. Even after I get married I'm probably living with them.

AL: Your parents move in with you? Or—

Thuy: They probably all move in, or something like that. Or if we buy two house, they're probably right next to me.

AL: Uh huh.

Thuy: . . . So what's the use. I'm trying to pick out a house that they have to walk at least 10 minutes to get there.

AL: Oh! [laughs]

Thuy: To get to my house.

AL: Ten minutes isn't that long.

Thuy: Have some time to clean up, get everything [inaud], get everything ready. [pause] But I don't think that's going to happen; I think they just going to live with me. . . . I don't mind, especially when I get married and have a family. It's good to have your parents taking care of everything else with you . . . they can help making the food, watching the kids. It's pretty good.

AL: Mmhmm.

Thuy: Mmm, I don't mind. [giggles]

Although Thuy experiences mild annoyance at her parents' close supervision, she plans to continue to live with her parents at least until and probably even after she gets married. As in the domain of dating and marriage, Vietnamese goals like *Taking care of my parents* and *Being taken care of by my parents* override any personal preferences Thuy might have with regard to where she will live.

Earlier in this chapter, I also presented case material exemplifying Thuy's average level of C4: Achievement Striving. Here I can add that that same interview excerpt also demonstrates the importance to Thuy of the Vietnamese goals *Taking care of my parents* and *Having a successful family*. In Vietnamese society and culture, getting a good education and a good job are the means to both of these goals. In order to take care of one's parents, one must get a good education so one can get a good job. Having a good job is also essential to having a successful family, and allows one to take care of one's parents both by providing for them financially and by honoring them by becoming respected and successful. While Thuy is not especially fond of dentistry, she is highly motivated to get through for the sake of her parents. Evidence for this comes from interviews like the following, in which Thuy associated her own academic and occupational achievement with her mother's happiness.

AL: How's your mom? Is she still working at the same place?

Thuy: Yeah. [pause] I'm going to try to finish my program on time. Because sometimes we couldn't pass the board exam and then it takes awhile. I want to pass the board on my first time so my mom can stay home, take vacation, travel. . . . When I get out [of dental school] I think [my mother is] able to, you know, early retirement. Stay home or travel or something like that.

In the above interview excerpt, my question about Thuy's mother's job led Thuy to explain to me that she is motivated to reach her career goals because of these goals' implications for her mother's well-being. While Thuy is not highly motivated to excel as a student or a dentist and does not express passion about her studies or future occupation, she does express a strong desire to get A's, get into college, get into dental school, pass her board exams, and get a good job—for Thuy these goals are self-evident necessities. In her career, her living arrangements, and her dating behavior, Thuy exhibits a Vietnamese pattern of goal striving that is in clear contrast to typical U.S. Americans, who tend to understand their career, dating, and other life choices in terms of personal talents, interests, and preferences. Thuy exemplifies the largely uncultured Generation 1.5 Californians, whose life activities and self-understandings are organized around Vietnamese cultural goals.

In contrast to Californians like Thuy, Generation 1.5 Vietnamese in North Carolina were much more acculturated. Some excerpts from my interviews with Mai, a Generation 1.5 North Carolinian, will demonstrate this. Like Thuy, Mai was in her early teens when she came with her family to the United States, and like Thuy, she was in her mid twenties at the time of our interviews. Unlike Thuy, who, under her parents' direction, followed a normative Vietnamese-American education and career path, Mai chose a college major and career based on her interests, even though her preference conflicted with her parents'. When I asked Mai to explain her choice to attend the University of North Carolina and to study art, her answer showed that she understood her choice as resulting from her own preference and decision, and to a lesser extent from pragmatism and sensitivity to Vietnamese norms.

AL: How did you decide on art?

Mai: . . . My teacher in my freshman art class, when he evaluated my project, he said my work is good. So I was, 'hmmm.' I wanted to do art, but people kept telling me how art is just not gonna make any money. So I realized that, and I thought well, maybe I'll try art and computer. Because I don't want just computer, writing code and stuff. So I just try web design. And I also thought, I've seen some artwork, not artwork, but web design work and animation, and I thought, I'd like to try that too, cause I wonder how it's done. Some looks pretty cool. Beautiful imagery and stuff. So I just go ahead and try.

During my participant observation in North Carolina, Mai frequently showed me her work and spoke about the projects she was working on in her art classes. As the above excerpt demonstrates, Mai pursued the art major because she was interested in trying it. Once she tried it she found art enjoyable and therefore stayed with it. Unlike Thuy, but like the typical U.S. American college student, Mai was pursuing the American cultural goal of *Pursuing a career that fits my interests and talents*. This was despite her parents' and grandparents' warnings that she was making a mistake and would not be able to secure as good a job as if she had majored in Engineering. While her decision to use her art major to become a web designer shows a pragmatic concern to get a stable job, Mai's assumption of the autonomy to choose what she would study and her resulting choice to major in art is unheard of among members of the Californian Generation 1.5.

Similarly, in the domain of Mai's living arrangements, Mai's goals were American, not Vietnamese. Her parents told her she should live at home, but she nevertheless moved out and lived on campus while attending college. Unlike Thuy, who internalized the Vietnamese goals of *Taking care of my parents* and *Being taken care of my parents*, Mai rejected these goals, and instead pursued the U.S. American cultural goal, *Being autonomous and independent*, as the following interview excerpt demonstrates. It begins with Mai explaining why she had chosen to move onto campus.

Mai: . . . When I first got out of high school I had to ask my parents if I could go anywhere and I had to ask my sister to take me places. That just got so— I got so— sick of it! . . . I just got so frustrated! Even when I was in high school and I'd gotten my license already, they still wouldn't let me drive around alone or with friends.

AL: Wow. Because they were worried about you?

Mai: Yeah. They're just overprotective. Which is really not fair. . . . After a semester at UNC I moved to campus just to try it out and that worked out pretty well. . . . And I can do things by myself; I don't have to like beg them. I could go out with friends more. After awhile they [my parents] just get used to that I guess. And after I move home, they just don't force me to not go out, whatever.

AL: Before you moved out and they were really strict with you, how did you interact with them? Did you try to fight it, or—

Mai: I tried to fight it a couple of times. A couple times when they would tell me not to go somewhere I would get really mad. Sometimes I would say something back, like, "you won't let me go even if you let my sister go." And I was just quiet, I would ignore them like for the rest of the week or something! (laughs) So the relationship was pretty bad, just on and off, just kinda like—I'd get mad at them for a week or so, then start talking to them again for a few days. Then when I ask to go somewhere else again, you know, fight again. (laughs). Yeah, it was pretty bad.

In this segment, Mai is critical of her parents ("it's not fair"), expresses frustration ("I just got so—sick of it"), is aware that her own wishes are in conflict with her parents', and tells of arguing with them—all elements absent in Thuy's discussions. Mai's desire to be autonomous is clear not only in her narrative, but in her actions. By moving to campus, even though campus was commuting distance from home, Mai released herself from her parents' restrictions and achieved her goal of autonomy.

Similarly, Mai followed U.S. American, not Vietnamese, goals, in her dating behavior. In spite of her family's desire for her to marry a Vietnamese American, Mai dated Ben, a Chinese American, treating dating and possibly marrying Ben as something that was completely her choice, not something she needed her parents' approval for. The following excerpt begins after Mai had told me that her mother and sister were teasing her about Ben.

AL: So they were just joking, they don't have any serious complaints about him.

Mai: No, not except that he's not Vietnamese so I can't marry him!

[AL and Mai laugh]

AL: Have they said that specifically to you?

Mai: Yeah, because when we were talking about [my sister's] marriage, it jumped over to me, saying you should marry a Vietnamese too, because of language difference and culture difference. Stuff like that. I consider it somewhat, but I still—I have a boyfriend right now, I can't just dump him because of that. (laugh) And not because you said so. I believe that I marry whoever I love. So, I don't care about [ethnicity] or anything. Yeah. But they just don't care.

Unlike Thuy, who emphasized the importance of marrying someone who would respect her parents and of whom her parents approved, Mai wanted to date someone with whom she could develop a romantic relationship and close friendship. Her relationship with Ben was a romantic friendship, not the pragmatic marital relationship that Thuy sought and that characterizes the marital relationship in Vietnam (Pham, 1999). Whereas for Thuy, finding the appropriate man to marry is a subgoal of the Vietnamese goal *Obeying my parents*, Mai's her dating behavior was guided by the U.S. American goal of *Having a close, loving, friendship with my romantic partner*.

In summary, a typical Generation 1.5 North Carolinian's goal striving, like Mai's, was organized around the desire to follow her own preferences and to differentiate from her parents: She wants to study art, move out, and develop a romantic relationship with someone who interests and attracts her. Mai is aware of Vietnamese goals, but these Vietnamese goals are not her internalized, personal goals. She knows that according to her parents, she should have studied engineering, lived at home until she is married, and marry a Vietnamese American. But unlike in Thuy's case, what Mai's parents want is less important to Mai than what she herself wants.

4.4. Models of Relationships Between Culture, Personality, and Social Environment among Vietnamese Americans

The following will offer some interpretations of the above culture and personality differences between Generation 1.5 Californians and Generation 1.5 North Carolinians. A demographic comparison of these groups indicates it is unlikely that these differences are due to demographic variables. For instance, the average number of years the Californians have been in the United States is 14.3, while the North Carolinian average is only 10.0. If number of years in the U.S. accounted for these findings, we would expect the exact opposite pattern, with the more acculturated North Carolinians having spent more time in the United States. One demographic pattern that warrants further investigation is that the Generation 1.5 North Carolinians are higher in socioeconomic status than the Californians (SES derived from education and income ranking).[10] We might wonder whether SES, rather than region and acculturation, is the variable of interest here. Certainly, SES, region, and acculturation are closely associ-ated variables. However, an analysis of NEO-IPIP results by SES showed few effects of SES, and did not show the pattern seen here. Other demographic variables show little or no difference between Generation 1.5 respondents in North Carolina and California.[11]

Still, we must be cautious in interpreting the above results, both because the low cell *n*'s make the tests of significance relatively weak, and because the results may reflect selection bias rather than true regional and generational differences. For instance, perhaps Generation 1.5 North Carolinians who are not Open to Experience were particularly unlikely to volunteer to take the questionnaire or be interviewed. The

---

[10]Roughly, the Californians reported an average annual household income in the $20-29,000 range, compared to the North Carolinians' average of $30-39,000. Similarly, the average highest level of education for a Californian was a two-year technical or trade degree, as compared to North Carolinians' average highest level of education, a four-year BA or BS.

[11]The Californian sample is 49% male; the North Carolinian sample is 50% male. The Californians are slightly older than the North Carolinians on average (28.5 vs. 23.8), but again, the pattern of findings does not match that which we would expect (Costa & McCrae, 1994) if it were simply an age effect.

following discussion notes where these results follow previously established relationships between immigration-related variables and offers speculative interpretations in the service of developing models to be tested in future studies.

As reviewed above, Generation 1.5 North Carolinians stand out from the other Vietnamese Americans in this study both in their higher level of acculturation and their higher levels of N and O. Assuming selection bias is ruled out, we can postulate both sociocultural and personality effects to explain this finding. The Region × Generation difference suggests the possibility that we are seeing the effects of differences in immigrant community composition. Recall that North Carolina's Vietnamese population is relatively sparse and does not form an ethnic enclave like that found in San Diego and greater Southern California. The Vietnamese community in San Diego is not only larger but also more cohesive than that in North Carolina. In North Carolina, in contrast, the Vietnamese community is more fragmented. Community functions exist (e.g. an annual Tet celebration) and there are social networks revolving around the Buddhist Temple in Raleigh, Vietnamese churches (both Catholic and Protestant), and Vietnamese language classes to which parents bring their children, but contact with other Vietnamese is less and with non-Vietnamese is greater.[12]

One way in which size and cohesiveness of the immigrant community may affect acculturation and personality is through its effect on the number of Vietnamese versus non-Vietnamese friends and relatives in the adolescents' peer group. North Carolinians were less likely than Californians to spend time and interact with same-age Vietnamese peers, either inside or outside of school. In her study of acculturation among Japanese children growing up in the U.S., Minoura (1992) found that density of interaction with American peers was highly correlated (.64) with the degree of internalization of U.S. American schemas for interpersonal relationships. Other variables strongly related to degree of internalization of U.S. American schemas were proficiency in English (.76) and age of entry (−.60). What we see in the present results, then, is a case in which English proficiency and age of entry are held constant, while density of interaction with Vietnamese vs. U.S. American peers varies greatly between the two regions. The result, as might have been predicted from Minoura's findings, is that Generation 1.5 North Carolinians are more acculturated than the Californians.

We might postulate that acculturation, in turn, leads to higher N and O. For example, we could speculate that the North Carolinians' high acculturation creates greater conflict in their relationships with their parents, who are relatively unacculturated. This conflict could, in turn, heighten Neuroticism (c.f. Juang, Lerner, McKinney, & von Eye, 1999). Another way in which acculturation could increase Generation 1.5 North Carolinians' N level is through a culturally-related social desirability effect, by which it is less acceptable in Vietnamese culture to be sad, angry, and so forth.

One framework for interpreting the negative correlation between Openness and

---

[12]This regional difference in type of ethnic community may also be related to the fact that North Carolinians' mean N (55.8) is higher than that of Californians ($t = 2.7$, $p = .008$). Density of social support is a factor known to be related to many mental health outcomes and has been suggested as an important factor in immigrants' adaptation (Rumbaut, 1989; Zhou & Bankston, 1994). Another possibility is that higher N discouraged secondary migration to California.

certain Vietnamese cultural goals is provided by Five-Factory Theory (McCrae & Costa, 1999) in its conceptualization of basic tendencies, like Openness, as being expressed in culturally particular ways. One psychological anthropological model of the culturally shaped expression of basic tendencies is the model of hyper- and hypocognition (Levy, 1984). Hypocognition is a state in which a basic tendency undergoes little or no cultural specification. The basic tendency may then manifest itself in a somewhat distorted or disguised form; it may be muted or suppressed, and the individual may be unaware of it or have no conceptual framework with which to understand it and no vocabulary to describe it. The opposite process, hypercognition, is the cultural proliferation of conceptual schemas related to a particular basic tendency. A related process, canalization (D'Andrade, 1992) is the specification of a motive by a cognitive schema, often a culturally learned goal.

Within this framework, it might be speculated that Vietnamese goals like *Obeying my parents* and *Being taken care of by my parents* are relatively incompatible with Openness, in that they do not canalize Openness-related motives and they inhibit the internalization of cultural goals that would have the capacity to canalize such motives.[13] An alternative speculation is that Vietnamese goals of traditionalism canalize motives related to negative Openness, the motive to pursue regularity and avoid change.

Similarly, we could posit that Openness is hypocognized or closedness is hypercognized. That is, there are many Vietnamese cultural goals that specify ways of behaving appropriately and perpetuating tradition and few that specify ways of pursuing something new. When Thuy, for example, finds she is attracted to a man of whom her parents disapprove, or experiences mild annoyance at her parents' control of her while she lives at home, she has no cognitive schemas that direct her to pay attention to these preferences. In a case like hers, not being open to her own experience (of attraction to Hien, of annoyance with her parents) might be an example of how the process of hypocognition could constitute low Openness.

A related speculation, turning to the U.S. American goals, is that American culture hypercognizes Openness, providing individuals with plentiful ways of enacting Openness motives. For example, a goal like *Pursuing a career that fits my interests and talents* could encourage the expression of Openness-related motives in that it specifies that one should both understand one's own interests and choose from among all available careers one that actualizes these interests. This is exemplified when Mai explains she ended up majoring in art as a result of "just trying it." While all humans share the propensity for this kind of exploratory behavior, American cultural goals specify ways of enacting such traits. And while all humans share the ability for self-reflection and understanding, U.S. American cultural goals emphasize this ability, specifying that Mai think about what she is good at, not good at, and what she enjoys, as she does in the above excerpt when talking about her enjoyment of web animation and her doubts about her painting and drawing skills.

The finding of a large difference in Openness between Generations 1 and 1.5 in North Carolina would seem to favor social explanations, however, non-immigrant Vietnamese norms would be needed to be more certain about it. If, for example, non-

---

[13]This is consistent with another of my findings, that none of my informants deeply internalized both Vietnamese and U.S. American cultural goals.

immigrant Vietnamese report levels of Openness close to the American norm, then we would look for explanations for the lower O of the Californian and Generation 1 North Carolinian Vietnamese Americans. If, in fact, these three groups represent average Vietnamese O levels, it would seem more likely that some aspect of the experience of Generation 1.5 North Carolinians has led to their higher Openness. Presently, we are without such data; it is therefore prudent to consider possible effects of Neuroticism and Openness on acculturation-related variables that might also explain the findings in question.

One sensible explanation is that being Open to Experience may make acculturation more likely. Being Open to Experience may make immigrants more likely to entertain new ideas (in this case, cultural models that differ from those one learned at Vietnam or in the home). Similarly, young adult immigrants who are Open to Experience may be more likely to associate with peers who are not from their own ethnic group, which in turn would increase exposure to and likelihood of acquisition of U.S. American cultural goals. Finally, it is important to note the possibility of a bi-directional causality in which personality and social environment mutually influence one another. Acculturation may heighten the expression of certain personality traits, and personality traits like Openness may heighten acculturation. Further, such causal relationships may be contingent on numerous other factors and therefore highly individually variable. That is, for one individual, high Openness may lead to acculturation, while for another individual, acculturation may lead to greater expression of Openness.

5. EXPLORING THE RELATIONSHIPS BETWEEN CULTURE, SOCIAL SYSTEMS, AND PERSONALITY: SOME CONCLUSIONS

This chapter has offered some speculative interpretations of the Vietnamese-American personality profile. In conclusion, it can be emphasized that because the study of personality traits and culture is in its early stages, and this chapter represents a preliminary study, it is important to consider the possibility of cultural influences on personality, personality influences on culture, and situations in which society, culture, and personality coexist in a system but do not change each other.

I urged the consideration of this latter model with respect to the finding that Vietnamese Americans tended to be slightly low on C facets like C4: Achievement Striving. Possible interpretations of this finding include cultural differences in scale use and domain-specific canalization of C4. I suggested the investigation of an alternative model, in which average levels of personality traits are put to work in a social system that leads to outcomes like the educational and economic success of Vietnamese Americans. In such a scenario, the social system and culture do not increase the amount of Achievement Striving in individuals, but simply put to use the extant Achievement Striving (and other traits) with greater efficiency than other social systems might. This model is consistent with a conclusion reached by one of the leading personality and culture researchers decades ago: that we cannot, as culture and personality scholars had originally thought, infer large amounts of some personality trait to be the cause of social outcomes (Spiro, 1961).

Recall here as well the finding that individual differences far outweigh inter- and intra-cultural differences. This finding, too, suggests that the Vietnamese family—and social systems in general—can accommodate human personalities of all kinds, and individuals of a broad range of personality profiles can accommodate the role and norm requirements of the Vietnamese family or of other social systems. This is not to say that in this scenario personality is unrelated to social outcomes, but rather, that an average level of Achievement Striving can be amplified by social systems and cultural schemas.

However, the fact that social systems can accommodate individual differences does not mean that human personality has no effect on social systems or cultures. A general social theory must recognize that human society, personality, and culture co-evolved, and indeed, anthropologists of personality and culture have theorized and studied the effect of personality on culture and society (Wallace, 1970). The influence of personality on society is rarely studied in contemporary anthropology, perhaps in part because of the current ascendancy of cultural constructionist theories, and also in part because of the difficulty of testing such models. A refreshing exception is a recent case study by Douglas Hollan (2000), who offers an analysis of how, in a changing social system, certain personality characteristics can become advantageous and might affect the direction taken as the social system continues to evolve.

Finally, this chapter presented models of cultural effects on personality, with special attention to models in which basic tendencies are shaped by culture. The metaphor "shaped by" is here used to refer to processes like canalization or hyper- and hypocognition, in which, for example, an Openness-related motivational state is either realized through the activation of a cultural goal that canalizes the Openness motive, or fails to influence behavior due to the lack of such a goal. Such models deserve to be tested in future studies, for they represent an advance over the previous culture-and-personality approach, which largely focused on mean differences in basic tendencies. Regardless of the direction of causality—whether, for example, high Openness increases Vietnamese Americans' acculturation or the acquisition of American schemas boosts Vietnamese Americans' expression of Openness—these models stress the view that in human experience and action, biologically based basic tendencies and culturally learned goals are intertwined.

As McCrae (2000) argued, our ability to conduct cross-cultural comparisons of personality factor structure and mean factor and facet levels represents an advance in the study of personality and culture. Similarly, this chapter has attempted to demonstrate how some recent theoretical and methodological advances in psychological anthropology will also benefit this project. The conceptualization and measurement of culture, too, has vastly improved since the days of the original culture and personality school. Less well-developed is the conceptualization and measurement of processes of culture-personality interaction, like hypocognition. Looking at the personality profile and participant observation findings together in this chapter proved useful in developing models of such relationships. Thus far, psychological anthropologists have relied mainly on person-centered ethnographic methodologies (e.g. Levy & Wellenkamp, 1989) to make inferences about processes like hyper- and hypocognition. In future studies, further collaboration between anthropologists and cross-cultural psychologists can lead to the development of better measures of these processes and designs for testing these models.

REFERENCES

Caplan, N. S., Choy, M. H., & Whitmore, J. K. (1989). *The boat people and achievement in America: A study of family life, hard work, and cultural values.* Ann Arbor, MI: University of Michigan Press.

Caplan, N. S., Choy, M. H., & Whitmore, J. K. (1991). *Children of the boat people: A study of educational success.* Ann Arbor, MI: University of Michigan Press.

"Chung yung." (1995). In J. Z. Smith, W. S. Green, J. J. Buckley, & American Academy of Religion (Eds.), *The HarperCollins dictionary of religion* (p. 269). San Francisco: Harper San Francisco.

Costa, P. T., Jr., & McCrae, R. R. (1992). *Revised NEO Personality Inventory (NEO-PI-R) and NEO Five-Factor Inventory (NEO-FFI) professional manual.* Odessa, FL: Psychological Assessment Resources.

Costa, P. T. Jr., & McCrae, R. R. (1994). Stability and change in personality from adolescence through adulthood. In C. F. Halverson, G. A. Kohnstamm, & R. Martin (Eds.), *The developing structure of temperament and personality from infancy to adulthood* (pp. 139-150). Hillsdale, NJ: Erlbaum.

D'Andrade, R. (1990). Culture and personality: A false dichotomy. In D. K. Jordan & M. J. Swartz (Eds.), *Personality and the cultural construction of society* (pp. 145-160). Tuscaloosa: University of Alabama Press.

D'Andrade, R. G. (1992). Schemas and motivation. In R. G. D'Andrade & C. Strauss (Eds.), *Human motives and cultural models* (pp. 23-44). Cambridge, England: Cambridge University Press.

D'Andrade, R. G. (1995). *The development of cognitive anthropology.* Cambridge, England: Cambridge University Press.

D'Andrade, R. (in press). Some methods for studying cultural models. In N. Quinn (Ed.), *How to find culture in language.* Cambridge, England: Cambridge University Press.

Daeg de Mott, D. K. (1997). Vietnamese Americans. In T. L. Gall (Ed.), *Worldmark encyclopedia of cultures and daily life: Volume 2. Americas* (pp. 442-444). Detroit: Gale.

De Vos, G. A. (1973). *Socialization for achievement: Essays on the cultural psychology of the Japanese.* Berkeley: University of California Press.

Flannery, W. P., Reise, S. P., & Yu, J. (2001). An empirical comparison of acculturation models. *Personality and Social Psychology Bulletin, 27,* 1035-1045.

Freeman, J. M. (1989). *Hearts of sorrow: Vietnamese-American lives.* Stanford, CA: Stanford University Press.

Freeman, J. M. (1995). *Changing identities: Vietnamese Americans, 1975-1995.* Boston: Allyn and Bacon.

Goldberg, L. R. (1999). A broad-bandwidth, public-domain, personality inventory measuring the lower-level facets of several five-factor models. In I. Mervielde, I. J. Deary, F. De Fruyt, & F. Ostendorf (Eds.), *Personality psychology in Europe. Vol. 7* (pp. 7-28). Tilburg, The Netherlands: Tilburg University Press.

Hollan, D. (2000). Constructivist models of mind, contemporary psychoanalysis, and the development of culture theory. *American Anthropologist, 102,* 538-550.

Juang, L. P., Lerner, J. V., McKinney, J. P., & von Eye, A. (1999). The goodness of fit in autonomy timetable expectations between Asian-American late adolescents and their parents. *International Journal of Behavioral Development, 23,* 1023-1048.

Kibria, N. (1993). *Family tightrope: The changing lives of Vietnamese Americans.* Princeton, NJ: Princeton University Press.

Leininger, A. (2000). *Questionnaires and participant observation: A comparison of the two research methods.* Unpublished manuscript, University of California, Los Angeles.

Levy, R. I. (1984). Emotion, knowing, and culture. In R. A. Shweder & R. A. LeVine (Eds.), *Culture theory: Essays on mind, self and emotion* (pp. 214-237). Cambridge, England: Cambridge University Press.

Levy, R. I., & Wellenkamp, J. C. (1989). Methodology in the anthropological study of emotion. R. Plutchik & H. Kellerman (Eds.), *The measurement of emotions* (pp. 205-232). San Diego, CA: Academic Press.

McCollum, C. (2000). *The cultural patterning of self-understanding: A cognitive-psychoanalytic approach to middle-class Americans' life stories.* Unpublished doctoral dissertation, Duke University.

McCrae, R. R. (1993). Agreement of personality profiles across observers. *Multivariate Behavioral Research, 28,* 25-40.

McCrae, R. R. (2000). Trait psychology and the revival of personality and culture studies. *American Behavioral Scientist, 44,* 10-31.

McCrae, R. R., & Costa, P. T. Jr. (1997a). Conceptions and correlates of openness to experience. In R. Hogan, J. A. Johnson, & S. R. Briggs (Eds.), *Handbook of personality psychology* (pp. 825-847). San Diego, CA: Academic Press.

McCrae, R. R., & Costa, P. T. Jr. (1997b). Personality trait structure as a human universal. *American*

Psychologist, 52, 509-516.

McCrae, R. R., & Costa, P. T. Jr. (1999). A Five-Factor Theory of personality. In L. A. Pervin & O. P. John (Eds.), *Handbook of personality: Theory and research* (2nd ed., pp. 139-153). New York: Guilford Press.

McCrae, R. R., Costa, P. T. Jr., del Pilar, G. H., Rolland, J.-P., & Parker, W. D. (1998). Cross-cultural assessment of the Five-Factor Model: The Revised NEO Personality Inventory. *Journal of Cross-Cultural Psychology, 29,* 171-188.

McCrae, R. R., Yik, M. S. M., Trapnell, P. D., Bond, M. H., & Paulhus, D. L. (1998). Interpreting personality profiles across cultures: Bilingual, acculturation, and peer rating studies of Chinese undergraduates. *Journal of Personality & Social Psychology, 74,* 1041-1055.

McCrae, R. R., Zonderman, A. B., Costa, P. T. Jr., Bond, M. H., & Paunonen, S. V. (1996). Evaluating replicability of factors in the Revised NEO Personality Inventory: Confirmatory factor analysis versus Procrustes rotation. *Journal of Personality and Social Psychology, 70,* 552-566.

Minoura, Y. (1992). A sensitive period for the incorporation of a cultural meaning system: A study of Japanese children growing up in the United States. *Ethos, 20,* 304-339.

Moore, C. C., Romney, A. K., Hsia, T.-L., & Rusch, C. D. (1999). The universality of the semantic structure of emotion terms: Methods for the study of inter- and intra-cultural variability. *American Anthropologist, 101,* 529-546.

Nguyen Ngoc Huy. (1998). The Confucian incursion into Vietnam. In W. H. Slote & G. A. De Vos (Eds.), *Confucianism and the family* (pp. 91-104). Albany, NY: State University of New York Press.

Parsons, T. (1966). *The structure of social action: A study in social theory with special reference to a group of recent European writers* (2nd ed.). New York: Free Press. (Original work published 1949)

Pham, V. B. (1999). *The Vietnamese family in change: The case of the Red River Delta.* Richmond, England: Curzon Press.

Quinn, N. (in press). How to reconstruct schemas people share from what they say. In N. Quinn (Ed.), *How to find culture in language.* Cambridge, England: Cambridge University Press.

Romney, A. K., Moore, C. C., & Rusch, C. D. (1997). Cultural universals: Measuring the semantic structure of emotion terms in English and Japanese. *Proceedings of the National Academy of Sciences of the United States of America, 94,* 5489-5494.

Rumbaut, R. G. (1989). Portraits, patterns, and predictors of the refugee adaptation process: Results and reflections from the IHARP panel study. In D. W. Haines (Ed.), *Refugees as immigrants: Cambodians, Laotians, and Vietnamese in America* (pp. 138-182). Totowa, NJ: Rowman & Littlefield Publishers.

Rumbaut, R. G. (1985). Mental health and the refugee experience: A comparative study of Southeast Asian refugees. In T. C. Owan (Ed.), *Southeast Asian mental health: Treatment, prevention, services, training, and research* (pp. 433-486). National Institute of Mental Health.

Rumbaut, R. G. (1991). The agony of exile: A study of the migration and adaptation of Indochinese refugee adults and children. In F. L. Ahearn & J. L. Athey (Eds.), *Refugee children: Theory, research, and services* (pp. 53-91). Baltimore, MD: Johns Hopkins University Press.

Shun, K.-L. (1995). Jen. In R. Audi (Ed.), *The Cambridge dictionary of philosophy* (p. 390). Cambridge, New York: Cambridge University Press.

Spiro, M. E. (1961). Social systems, personality, and functional analysis. In B. Kaplan (Ed.), *Studying personality cross-culturally* (pp. 93-127). Evanston, IL: Row, Peterson.

Strauss, C., & Quinn, N. (1997). *A cognitive theory of cultural meaning.* Cambridge, England: Cambridge University Press.

Tenhula, J. (1991). *Voices from Southeast Asia: The refugee experience in the United States.* New York: Holmes & Meier.

Wallace, A. F. C. (1970). *Culture and personality.* New York: Random House.

Werner, O., & Campbell, D. T. (1970). Translating, working through interpreters, and the problem of decentering. In R. Naroll & R. Cohen (Eds.), *A handbook of method in cultural anthropology* (pp. 398-420). Garden City, New York: The Natural History Press.

Wierzbicka, A. (1999). *Emotions across languages and cultures: Diversity and universals.* Cambridge, England: Cambridge University Press.

Yang, K., & Bond, M. H. (1990). Exploring implicit personality theories with indigenous or imported constructs: The Chinese case. *Journal of Personality and Social Psychology, 58,* 1087-1095.

Zhou, M., & Bankston, C. L. (1994). Social capital and the adaptation of the second generation: The case of Vietnamese youth in New Orleans. *The International Migration Review, 28,* 821-839.

Zhou, M., & Bankston, C. L. (1998). *Growing up American: How Vietnamese children adapt to life in the United States.* New York: Russell Sage Foundation.

AUTHOR NOTE

The findings reported here are part of my dissertation research, which was conducted in part with funding from a National Science Foundation Dissertation Improvement Grant and funding from the UCSD Department of Anthropology. I thank Roy D'Andrade for assistance with statistical analyses conducted here and for comments on earlier drafts. E.mail: arl@alumni.northwestern.edu

THE FIVE-FACTOR MODEL OF PERSONALITY

Measurement and Correlates in the Indian Context

P. H. LODHI, SAVITA DEO & VIVEK M. BELHEKAR

University of Pune, India

Abstract. Study I in this chapter reports an Indian (Marathi) adaptation of the Revised NEO Personality Inventory (NEO-PI-R), its psychometric evaluation, and gender differences based on data from 214 subjects. Factor analyses supported the Five-Factor Model and indicated factorial invariance across Indian and American cultures. The study also demonstrated the utility of oblique and orthogonal Procrustes rotations and multiple group factor analysis in evaluating the Five-Factor Model. Study II, employing 300 subjects, examined the Eysenckian correlates of the Indian (Marathi) NEO Five-Factor Inventory (NEO-FFI). The obtained correlations provide validity evidence for the NEO-FFI and its parent instrument, the NEO-PI-R.

Key words: Indian adaptation, EPQ-R, factor analysis, cross-cultural comparisons

1. INTRODUCTION

1.1. Personality Research in India

Research in personality is one of the most popular areas of psychological research in India. Early brief reviews of psychological research in India had been presented by S. C. Mitra (1955), Krishnan (1961), S. Sinha (1963), and Kapoor (1965). However, the first systematic and exhaustive survey of research in psychology was presented by the Indian Council of Social Science Research (S. K. Mitra, 1972a), hereafter referred to as the ICSSR first survey. S. K. Mitra (1972b) pointed out that 64% of all publications referred to in the ICSSR first survey were contributed in only four areas: personality, clinical, social, and experimental. As per this survey (S. K. Mitra, 1972b, p. xxi), during 1961 to 1969, the largest number of papers were published in the field of personality. The popularity of the field of personality has continued in India, as is evident from the subsequent surveys (Nandy & Kakar, 1980; Asthana, 1988; Naidu, 2001).

The factor analytic theories of personality, particularly the theories of Raymond B. Cattell and Hans J. Eysenck, have attracted quite a few Indian psychologists. The various tools developed by these psychologists have been extensively used in India either in the original form or in adapted or translated forms. An early review in this

227

regard is available in Shanmugam (1972). Use of the tests of Eysenck and Cattell still continues today in Indian research on personality and related areas, as is evident from subsequent reviews by Asthana (1988), Kulkarni and Puhan (1988), and Naidu (2001). The Five-Factor Model (FFM) of personality and its psycho-lexical analogue, the "Big Five" model, which emerged in the eighties and flourished in the nineties have not been sufficiently utilized in Indian research on personality, with a few exceptions. For example, Narayanan, Menon, and Levine (1995) examined personality taxonomies for Indian subjects by employing two emic (culture-specific) techniques—a free-descriptor method and a critical incident method—and concluded that their work "strongly supported the five-factor model, while also revealing certain culturally based departures" (p. 51).

Nandy and Kakar (1980) presented a review as well as their own analysis of the relationship between culture and personality in the Indian context. Prolonged infancy, the intimate ties between mother and son, mother's indulgence, identity development of the daughter centering around an evolving motherhood role in society, the significant role played by the female principle in the culture as a whole, the evolution of masculine identity, the need for constant availability (in the psychological sense) of the father who would be a mentor or guide, were some of the major issues discussed by Nandy and Kakar. Their treatment of these issues was influenced by the psychoanalytic orientation. J. B. P. Sinha (1982) conceptualized the Hindu identity (Hinduism is the major religion in India) as a product of three forces: (a) the intrapsychic structure conditioned by the indigenous religio-philosophical thinking; (b) the familial-social-institutional relationships; and (c) the contemporary Indian reality, especially economic poverty. While analyzing Indian culture, S. Sharma (1981) suggested that the Indian culture differs from other cultures on several dimensions, such as caste, socio-economic hierarchy, theory of *karma* and feudal system. These facets of our culture may be the major antecedents determining our behavior.

Asthana (1988), among other topics, reviewed the Indian work on socialization, social change and personality development, development of identity, and cross-cultural and sub-cultural studies. Indian culture is a very ancient culture characterized by a multiplicity of philosophical outlooks (sometimes contradictory), castes and creeds, languages and dialects spoken, and religions and customs followed. (For further details in respect of castes and Indian religio-philosophical schools, sources in Indian sociology, anthropology, and philosophy may be consulted: See Barlingay, 1998; Bayly, 1999; Ghurye, 1994; Murty, 1985; Radhakrishanan & Moore, 1957; and K. Sharma, 1986.) Indian society is quite often conceptualized as a traditional and conservative society. Nevertheless, in the last five decades of post-independence era, India has witnessed increased literacy and education; scientific, technological, industrial, and economic growth; a comparatively stable democratic system; the consequent socio-economic changes and increased urbanization; the increased impact of the media; and resulting changes in life style. A comprehensive treatment of personality in the Indian socio-cultural context would be required to take all these complexities into consideration. Many more scientific and empirical studies would be needed in this direction, although considering the complexity of the phenomena involved, designing such studies is not conceptually and methodologically an easy task.

1.2. Personality-and-Culture Studies

The emic/etic distinction is one of the central concepts in current thinking about cross-cultural research (Brislin, 1980). Research on personality and culture has been carried out in different contexts such as psychological anthropology, cross-cultural psychology, contextual social psychology, cultural psychology, and comparative psychiatry. McCrae (1998) argued that personality and culture studies have largely disappeared since 1960, though progress in trait psychology makes their revival feasible. In the context of personality-and-culture studies, McCrae (2001, p. 819) distinguished among transcultural research, intracultural research, and intercultural research. "*Transcultural* research focuses on identifying human universals such as trait structure and development; *intracultural* studies examine the unique expression of traits in specific cultures; and *intercultural* research characterizes cultures and their subgroups in terms of mean levels of personality traits and seeks associations between cultural variables and aggregate personality traits." Church (2000) remarked that two theoretical perspectives currently dominate research on culture and personality, the cross-cultural trait psychology approach, in which the trait concept is central, and the cultural psychology approach, in which the trait concept is questioned. Church reviewed the theory and research from both perspectives and proposed that the tenets of cultural psychology can be synthesized with the trait psychology approach, resulting in an integrated cultural trait psychology perspective.

In the last two decades, several cross-cultural studies have been conducted on the Eysenckian model of personality (Barrett & S. Eysenck, 1984; Laungani, 1985; S. B. G. Eysenck, Barrett, Spielberger, Evans, & H. J. Eysenck, 1986; Barrett, Petrides, S. B. G. Eysenck, & H. J. Eysenck, 1998; Ortet, Ibáñez, Moro, Silva, & Boyle, 1999). Laungani (1985, p. 217) concluded that "the organization of personality in India is sufficiently similar to that in England to make national comparisons feasible since identical dimensions underlie the personalities of Indian and English S's." The works of Barrett and S. Eysenck (1984) and Barrett et al. (1998) have included Indian data. Barrett et al. (1998, p. 805) concluded that their analyses "conclusively demonstrate a significant degree of factorial similarity with the U. K. data, across the 34 comparison countries."

Outside of India, a good deal of cross-cultural research has been carried out on the FFM. Reviewing work in the psycho-lexical research tradition, Saucier and Goldberg (1996) observed that the Big Five have been isolated in relatively similar form in lexical studies of American English, Dutch, and German, and pointed out that similar studies were underway in several languages. Saucier and Goldberg (2001) compared lexical studies in English and twelve other languages and concluded that the Anglo-Germanic Big Five is reproduced better in some languages than others. Although there are some culture-specific findings, in general the robustness of the FFM has been demonstrated across different cultures such as Chinese (McCrae, Costa, & Yik, 1996; Yik & Bond, 1993), Filipino (Katigbak, Church, Guanzon-Lapeña, Carlota, & del Pilar, 2000), French (McCrae, Costa, del Pilar, Rolland, & Parker, 1998), Greek (Tsaousis, 1999), South Korean (Piedmont & Chae, 1997), and Russian (Martin, Oryol, Rukavishnikov, & Senin, 2000). Angleitner and Ostendorf (2000) demonstrated the robustness of the FFM in German-speaking Switzerland, Austria, and former East and West Germany. McCrae et al. (1999) showed that age differences in the five factors of personality across the adult life span are parallel in samples from Germany, Italy, Portugal, Croatia and South Korea. Rolland (2000), on the basis of the data from sixteen cultures, claimed the cross-cultural validity of Neuroticism, Openness, and Conscientiousness. According to Rolland, Extraversion and Agreeableness, described as components of the interpersonal circumplex, appear to be more sensitive to cultural context. McCrae (2001) examined data from 26 cultures and showed that age and gender differences resembled those found in the American sample. An intercultural factor analysis yielded a close approximation to the FFM. On the methodological front, Caprara, Barbaranelli, Bermúdez, Maslach, and Ruch (2000) discussed multivariate methods for the comparison of factor structures in cross-cultural research and offered an illustration using the Big Five Questionnaire in Italian, American, Spanish, and German samples. Some theoretical analysis has been offered by McCrae and Costa (1996) and MacDonald (1998) that would explain the relative robustness of the FFM across different cultures. Certain authors (e.g., Eysenck, 1991; Block, 1995) have expressed their discontent with the FFM. However other authors like John and Srivastava (1999) have regarded it as "a major step ahead" (p. 131), though they, too, have pointed out some limitations.

1.3. Marathi Language and Maharashtra

When adapting any well-known non-Indian test or similar work in India, one is confronted with the fact that India is a multi-lingual country with many languages, sub-languages, and dialects. The 8th schedule of the constitution of India includes 18 languages, out of which 15 are the official languages of different Indian states (Silveira, 1998). In this work, we have adapted the NEO-PI-R in Marathi, one of the major languages in India. Marathi is an official language of the Maharashtra State, which has an area of 307,713 sq. kms. (9.36% of Indian area). According to provisional results of the latest census of India carried out in 2001 (Banthia, 2001), Maharashtra is the second largest populated state of India with a population of 96,752,247 (9.42% of Indian population). According to the 1991 census, 7.38% of the Indian population reported Marathi to be their mother tongue (Publications Division, Ministry of Information and Broadcasting, Government of India, 2001), making Marathi the fourth most widely spoken language in India. Assuming that the same percentage of people report Marathi as their mother tongue in the 2001 census also, and given the fact that many people in Maharashtra who do not report Marathi as their mother tongue can speak and understand Marathi, it seems safe to conclude that approximately 90 million people use Marathi in their day-to-day life.

Marathi belongs to the group of Indo-Aryan languages which are a part of the Indo-European family. Among the Indo-Aryan languages, Marathi is the southernmost. Like other Indo-Aryan languages, including Hindi, Marathi evolved from Sanskrit in different stages. According to Deshpande and Rajadhyaksha (1988), Marathi had been in use as a spoken language since about 600 A.D., and as a literary language since the 11th Century. Marathi had acquired a respectable place in the court life by the time of *Yadava* kings in 13th Century. The strong, powerful, and long literary tradition of Marathi has been traced by Deshpande and Rajadhyaksha (1988). Although Marathi draws a major part of its vocabulary from Sanskrit and its descendents, it has absorbed words from Kannad and Telugu, the languages of neighboring states. It has also absorbed words from Persian, Arabic, Turkish, Portuguese, and English. The script currently used in Marathi is Devanagari, a script also used by Hindi, the most widely spoken language in India. In fact, Marathi resembles Hindi to a considerable extent.

Although culture is a complex concept, the main stream Maharashtrian/Marathi culture is assumed to share the core characteristics of Indian culture. A good deal of excellent literature on the Marathi language, Maharashtra and its culture, and related aspects is available in the Marathi language. The English and Marathi bibliography in this regard is available in relevant entries in *Marathi Vishwakosh* (i.e. Marathi Encyclopedia, Vol.12, Joshi, 1985). Dastane (2000) can also be consulted for a working introduction to Maharashtra and Marathi.

1.4. Aims and Objectives

We have now presented a bird's-eye view of a) personality research in India; b) personality-and-culture studies employing the Eysenckian model and the FFM; and c) the Marathi language and Maharashtra State. With this background, we now specify the aims and objectives of this work, presenting two studies. Although different trait models have been extensively used in Indian research on personality and have yielded fruitful results (see the reviews quoted earlier), there is a paucity of research in India employing the FFM. As such, in the present chapter we intend to explore the validity of the FFM in the Indian context. For this purpose, we will present the psychometric properties of an adaptation of the NEO-PI-R and examine its factor structure in comparison to the normative American factor structure. We also intend to examine the relationship between the Eysenckian scales and the FFM scales. This would provide some validity data for the NEO-PI-R. We shall also explore gender differences in the FFM and Eysenck scales. We expect that gender differences would be small relative to the individual variation within genders, thus leading to low or medium effect sizes. The results obtained in the present study will also be compared with the results from other cultures. For the above purpose, two studies have been carried out and are reported here. The specific aims and objectives are listed below.

The aims and objectives of Study I are:

1) To present the Indian adaptation of the NEO-PI-R in Marathi and report its psychometric properties;
2) To examine gender differences on the NEO-PI-R scales;
3) To examine the factor structure of the NEO-PI-R in the Indian context; and
4) To compare the factor structure of the NEO-PI-R in Indian and American samples.

The aims and objectives of Study II are:

1) To examine the relationship between the Eysenck scales and the scales of a short

version of the NEO-PI-R, the NEO Five-Factor Inventory (NEO-FFI); and
2) To examine gender differences on the Eysenck and NEO-FFI scales.

2. STUDY I: AN INDIAN ADAPTATION OF THE NEO-PI-R

As pointed out above, there is a paucity of research in India employing the FFM. As
such, the first author of this chapter, who has keen interest in factor analytic theories of
personality and has done some work on the Eysenckian model, decided to initiate
research in this direction in his University. For this purpose, the development or
adaptation of a suitable tool for the assessment of five factors was necessary; hence the
present study, aimed at an adaptation of the NEO-PI-R and validation of the FFM, was
undertaken.

2.1. Marathi Adaptation of the NEO-PI-R: A Process

The NEO-PI-R measures five major dimensions of personality: Neuroticism (N),
Extraversion (E), Openness to Experience (O), Agreeableness (A), and Conscientiousness (C). Each of these dimensions (or domains) has been further conceptualized in
terms of six facet scales, thus yielding thirty facet scales in the NEO-PI-R (Costa &
McCrae, 1992). After studying the definition of each facet, all eight items were
translated as a set. This task was completed primarily by the second author and AP (see
Author Note), both being doctoral students in psychology. After translation, all the
items were rearranged according to the original order in the test booklet. Then the
translation and the original English inventory were given to two persons not familiar
with the NEO-PI-R (BK, contributory teacher in psychology and AJ, the University
teacher in English) for further comments and suggestions. Taking into account their
suggestions, the Marathi translation was edited by the first and second authors. The
comments of a Marathi language expert (VT) were invited on this translation, and the
translation was further edited. This Marathi translation was handed over to a psychologist (BRS) for backtranslation. This backtranslation was given to an English language
expert (SBG) for further comments. The two backtranslations were sent to the test
authors who provided some useful comments and suggested the revision of 24 items
(Nos. 7, 20, 21, 36, 47, 59, 89, 104, 111, 115, 125, 140, 142, 150, 159, 163, 170, 173,
198, 199, 205, 222, 223, 225). The revised translations of these 24 items and their backtranslations (by PHL, VT, SBG, and SD) were reviewed by the test authors and the
resulting inventory was approved as an authorized Marathi translation.

2.2. Method

Subjects. The subjects in Study I were 214 post-graduate students (graduate students in
American terminology; *Mean age* = 21.71 years, *SD* = 1.29) who were able to speak,
write, and understand Marathi comfortably. Of these subjects, 107 were males (*Mean
age* = 22.18 years, *SD* = 1.53) and the remaining 107 were females (*Mean age* = 21.25
years, *SD* = 0.75). This sample was drawn from ten University departments so that it
would be fairly heterogeneous.

Procedure. Subjects were administered the Marathi version of the NEO-PI-R in small groups ranging from 8 to 33. Subjects were told they could respond anonymously, but no one did. As an incentive to participate in the study, subjects were promised feedback if they were interested. While collecting the completed answer sheet from each subject, it was scanned for missing data. As a result, we had 107 and 112 complete answer sheets for the males and females, respectively. To have an equal number of cases for males and females, the data of five female subjects were omitted. After scoring was completed, subjects were given feedback in sealed envelopes using the form developed by Costa and McCrae (1992, p. 9); subjects were told they could contact the investigator for further clarification with respect to the feedback, if necessary. Quite a few subjects used this opportunity.

2.3. Results and Discussion

Descriptive statistics and internal consistency. Means and standard deviations are reported in Table 1 for the five domain scales and the 30 facet scales by gender and for the entire sample. Cronbach alphas for the full sample are also presented in Table 1. An examination of Table 1 reveals that internal consistencies for the domain scores of N and C are high (.88 and .90, respectively) and are comparable to those in the normative sample (Costa & McCrae, 1992). The alpha coefficients for the domain scores of E, O, and A are also satisfactory (Nunnally, 1981), although somewhat lower than the corresponding coefficients in the normative sample. Alpha coefficients for most of the facet scales (except O6: Values) should be regarded satisfactory in view of the fact that each is based on only eight items. The alpha coefficient for O6 is, however, quite low. In this context, it may be noted that Martin, Oryol, Rukavishnikov, and Senin (2000) and Piedmont and Chae (1997) encountered the problem of low reliability with the O6 facet when developing the Russian and Korean versions of the NEO-PI-R. The nature of the O6: Values scale needs to be further explored in the Indian context.

Gender differences. To evaluate gender differences in the 30 facet scales, one-way multivariate analysis of variance (MANOVA) was carried out with gender as an independent variable and the 30 facet scales as dependent variables. The domain scores were not included in this MANOVA since each domain score is completely linearly dependent on the respective facet scores. The suitability of MANOVA and the assumptions underlying it were carefully assessed following Norušis/SPSS Inc. (1990a), Tabachnick and Fidell (1989), and Huberty and Petoskey (2000). The MANOVA yielded a Wilks' Lambda (Λ) value of 0.71217. The transformation of Wilks' Lambda provided $F(30, 183) = 2.465$, $p < .001$. Since Wilks' Lambda is highly significant, multiple univariate F tests were carried out to identify the specific dependent variables whose means differed significantly by gender. For facet means showing significant gender differences, Cohen's d was also computed to assess effect size. The results indicated that there are no significant gender differences for 21 facet scales. Males, as compared to females, showed significantly higher means on the facet scales of Impulsiveness ($F = 4.82, p < .05; d = 0.30$), and Excitement-Seeking ($F = 8.10$, $p =$

Table 1. Descriptive Statistics and Alpha Reliabilities.

NEO-PI-R scale	Males		Females		Entire Sample		
	Mean	*SD*	*Mean*	*SD*	*Mean*	*SD*	Alpha
Domains							
N: Neuroticism	85.4	20.5	85.0	22.0	85.2	21.2	.88
E: Extraversion	106.4	15.4	107.8	15.8	107.1	15.5	.77
O: Openness to Experience	110.2	13.8	114.3	13.4	112.3	13.7	.73
A: Agreeableness	116.8	14.8	121.7	14.0	119.3	14.6	.75
C: Conscientiousness	119.1	21.9	124.5	18.5	121.8	20.4	.90
Facets							
N1: Anxiety	16.2	4.3	17.0	4.7	16.6	4.5	.60
N2: Angry Hostility	13.5	4.9	13.3	5.1	13.4	5.0	.63
N3: Depression	14.9	4.9	14.6	5.0	14.7	4.9	.65
N4: Self-Consciousness	15.6	4.7	15.2	4.5	15.4	4.6	.53
N5: Impulsiveness[a]	14.3	4.6	13.0	4.3	13.7	4.5	.54
N6: Vulnerability	10.9	4.4	11.9	5.5	11.4	5.0	.72
E1: Warmth	20.6	4.5	20.9	4.5	20.7	4.5	.66
E2: Gregariousness	16.9	4.9	18.2	5.4	17.5	5.2	.63
E3: Assertiveness	13.6	4.9	13.5	4.5	13.6	4.7	.68
E4: Activity	17.3	3.5	17.6	3.8	17.5	3.7	.37
E5: Excitement-Seeking[a]	17.1	4.3	15.5	4.1	16.3	4.2	.44
E6: Positive Emotions[a]	20.9	4.1	22.1	4.0	21.5	4.1	.55
O1: Fantasy	15.3	3.8	15.8	4.1	15.5	3.9	.44
O2: Aesthetics[a]	21.9	5.2	23.8	4.1	22.8	4.8	.70
O3: Feelings	20.9	3.8	21.2	3.8	21.0	3.8	.51
O4: Actions	14.9	4.0	15.7	3.7	15.3	3.9	.43
O5: Ideas	21.0	4.8	20.6	4.6	20.8	4.7	.67
O6: Values[a]	16.4	2.9	17.2	3.4	16.8	3.2	.10
A1: Trust	20.1	4.6	21.0	3.7	20.5	4.2	.61
A2: Straightforwardness[a]	20.2	5.1	22.1	4.2	21.2	4.7	.57
A3: Altruism[a]	21.1	3.7	22.7	3.3	21.9	3.6	.49
A4: Compliance	17.4	4.2	17.0	5.0	17.2	4.6	.49
A5: Modesty	16.5	3.6	17.0	3.6	16.8	3.6	.41
A6: Tender-Mindedness	21.5	3.9	21.9	3.9	21.7	3.9	.42
C1: Competence	20.0	4.4	20.3	3.7	20.2	4.0	.62
C2: Order[a]	19.6	5.4	21.4	4.8	20.5	5.2	.75
C3: Dutifulness	22.2	4.7	23.3	3.4	22.7	4.1	.57
C4: Achievement Striving	21.0	4.9	21.6	4.1	21.3	4.5	.65
C5: Self-Discipline	18.0	4.7	18.5	4.7	18.3	4.7	.65
C6: Deliberation[a]	18.2	4.0	19.5	4.0	18.9	4.0	.57

Note. N = 107 males, 107 females. [a]Facet scale showing significant gender differences.

.005; $d = 0.39$); and significantly lower means on Positive Emotions ($F = 4.46, p < .05$; $d = 0.29$), Openness to Aesthetics ($F = 8.93, p < .005$; $d = 0.41$) and Values ($F = 3.99$, $p < .05$; $d = 0.27$), and Straightforwardness ($F = 9.32, p < .005$; $d = 0.42$), Altruism ($F = 11.56, p = .001$; $d = 0.46$), Order ($F = 6.58, p < .05$; $d = 0.35$), and Deliberation ($F = 5.20, p < .05$; $d = 0.31$). It may be noted that all effect sizes are in the low to medium (0.27 to 0.46) range by Cohen's (1992) classification.

The obtained gender differences are either in line with previous findings or in the direction expected by us. Costa, Terracciano, and McCrae (2001) presented the results of secondary analysis of NEO-PI-R data from 26 cultures. They presented gender differences in three groups: U. S. adults, other culture college-age subjects, and other culture adults. The findings, in this chapter, of males being higher on Excitement-Seeking and females being higher on Positive Emotions, Aesthetics, Straightforward-ness, and Altruism are in line with the results reported by Costa et al. (2001) for all the three groups. The present finding that females are higher on Values is in line with Costa et al.'s result for the group of "other culture college subjects." Similarly, the present finding that females score higher on Order is in line with Costa et al.'s result for the group of "other culture adults." Although our finding that males score higher on Impulsiveness is contrary to Costa et al.'s results, it is not at all unexpected to us, because, during socialization in Indian culture, it is emphasized that females should control impulsiveness of the sort measured by this facet scale. Similarly, our finding that females are higher on Deliberation is also understandable in the Indian cultural context. Although the obtained gender differences are in line with either earlier findings or our expectations, it may be pointed out here that for 21 facet scales there are no significant gender differences and for the nine facet scales for which gender differences are statistically significant, the effect sizes are quite modest in magnitude (low to medium range). The gender differences reported by Costa et al. are also modest. Thus we conclude in line with Costa and McCrae (1992, p. 55), "For many purposes it would appear to be appropriate to use combined sex norms."

Domain correlations. The correlations among the five domain scales for the full sample, along with their significance levels, are reported in Table 2, below the diagonal. It may be noted that the correlation between N and C scales is $-.51$, the correlation

Table 2. Correlations Among the Five NEO-PI-R Domain Scales And Oblique Procrustes-Rotated Factors.

Scale	N	E	O	A	C
N		$-.04$	$-.13$	.18**	$-.22$**
E	$-.20$**		.22**	.16*	.23***
O	$-.12$	.38***		$-.08$	.18**
A	$-.15$*	.04	.05		.07
C	$-.51$***	.23***	.15*	.30***	

Note. Correlations among domains given below the diagonal; correlations among factors given above the diagonal. N = Neuroticism, E = Extraversion, O = Openness to Experience, A = Agreeableness, C = Conscientiousness. * $p < .05$. ** $p < .01$. *** $p < .001$.

between E and O scales is .38, and the correlation between A and C scale is .30. All other correlations, although some of them statistically significant by virtue of a sample size of 214, are quite small and of no practical consequence. The correlations among the five domain scales are quite similar to the correlations among the corresponding scales obtained by Costa and McCrae (1992) for the adult normative sample.

Incidentally, it may be noted that the application of *Box's M* test of homogeneity of variance-covariance matrices indicated that the variance-covariance matrices, based on the five domain scores, did not differ significantly between males and females (*Box's M* = 15.877, χ^2 = 15.477, *df* = 15, *p* = .42). As Marascuilo and Levin (1983) pointed out, this implies the equality of the two corresponding correlation matrices. Thus, there are no gender differences for the correlations among the five domain scales. This is a welcome feature.

Correlations of the NEO-PI-R domain scales with the NEO Five-Factor Inventory (NEO-FFI) scales. The NEO-FFI is a 60-item short version of the NEO-PI-R, with 12 items per scale. NEO-FFI scales were scored from the item data and correlated with the corresponding NEO-PI-R domain scores. These correlations were .86, .78, .79, .73, and .89, respectively, for the N, E, O, A, and C domains. Thus, the NEO-FFI can be used as a substitute to NEO-PI-R when the shorter version is needed.

Factor Analyses of the NEO-PI-R. The factor analyses reported here are motivated by two objectives: a) to assess the factorial invariance of the NEO-PI-R across the Indian and American cultures; and b) to evaluate the FFM. Obviously, the two objectives are interdependent. Initially, the 30 × 30 correlation matrix, based on the facet scales, was subjected to careful scrutiny for factorability (Norušis/SPSS Inc., 1990b; Tabachnick & Fidell, 1989). Principal components analysis was then performed. Both Cattell's scree test and Five-Factor Theory suggested a five-factor solution. Nevertheless, four-factor, five-factor, and six-factor varimax-rotated principal component solutions were obtained. The five-factor solution, explaining 53.2 per sent of total variance, was comparatively more interpretable. The factors maximally corresponding to the respective domains, were labeled accordingly for comprehension. The five-factor varimax solution is presented in Table 3.

The varimax solution approximates the American factor structure, except that the E and A factors are misaligned to some extent, and the highest loadings of two of the O scales (O4 and O6) are not on the intended factor (though these two facets load above .30 on the O factor also). These findings are not completely unexpected. As McCrae, Zonderman, Costa, Bond, and Paunonen (1996, p. 558) remarked, "exploratory analyses are not necessarily optimal for testing hypothesized models." In principal components analysis with varimax rotation—an exploratory factor analytic method— theory can at most suggest the number of factors to be rotated; neither extraction nor rotation is guided by theory. This can be a crucial issue, especially when the hypothesized structure is not simple. As McCrae, Zonderman et al. (1996, p. 558) noted, "small differences in the observed correlations can then yield large differences in the position of the axes, and the solutions may appear to be dramatically different."

Table 3. Factor Pattern Matrix for the NEO-PI-R Facet Scales: Varimax Rotation.

NEO–PI–R Facet	Factor					h^2
	N	**E**	**O**	**A**	**C**	
N1: Anxiety	**.77**	.01	.24	.12	−.11	.68
N2: Angry Hostility	**.61**	−.34	.07	−.30	−.13	.60
N3: Depression	**.66**	−.09	.11	.14	−**.43**	.66
N4: Self-Consciousness	**.67**	−.08	.05	.04	−.33	.57
N5: Impulsiveness	.39	.06	.08	−.31	−**.47**	.48
N6: Vulnerability	**.67**	.04	.13	.12	−**.45**	.68
E1: Warmth	−.10	**.76**	.18	−.08	.09	.64
E2: Gregariousness	.05	**.77**	−.01	−.03	−.08	.60
E3: Assertiveness	−**.41**	.10	.17	−**.57**	.21	.58
E4: Activity	−.17	.08	.08	−**.45**	.39	.40
E5: Excitement-Seeking	−.06	.20	.18	−**.47**	−.26	.37
E6: Positive Emotions	−.01	**.54**	**.47**	−.16	.18	.58
O1: Fantasy	.15	−.03	**.57**	−.10	−.22	.40
O2: Aesthetics	.08	.16	**.73**	.13	.13	.60
O3: Feelings	.05	.19	**.65**	−.17	.19	.53
O4: Actions	−**.45**	.03	.31	−.08	−.18	.33
O5: Ideas	−.32	.00	**.42**	−.28	.32	.46
O6: Values	−**.52**	−.30	.36	.15	−.19	.55
A1: Trust	−.27	.36	.06	.39	.07	.37
A2: Straightforwardness	.12	.01	.23	**.63**	.18	.49
A3: Altruism	−.17	**.46**	.31	.27	.34	.52
A4: Compliance	−.15	.34	−.03	**.62**	.03	.53
A5: Modesty	.01	−.04	−.10	**.47**	−.01	.23
A6: Tender-Mindedness	.38	**.41**	−.00	.32	.29	.49
C1: Competence	−.31	.11	.15	−.18	**.72**	.68
C2: Order	.10	.04	−.07	.15	**.73**	.57
C3: Dutifulness	−.12	.07	.14	.21	**.70**	.58
C4: Ach. Striving	−.09	.12	.06	−.09	**.76**	.61
C5: Self-Discipline	−.24	.07	−.05	−.07	**.77**	.66
C6: Deliberation	−.06	−.00	.06	.13	**.71**	.53

Note. $N = 214$. Loadings greater than .40 in absolute value are given in boldface.

McCrae, Costa, del Pilar, Rolland, and Parker (1998, p. 179) commented that "varimax rotation is designed to optimize simple structure and is not necessarily appropriate for the analysis of variables that show circumplex ordering, as do the facets of E and A." When the correlation matrices for two groups are separately factor analyzed and rotated, sometimes the apparent varying structure may merely represent "a rotational shift in the data due to sample-specific error" (Piedmont & Chae, 1997, p. 140). To overcome this problem, McCrae, Zonderman et al. (1996) suggested orthogonal Procrustes rotation as an alternative. McCrae, Zonderman et al. (1996), Piedmont and Chae (1997), McCrae, Costa, del Pillar et al. (1998), and Angleitner and Ostendorf

(2000) employed orthogonal Procrustes rotation toward the American normative factor pattern. In the context of the study of factorial invariance, Procrustes rotation has also been recommended by Mulaik (1972). As such, to assess the factorial similarity, the five-factor varimax solution was subjected to orthogonal Procrustes rotation (Schöne-mann, 1966; McCrae, Zonderman et al., 1996) to the American normative factor pattern (Costa & McCrae, 1992), and the results are presented in Table 4. Examination of various congruence coefficients reveal that there is a very high degree of similarity between the two factor patterns, thus demonstrating factorial invariance across the two cultures. The congruence coefficients for the five factors range from 0.89 to 0.97. The variable congruence coefficients are also quite satisfactory except for O6: Values and A6: Tender-Mindedness. The overall coefficient of congruence is 0.94.

Orthogonal and oblique Procrustes rotations to a hypothesized binary target matrix are underutilized for evaluating the FFM, although the possibilities are suggested by McCrae, Zonderman et al. (1996). (The hypothesized binary target matrix is formed by indicating the targeted loadings by unities and the non-targeted loadings by zeros.) The varimax solution presented in Table 3 was therefore also subjected to orthogonal (Schönemann, 1966) and oblique (Mulaik, 1972) Procrustes rotation to the hypothe-sized binary target matrix.

The results of both Procrustes rotations very clearly support the FFM.[1] Only E4: Activity had its highest loading on a non-intended factor, C. The intercorrelations among the oblique Procrustes-rotated factors are shown above the diagonal in Table 2. Although some are statistically significant in this large sample, all are quite low, and the five factors, for practical purposes, can be regarded as orthogonal. This is not a mathematical artifact imposed by an orthogonal method. In this context it may be pointed out that oblique Procrustes rotation has been strongly criticized by certain authors (e.g., Horn, 1967) because it can capitalize on chance considerably by introducing high obliqueness (i.e., high intercorrelations among factors) in the process of rotation. Horn, therefore, suggested examining the intercorrelations among oblique Procrustes-rotated factors. Since the intercorrelations among the factors obtained in the present analysis are quite low, this criticism is not applicable here.

Apart from maximum likelihood confirmatory factor analysis (CFA; discussed by McCrae, Zonderman et al., 1996, in the context of the NEO-PI-R) and allied methods from the LISREL family (Jöreskog & Sörbom, 1986) and Procrustes rotation methods, multiple group factor analysis (MGFA) also merits consideration as a technique of CFA. Several factor analysts like Guttman (1952), Harman (1970), and Gorsuch (1974) have emphasized the hypothesis testing role of MGFA. Nunnally (1981, p. 399) went so far as to claim that he was "sold" on the general usefulness of multiple group methods for performing CFA. Mulaik (1988, p. 273) also discussed MGFA in his chapter on CFA under the caption "revival of an old method." Retaining unities on the diagonal of the correlation matrix, we worked out oblique as well as the orthogonal MGFA solutions. The five MGFA factors explained 49.8 per cent of total variance. Thus the MGFA explained only 3.4 per cent variance less than the solutions based on principal components analysis, a method known for its efficiency in condensing the maximum variance. Both of them very clearly support the FFM.

---

[1]These matrices, and those from the MGFA analyses, are available from the first author.

Table 4. Factor Pattern Matrix for the NEO-PI-R Facet Scales:
Orthogonal Procrustes Rotation to Normative American Pattern.

NEO–PI–R Facet	N	E	O	A	C	VC[b]
			Factor			
N1: Anxiety	**.81**	.01	−.01	.15	−.03	.98**
N2: Angry Hostility	**.64**	−.14	−.04	**−.41**	−.02	.98**
N3: Depression	**.71**	−.12	−.06	.07	−.36	.98**
N4: Self–Consciousness	**.69**	−.08	−.12	−.01	−.26	.98**
N5: Impulsiveness	**.45**	.21	−.02	−.28	−.39	.97**
N6: Vulnerability	**.72**	.01	−.07	.10	−.39	.98**
E1: Warmth	−.11	**.73**	.06	.29	.05	.97**
E2: Gregariousness	.00	**.69**	−.15	.30	−.13	.88*
E3: Assertiveness	−.37	.37	.27	**−.42**	.22	.98**
E4: Activity	−.18	.29	.10	−.32	**.41**	.89*
E5: Excitement–Seeking	.02	**.41**	.19	−.34	−.21	.94**
E6: Positive Emotions	.07	**.62**	.34	.18	.19	.95**
O1: Fantasy	.34	.11	**.50**	−.05	−.14	.93*
O2: Aesthetics	.26	.19	**.62**	.29	.17	.95**
O3: Feelings	.20	.35	**.56**	.03	.25	.95**
O4: Actions	−.31	.11	**.43**	−.05	−.19	.90*
O5: Ideas	−.22	.19	**.48**	−.17	.35	.86*
O6: Values	−.35	−.29	**.55**	.02	−.20	.80
A1: Trust	−.28	.15	.06	**.51**	−.01	.99**
A2: Straightforwardness	.15	−.24	.15	**.61**	.15	.89*
A3: Altruism	−.15	.33	.24	**.51**	.28	.90*
A4: Compliance	−.18	.01	−.07	**.70**	−.06	.98**
A5: Modesty	−.03	−.26	−.10	.38	−.06	.87*
A6: Tender–Mindedness	.29	.22	−.21	**.50**	.26	.73
C1: Competence	−.34	.21	.17	−.02	**.70**	.99**
C2: Order	−.01	−.04	−.15	.22	**.70**	.95**
C3: Dutifulness	−.16	−.01	.11	.30	**.67**	.99**
C4: Ach. Striving	−.16	.16	.02	.06	**.74**	.95**
C5: Self–Discipline	−.34	.08	−.03	.04	**.73**	.99**
C6: Deliberation	−.12	−.05	.03	.19	**.69**	.92*
Congruence	.95**	.91**	.89**	.95**	.97**	.94**

Note. N = 214. Loadings greater than .40 in absolute value are given in boldface. VC = variable congruence. *Congruence higher than that of 95% of rotations from random data. ** Congruence higher than that of 99% of rotations from random data.

Intercultural comparisons. As in earlier research in other cultures, the present study has demonstrated the factorial invariance of the NEO-PI-R across Indian and American cultures. This permits meaningful intercultural comparisons in terms of the FFM. Factor scores can be computed for such a purpose using factor scoring weights of the normative U. S. sample. Costa and McCrae (1992, p. 7) have discussed the advantages of factor scores over the simple domain scores. McCrae (2001), in fact, obtained composite factor T-scores for 26 cultures including India (using our present data). Indians showed high factor scores on A (T-score = 56.7), and C (T-score = 55.7), low factor scores on E (T-score = 40.7) and average factor scores on N (T-score = 49.1) and O (T-score = 51.4). These findings are interesting. However, to what extent they reflect genuine Indian personality characteristics and to what extent they are sample specific is a matter of speculation. The sample for this study was drawn from the post-graduate students of University departments where the admission is quite competitive. The students in such departments are likely to be more conscientious than the average population. De Raad (2000) has presented a brief review on the role of conscientiousness in achievement in general and academic success and performance in particular. Wolfe and Johnson (1995) have indicated the role of Big Five Conscientiousness in prediction of college performance.

To clarify the results further, some findings relating Eysenckian Psychoticism, A, C, academic achievement and academic interest need to be recapitulated. McCrae and Costa (1985) reported that Psychoticism correlated –.45 and –.31 with A and C, respectively, and Costa and McCrae (1995) reported negative correlations of A and C with various components of Psychoticism derived from the Eysenck Personality Profiler scales (H. J. Eysenck & Wilson, 1991). Brand (1997, p. 23) remarked that modern workers invariably find Psychoticism linked to "disagreeableness." H. J. Eysenck and S. B. G. Eysenck (1976) have pointed out that Psychoticism correlates negatively with educational achievement and interest. High Psychoticism scorers would tend to drop out before they reach post-graduation level. Thus it can be expected that the post-graduate students would be low on Psychoticism and high on A and C. In view of the well established association between introversion and academic performance (Eysenck, 1969), post-graduate students are also expected to be comparatively introverted. Thus a post-hoc explanation can be offered for the findings about the Indian personality profile in terms of sample-specific characteristics, though an alternative possibility that, to some extent, it reflects a real phenomenon cannot be ruled out. As such, the generalizability of these findings needs to be assessed by fresh studies employing large and properly representative samples.[2]

To sum up, we have presented a reliable Marathi adaptation of the NEO-PI-R, with modest gender differences. The obtained factor pattern supports the FFM and shows quite a high degree of similarity to the normative American factor pattern, thus indicating factorial invariance. As such, the tool is ready for cross-cultural work. The study has also demonstrated the utility of oblique Procrustean rotation as well as multiple group factor analysis for evaluating the Five-Factor Model.

3. STUDY II: EYSENCKIAN DIMENSIONS OF PERSONALITY AND THE FIVE FACTORS

H. J. Eysenck and his collaborators have conceptualized personality in terms of three higher order factors—Extraversion (E), Neuroticism (N), and Psychoticism (P). In this study, we aim to investigate the Eysenckian correlates of the five factors, since

---

[2]See a comparison with a Telugu sample in McCrae (2002).

obtaining the theoretically expected correlations would provide validity evidence for our adaptation. We expect that the Eysenckian N and E scales would correlate with Costa and McCrae's N and E scales, respectively. As pointed out in Study I, McCrae and Costa (1985) reported Eysenckian P correlates negatively with A and C scales. Eysenck (1997) claimed that both A and C are primary rather than higher order factors, and both form part of his P factor. Although a critical appraisal of the controversy in this regard is beyond the scope of the present chapter, it would be legitimate to expect that in this study P would be negatively correlated with A and C scales. McCrae and Costa (1985) remarked that O is represented in the FFM but not in the Eysenckian system. For H. J. Eysenck, O is a dimension belonging to the intellectual domain. In either case it would be expected that O would show low correlations with Eysenckian dimensions.

The Eysenckian Lie (L) scale has multiple interpretations (Dicken, 1959; H. J. Eysenck & S. B. G. Eysenck, 1976; Jackson & Francis, 1999). As Lodhi and Thakur (1993, p. 122) remarked, "Much current research has shown that under conditions for high motivation to dissimulate, 'L' scale measures the degree of faking and under conditions for low motivation to dissimulate, it measures a trait of social conformity." According to McCrae and Costa (1983), social desirability scales assess "more substance than style." McCrae and Costa (1985) reported a correlation of .29 between C and L. Lodhi (unpublished) obtained a correlation of .69 between the Lie scale of the Revised Eysenck Personality Questionnaire (EPQ-R) and the Marlowe-Crowne Social Desirability Scale (Crowne & Marlowe, 1960), a measure of need for social approval. It is reasonable to think that a person high on social conformity or a need for approval would tend to behave in agreeable ways with others. As such, we expect the Eysenckian L scale to correlate positively with A and C.

3.1. Method

Subjects. The subjects in Study II were 300 undergraduate students (*Mean age* = 19.29 years, *SD* = 1.23) who were able to speak, write, and understand Marathi comfortably. Out of these subjects, 150 were males (*Mean age* = 19.47 years, *SD* = 1.33) and the remaining 150 were females (*Mean age* = 19.10 years, *SD* = 1.09). This sample was drawn from three faculties—Arts, Commerce, and Science—from two local colleges, so that it would be fairly heterogeneous.

Measures. The Marathi adaptation of the NEO-FFI (a 60 item version of the NEO-PI-R) was developed by selecting the corresponding items. As pointed out in Study I, NEO-FFI N, E, O, A, and C scales correlate .86, .78, .79, .73, and .89 with the corresponding NEO-PI-R scales, thus indicating that the NEO-FFI can be used as a substitute for the NEO-PI-R when a shorter version is needed.

A Marathi translation of the Revised Eysenck Personality Questionnaire (EPQ-R, S. B. G. Eysenck, H. J. Eysenck, and Barrett, 1985) had been developed by the first author and had yielded theoretically consistent results (Lodhi & Thakur, 1993). The Marathi translations as well as the original English versions of the various Eysenckian tests had provided satisfactory results in our previous studies (e.g., Lodhi, 1985, and Palsane &

Lodhi, 1979, Marathi translation of EPI Form A; Lodhi & Thomas, 1991, English JEPQ). Currently at our University, six doctoral students, under the supervision of the first author, are using Eysenckian tests, out of which four are using the Marathi translation of the EPQ-R.

. *Procedure.* The subjects were administered the NEO-FFI (Form S) and the EPQ-R in addition to a trial inventory, the results of which are not reported here. As an incentive to participate in the study, the subjects were promised feedback if they were interested. Feedback was provided to all subjects.

3.2. Results and Discussion

Descriptive statistics. Means and standard deviations are reported in Table 5 for nine personality scales (four EPQ-R scales and five NEO-FFI scales) for men, women, and the total sample.

Gender differences. To evaluate gender differences in the nine personality scales, one way MANOVA was carried out with gender as an independent variable and the nine personality scales as dependent variables. The MANOVA yielded a Wilks' Lambda (Λ) value of 0.71526. The transformation of Wilks' Lambda provided $F(9, 290) = 12.827$, $p < .001$. Since Wilks' Lambda is highly significant, multiple univariate F tests were carried out to identify specific personality scales whose means differed significantly by gender. For the personality scale means showing significant gender differences, Cohen's *d* has been reported to assess the effect size. The significant univariate F ratios and the corresponding effect sizes are presented in Table 5.

Gender differences in the Eysenckian scales are in the expected direction. Females scored higher on N and lower on P. These findings are in line with earlier findings for

Table 5. Descriptive Statistics for Nine Variables and Gender Differences.

Variables	Total		Males		Females		F	d
	Mean	*SD*	*Mean*	*SD*	*Mean*	*SD*	*F*	*d*
EPQ-R Scales								
Extraversion	15.84	3.57	15.97	3.69	15.71	3.46		
Neuroticism	12.72	4.92	11.65	4.95	13.78	4.68	14.62***	.44
Psychoticism	7.16	2.91	7.63	3.27	6.69	2.41	8.15**	.33
Lie	13.37	4.10	11.91	4.13	14.83	3.53	43.12***	.76
NEO-FFI Scales								
Neuroticism	20.33	6.05	19.83	6.13	20.83	5.95		
Extraversion	30.45	5.80	31.44	5.70	29.45	5.74	9.04**	.35
Openness	25.67	4.64	25.89	4.57	25.45	4.72		
Agreeableness	30.10	5.74	28.58	5.94	31.61	5.12	22.44***	.55
Conscientiousness	34.42	6.23	33.85	6.84	34.99	5.51		

Note. Only statistically significant $F(1, 298)$ ratios are reported. $*p < .05$. $**p < .01$. $***p < .001$.

this age group (H. J. Eysenck & S. B. G. Eysenck, 1975; S. B. G. Eysenck, H. J. Eysenck, & Barrett, 1985). The effect sizes are quite modest. Before commenting on the gender differences for the L scale, a cross-culturally interesting finding may be noted. The present sample has scored higher on the L scale than the British normative sample (S. B. G. Eysenck, H. J. Eysenck & Barrett, 1985). These findings are in line with earlier Indian findings (Ameerjan & Thimmappa, 1980; Lodhi, 1985; Laungani, 1985; Nighojkar, 2000), and can be explained in terms of "different social desirability of an item among different cultural groups" (Manaster & Havinghurst, 1972, p. 37) and higher social conformity in Indians, an explanation also offered by Laungani (1985). Returning to gender differences, females score higher than males on the L scale. Although this gender difference is in the direction reported by Laungani (1985), the effect size obtained here ($d = 0.76$) appears to be high. The causes of this gender difference appear to be culture and age specific; girls around 18 in this culture are expected to conform to social norms and regulations considerably more than boys. The gender difference for the NEO-FFI A scale is in line with Costa, Terracciano, and McCrae (2001). Costa et al. (2001) reported, in the context of NEO-PI-R E, that males are higher on certain facets and females are higher on others. In this study, for the overall E scale, males are slightly higher than the females, the effect size being modest ($d = 0.35$).

Correlations among nine personality scales. The application of *Box's M* test of homogeneity of variance-covariance matrices indicated that the variance-covariance matrices based on nine personality scales did not differ significantly between males and females (*Box's M* = 57.441, χ^2 = 55.629, df = 45, $p = .13$). This implies that the hypothesis of the equality of the two corresponding correlation matrices can be accepted.

The correlations among nine personality scales for entire sample along with their significance levels are reported in Table 6. The N and E scales of the NEO-FFI corre-

Table 6. Intercorrelations Among EPQ-R and NEO-FFI Scales.

Scale	1.	2.	3.	4.	5.	6.	7.	8.
EPQ-R								
1. E								
2. N	−.09							
3. P	.04	.21***						
4. L	−.02	−.18**	−.42***					
NEO-FFI								
5. N	−.09	.60***	.19***	−.19***				
6. E	.53***	−.17**	−.10	.04	−.17**			
7. O	.14*	−.09	−.17**	.04	−.19***	.19***		
8. A	−.01	−.30***	−.42***	.51***	−.37***	.20***	.07	
9. C	.14*	−.15**	−.33***	.46***	−.25***	.28***	.19***	.39***

Note. EPQ-R = Revised Eysenck Personality Questionnaire. NEO-FFI = NEO Five-Factor Inventory. E = Extraversion, N = Neuroticism, P = Psychoticism, L = Lie, O = Openness to Experience, A = Agreeableness, C = Conscientiousness. $N = 300$. *$p < .05$. **$p < .01$. ***$p < .001$.

late .60 and .53 with the corresponding Eysenckian scales, indicating the validity of the NEO-FFI scales. Moreover, if the longer NEO-PI-R scales were employed, these correlations would be expected to improve further. The correlations of A and C scales with the Eysenckian P are also in line with the previous findings, even the values of the correlation coefficients approximating the values reported by McCrae and Costa (1985). As expected, the O scale of the NEO-FFI has very low correlations with Eysenckian dimensions, although, due to large sample size, some are significant. The correlations of Eysenckian L scale with NEO-FFI A and C scales and the Eysenckian P scale are also in the expected direction. The high social conformity and approval need in Indians, evident from high L score in this study and the cultural stereotypes, and the reasonably high correlation of the L scale with A may also explain the finding of high A in Indians in intercultural comparisions (McCrae, 2001). Thus, practically all the correlations of the NEO-FFI scales with the Eysenckian scales are in the theoretically predicted directions, providing evidence for the validity of the NEO-FFI scales and their parent scales in the NEO-PI-R.

4. CONCLUDING COMMENTS AND FURTHER RESEARCH

In this chapter we have reported two studies. In the first we presented a reliable Indian (Marathi) adaptation of the Revised NEO Personality Inventory which shows generally modest gender differences. The obtained factor pattern supported the FFM and showed quite a high degree of similarity with the normative American factor pattern, thus indicating factorial invariance across the two cultures. The tool thus appears to be ready for cross-cultural work. Study I also demonstrated the utility of oblique and orthogonal Procrustes rotations to a hypothesized binary target matrix, as well as multiple group factor analysis for evaluating the Five-Factor Model. The second study examined the Eysenckian correlates of the Indian (Marathi) NEO Five-Factor Inventory (NEO-FFI). The obtained correlations provide validity evidence for the NEO-FFI scales and their parent scales in the NEO-PI-R.

Several research studies are in progress under the supervision of the first author utilizing the present Marathi adaptation. The first investigation deals with a comparative study of addicts and non-addicts employing Eysenckian and FFM measures. Brown-sugar (crude-heroin), alcohol, and nicotine addicts are examined in this work. The second study in progress relates to the personality of criminals, again employing the Eysenckian and Five-Factor Models. A third study is concerned with the personality correlates of creativity; the fourth intends to conduct a joint factor analysis of the two instruments. This study also aims to investigate the effects of experimentally induced response sets in assessing the five factors. These studies will provide validity evidence for the Indian (Marathi) adaptation of the NEO-PI-R. We also hope that these studies would make a modest contribution to the field of personality psychology, particularly the Five-Factor Theory.

REFERENCES

Ameerjan, M. S., & Thimmappa, M. S. (1980). A study of Lie scores in Eysenck Personality Inventory.

Psychological Studies, 25, 23-25.

Angleitner, A., & Ostendorf, F. (2000, July). *The FFM: A comparison of German speaking countries (Austria, Former East and West Germany, and Switzerland).* Paper presented at the XXVIIth International Congress of Psychology, Stockholm, Sweden.

Asthana, H. S. (1988). Personality. In J. Pande (Ed.), *Psychology in India: The state-of-the-art, Vol. 1. Personality and mental processes* (pp. 153-189). New Delhi: Sage Publications.

Banthia, J. K. (2001). *Census of India 2001, Series-1, India, Provisional population totals, Paper -1 of 2001.* Delhi: Registrar General and Census Commissioner, India.

Barlingay, S. S. (1998). *Reunderstanding Indian philosophy.* New Delhi: D. K. Printworld.

Barrett, P., & Eysenck, S. (1984). The assessment of personality factors across 25 countries. *Personality and Individual Differences, 5*, 615-632.

Barrett, P. T., Petrides, K. V., Eysenck, S. B. G., & Eysenck, H. J. (1998). The Eysenck Personality Questionnaire: An examination of the factorial similarity of P, E, N, and L across 34 countries. *Personality and Individual Differences, 25*, 805-819.

Bayly, S. (1999). *The new Cambridge history of India: IV. 3. Caste, society and politics in India from the eighteenth century to the modern age.* Cambridge: Cambridge University Press.

Block, J. (1995). A contrarian view of the five-factor approach to personality description. *Psychological Bulletin, 117*, 187-215.

Brand, C. R. (1997). Hans Eysenck's personality dimensions: Their number and nature. In H. Nyborg (Ed.), *The scientific study of human nature: Tribute to Hans J. Eysenck at eighty.* (pp. 17-35). Oxford: Pergamon.

Brislin, R. W. (1980). Translation and content analysis of oral and written material. In H. C. Triandis & J. W. Berry (Eds.), *Handbook of cross-cultural psychology: Methodology* (Vol. 2, pp. 389-444). Boston: Allyn & Bacon.

Caprara, G. V., Barbaranelli, C., Bermúdez, J., Maslach, C., & Ruch, W. (2000). Multivariate methods for the comparison of factor structures in cross-cultural research: An illustration with the Big Five Questionnaire. *Journal of Cross-Cultural Psychology, 31*, 437-464.

Church, A. T. (2000). Culture and personality: Toward an integrated cultural trait psychology. *Journal of Personality, 68*, 651-703.

Cohen, J. (1992). A power primer. *Psychological Bulletin, 112*, 155-159.

Costa, P. T., Jr., & McCrae, R. R. (1992). *Revised NEO Personality Inventory (NEO-PI-R) and NEO Five-Factor Inventory (NEO-FFI) professional manual.* Odessa, FL: Psychological Assessment Resources.

Costa, P. T., Jr., & McCrae, R. R. (1995). Primary traits of Eysenck's P-E-N system: Three- and five-factor solutions. *Journal of Personality and Social Psychology, 69*, 308-317.

Costa, P. T., Jr., Terracciano, A., & McCrae, R. R. (2001). Gender differences in personality traits across cultures: Robust and surprising findings. *Journal of Personality and Social Psychology, 81*, 322-331.

Crowne, D. P., & Marlowe, D. (1960). A new scale of social desirability independent of psychopathology. *Journal of Consulting Psychology, 24*, 349-354.

Dastane, S. (2000). *Glimpses of Maharashtra* (2nd ed.). Pune: Dastane Ramchandra.

De Raad, B. (2000). *The Big Five personality factors: The psycholexical approach to personality.* Seattle: Hogrefe and Huber Publishers.

Deshpande, K., & Rajadhyaksha, M. V. (1988). *A history of Marathi literature.* Delhi: Sahitya Akademy.

Dicken, C. F. (1959). Simulated patterns on the Edwards Personal Preference Schedule. *Journal of Applied Psychology, 43*, 372-378.

Eysenck, H. J. (1969). Research findings with the M. P. I. In H. J. Eysenck & S. B. G. Eysenck (Eds.), *Personality structure and measurement* (pp. 84-96). London: Routledge & Kegan Paul.

Eysenck, H. J. (1991). Dimensions of personality: 16, 5 or 3?—Criteria for a taxonomic paradigm. *Personality and Individual Differences, 12*, 773-790.

Eysenck, H. J. (1997). Personality and experimental psychology: The unification of psychology and the possibility of a paradigm. *Journal of Personality and Social Psychology, 73*, 1224-1237.

Eysenck, H. J., & Eysenck, S. B. G. (1975). *Manual of the Eysenck Personality Questionnaire (Junior & Adult).* London: Hodder & Stoughton.

Eysenck, H. J., & Eysenck, S. B. G. (1976). *Psychoticism as a dimension of personality.* London: Hodder & Stoughton.

Eysenck, H. J., & Wilson, G. D. (1991). *The Eysenck Personality Profiler.* London: Corporate Assessment Network.

Eysenck, S. B. G., Barrett, P., Spielberger, C., Evans, F. J., & Eysenck, H. J. (1986). Cross-cultural comparisons of personality dimensions: England and America. *Personality and Individual Differences*, 7, 209-214.

Eysenck, S. B. G., Eysenck, H. J., & Barrett, P. (1985). A revised version of the psychoticism scale. *Personality and Individual Differences*, 6, 21-29.

Ghurye, G. S. (1994). *Caste and race in India* (5th ed.). Mumbai: Popular Prakashan.

Gorsuch, R. L. (1974). *Factor analysis*. Philadelphia: W. B. Saunders.

Guttman, L. (1952). Multiple group methods for common factor analysis: Their basis, computation, and interpretation. *Psychometrika*, 17, 209-222.

Harman, H. H. (1970). *Modern factor analysis* (2nd ed.). Chicago: The University of Chicago Press.

Horn, J. L. (1967). On subjectivity in factor analysis. *Educational and Psychological Measurement*, 27, 811-820.

Huberty, C. J., & Petoskey, M. D. (2000). Multivariate analysis of variance and covariance. In H. A. Tinsley & S. D. Brown (Eds.), *Handbook of applied multivariate statistics and mathematical modelling* (pp. 183-208). San Diego: Academic Press.

Jackson, C. J., & Francis, L. J. (1999). Interpreting the correlation between Neuroticism and Lie scale scores. *Personality and Individual Differences*, 26, 59-63.

John, O. P., & Srivastava, S. (1999). The Big Five trait taxonomy: History, measurement and theoretical perspectives. In L. A. Pervin & O. P. John (Eds.), *Handbook of personality: Theory and research* (2nd ed., pp. 102-138). New York: Guilford.

Jöreskog, K. G., & Sörbom, D. (1986). *LISREL VI: Analysis of linear structural relationships by maximum likelihood, instrumental variables, and least squares methods* (4th ed.). Mooresville, IN: Scientific Software.

Joshi, L. (Ed.). (1985). *Marathi vishwakosh* [Marathi Encyclopedia] (Vol. 12). Mumbai: Maharashtra Rajya Marathi Vishwakosha Nirmiti Mandal.

Kapoor, S. D. (1965). *Psychological research in India: A commemoration volume in honour of Prof. S. S. Jalota*. Varanasi: Jalota Commemoration Volume Committee.

Katigbak, M. S., Church, A. T., Guanzon-Lapeña, M. A., Carlota, A. J. & del Pilar, G. J. (2000, July). *Indigenous Philippine dimensions and the Five-Factor Model*. Paper presented at the XXVIIth International Congress of Psychology, Stockholm, Sweden.

Krishnan, B. (1961). A review of contributions of Indian psychologists. In T. K. N. Menon (Ed.), *Recent trends in psychology* (pp. 190-222). Kolkata: Orient Longmans.

Kulkarni, S. S., & Puhan, B. N. (1988). Psychological assessment: Its present and future trends. In J. Pandey (Ed.), *Psychology in India: The state-of-the-art, Vol. 1. Personality and mental processes* (pp. 19-91), New Delhi: Sage Publications.

Laungani, P. (1985). National differences in personality: India and England. *Personality and Individual Differences*, 6, 217-221.

Lodhi, P. H. (1985). Performance on Lie scale in relation to Extraversion, Neuroticism and anxiety: A correlational and factorial study. *Bombay Psychologist*, 7, 77-85.

Lodhi, P. H., & Thakur, S. (1993). Personality of drug addicts: Eysenckian analysis. *Personality and Individual Differences*, 15, 121-128.

Lodhi, P. H., & Thomas, G. (1991). Effects of experimentally induced response sets in assessing Eysenckian dimensions of personality. *Personality and Individual Differences*, 12, 811-817.

MacDonald, K. (1998). Evolution, culture, and the Five-Factor Model. *Journal of Cross-Cultural Psychology*, 29, 119-149.

Manaster, G. J., & Havinghurst, R. J. (1972). *Cross-national research: Social psychological methods and problems*. Boston: Houghton Miffin Company.

Marascuilo, L. A., & Levin, J. R. (1983). *Multivariate statistics in the social sciences: A researcher's guide*. Monterey, CA: Brooks/Cole.

Martin, T. A., Oryol, V. E., Rukavishnikov, A. A., & Senin, I. G. (2000, July). *Applications of the Russian NEO-PI-R*. Paper presented at the XXVIIth International Congress of Psychology, Stockholm, Sweden.

McCrae, R. R. (1998, August). Trait psychology and the revival of personality-and-culture studies. In P. T. Costa, Jr. (Chair), *Personality traits and culture: New perspectives on some classic issues*. Symposium presented at the 106th convention of the American Psychological Association, San Francisco.

McCrae, R. R. (2001). Trait psychology and culture: Exploring intercultural comparisons. *Journal of Personality*, 69, 819-846.

McCrae, R. R. (2002). NEO-PI-R data from 36 cultures: Further intercultural explorations. In R. R. McCrae & J. Allik (Eds.), *The Five-Factor Model of personality across cultures* (pp. 105-125). New York:

Kluwer Academic/ Plenum Publishers.
McCrae, R. R., & Costa, P. T., Jr. (1983). Social desirability scales: More substance than style. *Journal of Consulting and Clinical Psychology, 51*, 882-888.
McCrae, R. R. & Costa, P. T., Jr. (1985). Comparison of EPI and Psychoticism scales with measures of the Five-Factor Model of personality. *Personality and Individual Differences, 6*, 587-597.
McCrae, R. R., & Costa, P. T., Jr. (1996). Toward a new generation of personality theories: Theoretical contexts for the Five-Factor Model. In J. S. Wiggins (Ed.), *The Five-Factor Model of personality: Theoretical perspectives* (pp. 51-87). New York: The Guilford Press.
McCrae, R. R., Costa, P. T., Jr., del Pilar, G. H., Rolland, J. P., & Parker, W. D. (1998). Corss-cultural assessment of the Five-Factor Model: The Revised NEO Personality Inventory. *Journal of Cross-Cultural Psychology, 29*, 171-188.
McCrae, R. R., Costa, P. T., Jr., Lima, M. P., Simões, A., Ostendorf, F., Angleitner, A., Marušić, I., Bratko, D., Caprara, G. V., Barbaranelli, C., Chae, J. H., & Piedmont, R. L. (1999). Age differences in personality across the adult life span: Parallels in five cultures. *Developmental Psychology, 35*, 466-477.
McCrae, R. R., Costa, P. T., Jr., & Yik, M. S. M. (1996). Universal aspects of Chinese personality structure. In M. H. Bond (Ed.), *The handbook of Chinese psychology.* Hong Kong: Oxford University Press.
McCrae, R. R., Zonderman, A. B., Costa, P. T., Jr., Bond, M. H., & Paunonen, S. V. (1996). Evaluating replicability of factors in the Revised NEO Personality Inventory: Confirmatory factor analysis versus Procrustes rotation. *Journal of Personality and Social Psychology, 70*, 552-566.
Mitra, S. C. (1955). Progress of psychology in India. *Indian Journal of Psychology, 30*, 1-21.
Mitra, S. K. (Ed.) (1972a). *A survey of research in psychology.* Mumbai: Popular Prakashan.
Mitra, S. K. (1972b). Psychological research in India. In S. K. Mitra (Ed.), *A survey of research in psychology* (pp. xvii-xxxiii). Mumbai: Popular Prakashan.
Mulaik, S. A. (1972). *The foundations of factor analysis.* New York: McGraw-Hill.
Mulaik, S. A. (1988). Confirmatory factor analysis. In J. R. Nesselroade & R. B. Cattell (Eds.), *Handbook of multivariate experimental psychology* (2nd ed., pp. 259-288). New York: Plenum Press.
Murty, K. S. (1985). *Philosophy in India: Traditions, teaching and research.* New Delhi: Motilal Banarasidass for Indian Council of Philosophical Research.
Naidu, R. K. (2001). Personality, self and life events. In J. Pandey (Ed.), *Psychology in India revisited: Developments in the discipline: Vol. 2. Personality and health psychology* (pp. 228-299). New Delhi: Sage Publications.
Nandy, A., & Kakar, S. (1980). Culture and personality. In U. Pareek (Ed.), *A survey of research in Psychology, 1971-76, Part I* (pp. 136-167). Mumbai: Popular Prakashan.
Narayanan, L., Menon, S., & Levine, E. L. (1995). Personality structure: A culture-specific examination of the Five-Factor Model. *Journal of Personality Assessment, 64*, 51-62.
Nighojkar, R. D. (2000). *A study of personality, attitude towards nuclearization and perceived challenges among military leaders.* Unpublished M. Phil. dissertation, University of Pune, Pune.
Norušis, M. J./SPSS Inc. (1990a). *SPSS/PC+ Advanced statistics 4.0 for the IBM PC/XT/AT and PS/2* (Computer program manual). Chicago: SPSS Inc.
Norušis, M. J./SPSS Inc. (1990b). *SPSS/PC+ Statistics 4.0 for the IBM PC/XT/AT and PS/2* (Computer program manual). Chicago: SPSS Inc.
Nunnally, J. C. (1981). *Psychometric theory* (2nd ed.). New Delhi: Tata McGraw-Hill.
Ortet, G., Ibáñez, M. I., Moro, M., Silva, F., & Boyle, G. J. (1999). Psychometric appraisal of Eysenck's revised Psychoticism scale: A cross-cultural study. *Personality and Individual Differences, 27*, 1209-1219.
Palsane, M. N., & Lodhi, P. H. (1979). Eysenck Personality Inventory scales and social desirability: A correlational and factorial study. *Psychologia, 22*, 236-240.
Piedmont, R. L., & Chae, J. H. (1997). Cross-cultural generalizability of the Five-Factor Model of personality: Development and validation of the NEO-PI-R for Koreans. *Journal of Cross-Cultural Psychology, 28*, 131-155.
Publications Division, Ministry of Information and Broadcasting, Government of India. (2001). *India 2001: A reference annual.* New Delhi: Author.
Radhakrishnan, S., & Moore, C. A. (Eds.). (1957). *A source book in Indian philosophy.* Princeton: Princeton University Press.
Rolland, J.-P. (2000, July). *Cross-cultural validity of the Five-Factor Model of personality.* Paper presented at the XXVIIth International Congress of Psychology, Stockholm, Sweden.
Saucier, G., & Goldberg, L. R. (1996). The language of personality: Lexical perspectives on the Five-Factor

LODHI, DEO & BELHEKAR

Model. In J. S. Wiggins (Ed.), *The Five-Factor Model of personality: Theroretical perspectives* (pp. 21-50). New York: The Guilford Press.

Saucier, G., & Goldberg, L. R. (2001). Lexical studies of indigenous personality factors: Permises, products and prospects. *Journal of Personality, 69,* 847-879.

Schönemann, P. H. (1966). A generalized solution of the orthogonal Procrustes problem. *Psychometrika, 31,* 1-10.

Shanmugam, T. E. (1972). Personality: A trend report. In S. K. Mitra (Ed.), *A survey of research in psychology* (pp. 266-337). Mumbai: Popular Prakashan.

Sharma, K. L. (Ed.). (1986). *Social stratification in India.* New Delhi: Manohar Publications.

Sharma, S. (1981). Key concepts of social psychology in India. *Psychologia, 24,* 105-114.

Silveira, D. M. (1998). *D. M. Silveira's India book.* Goa: Classic Publishers.

Sinha, J. B. P. (1982). The Hindu (Indian) identity. *Dynamic Psychiatry, 15,* 148-160.

Sinha, S. (1963). Progress of psychology. In *Fifty years of science in India.* Kolkata: Indian Science Congress Association.

Tabachnick, B. G., & Fidell, L. S. (1989). *Using multivariate statistics* (2nd ed.). New York: Harper and Row.

Tsaousis, I. (1999). The traits personality questionnaire (TPQue): A Greek measure for the five factor model. *Personality and Individual Differences, 26,* 271-283.

Wolfe, R. N., & Johnson, S. D. (1995). Personality as a predictor of college performance. *Educational and Psychological Measurement, 55,* 177-185.

Yik, M. S. M., & Bond, M. H. (1993). Exploring the dimensions of Chinese person perception with indigenous and imported constructs: Creating a culturally balanced scale. *International Journal of Psychology, 28,* 75-95.

AUTHOR NOTE

P. H. Lodhi, Head (Chairperson), Department of Psychology, University of Pune, India; Savita Deo and Vivek M. Belhekar, Research students, Department of Psychology, University of Pune.

We thank an anonymous reviewer for valuable comments. We also thank Amita Phadke (AP), Dr. Bala Kulkarni (BK), Dr. Aniket Jaware (AJ), Dr. Vidyagauri Tilak (VT), Dr. B. R. Shejwal (BRS), Dr. S. B. Gokhale (SBG), all associated with University of Pune, for their assistance in the process of translation. In the text, abbreviations in the parentheses are used. Correspondence concerning this article should be addressed to P. H. Lodhi, Department of Psychology, University of Pune, Pune - 411007, India. E-mail: phlodhi@unipune.ernet.in

PERSONALITY AND CULTURE

The Portuguese Case

MARGARIDA PEDROSO DE LIMA

Universidade de Coimbra

Abstract. The Revised NEO Personality Inventory (NEO-PI-R) is the best known operationalization of the Five-Factor Model. Its validity and comprehensiveness justify its translation into many different languages. In this chapter the author presents the results of a validation of the NEO-PI-R for the Portuguese population and analyzes and reflects about the characteristic features of Portuguese personality. Some qualitative data are presented and discussed. Finally, some theoretical comments are made about culture and its powerful relations to personality and trait expression.

Key-Words: NEO-PI-R, Five-Factor Model, personality, culture, Portuguese validation

1. INTRODUCTION

I am the one who stands astonished about its own personality; in this sense I believe myself a Portuguese [*Eu sou aquele que se espanta da própria personalidade, e creio-me portanto português*] (Negreiros, 1917).

Pervin (1990) characterized the field of personality by the great diversity of phenomena it studies—e.g., the interactions between structure and process, stability and change in personality. But from this multiplicity of problems some authors have emphasized one as the most challenging topic for the next decades: the relations between personality, its expression, and culture.

 Among the scientific advances that have contributed to renewed interest in this topic are the Five-Factor Model of personality and Five-Factor Theory (Costa & McCrae,

249

1992; McCrae & Costa, 1996). The Five-Factor Model (FFM) is a representation of the structure of personality in terms of the "Big Five" dimensions—Neuroticism (N), Extraversion (E), Openness to Experience (O), Agreeableness (A), and Conscientiousness (C)—that, in the nice metaphor of John (1990, p. 96) cover the OCEAN of personality. Although the FFM has solid empirical and statistical support, the recent proliferation of theoretical perspectives about the five factors has enriched the model (Wiggins, 1996). Five-Factor Theory, proposed by McCrae and Costa (1996), makes a distinction between inherited *basic tendencies*[1] such as the Big Five traits, which are viewed as independent of culture, and *characteristic adaptations* such as self-concepts and personal strivings, which are viewed as a joint function of basic tendencies and external influences such as cultural norms. In this sense "personality and culture are relatively independent forces that interact to shape people's lives" (McCrae, 2000, p. 10). If it can be demonstrated that the same structure of traits can be found in many quite different languages and cultures, the way is open to a new approach to personality-and-culture studies (McCrae, 2000).

In fact traits—defined as relatively stable and enduring individual differences in thoughts, feelings, and behaviors—have been described as the "core of personality" (McCrae & Costa, 1996) and "have provided the theoretical basis for most of the cross-cultural research on personality" (Church, 2000, pp. 651-652). The comprehensiveness of the FFM and the conceptual advances of Five-Factor Theory allow a dynamic view of the person in the context of cultural diversity.

Although culture-specific (emic) trait dimensions may exist, there is considerable support for the trait approach from studies of the cross-cultural comparability of personality dimensions. "The replication of fairly comparable dimensions, using both imported and indigenous approaches in a wide variety of cultures, provides one source of evidence for the viability of the trait concept across cultures" (Church, 2000, p. 656). In contrast to the cross-cultural trait psychology approach, in which the trait concept is central, in the cultural psychology approach the trait concept is questioned. Nevertheless, Church (2000, p. 653) proposed that "the tenets of cultural psychology, at least in their moderate forms, can be synthesized with the trait psychology approach, resulting in an integrated cultural trait psychology perspective."

Findings of replicable cultural mean differences in trait scores that conform to theory or expectations could provide another form of evidence for the cross-cultural viability of the Big Five dimensions. In this chapter I begin with a short presentation of the Portuguese version of the NEO-PI-R. I then analyze data comparing American and Portuguese samples and describe the main features of the personality of the Portuguese through a complementary analysis of the NEO-PI-R with qualitative data (literature and proverbs). Finally, I make some theoretical comments about culture and its powerful relations to personality and personality expression.

---

[1]"A number of theoretical perspectives are consistent with the existence of universal traits. These include biological theories of temperament and personality (e.g., Rowe, 1997), recent evolutionary theories (Buss, 1996; Hogan, 1996; McDonald, 1998), and McCrae and Costa's (1996) Five Factor Theory" (Church, 2000, p. 663).

2. THE PORTUGUESE VERSION OF THE NEO-PI-R

> Do we imagine that the FFM—or the NEO-PI-R
> —is the last word in personality assessment? Of
> course we do not. It is, we hope and believe, a
> serviceable model, a taxonomy adequate for the
> needs of a young science (Costa & McCrae, 1995,
> p. 217).

The Revised NEO Personality Inventory (NEO-PI-R; Costa & McCrae, 1992) is a concise (240-item) measure of the five major dimensions of personality and some of the more important traits or facets that define each domain. I chose to translate this instrument into the Portuguese language because it had been studied in several different cultures and used in cross-cultural research (e.g., McCrae et al., 1999). The NEO-PI-R was translated into Portuguese by several native speakers with training in psychology and knowledge of the English language. After completing the translation, a back-translation into English was prepared by a second translator and reviewed by the test authors. Revisions were made and re-reviewed. The resulting instrument was then administered to a sample of the population, as described below.

2.1. A General Description of Portuguese Culture

Portugal is located on the edge of Europe and has modernized more slowly than most West European countries. Significant industrialization began only in the 1950s, and democratic government was instituted in 1974. Despite their complex origins, the Portuguese population today is one of Europe's most homogeneous, the only important minority—about 2% of the population—being from Portuguese-speaking African countries. In recent years Portuguese society has been changing from conservative values to more open and democratic ones. Portugal belongs to the European Union, which influences the country politically, economically, and culturally.

Portuguese is one of the Romance languages, with a mixture of Arabic and other foreign idioms. Most of the population is Roman Catholic, but the society is essentially secular.

Education has been free and compulsory since the 19th century, and all children over the age of 6 must attend school for 9 years. Nevertheless, literacy is still a problem. The samples used here are better educated than average. The majority of the population lives in small towns and villages rather than large urban centers.

2.2. A Representative Sample

For the normative sample I selected a district (Leiria) which approximately matched the total Portuguese population on demographic variables (sex, age, marital status, education level), based upon the 1991 Portuguese Census (Instituto Nacional de Estatística, 1993). The subjects to be interviewed were then recruited from this district. The sample is composed of 2,000 participants, including 1,133 women and 861 men, aged 17 to 84. The full range of socioeconomic and educational levels was represented, but the participants were predominantly from the middle socioeconomic level and were somewhat better educated than the general Portuguese population (the mean years of formal education was 9.5, ranging from 0 to 20). Finally, the sample was younger than the general population.

Of the first 300 administrations, 81 were considered invalid because of missing or distorted data, applying the criteria presented in the NEO-PI-R *Manual* (Costa & McCrae, 1992). It became clear that problems with literacy and vision and the unfamiliarity of questionnaires were largely responsible for this high invalidity rate. Subsequently, the questionnaire was administered orally to participants who were unable to read it themselves or who requested help; about half the sample was tested this way, and no further invalid questionnaires were encountered. Although this customized data collection was time-consuming, it gave insights into the problematic ways respondents interpreted some items, and it allowed a more representative sample. Questionnaires were completed in a wide diversity of settings (e.g., at home, school, church, restaurant, on the street), and they were administered individually or in groups. A total of 2,000 questionniares were completed (Lima, 1997; Lima & Simões, 1997).

2.3. The Portuguese NEO-PI-R

2.3.1. Factor Structure

The factor structure of the Portuguese NEO-PI-R and its correspondence to the predictions of the Five-Factor Model can be examined on the level of items or facets. Varimax-rotated principal components were first examined. In the item-level analysis, five components corresponded to the five intended factors and explained 21% of the variance. Costa, McCrae, and Dye (1991) reported that 23% of the variance was accounted for by five factors in their item-level analysis.

When the 30 facets were factored, the first seven eigenvalues were 5.54, 4.29, 2.96, 2.04, 1.35, .96, and .90, clearly indicating the presence of five factors. Together, these factors accounted for 55% of the variance, slightly less than the 58% Costa et al. (1991) reported.

Table 1 presents results of a Procrustes rotation (McCrae, Zonderman, Costa, Bond, & Paunonen, 1996), based on a factor analysis of the total sample. It shows that all factors, and all variables, had statistically significant patterns of loadings and that the overall pattern was similar to the American structure. Nevertheless N5, E3, and E4 are relatively weak definers of their intended factors—in fact, E3 had a larger (negative) loading on A, and E4 had a larger loading on C. Comparisons of the Portuguese and American structures indicate that the scales show the same kind of factorial complexity in the two versions, although with a slightly different emphasis.

Supplementary analyses conducted on younger (17-20) and older (21-64) subsamples showed similar results. Varimax and oblique rotations closely resembled the results reported in Table 1.

Table 1. Procrustes Rotation of the Portuguese NEO-PI-R.

NEO-PI-R Facet	α	Principal Component					VCᵃ
		N	E	O	A	C	
N1: Anxiety	.57	**.77**	.05	−.04	.17	.14	.93*
N2: Angry Hostility	.57	**.65**	−.17	−.10	−.34	−.01	.95**
N3: Depression	.67	**.78**	−.11	−.18	.06	−.17	.96**
N4: Self-Consciousness	.54	**.71**	−.08	−.08	.06	−.19	.99**
N5: Impulsiveness	.45	.39	.33	.26	−.21	−.34	.93*
N6: Vulnerability	.64	**.65**	−.10	−.14	−.03	**−.42**	.99**
E1: Warmth	.57	−.10	**.65**	.09	**.41**	.20	.99**
E2: Gregariousness	.63	−.15	**.66**	.03	.07	−.10	.99**
E3: Assertiveness	.50	−.32	.34	.17	**−.47**	.17	.95**
E4: Activity	.26	.06	.33	.20	−.24	.34	.98**
E5: Excitement Seeking	.55	−.02	**.60**	.25	−.24	−.03	.96**
E6: Positive Emotions	.57	−.11	**.65**	.35	−.02	.04	.96**
O1: Fantasy	.67	.17	.34	**.61**	−.07	−.15	.95**
O2: Aesthetics	.70	.12	.21	**.64**	.15	.16	.97**
O3: Feelings	.53	.17	**.47**	**.53**	−.10	.17	.95**
O4: Actions	.37	−.16	.11	**.55**	.04	−.07	.98**
O5: Ideas	.72	−.05	.22	**.69**	−.17	.08	.94*
O6: Values	.37	−.07	.05	**.71**	.08	−.08	.94*
A1: Trust	.66	−.21	.34	−.08	**.54**	.01	.91*
A2: Straightforwardness	.52	−.02	−.26	.03	**.70**	.07	.94*
A3: Altruism	.60	−.03	**.42**	.06	**.60**	.28	.98**
A4: Compliance	.58	−.11	−.03	−.21	**.71**	.08	.96**
A5: Modesty	.59	.13	−.28	.11	**.66**	.05	.86*
A6: Tender-Mindedness	.39	.16	.12	.20	**.55**	.13	.94*
C1: Competence	.49	−.26	.28	.05	.06	**.63**	.97**
C2: Order	.57	.07	.03	.02	.02	**.69**	.94**
C3: Dutifulness	.61	−.03	.04	.02	**.40**	**.71**	.96**
C4: Achievement Striving	.53	−.06	.25	.11	−.04	**.74**	.99**
C5: Self-Discipline	.61	−.31	.03	.10	.12	**.73**	.96**
C6: Deliberation	.68	−.22	−.14	−.27	.26	**.56**	.93*
Factor Congruenceᵇ		.98**	.95**	.90**	.97**	.97**	.95**

Note: These are principal components from 2,000 respondents targeted to the American normative factor structure. Loadings greater than .40 in absolute magnitude are given in boldface. ᵃVariable congruence coefficient; total congruence coefficient in the last row. ᵇCongruence with American normative factor structure. *Congruence higher than that of 95% of rotations from random data. **Congruence higher than that of 99% of rotations from random data.

2.3.2. Internal Consistency and Item Analyses

Coefficient alpha for the 30 facet scales is given in the first column of Table 1. These values are low, even for 8-item scales. The median alpha is .57, compared to .71 in American data (Costa & McCrae, 1992). However, alphas for the longer domain scores were acceptable, ranging from .80 for E to .86 for C.

Item/total correlations showed that seven items clearly had problems, as seen by negative item/facet correlations. I therefore developed new versions of these items and administrated the revised instrument to a convenience sample of 240 subjects (138 men, 102 women, mean age = 27.5 yrs.) Item/facet correlations for the new items ranged from .33 to .70, all $p < .001$. This finalized version has been published (Lima & Simões, 2000).

2.3.3. Validity

Despite the rather limited internal consistency of the Portuguese version, when NEO-PI-R scales were correlated with alternative measures of similar constructs in the normative sample, they showed clear evidence of convergent and discriminate validity. The criterion instruments utilized were the Eysenck Personality Questionnaire (EPQ; Eysenck & Eysenck, 1975), the Vocational Interest Inventory (VII; Ferreira, 1991), the Satisfaction with Life Scale (SWLS; Diener et al., 1985), and the Aggression Questionnaire (AQ; Buss & Perry, 1992). These instruments had already been translated and studied within the Portuguese population.

The pattern of associations was consistent with hypotheses. For instance, N showed a negative correlation with SWLS ($r = -.39$; cf. Simões, 1992) and a positive correlation with EPQ N ($r = .75$); E showed a positive correlation with EPQ E ($r = .70$). Both A and C had small negative correlations with EPQ P ($rs = -.30, -.22$; cf. McCrae & Costa, 1985). N ($r = .35$) and especially N2: Angry Hostility ($r = .44$) were related to the AQ; O ($r = .38$) and especially O2: Aesthetics ($r = .42$) were related to the VII Artistic scale.

In conclusion, the present study indicates that the Portuguese version of the NEO-PI-R measures the same dimensions of personality in much the same manner as the American version. Both have good psychometric qualities and useful applications in different areas of psychology (e.g., Counseling, Clinical Psychology, and Psychiatry; Behavioral Medicine and Health Psychology; Vocational Counseling and Industrial/ Organizational Psychology; Educational Research; Lima, 1998, 1999). Finally, it seems that this inventory may be useful in understanding aspects of the Portuguese character and culture.

3. PERSONALITY AND CULTURE

All nations are mysteries; each one is the whole world alone [*as nações todas são mistérios cada uma é todo o mundo a sós*] (Fernando Pessoa).

Intercultural comparisons of the results from the American normative sample (Costa & McCrae, 1992) and the Portuguese normative sample reveal some profound similarities. McCrae and Costa (1997, p. 514) observed that the "cross-cultural and cross-language similarities in the structure of the NEO-PI-R seen in these samples are in many ways remarkable." With regard to mean levels, however, there are notable differences. Figure 1 presents a personality profile using age- and gender-adjusted Portuguese mean values (see McCrae, 2002, Table 3 and Appendix I) plotted against American norms. In interpreting this profile, it must be recalled that Americans have T-scores of 50 on all scales.

The profile in Figure 1 is a good beginning for the study of culture-specific manifestations of common dimensions of personality, such as the Big Five. But, as McCrae and Costa (1997, p. 515) argued, "it is also essential to recall that equivalence of factor structure does not in itself mean that different translations of an instrument are parallel forms. Raw scores may have very different interpretations in different cultures. . . . Determining whether individuals in one culture are really more introverted, trusting, or diligent than those in another is an arduous task." One approach to this task is by comparing the data obtained from psychological tests with different sources of information on a culture.

3.1. The Portuguese as Depicted in Literature

In this sense it is meaningful to study deeply the relation between the so-called Portuguese national character (*carácter nacional Português*) explicit in the literature and in some sociological writings, and the personality characteristics of the normative Portuguese sample identified through the NEO-PI-R. I will present some of these relations here.

As Figure 1 shows, the Portuguese sample obtained relatively high scores (when compared with the American normative sample) on N1: Anxiety, N3: Depression, N6: Vulnerability, and O2: Aesthetics. They scored relatively low on E3: Assertiveness, E6: Positive Emotions, O6: Values, and C1: Competence.

The high Depression and low Positive Emotion scores are certainly understandable. The depressive temperament is, in the opinion of writers and historians (Lourenço, 1999), one of the main features of the Portuguese. Soares (1995), referring to the Statistics of the European Community, pointed out that the Portuguese, compared with other countries, have little interest in life, and boredom is one of their characteristic states. The Portuguese writer Eça de Queirós (1933, p. 93) wrote: "tedium invaded the souls. Youth drags itself, old, from office tables to coffee tables. —I feel bored! Is the general voice" ("*o tédio invadiu as almas. A mocidade arrasta-se, envelhecida, das mesas das secretarias para as mesas dos cafés. — Ando aborrecido! é o coro geral*").

The low score on Openness to Values also makes sense. The Portuguese writer Antero de Quental commented that the Portuguese are not really open to new values and modernity: "there is in all of us, the more modern we would like to be, hidden, dissimulated, but not dead, a pious person, a fanatic or a Jesuit" ("*há em todos nós, por mais modernos que queiramos ser, há lá oculto, dissimulado, mas não inteiramente morto, um beato, um fanático ou um jesuíta*"; in Monteiro, 1993, p. 68).

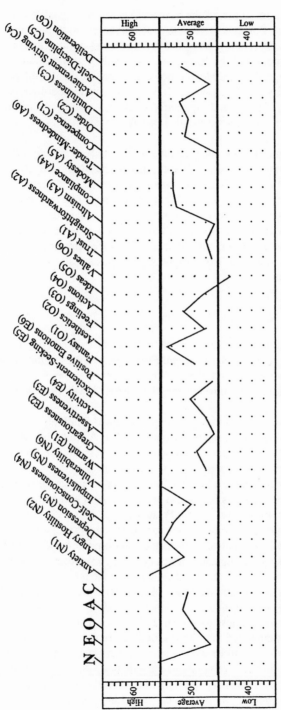

Figure 1. Mean NEO-PI-R profile for combined Portuguese sample relative to American norms (McCrae, 2002). Profile form reproduced by special permission of the Publisher, from the Revised NEO Personality Inventory, by Paul T. Costa, Jr., and Robert R. McCrae. Copyright 1978, 1985, 1989, 1992 by PAR, Inc. Further reproduction is prohibited without permission of PAR, Inc.

The Portuguese have also been characterized as lacking discipline and energy. Antero de Quental (1987, p.107) argued that "from the combative spirit of a conqueror nation we inherited a invincible horror of work and an intimate disdain to industry" (*"do espírito guerreiro da nação conquistadora herdámos um invencível horror ao trabalho e um íntimo desprezo pela indústria"*). Similarly, historian Fialho Gouveia (in Monteiro, 1993, p. 52) claimed that "every more or less energetic will makes us afraid . . . we wait all our life for that mysterious protector that will come on a misty morning and will set our table, give us a job, furnish our house, arrange us a rich marriage, but never coming, constantly impedes us of earning our life with a stable and hygienic work" (*"qualquer vontade medianamente enérgica nos faz medo...Aguardamos toda a vida por um fundo sebastiânico de raça, esse protector misterioso que numa manhã de névoa há-de vir pôr-nos a mesa, arranjar-nos um emprego, mobilar-nos a casa, casar-nos rico, e que não vindo nunca, constantemente nos impede de ganhar a vida por um trabalho fundo e higiénico"*).

The profile in Figure 1 is partially consistent with this depiction. Although Portuguese score about as high as Americans on C4: Achievement Striving and overall Conscientiousness, they are low in C1: Competence and C5: Self-Discipline. Combined with their low E3: Assertiveness and E4: Activity, these traits may account for the perception of passivity and helplessness.

The data presented here are speculative interpretations that should be studied in more detail. Nevertheless they point to the possibility of meaningful correspondences between the scores obtained through the NEO-PI-R and characterizations from literature and sociological studies, including work from different historical times. It seems that culturally distinct manifestations of common dimensions of personality can be encountered in both personality profile sheets and literary expressions of culture.

3.2. Personality and Proverbs

One of the more positive features of the Portuguese profile in Figure 1 is the high Openness to Aesthetics score. That is reflected in the literary traditions of Portugal, but also in the popular use of metaphorical speech in the form of proverbs. Their richness and diversity means that "for each occasion there is a proverb" (Machado, 1996, p. 5). The identification of a proverb, adage, or maxim relevant to each facet of the NEO Personality Inventory would be another way of providing evidence for the cross-cultural viability of the Five-Factor Model. It would confirm that these dimensions of personality correspond to indigenous Portuguese constructs.

This idea arose from collecting data, through interviews, from older people with low education levels. Often they would answer with proverbs, as if the idea of the question was present in an old sentence they knew well. For instance, for the item, "I rarely feel sad or depressed" of the N3: Depression facet, a person with low scores in N3 might answer, "Sadness doesn't pay debts." Or a low scorer in N5: Impulsiveness might respond with, "There are no vices man cannot resist." It is interesting that proverbs, like personality factors, are bipolar: For each idea present in a popular proverb there may be a counter proverb with the opposite idea. In Table 2 I present a Portuguese proverb relevant to each NEO-PI-R facet. As is often the case with poetry, many of these lines

Table 2. Portuguese Proverbs Relevant to NEO-PI-R Constructs.

NEO PI-R facet	Proverb
N1: Anxiety	Fear was left in mother's belly (R)
N2: Angry hostility	No use crying over spilt milk (R)
N3: Depression	Sadness doesn't pay debts (R)
N4: Self-consciousness	Troubles never trouble till trouble troubles you (R)
N5: Impulsiveness	There are no vices man cannot resist (R)
N6: Vulnerability	It is the last straw that breaks the camel's back
E1: Warmth	Who sees faces does not see hearts (R)
E2: Gregariousness	Better alone than in bad company (R)
E3: Assertiveness	Faint heart never won fair lady
E4: Activity	The more I run, the later I arrive (R)
E5: Excitement-seeking	Pleasures have their stings (R)
E6: Positive emotions	It never rains but it pours (R)
O1: Fantasy	Man does not live by bread alone
O2: Aesthetics	Taste can not be taught
O3: Feelings	Everyday is not Sunday
O4: Actions	Knowledge doesn't take the place of experience
O5: Ideas	So many men, so many minds
O6: Values	Don't be too sure
A1: Trust	Hope springs eternal in human breast
A2: Straightforwardness	Honesty is the best policy
A3: Altruism	Do what is right, come what way
A4: Compliance	Better come to an agreement than go to the law
A5: Modesty	Good wine needs no advertising
A6: Tender-mindedness	Who gives to the poor lends to God
C1: Competence	Perseverance is the mother of success
C2: Order	Practice makes perfect
C3: Dutifulness	Duty before pleasure
C4: Achievement Striving	He who does not look ahead finds himself left behind
C5: Self-discipline	There is no short cut to success
C6: Deliberation	Slow and steady wins the race

Note. Items marked with (R) are most relevant to the low pole of the facet.

lose a good deal in translation.

The qualitative analysis of the relation between personality constructs and the popular knowledge crystallized in literature and in proverbs points to the cultural expression of the traits in the FFM, the behavioral manifestations of universal traits across cultures. These analyses corroborate the importance of the FFM in the Portuguese culture.

3.3. Culture-specific Traits

It is also important to analyze the existence of unique traits that are culture-specific.

Again, literature can help point to some paths. It is said that the Portuguese have a trait that does not exist in other cultures, *Saudosismo*—a word without translation. Nevertheless the words *nostalgia* and *melancholia* have something in common with the word *saudade*; all refer to special nuances of our relation with temporality, memory, sensitivity, and eternity. *Saudade* is the expression of excessive love for everything not present; it is the tendency to imagine the past as paradise. It represents a nostalgia without an object, perhaps the heritage of a nation whose destiny was the sea, the voyage (Lourenço, 1999). The word-myth *saudade* evokes feelings of personal remoteness, the weight of sadness and bitterness, the remembrance of the abandoned house, the taste of honey and tears, the concrete consciousness of the temporality of our existence. But it is a pleasant melancholia and in this sense it is perhaps separate from the facet Depression, and it is worthwhile studying as a possible Portuguese-specific trait, or as a culturally-shaped characteristic adaptation for the expression of emotions. This emic position is compatible with the FFM and the Five-Factor Theory. These new conceptions of trait taxonomies, more comprehensive and more complex, mirror the tendencies of post-modern scientific paradigms that emphasize the necessity of understanding phenomena contextually and culturally. Perhaps the new theoretical and empirical settings will allow us to start thinking not just about traits, as a central concept in the study of personality, but about waves—dynamic traits in the OCEAN (John, 1990) of personality.

In conclusion, the study of individual differences through the universal Big Five also allows the study of idiosyncratic manifestations of traits across cultures and can provide a basis for the study of culture-specific traits and adaptations.

REFERENCES

Buss, D., & Cantor, N. (Eds). (1989). *Personality psychology: Recent trends and emerging directions.* New York: Springer-Verlag.

Church, A. T. (2000). Culture and personality: Toward an integrated cultural trait psychology. *Journal of Personality, 68,* 651-703.

Costa, P. T., Jr., & McCrae, R. R. (1992). *Revised NEO Personality Inventory (NEO-PI-R) and NEO Five-Factor Inventory (NEO-FFI) professional manual.* Odessa, FL: Psychological Assessment Resources.

Costa, P. T., Jr., & McCrae, R. R. (1995). Solid grounds in the wetlands of personality: A reply to Block. *Psychological Bulletin, 117,* 216-220.

Costa, P. T., Jr., McCrae, R. R., & Dye, (1991). Facet scales for Agreeableness and Conscientiousness: A revision of the NEO Personality Inventory. *Personality and Individual Differences, 12,* 887-898.

Eysenck, H. J., & Eysenck, M. W. (1985). *Personality and individual differences.* London: Plenum Press.

Ferreira, J. A. A. (1991). *The development and validation of a vocational interest inventory and its relationship to personality characteristic.* Coimbra: Ed. do autor.

Instituto Nacional de Estatística. (1993). *Censos de 91:* XII Recenseamento Geral da População, resultados pré-definitivos.

John, O. P. (1990). The "Big Five" factor taxonomy: Dimensions of personality in the natural language and in questionnaires. In L. A. Pervin (Ed.), *Handbook of personality: Theory and research* (pp. 66-100). New York: Guilford.

Lima, M. P. (1997). *NEO-PI-R Contextos teóricos e Psicométricos.* Tese de doutoramento, FPCE. UC., Coimbra.

Lima, M. P. (1998). Aplicações clínicas do modelo dos cinco factores, *Psiquiatria Clínica,* vol. 19 n°1.

Lima, M. P. (1998). A abertura à experiência, *Ensaios em homenagem a Joaquim Ferreira Gomes,* FPCE, Universidade de Coimbra.

Lima, M. P. (1999). Implicações do modelo dos cinco factores da personalidade em contextos educativos,

260   PEDROSO DE LIMA

Universidade de Coimbra.
Lima, M. P. (1999). Implicações do modelo dos cinco factores da personalidade em contextos educativos, *Investigar e Formar em Educação – Actas do IV da SPCE*, Aveiro.
Lima, M. P. & Simões, A. (1997). O Inventário da Personalidade NEO-PI-R: Resultados da aferição Portuguesa. *Psychologica, 18*, 25-46.
Lima, M. P. & Simões, A. (2000). *NEO-PI-R Manual Profissional*, 1ª edição, Lisboa: CEGOC.
Lourenço, E. (1999). *Portugal como destino seguido de Mitologia da Saudade*. Lisboa: Gradiva.
Machado, J. P. (1996). *O grande livro dos Provérbios*. Lisboa: Editorial Notícias.
McCrae, R. R. (2000). Trait psychology and the revival of personality-and-culture studies. *American Behavioral Scientist, 44*, 10-31.
McCrae, R. R. (2002). NEO-PI-R data from 36 cultures: Further intercultural comparisons. In R. R. McCrae & J. Allik (Eds.), *The Five-Factor Model of personality across cultures* (pp. 105-125). New York: Kluwer Academic/ Plenum Publishers.
McCrae, R. R., & Costa, P. T., Jr. (1985). Comparison of EPI and Psychoticism scales with measures of the Five-Factor Model of personality. *Personality and Individual Differences, 6*, 587-597.
McCrae, R. R., & Costa, P. T., Jr. (1996). Toward a new generation of personality theories: Theoretical contexts for the Five-Factor Model. In J.S. Wiggins (Ed.), *The Five-Factor Model of personality: Theoretical perspectives* (pp. 51-87). New York: Guilford.
McCrae, R. R., & Costa, P. T., Jr. (1997). Personality trait structure as a human universal. *American Psychologist, 52*, 509-516.
McCrae, R. R. & Costa, P.T., Jr. (1999). A Five-Factor Theory of Personality. In L. A. Pervin & O. P. John (Eds.), *Handbook of personality: Theory and research* (2nd. ed, pp. 139-153). New York: Guilford.
McCrae, R. R., Costa, P. T., Jr., Lima, M. P., Simões, A., Ostendorf, F., Angleitner, A., Marušić, I., Bratko, D., Caprara, G. V., Barbaranelli, C., Chae, J. H., & Piedmont, R. L. (1999). Age differences in personality across the adult lifespan: Parallels in five cultures. *Developmental Psychology, 35*, 466-477.
McCrae, R. R., Zonderman, A. B., Costa, P. T., Jr., Bond, M. H., & Paunonen, S. V. (1996). Evaluating replicability of factors in the Revised NEO Personality Inventory: Confirmatory factor analysis versus Procrustes rotation. *Journal of Personality and Social Psychology, 70*, 552-566.
Monteiro, P. F. (1993). A ideologia do carácter nacional Português. *Sociedade, Valores e Desenvolvimento*. Lisboa: FCSHUNL.
Pervin, L. A. (Ed.). (1990). *Handbook of personality: Theory and research*. New York: Guilford.
Queiróz, E. de (1933). *Uma campanha alegre*. Porto: Livraria Lello.
Quental, A. de (1987). *As causas da decadência dos povos peninsulares*. Lisboa: Ulmeiro.
Simões, A. (1992). *Desenvolvimento intelectual do adulto*, Unidade de Educação de Adultos, Braga.
Simões, A., Lima, M. P., et al., (2000). "O bem-estar subjectivo: estado actual dos conhecimentos." *Psicologia, Educação, Cultura*, nº2, Vol.IV.
Soares, M. G. (1995). Tão comuns que nós somos, *Semanário Expresso*, Suplemento Viva, 29, Setembro.
Wiggins, J. S. (Ed.). (1996). *The Five-Factor Model of personality: Theoretical perspectives*. New York: Guilford.

AUTHOR NOTE

Margarida Pedroso de Lima, Faculdade de Psicologia e de Ciências da Educação da Universidade de Coimbra, R. do Colégio Novo, 3000 Coimbra, Portugal. E-mail: mplima@fpce.uc.pt

APPLICATIONS OF THE RUSSIAN NEO-PI-R

THOMAS A. MARTIN,* PAUL T. COSTA, JR.,**
VALERY E. ORYOL,*** ALEXEY A. RUKAVISHNIKOV***
& IVAN G. SENIN***

*Susquehanna University, **National Institute on Aging, NIH, ***Yaroslavl State University

Abstract. This chapter reviews the development, revision, and use of the Russian-language version of the NEO-PI-R. Particular attention is given to items and facets that have proved least adaptable to the Russian context. Potential explanations for these difficulties are identified in Russian culture and in the current atmosphere of social, economic and political flux. Data on factor structure, cross-language equivalence, cross-observer validity, and one-year stability are reported.

Keywords: Test development, factor structure, bilingual studies, retest stability

1. INTRODUCTION

The Revised NEO Personality Inventory (NEO-PI-R; Costa & McCrae, 1992) has been translated into more than 30 languages, facilitating a resurgence of research on the interaction of personality and culture (McCrae, 2000). The Russian-language version of the NEO-PI-R extends the potential scope of such investigations to Russia and the Commonwealth of Independent States. These countries comprise a wide swath of Eastern Europe, Central Asia, and Siberia and are home to a correspondingly broad diversity of cultures. However, the effort to develop this instrument must be understood in the context of the historical development of psychological testing and personality research in the former Soviet Union, which differs in important respects from that of Western Europe and North America.

1.1. A History of Russian Psychological Testing and Personality Research

Soviet ideology and political history strongly influenced Russian psychology during the Twentieth Century (Gindis, 1992; Kozulin, 1984), and psychological testing was more powerfully affected than other psychological pursuits. As was true in Europe and North America, interest in testing developed rapidly in Russia during the early Twentieth

Century. The 1920s and early 1930s saw a period of extensive testing in industrial and educational settings. In both environments the purpose of testing was the measurement of individual differences. Psychologists studied successful workers and gifted students in order to identify the intellectual and personal characteristics that contributed to their success. The range of the tests in use at the time was quite broad, consisting of dozens of tests. In addition to the tests of Alfred Binet and modifications thereof, instruments developed by Grigory Rossolimo, Volfgang Mede, Genrih Piortkovskiy, Nikolai Levitov, and many others were popular. These techniques consisted mainly of tests of professional performance for adults and tests of developmental age and giftedness for children.

Personality *per se* was not a focus of the Russian pioneers of psychological testing, although some did create tests of moral development (Brushlinskiy, 1997). Since Soviet psychology directed psychologists' attention to research primarily on such processes as sensation, perception, attention, memory, thought, psychomotor functions, and expression of temperament, discussions of motivation and personality structure tended to be highly theoretical and did not spawn methods of personality assessment.

Promotion and validation of testing in Russia were central to the activities of such psychologists as Grigory Rossolimo, Michail Bernstein, and Pavel Blonskiy. Testing became especially active at the time of the first conference on educational psychology in April, 1927, which featured discussions of tests and their interpretation. In May of the same year, Moscow-based psychologists involved in testing formed a team to develop a broad prospectus for their work. Throughout the country educational psychologists conducted applied testing in children's clinics, schools, and laboratories. By this time the field was sufficiently robust to support the publication of several collections of tests.

By the middle of the 1930s, however, applied psychology came under concerted political attack. The campaign against educational psychology was especially intense. In 1936 the Central Committee of the Communist Party issued an infamous decree entitled "On Perversions in Educational Psychology in the People's Ministry of Education." In that document, educational psychology was declared a pseudoscience, a practice hostile to the Party, a form of mental abuse of children, and a detriment to the Soviet state (Brushlinskiy, 1997; Petrovskiy, 1967).

The demise of educational psychology was caused by several factors. The "old Bolsheviks" who had supported or at least tolerated educational psychology and psychological testing had been swept away by Iosif Stalin's brutal consolidation of power. Furthermore, educational psychology failed to fulfill an essential mission assigned to the social sciences by the Soviet state: validation of the ideology of Bolshevism (Brushlinskiy, 1997). Studies of the intellectual achievements of Soviet schoolchildren had compared them unfavorably to their American counterparts, children from working and peasant families were reported to exhibit lower rates of mental development than the children of the intelligentsia, and data on national differences in intelligence had been published. These results, however we might interpret them now, did not comply with the imperative of *partiinost* (being a loyal member of the Party). Furthermore, the fact that unqualified examiners increasingly used psychological tests played a role in the destiny of educational psychology. Assessment laboratories employed a great number of government administrative workers, teachers, physicians, and engineers who believed that assessment did not require any specialized training. The practice of entrusting assessment activities to untrained examiners precipitated widespread abuse of tests and degraded the scientific prestige of psychological measurement in the eyes of Party officials.

Following the 1936 ruling, the Party closed all psychological assessment centers and laboratories, banned publications, and eliminated academic degrees in the field (Petrovskiy, 1967). Leading specialists in applied psychology were arrested, exiled, tortured, and killed. Psychological testing as a research and diagnostic tool disappeared entirely.

The Great Patriotic War (World War II) was a period of enormous difficulty for the people of the Soviet Union. However, it posed an opportunity for its remaining psychologists to turn their attention to matters somewhat related to personality. The primary line of inquiry addressed traits that contributed to the success of soldiers and officers. The seminal research in this field was that of a famous Russian psychologist, Boris Teplov, who identified the personality traits of effective high-ranking officers. In addition, he described a broad spectrum of desirable traits of soldiers, such as patriotism, loyalty to the ideas of Bolshevism, bravery, courage, discipline, and endurance. Although formal testing was prohibited, observation, query, and expert evaluation were employed to study these attributes. This line of work rehabilitated psychology in the eyes of the public, improved perceptions of psychology held by top Party officials, and reduced the fear among psychologists that they might meet the fate of their colleagues who had practiced educational psychology and psychological testing.

The political "thaw" initiated by Nikita Khruschev in 1956 may be regarded as the beginning of an era in which psychology in general and the study of personality in particular were gradually released from the constraints of political ideology. By the 1960s Soviet psychologists began to work more actively to develop broad conceptions of personality. The discussion of foreign theories of personality and the formulation of original personality theories characterize this period. Notable figures in this movement were Sergei Rubinstein, Boris Ananiev, Konstantin Platonov, and others. The trend developed further in the mid-1980s as Mikhail Gorbachev launched perestroika, manifesting itself in Soviet psychologists' aspirations to study personality in ways that acknowledged global theoretical conceptions and in the growing popularity of humanistic psychology.

This period also saw a surge of interest in adopting Western methods of psychological measurement (Burlachuk & Morozov, 1989; Melnikov & Yampolskiy, 1985). Russian psychologists renewed the active use of psychological tests as a primary tool for studying personality traits. The personality questionnaires of Hans Eysenck, the 16PF of Raymond Cattell, and the MMPI (the first Russian version of which was designed by Fedor Berezin in 1967) were the most popular tests. Some more recent research has demonstrated that the Five-Factor Model can be replicated in Russian samples (Digman & Shmelyov, 1996; Paunonen et al., 1996).

The attempts of Russian psychologists to develop their own typologies of personality inevitably led them to design their own personality questionnaires, as well. For example, in 1970 Andrei Lichko developed a personality questionnaire for defining types of psychopathy in adolescence.

The adaptation of foreign tests and attempts to develop indigenous tests led to the emergence of groups of psychologists in several cities who were devoted to developing, validating, and employing tests. These psychologists were Konstantin Gurevich, Vladimir Druzhinin, Vladimir Rusalov, and Alexandr Shmelyov in Moscow; Verner Gayda, Alexandr Zakharov, and Andrei Lichko in St. Petersburg; and Leonid Burlachuk in Kiev. Businesses engaged in publishing tests also emerged by the late 1980s due to the liberalization of laws governing private enterprise. Many of these businesses were engaged in selling pirated foreign tests that had received only casual translation, and most are no longer operating. At present, three firms in Russia specialize in adapting and publishing psychological tests: Imaton in St. Petersburg, Psychodiagnostika in Yaroslavl, and Smisl in Moscow. The Russian authors of this article are partners in Psychodiagnostika.

2. THE RUSSIAN NEO-PI-R

The Russian NEO-PI-R is one product of a Russian-American academic exchange between Yaroslavl State University in Russia and Susquehanna University in Pennsylvania arranged just prior to the dissolution of the Soviet Union in 1991. The first faculty delegation from Susquehanna University visited Yaroslavl in June, 1992. The delegation included the first author of this chapter, Tom Martin, who was hosted by the third author, Valery Oryol. Dr. Oryol then traveled to Susquehanna University in March, 1993. As often happens, these exchanges concluded with an attempt by the participants to identify issues of mutual interest and means of working together in the future. Our shared interest in test development led us to pursue a collaborative project of this sort. We selected the NEO-PI-R because its applicability to a broad range of inquiry in psychology had been amply demonstrated, and it was rapidly gaining international acclaim. Our goal was to develop a research tool that would encourage other international collaborations, conform to the highest principles of test development, and recognize international standards for the protection of intellectual property. The project was launched in late 1993 by requesting permission from Psychological Assessment Resources to undertake the work.

2.1. Development and Revision

Martin et al. (1997) described our approach to the translation of the NEO-PI-R into the Russian language. We attempted to remain faithful to the original content of the NEO-PI-R and to preserve its casual tone and modest reading difficulty. However, adaptations of a variety of sorts were necessary, including replacing single English words with Russian phrases, adapting American English colloquial expressions to their Russian semantic equivalents, and replacing a few items that were inescapably culturally bound. (In the latter case, for example, "I wouldn't enjoy vacationing in Las Vegas" was replaced with a related item we judged to preserve the original item's meaning, "I would not like going to a casino.") An item analysis based on the protocols of 178 participants identified 64 items that met our psychometric criterion for revision, operationalized as an item-facet or item-domain correlation that fell below .20. Never-

Table 1. Comparison of Internal Consistency Coefficients of the
Russian and English NEO-PI-R.

Domain/Facet	Draft 1[a]	Draft 2[b]		U. S.[c]
	α	Items[d]	α	α
Neuroticism	.88	15	.89	.92
N1: Anxiety	.66	2	.76	.78
N2: Angry Hostility	.60	4	.73	.75
N3: Depression	.67	3	.66	.81
N4: Self-Consciousness	.62	1	.61	.68
N5: Impulsiveness	.64	5	.65	.70
N6: Vulnerability	.70	0	.64	.70
Extraversion	.91	7	.90	.89
E1: Warmth	.68	2	.68	.73
E2: Gregariousness	.77	2	.80	.72
E3: Assertiveness	.68	1	.77	.77
E4: Activity	.77	0	.76	.63
E5: Excitement-Seeking	.72	2	.64	.65
E6: Positive Emotions	.77	0	.74	.73
Openness to Experience	.86	12	.85	.87
O1: Fantasy	.74	1	.74	.76
O2: Aesthetics	.76	1	.73	.76
O3: Feelings	.65	1	.68	.66
O4: Actions	.60	3	.61	.58
O5: Ideas	.70	0	.66	.80
O6: Values	.40	6	.47	.67
Agreeableness	.85	19	.86	.86
A1: Trust	.67	3	.70	.79
A2: Straightforwardness	.64	3	.71	.71
A3: Altruism	.66	1	.65	.75
A4: Compliance	.60	4	.62	.59
A5: Modesty	.74	1	.72	.67
A6: Tender-Mindedness	.34	7	.43	.56
Conscientiousness	.87	12	.91	.90
C1: Competence	.56	3	.55	.67
C2: Order	.67	2	.68	.66
C3: Dutifulness	.68	2	.70	.62
C4: Achievement Striving	.70	2	.73	.67
C5: Self-Discipline	.68	1	.76	.75
C6: Deliberation	.68	2	.73	.71

[a]$N = 178$. [b]$N = 350$. [c]From Costa & McCrae, 1992. $N = 1,539$. [d]Number of items revised in Draft 2.

theless, the alpha coefficients for the domains and the factor structure of the translated test corresponded well to the original NEO-PI-R.

A 278-item version of the Russian NEO-PI-R was developed which replaced 64 items with new translations of the English items. An additional 38 items were appended to the end of the test. These were mostly alternative translations of items that were judged to be problematic, for which two or three equally plausible renditions of the item were generated. A few alternatives were also included for items that were identified subjectively; we thought the item might perform even better if modified in some way. In the latter case, the original item was left in place and the putative improvement appended to the end of the test. The first 240 items followed the order typical of the NEO-PI-R, presenting in sequence items from the N, E, O, A, and C domains. The final 38 items were arranged in a random order, so did not employ the domain sequence of earlier items.

The 278-item version was administered to 350 participants in Yaroslavl and surrounding regions of Central Russia. They were university students, medical students, and workers in educational, industrial, and commercial enterprises. The 208 females and 142 males ranged in age from 16 to 63 years ($M = 28.7$). If alternative items correlated more strongly with the applicable facet and domain, they were selected for inclusion in the test and their data substituted for the earlier item.

Table 1 compares the internal consistency of the two drafts of the Russian NEO-PI-R with the published values for the original English NEO-PI-R. In addition, the third column of the table lists the number of items of the first draft that were replaced by new renditions of the item or an alternative item that proved to be superior to the original translation. These were 65 in number. In most cases, the revision of items improved the internal consistency of the facet in question. However, four facets proved particularly difficult. They were N3: Depression, O6: Values, A6: Tender-Mindedness, and C1: Competence. These facets follow two patterns. In the first instance, the internal consistency of N3 and C1 were unaffected by our revisions, and fail to approach the reliability of the original facets. This is particularly notable in the case of N3, the most consistent facet of the English version. The alpha coefficients of O6 and A6 did respond modestly to our revisions, but remain substantially lower than those of their English counterparts.

The two questions in N3 that challenged us were 101 and 131. The back translations of item 101 in the first draft read "On occasion I have experienced strong feelings of guilt or shame," and in the second version "I experience the feelings of guilt and sin." The second problematic item was translated "When something goes wrong I tend to blame myself" in the first draft and "I am inclined to blame myself for all of my failures" in the second draft. Neither revision performed well. It is our belief that guilt and self-censure are not so prevalent in the Russian manifestation of depression as are the experiences tapped by other NEO-PI-R items: loneliness, sadness, worthlessness, poor self-esteem, hopelessness, and discouragement in the face of challenge. The American emphasis on individual responsibility and some religious conceptions of depression teach that depression is a personal and spiritual failing of the person so affected. By contrast, Russians are far less likely to consider depression in moral and religious terms. Moreover, daily experience in the Soviet Union and in contemporary Russia has taught individuals to recognize that many problems in living are caused by difficult circumstances rather than personal deficiencies. Therefore, Russians may be more likely than Americans to make external attributions when something does not go well. This explanation is consistent with the cross-cultural literature on attribution

(Oyserman, Coon, & Kemmelmeier, 2002), which suggests that people in collectivistic cultures like Russia (Hofstede, 2001) are more prone to use external attributions.

Competence is the facet of the Conscientiousness domain that was least internally consistent. Although not evident from the unchanged alpha coefficient, two of the three revised items yielded acceptable item-facet and item-domain correlations. The remaining problematic item (#35) was translated "I don't take my civic duties such as voting very seriously," and "I don't pay much attention to such civic obligations as, for example, voting" in the first and second drafts, respectively. This has an obvious relationship to the historic and contemporary political environment in Russia. Competence is intended to measure the degree to which people perceive themselves as "capable, sensible, prudent, and effective" (Costa & McCrae, 1992, p. 18). In the Russian environment, concern with political matters and voting in particular is unlikely to be viewed as an expression of competence. More generally, Martin et al. (1997, p. 4) noted that:

> . . . in Russian language and usage, the qualifier "competent" is typically applied to well educated persons who are, moreover, well informed on a specific subject. While there may be overlap in these constructs, the discrepancies in the meaning of competence across languages and cultures may have curtailed the internal reliability of C1.

Despite our awareness of these differences in the connotations of competence at the time of the revisions, we may not have overcome this linguistic challenge.

The Values facet of the Openness domain yielded one of the lowest alpha coefficients in the first phase of test development. Six of its eight items met our criteria for revision. Given the performance of the first-draft items, two new translations of most items were prepared, and the alternative with the better performance was selected for inclusion in the test. These efforts produced a modest improvement in the facet's internal consistency, but one that falls short of the standard set by the original English version. It is our conclusion that the problem lies with the original content of the scale, and with the difficulty Russian participants experienced in responding to these questions in the circumstances that prevailed in 1997. The fluid sociopolitical environment of the decade had called into question the fundamental values by which Russians guided their lives. Whether or not one was temperamentally inclined "to reexamine social, political, and religious values" (Costa & McCrae, 1992, p. 18), one was compelled to engage in such reexamination or to set aside these considerations as hopelessly complex and relative. We suggest that these NEO-PI-R questions assume a relatively stable sociopolitical environment. It may be that this assumption cannot be appreciated fully until the instrument is used in a society undergoing rapid and dramatic change. As the situation in Russia stabilizes, it may be that the internal consistency of this facet will improve.

Tender-Mindedness, the last facet of the Agreeableness domain, presented a similar challenge to us. It is intended to measure "attitudes of sympathy and concern for others" (Costa & McCrae, 1992, p. 18). Seven of eight items required revision; two new translations were prepared for most of them. The resulting improvement in internal consistency of the facet was modest. Again, we attribute this outcome to an interaction of the content of the facet with the ongoing political, social, and economic change in Russia. An ideology that purported to meet the needs of all has been swept away, so means of expressing concern for others must be reformulated. In a more stable socio-political framework, such as that in the United States, people readily identify themselves as favoring more or less action to meet human needs than is accomplished by the *status quo*. The participants in this research, who are of modest socioeconomic standing and must themselves respond to the exigencies of earning a living in the new era, are unlikely to be as settled in their opinions as are their American counterparts. Again, it will be interesting to see whether the internal consistency of this facet will increase as the socioeconomic environment in Russia becomes more secure.

Despite the difficulties with four of 30 facets, we believe the revised Russian NEO-PI-R performs well. Domain internal consistency is robust, and facet alpha coefficients approximate those of the English version. Moreover, Table 2 displays the factor structure of the revised test, which is quite similar to that of the original NEO-PI-R (Costa & McCrae, 1992). A final version incorporating the best items has been prepared, and is now in use in our ongoing research.

2.2. Studies Employing the Russian NEO-PI-R

Before the first draft of the Russian NEO-PI-R could be revised, Anna Krylova collected data for her diploma thesis comparing the personalities of Russian and Nentsy young adults (Draguns, Krylova, Oryol, Rukavishnikov, & Martin, 2000). The Nentsy are indigenous to a large area of the European and Siberian Arctic. Their language, folklore, and traditions are quite distinct from the Slavic culture of Central Russia. Nomadic reindeer herding remains the livelihood of some Nenets, while others were collectivized into permanent residences during the Soviet era. This study is of interest because it compares mean personality characteristics of young adults raised in a small, traditional ethnic group with those of their peers from the dominant modern culture of Russia. Participants were 80 Nentsy students from secondary and technical schools in the Yamal-Nentsy National District and 80 university and technical school students in Yaroslavl. All Nentsy students were fluent in Russian, as this was the sole language in which they were taught. Nentsy participants scored significantly lower on all facets of Openness to Experience, three facets of Extraversion (Warmth, Gregariousness, and Assertiveness), and on the Straightforwardness facet of Agreeableness. They scored significantly higher on the Angry Hostility and Self-Consciousness facets of the Neuroticism domain. While the article identifies a number of reasons to interpret these results with some caution, the study nonetheless demonstrates the applicability of the NEO-PI-R for investigations of small, traditional cultures.

The data collected for the purpose of the second item analysis were analyzed by Costa et al. (2000) for age-related trends and compared with American, Japanese, and Estonian trends, as well as those reported earlier for Germany, Italy, Portugal, Croatia, and South Korea. They found that, in the cross-sectional samples of most cultures, N, E, and O correlated negatively with age, while A and C correlated positively with age. The Russian data followed this pattern as well, with the exception of Neuroticism. As with the Estonian sample, Russian participants showed no significant age differences in Neuroticism.

Two individuals who are not directly involved in our research group have explored

Table 2. Factor Structure of the Russian NEO-PI-R.

NEO–PI–R Facet Scale	Varimax–Rotated Principal Component				
	N	**E**	**O**	**A**	**C**
N1: Anxiety	**.86**	.00	.07	.09	.06
N2: Angry Hostility	**.70**	.08	−.13	−.33	−.10
N3: Depression	**.61**	−.25	.16	.08	−.17
N4: Self–Consciousness	**.74**	−.12	.02	.11	.15
N5: Impulsiveness	**.40**	**.43**	−.05	−.24	**−.41**
N6: Vulnerability	**.67**	.08	−.18	.12	−.33
E1: Warmth	−.09	**.75**	.04	.34	.10
E2: Gregariousness	−.07	**.81**	−.14	.23	−.16
E3: Assertiveness	−.26	**.49**	.00	−.34	.27
E4: Activity	.00	**.62**	.04	−.14	.28
E5: Excitement Seeking	−.15	**.41**	.23	−.17	−.24
E6: Positive Emotions	.03	**.60**	.30	.03	.00
O1: Fantasy	.19	.01	**.55**	−.06	−.36
O2: Aesthetics	.12	−.06	**.78**	.18	.25
O3: Feelings	.31	.14	**.67**	−.02	.00
O4: Actions	−.13	.12	**.60**	.14	−.25
O5: Ideas	−.17	−.27	**.85**	−.08	.18
O6: Values	−.21	−.02	.38	.00	−.18
A1: Trust	−.05	.35	.00	**.73**	−.09
A2: Straightforwardness	.05	−.18	−.07	**.69**	.05
A3: Altruism	.08	**.40**	.07	**.64**	.22
A4: Compliance	−.22	−.22	.17	**.74**	−.04
A5: Modesty	.13	−.17	−.10	**.54**	.12
A6: Tender–Mindedness	.27	.28	−.04	**.64**	−.08
C1: Competence	−.06	.21	−.08	−.18	**.77**
C2: Order	.02	.03	−.07	.02	**.71**
C3: Dutifulness	.17	−.05	.11	.22	**.76**
C4: Achievement Striving	−.02	.34	.06	−.22	**.72**
C5: Self–Discipline	−.10	.07	−.02	.06	**.78**
C6: Deliberation	−.13	−.25	.04	.08	**.70**

Note. $N = 350$. Loadings that equal or exceed .40 appear in bold type.

the equivalency of the Russian-language NEO-PI-R with the Estonian and English versions of the test. Each did so by testing fluently bilingual subjects with two versions of the NEO-PI-R, one in each language. Konstabel (1999) administered the Estonian and Russian versions to 60 individuals, 31 of whom had learned Estonian as their first language. Twenty learned Russian as their primary language and the remainder either

Table 3. Cross-Language Validity Coefficients and One-Year Retest Stability
For the Russian NEO-PI-R.

| | Cross-language *r* with | | One-year r_{tt} | |
Domain/Facet	Estonian[a]	English[b]	Form S	Form R
Neuroticism	.93	.95	.84	.79
N1: Anxiety	.80	.82	.84	.69
N2: Angry Hostility	.74	.80	.79	.79
N3: Depression	.83	.90	.78	.79
N4: Self-Consciousness	.82	.84	.68	.66
N5: Impulsiveness	.78	.72	.75	.70
N6: Vulnerability	.82	.93	.78	.76
Extraversion	.88	.96	.84	.88
E1: Warmth	.82	.89	.71	.79
E2: Gregariousness	.83	.89	.81	.86
E3: Assertiveness	.87	.94	.76	.70
E4: Activity	.78	.84	.78	.84
E5: Excitement-Seeking	.80	.73	.81	.71
E6: Positive Emotions	.88	.92	.81	.78
Openness to Experience	.85	.88	.89	.81
O1: Fantasy	.84	.86	.80	.81
O2: Aesthetics	.83	.87	.80	.76
O3: Feelings	.65	.86	.82	.68
O4: Actions	.72	.76	.71	.65
O5: Ideas	.78	.87	.88	.84
O6: Values	.58	.65	.62	.68
Agrèeableness	.93	.92	.86	.65
A1: Trust	.88	.83	.77	.70
A2: Straightforwardness	.81	.85	.70	.65
A3: Altruism	.81	.85	.83	.71
A4: Compliance	.83	.81	.65	.57
A5: Modesty	.87	.79	.79	.64
A6: Tender-Mindedness	.68	.86	.77	.56
Conscientiousness	.88	.98	.85	.78
C1: Competence	.69	.91	.78	.56
C2: Order	.76	.88	.78	.78
C3: Dutifulness	.73	.75	.81	.71
C4: Achievement Striving	.72	.84	.78	.86
C5: Self-Discipline	.88	.76	.84	.68
C6: Deliberation	.84	.85	.78	.75

Note. Form S = self-reports, Form R = spouse ratings. *N* = 60 for stability coefficients. [a]From Konstabel (1999, pp. 16-17), *N* = 60. [b]From Simakhodskaya (2000, pp. 2-3), *N* = 42.

reported they had learned Estonian and Russian simultaneously or had learned another Baltic language before mastering Estonian and Russian. Konstabel found that the cross-language validity coefficients of domain scores ranged from .85 to .93. The median validity coefficient for facet scores was .81, with a range from .58 to .88 (see Table 3). In general, the facets for which he observed low correlations were ones for which relatively low internal consistency has been observed for Russian or Estonian samples. The factor structures of the Estonian and Russian versions were nearly identical, although he noted different patterns of secondary loadings for O3: Feelings. He also observed that responses to the Russian-language version yielded higher Neuroticism and lower Agreeableness domain scores, higher N6: Vulnerability and O4: Actions facet scores, and lower A1: Trust and A4: Tender-Mindedness scores. Taken as a whole these results support the semantic equivalence of the instruments but raise the likelihood that scalar equivalence between the Russian and Estonian versions cannot be assumed.

Simakhodskaya (2000) administered the Russian and English versions of the NEO-PI-R to 42 participants, all of whom had immigrated to the United States from the Commonwealth of Independent States. She reported domain cross-language validity coefficients ranging from .88 to .98, and facet validity coefficients of .65 to .94. The median validity for facet scores in this study was .85. These coefficients are rather robust. Even the lowest coefficient, that of .65 for the O6: Values facet, rises to .79 when corrected for attenuation of the English criterion. Inspection of Table 3 indicates that the reported Russian/English cross-language validity coefficients are generally higher than are Russian/Estonian coefficients. This observation is likely attributable to the fact that semantic drift in two translations has contributed error variance to the Russian/Estonian coefficients, while Russian/English coefficients are affected by the vagaries of only a single translation process.

Simakhodskaya (2000) did not report the domain or facet means necessary to evaluate the scalar equivalence of the Russian and English versions of the NEO-PI-R. However, she did explore the capacity of the NEO-PI-R in both of these versions to predict the acculturation of immigrants. Acculturation was assessed with the Language, Identity, and Behavioral Acculturation Scale (LIB; Birman, 1997). This instrument measures acculturation to Russian and American cultures via general acculturation indexes for each culture. It also yields subscale scores for language, identity, and behavioral acculturation to each culture. American acculturation by the immigrants in this sample correlated significantly with the Conscientiousness domain and the C1: Competence and C4: Achievement Striving facets of both the Russian and English versions of the NEO-PI-R. These correlations were positive and of moderate magnitude ($rs = .48$ to .65). Additionally, Simakhodskaya reported significant correlations between the Conscientiousness domain and several facet scales of the NEO-PI-R with American Behavior Acculturation, English Language Competency, and American Identity subscales of the LIB. While these coefficients are interesting, they must be interpreted with extreme caution as she apparently reviewed 210 correlations (35 domains and facets × two NEO-PI-R versions × three LIB subscales) to identify the 18 significant coefficients. Even with a $p < .01$ criterion, the aggregate probabilities suggest that several of these relationships are due to chance alone. Nevertheless, C1: Competence

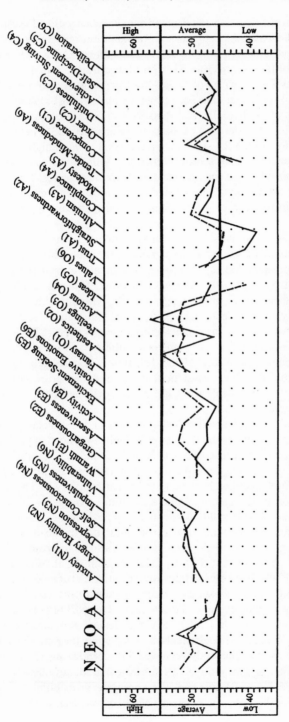

Figure 1. Mean NEO-PI-R profile for college age Russian women (solid line) and men (dashed line) relative to American norms. Profile form reproduced by special permission of the Publisher, from the Revised NEO Personality Inventory, by Paul T. Costa, Jr., and Robert R. McCrae. Copyright 1978, 1985, 1989, 1992 by PAR, Inc. Further reproduction is prohibited without permission of PAR, Inc.

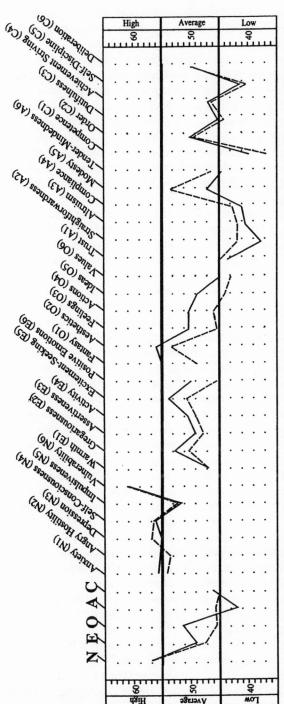

Figure 2. Mean NEO-PI-R profile for adult Russian women (solid line) and men (dashed line) relative to American norms. Profile form reproduced by special permission of the Publisher, from the Revised NEO Personality Inventory, by Paul T. Costa, Jr., and Robert R. McCrae. Copyright 1978, 1985, 1989, 1992 by PAR, Inc. Further reproduction is prohibited without permission of PAR, Inc.

was consistently related to all LIB subscales. Competence (and overall Conscientiousness) may contribute to adaptation in a new culture, or successful acculturation may promote a sense of competence.

While we have yet to generate evidence for the scalar equivalence of the English and Russian versions of the NEO-PI-R, we have plotted mean Russian factor and facet scores against American norms. The 350 participants in the second item analysis study were divided by age and sex. Young participants were defined as those who were 16 to 21 years of age. Older participants were 22 years of age or older. Figure 1 plots younger women ($n = 98$) and men ($n = 30$) against American college student norms; Figure 2 plots older women ($n = 190$) and men ($n = 112$) against American adult norms. Inspection of these plots reveals that older Russian men and women exhibit higher Neuroticism scores than younger Russians or Americans in either age group. The most notably elevated facet of this domain is N6: Vulnerability. C5: Self-Discipline also shows an age-related pattern, although less extreme and in the direction of lower scores for older participants. All participants scored lower than their American counterparts on A2: Straightforwardness, A3: Altruism, and C1: Competence.

In the absence of information on the scalar equivalence of these instruments, any interpretation of the observed differences must be regarded as speculative, because one cannot discriminate clearly between translation-induced differences and cultural differences in response to facets or domains. Nonetheless, several related lines of evidence suggest the potential for cultural differences that should be evaluated in future studies. The higher Neuroticism scores converge with the findings of Lynn and Martin (1995) that Russians exhibit higher Neuroticism scores on the Eysenck Personality Questionnaire. Moreover, as noted in Costa et al. (2000), Neuroticism scores generally decrease with age in other countries, suggesting that this pattern reveals something unique to Russian participants rather than semantic drift in the translation process. Certainly the dramatic ideological, political, and economic changes of recent years in Russia may play some role in this observation, since the young may be less disrupted by the changes and better positioned to benefit from them. Older adults, on the other hand, have often seen their standard of living deteriorate, the verities by which they organized their lives overturned, and prospects for security in old age diminished. These may fuel feelings of alienation, discouragement, and vulnerability in older Russian adults to a degree that is not shared by their counterparts in other countries or by younger Russians. This interpretation converges with the factor analytic finding of Lynn and Martin (1995) that national per capita income across 37 countries has a strong negative loading on a factor they interpret as neuroticism.

It is also interesting to note that A3: Altruism and C1: Competence are identified by Simakhodskaya as NEO-PI-R facets that correlate positively with the American Behavior subscale of the LIB, and that C1 correlates positively with the English Language and American Identity subscales as well. This suggests that these facets are sensitive to behavior and patterns of thinking that differ in the two cultures, or at least that the operational definitions of American behavior and identity represented in the LIB are associated with the constructs measured by A3 and C1. Again, this may be a fruitful line of inquiry for future research. The remaining facets which differ in the plots, A2: Straightforwardness and C5: Self-Discipline, are less accessible to speculative analysis. Yet, as facets in the same domains as A3 and C1, they likely pick up some of the same variance and may also be sensitive to differences in Russian and American culture.

Finally, a recent pilot study by our research group examined the one-year stability and cross-observer validity of the Russian NEO-PI-R. Thirty married couples in Yaroslavl, Russia, participated in the study. The age of participants ranged from 20 to 55, with a mean age of 39.6 for men and 38.3 for women. Thirty-four participants (56.7%) had earned a university degree. Each individual completed the self-report version (Form S) of the NEO-PI-R and rated his or her spouse using Form R of the NEO-PI-R. The same couples were retested approximately one year later. Stability coefficients for domain scores ranged from .65 to .89. Facets yielded stability coefficients from .56 to .88 (see Table 3).

Computation of the Index of Profile Agreement (I_{pa}; McCrae, 1993) from the domain scores of paired Form S and Form R profiles indicated that 80.8% of them exceeded zero, the minimum value for inferring profile agreement. Also computed were Coefficients of Profile Agreement (r_{pa}), a transformation of the I_{pa} that yields coefficients resembling correlation coefficients. The median r_{pa} for the sixty pairs of profiles was .47. Consensual validity coefficients were significant for each domain: N ($r = .43, p < .0001$), E ($r = .50, p < .0001$), O ($r = .45, p < .0001$), A ($r = .31, p < .0006$), and C ($r = .35, p < .0001$). While these results are based on the profiles of a limited number of subjects, they suggest that the stability and consensual validity of the Russian NEO-PI-R will prove to be acceptable for an instrument of this type.

3. CONCLUSION AND FUTURE DIRECTIONS

The studies reviewed above demonstrate that the Russian-language NEO-PI-R is a reliable instrument with a factor structure very similar to that of the original NEO-PI-R. While additional work is necessary to further document its validity and to restandardize it for general use, we are confident that these tasks can be accomplished in the foreseeable future.

Our research with the Russian NEO-PI-R remains quite active. We are currently working with colleagues at the National Institute on Aging to test 400 pairs of Russian subjects, both marital and sibling pairs, in the first phase of a longitudinal study of personality development. Possibilities for future research include exploring the interaction of personality and culture by testing members of relatively assimilated ethnic groups that nonetheless maintain a distinctive language and culture (for example, Tatars), examining differences between practitioners of various professions, and investigating the relationship between personality and burnout.

We believe that the NEO-PI-R also holds promise for use by many psychologists in Russia and the Commonwealth of Independent States. At present there are no well-validated personality tests that have been developed originally in the Russian language, nor are there other authorized translations of comprehensive tests of normal personality that were developed outside of Russia. As psychologists come to appreciate the value of the Russian-language NEO-PI-R, we believe that it will receive extensive use.

REFERENCES

Birman, D. (1997). *The adjustment of Russian students at Pikesville High School, Pikesville, MD.* Refugee Mental Health Program, Center for Mental Health Services, Substance and Mental Health Services Administration, Rockville, MD.

Brushlinskiy, A.B. (Ed.). (1997). *Психологическая наука в России XX века: Проблемы теории и истории [Psychological science in Russia of the twentieth century: Problems of theory and history].* Moscow: Psychological Research Institute of the Russian Academy of Sciences.

Burlachuk, L. F., & Morozov, S. A. (1989). *Словарь-справочник по психодиагностике [Reference dictionary in psychodiagnostics].* Kiev: Naukova Dumka.

Costa, P. T., & McCrae, R. R. (1992). *Revised NEO Personality Inventory (NEO-PI-R) and NEO Five-Factor Inventory (NEO-FFI) professional manual.* Odessa, FL: Psychological Assessment Resources.

Costa, P. T., Jr., McCrae, R. R., Martin, T. A., Oryol, V. E., Senin, I. G., Rukavishnikov, A. A., Shimonaka, Y., Nakazato, K., Gondo, Y., Takayama, M., Allik, J., Kallasmaa, T., & Realo, A. (2000). Personality development from adolescence through adulthood: Further cross-cultural comparisons of age differences. In V. J. Molfese & D. Molfese (Eds.), *Temperament and personality development across the lifespan* (pp. 235-252). Hillsdale, NJ: Lawrence Erlbaum Associates.

Digman, J.M. & Shmelyov, A. (1996). The structure of temperament and personality in Russian children. *Journal of Personality and Social Psychology, 71,* 341-351

Draguns, J. G., Krilova, A. V., Oryol, V. E., Rukavishnikov, A. A., & Martin, T. A. (2000). Personality characteristics of the Nentsy in the Russian arctic: A comparison with ethnic Russians by means of NEO-PI-R and POI. *American Behavioral Scientist, 44,* 126-140.

Gindis, B. (1992). Soviet psychology on the path of perestroika. *Professional Psychology: Research and Practice, 23,* 114-118.

Hofstede, G. (2001). *Culture's consequences: Comparing values, behaviors, institutions, and organizations across nations* (2nd ed.). Thousand Oaks, CA: Sage.

Konstabel, K. (1999). *A bilingual retest study of the Revised NEO Personality Inventory: A comparison of Estonian and Russian versions.* Unpublished master's thesis, University of Tartu, Estonia.

Kozulin, A. (1994). Psychology in utopia: Toward a social history of Soviet psychology. Cambridge, MA: MIT Press.

Lynn, R., & Martin, T. (1995). National differences for thirty-seven nations in Extraversion, Neuroticism, Psychoticism, and economic, demographic, and other correlates. *Personality and Individual Differences, 19,* 403-406.

Martin, T. A., Draguns, J. G., Oryol, V. E., Senin, I. G., Rukavishnikov, A. A., & Klotz, M. L. (1997, August). *Development of a Russian-language NEO-PI-R.* Poster session presented at the 105th Annual Meeting of the American Psychological Association, Chicago.

McCrae, R. R. (1993). Agreement of personality profiles across observers. *Multivariate Behavioral Research, 28,* 13-28.

McCrae, R. R. (2000). Trait psychology and the revival of personality and culture studies. *American Behavioral Scientist, 44,* 10-31.

Melnikov V., & Yampolskiy, L. (1985). *Введение в экспериментальную психологию личности [Introduction to experimental psychology of personality].* Moscow: Prosveschenie.

Oyserman, D., Coon, H. M., & Kemmelmeier, M. (2002). Rethinking individualism and collectivism: Evaluation of theoretical assumptions and meta-analyses. *Psychological Bulletin, 128,* 3-72.

Paunonen, S. V., Keinonen, M., Trzebinski, J., Forsterling, F., Grishenko-Roze, N., Kouznetsova, L., Chan, D. W. (1996). The structure of personality in six cultures. *Journal of Cross-Cultural Psychology, 27,* 339-353.

Petrovskiy, A. V. (1967). *История советской психологии [History of Soviet psychology].* Moscow: Prosveschenie.

Simakhodskaya, Z. (2000, August). *Russian revised NEO-PI-R: Concordant validity and relationship to acculturation.* Poster session presented at the 108th Annual Meeting of the American Psychological Association, Washington, DC.

AUTHOR NOTE

Thomas A. Martin is an Associate Professor of Psychology at Susquehanna University. He is a clinical psychologist whose interests include test development and personality assessment. Paul T. Costa, Jr., is Chief, Laboratory of Personality and Cognition, National Institute on Aging. Valery E. Oryol is Dean of the Faculty of Psychology at Yaroslavl State University. He is an industrial psychologist with a primary interest in professional deformation (i.e., burnout). The late Alexey A. Rukavishnikov was an Assistant Professor of Psychology at Yaroslavl State University. His interests included psychological testing and the assessment of burnout. Ivan G. Senin is an Associate Professor of Psychology at Yaroslavl State University. His interests are psychological testing, measurement of values, and industrial psychology.

This research was supported originally by grants from the Faculty Development and Research Committee of Susquehanna University. It has been supported in part by a contract with the Laboratory of Personality and Cognition of the National Institute on Aging and a grant from the International Research & Exchanges Board, with funds provided by the U.S. Department of State (Title VIII program) and the National Endowment for the Humanities. We thank these organizations for their support. They are not responsible for the views expressed. Many thanks to Vadim V. Vilgelmi, whose outstanding first translation of the NEO-PI-R into the Russian language laid the foundation for our later success. Thanks, too, to Juris G. Draguns, Emeritus Professor of Psychology at The Pennsylvania State University, who was of great assistance to the authors in the process of item revision. Correspondence concerning this chapter should be addressed to Thomas A. Martin, Susquehanna University, 514 University Avenue, Selinsgrove, PA 17870. E-mail: tmartin@susqu.edu

SECTION III: METHODOLOGICAL AND THEORETICAL PERSPECTIVES

By and large, the previous chapters in this book have shown a free-wheeling, speculative, exploratory spirit that the Editors frankly encouraged. Within the past decade an impressive body of data has shown that personality inventories can be translated and used meaningfully in other cultures. Given these initial successes, it seems reasonable to press on in the quest for new insights, especially in the area of intercultural comparisons. Some new directions will ultimately turn out to be fruitless or misguided, but in the meantime we will have learned much, quickly.

However, it is also useful to recall from time to time the limitations in our methods and the possibility of alternative, artifactual interpretations. Poortinga, Van de Vijver, and Van Hemert do an admirable job of offering this sobering assessment of the work in this book. They review the hard-won insights of cross-cultural methodologists and use them as the basis of a critique of the present body of research. Perhaps most important, they offer suggestions for superior research methods and alternative hypotheses that can and should be tested in future intercultural research.

The final chapter puts cross-cultural research into the perspective of Five-Factor Theory. FFT was developed to account for the results of longitudinal studies of middle-class Americans, but it is a very general model of the personality system and its functioning. In FFT personality traits are seen as the psychological reflection of biological bases, and to the extent that human biology transcends culture, FFT expects that personality traits will, too. Is FFT supported or undermined by cross-cultural research to date? And if we adopt FFT, what can we make of cross-cultural findings? These are among the most interesting questions in the field of personality psychology today.

CROSS-CULTURAL EQUIVALENCE
OF THE BIG FIVE

A Tentative Interpretation of the Evidence

YPE H. POORTINGA,*' † FONS J. R. VAN DE VIJVER*
& DIANNE A. VAN HEMERT*

*Tilburg University, the Netherlands, †Catholic University of Leuven, Belgium

Abstract. This chapter examines cross-cultural evidence on the Five-Factor Model (Big Five dimensions) and other dimensional representations of personality (like the Eysenck model) in the light of distinctions between various forms of psychometric equivalence. In the first section we give an overview of types of inequivalence and associated forms of cultural bias. In the following three sections we look at evidence concerning three categories: structural equivalence, metric equivalence, and full score equivalence. Dimensions of personality replicate reasonably well across cultures. However, metric and full score equivalence are questionable. In a final section we discuss implications for trait theory. The findings of structural equivalence suggest that a common set of dimensions may reach across cultures to represent personality. The absence of empirical evidence for equivalence in score patterns and levels of scores makes the interpretation of quantitative cross-cultural differences on the dimensions rather tentative.

Keywords: Psychometric equivalence, factor structure, full score equivalence

1. INTRODUCTION

Two main findings emerge from this volume. The first is that each of the five dimensions of the Five-Factor Model (FFM) of personality can be recovered quite consistently across a broad range of literate societies. The second finding is that quantitative differences in scores on each of these dimensions are difficult to link to psychological characteristics of culture. Together these two results define the scope for this chapter.

Our perspective is mainly psychometric, raising questions about the interpretation of the body of findings in this book and elsewhere. The discussion is guided by a focus on cross-cultural comparability (or equivalence) of scores. It has long been recognized that behavior similar in appearance need not have the same meaning cross-culturally and that this also holds for answers on personality questionnaire items. One powerful expression of this principle is given by Przeworski and Teune (1970, p. 92) who argued: "For specific observation a belch is a belch and nepotism is nepotism. But within an inferential framework a belch is an 'insult' or a 'compliment' and nepotism is 'corruption' or 'responsibility'."

This example can be used to illustrate three approaches to cross-cultural comparison (Berry, Poortinga, Segall, & Dasen, in press). From a relativist point of view, it can be argued that the statement only seemingly makes sense. Probably the meaning of a belch in so far as it refers to a bodily event is similar across cultures. However, it is implied that the inferential categories of "insult" and "compliment," as well as of "corruption" and "responsibility" are also common across cultures. Most relativists would dispute this. In their perspective the typically human aspects of behavior are essentially cultural, and it does not make sense to separate psychological functioning from cultural context (Denzin & Lincoln, 2000; Miller, 1997).

The opposite perspective is taken by those with absolutist views. They would argue that Przeworski and Teune are probably overemphasizing differential meanings of belches or nepotism. Also in Western societies a little burp after a copious dinner, even though not encouraged, is a sign that one has eaten well, and to the best of our knowledge, nowhere is it mandatory as an expression of appreciation. Equally, a civil servant in a low-income society may be pressured to help members of his family or neighborhood, but others who fall short of the benefits are unlikely to be pleased with such positive discrimination. In other words, the example could be more rhetorical than real (see Eibl-Eibesfeldt, 1989, for similar arguments).

A middle-of-the-road position, and the one taken in this chapter, is that psychological functions are unlikely to show much cross-cultural variation; i.e., "insult," "compliment," "corruption," and "responsibility" should have an almost identical meaning across cultures. But the manifestations, the expressions of insults and compliments (as in a belch) or social responsibility (as in preferential treatment of your family) may be context dependent. In this latter approach, called universalism or psychological universalism by Berry et al. (in press), validity of inferences is a matter of empirical evidence. Researchers have to demonstrate the validity of their interpretations of cross-cultural similarities and differences in data. This intermediate position has two implications for the cross-cultural study of personality. First, as the above example indicates, personality may show absolutist and relativist characteristics, depending on, among other things, the level of generality at which personality is studied. Second, statements about the universality of personality characteristics can and should be empirically tested. We reject any position implied by absolutists and relativists in which either the universality or the cultural specificity of traits is merely assumed.

In the following sections we first outline an approach to the cross-cultural equivalence of data as a crucial concept in the interpretation of cross-cultural data. In particular we make distinctions between three hierarchically ordered forms or levels, called structural equivalence, metric equivalence, and full score equivalence (Van de Vijver & Leung, 1997a, b). Thereafter we examine empirical evidence pro and con each form of equivalence, mainly in cross-cultural data collected with the NEO-PI-R. The equivalence of personality characteristics at individual and country level is also discussed. In the final section we draw attention to some implications of the findings.

2. CROSS-CULTURAL EQUIVALENCE: AN OVERVIEW

In the analysis of equivalence of a cross-cultural data set, psychometric conditions are investigated that presumably should be satisfied by data that are equivalent across cultures, but not by data that are lacking equivalence. One such condition is that the relative difficulty of the items in an instrument should be approximately the same cross-culturally. Another condition is that patterns of correlations between items should be similar (Poortinga, 1971). Initially equivalence was almost treated as dichotomous. The main objective was to decide whether or not scores (more often than not ability tests) obtained by samples from other cultures could be interpreted in the same way as scores obtained within the culture from which an instrument originated. However, one can take a more differentiated view; four extensions of the original thinking on equivalence are mentioned below.

First, equivalence should be studied as a function of the inferences that a researcher wants to derive from the data, rather than as a characteristic of an instrument (Poortinga & Malpass, 1986). For example, one can think of an arithmetic test with simple addition and subtraction items for young children. If between-country differences in score distributions are found, these are likely to reflect valid differences in achievements. More questionable would be inferences to the effect that children in the two countries differ in arithmetical aptitude (i.e., the ability to learn arithmetic), and very few would see the finding as support for differences in inborn intellectual capacity between the two nations. One way to look at these various interpretations is in terms of levels of generalization (Cronbach, Gleser, Nanda, & Rajaratnam, 1972). According to general-izability theory, an instrument forms a sample from the entire collection of possible measurements that might have been taken to represent the domain of interest (called by Cronbach the "universe of generalization"). In the example, achievement in arithmetic, aptitude, and general intelligence would form three universes of generalization.

Two questions arise in relation to generalizability or interpretation of cross-cultural data. The first is whether the domain of generalization is shared by the cultural popula-tions concerned. For example, it is questionable whether arithmetical skill is an approp-riate notion to use in a non-literate society. It should be clear that any comparison logically collapses if there is cross-culturally no domain identity. In psychometric analyses of equivalence, domain identity is a working assumption for which the researcher tries to find support.

Assuming domain identity, a second question arises, pertaining to domain represen-tation by an instrument. For the addition or subtraction of two one-digit numbers it is easy to list all the elements in the relevant domain of arithmetic and to draw a more or less representative sample of items for an achievement test. In the case of personality traits and similar hypothetical constructs a listing of all behaviors that belong to such domains is impossible. The common strategy is to develop scales that presumably capture core elements of such constructs. According to Poortinga and Malpass (1986) a further distinction can be made in hypothetical constructs according to the level of generalization or inclusiveness. For more narrowly defined constructs, like the facets in the FFM, cross-cultural equivalence can still be examined fairly rigorously. However, as a domain is more inclusive and more poorly demarcated conceptually, it becomes increasingly difficult to think of a measurement procedure as fully representative of that domain. Moreover, it becomes increasingly difficult to demonstrate that the items sampled are an adequate representation.

A second extension in the analysis of equivalence concerns the interpretation of information in cross-cultural data sets that points to inequivalence. Initially an observed lack of equivalence was taken as evidence either that an instrument should be improved or that a meaningful comparison was out of the question. The former interpretation typically leads to the removal of items for which evidence of cultural bias is found. In the latter interpretation bias is seen as an indication that items have not been sampled from a cross-culturally corresponding domain or universe, thus precluding comparison. However, it is also possible to consider bias as systematic variance that needs to be explained and to search for variables that can account for observed inequivalence (Poortinga & Van de Vijver, 1987). Thus, cultural bias need no be treated simply as a nuisance (which it is when a researcher is aiming at making a specific comparison); it can also be treated as a reflection of cultural differences that require further analysis and explanation.

A third extension in thinking has to do with distinctions between different levels of data aggregation, particularly the individual and the country level. The central argument is that there is no reason why group differences in score distributions should be interpreted in the same way as individual differences. One illustration of this well-known issue mentions a population in which individual body height is influenced by genetic factors and by nutrition, such as consumption of milk. Suppose samples are drawn from this population that differ in milk consumption. Between-sample differences in average height are then a matter of diet, but individual variation within each sample could be due to inherited traits (Furby, 1973). Techniques for multilevel analysis are known, especially from research in education (e.g., Goldstein, 1987; Muthén, 1991), but have been rarely applied in cross-cultural psychology, even though the issue has been recognized (Hofstede, 1980, 2001; Leung & Bond, 1989). Van de Vijver and colleagues (Van de Vijver & Leung, 2001; Van de Vijver & Poortinga, 2002) have argued that data at different levels of aggregation can be compared if it can be established that they meet conditions for equivalence. In more general terms, the study of multilevel and of cross-cultural equivalence follows the same logic. Thus, similarity of factor analytic structures at individual and country level points to the equivalence of the factors at both levels; conversely, dissimilarity of structures implies that individual- and country-level differences have a different psychological meaning.

For the purpose of the present chapter a fourth extension in thinking about equivalence is the most relevant, namely distinctions between various levels of equivalence. For example, a scale can be measuring anxiety (qualitative) in two cultures, but this does not imply that identical scores in two cultures indicate the same standing (quantitative) on the underlying trait. Various categorizations of levels of equivalence are possible (e.g., Poortinga & Van de Vijver, 1987; Poortinga, 1989). Like other authors of this book (Church & Katigbak, 2002; McCrae, 2002), we use in this chapter the three categories distinguished by Van de Vijver and Leung (1997b; 2001), namely *structural equivalence, metric equivalence* and *full score equivalence*. Findings on the cross-cultural equivalence of the NEO-PI-R and, occasionally, other trait traditions are discussed in the three following sections.

2.1. Structural Equivalence

To distinguish between levels of equivalence it is convenient to think of joint scaling properties that the score variable of an instrument has in common across different cultures. When an instrument measures the same construct across cultures, the scores are said to be structurally equivalent. This is a minimum requirement for any kind of comparison. The joint properties are limited to qualitative aspects; the scale of the scores pertains cross-culturally to the same domain or construct. However, units of measurements (steps on a Likert response scale or the test score scale) may be different across cultures. In other words, if an instrument is structurally equivalent for two cultures A and B, and if it measures anxiety in culture A, then it will also measure anxiety in culture B. However, numerically equal scores may well reflect higher (or lower) anxiety in the one culture than in the other culture.

Structural equivalence is usually examined by means of correlational procedures.[1] In practice these analyses often take items as separate variables, while reducing the correlation matrix by means of exploratory factor analysis. The key question is whether factor structures derived for different groups can be considered similar. Various procedures can be followed. One can just inspect the patterns and decide ad hoc whether or not they look alike. A more formal procedure is to take the structure of one group (usually the one from where an instrument originates) or a theoretical model as a standard. This standard can serve as a target to which other structures are rotated (Procrustes rotation). Factorial agreement or congruence can be calculated by means of various statistics of which Tucker's phi (φ) is the best known. Uncertainty arises from the fact that the distribution of φ is unknown; consequently levels of confidence for values of φ cannot be determined. In the literature a minimum value of .85 or .90 is recommended for factor similarity. Especially when using empirically derived structures based on two groups, we consider the value of .90 as a minimum, because solutions may capitalize on shared error variance (Bijnen, Poortinga, & Van der Net, 1986; Van de Vijver & Poortinga, 1994; for more information see McCrae, Zonderman, Costa, Bond, & Paunonen, 1996; Van de Vijver & Leung, 1997b; Zegers & ten Berge, 1985). Recently, a bootstrap procedure has been proposed that makes it possible to examine the statistical significance of φ (Chan, Ho, Leung, Chan, & Yung, 1999).

Other multivariate techniques are available, such as multidimensional scaling and structural equation modeling (Van de Vijver & Leung, 1997b). One form of structural equation modeling is confirmatory factor analysis. This allows for a series of testable conditions that are hierarchically ordered and impose increasing constraints on joint scaling properties across cultures (e.g., Marsh & Byrne, 1993). (Such analyses pertain also to the other two levels of inequivalence that we discuss in the next two sections.) Compared to exploratory factor analysis, confirmatory factor analysis tends to result in lower estimates of cross-cultural invariance and a poorer fit of empirical data to theoretical models (e.g., Katigbak, Church, & Akamine, 1996; McCrae et al., 1996; Caprara, Barbaranelli, Bermudez, Maslach, & Ruch, 2000). This most likely has to do

---

[1]Strictly speaking this requires a linear relationship between scales (while the definition of structural equivalence does not require this). In practice this is not a serious limitation except in the case of curvilinear scales, but these hardly ever occur in the study of personality traits.

with various statistical issues. For example, compared to exploratory factor analysis, confirmatory analyses have a large power to detect small model misspecifications (e.g., deviations of multivariate normality of item score distributions). In personality research the number of indicators per factor is large, compared to what is common in the literature on structural equation modeling, which could lead to an accumulation of small errors and to a poor model fit. Confirmatory factor analysis is based on covariance matrices, while exploratory factor analysis models correlation matrices; the latter procedure is more lenient as it does not contain metric information. Finally, similarity in wording or in the life domain items pertain to, can lead to substantial and correlated residual variance components. Therefore, structural equivalence of the FFM tends to be considered mainly in the light of findings derived from exploratory factor analyses, and we shall follow this tradition.

There are two main reasons why the administration of an instrument like the NEO-PI-R in a non-Western country will not lead to a similar factor structure cross-culturally. The first reason is substantive. If what is called "personality" is imagined as a kind of pie, it is possible that the pie in Western groups differs from that of (some) non-Western, particularly preliterate, societies. One might even ask whether the notion of personality, centering on the idea of the individual as a person separate from others, makes sense everywhere (Shweder & Bourne, 1984). In an extensive discussion, Church (2000) shows why such a position is difficult to maintain. For us the relative ease of translation of most personality questionnaire items in various languages (e.g., McCrae, 2000), and the preponderance of evidence pointing to large-scale similarities (see below) is incompatible with the idea that the pie of personality would be made up of largely different ingredients cross-culturally, let alone the suggestion that in some societies there might be no pie at all.

The second reason for not finding structural equivalence has to do with various aspects of method. If indeed an identical psychological process or function can find expression in different behaviors across cultures, it is quite possible that a separate item, or even a set of items forming a scale, is unequally representative of the construct. Moreover, if cultures differ in *traitedness* (the extent to which traits play a role in self descriptions and attributions to actors; Church, 2000; Triandis, 1995), one can expect systematic differences in the ease with which these can be assessed. Continuing with our metaphor, we might say that instruments are cutting an in-itself-cross-culturally identical pie somewhat differently.

There are now numerous culture-comparative studies based on the NEO-PI-R (for references see McCrae, 2001; Rolland, 2002). In general, the five dimensions of the FFM that were identified originally in the USA are also found elsewhere, including non-Western societies. Congruence coefficients are often impressive. Like many others, we consider this to be a major finding that in all likelihood imposes important constraints on the associations between cultural contexts and the make-up of person-ality. At the same time, replication of the precise FFM structure is quite frequently less than perfect. In the present volume examples can be found, as well as reasons for inequivalence such as difficulties in translation (see, e. g., Piedmont, Bain, McCrae, & Costa, 2002). In the following paragraphs we selectively mention some related findings, going beyond the FFM.

A complementary body of evidence derives from lexical studies, mainly conducted with person-descriptive adjectives. For research in different countries adjectives are sampled from the local vocabulary; thus, the item sets are obtained independent from each other. One recent review (Saucier & Goldberg, 2001) discussed data from 13 languages. They examined models ranging from one to seven factors. Inspection of factor content showed a reasonably good replicability of all Big Five factors across Germanic languages. With other languages (e.g., Eastern European and Korean) support was less clear, or even problematic. For three of the FFM factors (Extraversion, Agreeableness, and Conscientiousness) evidence is consistent; when a larger number of factors is extracted, Agreeableness tends to split before an additional FFM factor emerges. It is regrettable that in lexical studies factors often are not rotated to each other or to a common structure. In one study in which precise congruence coefficients with English were reported for Dutch, German, Hungarian, Italian, Czech, and Polish structures based on translation equivalent terms for each of the Big Five factors, these coefficients stayed on average well below the value of .90 (De Raad, Perugini, Hřebíčková, & Szarota, 1998).

In various countries personality inventories have been constructed on the basis of locally generated item pools, without reference to existing instruments. In the non-Western world this development has been particularly pursued in the Philippines (Enriquez, 1990). Factor structures derived from local instruments do not always correspond to the Big Five; again, this is not very informative, unless it has been investigated how well a common structure will fit the data. On the basis of a number of studies in the Philippines, Guanzon-Lapeña, Church, Carlota, and Kagitbak (1998) organized constructs in accordance with the FFM. They concluded that "our allocation of dimensions to the Big Five domains suggests two things: (a) Each of the Big Five domains is represented by one or more dimensions from each of the indigenous instruments; and (b) None of the indigenous dimensions is so culturally unique that it is unrecognizable to non-Filipinos, or that it cannot be subsumed, at least conceptually, under the Big Five dimensions" (p. 265). They continued: "This is not to say, however, that there are no cultural differences reflected in the flavor or focus of the dimensions considered most salient to assess in the Philippine context."

Research on congruence of FFM factors with data from a Chinese instrument has been reported by Cheung and Leung (1998) and by Cheung et al. (2001). Data analyses mainly take the form of confirmatory factor analysis on data sets in which an indigenous Chinese instrument and the NEO-PI-R are both administered to the same respondents. In separate studies four or five of the Big Five factors were replicated, but also an additional factor was identified consistently, labeled Interpersonal Relatedness. Harmony, "face" and relationship orientation are facets of this factor. Filial piety, which is much emphasized in Chinese society, was significantly predicted by scales for harmony and social relationships even after controlling for the effects of the Big Five factors (Zhang & Bond, 1997, cited by Cheung & Leung, 1998). This indicates that a culture-specific factor beyond the Big Five can have some relevance. On the other hand, the Interpersonal Relatedness factor has also been replicated in a multiethnic sample in Hawaii, tentatively suggesting that Interpersonal Relatedness is an aspect of personality that should be added elsewhere to a comprehensive personality inventory.

In indigenous conceptualizations cultural specificity is pursued explicitly (e.g., Sinha, 1997). Interpersonal Relatedness, if ultimately not found in Western samples, is an example of a broad and rather inclusive dimension. But there are numerous person-descriptive concepts in many languages that do not translate directly into English or other West-European languages. Examples include: *anasakti* or detachment in India (Pande & Naidu, 1992); *philotimo,* or behaving towards one's group members as one should in Greece (Triandis & Vassiliou, 1972); and *machismo,* one of the Historic Sociocultural Premises distinguished by Diaz-Guerrero (1993) in Mexico. The mere fact that a notion is indicated by a local term does not say much about its status. Thus, it could be said that *machismo* is hardly an exclusively Mexican male trait, but at the same time it may be more sharply present in gender relations in Mexico than in other countries. Similarly, *anasakti* is a fairly central notion in Hindu religion, which is a strong determinant of all kinds of cultural practices in India and thus may color Indian personality. Also, Greek subjects when describing themselves as *philotimo* in question-naires may refer to a class of situations that require socially responsible behavior. These interpretations will remain unclear until there have been more studies in which such concepts are examined cross-culturally.

An attempt to identify differences in factor structures and to link these to culture characteristics can be found in the work of Konstabel, Realo, and Kallasmaa (2002). Calculating the angular degree between the Procrustes and varimax locations of the Extraversion and Agreeableness factors in 22 samples, Kallasmaa, Allik, Realo and McCrae (2000) had found a significant correlation of this angle with some ratings (though not with other ratings) of individualism-collectivism. Konstabel et al. have extended this work by examining the relationship between Impulsiveness and the two FFM dimensions of Extraversion and Conscientiousness. Again, some relationships were found. We consider the evidence too premature to draw firm conclusions. However, it should be clear that substantial and meaningful differences in the geometric configuration of factors point to structural inequivalence and to the cross-cultural non-identity of FFM dimensions.

We can throw our net a bit wider by considering other trait questionnaire traditions beyond the FFM. The most obvious choice is Eysenck's theory postulating three per-sonality dimensions (the Giant Three) that are assessed by the Eysenck Personality Questionnaire (EPQ; Eysenck & Eysenck, 1975), in which a Lie Scale has also been included. In a cross-cultural analysis with data collected in 34 countries, Barrett, Petrides, Eysenck, and Eysenck (1998) demonstrated that on average the factor similarity of the other 33 countries in their data set with the UK factors was high, at least for Extraversion (EPQ-E) and Neuroticism (EPQ-N). For Psychoticism (EPQ-P) and for the Lie Scale (EPQ-L) the average indices of factor similarity stay just below the value of .90. Thus, the analysis by Barrett et al. shows the same kind of results as found for the NEO-PI-R and other instruments of the FFM family. Moreover, various studies have shown substantial to high correlations between instruments in the two traditions, at least for Neuroticism and Extraversion, the two like-named factors (e.g., Costa & McCrae, 1995; Avia, et al., 1995; Saggino, 2000; Draycott & Kline, 1995). This is part of a general trend, noted by, among others, Paunonen and Ashton (1998), that personality inventories mostly show replicable factors across cultures.

However, when we examined relationships between the NEO-PI-R and the EPQ at country level we encountered some puzzling results. McCrae (2001, 2002) claimed structural equivalence of the Big Five at individual and country level. A meta-analysis was carried out on the four scales of the EPQ, on the basis of 153 studies with 333 samples, including 38 countries (Van Hemert, Van de Vijver, Poortinga, & Georgas, in press). We found some of the scales of the EPQ to be equivalent at both levels. The EPQ-E and the EPQ-N proved to have a similar meaning across levels. However, equivalence of the EPQ-P and the EPQ-L scales could not be demonstrated. By implication, one might expect at least the Neuroticism and Extraversion scales from both questionnaires to be correlated, as indeed was found by McCrae (2001, 2002) with EPQ data taken from Lynn and Martin (1995). We replicated that analysis using the country-level EPQ scores of the extensive meta-analysis by Van Hemert et al., while country-level Big Five scores were taken from McCrae (2002). There was overlap for 18 countries. Table 1 shows intercorrelations of the NEO-PI-R and EPQ. The correlation of the two Neuroticism scales was substantial and in the expected direction. However, for the Extraversion scales the correlation was $r = .19$ (n.s.), which casts serious doubts on the similarity of meaning of the scales at country level. The interpretation is further complicated by a closer inspection of the other correlations in the table. The EPQ-E showed a significant correlation of $r = -.62$ ($p < .05$) with the NEO-PI-R Neuroticism scale, while the EPQ-P correlated $r = -.64$ ($p < .05$) with the NEO-PI-R Extraversion scale, and the EPQ-N had a negative correlation with Agreeableness of $r = -.53$ ($p < .05$), and with Extraversion of $r = -.47$ ($p < .05$). A substantive reason for the significance of these correlations is difficult to see. It has been argued that at the individual level Eysenck's Psychoticism factor may be a combination of low Agreeableness and Conscientiousness (e.g., Barrett, 1999; Costa & McCrae, 1995; Draycott & Kline, 1995); however, the present analysis shows that at country level this reasoning does not hold. Looking at the Extraversion items in the EPQ and NEO-PI-R, we found them to be quite different. The EPQ-items relate mainly to gregariousness. The NEO-PI-R Extraversion facets also include assertiveness, activity and excitement-seeking, which seem more reminiscent of a somewhat dominant manager than of a person who enjoys the presence of others.

Finally, there was a substantial correlation between EPQ-L and NEO-PI-R Conscientiousness ($r = .54, p < .05$). This finding is relevant to a long-standing debate about the meaning of social desirability (Lie scale) at the individual level. McCrae and Costa (1983, 1985) have interpreted Lie Scale scores in terms of substantive personality

Table 1. Correlations between Eysenck Personality Questionnaire Scales And NEO-PI-R Factors.

	Factor				
	N	E	O	A	C
EPQ–P	.36	−.64**	.09	−.08	.26
EPQ–E	−.62**	.19	.00	.34	.19
EPQ–N	.63**	−.47*	.12	−.53*	.16
EPQ–L	.20	−.40	−.23	−.07	.54*

Note. $N = 18$; for the EPQ-L $N = 17$; *$p < .05$. **$p < .01$.

dimensions. In Eysenck's theory, social desirability is mainly taken as a tendency to provide a distorted picture of reality by respondents so as to protect or enhance a public image (hence the term Lie Scale). If the same reasoning can be applied at country level, the significant correlation of the EPQ-L with Conscientiousness seems to be more in line with Eysenck's interpretation.

Corollaries derived from the claimed cross-level equivalence of the Big Five and at least two of the Eysenck factors are poorly supported. Why do the country-level scales correlate in such an unexpected way? First, the bias techniques used by McCrae and Van Hemert et al. have a low power and may have left sources of inequivalence undetected. It is widely documented that item bias tests used in education and mental testing (e.g., Holland & Wainer, 1993) are more powerful than the factor-analytic procedures used in cross-cultural personality research. Second, the strong and unexpected correlations of Table 1 suggest that aggregation alters the meaning of at least some scales.

To summarize, the overall picture emerging from this brief review of evidence on structural equivalence is that dimensional structures show unmistakable evidence of similarity cross-culturally over a wide range of literate countries. However, it seems premature to consider any configuration of dimensions as definite. Across levels of aggregation and across traditions of research, labels for facets and dimensions do not carry precise meanings. Moreover, new measurements with sets of items from other cultures may lead to (perhaps minor) domains of personality that are not adequately covered by the NEO-PI-R or related instruments. This becomes a distinct possibility in non-Western samples. On the other hand, the results would probably have been more consistent if in all studies exploratory factor analyses had been carried out, followed by Procrustes rotation to a common target. All in all, the evidence of structural equivalence of personality traits at individual level appears to be sufficient not to preclude a meaningful examination of other levels of equivalence. The structural equivalence of country-level personality differences is more questionable.

2.2. Metric Equivalence

The second level distinguished by Van de Vijver and Leung (1997a, b) is metric equivalence. When this level is satisfied a measurement scale not only reflects the same dimension across cultures, but the metric of the scale (i.e., the distance between scale points) is also the same. An analog is provided by the temperature scales of Celsius and Kelvin; an increase or decrease in temperature leads to the same change in values on both scales. (Please note that by the same reasoning, the Celsius and Fahrenheit scales are not metrically equivalent.) Metric equivalence is relevant in studies where one is interested in the interpretation of patterns of differences between variables, or in patterns of change between measurement occasions. The factor analytic procedures used in the study of the Big Five and Giant Three are based on cross-cultural comparisons of correlations. These procedures do not employ information about the measurement unit. Therefore, exploratory factor analysis, followed by target rotation, cannot provide a test of metric equivalence.

We can clarify the relevance of metric equivalence by mentioning non-trait related sources of variance that are likely to affect test score levels but not necessarily factor structures. Three clusters of such sources have been distinguished: sample bias, instrument bias, and administration bias (Van de Vijver & Tanzer, 1997). The first refers to unrepresentativeness of samples, often consisting of students who vary across populations in representativeness for socioeconomic status, education, gender composition, etc. Instrument bias has to do with characteristics that are shared by the items, such as response styles. Finally, administration bias can result from differences in instructions (e.g., emphasis on carefulness) and testing conditions, differences in scrupulousness between groups of respondents, etc. The most obvious threat to metric equivalence in personality inventories probably results from response styles such as social desirability, acquiescence, and extremity set.

Effects of response styles, like extremity set and acquiescence, may well be more or less the same for most or even all dimensions and facets of a multiscale questionnaire like the NEO-PI-R, since the same response scale is used for all items. Thus, a probable explanation for the differences between countries in standard deviations reported by McCrae (2002) is some form of response set. This also is the case for differences in the average score over all five FFM dimensions that was found to be lower in Czech, Slovak, and Polish samples than in the normative data in the USA (Hřebíčková et al., 2002; see also McCrae, 2002). However, the social desirability of various facets and dimensions may differ and this could lead to a pattern of differences in mean scores across facets or dimensions. There are quite a few studies suggesting that in countries with high GNP (and thus high levels of education) social desirability plays a lesser role than in low-income countries (Van Hemert et al., in press). For country-level data this is suggested by the substantial correlation ($r = .54$, $p < .05$) between NEO-PI-R Conscientiousness and the EPQ Lie-scale reported in the previous section.

Further evidence about generalized response tendencies arises from a series of studies reported by Williams, Satterwhite, and Saiz (1998). They found a difference between two sets of countries labeled as individualist and collectivist, in the relationship between favorability ratings (akin to Osgood's evaluation dimension) of the items of the Adjective Check List (ACL; Gough & Heilbrun, 1983) and ratings of psychological importance for these items. In the collectivist countries only adjectives with high favorability ratings (*kind, sincere, sociable*) received high ratings of psychological importance, while items with low favorability (*deceitful, irresponsible, selfish*) were considered of low importance. In individualist countries items with low favorability ratings had substantial importance ratings. So, in the former countries the relationship between the psychological importance of trait descriptive adjectives and their favorability was more or less linear, while in the latter countries a U-curve was found. It might be argued that the ACL is not the same instrument as the NEO-PI-R. However, Goodman and Williams (1996, cited in Williams et al., 1998) found that the items of the NEO-FFI which are indicative of each FFM dimension received higher favorability ratings (in the U.S.) than items that are counterindicative of each dimension (with the Neuroticism scale reversed and labeled as Emotional Stability). Moreover, under "faking good" instructions substantially higher scores were obtained than under "faking bad" instructions on all five FFM dimensions, again with the Neuroticism scale reversed.

292   POORTINGA, VAN DE VIJVER & VAN HEMERT

In summary, evidence on metric equivalence of personality questionnaires is scarce. Effects of response tendencies have been established; consequently, profiles of scores may not merely reflect patterns of higher and lower standing on various trait dimensions. Of course, response tendencies themselves may have psychological significance, but they can hardly be identified with the trait(s) targeted by a dimension or facet.

2.3. Full Score Equivalence

This level of equivalence implies that a score has precisely the same meaning, even quantitatively, in terms of an interpretation, independent of the cultural background of the respondent from whom that score was obtained (Van de Vijver & Leung, 1997a,b). Full score equivalence (or comparability) implies that a joint scale exists for which all scaling properties are the same in the cultural populations to be compared. The difference from metric equivalence is that in case of full score equivalence there is also a joint zero point.

In the absence of common external standards for different cultural groups it is difficult to establish whether or not a difference in score distributions is valid (and shows full score equivalence), or is due to some biasing factor. One might reverse this point and argue that if equivalence cannot be established, it is equally impossible to establish inequivalence. It can be seen as a pragmatic strategy of interpreting score differences at face value, especially if they are in agreement with other information about how cultures differ. We mention three reasons to question this strategy: (a) the presence of item bias, (b) the inability of experts to provide valid estimates of country differences in questionnaire score levels of facets or dimensions, and (c) the post hoc character of supporting evidence in explanations of cross-cultural differences in scores.

Most analyses are at the level of dimensions or sometimes facets. It is not surprising to find evidence of item bias, or differential item functioning (DIF), for separate items; after all, cross-cultural differences are most evident at the level of specific cultural rules and practices. An extensive analysis of item bias has been provided by Huang, Church, and Katigbak (1997). In a comparison of Filipino and American college students they found with different statistical procedures that approximately 40% of NEO-PI items were biased. However, when biased items were removed there was a substantial reduction in the number of facets showing a significant cross-cultural difference as well as in the size (η^2) of most of these differences. Effects of item bias may average out, but the findings by Huang et al. suggest that the scales in the NEO-PI are probably too short to make such averaging effective. In any case, the results show that it is less than prudent to interpret cross-cultural differences at face value.

The second reason for hesitation follows from findings reported by McCrae (2001). He made an attempt to validate country score levels in terms of judgments of experienced researchers in cross-cultural psychology and cultural anthropology. From a 26-culture data set, he derived five lists, each mentioning the countries with the seven highest and the seven lowest scores on one of the Big Five dimension. The judges had to indicate for each of the five lists which Big Five dimension was represented. They found the task exceedingly difficult and some declined to answer. Those who answered did not do clearly better than chance. Hřebíčková et al. (2002) derived hypotheses about expected levels in NEO-PI-R scores from various written sources for their Czech, Polish, and Slovak samples, but found very limited support in the actual score profiles. Church and Katigbak (2002) report a study in which judges with first-hand experience of the U.S. and the Philippines were asked to rate whether Americans or Filipinos would exhibit more of each of the facets of the NEO-PI-R. In a number of instances high agreement between judges was found, and these differences also tended to be in agreement with differences between the two countries found in the literature. However, correlations between judges' estimates and actual questionnaire score levels were virtually negligible. These findings concur with the idea that perceived national characteristics of personality reside, at least to an important extent, in the eye of the beholders (Poortinga & Girndt, 1997). They also replicate findings of studies of item bias in mental tests, in which experts and statistical procedures only agree on the presence of bias if its effect is substantial. For items with small bias effects the two sources tend not to agree (Van de Vijver & Leung, 1997b).

This brings us to the third point, i.e., the tendency in the literature to make sense out of observed differences. Typically such differences are not predicted but first observed and then interpreted post hoc. The chapters of this book contain several examples of how researchers attempt to grasp the meaning of culture-specific findings. For example, Leininger (2002) confronts findings with the narrative of an informant. In other chapters supportive evidence from various sources is mentioned to explain why scores on dimensions and facets happen to deviate from the results obtained in the U.S. (e.g., Gülgöz, 2002; Lima, 2002; Martin, Costa, Oryol, Rukavishnikov, & Senin, 2002). Apart from the fact that such comparisons may reflect cultural specificities of the U.S., one should keep in mind Donald Campbell's warning that for ad hoc findings there can be a variety of cultural antecedents (cf. Segall, Dasen, Berry, & Poortinga, 1999).

One way to acquire a more solid database is to enlarge the number of countries. The correlations in Table 2 are based on the same data set as those reported in Table 1, supplemented with country-level indicators of economic and ecological context from a data set analyzed by Georgas, Van de Vijver, and Berry (2002). The Economy factor is a composite of indicators like GNP, energy consumption, and calorie intake. The Ecology factor encompasses highest and lowest average temperature and precipitation. Also included in Table 2 are a score for subjective well-being (Diener, Diener & Diener, 1995) and the Hofstede (1980, 2001) dimensions (Power Distance, Individualism, Masculinity, Uncertainty Avoidance and Long-Term Orientation). Except for the last three rows, all the variables have to do with a cluster of industrialization, income, and education (also called modernization) that distinguishes the Western world from the Majority world. This is immediately clear for the first two rows of the table, and for the ecology index. The relationship of Well-Being, based on Diener et al. (1995), also seems plausible. As far as the Hofstede dimensions are concerned, it should be noted that Power Distance and Individualism in the original analysis came out as a single bipolar factor that was highly correlated with GNP. It should be noted that part of Table 2 has been copied from McCrae (2002).

The clearest pattern of correlations in Table 2 is between the EPQ-Lie scale and the

Table 2. Correlations between NEO-PI-R and EPQ Scales and Context Variables.

Context Variable	NEO-PI-R						EPQ				
	N_c	N	E	O	A	C	N_c	P	E	N	L
GNP	24	-.15	.54**	.24	-.04	-.66**	38	-.19	.11	-.06	-.67**
Economy Factor	24	-.21	.65**	.21	-.02	-.62**	38	-.23	.10	-.04	-.64**
Ecology Factor	24	.05	-.69**	-.25	.46*	.61**	38	.07	.05	-.11	.69**
Subjective Well-Being	19	-.43	.59**	.23	.28	-.10	30	-.41*	.29	-.23	-.57**
Power Distance	35[a]	.28	-.58***	-.40*	.19	.52**	23	.26	-.39	.25	.58**
Individualism	35[a]	-.12	.64***	.34*	-.07	-.30	23	-.11	.18	.05	-.68**
Long-Term Orientation	25[a]	.08	-.51**	-.16	.11	-.04	12	.49	-.70*	.25	.54
Masculinity	35[a]	.55*	-.27	.37*	-.32	.06	23	.47*	-.04	.63**	-.17
Uncertainty Avoidance	35[a]	.58**	.03	.31	-.56**	-.25	23	.14	-.05	.23	.30

Note. N_c = Number of countries. N = Neuroticism. E = Extraversion. O = Openness. A = Agreeableness. C = Conscientiousness. P = Psychoticism. L = Lie Scale. *p < .05. **p < .01.
[a]Cell entries for the NEO-PI-R were obtained from McCrae (2002).

affluence-related variables. The pattern of positive and negative correlations is the same for Conscientiousness, and, with lower values, for Agreeableness and Neuroticism Moreover, with reversed sign we find a corresponding pattern also for FFM Extraversion (including a substantial correlation with GNP) and for Openness to Experience. For the three factors in the Eysenck tradition only one significant correlation (between Well-Being and Psychoticism) with an economy-related variable is observed. This confirms that the EPQ and the NEO-PI-R may not be equivalent when scores are aggregated at the country level. Although the correlations of the economic variables with the EPQ scales are lower than with some of the Big Five dimensions, the patterns of positive and negative entries show some similarity (with three exceptions, one for EPQ-E and two for EPQ-N). However, we find these post hoc results for the EPQ too weak to warrant further interpretation.

In the three bottom rows of Table 2 where a link with economic indicators is less plausible, the same pattern of positive and negative signs of the earlier rows can be observed for Long-Term Orientation. For Masculinity and Uncertainty Avoidance the pattern is not interpretable in terms of the economic indicators.[2] The significant correlations between Masculinity and both Neuroticism scales, combined with the low correlations of GNP-related variables, point to the possibility that there are context variables that are not even weakly linked to this cluster. Of course, even for the FFM dimensions where the pattern is clearest, not all variance can be attributed to aspects of affluence.

There are various kinds of explanations to deal with the patterns of correlations in Table 2. The first is that the correlations reflect a pervasive ecocultural dimension (Berry, 1976; Berry et al., in press), either of a substantive or a method-related nature (or perhaps both). A clear example of the former kind of interpretation is in terms of cultural syndromes (Triandis, 1996), such as individualism-collectivism. This single distinction has been used to explain a host of cross-cultural differences, including differences on FFM dimensions.

Another possibility is that the observed parallels in patterning of the various Big Five dimensions are coincidental and that each of them has to be explained in terms of quite different psychological functions or mechanisms. Thus, the differences in level of Agreeableness may have to do with a lower conformity in more wealthy societies that can better afford the risks of individuals making costly mistakes (cf. Bond & Smith, 1996). Differences in Extraversion, as operationalized in the NEO-PI-R, could possibly reflect a growing emphasis on self-expression in post-industrialized societies, as suggested by Bell (1976; cf. Inglehart & Baker, 2000). A still broader scope for interpretation arises if constituents like religion are peeled off from the highly confounded variable of national wealth. For example, Georgas et al. (2002) found that power and hierarchy tend to be positively associated with self-declared religious denomination. Combined with the present findings this could be interpreted as implying

---

[2]Absence of a consistent pattern of correlations for Masculinity and Uncertainty Avoidance may also have to do with the stability of these dimensions. In an extensive replication Merritt (2000) found in a 19-country study a correlation of $r = .25$ with the original values for Masculinity and $r = .16$ for Uncertainty Avoidance.

that Agreeableness and Conscientiousness are personality characteristics that are part of these power-regulating mechanisms in society.

A quite different interpretation is in terms of method-related factors. Such an interpretation might point out that the answers of well-educated respondents in affluent societies are perhaps less influenced by normative concerns and/or social desirability. A tendency such as that found by Williams et al. (1998) that in less industrialized societies negative trait adjectives (and inventory items?) are seen as less important, would also fit a general pattern of differences. Perhaps the clear correlations with the EPQ-L (social desirability) make this latter interpretation the more prudent one, at least as long as metric and full score equivalence of the NEO-PI-R have not been more extensively investigated.

In summary, there is a persistent tendency among authors to make sense of cross-cultural differences. We are not the first to question full score equivalence of NEO-PI-R scores. Among others, McCrae, Yik, Trapnell, Bond, and Paulhus (1998) have warned that observed quantitative differences in single trait score variables are not really interpretable even when conditions for structural equivalence are reasonably met. We would argue that this is not just a conservative position, but the only tenable one, given what we currently know about cross-cultural equivalence of questionnaires like the NEO-PI-R.

3. IMPLICATIONS FOR TRAIT THEORY

The evidence on structural equivalence of the NEO-PI-R is strong enough to conclude that the search for universal dimensions of personality is a meaningful pursuit. At the same time it seems premature to claim for any constellation of trait dimensions that it forms an optimal and exhaustive representation of personality. The congruence of dimensions across cultures is too far from perfect and the shifts in meaning across aggregation levels shown in Table 1 are too poorly understood to substantiate such claims. Nevertheless, for further cross-cultural research on personality traits, dimensional identity is not merely a working assumption anymore, but a sound starting point. We see as the most important next step an extension of the range to include societies that are preliterate or where the level of school education is low. Most likely this will imply that new items will have to be written, and perhaps that other methods of data collection have to be employed beyond self-report questionnaires. A broad database is needed to further substantiate the claims of universality that are part of personality theories like Five-Factor Theory (McCrae & Costa, 1996).

In a longer time perspective cross-culturally invariant dimensions are perhaps also needed to examine possible biological factors underlying person-typical behavior. Research on quantitative trait loci theoretically holds promise (Plomin & Caspi, 1998; Plomin, DeFries, & McClearn, 1997), but there seems to be a long way to go before personality dimensions can be validated against biological data. Even then a psychological database is needed and culture-comparative studies appear to be an important way of validating our knowledge on individual biosocial functioning.

We have argued quite extensively that the metric of the response scales as employed by different cultural samples may not be the same. Systematic differences in standard deviations reported by McCrae (2002) also point in this direction. More generally, the likelihood of differences in response styles makes a simple interpretation of score patterns doubtful. This holds even more strongly for any interpretation that presumes full score equivalence. The consistent patterns of correlations in Table 2 for the EPQ-L suggest that score levels across countries are influenced by affluence. It may not be superfluous to add that affluence could have an impact on both substance and style in responses to personality questionnaires. The data of Table 2 suggests that an increase in affluence may lead to higher scores in Extraversion; individuals in more affluent countries may feel less restraint to express their opinions. In addition, affluence may well influence response styles. The consistent relationships we found between the Lie Scale and indicators of affluence are in line with this interpretation. There is a clear need to further validate observed country score differences.

Although issues of equivalence are an important impediment for the interpretation of observed differences in score levels, they often can be avoided or transcended. We have argued for a long time that lack of equivalence in its own right is a source of information about cross-cultural differences (e.g., Poortinga & Van de Vijver, 1987; Poortinga, Van de Vijver, Van de Koppel & Joe, 1987). By extending one's research design with variables that potentially can explain cross-cultural variance (related to more substantial interpretations of cross-cultural differences and/or to response styles), alternative hypotheses about the meaning of differences can be tested.

Maybe the time has come to extend the notion of cross-cultural invariance from structural relationships to patterns and levels of scores. This would involve a working hypothesis to the effect that the distribution of scores on basis personality dimensions is the same in each culture, until there is sufficient evidence to the contrary. Thus, the notion of universalism would include quantitative aspects of basic personality dimensions. This may not be as far-fetched as it seems. In cross-cultural research on perception and cognition earlier theories on cross-cultural differences in major functions have long been abandoned. For example, the suggestion that there could be population differences in general intelligence (often represented by the notion of g) is summarily rejected by many cross-cultural researchers (cf. Berry et al., in press). In any case, an explicit strategy of looking for similarities could be a good antidote against the common belief that people in different cultures are psychologically different because they do different things (Poortinga, 2001).

Moreover, it is theoretically not clear why basic personality differences should be anticipated. If personality dimensions such as the Big Five indeed are universal and even may have a biological basis, as is sometimes suggested (e.g., McCrae & Costa, 1996), it is questionable whether anything more than minor differences in score distributions can be expected across cultures, even at a global level. Perhaps the most likely state of affairs is that there are only small (quantitative) differences in major trait dimensions between global regions of the world and virtually none at any smaller geographical and cultural scale. This is not to say that personality traits are immune to genetic selection. However, to the best of our insight not a single ecological or sociocultural factor has been identified that can be said to push genetic selection on any of the Big Five dimensions and that might have done so consistently for numerous generations.

4. CONCLUSION

If one looks at the history of cross-cultural research in different areas of psychology there emerges a fairly common pattern. Initially large differences in psychological functioning are postulated and observed. When more sophisticated research methods are applied, culture loses its status as a mega-variable and more precise and less general factors are identified. Cross-cultural research on personality is no exception (Poortinga & Van Hemert, 2001). Early students of culture-and-personality like Benedict tended to characterize an entire cultural group in terms of a single aspect of personality. As far as trait traditions are concerned cross-cultural differences are now mainly studied in terms of dimensions like the Big Five or the Giant Three. Such dimensions replicate at least moderately well across cultures, even though the optimal dimensional representation may yet have to be established. When it comes to quantitative differences we are more pessimistic about the validity of most findings. There is reason to doubt the metric and full score equivalence of personality questionnaires like the NEO-PI-R.

In a sense we have taken the position of devil's advocate in this chapter. As cross-cultural psychologists we do not doubt the importance of cultural context for behavior. But the questions of how culture is important and at what level of inclusiveness can so far only be answered very tentatively. The structural similarities resulting from research with the NEO-PI-R and other questionnaires already have imposed constraints on how we should look at the nature and extent of cross-cultural differences in personality. We expect that a sharper picture will gradually emerge from further culture-comparative research, especially if preliterate societies are included on a much larger scale than has so far been the case.

Two hesitant conclusions may serve as a slightly provocative summary of this chapter. First, substantial evidence of cross-cultural invariance of structural relationships has been found. This evidence indicates that at least the personality dimensions examined tend to be universal and this justifies the further search for additional universal dimensions. Second, frequent differences in score levels have been reported, but the validity of such claims has to remain tentative as long as metric equivalence and full score equivalence remain questionable.

REFERENCES

Avia, M. D., Sanz, J., Sánchez-Bernardos, M. L., Martínez-Arias, M. R., Silva, F., & Graña, J. L. (1995). The Five-Factor Model – II. Relations of the NEO-PI with other personality variables. *Personality and Individual Differences, 19,* 81-97.

Barrett, P. T. (1999). Rejoinder to: The Eysenckian personality structure: A 'Giant Three' or 'Big Five' model in Hong Kong? *Personality and Individual Differences, 26,* 175-186.

Barrett, P. T., Petrides, K. V., Eysenck, S. B. G., & Eysenck, H. J. (1998). The Eysenck Personality Questionnaire: An examination of the factorial similarity of P, E, N, and L across 34 countries. *Personality and Individual Differences, 25,* 805-819.

Bell, D. (1976). *The cultural contradictions of capitalism.* New York: Basic Books.

Berry, J. W. (1976). *Human ecology and cognitive style: Comparative studies in cultural and psychological adaptation.* New York: Sage/Halsted.

Berry, J. W., Poortinga, Y. H., Segall, M. H., & Dasen, P. R. (in press). *Cross-cultural psychology: Research and applications.* Cambridge: Cambridge University Press.

Bijnen, E. J., Poortinga, Y. H., & Van der Net, T. Z. J. (1986). On cross-cultural comparative studies with the

Eysenck Personality Questionnaire. *Journal of Cross-Cultural Psychology, 17,* 3-16.

Bond, R., & Smith, P. B. (1996). Culture and conformity: A meta-analysis of studies using Asch's line judgment task. *Psychological Bulletin, 119,* 111-137.

Caprara, G. V., Barbaranelli, C., Bermudez, J., Maslach, C., & Ruch, W. (2000). Multivariate methods for the comparison of factor structures. *Journal of Cross-Cultural Psychology, 31,* 437-464.

Chan W., Ho, R. M., Leung, K., Chan, D. K.-S., & Yung, Y.-F. (1999). An alternative method for evaluating congruence coefficients with Procrustes rotation: A bootstrap procedure. *Psychological Methods, 4,* 378-402.

Cheung, F. M., & Leung, K. (1998). Indigenous personality measures: Chinese examples. *Journal of Cross-Cultural Psychology, 29,* 233-248.

Cheung, F. M., Leung, K., Zang, J. X., Sun, H. F., Gan, Y. Q., Song, W. Z., & Xie D. (2001). Indigenous Chinese personality constructs: Is the Five-Factor Model complete? *Journal of Cross-Cultural Psychology, 32,* 407-433.

Church, A. T. (2000). Culture and personality: Toward an integrated cultural trait psychology. *Journal of Personality, 68,* 651-703.

Church, A. T., & Katigbak, M. S. (2002). The Five-Factor Model in the Philippines: Investigating trait structure and levels across cultures. In R. R. McCrae & J. Allik (Eds.), *The Five-Factor Model of personality across cultures* (pp. 129-154). New York: Kluwer Academic/Plenum Publishers.

Costa, P. T., Jr., & McCrae, R. R. (1995). Primary traits of Eysenck's P-E-N system: Three and five-factor solutions. *Journal of Personality and Social Psychology, 69,* 308-317.

Cronbach, L. J., Gleser, G. C., Nanda, H., & Rajaratnam, N. (1972). *The dependability of behavioral measurements.* New York: Wiley.

De Raad, B., Perugini, M., Hřebíčková, M., & Szarota, P. (1998). Lingua Franca of personality: Taxonomies and structures based on the psycholexical approach. *Journal of Cross-Cultural Psychology, 29,* 212-232.

Denzin, N. K., & Lincoln, Y S. (Eds.). (2000). *Handbook of qualitative research* (2nd ed.). Thousand Oaks, CA: Sage.

Diaz-Guerrero, R. (1993). Mexican ethnopsychology. In U. Kim & J. W. Berry (Eds.), *Indigenous psychologies: Research and experience in cultural context* (pp. 44-55). Newbury Park, CA: Sage.

Diener, E., Diener, M., & Diener, C. (1995). Factors predicting the subjective well-being of nations. *Journal of Personality and Social Psychology, 69,* 851-864.

Draycott, S. G., & Kline, P. (1995). The Big Three and the Big Five—the EPQ-R vs. the NEO-PI: A research note, replication and elaboration. *Personality and Individual Differences, 18,* 801-804.

Eibl-Eibesfeldt, I. (1989). *Human ethology.* New York: Aldine de Gruyter.

Enriquez, V. G. (Ed.). (1990). *Indigenous psychologies.* Quezon City, The Philippines: Psychology Research and Training House.

Eysenck, H. J., & Eysenck, S. B. G. (1975). *Manual of the Eysenck Personality Questionnaire.* London: Hodder and Stoughton.

Furby, L. (1973). Implications of within-group heritabilities for sources of between-group differences: IQ and racial differences. *Developmental Psychology, 9,* 28-37.

Georgas, J., Van de Vijver, F. J. R., & Berry, J. W. (2002). *Ecosocial indicators and psychological variables in cross-cultural research.* Unpublished manuscript, University of Athens, Greece.

Goldstein, H. (1987). *Multilevel models in educational and social research.* London: Griffin.

Gough, H. G., & Heilbrun, A. B. (1983). *The Adjective Check List* (1983 ed.). Palo Alto, CA: Consulting Psychologists Press.

Guanzon-Lapeña, M. A., Church, A. T., Carlota, A. J., & Katigbak, M. S. (1998). Indigenous personality measures: Philippine examples. *Journal of Cross-Cultural Psychology, 29,* 249-270.

Gülgöz, S. (2002). Five-Factor Theory and the NEO-PI-R in Turkey. In R. R. McCrae & J. Allik (Eds.), *The Five-Factor Model of personality across cultures* (pp. 175-196). New York: Kluwer Academic/Plenum Publishers.

Hofstede, G. (1980). *Culture's consequences.* Beverly Hills, CA: Sage.

Hofstede, G. (2001). *Culture's consequences* (2nd ed.). Beverly Hills, CA: Sage.

Holland, P. W., & Wainer, H. (Eds.). (1993). *Differential item functioning.* Hillsdale, NJ: Erlbaum.

Hřebíčková, M., Urbánek, T., Čermák, I., Szarota, P., Ficková, E., & Orlická, L. (2002). The NEO Five-Factor Inventory in Czech, Polish, and Slovak contexts. In R. R. McCrae & J. Allik (Eds.), *The Five-Factor Model of personality across cultures* (pp. 53-78). New York: Kluwer Academic/Plenum Publishers

Huang, C. D., Church, A. T., Katigbak, M. S. (1997). Identifying cultural differences in items and traits:

Differential item functioning in the NEO Personality Inventory. *Journal of Cross-Cultural Psychology, 28*, 192-218.

Inglehart, R., & Baker, W. E. (2000). Modernization, cultural change, and the persistence of traditional values. *American Sociological Review, 65,* 19-51.

Kallasmaa, T., Allik, J., Realo, A., & McCrae, R. R. (2000). The Estonian version of the NEO-PI-R: An examination of universal and culture-specific aspects of the Five-Factor Model. *European Journal of Personality, 14*, 265-278.

Katigbak, M. S., Church, A. T., & Akamine, T. X. (1996). Cross-cultural generalizability of personality dimensions: Relating indigenous and imported dimensions in two cultures. *Journal of Personality and Social Psychology, 70*, 99-114.

Konstabel, K., Realo, A., & Kallasmaa, T. (2002). Exploring the sources of variations in the structure of personality traits across cultures. In R. R. McCrae & J. Allik (Eds.), *The Five-Factor Model of personality across cultures* (pp. 29-52). New York: Kluwer Academic/Plenum Publishers.

Leininger, A. (2002). Vietnamese-American personality and acculturation: An exploration of relationships between personality traits and cultural goals. In R. R. McCrae & J. Allik (Eds.), *The Five-Factor Model of personality across cultures* (pp. 197-225). New York: Kluwer Academic/Plenum Publishers.

Leung, K., & Bond, M. H. (1989). On the empirical identification of dimensions for cross-cultural comparison. *Journal of Cross-Cultural Psychology, 20,* 133-151.

Lima, M. P. (2002). Personality and culture: The Portuguese case. In R. R. McCrae & J. Allik (Eds.), *The Five-Factor Model of personality across cultures* (pp. 249-260). New York: Kluwer Academic/Plenum Publishing.

Lynn, R., & Martin, T. (1995). National differences for thirty-seven nations in extraversion, neuroticism, psychoticism and economic, demographic and other correlates. *Personality and Individual Differences, 19,* 403-406.

Martin, T. À., Costa, P. T., Jr., Oryol, V. E., Rukavishnikov, A. A., & Senin, I. G. (2002). Applications of the Russian NEO-PI-R. In R. R. McCrae & J. Allik (Eds.), *The Five-Factor Model of personality across cultures* (pp. 261-277). New York: Kluwer Academic/Plenum Publishers.

Marsh, H. W., & Byrne, B. M. (1993). Confirmatory factor analysis of multigroup-multimethod self-concept data: Between-group and within-group invariance constraints. *Multivariate Behavioral Research, 28,* 313-349.

McCrae, R. R. (2000). Trait psychology and the revival of personality and culture studies. *American Behavioral Scientist, 44,* 10-31.

McCrae, R. R. (2001). Trait psychology and culture: Exploring intercultural comparisons. *Journal of Personality, 69,* 819-846.

McCrae, R. R. (2002). NEO-PI-R data from 36 cultures: Further intercultural comparisons. In R. R. McCrae & J. Allik (Eds.), *The Five-Factor Model of personality across cultures* (pp. 105-126). New York: Kluwer Academic/ Plenum Publishers.

McCrae, R. R., & Costa, P. T., Jr. (1983). Social desirability scales: More substance than style. *Journal of Consulting and Clinical Psychology, 51,* 882-888.

McCrae, R. R., & Costa, P. T., Jr. (1985). Comparison of EPI and Psychoticism scales with measures of the Five-Factor Model of personality. *Personality and Individual Differences, 6,* 587-597.

McCrae, R. R., & Costa, P. T., Jr. (1996). Toward a new generation of personality theories: Theoretical contexts for the Five-Factor Model. In J. S. Wiggins (Ed.), *The Five-Factor Model of Personality: Theoretical perspectives* (pp. 51-87). New York: Guilford Press.

McCrae, R. R., Yik, M. S. M., Trapnell, P. D., Bond, M. H., & Paulhus, D. L. (1998). Interpreting personality profiles across cultures: Bilingual, acculturation, and peer rating studies of Chinese undergraduates. *Journal of Personality and Social Psychology, 74,* 1041-1055.

McCrae, R. R., Zonderman, A. B., Costa, P. T., Jr., Bond, M. H., & Paunonen, S. V. (1996). Evaluating replicability of factors in the Revised NEO Personality Inventory: Confirmatory factor analysis versus Procrustes rotation. *Journal of Personality and Social Psychology, 70,* 522-566.

Merritt, A. (2000). Culture in the cockpit: Do Hofstede's dimensions replicate? *Journal of Cross-Cultural Psychology, 31,* 283-301.

Miller, J. G. (1997). Theoretical issues in cultural psychology. In J. W. Berry, Y. H. Poortinga, & J. Pandey (Eds.), *Handbook of cross-cultural psychology* (2nd ed., Vol. 1, pp. 85-128). Boston: Allyn and Bacon.

Muthén, B. O. (1991). Multilevel factor analysis of class and student achievement components. *Journal of Educational Measurement, 28,* 338-354.

Pande, N., & Naidu, R. K. (1992). Anasakti and health: A study of non-attachment. *Psychology and Develop-*

ing Societies, 4, 91-104.

Paunonen, S. V., & Ashton, M. C. (1998). The structured assessment of personality across cultures. *Journal of Cross-Cultural Psychology, 29,* 150-170.

Piedmont, R. L., Bain, E., McCrae, R. R., & Costa, P. T., Jr. (2002). The applicability of the Five-Factor Model in a Sub-Saharan culture: The NEO-PI-R in Shona. In R. R. McCrae & J. Allik (Eds.), *The Five-Factor Model of personality across cultures* (pp. 155-174). New York: Kluwer Academic/Plenum Publishers.

Plomin, R., & Caspi, A. (1998). DNA and personality. *European Journal of Personality, 12,* 387-407.

Plomin, R., DeFries, J. C., & McClearn, G. E. (1997). *Behavioral genetics: A primer* (3rd. ed.). New York: Freeman.

Poortinga, Y. H. (1971). Cross-cultural comparison of maximum performance tests: Some methodological aspects and some experiments. *Psychologia Africana,* Monograph Supplement, No. 6.

Poortinga, Y. H. (1989). Equivalence of cross-cultural data: An overview of basic issues. *International Journal of Psychology, 24,* 737-756.

Poortinga, Y. H. (2001, April). *Coherence of culture and generalizability of data: Two questionable assumptions in cross-cultural psychology.* Invited address, Nebraska Symposium on Motivation, Lincoln, Nebraska.

Poortinga, Y. H., & Girndt, T. (1996). Gibt es einen Nationalcharakter? [Does national character exist?] In H. Süssmuth (Ed.), *Deutschlandbilder in Dänemark und England, in Frankreich und den Niederlanden* (pp. 124-139). Baden-Baden: Nomos.

Poortinga, Y. H., & Malpass, R. S. (1986). Making inferences from cross-cultural data. In W. J. Lonner & J. W. Berry (Eds.), *Field methods in cross-cultural research* (pp. 17-46). Beverly Hills, CA: Sage.

Poortinga, Y. H., & Van de Vijver, F. J. R. (1987). Explaining cross-cultural differences: Bias analysis and beyond. *Journal of Cross-Cultural Psychology, 18,* 259-282.

Poortinga Y. H., & Van Hemert, D. A. (2001). Personality and culture: Demarcating between the common and the unique. *Journal of Personality, 69,* 1033-1060.

Poortinga, Y. H., Van de Vijver, F. J. R., Joe, R. C., & Van de Koppel, J. M. H. (1987). Peeling the onion called culture. In Ç. Kagitçibaşi (Ed.), *Growth and progress in cross-cultural psychology* (pp. 22-34). Lisse: Swets & Zeitlinger.

Przeworski, A., & Teune, H. (1970). *The logic of comparative social inquiry.* New York: Wiley.

Rolland, J.-P. (2002). Cross-cultural generalizability of the Five-Factor Model of personality. In R. R. McCrae & J. Allik (Eds.), *The Five-Factor Model of personality across cultures* (pp. 7-28). New York: Kluwer Academic/Plenum Publishers.

Saggino, A. (2000). The Big Three or the Big Five? A replication study. *Personality and Individual Differences, 28,* 879-886.

Saucier, G. & Goldberg, L. R. (2001). Lexical studies of indigenous personality factors: Premises, products, and prospects. *Journal of Personality, 69,* 847-880.

Segall, M. H., Dasen, P. R., Berry, J. W., & Poortinga, Y. H. (1999). *Human behavior in global perspective: An introduction to cross-cultural psychology* (2nd ed.). Boston: Allyn and Bacon.

Shweder, R. A., & Bourne, E. J. (1984). Does the concept of the person vary cross-culturally? In R. A. Shweder & R. LeVine (Eds.) *Culture theory* (pp. 158-199). New York: Cambridge University Press.

Sinha, D. (1997). Indigenizing psychology. In J. W. Berry, Y. H. Poortinga, & J. Pandey (Eds.), *Handbook of cross-cultural psychology. Vol. 1. Theory and method* (2nd ed., pp. 129-169). Boston: Allyn and Bacon.

Triandis, H. C. (1995). *Individualism and collectivism.* Boulder, CO: Westview.

Triandis, H. C. (1996). The psychological measurement of cultural syndromes. *American Psychologist, 51,* 407-415.

Triandis, H. C., & Vassiliou, V. (1972). A comparative analysis of subjective culture. In H. C. Triandis (Ed.), *The analysis of subjective culture* (pp. 299-335). New York: Wiley.

Van de Vijver, F. J. R., & Leung, K. (1997a). Methods and data analysis of comparative research. In J. W. Berry, Y. H. Poortinga, & J. Pandey (Eds.), *Handbook of cross-cultural psychology. Vol 1. Theory and method* (pp. 257-300). Boston: Allyn and Bacon.

Van de Vijver, F. J. R., & Leung, K. (1997b). *Methods and data analysis for cross-cultural research.* Newbury Park, CA: Sage.

Van de Vijver, F. J. R., & Leung, K. (2001). Personality in cultural context: Methodological issues. *Journal of Personality, 69,* 1007-1032.

Van de Vijver, F. J. R., & Poortinga, Y. H. (2002). Structural equivalence in multicultural research. *Journal of Cross-Cultural Psychology, 33,* 141-156.

Van de Vijver, F. J. R. (1994) Methodological issues in cross-cultural studies on parental rearing behavior and psychopathology. In C. Perris, W. A. Arrindell, & M. Eisemann (Eds.), *Parenting and psychopathology* (pp. 173-197). New York: Wiley.

Van de Vijver, F. J. R., & Tanzer, N. K. (1997). Bias and equivalence in cross-cultural assessment: An overview. *European Review of Applied Psychology, 47,* 263-279.

Van Hemert, D. A., Van de Vijver, F. J. R., Poortinga, Y. H., & Georgas, J. (in press). Structure and score levels of the Eysenck Personality Questionnaire across individuals and countries. *Personality and Individual Differences.*

Williams, J. E., Satterwhite, R. C., & Saiz, J. L. (1998). *The importance of psychological traits: A cross-cultural study.* New York: Plenum.

Zegers, F. E., & ten Berge, J. M. F. (1985). A family of association coefficients for metric scales. *Psychometrika, 50,* 17-24.

AUTHOR NOTE

Ype H. Poortinga is part-time professor of cross-cultural psychology at Tilburg University and at the Catholic University of Leuven. Fons J. R. Van de Vijver is professor of cross-cultural psychology at Tilburg University. Dianne A. Van Hemert is working on her PhD at Tilburg University. E-mail: Y.H.Poortinga@kub.nl

A FIVE-FACTOR THEORY PERSPECTIVE

JÜRI ALLIK* & ROBERT R. MCCRAE**

*University of Tartu, **National Institute on Aging, NIH*

Abstract. Five-Factor Theory (FFT) is a conceptualization of the personality system that identifies traits as abstract Basic Tendencies rooted in biology. In this chapter, FFT is examined in relation to recent findings in cross-cultural psychology reported in this volume. FFT correctly predicts the universality of personality structure, maturation, and gender differentiation. FFT suggests that differences in the mean levels of traits across cultures may be due to differences in the distribution of trait-related alleles, and that cultural differences may be the effect, rather than the cause, of trait level differences. Reports of substantial cohort and acculturation effects pose challenges to FFT and provide special opportunities for future research.

Keywords: Personality theory, personality traits, culture, personality-and-culture research

1. FIVE-FACTOR THEORY

In contrast to the Five-Factor Model (FFM; McCrae & John, 1992), which is in an empirical generalization about the covariation of personality traits, Five-Factor Theory (FFT; McCrae & Costa, 1996, 1999) is an attempt to conceptualize recent findings about personality traits in the context of the development and operation of the whole personality system. FFT describes how biology and culture interact in the development of habits, attitudes, values, roles, and relationships, which express both the individual's traits and the press of the social environment. The components of FFT are familiar; what is distinctive is the role assigned to each in personality functioning.

FFT originated in efforts to understand the extraordinary stability of personality traits across periods of many years (Costa & McCrae, 1994a): Longitudinal research had shown that decades of life experience appear to have little systematic impact on basic personality traits. Combined with findings from behavior genetic studies that had shown a powerful effect of genes and a vanishingly small effect of the shared environment (Riemann, Angleitner, & Strelau, 1997), these observations led to the proposal that traits are endogenous dispositions, relatively untouched by life experience. That theory certainly explains the findings of longitudinal stability and heritability; in this chapter we consider how well it squares with cross-cultural results, and what it suggests for future research on personality and culture.

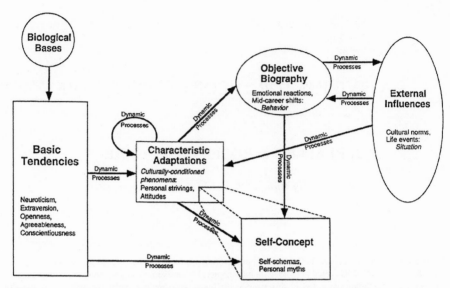

Figure 1. A representation of the personality system, with categories of variables, specific examples, and arrows indicating causal pathways. Adapted from McCrae & Costa, 1999.

1.1. The Personality System

Figure 1 represents personality as a system. The chief inputs are *Biological Bases* and *External Influences*—the organism and the environment. The ultimate output is labeled the *Objective Biography*; it is the cumulative record of a person's acts and experiences. At any one point in time it represents the individual's behavior. More novel and interesting are the distinctions made within the system, specifically, the distinction between *Basic Tendencies* and *Characteristic Adaptations*.

At issue is the definition of *traits*. Phenotypically, traits can be described as enduring tendencies to think, feel, and behave in consistent ways: Extraverts talk a lot, in many situations; conscientious people are methodical and persistent over long periods of time. Some theorists have equated traits with the behavior itself (Buss & Craik, 1983); others have identified traits as broad habits that account for consistencies in behavior (Pervin, 1994). By contrast, FFT asserts that traits are much deeper constructs: Basic Tendencies, rooted in biology, that are not directly accessible either to observation or to introspection. It is precisely because they are so deeply grounded in the organism that they resist the shaping influences of the environment.

How, then, do they operate? According to FFT, they interact with the environment in shaping those psychological structures that directly guide behavior: Habits, values, plans, skills, scripts, schemas, relationships. These are called Characteristic Adaptations; they are *characteristic* because they reflect the individual's underlying dispositions, and they are *adaptations* because they are designed to respond to the requirements of the environment. For example, an extravert might find that she enjoys talking to people; learn the techniques of a good salesman; and take a job selling insurance. What she does during most of the day is a direct reflection of her occupational role, but indirectly it expresses her Extraversion.

Perhaps the most studied aspect of Characteristic Adaptations is the *Self-Concept*, an acquired view of the self based on life experience and social feedback. It, too, can be shaped by traits, as when an individual high in Neuroticism ignores his talents and accomplishments and builds a self-image around his perceived faults. The Self-Concept is of special significance because it is the source of information that people draw on when completing personality questionnaires.

1.2. The "Dogma" of Endogenous Influences

Once the constructs are understood, most of FFT in not controversial: Who would dispute, for example, that people develop value systems which help to guide behavior in relevant situations? But FFT distinguishes itself from almost all other personality theories by its claim that traits are strictly endogenous, changing only in response to intrinsic maturation or other biological inputs. In addition to genes, these biological influences include intrauterine hormones, brain injury and illness, psychopharmacological interventions, and aging processes.

McCrae and Costa (1999) do not suppose that this postulate is literally true—that the environment never has any effect whatsoever on traits—but they do believe that it is a parsimonious first approximation to the truth. It accounts for the stability of personality in adulthood (McCrae & Costa, in press), the limited role of parental influence (Rowe, 1994), even the existence of human-like personality traits in other animals (Gosling, 2001).

Perhaps more important, it provides a clear basis for formulating testable hypotheses. Almost any set of findings would be compatible with a theory that allows a mix of biological and environmental influences. But the principle of strictly endogenous influences makes clear predictions and suggests novel interpretations in many cases. It serves as a what Francis Crick (1990) called a scientific "dogma." These "are speculative and so may turn out to be wrong. Nevertheless, they help to organize more positive and explicit hypotheses. If well formulated, they act as a guide through a tangled jumble of theories. Without such a guide, any theory seems possible" (p. 109).

One characteristic feature of Crick's dogmas is that they can be formulated in terms of a fundamental prohibition. For example, one of the most basic dogmas of physics postulates that no material particle can travel faster than the speed of light. Analogously, the central dogma of molecular biology postulates that genetic information flows only outward from DNA to RNA to protein. Although this postulate was eventually proved wrong by the discovery of retroviruses, in which information is transferred from RNA to DNA, it served as an exquisite guiding principle for the whole field of molecular biology. The central dogma of FFT postulates that there is no "transfer" from culture and life experience to basic personality traits. Postulating this as a general heuristic principle stimulates the search for conditions—apparently not very frequent ones—where this general postulate is violated. An analysis of these special circumstances should lead to a deeper understanding of the origins of traits.

1.3. FFT and Personality Assessment

Because traits are not directly observable, knowledge about their properties must be inferred from information about people's concrete habits, attitudes, preferences, and social skills. In other words, personality traits can be assessed only through asking questions about Characteristic Adaptations. Because Characteristic Adaptations are shaped by both traits and the environment, these trait indicators are inherently fallible. Belonging to a fundamentalist religion may be an indicator of experiential closedness (Streyffeler & McNally, 1998), but it may also be the result of growing up in a fundamentalist community. The general strategy for dealing with this ambiguity is by averaging across a large pool of items, covering many different manifestations of a trait.

The relevant Characteristic Adaptations can be assessed by direct observation; or by observer ratings, in which the acquired knowledge of the informant is utilized; or by self-reports, which are based on the Self-Concept.[1] It is well-known that the Self-Concept is not infallibly accurate, and personality researchers are painfully aware that respondents are sometimes less than candid in their answers. Given the length of the inferential chain from self-reports through the Self-Concept through Characteristic Adaptations to Basic Tendencies, it is remarkable that personality measures work at all (cf. Funder, 1989). But the success of trait psychology in predicting real life outcomes (Barrick & Mount, 1991) and the convergence of personality scores across observers (Funder, Kolar, & Blackman, 1995) and separated twins (Tellegen et al., 1988) provide ample evidence that they do.

When personality information has been gathered, it must be interpreted relative to some normative group. If groups or individuals from two different cultures are to be compared, an entirely new set of difficult issues arises. Is a given Characteristic Adaptation an equally valid trait indicator in two cultures? Praying five times a day would be seen as strong evidence of piety in America, but means virtually nothing in Saudi Arabia, where it is compulsory. Is the Self-Concept systematically biased? Americans are said to self-enhance, whereas Japanese do not (Heine, Lehman, Markus, & Kitayama, 1999). Lodhi, Deo, and Belhekar (2002) argue that socially desirable responding is more pronounced in India than America, leading to inflated scores on desirable personality traits. All these issues need to be borne in mind when considering cross-cultural comparisons.

In principle, FFT offers a way around all these difficulties: One could measure the biological bases and infer trait levels from these. At present, we do not know what the underlying biology is, nor have we made much demonstrable progress since 1967, when Eysenck published his landmark volume. If and when the genes or neuropsychic structures or neurohormones that underlie personality traits are identified, it will lead to a revolution in personality assessment with profound implications for cross-cultural comparisons.

---

[1]When we ask respondents to tell us directly about their traits, as on adjective rating scales, we are asking them to make inferences based on their knowledge of their Characteristic Adaptations. People do not have direct, intuitive knowledge of their trait standing.

2. PERSONALITY-AND-CULTURE RESEARCH

The classic field of culture and personality research, as practiced by such anthropologists as Benedict, Mead, and Linton, was based on the premise that culture shaped personality, largely through child-reading practices. It may seem that by denying the direct influence of culture on personality traits, FFT has abandoned interest in the personality-and-culture relationship. But traits can be expressed only in interaction with the environment, by developing Characteristic Adaptations that change over time in response to biological maturation and changes in the environment. The interaction of personality traits with the cultural environment constitutes a major subject for personality-and-culture research, but a different set of questions arise in the framework of FFT: How do different personality types adapt to various cultures? How do specific personality traits support cultural practices in the societies in which people live? Can cultures speed up or slow down the intrinsic course of maturation? Perhaps most crucially, FFT makes it reasonable to reverse the classic causal scheme and ask if personality traits in the aggregate and over time can shape culture. Would a society of introverts develop different customs and traditions than a society of extraverts?

In an effort to systematize these kinds of questions, McCrae (2000) proposed that analyses could be conducted on three levels. *Transcultural* analyses look for universals in personality that transcend cultural differences. *Intracultural* analyses examine the specific expression of traits in a given culture; in the language of FFT, they are concerned with cultural differences in Characteristic Adaptations. *Intercultural* analyses compare cultures on aggregate trait characteristics (typically means), and study their relations to features of culture. Rolland's (2002) chapter on the generalizability of the FFM is a clear instance of a transcultural analysis; Konstable, Realo, and Kallasmaa's (2002) search for variations in trait structure is an intercultural analysis. Lima (2002) discusses boredom as a typically Portuguese manifestation of high Neuroticism (N) and low Extraversion (E) in what might be considered an intracultural analysis.

2.1. Transcultural Evidence Supporting FFT

Transcultural analyses are most directly relevant to an evaluation of FFT. If, as FFT asserts, N, E, Openness to Experience (O), Agreeableness (A), and Conscientiousness (C) are biologically-based aspects of human nature, then they must be universal: One species, one structure. A decade ago that would have been a doubtful proposition at best (Juni, 1996), but a variety of studies have now made it clear that, even with imperfect measuring instruments, the FFM can be detected in all cultures (McCrae & Costa, 1997; Paunonen, 1996). Related individual difference variables, such as emotions (Yik, Russell, Ahn, Fernández Dols, & Suzuki, 2002) and values (Schwartz, 1992) also appear to be universal, perhaps in part because they are related to species-wide Basic Tendencies.

Studies in the United States show that there are small but consistent changes in the mean levels of personality traits across the adult life span. When college students are compared to older adults, adults score higher on A and C but lower on N, E, and O (Costa & McCrae, 1994b). These changes cannot be attributed to cohort differences, because similar trends can be observed in longitudinal studies (e.g., McGue, Bacon, & Lykken, 1993). According to FFT, these are intrinsic maturational changes, tied to some kind of biological clock. If so, then they ought to be observed everywhere; and in fact, cross-cultural studies have revealed the same patterns of development in very different cultures, including several non-Western societies (Costa, McCrae et al., 2000; McCrae et al., 1999). These are particularly impressive findings because different countries have had different recent histories that might have been expected to leave distinctive marks on successive cohorts. But personality traits are transhistorical as well as transcultural: Chinese generations that endured the Cultural Revolution show the same age differences as middle-class Americans (Yang, McCrae, & Costa, 1998).

Lynn and Martin (1997) noted that women obtained higher mean scores on N in all 37 nations where the results of the Eysenck Personality Questionnaire were available. Men scored higher than women on E in 30 countries and on Psychoticism in 34 countries. Secondary analyses of Revised NEO Personality Inventory data from 26 cultures (total $N = 23,031$) confirmed that women report themselves to be higher in N and A, whereas men are higher in Assertiveness and Openness to Ideas (Costa, Terracciano, & McCrae, 2001). These findings are clearly consistent with the universality demanded by FFT. However, that study also showed that the magnitude of sex differences was smaller in traditional cultures (e.g., Zimbabwe) than in modern, progressive nations (e.g., Belgium). That finding, initially counterintuitive, cannot be directly explained by FFT, but it is not necessarily inconsistent with it. Costa et al. (2001) argued that the effect might be accounted for by attribution processes: In traditional cultures, men and women attribute their masculine and feminine traits to role requirements, and thus do not incorporate them into their Self-Concepts. FFT predicts that observers from outside traditional cultures (and thus not prone to the same attribution error) would rate traditional women as clearly higher in N and A than their male compatriots. This is a testable hypothesis derived from FFT.

2.2. A Political Experiment

FFT makes the bold claim that environmental interventions cannot alter personality traits (although they can certainly change Characteristic Adaptations and the resulting behavior). But changing human nature has long been a goal of religions and governments, and many political systems have tried to create a new type of personality to fit their ideological objectives. How successful have these experiments been? In this respect it is very instructive to compare people living in Eastern and Western Germany, because between 1945 and 1989 they lived under dramatically different political systems. Did Communist control of education, law, the mass media, and the economy result in a new *Homo Sovieticus* in the German Democratic Republic? If so, it should be possible to detect differences between East and West German personality profiles. Note that this is an elegant natural experiment: Before 1945, the "participants" shared a common ancestry, language, culture, and history; they were assigned to one of two conditions by accidents of geography that must have approximated randomization. When Anglietner and Ostendorf (2000) administered the German NEO-PI-R to large (Ns = 2,174; 5,234) Eastern and Western German samples, they found identical factor structures. More tellingly, they also showed very similar mean levels: East Germans scored about one-fifth standard deviation lower than West Germans on O, but did not differ on any of the other factors. These surprising findings are precisely what FFT would predict.

3. FFT AND INTERCULTURAL COMPARISONS

Analyses at the *intercultural* level compare cultures with respect to traits and seek associations between traits and features of culture. Most often, mean levels of traits have been the focus of interest, but one could also ask about cultural differences in standard deviations of trait scores (McCrae, 2002), or in the alignment of factors (Konstabel et al., 2002). FFT does not make direct predictions about intercultural comparisons. Nothing in the theory leads one to expect that Russians will be higher in N than Swedes, or that mean national level of E should be associated with cultural individualism. But FFT does provide a way of interpreting whatever findings are observed, and these interpretations are, in principle, subject to empirical test.

As Poortinga, Van de Vijver, and Van Hemert (2002) make clear, intercultural comparisons are fraught with interpretive perils. There are many reasons why raw scores on translations of an instrument might not be comparable, and most psychologists do not gather probability samples that would be truly representative of the cultures they hope to compare. Nevertheless, as McCrae (2002) has shown, comparisons of available data produce meaningful, often striking, results. We will discuss three of them—culture-level factor structure, cultural correlates, and geographical distribution—from the perspective of FFT. First, however, we need to address the problem of national character as it bears on the interpretation of scores.

3.1. Judgments of National Character

If there are systematic differences in the levels of personality traits in different cultures, one might expect that they would have been noticed by now. And in fact, people have long claimed that societies can be described in terms of distinctive national characters. Descriptions of national character might be based on scholarly study (e.g., Benedict, 1946), or might simply reflect popular prejudice. National stereotypes are often shared by nations and their neighbors (Peabody, 1985), and they are very resistant to change (Peabody & Shmelyov, 1996).

Until recently, the accuracy of judgments of national character could not be assessed, because there was no standard (other than consensus) against which they could be evaluated. But the personality data described in this volume give at least one way to judge accuracy: Do perceptions of national character correspond to mean levels of personality traits?

McCrae (2001) asked eight prominent cross-cultural psychologists to identify the personality factor that had been used to rank 26 cultures based on their mean NEO-PI-R scores. He asked, for example, which personality factor is lowest among Hong Kong Chinese and South Koreans, but highest among Norwegians and Americans? Rather surprisingly, these experts all considered this a difficult task and were unable to identify factors at a better-than-chance level.

Hřebíčková et al. (2002) searched the literature for speculations about the national character of Czechs, Poles, and Slovaks, but these characterizations did not agree well with the means of self-reported data. For example, contrary to the belief that Polish people are traditional and closed, Polish adolescents rated themselves as most open in comparison with Czechs and Slovaks. On the other hand, Lima (2002) found some support for writers' views of the Portuguese in the mean levels of her NEO-PI-R data.

The most focused and systematic attempt to compare national stereotypes with the means of self-reported personality traits was undertaken by Church and Katigbak (2002). In this study, 43 judges who had lived in both the Philippines and the United States for a considerable time, rated whether Filipinos or Americans would tend to show a particular trait more. These bicultural judges were in high agreement with each another, but were not consistent with the mean NEO-PI-R profiles.

It is possible to fault the methodology of these studies. McCrae's (2001) judges may not have been familiar with all 26 cultures; Church's trait descriptions may not have matched the NEO-PI-R constructs exactly. But the strong preponderance of negative findings suggests that mean trait levels and national stereotypes are not alternative measures of the same construct. Why not? What do they each represent?

One attractive interpretation is to discount beliefs about national character as a form of mythology (cf. Pennebaker, Rime, & Blankenship, 1996). National stereotypes may be historical accidents, or self-serving attributions, or totems that serve the function of cementing group identity, rather than veridical accounts of aggregate personality traits. Indeed, it seems unrealistic to expect that people could reach correct judgments of mean personality profiles. The measured differences are rather small for most traits, and it may be impossible for individuals to perceive them accurately (Stricker, 2000). It is unclear how individuals make a composite judgment of a large body of people (most of whom they have never met), and we have long known that statistical predictions are more accurate than clinical judgments (Meehl, 1954) and do not necessarily agree with them.

On the other hand, Church and Katigbak (2002) make a good point when they note that "the backgrounds of our bicultural judges would seem to be fairly ideal for their task. Thus, if their judgments of average cultural differences are not valid, it is not clear whose judgments would be" (p. 149). Echoing cautions raised by Poortinga et al. (2002), they conclude from these findings that mean level comparisons across cultures must be viewed with skepticism.

The research agenda here is clear. Replications of Church and Katigbak's study should be conducted in a wide variety of cultures. That information would allow a definitive test of the concordance of mean levels and national stereotypes, but it would also allow far more informative analyses. For example, it might be the case that certain domains or facets consistently show convergence, whereas other do not; a comparison of the two might suggest reasons. National stereotypes, gathered within the comprehensive framework of the Five-Factor Model, could also be used in intercultural comparisons: Are they geographically ordered? Do they have culture-level correlates? Finally, one could test the relative predictive utility of judgments and assessed means: Which tells us more about industrial production or rates of homicide or artistic styles?

Pending a resolution of these issues, we can return to a consideration of measured mean trait scores and their interpretation from the perspective of FFT.

3.2. The Culture-Level Factor Structure

McCrae (2001, 2002) reported culture-level factor analyses of NEO-PI-R facet scores. In these analyses, aggregate data from college age and adult men and women were treated as cases. The resulting factors reflect the covariation of traits across cultures. As Bond (2001) has noted, there is no logical requirement that this structure will have any resemblance to the factor structure observed when individual data are analyzed. We might, for example, find that cultures tend to promote either emotional or intellectual approaches to exploring the world, but not both. In that case, a culture-level factor might emerge contrasting Openness to Feeling with Openness to Ideas—traits that are positively related at the individual level.

In fact, however, the observed culture-level factors closely resemble individual-level factors, and can readily be interpreted as N, E, O, A, and C. There are three possible explanations for this intriguing finding, and all deserve attention.

Artifact. A first possibility is that mean trait levels do not in fact covary meaningfully across cultures; instead, the observed factor structure results from the operation of response biases. For example, all the Neuroticism items of the Eysenck Personality Questionnaire (Eysenck & Eysenck, 1975) are keyed in the positive direction; an intercultural factor analysis of those items might uncover a factor resembling N simply because cultures vary systematically on acquiescent response tendencies. That interpretation cannot be applied to the NEO-PI-R, however, because all scales (in all translations) are roughly balanced to control the effects of acquiescence. Again, as discussed in McCrae (2002), extreme versus neutral responding is unlikely to explain either mean levels or covariation of traits.

Social desirability, however, is a more promising candidate. Lodhi, Deo, and Belhekar (2002) suggest that high A scores among Marathi-speaking Indians might be due to socially desirable responding. If social desirability affects all—and only—facets of A, then cultural variation on this response tendency would tend to create an A factor. It is possible that this accounts in part for the observed structure, but it cannot account for it completely. If intercultural factor structure were nothing but social desirability, we would expect a single evaluative factor (contrasting N with E, O, A, and C) or perhaps two factors, corresponding to Positive Valence (E and O) and Negative Valence (N vs. A and C; McCrae & Costa, 1999). There is no obvious way in which familiar response styles could give rise to the culture-level FFM.

Cultural mechanisms. The culture-level factor structure could be the result of cultural influences that mimic sources of structure at the individual level (McCrae, Jang, Livesley, Riemann, & Angleitner, 2001). In this interpretation, differences in trait levels across cultures are real, and they are created by cultural processes. For example, Openness to Ideas and Openness to Feelings may covary because some cultures encourage

Openness in general, whereas others discourage it. Indeed, the appearance of a culture-level FFM seems to imply that any cultural influences must operate on a factor-by-factor basis. Perhaps the same child-rearing practices that foster need for achievement also encourage caution and deliberation, leading to high C; perhaps the same kinship systems that inhibit gregariousness also inhibit cheerfulness, leading to low E.

It must be stressed that, at present, no one has demonstrated that child-rearing practices or kinship systems or any other features of culture in fact influence the mean levels of traits. Rohner and colleagues (e.g., Rohner & Britner, 2002) have gathered an impressive array of evidence to show that perceived parental rejection is associated with poorer psychological adjustment around the world, but the causal order is not clear: Perhaps individuals high in N misperceive their parents to have been rejecting even when they were not; perhaps parents of high N children come to reject them because they are so difficult. These alternative interpretations are consistent with FFT, which provides another explanation for the factor structure.

Endogenous influences. A simple explanation for the culture-level FFM can be derived from FFT. People living in the same culture by and large share a common ancestry, and thus genetic similarity. The alleles that shape personality factors may be more common in some of these populations than others, and we know from studies of individuals that facets that define the same factor are genetically related (McCrae et al., 2001). Thus, the Agreeableness factor emerges in culture-level analyses because societies differ in the distribution of Agreeableness-related genes.

Poortinga et al. (2002) have argued that a genetic explanation for group differences in personality traits is unlikely, because there is no compelling reason why certain traits would be differentially selected in different groups. But Tooby and Cosmides (1990) have hypothesized that, within the normal range, personality traits are of no evolutionary significance, and are thus perpetuated as genetic noise. Random fluctuations in personality-related genes in ancestral populations may have been preserved and transmitted to contemporary cultures.

3.3. Cultural Correlates

If culture does not affect the mean levels of personality traits, then we might find no association between features of culture and mean levels of traits. Indeed, this is precisely what Angleitner and Ostendorf (2000) reported when they examined the former East and West Germanys. Long-standing differences in religion, educational policies, and political ideology had no lasting impact on NEO-PI-R scores. But that situation was imposed on the people of Germany by conquering nations. Where institutions and customs have evolved naturally, some association is possible, according to FFT, because personality traits may help shape culture.

Consider, for example, the correlations McCrae (2002) reported for Hofstede's (2001) Power Distance dimension. Groups low in E and O and high in C scored high on Power Distance, implying that their members had a high tolerance for status differences and preferred a hierarchical structure in society, with some people giving orders and some taking them. This would appear to be a natural social organization for people who are closed and conscientious, because it is both predictable and efficient. The preponderance of introverts would also be consistent with the fact that in hierarchical organizations there are always more people taking orders than giving them—a situation more tolerable for introverts than extraverts.

It remains to be seen how such fit between aggregate personality and social structure develops. Presumably trial and error is involved; structures that work well are retained, whereas those that do not are discarded. Social structures may develop on small scales, perhaps within the family, and become a model for larger organizational patterns (as filial piety became the model for ministers' relations to the emperor in Confucian societies; Gabrenya & Hwang, 1996).

There is one way, consistent with FFT, that cultural patterns could contribute to the personality profiles of nations: Individuals may be selected in or out. Extraverts lost in the lower levels of a hierarchy in a high Power Distance society may decide to try their luck elsewhere; individuals low in C may be forced out. Draguns, Krylova, Oryol, Rukavishnikov, and Martin (2000) speculated that the closedness and introversion of their reindeer-herding sample may have been due to self-selection, as more adventurous members of the group left for more interesting climates. It is known that extraverts are more susceptible to boredom and higher in excitement seeking than introverts, and thus perhaps more willing to take the risks of emigration. Lynn (1981) noted that nations like Australia, Canada, and the United States, whose populations are almost entirely made up of relatively recent immigrants, tend to have higher E scores than the European countries from which the emigrants largely came. The effects of self-selection were not seen in Angleitner and Ostendorf's (2000) study of East Germany, presumably because it was infamously prohibited.

We wish to make it clear that we are not claiming that personality traits are the only or even the most important influence on social structure and other cultural patterns. Obviously, climate, economics, religion, and the fortunes of war all have powerful influences on customs and institutions and on the resulting conduct of life. Only over long time periods and in favorable circumstances would one expect to see effects of aggregate personality traits.

3.4. The Geography of Personality

Although the Hofstede dimensions are linked to a wide variety of outcomes and national characteristics, they are ultimately based on self-report responses, and it might be argued that response biases create the correlations with personality measures. The same shared social desirability biases that lead people in some cultures to describe themselves as conscientious may also lead them to endorse high Power Distance values. It would be useful to have correlates that entirely avoid issues of method variance.

Geographical location is one, and several studies have shown that personality traits are organized geographically. Costa et al. (2001) reported that European countries differed from Asian and African countries in the degree of gender differentiation. McCrae (2002) showed a similar pattern with trait variances, which are larger in Europe. Allik and McCrae (2001) showed more detailed associations between psychological and physical proximity. They used cluster analysis to identify similarities among personality profiles in 26 cultures. Pairs of cultures with closest profiles included Spain and Portugal, Indonesia and the Philippines, Zimbabwe and Black South Africa, and Taiwan and South Korea. These associations are remarkable when it is considered that different languages and often different sampling methods were used in each country.

Geographically adjacent cultures often share both geophysical features, like climate, and cultural features, like religion or language family. In addition, however, they are likely to share ancestry and thus to have overlapping gene pools (Cavalli-Sforza, Menozzi, & Piazza, 1994). Psychologists in general have a long-standing bias toward environmental explanations, and most would probably favor a cultural account of these findings. But FFT holds that the genetic similarities are the more likely sources of personality similarities, and as we have seen, FFT is strongly supported by several lines of evidence, including many of the findings of cross-cultural studies.

A direct test of this view provides modest support. Cavalli-Sforza et al. (1994) provide data on *genetic distances* between cultures, which are determined by similarity in the distribution of a variety of alleles. By and large, these genetic distances correspond to known patterns of human migration. From the data in Table 3 of McCrae (2002) we can calculate personality profile distances, most simply as the Euclidean distance between the five factor scores. Genetic distances are given by Cavalli-Sforza et al. for 16 of the cultures in McCrae; the correlation between genetic and personality profile distances across the 120 pairs of cultures is $r = .19, p < .05$. When Yugoslavia, which is identified as an outlier by Cavalli-Sforza et al. (1994, p. 268), is omitted, the correlation rises to $r = .24, N = 105, p < .05$. These correlations are modest in part because there is relatively little genetic differentiation within European countries, and correspondingly little variation in mean personality levels. If the analysis were conducted on samples from around the world, larger associations would probably be found.

Of course, even very large correlations would not prove causal associations. Genetically related groups tend to share geography, history, and culture as well as genes, and genetic distance may simply serve as a marker of cultural distance.

3.5. Ethical Considerations

It is not possible to discuss the idea of genetic differences among human groups without acknowledging the potential for its misuse. Historically, traits attributed to despised minorities have been used to justify enforced sterilization, slavery, and genocide. It is common to ascribe undesirable traits to members of other cultures, but to suggest that they are genetically based seems further to imply that there is no hope that they will change. In this way, psychology may unwillingly give ammunition to racists.

If there were no mean level differences in traits across cultures, or if the data were clearly uninterpretable, we would have been spared the task of dealing with these issues. But there are meaningful differences, and it is scientifically possible, even likely, that these are due in some degree to genetics. Personality psychologists need to learn how to evaluate such claims cautiously but thoroughly, and to begin to deal with the ethical implications if they are in fact supported. It is probably only a matter of time before someone identifies a gene linked to a trait and demonstrates that the distribution of the gene alleles differs across cultures (cf. Gelernter, Kranzler, & Satel, 1999).

Questions will then arise about the implications for social behavior, and if we psychologists are not prepared to answer them, someone else will—someone who may be less scientifically informed, and perhaps less well-intentioned, than we are.

Any suggestion that there may be biologically-based differences in personality between two groups should be properly qualified, noting the limitations of the available evidence. That is, of course, true of any scientific conclusion, but special care is needed here. FFT suggests that different personality profiles across cultures may result from differences in the distribution of trait-related alleles. But that is only one possible interpretation of the evidence, and we must be clear that the question is far from settled.

In justifying intercultural comparisons, McCrae (2002) relied on the principle that errors in some datasets are likely to average out when comparisons are made across a range of cultures. This is a reasonable assumption, but it must be kept in mind that the resulting conclusions apply only at a general level. There is considerable evidence that Asian cultures are lower in Extraversion than European cultures, but the evidence that Chinese are less extraverted than Danes is much weaker.

Any discussion of cultural differences must also point out the magnitude of the effects and the range of individual differences within cultures. The factor means in McCrae (2002) have standard deviations ranging from 2.65 to 3.72 T-score points, or about one-third the magnitude of individual differences within cultures. Even if our characterizations of cultures' personality profiles were perfectly accurate, knowing a person's culture would tell us rather little about his or her own personality profile. Stereotypes should not be applied to individuals.

Finally, it must be emphasized that behavior, the Objective Biography, is not determined solely or even principally by personality traits. Since the person–situation debate, personality psychologists have been sensitized to the fact that traits typically account for only a small portion of the variance in behaviors. This is *a fortiori* true of aggregate personality traits and the behavior of groups. If we judged Vietnamese Americans by their low C scores, we might anticipate poor performance in school and at work; in fact, because of their cultural background, they have succeeded admirably (Leininger, 2002).

4. CHALLENGES TO FIVE-FACTOR THEORY

Not all cross-cultural findings offer clear support to FFT—indeed, some appear flatly to contradict it. An examination of these cases is likely to be particularly informative about FFT and the interpretations of cross-cultural results that it suggests. Two of the most important are cohort effects and secular trends, and effects of acculturation on personality traits. At present, neither line of research provides decisive evidence against FFT, but both pose clear challenges.

4.1. Birth Cohort Effects and Secular Trends

Societies and cultures are not frozen; they continuously change and evolve. For example, in the United States each successive generation during the last fifty years spent less time reading newspapers, working on community projects, and visiting their friends, and more time watching television (Putnam, 2000). Similar changes can be observed all over the world where people have, in the last few decades, become sub-jectively happier, less concerned about money, and somewhat less obedient to tradi-tional authorities (Inglehart, 1997; Inglehart & Baker, 2000). Do these global societal changes affect personality traits?

There are some hints that they might. McCrae (2002) reported on the similarity of personality scores across gender and across age groups. Mean levels on the five factors were strongly correlated when men were compared with women of the same age and culture ($rs = .77$ to $.88$); the correlations were weaker when adults were compared with college-age samples ($rs = .48$ to $.81$). These smaller correlations might be due to cohort effects that vary by culture.[2]

Adult developmentalists (Schaie & Labouvie-Vief, 1974) have long been con-cerned with generational effects, which have been shown to have a powerful influence on cognitive functioning. Until recently, personality traits appeared to be largely immune to cohort effects: Age differences in the mean levels of adult personality traits are small, and can be accounted for by known maturational changes in trait levels (McCrae & Costa, in press). But Twenge (2000, 2001) has recently reported meta-analyses that claim to find dramatic cohort effects on N and E: American college students have increased in both N and E by nearly a full standard deviation over the past half century.

If these findings are not artifactual, they appear to constitute a falsification of the dogma of endogenous influences. Changes in population genetics over the past fifty years are not sufficient to account for such large effects, and it seems unlikely that changes in health or diet would increase N and E (although they have had profound effects on physical characteristics such as stature in the period since the Industrial Revolution; Cavalli-Sforza et al., 1994). The source would seem to be the psychological impact of the environment.

But Twenge's data are puzzling. Cross-sectional studies of adults born in the same time period as the subjects in her analyses ought to show profound age differences: Later-born (and thus younger) men and women ought to be much more extraverted and neurotic. In fact, the differences, although in the right direction, are tiny in magnitude (Costa et al., 1986), and replicate tiny longitudinal increases (Costa, Herbst, McCrae, & Siegler, 2000). If the cohort effects reported by Twenge in college students actually occurred, they seem to have evaporated by the time the students reached adulthood.

Artifactual explanations are also possible. Most of the studies Twenge (2000) reviewed used the Eysenck N scales, which are keyed exclusively in the positive direc-tion. If acquiescence became more widespread over the past half-century, that could account for the findings. Again, changes may have occurred in social desirability. Perhaps admitting to signs of anxiety or depression was less acceptable in the 1950s than in the 1990s. Until all these possibilities are sorted out, the question of cohort effects will remain a mystery.

---

[2]However, they might also be due to sampling biases. Men and women were always sampled from the same population (e.g., all were college students, or all were community members), whereas the two age groups might represent somewhat different populations (e.g., students vs. community members).

4.2. Acculturation Studies

Most cross-cultural studies cannot shed light on the relative importance of nature and nurture in personality development, because most societies consist of individuals who share both biological ancestry and culture. Acculturation studies, however, offer a way to unconfound these two: Immigrants are often assimilated into a new culture long before they lose their genetic ethnic identity. According to FFT, ancestry ought to be more important than the current social environment in shaping personality dispositions.

Leininger (2002) touches on possible acculturation effects in her Vietnamese-American sample, but the design is not ideal. Because data are not available from respondents in Vietnam, the only possible comparisons are between two generations of Vietnamese Americans and between subsamples who live in traditional versus Americanized communities, and these comparisons are complicated by age differences and the possibilities of self-selection.

Although there is a large literature on the psychology of acculturation, there appears to be only a single study in which individuals of the same age but different levels of acculturation are compared on personality traits.[3] McCrae, Yik, Trapnell, Bond, and Paulhus (1998) examined personality profiles in Chinese undergraduates in Hong Kong and Vancouver. Recent immigrants to Canada closely resembled their compatriots in Hong Kong. Ethnic Chinese born in Canada also shared many feature of the Hong Kong personality profile: Compared to European Canadians, they scored higher on Anxiety, Self-Consciousness, and Vulnerability, and lower on Assertiveness, Activity, and Excitement Seeking. These findings are consistent with FFT and its emphasis on endogenous determinants of personality.

But there were also significant acculturation effects. Canadian-born Chinese were higher than recent immigrants in E, O, and A when self-reports of personality were examined; when rated by Chinese acquaintances, the effects were replicated for E and O, and for the Trust, Altruism, and Tender-Mindedness facets of A.

Analyses of self-report data also suggested acculturation effects for Vulnerability, which was higher for recent immigrants, and Competence, which was lower. That finding was not replicated in peer rating data. The resolution of this discrepancy was found when the data were analyzed by the status of the rater: Peer raters who were recent immigrants from Hong Kong rated targets higher in Vulnerability and lower in Competence regardless of the target's place of birth. It appears that these two facets are susceptible to social judgment effects. Hong Kong residents appear to have a different, and harsher, standard by which to judge Competence. What changes with acculturation is not standing on the real personality trait, but the standards by which it is judged. Social standards are, of course, Characteristic Adaptations, and their modification by culture is understandable within FFT.

The increases in E (especially Warmth, Excitement-Seeking, and Positive Emotions), O, and facets of A cannot be explained by the social judgment mechanism, and constitute a challenge to FFT. If we wish to retain FFT without modification, we would need to interpret these changes as artifacts. One possibility is that the individual items

---

[3]Tsai and Pike (2000) examined acculturation effects on MMPI-2 clinical scales, and found that more acculturated Asians more closely resembled Americans.

of the NEO-PI-R have a different significance in different cultural contexts: Perhaps the Characteristic Adaptations we assess do not have quite the same implications for inferring Basic Tendencies in Hong Kong and in Canada. A plausible example of this is altruistic behavior. Being helpful to strangers is a clear indicator of Agreeableness in individualistic cultures, but not in collectivistic cultures (McCrae et al., 1998). There, resources are saved for the family or other in-group members. The same amount of generosity may be present in the two cultures, but it is distributed differently. In this interpretation, Chinese do not become more agreeable with time in Canada; they simply express their Agreeableness in a more Canadian way.

That proposal saves the dogma of endogenous origins, but at the cost of conceding that the personality profiles collected across cultures are subject to distortions.[4] It is, of course, not surprising that some distortions appear when an instrument is translated and imported into a very different context; the question is, how serious are they? The errors cannot be both large and random, rendering the data meaningless, or else we would not find culture-level correlates. And if the distortions are small, then they can probably be safely disregarded.

It is possible, however, that the distortions are large and systematic, and that culture-level correlates are spurious. What, aside from real differences, could account for the fact that Europeans portray themselves as extraverts, whereas Asians respond like introverts? Perhaps E is more highly valued in individualistic cultures; or perhaps attribution is the mechanism (cf. Costa et al., 2001): Asians living in close social groups may attribute sociability not to themselves, but to their collectivistic circumstances. They may act like extraverts, but believe it is their duty rather than their disposition.

An alternative solution to the problems posed by the McCrae et al. (1998) study is to modify FFT, by acknowledging that some External Influences can affect personality traits. *Culture* in fact refers to a huge class of External Influences that affect every aspect of one's life. It is not implausible to think that so pervasive and powerful an environmental manipulation as acculturation could reshape one's Basic Tendencies. The problem would be to determine which aspects of acculturation are operative. Most of the events one experiences in a lifetime do not appreciably change personality traits (McCrae & Costa, in press)—why would changing cultures?

This chain of speculations illustrates the kind of thinking that must go on as we progress in understanding personality and culture. But it would be absurd to reach any conclusions based on a single study. Acculturation studies are powerful tools, but we will be in a much better position to use them when we have a broad body of research on which to reflect.

REFERENCES

Allik, J., & McCrae, R. R. (2001). *The geography of personality traits: Patterns of trait profiles across 26 cultures.* Unpublished manuscript, University of Tartu.

Angleitner, A., & Ostendorf, F. (2000, July). *The FFM: A comparison of German speaking countries (Austria, Former East and West Germany, and Switzerland).* Paper presented at the XXVIIth International Congress of Psychology, Stockholm, Sweden.

---

[4]Indeed, from the perspective of a Five-Factor Theory purist, data for different ethnic groups should probably be collected only from third-generation Americans, who would all interpret the items in American fashion.

Barrick, M. R., & Mount, M. K. (1991). The Big Five personality dimensions and job performance: A meta-analysis. *Personnel Psychology, 44*, 1-26.
Benedict, R. (1946). *The chrysanthemum and the sword: Patterns of Japanese culture.* Boston: Houghton Mifflin.
Bond, M. H. (2001). Surveying the foundations: Approaches to measuring group, organizational, and national variation. In M. Erez & U. Kleinbeck (Eds.), *Work motivation in the context of a globalizing economy* (pp. 395-412). Mahwah, NJ: Erlbaum.
Buss, D. M., & Craik, K. H. (1983). The act frequency approach to personality. *Psychological Review, 90*, 105-126.
Cavalli-Sforza, L. L., Menozzi, P., & Piazza, A. (1994). *The history and geography of human genes.* Princeton, NJ: Princeton University Press.
Church, A. T., & Katigbak, M. S. (2002). The Five-Factor Model in the Philippines: Investigating trait structure and levels across cultures. In R. R. McCrae & J. Allik (Eds.), *The Five-Factor Model of personality across cultures* (pp. 129-154). New York: Kluwer Academic/Plenum Publishers.
Costa, P. T., Jr., Herbst, J. H., McCrae, R. R., & Siegler, I. C. (2000). Personality at midlife: Stability, intrinsic maturation, and response to life events. *Assessment, 7*, 365-378.
Costa, P. T., Jr., & McCrae, R. R. (1994a). "Set like plaster"? Evidence for the stability of adult personality. In T. Heatherton & J. Weinberger (Eds.), *Can personality change?* (pp. 21-40). Washington, DC: American Psychological Association.
Costa, P. T., Jr., & McCrae, R. R. (1994b). Stability and change in personality from adolescence through adulthood. In C. F. Halverson, G. A. Kohnstamm & R. P. Martin (Eds.), *The developing structure of temperament and personality from infancy to adulthood* (pp. 139-150). Hillsdale, NJ: Lawrence Erlbaum Associates.
Costa, P. T., Jr., McCrae, R. R., Martin, T. A., Oryol, V. E., Senin, I. G., Rukavishnikov, A. A., Shimonaka, Y., Nakazato, K., Gondo, Y., Takayama, M., Allik, J., Kallasmaa, T., & Realo, A. (2000). Personality development from adolescence through adulthood: Further cross-cultural comparisons of age differences. In V. J. Molfese & D. Molfese (Eds.), *Temperament and personality development across the life span* (pp. 235-252). Hillsdale, NJ: Erlbaum.
Costa, P. T., Jr., McCrae, R. R., Zonderman, A. B., Barbano, H. E., Lebowitz, B., & Larson, D. M. (1986). Cross-sectional studies of personality in a national sample: 2. Stability in Neuroticism, Extraversion, and Openness. *Psychology and Aging, 1*, 144-149.
Costa, P. T., Jr., Terracciano, A., & McCrae, R. R. (2001). Gender differences in personality traits across cultures: Robust and surprising findings. *Journal of Personality and Social Psychology, 81*, 322-331.
Crick, F. (1990). *What mad pursuit: A personal view of scientific discovery.* London: Penguin.
Draguns, J. R., Krylova, A. V., Oryol, V. E., Rukavishnikov, A. A., & Martin, T. A. (2000). Personality characteristics of the Nentsy in the Russian Arctic. *American Behavioral Scientist, 44*, 126-140.
Eysenck, H. J. (1967). *The biological basis of personality.* Springfield, IL: Charles C Thomas.
Eysenck, H. J., & Eysenck, S. B. G. (1975). *Manual of the Eysenck Personality Questionnaire.* San Diego: EdITS.
Funder, D. C. (1989). Accuracy in personality judgment and the dancing bear. In D. M. Buss & N. Cantor (Eds.), *Personality psychology: Recent trends and emerging directions* (pp. 210-223). New York: Springer-Verlag.
Funder, D. C., Kolar, D. C., & Blackman, M. C. (1995). Agreement among judges of personality: Interpersonal relations, similarity, and acquaintanceship. *Journal of Personality and Social Psychology, 69*, 656-672.
Gabrenya, W. K., Jr., & Hwang, K.-K. (1996). Chinese social interaction: Harmony and hierarchy on the Good Earth. In M. H. Bond (Ed.), *The handbook of Chinese psychology* (pp. 309-321). Hong Kong: Oxford University Press.
Gelernter, J., Kranzler, H., & Satel, S. L. (1999). No association between D-2 dopamine receptor (DRD2) alleles or haplotypes and cocaine dependence or severity of cocaine dependence in European- and African-Americans. *Biological Psychiatry 45*, 340-345.
Gosling, S. D. (2001). From mice to men: What can we learn about personality from animal research? *Psychological Bulletin, 127*, 45-86.
Heine, S. J., Lehman, D. R., Markus, H. R., & Kitayama, S. (1999). Is there a universal need for positive self-regard? *Psychological Bulletin, 106*, 766-794.
Hofstede, G. (2001). *Culture's consequences: Comparing values, behaviors, institutions, and organizations across nations* (2nd ed.). Thousand Oaks, CA: Sage.

Hřebíčková, M., Urbánek, T., Čermak, I., Szarota, P., Ficková, E., & Orlická, L. (2002). The NEO Five-Factor Inventory in Czech, Polish, and Slovak contexts. In R. R. McCrae & J. Allik (Eds.), *The Five-Factor Model of personality across cultures* (pp. 53-78). New York: Kluwer Academic/Plenum Publishers.

Inglehart, R. (1997). *Modernization and postmodernization: Cultural, economic, and political change in 43 societies.* Princeton, NJ: Princeton University Press.

Inglehart, R., & Baker, W. E. (2000). Modernization, cultural change, and the persistence of traditional values. *American Sociological Review, 65,* 19-51.

Juni, S. (1996). Review of the Revised NEO Personality Inventory. In J. C. Conoley & J. C. Impara (Eds.), *12th Mental Measurements Yearbook* (pp. 863-868). Lincoln: University of Nebraska Press.

Konstabel, K., Realo, A., & Kallasmaa, T. (2002). Exploring the sources of variations in the structure of personality traits across cultures. In R. R. McCrae & J. Allik (Eds.), *The Five-Factor Model of personality across cultures* (pp. 29-52). New York: Kluwer Academic/Plenum Publishers.

Leininger, A. (2002). Vietnamese-American personality and acculturation: An exploration of relationships between personality traits and cultural goals. In R. R. McCrae & J. Allik (Eds.), *The Five-Factor Model of personality across cultures* (pp. 197-225). New York: Kluwer Academic/Plenum Publishers.

Lima, M. P. (2002). Personality and culture: The Portuguese case. In R. R. McCrae & J. Allik (Eds.), *The Five-Factor Model of personality across cultures* (pp. 249-260). New York: Kluwer Academic/Plenum Publishing.

Lodhi, P. H., Deo, S., & Belhekar, V. M. (2002). The Five-Factor Model of personality: Measurement and correlates in the Indian context. In R. R. McCrae & J. Allik (Eds.), *The Five-Factor Model of personality across cultures* (pp. 227-248). New York: Kluwer Academic/Plenum Publishers.

Lynn, R. (1981). Cross-cultural differences in Neuroticism, Extraversion and Psychoticism. In R. Lynn (Ed.), *Dimensions of personality: Papers in honor of H. J. Eysenck* (pp. 263-286). Oxford: Pergamon Press.

Lynn, R., & Martin, T. (1997). Gender differences in Extraversion, Neuroticism, and Psychoticism in 37 countries. *Journal of Social Psychology, 137,* 369-373.

McCrae, R. R. (2000). Trait psychology and the revival of personality and culture studies. *American Behavioral Scientist, 44,* 10-31.

McCrae, R. R. (2001). Trait psychology and culture: Exploring intercultural comparisons. *Journal of Personality, 69,* 819-846.

McCrae, R. R. (2002). NEO-PI-R data from 36 cultures: Further intercultural comparisons. In R. R. McCrae & J. Allik (Eds.), *The Five-Factor Model of personality across cultures* (pp. 105-126). New York: Kluwer Academic/ Plenum Publishers.

McCrae, R. R., & Costa, P. T., Jr. (1996). Toward a new generation of personality theories: Theoretical contexts for the Five-Factor Model. In J. S. Wiggins (Ed.), *The Five-Factor Model of personality: Theoretical perspectives* (pp. 51-87). New York: Guilford.

McCrae, R. R., & Costa, P. T., Jr. (1997). Personality trait structure as a human universal. *American Psychologist, 52,* 509-516.

McCrae, R. R., & Costa, P. T., Jr. (1999). A Five-Factor Theory of personality. In L. A. Pervin & O. P. John (Eds.), *Handbook of personality: Theory and research* (2nd ed., pp. 139-153). New York: Guilford.

McCrae, R. R., & Costa, P. T., Jr. (in press). *Personality in adulthood: A Five-Factor Theory perspective.* New York: Guilford.

McCrae, R. R., Costa, P. T., Jr., Lima, M. P., Simões, A., Ostendorf, F., Angleitner, A., Marušić, I., Bratko, D., Caprara, G. V., Barbaranelli, C., Chae, J.-H., & Piedmont, R. L. (1999). Age differences in personality across the adult life span: Parallels in five cultures. *Developmental Psychology, 35,* 466-477.

McCrae, R. R., Jang, K. L., Livesley, W. J., Riemann, R., & Angleitner, A. (2001). Sources of structure: Genetic, environmental, and artifactual influences on the covariation of personality traits. *Journal of Personality, 69,* 511-535.

McCrae, R. R., & John, O. P. (1992). An introduction to the Five-Factor Model and its applications. *Journal of Personality, 60,* 175-215.

McCrae, R. R., Yik, M. S. M., Trapnell, P. D., Bond, M. H., & Paulhus, D. L. (1998). Interpreting personality profiles across cultures: Bilingual, acculturation, and peer rating studies of Chinese undergraduates. *Journal of Personality and Social Psychology, 74,* 1041-1055.

McGue, M., Bacon, S., & Lykken, D. T. (1993). Personality stability and change in early adulthood: A behavioral genetic analysis. *Developmental Psychology, 29,* 96-109.

Meehl, P. E. (1954). *Clinical versus statistical prediction: A theoretical analysis and review of the evidence.* Minneapolis, MN: University of Minnesota Press.

Paunonen, S. V., Keinonen, M., Trzebinski, J., Forsterling, F., Grishenko-Roze, N., Kouznetsova, L., Chan, D. W. (1996). The structure of personality in six cultures. *Journal of Cross-Cultural Psychology, 27,* 339-353.

Peabody, D. (1985). *National characteristics.* New York: Cambridge University Press.

Peabody, D., & Shmelyov, A. G. (1996). Psychological characteristics of Russians. *European Journal of Social Psychology, 26,* 507-512.

Pennebaker, J. W., Rime, B., & Blankenship, V. E. (1996). Stereotypes of emotional expressiveness of Northerners and Southerners: A cross-cultural test of Montesquieu's hypotheses. *Journal of Personality and Social Psychology, 70,* 372-380.

Pervin, L. A. (1994). A critical analysis of current trait theory. *Psychological Inquiry, 5,* 103-113.

Poortinga, Y. H., Van de Vijver, F., & Van Hemert, D. A. (2002). Cross-cultural equivalence of the Big Five: A tenative interpretation of the evidence. In R. R. McCrae & J. Allik (Eds.), *The Five-Factor Model of personality across cultures* (pp. 281-302). New York: Kluwer Academic/Plenum Publishers.

Putnam, R. D. (2000). *Bowling alone: The collapse and revival of American community.* New York: Simon & Schuster.

Riemann, R., Angleitner, A., & Strelau, J. (1997). Genetic and environmental influences on personality: A study of twins reared together using the self- and peer report NEO-FFI scales. *Journal of Personality, 65,* 449-475.

Rohner, R. P., & Britner, P. A. (2002). Worldwide mental health correlates of parental acceptance-rejection: Review of cross-cultural and intracultural evidence. *Cross-Cultural Research: The Journal of Comparative Social Science, 36,* 15-47.

Rolland, J.-P. (2002). Cross-cultural generalizability of the Five-Factor Model of personality. In R. R. McCrae & J. Allik (Eds.), *The Five-Factor Model of personality across cultures* (pp. 7-28). New York: Kluwer Academic/Plenum Publishers.

Rowe, D. C. (1994). *The limits of family influence: Genes, experience, and behavior.* New York: Guilford.

Schaie, K. W., & Labouvie-Vief, G. (1974). Generational vs. ontogenetic components of change in adult cognitive behavior: A fourteen-year cross-sequential study. *Developmental Psychology, 10,* 305-320.

Schwartz, S. H. (1992). Universals in the content and structure of values: Theoretical advances and empirical tests in 20 countries. In M. P. Zanna (Ed.), *Advances in experimental social psychology* (Vol. 25, pp. 1-65). New York: Academic Press.

Streyffeler, L. L., & McNally, R. J. (1998). Fundamentalists and liberals: Personality characteristics of Protestant Christians. *Personality and Individual Differences, 24,* 579-580.

Stricker, L. A. (2000). Using just noticeable differences to interpret test scores. *Psychological Methods, 5,* 415-424.

Tellegen, A., Lykken, D. T., Bouchard, T. J., Jr., Wilcox, K. J., Segal, N. L., & Rich, S. (1988). Personality similarity in twins reared apart and together. *Journal of Personality and Social Psychology, 54,* 1031-1039.

Tooby, J., & Cosmides, L. (1990). On the universality of human nature and the uniqueness of the individual: The role of genetics and adaptation. *Journal of Personality, 58,* 17-68.

Tsai, D. C., & Pike, P. L. (2000). Effects of acculturation on the MMPI-2 scores of Asian American students. *Journal of Personality Assessment, 74,* 216-230.

Twenge, J. M. (2000). The Age of Anxiety? Birth cohort change in anxiety and Neuroticism, 1952-1993. *Journal of Personality and Social Psychology, 79,* 1007-1021.

Twenge, J. M. (2001). Birth cohort changes in Extraversion: A cross-temporal meta-analysis, 1966-1993. *Personality and Individual Differences, 30,* 735-748.

Yang, J., McCrae, R. R., & Costa, P. T., Jr. (1998). Adult age differences in personality traits in the United States and the People's Republic of China. *Journal of Gerontology: Psychological Sciences, 53B,* P375-P383.

Yik, M. S. M., Russell, J. A., Ahn, C.-K., Fernandes Dols, J. M., & Suzuki, N. (2002). Relating the Five-Factor Model of personality to a circumplex model of affect: A five language study. In R. R. McCrae & J. Allik (Eds.), *The Five-Factor Model of personality across cultures* (pp. 79-104). New York: Kluwer Academic/ Plenum Publishers.

AUTHOR NOTE

Address correspondence to Jüri Allik, Department of Psychology, University of Tartu, Tiigi 78, Tartu 50410, Estonia. E-mail: jyri@psych.ut.ee

AUTHOR INDEX

A

Ahn, C., 5, 79, 82, 84, 87, 307
Akamine, T. X., 10-12, 14, 16, 30, 132, 285
Allen, W., 158
Allik, J., 1-3, 7, 17, 30, 37, 40-41, 83, 107,
    147, 288, 303, 313
Allport, G. W., 11
Almagor, M., 11, 82, 147
Ameerjan, M. S., 243
Amelang, M., 2
Ananiev, B. 263
Angleitner, A., 7, 9, 14, 20-21, 30, 43, 54, 61,
    64, 106, 170, 229, 237, 303, 311-313
Ashton, M. C., 12, 14, 130, 288
Asthana, H. S., 227-228
Avia, M. D., 84, 107, 288
Aygün, Z. K., 186

B

Bacon, S., 307
Bain, E., 35, 115, 127, 155, 286
Baker, W. E., 295, 315
Balcı, Z., 176
Bankston, C. L., 198, 209, 212, 219
Barbaranelli, C., 11, 17, 62-63, 74, 156, 230,
    285
Barlingay, S. S., 228
Barrett, P. T., 14, 17, 105, 147, 229, 241, 243,
    288-289
Barrick, M. R., 22, 306
Barter, J., 83
Bayar, B., 176
Bayly, S., 228
Belhekar, V. M., 109, 128, 188, 306, 311
Bell, D., 295
Benedict, R., 306, 309
Benet-Martínez, V., 9, 11, 62, 67, 170
Benjafield, J., 171
Benne, A., 62
Bennett, A. B., 12, 132
Ben-Porath, Y. S., 82, 147
Bergman, H., 107
Bermudez, J., 74, 230, 285
Bernard, J., 56
Berne, S. L., 161
Bernstein, M., 262
Berry, J. W., 10, 30, 100, 158, 192, 282, 293,
    295, 297
Binet, A., 262
Birman, D., 271
Blackman, M. C., 306

Blankenship, V. E., 310
Blatný, M., 56
Blickle, G., 22
Blitz, R. C., 187
Blonskiy, P., 262
Bobrownicka, M., 54
Bond, M . H., 2, 9-11, 13, 21, 30, 32, 36, 40,
    106, 110, 114, 133, 149, 156-157, 202,
    206, 229, 236, 252, 284-285, 287, 296,
    311, 317
Bond, R., 295
Borgogni, L., 11, 62-63, 156
Borkenau, P., 2, 11, 57, 60, 73-74, 156
Boski, P., 71
Botwin, M. D., 9
Bourne, E. J., 286
Boyle, G. J., 229
Brand, C. R., 7, 240
Bratko, D., 12, 16, 17
Brief, D. E., 147
Briggs, S. R., 7
Brinkmeier, H., 62
Brislin, R. W., 229
Britner, P. A., 312
Brokken, F. B., 2
Brown, K. W., 83
Brownbridge, G., 83
Browne, M. W., 89, 91
Brunas-Wagstaff, J. 49
Brushlinskiy, A. B., 262
Bulatao, J. C., 146, 150
Burke, P. J., 12, 16, 133, 147
Burlachuk, L. F., 263, 264
Buss, A. H., 254
Buss, D. M., 9, 36, 130, 250, 254, 304
Butcher, J. N., 14, 16
Byrne, B. N., 285

C

Campbell, D. T., 204, 293
Caplan, N. S., 198, 209-210, 212
Caprara, G. V., 9, 11, 63-63, 74, 107, 230, 285
Carlota, A. J., 130, 132, 229, 287
Carroll, J. M., 88
Carver, C. S., 83
Caspi, A., 296
Cassaretto, M., 35, 107
Cattell, H. E. P., 16
Cattell, R. B., 7, 139, 227-228, 236, 263
Cavalli-Sforza, L. L., 314, 316
Čermák, I., 53, 56, 62, 64
Chae, J. H., 9, 12, 14, 17-18, 30, 35, 37, 40,

Fossum, T. A., 83
Freeman, J. M., 198-199
Freeman, M. A. 40
Fujita, F., 80, 83, 95
Funder, D. C., 306
Furby, L., 284
Furnham, A., 36

G

Gabrenya, W. K., 313
Gayda, V., 264
Geary, D. C., 9, 11, 14
Gelernter, J., 314
Gelfand, M. J., 40
Georgas, J., 30, 289, 293, 295
Gerong, A., 191
Ghurye, G. S., 228
Gillette, C. S., 83
Gindis, B., 261
Girndt, T., 293
Gleser, G. C., 283
Goldberg, L. R., 7-12, 14-15, 54-55, 62-64, 67, 69, 79, 135, 148, 177-178, 182, 197, 199, 204, 229, 287
Goldman, S. L., 95
Goldstein, H., 284
Gondo, Y., 30, 34-35, 84
Gorbachev, M. S., 263
Gorsuch, R. L., 238
Gosling, S. D., 305
Gough, H. G., 157, 161, 176, 291
Gouveia, F., 257
Green, D. P., 95
Greenfield, P. M., 131
Grimm, S. D., 136-137
Grob, A., 80
Grosjean, F., 194
Gross, J. J., 83
Guanzon-Lapeña, M. A., 21, 130, 132, 229, 287
Guilford, J. S., 1
Gülgöz, S., 106-107, 127, 175, 191, 293
Gurevich, K., 264
Gurtman, M. B., 20-21
Guthrie, G. M., 12, 132
Guttman, L., 238
Gwanzura, F., 156

H

Halim, L., 107
Hamada, W. C., 105
Han, K., 16
Harman, H. H., 238
Haven, S., 17-18, 110
Havinghurst, R. J., 243

Haynes, O. M., 83
Heaven, P. C. L., 11-12, 156, 160, 170
Heilbrun, A. B., 157, 161, 176, 291
Hendriks, A. A. J., 9, 14, 62-63
Herbst, J. H., 316
Heuchert, J. W. P., 43, 157, 160, 184, 192
Ho, D. Y. F., 130
Ho, E. K. F., 84
Ho, R. M., 285
Hoekstra, H. A., 9, 12, 17, 35, 107
Hoffman-Chemi, A., 147
Hofstede, G., 31, 36, 39- 41, 44, 71, 106, 110, 112-114, 267, 284, 293, 312-313
Hofstee, W. K. B., 9, 12-13, 63
Hollan, D., 222
Holland, P. W., 290
Holton, R., 193-194
Hong, S., 166
Horn, B. S., 157, 160
Horn, J. L., 110, 238
Hřebíčková, M., 5, 55-56, 62, 64, 74, 116, 291-292, 309
Hsia, T.-L., 204
Huang, C. D., 138, 148-149, 292
Hui, C. H., 31
Huntington, S. P., 54
Huss, J., 69
Hwang, K.-K., 313
Hyhlík, F., 70

I

Ibáñez, M. I., 229
İmamoğlu, O., 186
Imuta, H., 30, 34
Inglehart, R., 36, 116, 295, 315
Ishihara, O., 30, 34
Izard, C. O., 83

J

Jaccard, J., 95
Jackson, C. J., 241
Jackson, D. N., 2, 12, 30, 132, 139, 156
Jakobson, R., 53
Jang, K. L., 106-107, 311
Jensen, S. M., 82
Jin, P., 9, 12, 35, 133, 184, 192
Joe, R. C., 297
John, O. P., 1, 7-9, 20, 54, 62, 64, 67, 69, 74, 79, 170, 230, 250, 259, 303
Johnson, S. D., 240
Joiner, J. T., Jr., 82
Jónsson, F. H., 9, 12, 14, 17, 21, 35, 161
Jöreskog, K. G., 238
Joshi, L., 231
Juang, L. P., 219

SUBJECT INDEX

A

Acculturation, 149, 197, 201, 209, 212-214, 218, 219, 221, 222, 271, 274, 304, 316-318
ACL. *See* Adjective Check List
Acquiescent response tendencies, 95, 137, 291, 312, 317
Adjective Check List, 155, 157, 161, 168-170, 176, 182, 291
Adolescents, 53, 56, 61, 69, 72-75, 106, 128, 219, 310
Adults, 69, 106, 109, 127, 139, 177, 180, 184-186, 188, 199, 206, 208-209, 212, 235, 262, 268, 272, 307, 316
Affect, 5, 71, 79-80, 82-83, 85-91, 93-101, 160, 204, 206, 219, 222, 291, 312, 316, 318
Age differences, 109, 127, 157, 170, 185, 229, 268, 308, 316-317
Anthropological perspective, 7, 10, 105, 127, 160, 220-221, 204, 206, 222
Attribution, 90, 266-7, 286, 310

B

Backtranslation, 56, 133, 137, 160-161, 179, 200, 204, 206, 232, 266
BFQ. *See* Big Five Questionnaire
Bicultural judges, 127, 129, 138-139, 141-143, 146, 149-150, 310
Big Five (*See also* Five-Factor Model), 7, 10-11, 15, 21, 36, 53, 55, 62-65, 68, 72-73, 80, 94, 130-132, 135-136, 148, 228-229, 240, 250, 255, 259, 281, 287, 289-290, 292, 295, 297-298
Big Five Inventory, 62
Big Five Questionnaire, 62-65, 68, 74, 230
Bilingual studies, 30, 106, 155, 157, 160-161, 163, 175, 189, 191-192, 200, 206, 261, 269

C

California Psychological Inventory, 176
CBFM. *See* Czech Big Five Markers
CIRCUM program, 89, 91, 93, 94, 96
Circumplex models, 12, 21, 79-80, 82, 89-91, 94, 99, 135, 237
Clinical applications, 22, 62, 139, 176, 179, 227, 310, 317
Cognitive schema, 201, 220
Cohort effects, 185, 315-316
Collectivistism. *See* Individualism-

Collectivism
Confirmatory factor analysis, 88, 133, 238, 285, 287
Cross-cultural differences, 12, 16, 29, 74, 281, 292, 295-298
Cross-cultural generalizability, 7, 9, 14-15, 21-22, 170
Cultural context, 3, 7, 10-11, 13, 17, 19, 21, 30, 155, 175, 189, 228, 230, 235, 282, 298
Cultural goals, 201, 207, 216, 219-221
Cultural psychology, 2, 10, 30-31, 130, 148, 155, 229, 250, 284, 292, 303
Cultural schemas, 201, 222
Czech Big Five Markers, 53, 62-65, 68, 74

D

Decentered translation, 204
Discriminant validity, 2, 53, 62, 65, 67, 169

E

Ecological fallacy, 31
Emic perspective, 7, 10-11, 13-15, 20-21, 100, 130-131, 135-137, 139, 147-148, 156, 228-229, 250, 257, 259, 264, 268, 287-288
Emotion. *See* Affect
EPQ. *See* Eysenck Personality Questionnaire
EPQ-R. *See* Eysenck Personality Questionnaire
ESTCOL scale, 41
Ethical considerations in intercultural comparisons, 314
Ethnocentrism, 117, 147
Etic perspective, 7, 10-11, 13-16, 20, 80, 100, 137, 147-148, 157, 229
Evolutionary perspectives, 130
Eysenck Personality Questionnaire, 110, 112-113, 176, 185, 227, 241-243, 254, 274, 288-291, 293, 295-296, 308, 311

F

Factor structure. *See* Personality factor structure
FFM. *See* Five-Factor Model
Five-Factor Personality Inventory, 62-65, 67-69, 74
FFT. *See* Five-Factor Theory
Five-Factor Model, 1-3, 5, 7-16, 21-22, 29-30, 53-55, 62, 64, 74, 79-80, 83-84, 87, 91, 93, 95-96, 99-101, 105-106, 116, 127, 129-133, 135-140, 146-148, 155-157, 160-